ISBN 978-1-334-60114-9
PIBN 10709088

1 MONTH OF
FREE
READING

at
www.ForgottenBooks.com

By purchasing this book you are eligible for one month membership to ForgottenBooks.com, giving you unlimited access to our entire collection of over 700,000 titles via our web site and mobile apps.

To claim your free month visit:
www.forgottenbooks.com/free709088

English
Français
Deutsche
Italiano
Español
Português

www.forgottenbooks.com

Mythology Photography **Fiction**
Fishing Christianity **Art** Cooking
Essays Buddhism Freemasonry
Medicine **Biology** Music **Ancient
Egypt** Evolution Carpentry Physics
Dance Geology **Mathematics** Fitness
Shakespeare **Folklore** Yoga Marketing
Confidence Immortality Biographies
Poetry **Psychology** Witchcraft
Electronics Chemistry History **Law**
Accounting **Philosophy** Anthropology
Alchemy Drama Quantum Mechanics
Atheism Sexual Health **Ancient History**
Entrepreneurship Languages Sport
Paleontology Needlework Islam
Metaphysics Investment Archaeology
Parenting Statistics Criminology
Motivational

REPORTS

OF

CASES ARGUED AND DETERMINED

IN THE

SUPREME COURT

OF THE

STATE OF WISCONSIN,

WITH

TABLES OF THE CASES AND PRINCIPAL MATTERS.

FREDERIC K. CONOVER,
OFFICIAL REPORTER.

VOLUME 73.

DECEMBER 4, 1888 — MARCH 12, 1889.

CHICAGO:
CALLAGHAN & COMPANY,
LAW BOOK PUBLISHERS.
1889.

DAVID ATWOOD,
PRINTER AND STEREOTYPER,
MADISON. WIS.

JUDGES OF THE SUPREME COURT

OF THE

STATE OF WISCONSIN.

DURING THE PERIOD COMPRISED IN THIS VOLUME.

ORSAMUS COLE,   CHIEF JUSTICE.

WILLIAM P. LYON, ⎫

DAVID TAYLOR,   ⎬ ASSOCIATE JUSTICES.

HARLOW S. ORTON, ⎮

JOHN B. CASSODAY, ⎭

Attorney General,   CHARLES E. ESTABROOK.

Clerk,   -   -   -   CLARENCE KELLOGG.

ERRORS NOTED IN PREVIOUS VOLUMES.

VOL. 68.

Page 497. The date under title of case should read: *March 5 — March 22, 1887.*

VOL. 70.

Page 558, line 25. For sec. 3, read sec. 1.

TABLE

NAMES OF CASES

REPORTED IN THIS VOLUME.

---

b

TABLE OF CASES

CITED BY THE COURT.

N. B.—The abbreviation W. is used for Wisconsin Reports.

IN MEMORIAM.

DEATH OF MONTGOMERY M. COTHREN.

On the 8th day of January, 1889, the Honorable Moses M. Strong addressed the court as follows:

May it please the Court.— At a meeting of the members of the bar of the fifth judicial circuit, held at the court house in Darlington on the 6th of December, 1888, for the purpose of taking appropriate action relative to the death of Hon. MONTGOMERY M. COTHREN, Moses M. Strong was called to preside, and the committee appointed for that purpose reported the following resolutions:

" *Whereas*, on October 27th, 1888, at his farm home near Calamine in this county, Hon. MONTGOMERY M. COTHREN died, aged sixty-nine years, after the fullness of legal honors and of official trusts had illustrated not only his own character but the early history of the state;

" We surviving members of the bar of Southwestern Wisconsin unite in grateful memory as well as in affectionate testimonial not only to his character as a man, to his broad and comprehensive intellect, to his fearless probity as judge, to his luminous sense of duty and patriotism, and to his profound knowledge of the law united with noble generosity of heart;

" *Resolved*, that in the death of Judge COTHREN one of the most illustrious members of the bar has been removed;

" *Resolved*, that while we mourn the loss of our professional brother and friend, we yet rejoice to know from his example that poverty in youth is no wall, that friendless beginnings are no discouragement, that mighty difficulties are no impediment which energy and enthusiasm, a sound brain and a stout heart, may not completely overcome and achieve for the possessor most enduring victory at last;

" *Resolved*, that while about his knees loving and grateful grandchildren shall gather never again, either to share his fatherly kiss, to receive his welcome, to hear his tender counsel, or to catch his smile;

c

we to them and to his bereaved wife bespeak from saddened eyes and full hearts our sympathy at their irreparable loss, and our mutual grief at his, our honored brother's, death;

"*Resolved*, that the proceeding of this bar meeting, together with a memorial address to be prepared by Hon. Moses M. Strong, president of the bar association of this judicial circuit, be forwarded to the family of the deceased, and be presented by him to the circuit court of this county, and to the supreme court of this state at its next term, with a request that they be entered on the records of those courts respectively."

Interesting and eloquent remarks were made by James R. Rose, Calvert Spensley, Philo A. Orton, William E. Carter, Henry S. Magoon, and David S. Rose, which exhibited a deep sense of the loss which the bar had sustained in the demise of their professional brother; which portrayed his elevated character as a lawyer, a legislator, a judge, a citizen, and a man, and the sympathy felt by the members of the bar for his afflicted family; whereupon the resolutions were unanimously adopted.

When I reflect that he of whom it becomes my duty, in compliance with the resolution of the bar, to address this court *in memoriam*, was nearly nine years younger than myself, with every appearance, until shortly before his death, of having as long a lease of life, I cannot withhold the reflection that, judging by the expectations of longevity, the relations we now sustain to each other should be reversed, and that it would be more in harmony with the ordinary laws of nature that he should ask that the mantle of charity be spread over the short-comings of *my* protracted and — compared with what it might have been — unprofitable life, than that I should attempt to portray the eminent and beautiful features of *his*. But the Omniscient Disposer of events has ordered otherwise, and his will must be done on earth as it is in heaven, and I shall therefore attempt to perform the duty devolving upon me by the resolutions of the members of the bar, in a spirit of impartiality, tempered though it may be by a feeling of warm regard.

Judge COTHREN, as a brief reference to the earlier years of his life abundantly demonstrates, was pre-eminently a *self-made man*. Born in Yates county in the state of New York on the 18th of September, 1819, of worthy parents, their moderate pecuniary circumstances did not admit of their providing for their son other educational advantages than such as were furnished by the common schools of the vicinity. When ten years of age, his father removed with his family in 1829 to the state of Michigan, then the frontier of the "far West," where educational facilities were more limited than those he had left behind him. Here he remained for nine years, until 1838, assisting his father in opening up and cultivating the farm upon which he had located, devoting the little time which this duty left at his command in acquiring such an education as the circumscribed opportunities of his situation in so new a country rendered possible. Here also he spent a part of his time in studying the elementary principles of that profession of which he then little thought he was to become so distinguished a member.

He had now attained the age of nineteen years, and had made such use of the limited educational advantages within his reach that he felt qualified to undertake the education of others in elementary studies, and left Michigan for Wisconsin with the purpose of teaching school and at the same time of pursuing the study of his chosen profession of the law to such an extent as his pedagogical duties would admit. On his way to Wisconsin he reached Rock river near Rockford, where he had some acquaintances with whom he spent a year or more, and then went to New Diggings in Wisconsin, where when about twenty years of age he entered upon the business of school teaching, continuing at the same time the study of law. He continued to be thus

occupied until 1843, when having been chosen clerk of the
board of county commissioners of Iowa county, which then
embraced La Fayette county — the whole being then under
the old county system of government,— he removed to
Mineral Point, then the county seat, where he ever after
made his home.

That year (1843) he was admitted to the bar in the
United States district court, over which Chief Justice DUNN
presided. He soon after formed a law-partnership with
Hon. Parley Eaton, and the firm of Eaton & Cothren
very soon had an extensive practice, and the junior member
of the firm at once attained a high standing at the bar,
which grew more and more with increasing years and was
marked by a corresponding success.

In 1847 Mr. COTHREN was elected a member of the house
of representatives in the territorial legislature. The session
that year was very short, extending only from the 17th to
the 27th of October, and was confined almost entirely to
making provision for a second convention to form a state
constitution — that adopted by the first convention having
been rejected. The next session was more important and
longer, having extended from the 7th of February to the
13th of March, 1848, and was the last session of the territorial legislature, the present constitution having been ratified by a vote of the people on the same 13th of March.
In 1848 he was elected a member of the state senate to represent the then 5th senate district, embracing the counties
of Iowa and Richland. He held this office from January
1, 1849, until January 1, 1851. During this period legislative work was performed of the greatest importance to the
new state. In 1848 a commission of three lawyers had been
created to collate and revise all the public acts of the state
of a general and permanent nature, and to report at the
next session of the legislature. The commissioners, not
having been able to complete the revision, reported it so

far as completed, and a joint committee of nine members was appointed to co-operate with the commission in the completion of the revision. Mr. COTHREN, being chairman of the judiciary committee of the senate, was appointed a member of the committee, and became its chairman, and the result of the combined action of this committee and the commission was the "Revised Statutes of 1849." Much other important legislation was had during this term, which the occasion does not admit of mentioning more particularly.

In 1852, the term for which Judge JACKSON had been elected as judge of the 5th judicial circuit being about to expire, Mr. COTHREN was nominated by the Democratic party of the circuit as his successor, and was elected by a large majority over his opponent. He performed the duties of the office for six years, when in 1858 he was re-elected without opposition and held the office during the term until January 1, 1865, when he retired from the bench and resumed the practice of his profession with signal success.

In 1852, Judge COTHREN was nominated by the Democratic party and elected as one of the electors at large for president and vice president, and with his colleagues in the electoral college cast the five votes of Wisconsin for Franklin Pierce and William R. King.

In 1863, he was nominated at a state convention of the Democratic party for the office of chief justice of the supreme court, but was defeated by Chief Justice L. S. DIXON.

After a service of twelve years upon the bench, he continued his law practice for the next twelve years, when he was again called by a numerous non-partisan assemblage to become once more a candidate for the office of circuit judge. The Republican party had placed a candidate in nomination, and an independent candidate had been self-announced. The hold which the former judge had secured upon the confidence of the people, the satisfaction which he had given upon the bench, and his wonderful personal popularity overcame all opposition, and he was elected in April, 1876, and again served upon the bench with unabated acceptance from January 1, 1877, until January 1, 1883, when he again, resumed the practice of law, which he continued until death terminated his professional labors.

In September last he was nominated as the Democratic candidate for state senator, and accepted the nomination, but his death ten days before the election removed him from the political contest.

He was married August 24, 1848, to Miss Esther Maria Pulford, who still survives him. The birth of six children resulted from this marriage — two sons and four daughters, — all of whom survive their father except one daughter, who died in infancy. To this grief-stricken family, any attempt upon this occasion to assuage their sorrow would be opening afresh the wounds of their lacerated feelings, and only tend to add poignancy to the overwhelming suffering with which they are already so severely afflicted.

To give expression in an address of this character to the whole flood of thoughts, portraying the characteristics of the deceased, which unbidden crowd themselves upon our consideration, would swell it to an unpardonable length. It is to his character as a lawyer and the cognate functions of judge, that the proprieties of the present occasion seem to demand that this address should primarily relate.

The prominent defect in the character of Judge COTHREN as a lawyer, was that his professional, like his scholastic, education had been fragmentary and without system. He had none of the advantages of law schools or lectures, nor even the benefit of a regular course of study under the supervision of any competent lawyer. Notwithstanding these embarrassments, which he alone appreciated at their full importance, the uncommon strength of his native intellect, his quick intuitive perception, and his ready faculty of making the appropriate application of the proper legal principle to each case as it arose, enabled him to overcome the latent defects of his professional education to such an extent that to the layman and 'to the superficial lawyer genius had the appearance of education, and tact and intuitive perception effectually concealed any lack of professional education. It was in the trial of jury cases, the examination of witnesses, and in arguments to the jury, that Judge COTHREN won his principal distinction as a lawyer. To his intellectual and perceptive faculties, to his genius and tact, were added a wonderful knowledge of human nature and of the influences which affect human action. The confidence which was reposed in his integrity and his unswerving devotion to truth and honesty by all with whom he came in contact was unlimited. His warm sympathy with all the better feelings of our nature permeated his whole life. His generous and noble nature and his universal self-sacrificing love of his fellow men seemed to attach all to him. These elements of his character gave to him such an influence over the hearts of witnesses, jurors, and all whose concurrent thought and action he desired, that his power over them may most appropriately be called magnetic. Possessing these faculties he supplemented them in arguing a cause to the jury by an intelligent and attractive mode of arranging for their consideration the issues presented by the case; a clear and fair statement of the facts and evidence of facts existing in the case, as well against him as in his favor; and superadded to which he made the most powerful arguments, sustained by analytical and synthetical reasoning, of which the case admitted. His arguments were always adorned with finished rhetoric and fervid eloquence. It was thus that Judge COTHREN attained the distinction of being a great power at the bar; a power which caused suitors to desire to retain his professional services, and which always inspired counsel to whom he was opposed with a knowledge, if not a fear, that to cope with him demanded their utmost efforts.

As distinguished as he was at the bar, the elevated standing which Judge COTHREN attained upon the bench during the eighteen years in which he adorned it, transcended, in those proud characteristics which mark the able and the just judge, the splendid fame which was attained in his career as a lawyer.

Called to the bench at the early age of thirty-three, with only nine years practice at the bar, it would have been wonderful indeed if the manner in which he discharged the duties of his novel position had not elicited criticism. He had from the beginning of his term a modest diffidence of his ability, but it was overweighed by a sensitive consciousness of the integrity of his intentions and an inflexible determination that truth and justice should be his guiding star, which under all circumstances he would impartially follow without fear or favor, and that he would administer the law as he understood it, according to the best lights which had been vouchsafed to him. This determination, upon which he ever acted, always sustained him, and if it led him into any error, he knew and all knew that it was of a character which is ever liable to result from the infirmities and ignorance of the most perfect of men. To parties litigant every reasonable opportunity was always afforded of presenting their whole cause of action or their whole line of defense. To attorneys and counsel the judge, while careful to maintain the observance of the duty due from them to the bench, was as scrupulously observant of every right and courtesy due to the members of the bar. He appeared to act upon the apothegm of Lord Bacon in his essays, that "patience and gravity of hearing is an essential part of justice, and an overspeaking judge is no well-tuned cymbal. It is no grace to a judge first to find that which he might have heard in due time from the bar; or to show quickness of conceit in cutting off evidence or counsel too short." To jurors he was (to quote Bacon again) "a light to open their eyes, but not a guide to lead them by their noses." His charges were always fair and perspicuous, and, if exceptionable, a fair bill of exceptions could always be obtained, as it could upon all questions arising in the progress of the trial. Witnesses were always protected by the judge from any improper or impertinent examination.

In regard to his judicial duty to the people and the state, the judge never forgot the conclusion of the Roman twelve tables, "*salus populi suprema lex.*" It is no reflection upon any of the numerous judges who have from time to time, during the last forty years, adorned the bench in the numerous circuits of the state, to say that all in all, considering the various elements which enter into the character of the perfect judge, the subject of this address was the peer of the most eminent. It is of course impracticable on this occasion to make further reference in detail to evidences which might be adduced to sustain this judgment, and the proper estimate of the character of Judge COTHREN as a lawyer and a judge must be left to the impartial verdict of a just public sentiment.

Independently of his judicial character, much might be justly said in eulogy of him as a man; but the proprieties of this occasion must necessarily greatly restrict what shall be written in that regard.

The most predominant trait in the character of Judge COTHREN — the one uniformly recognized as such by all his large circle of friends — was his charity, in the most enlarged meaning of the word. That charity which "suffereth long, is kind, envieth not, vaunteth not itself, is not puffed up, seeketh not her own, is not easily provoked, thinketh no evil, rejoiceth in the truth, beareth all things,

believeth all things, hopeth all things, is the bond of per-
fectness and the end of the commandment." This Apostolic definition of charity presents as perfect a picture of
the life of our subject as can be drawn. If any single feature of this picture were to be selected from the others as
most expressive of his character, it would be " thinketh no
evil." So far from indulging in expressions of malice or
unkindness to any, it was his uniform habit to speak well
of all, and, if that could not be done with conscientious regard for truth, to give them the charity of his silence. But
his charity, in the more popular and limited sense of benef-
icence, was great and characteristic. He visited the sick,
clothed the naked, fed the hungry, and never refused charitable aid to the deserving poor.

His uniform unswerving integrity was a marked feature
of his character, not alone in the more restricted sense of
fidelity to his pecuniary obligations, but with reference to
all his duties to society and his fellow-men.

While he had that dignity of character which always
commanded the respect and appreciation of all who met
him, he was one of the most approachable and social of
mankind, and enjoyed the kindest regards of hosts of
friends. To young men, and especially to young lawyers,
he extended the kindest consideration and the assistance of
his friendly counsel and advice.

It would seem to be a consequence that a man possessing
the commendable traits of character which we have attempted to describe should develop the religious element.
This natural sequence resulted. Brought up in the faith of
the Presbyterian sect from early youth, he was always influenced by religious sentiments. In 1857 he was confirmed
by the sainted Bishop Kemper in the Protestant Episcopal
Church, but did not continue such relation to it permanently. Subsequently at one time he was strongly inclined
to become attached to the Roman Catholic Church, but

never gave practical effect to his inclinations. Soon after he took up the study of Swedenborg's writings, and was so deeply interested in them that he became a firm believer in his doctrines and a sincere disciple of his faith, which he openly avowed and consistently practiced until by his death he found the opportunity of determining their truth. He was a firm believer "in the communion of saints, the forgiveness of sins, the resurrection of the body, and the life everlasting." In this belief he lived, in this belief he died.

Judge Cothren was a man of vigorous constitution, and as a rule was in the enjoyment of robust health. It was however observed by his friends, and he was conscious of it, that during the last year his health and strength were sensibly impaired. The last term of court which he attended was the October term of the circuit court of Iowa county. He was there engaged for the defense in a homicide trial, upon which occasion it was obvious that his physical powers were greatly affected, although he complained of no special ailment. Soon after he went to his farm home near Calamine, where his wife and two daughters were, and was compelled by his disease to take his bed. His trouble soon developed into a serious inflammation of the bowels, which he immediately became conscious must result in death. After a few days the disease became in a great measure assuaged, so that he was relieved of the awful pains which he had endured, but his vital energies had become so much impaired that his system could not yield to the influence of stimulants, and after two days of comparatively painless rest, during which his mental faculties appeared unimpaired, his heart ceased to beat, and his spirit passed to that

> "undiscovered country, from whose bourn
> No traveler returns."
> "Tired he sleeps, and life's poor play is o'er."

Death of Montgomery M. Cothren.

Mr. Justice Orton, on behalf of the court, responded as follows:

The duty and honor of responding to your resolutions in memory of our deceased brother, which we most cordially indorse, have been assigned to me by the chief justice, but certainly not because I am more competent to discharge that duty than any one of the other members of this court, except possibly by reason of my long acquaintance and intimate relations with Judge Cothren. But even in this respect I can claim but slight superior qualification, for all of the old lawyers and judges of this state have known Judge Cothren almost as well personally, and his reputation and standing as a lawyer and a judge quite as well; for he has been one of the most eminent and honored of our citizens, legislators, lawyers, and judges, and a commanding figure in our history for over forty years.

The southwestern portion of the state was settled at an early day, in consequence of its mineral resources, and attracted a very able class of men of all professions and other kinds of business, and especially a very learned and highly qualified class of lawyers, from the older states, east and south. The legal business of such a region is generally more important by reason of the amount in controversy and the high rate of professional compensation, and these are inducements to the ablest members of the profession (and the services of only such are sought), and it is well known that such a region has a very able bar, and consequently very able judges. This district of our own state was no exception to this rule, and from an early day Mineral Point was one of its most important places of business, and the subject of these memorial exercises was one of the earliest and ablest members of its bar, and he remained there until his death, one of the most honored and respected and now deeply lamented of its citizens.

I need only to mention the names of some of the mem-

bers of the Mineral Point bar, to show the high rank it
bore in comparison with others of the west: Judges Dunn,
Crawford. Jackson, and Cothren, the venerable General
Smith, Governor Washburn, and last but not least the Hon.
Moses M. Strong, who still remains amongst us, the Nestor
of the Wisconsin bar. Judge Jackson has lived "to crown
a life of labor with an age of ease." The others have gone
to another world with about the same proportion of the
old lawyers in other parts of the state. It is a saddening
thought that nearly all of that splendid galaxy of lawyers
who commenced practice with Judge Cothren over forty
years ago have with him gone to their everlasting home.
They were all of them, with but very few exceptions, young
then, as a large majority of the present bar is now, and
they have left noble examples of character, ability and success, which may be imitated but will not be excelled. It
is enough to say that the lamented Cothren was one of
the most distinguished and promising of that old bar of
the state, and like the others continued all his life, by reading, practice, and experience, to grow in knowledge and
maturity of judgment, until he ranked high as a jurist in
the great body of American lawyers. I have known him
well in all his public and his private life, and when I speak of
him from that knowledge I feel sure that my judgment of
him will be approved by all who knew him as well.

Judge Cothren had strong and well marked personali-
ties. His intellect was naturally well balanced, and by
education it did not lose its symmetry. His judgment controlled his other faculties in all of the practical affairs of
life. He had a keen sense of right and wrong, and he was
honest and extremely conscientious. He was positive and
independent in his opinions, because they were deliberately
and candidly formed. He was kind and tender in his af-
fections, and his personal friendships were very strong and
his fidelity everlasting. He was dignified and courteous in

manner, but without the least appearance of self-apprecia-
tion or conceit. In short he was a perfect gentleman in all
his intercourse with others. He extended and perfected a
good education by a taste and habit of reading, and his
knowledge in all departments of intellectual acquirement
was comprehensive and accurate. He was thoughtful and
somewhat reserved, but never morose. He was naturally
and intensely religious, and had much of that faith which
is "the substance of things hoped for and the evidence of
things not seen," and was fond of metaphysical investigation.

As a lawyer he was a profound reader of the books, and
reasoned from principle, and had an intuitive knowledge of
the law from its justice. Having been educated for the
bar at a time when a long reading of the common law and
a thorough knowledge of its principles were the conditions
of admission, he acquired a love and veneration for those
grand old rules and systems which are the perfection of
reason and the accumulated wisdom of the ages. He loved
and honored his profession with an unchangeable devotion,
and never violated its ethics or its amenities. As a practicing lawyer he brought to the trial of his causes the very
highest skill and the best judgment. He had every step in
progress full in view, and was never taken by surprise. As
an advocate before the court or jury he had few equals. In
his brief, terse, but comprehensive, arguments he never
wandered from or omitted the points which were material.
He was indeed eloquent, and moved both court and jury
by the irresistible charms of his oratory, and the clear,
shrill tones of his musical voice held the ear spell-bound as
they arose higher and louder to the rounded periods of his
rhetoric. As a legislator both in territory and state he was
wise, judicious, and influential, and did much in forming
the institutions of the state. As a judge, thrice elected in
one of the most intelligent circuits of the state, he had the

very highest qualifications, and his decisions were always impartial and generally correct. He was kind and courteous to the bar, as he was to everybody, but was firm and decisive in his rulings and judgments.

Judge COTHREN left his indelible impress upon his times and his state, as one of their most distinguished and long-remembered benefactors and jurists. But he has left us and gone to his reward where rewards and judgments are always impartial and just. Sad to say, he has gone to join the great majority of his former associates. It seems but a very short time ago that he appeared before this court in the full vigor of his perfected manhood, and made a clear, pleasing, cogent, and eloquent argument of his cause. Like all other men he had his frailties of life, but this is no occasion to "draw [them] from their dread abode."

These proceedings will be placed upon the records of this court as a perpetual memorial of our deceased brother.

CASES DETERMINED

August Term, 1888.

BARNES, Respondent, vs. STACY and another, Appellants.

November 8 — December 4, 1888.

Liens: Pleading: Separate contracts: Mingling causes of action: Indefiniteness.

In an action to enforce a lien for machinery and materials furnished and labor performed, a complaint to which is annexed a copy of an agreement under which certain specified articles were to be furnished for a certain price, and a bill of particulars of all charges, including, as one item, the articles furnished under the specific contract, is *held* to be sufficiently definite and certain, although it does not state separately a cause of action for the articles furnished under the written agreement, and one for the other articles furnished and labor performed.

APPEAL from the Circuit Court for *Shawano* County. Action to enforce a lien for machinery and materials furnished and labor performed. The complaint, after alleging the partnership of the defendants in the business of manufacturing lumber, and that the plaintiff was the proprietor of a general machine shop and foundry, alleges that in the spring of 1887 the defendants' saw-mill was destroyed by fire; that on or about June 15, 1887, the plaintiff entered into an agreement with the defendants to sell and deliver to them such machinery as they might want in the rebuilding of their said saw-mill, and to repair and re-

VOL. 78 — 1

fit for use such of the old machinery as they might want
refitted and repaired; that as to a portion of said machinery (to wit, one set of Gowen head blocks, three in number;
Gowen set works; 24 feet of carriage, with 6 trucks and
shafts with boxes for the same; 30 feet of rack stick,
with heavy segments for same; one pinion, and 120 feet of
track, and one wood saw husk) the price therefor was to be
$450; that the balance of the machinery or materials used
in repairing the same was to be furnished and the work
thereon performed by the plaintiff for what they were reasonably worth; and that a memorandum of agreement
with reference to the machinery to be furnished for said
sum of $450 was made and signed by the parties, and a
copy thereof is attached to the complaint, marked " Exhibit A."

The complaint further alleges that, pursuant to said agreement and at the special instance and request of the defendants thereafter, the plaintiff sold and delivered to the
defendants certain machinery, including that described in
Exhibit A., and used materials and performed labor in repairing machinery for them, which machinery was used in
rebuilding and now forms a part of said saw-mill; that the
value of the machinery thus sold and the materials used
and labor performed (including that for which a price had
been agreed upon as before stated) was $928.77; and that
a full and complete statement of the same is attached to
Exhibit B. (plaintiff's petition for a lien), which is annexed
to and made a part of the complaint; that of said sum of
$928.77 a balance of $760.57 is still due and payable to the
plaintiff.   The complaint contains further allegations showing that the plaintiff has taken the requisite steps to entitle him to the lien sought to be enforced.

Exhibit A., annexed to the complaint, was as follows:
" JUNE 21, 1887.   *W. H. Stacy & Co.*— GENTLEMEN: I will
furnish you the following: One set of Gowen head blocks,

three in number, also Gowen set-works; the above are second-hand, but thoroughly repaired; also 24-feet carriage, with six sets of trucks, and shafts to be 2-inch iron, wheels 14 inches, with boxes for same; also 30 feet of rack stick, with heavy segments for the same; one pinion for same; 60 feet of V inch 1 and ½ track and 60 feet flat track; also one wood saw husk, W. H. Stacy & Co. to furnish all the irons which can be used from old husk to be placed on new husk. The above work to be done in good, workmanlike manner, and on or before 30 days from the above date; consideration, $450,— $200 to be paid upon delivery, and balance in 60 days from delivery. W. H. Stacy & Co. agree to deliver job at Birnamwood. Scrap iron for $10 a ton. J. A. BARNES. W. H. STACY & Co. *Birnamwood, Wis.*"

The bill of particulars annexed to Exhibit B. contained one item as follows: "To head block, carriage truck, trucks, husk, etc. (contract), $450."

The defendants moved that the complaint be made more definite and certain, on the grounds (1) that it improperly commingles into one count or statement of cause of action two or more causes of action which should be stated separately; that if any causes of action exist they are upon independent, separate agreements, to wit, an agreement made in writing, and an oral or implied contract; that the complaint does not state when and where articles claimed for were delivered, whether all at one time or not, and it fails to set forth definitely and with sufficient certainty what articles were delivered under the memorandum of agreement, Exhibit A.; (2) that in what purports to be a statement of an account, annexed to Exhibit B., the charges for hours of work and materials used in the articles made are so mingled together that the cost or charges made for any particular article of machinery therein named cannot be ascertained with certainty so as to see if the charges for

the same are what it is reasonably worth as a finished piece
of machinery ready for use. From an order denying the
motion the defendants appeal.

For the appellants there was a brief by *Houghton &
Thorn*, and oral argument by *G. T. Thorn.*

For the respondent there was a brief by *Hicks & Phillips*, and oral argument by *M. C. Phillips.*

Cole, C. J. There is no difficulty in understanding what
claims are relied on as a cause of action for which a lien
is sought. The plaintiff evidently seeks to recover or have
a lien for the machinery furnished under the letter or written agreement of June 21, 1887, the price of which was
agreed upon at $450. He also seeks to recover and have a
lien for other materials furnished and services rendered
upon machinery placed in the mill, for the amount which
these materials and services were reasonably worth. These
materials and services are set forth in the bill of particulars
which is attached to and made a part of the complaint.
It is true, this bill of particulars contains the aggregate
charge for the machinery furnished upon the written contract; but this could not have misled any one, as the item
itself refers to a contract, thus giving an explanation of the
charge. In respect to the other materials furnished and
services rendered the bill of particulars contains all necessary information as to the nature of the article and time
of service which was essential to enable the defendants to
make their defense. The different claims might have been
kept more distinct in the complaint, and not mingled together as they are to some extent; but still there is no
difficulty whatever in ascertaining with certainty the precise nature of the claims which the plaintiff is to recover
upon and have a lien for. Of course, the special agreement will control as to the price of all machinery furnished
under it; and as to the other materials and services the

plaintiff can recover only what he shows they are reasonably worth. But the complaint states, with reasonable certainty, the facts relating to each claim or cause of action. It is not possible for the defendants to be embarrassed in making their defense.

The motion to make the complaint more definite and certain was properly denied.

By the Court.— The order of the circuit court is affirmed.

SCHRIBER, Appellant, vs. THE TOWN OF RICHMOND, Respondent.

November 8 — December 4, 1888.

(1) Town orders: Presentation for audit. (2) Limitation of actions: When statute begins to run: Demand. (3) De minimis non curat lex. (4) Judgment dismissing instead of abating action: Immaterial error.

1. Under sec. 824, R. S., as amended by ch. 163, Laws of 1882, where one town has become liable upon orders issued by another, no action can be maintained thereon against the town so becoming liable unless a claim thereon has been filed with its town clerk to be laid before the town board of audit.

2. Although, before the enactment of ch. 240, Laws of 1881, an action on a town order could be maintained only after demand and refusal of payment, yet the statute of limitations began to run from the date of the order, not from the date of the demand. [The court inclines to the opinion, but does not decide, that the effect of ch. 240. Laws of 1881, so far as the statute of limitations is concerned, is only to extend the period of limitation thirty days.]

3. An action upon sixty-eight town orders for about $2.000 was barred by the statute of limitations as to all but one order for $15. The judgment dismissed the action. In the argument on appeal no special point was made as to that one order as distinguished from the others. *Held*, that the judgment would not be reversed for an error affecting a sum so comparatively small.

4. The entry of judgment dismissing an action upon the merits instead of abating it is an immaterial error where another action would be barred by the statute of limitations and it is manifest that that defense would be interposed.

APPEAL from the Circuit Court for *Shawano* County.

The action is upon sixty-eight town orders, drawn in due form by the chairman of the board of supervisors and town clerk of the town of Langlade, upon the treasurer of that town, amounting in the aggregate to about $2,000; and bearing different dates between March 30, 1880, and May 14, 1881.

On May 25, 1883, all the territory then included in the town of Langlade was, by the proper county board of supervisors, duly annexed to and made a part of the town of *Richmond*, the defendant, and remained a part of that town until the spring of 1885, when, under ch. 137, Laws of 1885, the same territory was detached from *Richmond* and organized as the town of Langlade. The plaintiff, *Schriber,* afterwards brought an action against the new town of Langlade on the same orders here in suit, and on appeal this court held that such new town was not, but the town of *Richmond* was, liable on such orders. *Schriber v. Langlade,* 66 Wis. 616. Hence this action.

The orders in suit were never presented to the treasurer of the original town of Langlade for payment, nor to the town board of *Richmond* for audit, but were presented to the treasurer of *Richmond*, November 13, 1886, for payment. This action was commenced December 18, 1886. The complaint counts upon the sixty-eight town orders above mentioned. The defendant town answered, in abatement of the action, that a claim for the payment of such orders had never been filed with its clerk to be laid before its town board of audit; and also answered the six years statute of limitations in bar of the action.

A jury was waived, and the cause was tried by the court. The findings are for the defendant on the answer in abatement, and also on the answer of the statute of limitations, except as to fourteen of the orders. It was also found that some of the fourteen orders thus excepted are void. The matters thus found in bar of the action cover all the orders in suit, except six aggregating about $176. The matters found in abatement cover the whole sixty-eight orders. The plaintiff appeals from the judgment dismissing his complaint on the merits of the action, with costs.

For the appellant there was a brief by *Houghton & Thorn*, and oral argument by *F. W. Houghton*. They contended, *inter alia*, that a demand is necessary to the accruing of a cause of action on town orders, and that therefore the statute of limitations does not begin to run until such demand is made. Wood on Lim. of Act. secs. 117, 118, 125; R. S. sec. 4249; Laws of 1881, ch. 240; *Packard v. Bovina*, 24 Wis. 382; *Keithler v. Foster*, 22 Ohio St. 27; Angell on Lim. 96; *Codman v. Rogers*, 10 Pick. 120; *Rhind v. Hyndman*, 54 Md. 527; *Stanton v. Stanton*, 37 Vt. 411; *Thorpe v. Booth*, Ryan & M. 388; *Holmes v. Kerrison*, 2 Taunt. 323; *Brown v. Rutherford*, 42 L. T. R. (N. S.), 659; *Little v. Blunt*, 9 Pick. 490; Dillon on Mun. Corp. 505, and note 2.

For the respondent there was a brief by *M. J. Wallrich* and *Geo. G. Greene*, and oral argument by *Mr. Greene*. They argued, among other things, that the terms of a town order do not require presentation. Its necessity springs, not from any contract, but from the provisions of law for auditing and paying the public debt. When presentation of a claim, or any other preliminary step, is thus required *by law* before action, the cause of action *accrues* when the plaintiff can, at will, take the step and bring the action. *Baxter v. State*, 17 Wis. 588; *Goldman v. Conway Co.* 10 Fed. Rep. 888; *Dewey v. Lins*, 57 Iowa, 235; *Hintrager v. Traut*, 69 id. 746; *Baker v. Johnson Co.* 33 id. 151; *Arapahoe v. Albee*, 38 N. W. Rep. (Neb.), 737; *Hostetter v. Hollinger*, 117 Pa. St. 606; *Brehm v. Mayor*, 104 N. Y. 186; *Palmer v. Palmer*, 36 Mich. 487; *Litchfield v. McDonald*, 35 Minn. 167; *Prescott v. Gonser*, 34 Iowa, 175; *Dorland v. Dorland*, 66 Cal. 189; *Burleigh v. Rochester*, 5 Fed. Rep. 667.

Lyon, J. I. The first question to be determined is whether the defense in abatement of the action should have been sustained. That is to say, was it essential to the plaintiff's right of action that the town orders in suit should have been previously filed with the town clerk of *Richmond*, the defendant town, to be laid before the town board of audit of that town? It is claimed on behalf of defendant that such filing thereof is essential to the right of action under sec. 824, R. S., which reads as follows: "No action upon any claim or cause of action for which a money judgment only is demandable, shall be maintained against any town, unless a statement of such claim shall have been filed with the town clerk, to be laid before the town board of audit, nor until ten days after the next annual town meeting thereafter."

We think a fair construction of the above statute excludes from its operation town orders regularly issued by the proper authorities of the town on behalf of which the same were issued. The object of the statute was to protect towns from suits upon claims payable in money, until the town board, or, in case of its refusal to allow such demands, the town meeting, may act upon such claims. In the case of a valid town order, the board or town meeting must necessarily have passed upon and allowed the claim before the order was issued, and there is no necessity that the board act upon the order. In this view, ch. 163, Laws of 1882, was enacted, amending sec. 824, R. S., by inserting immediately after the word "demandable" these words: "Except upon town orders, bonds, coupons, or written promises to pay any sum of money." All these instruments, if valid, must have been executed by the proper town officers; and the consideration thereof, or the indebtedness they represent, must have been subjected to the scrutiny of the town meeting, the electors, or the town board. Probably the amendment of 1882 does not change the provisions of sec. 824, but only makes that section express what would otherwise have been implied.

The question remains, however, whether, in a case like this, where the orders in suit were issued by one town and the liability thereon (if the orders are valid) is thrown upon another, the orders must be presented to the town board of the latter town for allowance before an action on them against such town can be maintained. We think this question must be answered in the affirmative. In the present case the town of Langlade issued the orders in suit, but, if there is any liability upon them, the same has been laid upon the defendant town of *Richmond* by the action of the county board of supervisors. The claims or demands upon which the orders were based have never been subjected to the scrutiny of the town board or town meeting of *Richmond*, and that board has had no opportunity to inquire into the validity of the orders. They may be void for many reasons. For example, some or all of them may have been issued without the authority of the town board, or for an unauthorized or illegal purpose, or they may have been paid by the town which issued them. The plain object of the statute above quoted is, as already intimated, to give the town board, or town meeting, as the case may be, an opportunity to ascertain whether the orders are valid and binding obligations against the town before it shall be subjected to a suit upon them. (See Revisers' note to sec. 824.) Moreover, the town treasurer of *Richmond* had no authority to pay the orders on presentation. He could lawfully pay only orders issued by the proper officers of that town. Hence the necessity that the orders should go to the town board of *Richmond* for audit, like other claims against the town, to the end that, if allowed, town orders should be issued therefor which the treasurer of *Richmond* is authorized to pay.

Hence we are constrained to construe the exception of

town orders in the amended sec. 824 to mean only those orders issued by the town sought to be charged with their payment, and that where the orders were issued by another town, as in this case, the claim thereon is within the spirit and language of sec. 824, and must be filed with the town clerk, to be laid before the board of audit of the town upon which such liability has been cast, before an action can be lawfully commenced thereon against such town.

It is conceded that no claim founded upon the orders in suit was ever so filed. Hence this action cannot be maintained. All this, however, is only matter in abatement of the action, which would not interfere with the right to bring another action after complying with the statute. Were this all there is of the case, the judgment would necessarily have to be reversed; for it dismisses the complaint on the merits of the action, which is a judgment in bar of this or any future action upon the orders.

II. We are thus brought to the question, Does the record disclose any sufficient grounds for upholding the judgment in its present form? This involves a consideration of the effect of the statute of limitations upon the orders in suit.

Ch. 240, Laws of 1881, provides that "no action shall hereafter be brought upon any county, city, town, or school order until the expiration of thirty days after a demand for the payment of the same shall have been made." This chapter became a law, April 7, 1881. Before that date there does not seem to have been any special statutory provision on the subject. It was held, however, in *Packard v. Bovina*, 24 Wis. 382, decided in 1869, that under general rules of law no action could be maintained against a town on a town order drawn upon its treasurer, until after the order had been presented for payment to the treasurer and payment thereof refused. This case settled the law as it stood before the enactment of ch. 240, Laws of 1881, to be that a town order was payable on demand and only on demand. Such was the law when all of the orders in suit were issued, save one for $15, dated May 14, 1881.

The six years statute of limitations commences to run when the cause of action accrues. R. S. secs. 4219, 4222. The question here is, Did the cause of action accrue on the orders in suit when they were issued in 1880 and 1881, or not until payment thereof was actually demanded, November 13, 1886? We think this question is answered by the judgments of this court in *Baxter v. State*, 17 Wis. 588, and *Curran v. Witter*, 68 Wis. 16. In the first of these cases it was argued that because the statute required a party to present his claim to the legislature before bringing a suit thereon against the state, the cause of action does not accrue, and hence the statute of limitations does not commence to run, until the claim is so presented. This court negatived that proposition, and held that the cause of action accrues when a debt exists which the state owes and ought to pay, without regard to the time when the claim was so presented. Mr. Justice PAINE, delivering the opinion of the court, said that this provision of the statute did not constitute " any element of the cause of action within the scope and object of the statute of limitation. It was a mere condition to the bringing of a suit imposed by law for the protection of the state from unnecessary costs. If a debt existed, it existed entirely independent of such presentation of the claim. It existed as soon as a claim accrued which the state owed and ought to pay. And then it was that the cause of action accrued. True, the party had to present his claim before bringing his suit, but such presentation partook of the nature of the remedy. It was a preliminary proceeding, required of him in order to avail himself of the remedy." This judgment has never been questioned here, and stands as the law of this state. The decision was made under a limitation statute like the one

now in force, and the case, in principle, is strikingly like '
the present case. See Laws of 1861, ch. 282.

Curran v. Witter, 68 Wis. 16, was an action upon a certificate of deposit, payable to the order of the depositor on
the return of the certificate properly indorsed. The action
was brought sixteen years after the date of the certificate,
and it had never been presented for payment until shortly before the action was commenced. It was held that the cause
of action accrued at the date of the certificate, and hence that
the statute of limitation had run against it. The opinion
concedes that courts of great authority have held that in
such a case the statute does not commence to run until the
date of demand, but this court was of the opinion that the
reasons in favor of holding that the statute commenced to
run from the date of the certificate accorded best with the
objects sought to be attained by the enactment of the statute of limitation. It was there said that such a certificate,
payable on demand, was the equivalent of a promissory
note so payable; and although in *Packard v. Bovina,* 24
Wis. 382, a town order was likened to a bill of exchange
or check, we think (if there is any difference) it is nearer
like a certificate of deposit or a promissory note payable
on demand, save the quality of negotiability.

Applying the doctrine of the above cases to the present
case, it must be held that the statute of limitations had
fully run against each of the orders in suit (or at least
against all but the order of May 14, 1881) on the expiration of six years from the date of the orders. It follows
that the statute had run against all but fourteen of the
orders in suit when the action was commenced, and that it
ran against the fourteen orders, or at least thirteen of them,
before the trial, which commenced November 30, 1887.

As to the order of May 14, 1881, the only one issued
after ch. 240, Laws of 1881, took effect as a law, we have

only to say, without deciding the point, that we are strongly inclined to the opinion that the effect of ch. 240, so far as the statute of limitation is concerned, is only to extend the period of limitation thirty days. Such was held to be the effect of a like statute upon a note payable at a given time after demand, in *Palmer v. Palmer*, 36 Mich. 487. The opinion, which is by Mr. Justice CAMPBELL, contains a very able presentation of that view of the law. We prefer, however, to leave that question open for further argument and deliberation when a case shall arise involving it.

Considering the amount involved in the present case, the number of orders in suit, the trifling sum for which the order of May 14, 1881, was issued, and the fact that no special point was made in the argument upon such order as distinguished from the others, we feel justified in applying to it the maxim *de minimis non curat lex*, and hence we make no distinction between it and the other sixty-seven orders against which the statute of limitations has certainly run.

It may be said that because fourteen of the orders were not barred by the statute when the action was commenced, as to those orders, or at least as to six of them which were not held invalid on other grounds, the judgment should have been in abatement only; thus leaving the plaintiff at liberty, after filing his claim with the town clerk of the defendant town to be laid before the board of audit, to commence a new action thereon. But it is manifest that such privilege would be of no benefit to the plaintiff. The defendant is now here pleading the statute of limitations as a defense to those orders, and the presumption is quite irresistible that in such new action the same defense would be interposed, and it would certainly be fatal to the action. It is idle to reverse this judgment as to those orders, when it is perfectly obvious that a trial would result in the same judgment. We think the case comes within the statutory

rule so often applied, to the effect that no judgment shall
be reversed or affected by reason of any error or defect in
the proceedings which do not affect the substantial rights
of the adverse party. R. S. sec. 2829.

By the Court.— The judgment of the circuit court is
affirmed.

STACY, Respondent, vs. BRYANT and others, imp., Appellants.

November 8 — December 4, 1888.

LIENS: LOGS AND TIMBER. *(1) Lien for supplies placed on sale. (2) Description of logs: Amendment.*

1. Under secs. 1, 2, ch. 469, Laws of 1885, the vendor of supplies to be
   used in a logging camp, and which were in fact used in such camp
   by the vendees in getting out logs, is entitled to a lien on the logs
   for the amount due, although the supplies, before being so used,
   were placed by the vendees in their store to be sold at a profit to
   their employees and others.

2. In an action to enforce a lien upon logs the description of the logs
   in the complaint and the petition for a lien may be amended to
   conform to the evidence which was admitted without objection,
   when it is evident that the defendant is not surprised by such
   amendment and no injustice is done thereby.

APPEAL from the Circuit Court for *Langlade* County.
The case is sufficiently stated in the opinion. The defendants *S. Bryant, R. W. Pierce,* and *O. H. Pierce* appeal
from a judgment in favor of the plaintiff.

For the appellants there was a brief by *Lynch & McCarthy,*
and oral argument by *Thomas Lynch.*

For the respondent there was a brief by *F. M. Guernsey,*
attorney, and *Gerrit T. Thorn,* of counsel, and oral argument by *Mr. Thorn.*

TAYLOR, J. The respondent commenced his action in
the circuit court against M. Miller and E. Neff, to recover

for a bill of feed, flour, butter, etc., sold by him to said Miller & Neff, about the 30th of January, 1886. The price of the goods sold, including freight paid by respondent, was $646.72; and in said action the respondent claimed a lien for the value of the goods sold upon a lot of saw-logs owned by the appellants, *Bryant, Pierce & Pierce*, and so the appellants were made parties to the action.

The respondent claims that the goods were sold to Miller & Neff upon the statement of Neff that he wanted the bill of goods for his lumber-camp, and that he sold him the goods as supplies for that purpose. The evidence on the part of the plaintiff shows that at the time said goods were sold and delivered to said Miller & Neff they were engaged in getting out and banking the logs of the appellants which were attached in this action. The evidence on the part of the plaintiff tends to prove that the goods were used by the mén and teams in the employ of Miller & Neff, while they were at work in cutting, hauling, and banking the logs of the appellants which were attached in this action. It is admitted by the learned counsel for the appellants that the bill of goods sold, which consisted of flour, feed, and butter, were supplies, within the meaning of secs. 1, 2, ch. 469, Laws of 1885, and if they were in fact used by Miller & Neff in feeding the men and teams employed by them in cutting, hauling, and banking the logs in question, and were sold by the respondent to said Miller & Neff for the purpose of being used in that way, then the respondent was entitled by law to a judgment in his favor, subjecting the said logs to the payment of said claim.

The defense the appellants made upon the trial was (1) that the said Miller & Neff at the time in question were merchants dealing in the kind of merchandise sold by the respondent to them, and that the respondent sold the goods to them, not for the purpose of being used by them in getting out the logs in question or any other logs, but to go into the store of said Miller & Neff, to be sold out at retail by them as any other goods kept by them for sale; and (2) that such goods, or the greater share of them, were sold by said Miller & Neff at retail from their store, to persons other than those then in their employ and engaged in cutting, hauling, and banking said logs of the appellants; (3) that a large part of said bill of goods was used in boarding and paying off men in the employ of Miller & Neff, not at the time engaged in work upon the logs in question.

Upon this appeal these questions of fact have been fully presented by the learned counsel for the appellants, and this court is asked to reverse the verdict of the jury on the ground that it is wholly unsupported by the evidence, or, if not wholly unsupported, that the great preponderance of the evidence is against the verdict. A motion to set aside the verdict was made by the appellants in the court below upon this ground, and denied by the trial court, and exceptions taken.

Upon a careful reading of the evidence we find that, while there is considerable direct evidence and much circumstantial evidence tending to establish the contention of the learned counsel for the appellants, we also find that the evidence of the respondent and that of Neff and Rockafeller, the book-keeper of Miller & Neff, certainly sustains the verdict of the jury. It is therefore clear that the learned circuit judge was bound to submit these questions of fact in the case to the consideration of the jury, and, the jury having found in favor of the case as made by the plaintiff's evidence, and the learned circuit judge having refused to set aside the verdict as against the evidence or as against the great preponderance of the evidence, according to well-established rules this court ought not to reverse the judgment upon that ground.

It is further claimed that the court erred in refusing to give the following instructions asked by the appellants:

"*First.* If you find that the supplies were bought by Miller & Neff for the purpose of putting them in their store and retailing them at a profit to their employees generally, and to the customers of their store at a profit, and the supplies were so sold, then the plaintiff is not entitled to a lien in this case." Refused by the court, and the defendants excepted. "*Second.* If you find that the supplies were bought and taken to the store of Miller & Neff in the usual way by them as merchandise, and were kept on exhibition for sale at a profit to their employees and others in the usual way, then the plaintiff is not entitled to a lien." Refused by the court, and defendants excepted. "*Third.* The plaintiff must prove the use to which the supplies were put, and that they were used as supplies within the meaning of the law." Refused by the court, and the defendants excepted.

The first instruction asked probably stated the law applicable to the case; but the refusal to give it, as well as to give the third instruction, was not error, because they had been substantially given by the learned circuit judge in his general charge, and it was unnecessary to repeat them at the request of the appellants. The second instruction asked was properly refused, as not presenting the law of the case. If the goods were sold by the plaintiff for the purpose of being used in the logging camp, and were in fact used in such camp by the vendees, the respondent would be entitled to his lien, although the vendees may have placed them in their store for sale before they were so used. The learned circuit judge instructed the jury that the respondent could only have a lien upon the logs of the appellants for the value of the supplies furnished to Miller & Neff which were actually used by them in paying for work of men and teams in getting out the logs, and in feeding the men and teams so employed by them in the logging business in getting out the logs of the appellants. Upon the other question he instructed the jury as follows: "If you find from a fair preponderance of the evidence that Miller & Neff, at the time these supplies were furnished by the plaintiff, were engaged in keeping a general store for the general purpose of trade; that they were also engaged in building a mill or repairing it, and in lumbering; that *Stacy*, the plaintiff, knew it, and furnished these supplies to Miller & Neff upon their own credit alone, and for the purpose of their general trade business,— you will find that the plaintiff is not entitled to any lien at all upon the property described in the complaint, and will use form No. 2 for your verdict." This instruction is substantially as requested by the appellants.

The case seems to have been fairly submitted to the jury upon the evidence, and, there being sufficient evidence in the case to sustain a verdict for the respondent, this court will not reverse it on appeal.

It is also alleged as error that the logs were not sufficiently described in the complaint or in the petition for a lien filed by the respondent and offered in evidence on the trial, and that the court erred in allowing the plaintiff to amend his complaint and petition for a lien after the evidence in the action had been received. The record shows that the following proceedings were had on the trial: "After the testimony of both plaintiff and defendant had closed, and before arguments were made to the jury, plaintiff, by his counsel, moved the court to amend the petition and claim for lien on the logs, which petition was filed May 20, 1886, so as to make the description of the logs described therein conform to the proofs taken and read as follows, to wit:" (Here follows a particular description of the logs upon which it is claimed the supplies furnished by the plaintiff were expended). The court allowed the amendment, and the defendants excepted.

The claim for a lien, and the original complaint, described the logs simply as "about 1,500,000 feet of pine saw-logs and timber, end-marked and stamped M. B." The appellants had answered to the complaint; and made no objection on the trial to the insufficiency of the plaintiff's complaint or to the introduction of his evidence, except that the appellants objected to the introduction of the petition for a lien, which the respondent, at the close of his testimony, offered in evidence. The objection was that the logs were insufficiently described therein. This objection was overruled, and the defendants excepted. After the plaintiff rested his case the appellants moved to nonsuit the plaintiff on the sole ground that he did not prove that his action was commenced within four months after a lien was filed. Under the circumstances it is evident that the appellants were in no way misled by the generality of the description of the logs in the complaint and petition for a lien, and there was therefore no error in allowing the amendment, as permitted by the court. That the petition for a lien may be amended is fully established by the decisions of this court. *Witte v. Meyer*, 11 Wis. 295; *Brown v. La Crosse C. G. L. & C. Co.* 16 Wis. 555; *Challoner v. Howard*, 41 Wis. 355; *White v. Dumpke*, 45 Wis. 454; *Halpin v. Hall*, 42 Wis. 176, 181; *Sherry v. Schraage*, 48 Wis. 93; *Huse v. Washburn*, 59 Wis. 414; *Jacubeck v. Hewitt*, 61 Wis. 96; *Edleman v. Kidd*, 65 Wis. 18, 23. Sec. 3339, R. S., requires the plaintiff to allege in his complaint a description of the property against which he claims a lien. This allegation of the complaint is amendable in the same manner as any other allegation, and, when the evidence is admitted without objection, the courts may amend it to conform to the proofs in any case when it is evident the defendant is not surprised by such amendment and no injustice is done thereby.

By the Court.— The judgment of the circuit court is affirmed.

McDonald, Appellant, vs. Bryant, Garnishee, etc., Respondent.

November 9 — December 4, 1888.

(1) Contracts: Modification: Part performance: Apportionment: Waiver of complete performance. (2) Reference: Compensation of referee: Stipulation.

1. By the terms of a written contract the defendants were to cut and haul to their saw-mill all the down timber and slashings on lands of the garnishee and manufacture the same into timber and shingles, and for all lumber so manufactured and safely piled in their mill-yard the garnishee was to pay them $6 per thousand feet. Defendants cut and hauled a large quantity of logs and put them in their pond, but, before any of them were sawed into lumber, their mill was burned. *Held:*

    (1) A finding of the trial court that the contract had not been modified so that the defendants should be paid a certain sum for getting out and hauling the logs, irrespective of sawing them into lumber, is sustained by the evidence, although it appears that the garnishee had made advances to aid in getting out the logs.

    (2) The contract was entire, and there could be no recovery *quantum meruit* for its part performance in getting out the logs.

    (8) The fact that the garnishee took possession of the logs more than a year after the defendants had abandoned them and were insolvent, does not show a waiver of complete performance of the contract.

2. Under a stipulation in a garnishment proceeding "that the referee herein on the trial of the issue against the garnishee shall receive $10 per day for his services as such referee, in lieu of any and all other fees or perquisites," it is *held* that the *per diem* compensation of the referee was not limited to the time actually occupied by the trial itself.

APPEAL from the Circuit Court for *Langlade* County. Garnishment. The principal facts are stated in the opinion. The plaintiff appeals from a judgment in favor of the garnishee.

Before the commencement of the trial the parties entered into the following stipulation: "It is hereby stipulated and agreed by and between the plaintiff and garnishee above named that the referee herein on the trial of the issue against the garnishee shall receive $10 per day for his services as such referee, in lieu of any and all other fees or perquisites, and that the amount of such fees may be taxed as disbursements in this case." The trial occupied seven days. Upon the taxation of costs the garnishee sought to tax the compensation of the referee for ten days, and the plaintiff objected to the allowance for more than seven days. The clerk taxed for ten days and, on motion for review, this taxation was affirmed by the court. The affidavits on behalf of the plaintiff set forth that in the negotiations concerning the referee's fees two propositions were made, (1) that the referee should have a *per diem* of $5 and charge both for trial and for making up the report, and (2) that the *per diem* should be $10 *for trial only*, and that to cover all charges; and that the latter was agreed upon and inserted in the stipulation.

For the appellant there were briefs by *Colman & Sutherland,* and oral argument by *Elihu Colman.* They contended, *inter alia,* that the garnishee had waived the conditions of the written contract as to the logging (1) by agreeing to advance money on the logging, (2) by making payments on the same, and (3) by taking possession of the logs. The conditions of a written contract may be waived by parol. Bishop on Cont. ch. 29; *Barton v. Gray,* 57 Mich. 622; *Delaney v. Linder,* 22 Neb. 274; *Ruege v. Gates,* 71 Wis. 634; 13 Pick. 446; *Cummings v. Arnold,* 3 Met. 488, 37 Am. Dec. 155; *Emerson v. Slater,* 22 How. 28; *Kennebec Co. v. Augusta Ins. & B. Co.* 6 Gray, 204; *Deshazo v. Lewis,* 24 Am. Dec. 769. Payment on contract is a waiver of agreement to pay only on completion, and a waiver of the contract. *Keller v. Oberreich,* 67 Wis. 282; *Woodworth v. Hammond,* 19 Neb. 215; *Aldrich v. Price,* 57 Iowa, 151; *Stylow v. Wis. O. F. M. L. Ins. Co.* 69 Wis.

224; *Button v. Russell*, 55 Mich. 478; *McFadden v. Wetherbee*, 29 N. W. Rep. (Mich.), 881. Possession of the logs by
the garnishee is a waiver of the contract, and estops him
from setting up the original contract. *Jones v. Pashby*, 35
N. W. Rep. (Mich.), 152; *Young v. Hunter*, 6 N. Y. 203.
The logs being in the possession of the garnishee at the
commencement of the garnishee action, he would be liable
under secs. 2752–2768, R. S., and plaintiff could recover
on *quantum meruit* even if there were no special contract
as to the price per thousand. *Taylor v. Williams*, 6 Wis.
363; *Pickett v. School Dist.* 25 id. 559; *Trowbridge v. Barrett*, 30 id. 661; *Bishop v. Price*, 24 id. 480; *Hayward v.
Leonard*, 7 Pick. 180. A party having voluntarily taken a
benefit under work done by another must respond *quantum
meruit*. 2 Parsons on Cont. 523; *Dermott v. Jones*, 2 Wall.
1; 23 How. 220. Equity will interpose in behalf of the
plaintiff in this action. The proceeding is an equitable one.
First Nat. Bank v. Knowles, 67 Wis. 373. An intention
that the compensation should depend on full performance
ought to be clearly expressed. 2 Suth. on Dam. 469; *Leonard v. Dyer*, 26 Conn. 177. The defendants were excused
from full performance because prevented by an act of God,
their mill having been burned without fault on their part.
Chase v. Barrett, 4 Paige, 148.

For the respondent there was a brief by *Lynch & McCarthy*, and oral argument by *Thos. Lynch*.

ORTON, J. The appellant commenced an action against
the defendants, Miller & Neff, and finally obtained judgment therein for the sum of $2,585.11, and in the mean
time garnished the respondent, who took issue by denying
all liability to the defendants, and the issue was submitted
to John E. Martin, Esq., as a referee, for trial. In February, 1885, it appears, the firm of Miller & Wright owned a
steam saw-mill, and the respondent garnishee owned pine-

lands in the vicinity, and they commenced a series of business transactions in respect mostly to logs and lumber advances and payments; and in May of that year Wright sold out his interest in the partnership property and business to E. M. Neff, who assumed all of his liabilities and contracts as a member of the firm. From that time Miller & Neff continued business transactions with the respondent, and to operate the steam saw-mill. The mill was run by the firm until January, 1886, and afterwards by Neff alone until July, when it was burned.

On hearing the evidence the referee stated an account between the defendants and respondent, with various appropriate findings which need not be specially noticed, and made the sum total of the defendants' account $21,575.56, and the sum total of the respondent's account of payments, etc., $19,502.11. On motion of the respondent the circuit court modified the report of the referee, and found that two large items of the defendants' account were not chargeable to the respondent garnishee. These two items deducted from the defendants' account, the defendants owe the respondent a balance of $3,116.31, instead of the respondent owing the defendants a balance of $2,073.45, as found by the referee, so that these two items only need to be considered.

The first one of $4,200, allowed to the defendants, arises from a certain written contract between the respondent and Miller & Wright, by their names, Mathew Miller and N. S. Wright, and under seal, dated February 25, 1885, by which Miller & Wright were to cut and haul to their saw-mill all the down timber and pine slashings on certain lands of the respondent, and all the slashings and windfalls that he might buy on other land, *and to manufacture the same into lumber and shingles* as the respondent might from time to time direct. For all the shingles of the grade of "Star A Star," which they should manufacture and deliver on the railroad track, and branded as directed, the respondent was to pay them $1.50 per thousand, payable monthly, but not more than fifty cents per thousand per day; *and for all the lumber so manufactured by the defendants out of said timber and mill, and safely piled in their mill-yard, the respondent was to pay them $6 per thousand feet.* All the timber not sawed into lumber, and that would not make shingles of the above grade, should belong to the defendants. The firm of Miller & Wright, and afterwards of Miller & Neff, made shingles of a large amount, and received payment therefor as charged in the mutual accounts and adjusted by the referee, and they cut and hauled, and put into their pond, 1,400,000 feet of logs to be sawed in their mill; but before any of them were sawed into lumber the mill was burned. In the mean time the respondent made advances to the defendants to aid them in getting out the logs, which were charged and adjusted in said accounts. In respect to these logs there was the principal controversy in the case. The defendants claimed that the written contract above set out had been modified and changed by subsequent agreement, to the effect that they should be paid at the rate of $3 per thousand for getting out and hauling the logs, irrespective of sawing them into lumber. On this question the parties and other witnesses testified, and the respondent unqualifiedly denied that any such change of the written contract had ever been made, or that it had ever been changed in any respect whatever. It is contended that the circumstances confirm this claim of the defendants and their testimony in that behalf, such as the payment from time to time of different sums somewhat proportionate to the logs so got out at the rate of $3 per thousand. But this is explained by the respondent that the defendants were short of means, and asked for advances on the contract, which were made as a mere favor, and that no price per thousand for getting out the logs was ever fixed or talked about, and that he was careful and endeavored not to make advances to exceed what would be safe on the whole contract. The referee found that the written contract had been so changed, and charged the respondent for getting out and hauling 1,400,000 feet of logs at $3 per thousand, making the sum of $4,200. The circuit court found otherwise, and that the written contract was entire, and not apportionable, and had never been changed or modified. We have examined the evidence, and we are inclined to agree with the circuit court on the question as an original proposition. It is a question, however, on conflict of evidence, and to some extent of credibility, and in such case we ought not to disturb the finding of the circuit court unless there is a very clear preponderance of the evidence against it, and such, in our opinion, is not the case. This pretext of a change of the written contract in this respect appears much like an afterthought to meet the new conditions caused by the burning of the saw-mill.

But in case the written contract had not been so changed, the learned counsel of the appellant contends that the contract itself is such that in equity it may be apportioned and the plaintiff recover for its part performance in getting out the logs, on the basis of a *quantum meruit*. If there ever was an *entire* contract, or one could be made, it is this one. It is only " after all the lumber [is] so manufactured by the [defendants] out of said timber and mill, and safely piled in [their] mill-yard," that the respondent "agrees to pay the [defendants] the sum of $6 per thousand feet." It is impossible to apportion it without making a new contract for the parties. The logs are left in the defendants' pond, and at great expense have to be taken to some other mill to be manufactured, or sold at great loss where they are, and it seems that such expense would likely exceed the entire contract price. The manufacture of the logs into lumber is the important and material stipulation of the contract, and its piling safely in the mill-yard is the event on which depended the payment of $6 per thousand feet, or the condition of such payment. We think it can be said that but for these conditions, the sawing and piling, the contract would not have been made. There can be no doubt that the plaintiff's right to recover anything on this contract depends upon its full performance according to its terms. *Warren v. Bean*, 6 Wis. 120; *Jennings v. Lyons*, 39 Wis. 553; *Koplitz v. Powell*, 56 Wis. 671; *Cook v. McCabe*, 53 Wis. 250; *Hoffman v. King*, 70 Wis. 372; *Keller v. Oberreich*, 67 Wis. 282; *Oakley v. Morton*, 11 N. Y. 25. The principle has become elementary, and authorities are not necessary on the question whether this contract is apportionable, for it is utterly impossible to apportion it in the condition in which the logs were left upon this part performance, and by paying any regard to the contract terms of payment.

It is contended that the respondent waived complete performance of the contract by taking possession of the logs. It seems that he took possession of the logs over a year after the defendants had abandoned them and were insolvent. The logs were his property, and he had a right to take possession of them and save himself from loss to some extent if he could.

The other item allowed as a credit to the defendants by the referee, and which was disallowed by the court, was of property mortgaged by Miller & Neff to the respondent to secure $1,500 for money borrowed, and which was taken possession of and sold by the respondent under the mortgage. The property was of the value of $925, and one year's interest of $64.75 was added to this amount by the referee, as if the property had been unlawfully taken or wrongfully converted. This loan and mortgage appear to have been independent of the other dealings between the parties, and not the subject of their mutual accounts. The referee found that the mortgage had been paid before the property was so taken and sold. The evidence on that question was in conflict, and the circuit court found that nothing whatever had been paid upon it, and that the mortgage debt was still a valid claim against the defendants, and deducted $989.75, the value of the property and said interest, from their charges against the respondent. We think that the circuit court found correctly that the mortgage had not been paid.

There may be some other items of the defendants' account disallowed by the court, but it is unnecessary to consider them, as the two already disposed of make the defendants largely in debt to 'the respondent. The amount of such indebtedness is not material. It is sufficient for this case that the respondent, as garnishee, is not indebted to the defendants in any sum whatever. We see no reason for revising the allowance by the clerk to the referee.

By the Court.— The judgment of the circuit court is affirmed.

BAXTER, RESPONDENT, vs. DAY and another, Appellants.

November 9 — December 4, 1888.

Parties: Interpleader.

Sec. 2610, R. S. (providing that a defendant against whom an action is pending upon a contract may apply for an order substituting in his place a person, not a party to the action, who makes against him a demand for the *same debt),* does not apply to a defendant sued for the purchase price of logs to which the persons sought to be substituted claim title adverse to that of his vendor, the plaintiff.

APPEAL from the Circuit Court for *Langlade* County. The following statement of the case was prepared by Mr. Justice CASSODAY:

November 18, 1886, the plaintiff purchased of Gabe

Bouck 160 acres of land described and took an ordinary land contract therefor. Subsequently the plaintiff sold to the defendants a certain quantity of pine saw-logs from said land. January 11, 1888, this action was commenced for the purchase price of said logs, which the defendants concede has not been paid. The only reason given for such nonpayment is that Hale and Shipley claim that they bought the logs of one Baker for value, and were the owners of the same; that the plaintiff never had any title or right thereto; that Hale and Shipley, by reason of such ownership, had demanded payment for such logs of the defendants. Upon affidavits and answer showing such facts, the defendants moved the court, February 7, 1888, for an order making said Hale and Shipley parties defendant for and in the place of these defendants; and that upon the defendants paying into court the amount claimed in the plaintiff's complaint, which they were ready and willing to do, they be discharged from all further liability in the action. Upon the hearing of that motion an order was entered denying the same, with $10 costs. From that order the defendants appeal.

The cause was submitted for the appellants on the brief of *Thos. Lynch*, and for the respondent on that of *W. F. White*.

CASSODAY, J. If the defendants were entitled to have Hale and Shipley made parties defendant in the place of themselves, then it was by virtue of sec. 2610, R. S., as amended by ch. 41, Laws of 1883. The clause of that section which may be urged as applicable with most plausibility is this: "A defendant, against whom an action is pending *upon a contract*, or for specific real or personal property, or for the conversion thereof, may, at any time before answer, upon affidavit that a person, not a party to the action, and without collusion with him, *makes against him a demand for the same debt* or property, . . . ap-

McGrath vs. The Village of Bloomer.

ply to the court for an order to substitute such person in his place, and discharge him from liability to either party, on his depositing in court the amount of the debt, or delivering the property or its value to such person as the court may direct; and the court may in its discretion make the order." This is not an action "for specific real or personal property, or for the conversion thereof." It is, however, an action "upon a contract." But in such an action the defendant has no right to such interpleader, unless "a person not a party to the action . . . makes against him a demand for the *same debt*." Hale and Shipley have made no claim to the contract price of the logs which the defendants agreed to pay the plaintiff. Their claim, if any, is based upon their alleged ownership of the logs. Their remedy, if any, is manifestly to replevy the logs, or in an action for their wrongful conversion. In neither action could they make "a demand for the same debt" which this action is brought to recover. The case is not, therefore, within the statute.

By the Court.— The order of the circuit court is affirmed.

McGRATH, Respondent, vs. THE VILLAGE OF BLOOMER, Appellant.

November 9 — December 4, 1888.

(1) Instructions to jury. (2) Defective sidewalk: Court and jury. (3) Special verdict. Discretion.

1. It is not error to refuse to give instructions the substance of which has been given in the general charge.
2. It is not error for the trial court to assume that an excavation several feet deep in the line of a sidewalk is a defect in the walk unless properly guarded.
3. The trial court may, in its discretion, submit for a special verdict questions material to the issues.

APPEAL from the Circuit Court for *Chippewa* County.
The facts will sufficiently appear from the opinion. The
plaintiff had a verdict for $700, and from the judgment
thereon the defendant appeals.

The cause was submitted for the appellant on the brief
of *C. D. Tillinghast*, attorney, and *Marshall & Jenkins*, of
counsel, and for the respondent on that of *D. Buchanan, Jr.*

Cole, C. J. This is an action for personal injuries sustained by the plaintiff in falling into an excavation on the
line of the sidewalk in the defendant village, which, it is
claimed, was not properly guarded to prevent accidents to
persons traveling on the walk. The plaintiff fell into the
excavation in the night time.

The first error assigned for a reversal of the judgment is
that the court below erred in its charge to the jury, and in
refusing instructions asked on the part of the defendant.
The charge of the court is lengthy, covering several pages
of printed matter, and, while a number of exceptions are
taken to it, yet we think it is unobjectionable. The instructions of the defendant were handed to the court after it
had concluded its charge to the jury. They may have been
refused for that reason. However that may be, we think
there was no error in refusing to give them. They relate
generally to the degree of care which a traveler must exercise in passing along the sidewalk in the night time. But
upon that point the charge is full and explicit. The court
told the jury, in substance, that if there was any want of
ordinary care on the plaintiff's part, which contributed to
his fall into the hole in the sidewalk, there could be no recovery, even though the village authorities were negligent
in failing to place a sufficient barrier at the place to prevent
accidents. This idea was pressed upon the jury, and the
meaning of the words "ordinary care" defined. The jury
were told that "ordinary care" meant such care as men of

ordinary prudence would exercise under like circumstances, and that if the plaintiff failed in the exercise of that degree of care in any measure there could be no recovery. There can be no doubt but that the jury were fully instructed upon the question of contributory negligence, and they found that the plaintiff was not guilty of any want of ordinary care which contributed to his fall into the hole near the sidewalk. Such being the case, it was not necessary to give further instructions upon that question, and error cannot be assigned on the refusal of the court to give them. The appellant's counsel is clearly mistaken in assuming that the question of ordinary care on the part of the traveler was excluded from the consideration of the jury. It was repeatedly stated in different forms in the charge that the slightest want of ordinary care on the part of the plaintiff would defeat a recovery. The court fairly submitted the question whether there was a sufficient barrier or guard put up at the hole to prevent a person exercising proper care from falling into it. It is true, the court assumed that such a hole, which the evidence showed to be several feet deep and quite large, was a defect in the walk if not properly guarded, and there can be no doubt about the correctness of that view of the law. Such a hole, if not guarded, would be eminently dangerous to life and limb, and would call for the exercise of most extraordinary vigilance and care on the part of a traveler to avoid falling into it in the night time. This is too obvious to require comment.

The next error assigned is the refusal of the court to grant a new trial. This point, we think, is not well taken. The case seems to have been fairly tried, and it is not claimed there was any error either in the admission or rejection of testimony. There was some conflict in the evidence as to whether a man of ordinary care and prudence would have seen the hole and avoided it; also whether the timber placed on the walk in front of the excavation constituted a sufficient barrier or protection. These were clearly questions of fact for the jury to determine upon the evidence. There is ample testimony to support the verdict, and it is impossible to say the court erred under the circumstances in not granting a new trial.

It is further claimed that the court erred in submitting certain questions to the jury for a special verdict. It was clearly discretionary with the court to submit questions material to the issues involved. The questions submitted were, first, whether there was any want of ordinary care on the plaintiff's part which contributed to the injury; whether the hole near the sidewalk, into which he fell, was properly protected by a sufficient barrier; whether the village authorities were chargeable with notice of this defect; and, finally, the question of damages. The answers to all these questions were in favor of the plaintiff.

Upon the whole record, we see no reason for disturbing the judgment. It is therefore affirmed.

By the Court.— Judgment affirmed.

<hr />

GOUGH, Appellant, vs. ROOT, Respondent.

November 9 — December 4, 1888.

Attorney and client: Compensation: Special contract: Court and jury.

In an action by an attorney for a balance claimed to be due for several distinct services, the defendant alleged a contract whereby, for all of the services except one, the plaintiff was to receive nothing unless successful, and that he was unsuccessful. On the trial it appeared that such alleged contract could have related to but one of the services rendered. *Held*, that it was error to instruct the jury that it was for them to determine to what services the contract, if made, applied.

Gough vs. Root.

APPEAL from the Circuit Court for *Chippewa County.*

The plaintiff is an attorney at law, and brings this action to recover compensation for professional services rendered by him for the defendant under the following circumstances:

In 1872 the defendant commenced an action against one Phillips in the circuit court, and in 1873 recovered judgment therein. An execution on the judgment was issued in 1874, by virtue of which certain lands were sold by the sheriff and bid in by *Root* for the amount of the judgment. *Root* thereupon satisfied the judgment of record. In 1877 the sheriff conveyed such lands to *Root*, pursuant to the certificate issued to him on the execution sale. The land remained in the possession of Phillips; and *Root*, being unable to obtain possession thereof, employed the plaintiff in 1881 to obtain a writ of assistance to put him in possession of the land. The writ was duly issued; but before the same was executed Phillips commenced an action to set aside the sheriff's deed as to one lot thereby conveyed, for certain alleged irregularities, and also on the ground that the lot in controversy was his homestead. A preliminary injunction was issued in that action, restraining the execution of the writ of assistance. *Root* thereupon employed the plaintiff to defend the action, and the plaintiff did so. Phillips prevailed in the action, and judgment was rendered therein, setting aside and vacating the sheriff's deed as to such lot. The plaintiff thereupon prepared a bill of exceptions in the case, at the request of *Root*, and obtained a settlement thereof by the circuit judge. The defendant then retained the plaintiff to take an appeal from the judgment against him and to argue the same in this court. The parties made a special contract in writing fixing the compensation of the plaintiff for his services on such appeal. The contract is as follows: "It is hereby agreed, by and between *Franklin Root*, party of the first part, and *Arthur Gough*, party of the second part, that the first party hereby agrees to pay the party of the second part $50 as fees for his services in taking an appeal to the supreme court in the case of Jackson Phillips against *Franklin Root;* said first party also to pay his own printing, and the expenses of the second party to Madison in case said first party desires the case to be orally argued." The plaintiff took the appeal, and at *Root's* request argued the cause in this court. The judgment of the circuit court was affirmed. 68 Wis. 128. The defendant *Root* then employed the plaintiff to procure the vacation of the satisfaction of the original judgment in *Root v. Phillips*, and to investigate the records in the register's office, to ascertain whether Phillips had any real estate upon which he might levy an *alias* execution issued on that judgment. The plaintiff rendered these services. Subsequently, the defendant and Phillips negotiated a settlement of the whole matter in controversy between them, and Phillips paid *Root* $500 in accordance with such settlement.

In his complaint the plaintiff admits the receipt of $110, paid him by the defendant on account of the aforesaid services, and claims a balance still due him of $135. The defendant alleges, in his answer, that he has paid the plaintiff $123.50 on account of such services. He also alleges that all of the above services, except those connected with the appeal to this court, were rendered under a special contract between the parties to the effect that if the plaintiff did not succeed in putting the defendant in possession of the lot in controversy he should receive nothing for his services; and that he failed so to get possession of the lot for defendant. He also alleges that he has overpaid the plaintiff $70, in excess of what he is legally bound to pay him for such services.

The trial resulted in a verdict and judgment for the defendant. A motion for a new trial was denied. The testimony and the rulings of the court on the trial are sufficiently stated in the opinion. The plaintiff appeals from the judgment.

Arthur Gough, appellant, in person.

John Randall, for the respondent.

The following opinion was filed December 4, 1888:

LYON, J. The principal questions litigated on the trial were whether the alleged contract that the plaintiff should receive nothing for his services unless he succeeded in obtaining possession for the defendant of the land in controversy in the action of *Phillips v. Root*, was actually made; and, if so, how much of the services rendered by the plaintiff is covered by such contract.

The services for which the plaintiff claims compensation in this action may be classified as follows: (1) Obtaining the writ of assistance; (2) defending the case of *Phillips v. Root;* (3) settling a bill of exceptions therein; (4) appealing that case to this court, and arguing the appeal; (5) procuring the vacation of the satisfaction of judgment in *Root v. Phillips;* and (6) examining records to ascertain what property was held by *Phillips* out of which the judgment in the last case might be collected. The written contract, set forth in the above statement of facts, fixed the compensation for services rendered in the appeal to this court at $50 and expenses. Such expenses were proved to be a little over $30. The undisputed evidence shows that the services of the plaintiff in procuring the writ of assistance were not included in such alleged contract. The defendant so testified, and there is no proof to the contrary. Manifestly, the services in setting aside the satisfaction of judgment in *Root v. Phillips*, and in the examination of the records as aforesaid, were not included in the alleged contract, for the reason that those services were rendered after it was settled by the judgment of this court that the defendant had no valid claim upon the land in controversy in *Phillips v. Root*, and, of course, had no reference to obtaining possession of that land for the defendant. Hence, the only services to which which that contract could relate were those rendered by the plaintiff in the action of *Phillips v. Root*, before it was appealed to this court. The testimony tends to show that the value of the plaintiff's services for which, in any view of the case, he is entitled to compensation, including his expenses on the appeal, exceeds the sum which the defendant claims to have paid the plaintiff on account of such services.

The circuit judge submitted to the jury the question as to whether the alleged contract was made, and, if made, to what services it applied, without any restriction or limitation whatever. Thus the jury were left free to find that such contract covered all the services of the plaintiff, except those rendered on the appeal. It is certain that the jury found the contract was entered into by the parties, and that it covered and included a portion, if not all, of the services for which, as we have already seen, the plaintiff is entitled to compensation, exclusive of those rendered on the appeal. Instead of instructing the jury, as he did, that it was for them to determine to what services the contract applied, the judge should have instructed them that it could only apply to services rendered in the action of *Phillips v. Root* before the appeal. For this error a new trial should have been granted. For these reasons, the judgment of the circuit court is reversed, and the cause will be remanded for a new trial.

By the Court.— Ordered accordingly.

The following opinion was filed February 19, 1889:   ·

LYON, J. The judgment of the circuit court herein was reversed December 4, 1888. On January 18, 1889, defendant's attorney served on the plaintiff notice of a motion for February 1, for leave to move for a re-argument of the cause. It is founded upon the affidavit of the defendant and his attorney, in which they attempt to excuse their failure to move for such re-argument within the time limited therefor by the rules of this court. The attempt is a signal failure. ·

Rule XX gave the defendant until January 3 to file his motion, and ten days thereafter in which to serve his argument thereof. Both he and his attorney must have known that this court had reversed the, judgment of the circuit court, very soon after December 4, and could have obtained a copy of the opinion or learned its contents in a very few days thereafter, and would have done so had they exercised reasonable diligence. The excuse is that there was diphtheria in defendant's family, and he and his attorney could not safely meet until too late to move for a re-argument. Defendant lived near the city of Chippewa Falls, and obtained his mail there, and it is sought by the affidavits to convey the idea to us that from December 4, 1888, for a period of more than thirty days thereafter, defendant was secluded at home and inaccessible to his attorney. It is proved that he was in that city several times during such thirty days, and hence the affidavits tend to convey a false impression.

Because of such unexcused laches, the motion is denied.

We take this opportunity to correct an error in the opinion herein to which our attention is called in the motion papers, but which does not affect the determination of the appeal. It is said in the opinion that the jury were left free to find that the contingent contract for services, alleged by defendant, covered all the services rendered by the plaintiff except those rendered on the appeal. This is an error. After instructing the jury as stated in the opinion, the court did say to them: "Still it could not go beyond the subsequent written agreement; to that time it might go." The infirmity in the instruction, even thus qualified, is, that it left the jury free to find (as they undoubtedly did) that the contingent contract covered the services of plaintiff in suing out the writ of assistance, which services the plaintiff testified were worth $59, and the value thereof was not controverted. The defendant himself testified that such services were not included in the alleged contingent contract. Had this sum been allowed the plaintiff, the verdict would necessarily have been for him in some amount.

It should be further observed that, after stating the above limitation upon the alleged contingent contract and after charging the jury at considerable length on certain of plaintiff's charges for services, the court returned to the consideration of the scope and extent of such contract, and again charged without limitation, thus: "As I said, you will determine whether there was a verbal agreement between the parties, and, if so, what it was *and how far-reaching in its effects.*" If not contradictory, the charge certainly had a tendency to mislead, and probably did mislead, the jury to the prejudice of the plaintiff. Hence the judgment was properly reversed for that reason, even though no positive error had been committed.

By the Court.— The motion is denied with $10 costs and clerk's fees.

MIDDLETON and another, Respondents, vs. JERDEE and another, Appellants.

November 10 — December 4, 1888.

False representations: Instructions to jury: Reversal of judgment: Immaterial error: Nominal damages.

1. In an action for false representations alleged to have been made to induce the plaintiffs to lease land from the defendants, an instruction that if the defendants in making the contract for the lease made positive statements as to the character of the land, etc., without knowing them to be true, and they were not true and were relied upon by the plaintiffs, then the plaintiffs could recover, is *held* fairly to imply that such statements must have been made for the purpose of inducing the plaintiffs to enter into the lease, and the failure expressly so to state will not work a reversal of the judgment where such instruction was immediately followed by others to the effect that there could be no recovery unless the false representations were made with intent to deceive.

2. Where the plaintiff recovers substantial damages upon one cause of action and merely nominal damages upon another, the judgment will not be reversed on defendant's appeal for an error relating only to the nominal recovery, if that recovery does not affect the question of costs.

APPEAL from the Circuit Court for *Rock* County.

The case is sufficiently stated in the opinion. The defendants appeal from a judgment in favor of the plaintiffs.

For the appellants there was a brief by *Rufus B. Smith,* attorney, and separate briefs by *Lamb & Jones,* of counsel, and the cause was argued orally by *F. J. Lamb* and *Rufus B. Smith.*

For the respondents there was a brief by *John M. Olin* and *Pinney & Sanborn,* and oral argument by *A. L. Sanborn* and *John M. Olin.* To the point that a positive statement of fact, made without knowing it to be true, is fraudulent, they cited, besides cases cited in the opinion: *Haycraft v. Creasy,* 2 East, 103; *Pawson v. Watson,* Cowp.

788; *Evans v. Edmonds*, 13 C. B. 786; *Grim v. Byrd*, 32 Gratt. 293; *Goodwin v. Robinson*, 30 Ark. 535; *Taylor v. Ashton*, 11 Mees. & W. 401; *Case v. Ayers*, 65 Ill. 142; *Woodruff v. Garner*, 27 Ind. 4; *Frenzel v. Miller*, 37 id. 2; *Hammons v. Espy*, 1 Wils. (Ind.), 536; *Foard v. McComb*, 12 Bush, 723; *Doyle v. Hort*, 4 L. R. (Irish), 661; *Webster v. Bailey*, 31 Mich. 36; *Beebe v. Knapp*, 28 id. 53; *Coleman v. Pearce*, 26 Minn. 123; *Brownlee v. Hewitt*, 1 Mo. App. 360; *Pomeroy v. Benton*, 57 Mo. 531; *Nugent v. C., H. & I. S. L. R. Co.* 2 Disney (Ohio), 302; *Bower v. Fenn*, 90 Pa. St. 359; *Parmlee v. Adolph*, 28 Ohio St. 10; *Davis, M. & Co. v. Betz*, 66 Ala. 206; *Atwood's Adm'r v. Wright*, 29 id. 346; *Waters v. Mattingly*, 1 Bibb, 244; *Snyder v. Findley*, 1 N. J. Law, 48; *Mitchell v. Zimmerman*, 4 Tex. 75; *Cabot v. Christie*, 42 Vt. 121; *Stone v. Denny*, 4 Met. 151; *Litchfield v. Hutchinson*, 117 Mass. 195.

TAYLOR, J.   This action was brought by the respondents to recover damages of the appellants for alleged false and fraudulent representations made by the appellant *Mons P. Jerdee*, who acted as agent of *Ole P. Jerdee*, in leasing to the respondents a farm belonging to said *Ole P. Jerdee*. The evidence shows that the lease was made by the respondents in January, at a time when the farm was covered with a foot and more of snow; that the plaintiffs had no knowledge of the real character of the farm previous to the time of making the lease; and that, although they went upon the farm on the day the lease was made with *Mons P. Jerdee*, the whole surface thereof was so deeply covered with snow that they could not tell how much was plow-land, nor could they tell anything about the character of the marsh land or plow-land; and they allege that they depended entirely upon the representation made by *Mons P. Jerdee* as to the quantity and character of the plow-land, as well as to the character and quality of the marsh land.

On the trial the plaintiffs gave evidence which tended to show that the quantity and quality of the plow-lands, as well as the quality of the marsh lands, were materially different from what they were represented to be by the defendant *Mons P. Jerdee;* and also showing that the real rental value of the farm was much less than the rent they had agreed to pay by their lease, and which they were in fact compelled to pay. They also show that they went upon the farm while the snow was still on the ground and before they could determine that the character of the farm had been misrepresented to them, and that when they discovered its real character it was too late for them to abandon it and take another farm for the season. On the trial the plaintiffs recovered a judgment against the defendants.

The only errors relied upon by the appellants on this appeal are such as relate to the instructions given to the jury by the circuit judge.

The appellants duly excepted to the following instruction given to the jury, viz.: "If you find that the defendant *Mons P. Jerdee*, in making the contract for the lease, made positive statements as to the character of the farm, the number of acres of plow-land, or the character of the marsh, or the number of acres of good marsh, and made such statements without knowing them to be true, and they were not true and were relied upon by the plaintiffs, then the plaintiffs are entitled to recover."

The appellants also excepted to certain instructions of the court as to the validity of what was spoken of on the trial as the chattel-mortgage clause in the lease, under which the defendants had seized certain property of the plaintiffs and threatened to sell the same for the payment of the rent reserved in the lease. The circuit court held that the tenants could revoke this clause at their pleasure, and that a seizure by the landlord of the tenants' property under this clause, after the tenants had notified him that

they revoked it, was a trespass. We do not deem it necessary to pass upon the correctness of the ruling of the
learned circuit judge upon this question in this case, as it
appears that the plaintiffs recovered but nominal damages —
six cents — for the alleged seizure of the tenants' goods
after such alleged revocation. If the respondents are entitled to hold their judgment for the substantial damages
awarded them by the jury resulting from the alleged false
and fraudulent representations made by the defendants in
regard to the character of the land leased by the plaintiffs
from the defendants, then such judgment will not be reversed because the judgment may have included in it the
six cents nominal damages awarded them for the seizure of
their property by the defendants, even though such seizure
may have been lawful. The rule *de minimis non curat lex*
applies, as the question of costs does not depend upon the
recovery of said six cents damages.

The criticism made by the learned counsel for the appellants upon the instruction above quoted, and to which
exception was taken, is that under it the jury might find in
favor of the plaintiffs although they should be of the
opinion that no fraud had been committed or intended by
the defendants or either of them in making such representations. It is insisted that no allegations are made in the
complaint upon which a recovery can be had upon proof
of such facts; and, if such allegations had been made in
the complaint, that it would not have constituted a cause
of action, for the reason that, all the negotiations for making the lease having terminated in the written lease, no
mere verbal statements made by the parties during such
negotiations can be relied upon as constituting a cause of
action upon contract, as the law holds that they are all
merged in the written contract or waived by the parties:
and that in order to recover in this action the plaintiffs
must show that the defendants made some fraudulent repre-

sentations for the purpose of inducing the plaintiffs to enter into the lease afterwards executed by them.

Upon this question there is no dispute between the learned counsel for the respective parties. Whether the learned counsel for the appellants have stated the law correctly in their criticism and contention, as above stated, it is wholly unnecessary to decide in this case. The plaintiffs have in their complaint clearly set forth the representations alleged to have been made by the defendants, and they allege that they were made by the defendant *Mons P. Jerdee* knowing the same to be false, and with the intent to induce the plaintiffs to enter into the lease, and that they relied upon the truth of such representations. It is probable that the instruction is not applicable either to the allegations in the complaint or to the evidence offered on the trial. From an examination of the evidence it appears to me that there is very little, if any, evidence to which the instruction is applicable. The complaint, and the evidence in its support given on the part of the plaintiffs, makes out a case of false representations made knowing them to be false; and I do not understand that the evidence of *Mons P. Jerdee* tends to show that he did not know the falsity of the representations made, if made as alleged by the plaintiffs.

The instruction excepted to is defective, if defective at all, in not further stating that the representations were made with the intent to induce the plaintiffs to enter into the lease. That the learned circuit judge understood that the instruction as given was equivalent to such instruction, is evident from the fact that he immediately followed it by an instruction which clearly embodied that idea. This instruction reads as follows, and was given at the request of the defendants, viz.: "There can be no recovery unless *Mons P. Jerdee* represented as true a material matter which he at the time knew to be false or did not have

reason to believe to be true, and made the representation
in such a way or under such circumstances as to induce a
reasonable man to believe that it was true, and it was meant
to be acted upon, and the plaintiffs, believing it to be true,
acted upon their faith in it, and by so acting sustained
damages." This latter instruction perhaps more clearly
presents the idea that the material statement made must
be made with an intent to induce the opposite party to
enter into the proposed contract than the first instruction.
We do not think the two instructions are so inconsistent
with each other as to have in any way misled the jury,
especially in view of the very clear manner in which the
learned circuit judge afterwards in his general charge submitted the case to the jury upon the case as alleged in the
complaint and as presented by the evidence on the trial.

The learned circuit judge, after stating to the jury the
substance of the complaint in the case and the answer of
the defendants, then adds: "If one person represents to another *as true that which he knows to be false*, and makes the
representation in such a way and under such circumstances
as to induce a reasonable man to believe that the matter
stated is true, and the representation is meant to be acted
upon, and the person to whom the representation is made,
believing it to be true, acts upon the faith of it and suffers
damage thereby, this is fraud sufficient to constitute an action for deceit." Then, after stating that expressions of
opinion as to what will occur in the future are not actionable, he says: "But if *Mons P. Jerdee* said there was fifty
acres of good marsh on this farm, and there was in fact only
fourteen, this statement, if he knew it to be false and he
made it to deceive the plaintiffs, would form the basis of an
action for fraud." "So, if he had said that the meadow
land on his farm had produced one hundred tons of good
hay per year which had been sold at seven dollars a ton,
and he knew such statement to be false, and he made it to

deceive, this would be a false and fraudulent statement."
"Every false affirmation does not amount to a fraud. To
constitute a fraud, a knowledge of the falsity of the representations must be shown to have existed in the minds of
the persons making them at the time such representations
were made. Material representations made by *Mons P.
Jerdee* to the plaintiffs, or either of them, when negotiating
with them for leasing the farm, of matters assumed to be
within his personal knowledge, are false and fraudulent in
a legal sense, if made with intent to deceive the plaintiffs,
if untrue, and are relied on by the plaintiffs to their damage, although *Mons P. Jerdee* did not know them to be
untrue."

Although exceptions to most of these instructions were
taken on the trial, none of them are relied upon as errors
in this court. These instructions are certainly as favorable
to the defendants as the law and the evidence in the case
would warrant. The last instruction above quoted is substantially the same as the one given at the request of the
defendants and above referred to, and their correctness is
fully sustained by the decisions of this and other courts.
Cotzhausen v. Simon, 47 Wis. 103; *McClellan v. Scott*, 24
Wis. 81; *Risch v. Von Lillienthal*, 34 Wis. 250; *Miner v.
Medbury*, 6 Wis. 295; *Bird v. Kleiner*, 41 Wis. 134; *Wells
v. McGeoch*, 71 Wis. 196, 225-231; *Davis v. Nuzum*, 72
Wis. 439: and numerous other cases from other courts,
cited in the brief of the respondents. The last instruction
is in all material respects like the one excepted to by the
defendants, and which they allege is erroneous. The only
difference is that in the last it is expressly stated that the
representation must be made with intent to deceive, and in
the first the idea that the statement must be made with intent to deceive or to induce the plaintiffs to enter into the
lease is clearly implied. The language of the instruction is
"that if you find that the defendant *Mons P. Jerdee*, in
making the contract for the lease, made positive state-

ments," etc. We think it is fairly implied from this language that the statements made in such case would necessarily be made for the purpose of inducing the plaintiffs to
enter into the lease, and so are brought within the rule contended for by the learned counsel for the defendants. But,
if there be doubt about the real construction which this instruction should receive, we are very clear that, under the
pleadings, the evidence in the case, and other instructions
given concerning the correctness of which there is no question made, the defendant were not prejudiced by it, and the
judgment should not be reversed for that reason.

By the Court.— The judgment of the circuit court is
affirmed.

PALMER, Respondent, vs. HAWES, imp., Appellant.

November 10 — December 4, 1888.

*Promissory notes: Corporations: Collateral security: Pledge of corpo-
rate stock of officer of corporation: Negligence: Depreciation: False
representations.*

1. Where shares of stock in a corporation are pledged as collateral security to a note, the payee of which is a director and officer of
such corporation, the negligence of the payee in the performance
of his duties as such director and officer, whereby the stock depreciated or became worthless, is no defense to an action by him on
the note. So *held* where the defense was sought to be interposed
by one who indorsed the note at the time of its execution and who
owned a part of the stock pledged.

2. In such action it was alleged that some months after the stock was
so pledged the plaintiff had falsely represented to the indorser
that the affairs and business of the corporation were in good condition, when in fact they were being so carelessly and wastefully
managed by the plaintiff and the other officers that the stock was
rapidly depreciating; that the indorser relied on such representations and was thereby lulled into inactivity and rest concerning
her liability on the note when, but for such representations, she
might have secured herself from loss. *Held*, that such facts did
not constitute a defense.

APPEAL from the Circuit Court for *Rock* County.

The following statement of the case was prepared by Mr. Justice CASSODAY:

, The complaint is, in effect, upon a promissory note bearing date January 20, 1886, made by the defendant Williamson, and indorsed at the same time by the appellant, *Cornelia J. Hawes,* for $7,000, due one year after date, with interest at eight per cent., and which note was duly presented for payment at the maturity thereof, but the same was not paid, and was thereupon protested for nonpayment, and the appellant duly notified thereof; that the plaintiff is the lawful owner and holder thereof, and has been ever since January 20, 1886; and that no part thereof has been paid, etc.

The appellant separately answered, and for a defense relies wholly upon that portion of the answer of which the following is the substance: That the note was given by Williamson in payment for capital stock in the Wisconsin Shoe Company, a corporation organized under the laws of this state, doing business in Janesville; that, at the time of such giving and indorsing the note, Williamson delivered to the plaintiff 100 shares of such stock, of the par value of $100 each, as collateral security to the said note; that, at the time of such indorsement, the appellant owned in her own right 180 shares of such stock, and has ever since; that the plaintiff holds thirty shares thereof as collateral security to said note; that said company was January 20, 1886, and for a long time prior thereto had been, engaged in the manufacture and sale of boots, shoes, etc., at Janesville; that the capital stock of said company was $80,000; that the plaintiff was a stockholder, director, and vice-president of said corporation, January 20, 1886, and for a long time prior thereto and since; that it was the duty of the plaintiff, as such director and officer, to superintend and supervise and manage the affairs of said company, and to

protect the interests of all the stockholders therein; that
the appellant, in indorsing said note, relied upon said collateral security so furnished by Williamson to pay said
note, and upon the plaintiff, as such director and officer, to
see that said stock was maintained at a par value, so as to
be ample security,—all of which was well known to the
plaintiff; that the plaintiff, together with the other officers
and directors of the company, so carelessly, negligently,
and wrongfully managed, controlled, and supervised the
affairs of the company that the stock was thereby depreciated in value until it is almost if not entirely worthless
and has no market value whatever; that the stock and
such security have thus become worthless and of no value
through the negligence and carelessness of the plaintiff;
that the plaintiff failed and wholly neglected to perform
his duty as an officer of the company, to the great damage
of the appellant and to the entire loss of the 100 shares of
stock so held by him as collateral; that in July, 1886, the
plaintiff falsely represented to the appellant that the company was doing a good business and its affairs were in a
good condition; that at the same time such affairs were
being managed in a careless, negligent, and wasteful manner by the plaintiff and the other officers thereof, and the
stock was then being rapidly depreciated in value through
such careless and negligent management; that the appellant
relied upon such representations, and was thereby lulled
into inactivity and rest concerning any liability on said
note; that the appellant would have been able and would
have secured herself against loss by reason of such indorsement, but for such false representations so made by the
plaintiff; that from that time on the company continued to
lose money, and the assets of said company continued to
be lost through the carelessness and negligence of the
plaintiff, until said stock became almost if not entirely
worthless; that if the plaintiff had managed the affairs of

the company in a careful and prudent manner the 100 shares so held by him from Williamson would more than have paid said note, and there would have been no necessity to resort to the thirty shares from the appellant; but, as it is, she has lost said thirty shares.

To such defense the plaintiff demurred on the ground that the facts stated were insufficient to constitute a defense. There were other grounds of demurrer, and to other portions of the answer, but none of them were relied upon on this appeal. The court sustained the demurrer, with leave to the appellant to amend her answer within twenty days, on payment of $10 costs. From that order *Mrs. Hawes* appeals.

For the appellant there was a brief by *Fethers, Jeffris & Fifield*, and oral argument by *M. G. Jeffris*. They contended, *inter alia*, that it was a good defense that the collateral security became worthless through the negligence of the plaintiff. *Plant's Mfg. Co. v. Falvey*, 20 Wis. 200; *Charter Oak L. Ins. Co. v. Smith*, 43 id. 329; *Marschuetz v. Wright*, 50 id. 175; *Cullum v. Emanuel*, 1 Ala. 23; *Hurd v. Spencer*, 40 Vt. 581; *Strange v. Fooks*, 9 Jur. (N. S.), 943. The false representations made by the plaintiff operated as a discharge of the surety. *Baker v. Briggs*, 8 Pick. 122; *Carpenter v. King*, 9 Met. 511; *Harris v. Brooks*, 21 Pick. 195.

For the respondent there was a brief by *George Sutherland*, attorney, and *Winans & Hyzer*, of counsel, and oral argument by *John Winans*.

CASSODAY, J. It is alleged in the answer that the note was given to the plaintiff in payment for capital stock of the company, which was of par value at the time. Since it was indorsed by the appellant before it was so delivered to the plaintiff, there could be no question but what the indorsement was based upon a good and valuable consideration paid at the time. It is alleged in the answer that the plaintiff took the 100 shares of such stock from the maker and the thirty shares from the appellant, to hold as collateral security to the note. As such custodian of such stock, the plaintiff undoubtedly owed several duties to the appellant. He was required to safely guard such custody. There is no pretense that he did not. The only other thing he could do, apparently, was to sell the stock and apply the proceeds thereof in payment on the note. But no request nor agreement to that effect is alleged. Without such request or agreement the plaintiff was under no obligation to' sell. *Harris v. Newell,* 42 Wis. 690 *et seq.; Gardner v. Van Norstrand,* 13 Wis. 543; *O'Neill v. Whigham,* 87 Pa. St. 394; *Monroe Co. v. Otis,* 62 N. Y. 89; Cook on Stocks, § 476. The mere decline in the value of the stock while so being held by the plaintiff is no ground of defense. *Ibid.*

It is alleged, in effect, that some six months after the plaintiff obtained such stock he falsely represented to the appellant that the affairs and business of the company were in good condition, whereby she was lulled into inactivity and rest concerning her liability on the note. But that is no ground for defending against the note, nor of any action against the plaintiff, since the appellant parted with nothing on the faith of such representations.

But the ground most relied upon as a defense is the alleged carelessness and negligence of the plaintiff as a director and officer of the corporation which issued such stock so held as collateral, whereby the same became substantially worthless. There are cases where general allegations of carelessness and negligence in the performance or nonperformance of some specific act have been held good on demurrer. *Young v. Lynch,* 66 Wis. 514. But it is very doubtful whether such general allegations, without reference to any specific act, as here, constitute actionable negligence. *Cahill v. Layton,* 57 Wis. 614; *Pratt v. Lincoln Co.* 61 Wis.

66; *Williams v. Williams,* 63 Wis. 72; *Stone v. Oconomowoc,*
71 Wis. 159; *Brown v. Phillips,* 71 Wis. 254.   Assuming,
for the purposes of this case, however, that the allegations
of carelessness and negligence, though general, are nevertheless in that respect sufficient, still we are unable to hold
that they are available to the appellant as a defense in this
action.   The difficulty with such defense is in attempting
to hold such director and officer responsible for such alleged
misconduct directly to an individual stockholder.   While
the careless and negligent conduct of directors and officers
of a private corporation may injuriously affect the respective stockholders, yet they are primarily answerable for
such conduct to, through, or on behalf of such corporation,
and not directly to an individual stockholder.   Thus it has
been held by this court, upon careful deliberation, that a
stockholder of such corporation cannot maintain an action
in his own name against the officers thereof for the fraudulent act or waste of the corporate property, unless the corporation or its officers, upon being requested, refuse to
prosecute such action, or unless it appears that such a request would be useless.   *Doud v. W., P. & S. R. Co.* 65
Wis. 108.   An averment of such requisites is essential to
the pleading; otherwise it is bad on demurrer.   *Ibid.*   The
authorities in support of such ruling are numerous.   *Hersey
v. Veazie,* 24 Me. 9, 41 Am. Dec. 364; *Smith v. Hurd,* 12 Met.
371, 46 Am. Dec. 690; *Hodges v. New England Screw Co.* 1
R. I. 312, 53 Am. Dec. 624; *Brown v. Vandyke,* 8 N. J. Eq.
795, 55 Am. Dec. 250; *Greaves v. Gouge,* 69 N. Y. 154;
Hawes v. Oakland, 104 U. S. 450; *Conway v. Halsey,* 44 N.
J. Law, 462; *Abbott v. Merriam,* 8 Cush. 588.   While such
stockholder has an indirect remedy for such official misconduct by, through, or against the corporation, in behalf of
all stockholders, yet he has no right of personal action for
damages on account thereof against such individual director
or officer, notwithstanding such conduct may have had

the effect of depreciating the value of his stock. *Smith v. Hurd, supra; Conway v. Halsey, supra.* The reasons for such rulings are obvious. Such directors and officers are the trustees and agents of the corporation, and not in legal privity with the respective stockholders. Such misconduct primarily concerns and affects the corporation; and although a stockholder may be indirectly affected in the manner indicated, yet it necessarily affects all stockholders alike, and is therefore a matter in which all are equally concerned.

For these and other reasons which might be given we are forced to the conclusion that the answer fails to state facts sufficient to constitute a defense.

By the Court.— The order of the circuit court is affirmed.

CARROLL, Respondent, vs. LITTLE, Appellant.
CARROLL, Appellant, vs. LITTLE, Respondent.

November 12 — December 4, 1889.

Appeal to S. C.: Findings: Review of evidence: Sufficiency of exceptions: Printed case: Partnership: Accounting: Interest.

1. Where the violation by one partner of the partnership agreement has caused great confusion and conflict in the accounts, findings of a referee and the trial court, in an action for an accounting, against allowing items in favor of such partner, will not be disturbed unless contrary to the clear weight of evidence.

2. In such a case, it not being shown that an item for which the appellant was entitled to credit was overlooked by the referee in footing up the various sums in the statement of an account, the court declines to disturb the account stated.

3. An exception "to the allowance of each and all the items mentioned in Schedule A, and the charging of each of them to the defendant," where such schedule contains a large number of items many of which are not disputed, is not sufficiently specific, and the court will not review the evidence thereon.

4. The printed case herein containing a mass of immaterial testimony, but as to the points in dispute being so lacking in fullness and accuracy that resort must be had to the manuscript bill of exceptions, this court declines to review the alleged errors.

5. The allowance of interest in taking partnership accounts depends upon the circumstances of each particular case. Upon the facts in this case, there having been no agreement between the parties as to allowing or charging interest prior to the ascertainment of balances, it is *held* that the plaintiff should have interest on the amount found due him from the commencement of the suit.

APPEAL from the Circuit Court for *Rock* County.

Action for the dissolution of a partnership and for an accounting. The facts will sufficiently appear from the opinion. Both parties appeal from the judgment.

For the plaintiff there were briefs by *A. Hyatt Smith*, attorney, and *M. G. Jeffris*, of counsel, and oral argument by *Mr. Jeffris*. They argued, among other things, that the defendant should have been charged with interest on the sum of money which he had in his hands belonging to the firm from the day they ceased to do business to the date of the report of the referee. *Crabtree v. Randall*, 133 Mass. 552; *Gridley v. Conner*, 2 La. Ann. 87; *Hite v. Hite*, 1 B. Mon. 177–180. Indeed, he should be charged with interest from the time he received the money and, contrary to the partnership agreement, deposited it in his own name or converted it to his own use. *Dunlap v. Watson*, 124 Mass. 305; *Washburn v. Goodman*, 17 Pick. 519; 1 Suth. on Dam. 534, 596; *Honore v. Colmesnil*, 7 Dana, 199; *Taylor v. Young's Adm'rs*, 2 Bush, 428; *Stoughton v. Lynch*, 2 Johns. Ch. 210. Interest should be allowed to the plaintiff on the sum that was due him from the firm from the time the partnership ceased to do business until the date of the referee's report. See authorities cited above. A partner is entitled to interest on the advances to the firm. *Morris v. Allen*, 14 N. J. Eq. 44; *Ex parte Chippendale*, 4 DeG., M. & G. 36; *In re German Mining Co.* 19 Eng. L. & Eq. 591.

For the defendant there was a brief by *John Winans* and *Smith & Pierce*, and oral argument by *C. E. Pierce.*

Cole, C. J.   These are cross-appeals from the same judgment.   The parties formed a partnership for the purpose of buying and selling live-stock, sheep, and swine, etc.,— the profits to be shared equally.   The partnership commenced about October 10, 1876, and continued to February 24, 1879, when they ceased doing business by mutual consent.   The action is for a dissolution of the partnership, and for an accounting as to the partnership transactions.   The cause was referred to a referee, to hear, try, and determine.   On the hearing of the testimony the referee allowed some items in the account of the respective parties which the other side objected to and claims should not have been allowed; while he disallowed other items, which each claimed he should have been credited with.

The referee, among other things, found that the parties agreed that their bank-account should be kept at the First National Bank of Janesville, in the name of the plaintiff. *Carroll;* that all funds of the firm should be deposited there, and that the plaintiff should draw all the checks, and keep the books of the partnership transactions; that the defendant, *Little,* should attend to the shipments and sales of cattle; that the plaintiff's bank-book with said bank was adopted as the bank-book of the firm, and that the firm deposits which were made in the said bank were entered upon this book; that no other firm books were kept except this bank-book, check-books, and auction-book. The referee also found that in making sales of the property of the firm the defendant did, contrary to the partnership agreement, appropriate to his own use large sums of the money of the firm, part of which he deposited in his own name in the bank, without the knowledge of *Carroll,* and that this caused great confusion and conflict in the accounts, rendering it difficult to ascertain how much of said money was restored to the firm and how much still remained in the possession of the defendant. These findings as to the manner in which the accounts of the firm were kept, and of the failure of the defendant to deposit in the bank all firm money which came into his hands from the sales of cattle, are conclusively established and warranted by the evidence. The true state of the accounts could have been readily ascertained had the defendant reported all sales of firm property and made deposits of firm money as he should have done. If he is not credited in the accounting with all items which should have been allowed him, or items have been disallowed which he should have had credit for, it is attributable mainly to his own fault in not observing the agreement. Under the circumstances, no claim should be allowed in his favor which is not established by satisfactory proof; and, where the findings of the referee and of the circuit court are against allowing any item in his favor, such findings will not be disturbed unless it appears they were contrary to the clear weight of evidence. Plausible arguments or ingenious inferences cannot destroy them, nor can they be set aside on mere probabilities. The application of these general remarks will be apparent as we proceed in the examination of the case.

We will first consider the appeal of the defendant; and as to that appeal it is objected that he has taken no such exception to the findings of the referee and of the circuit court as will enable us to review the points he makes. He claims that he was erroneously charged with certain items in the accounting, and failed to receive credit for other items, so that he was brought in debt to the firm, when he should not have been on a fair and just accounting. There are two schedules annexed to the report of the referee, each stating a great number of items of debit and credit which the referee found each partner should be charged

with. The defendant excepted to the report of the referee,
and renewed his objections in the circuit court to so much
of the report as reads as follows: [then quoting two or
three pages of the report, including the schedules]. Of
course such an exception furnishes no information as to
what items or charges in the schedules the defendant objects to, and amounts to nothing more than a general exception. As the counsel on the other side observes, the
defendant might as well have excepted to everything the
referee found and to everything he did not find, as to except in this manner. How could counsel on the other side
know what item or charge in the account was controverted,
or what item or credit it was claimed had been improperly
disallowed upon the evidence. The practice adopted was
a most vicious one, and contrary to the decisions of this
court, which hold that we will not, on a general exception,
attempt to review the evidence or findings unless they are
entirely erroneous. That cannot be said of the findings
here, for most of the items in the schedules are undisputed
and indisputable. Therefore an exception " to the allowance of each and all the items mentioned in Schedule A,
and the charging of each of them to the defendant," can
have no other effect than a general exception to the schedule or statement of the account. It would be intolerable
practice for the court to be required to review evidence
upon such an exception. But, were the exceptions ever so
good and specific, we still would not undertake the labor of
reviewing the evidence upon the case which has been prepared for us; for the case contains hundreds of folios of
testimony immaterial so far as any question arising on this
appeal is concerned, and it is not full and accurate as to
the items in dispute. Resort must be had to the manuscript bill of exceptions to ascertain the real facts in respect
to these items. Consequently we shall not attempt to go
over the alleged errors in the items charged the defendant

or disallowed him in the accounting, both for the reason that the printed case is imperfect, and because there are no sufficient exceptions taken to enable us to review the evidence in respect to these items, under the rules which have been adopted by this court on that subject. So we affirm, without further remark, the decision of the circuit court, which found that the defendant had, when the firm ceased doing business, the sum of $4,586.73 belonging to the partnership and for which he must account. This disposes of the defendant's appeal, by affirming that part of the judgment from which his appeal was taken.

As to the plaintiff's appeal, the court below found and adjudged that he recover against the defendant judgment for the sum of $3,288.35, the balance of money due him from the firm, and also the sum of $649.19 for his share of the profits, making in the aggregate the sum of $3,937.54, with interest on said balance of $3,288.35 from the date of the report of the referee to the day of the entry of judgment. It is insisted that the plaintiff was entitled to interest on the amount due him from the firm from the date it ceased doing business, February 24, 1879. It is said that the money has been wrongfully withheld from the plaintiff from that time. We are unable to concur in that view as to allowing interest. We think the plaintiff should have interest on the amount found due him from the commencement of the suit, August 18, 1884. This is the more equitable rule, and is more in harmony with our decisions in respect to allowing interest on unsettled accounts. It is said the amount which the defendant owed the firm could have been computed and ascertained the very day it ceased doing business, therefore he ought to be charged with interest from that date. But many items in the partnership account were in dispute, and have remained so to this time, and the account may be said to have been an unsettled one. In *Gilman v. Vaughan*, 44 Wis. 646, this rule is laid down:

that, generally, interest will not be allowed upon partnership accounts until a balance has been struck on settlement between the parties, unless the parties have otherwise agreed or acted in the management of their business. It is not found that there was any agreement as to allowing or charging interest on partnership accounts prior to the ascertainment of the balances; and, as the balance here was uncertain, we think it more equitable to allow interest from ' the commencement of the suit. No unbending rule can be laid down on this subject, but each case must stand much on its own facts and circumstances. "The allowance or disallowance of interest in taking partnership accounts depends upon the circumstances of each particular case, and cannot be governed by any fixed rules." Note 1, to sec. 182, Story on Partn. So, in this case, we consider it equitable to allow the plaintiff interest from the commencement of the suit, and the judgment of the circuit court must be modified in that regard.

The plaintiff insists that the court erred in not charging the defendant with the two items of $299.60 and $112, received in October, 1876. This money was derived from the sale of stock which *Carroll* owned. The defendant admits the receipt of the money, and that it belonged to *Carroll*, but says he paid it over to him. This the plaintiff denies; but there is a conflict of testimony, and we cannot disturb the finding of the court in reference to it. The same remark may be made about giving the defendant credit for $245.82 under date of November 9, 1876, and also a credit for $621 under date of December 5, 1877. The evidence in regard to these credits is considerably confused, and it is impossible to say that the finding of the referee and court is contrary to the clear weight of testimony.

As to the charge of $317.43, allowed the defendant for the pasturage of the firm stock, the defendant testified that the understanding was that he should have pay for keeping it. It is not pretended there was any such understanding as to the stock the plaintiff kept. It is true, the plaintiff denies that there was any understanding that either should charge or be paid for pasturage of the firm stock. But here again is a conflict of testimony, which was practically decided against the plaintiff on the hearing, and the account must stand in that particular.

It is further claimed that there was error in not giving the plaintiff a credit for $102.56, under date of April 16, 1878. It is said the plaintiff gave a list of items of his own money that came from rents which were deposited for the benefit of the firm, and which was used by it in its business. We have examined the manuscript bill of exceptions and the bank-book, and find that such a deposit was proven; but whether this item was overlooked by the referee in footing up the various sums we cannot say, and, as error must be shown, we conclude that the account must stand as stated.

But the judgment of the circuit court must be reversed, and the cause remanded with directions to that court to allow the plaintiff interest from the commencement of the suit to the entry of judgment.

By the Court.— It is so ordered.

CRICHTON, Appellant, vs. CRICHTON, Respondent.

November 13 — December 4, 1888.

DIVORCE. *(1, 2) Cruelty: Drunkenness: Evidence. (3) Condonation: Revival of injuries. (4) Appeal to S. C.: Alimony.*

1. The testimony on behalf of the plaintiff in this case — tending to show, among other things, that the defendant is an habitual drunkard, and, when intoxicated, is violent, profane, and grossly inde-

Crichton vs. Crichton.

cent in his language and conduct; that he has frequently applied vile epithets to his wife and their daughters, and has threatened to kill her and them; and that on several occasions he has pushed her about in anger, handling her roughly — is *held*, if true, to show a case of cruel and inhuman treatment, within the meaning of subd. 5, sec. 2356, R. S.

2. Though the testimony of the parties is in conflict, and there is corroborating testimony on each side, the unimpeached testimony of the three children of the parties in support of the allegations of cruelty and habitual drunkenness is *held* to create such a clear preponderance of evidence against the findings of the trial court that its judgment denying a divorce is reversed.

3. After condonation, former injuries will be revived by subsequent similar misconduct.

4. Questions of allowances, alimony, or division of estate, will not be considered by this court until they have been passed upon by the trial court.

APPEAL from the Circuit Court for *Rock* County.

The facts are sufficiently stated in the opinion.

William Street, for the appellant, to the point that mental suffering, cruel and wicked words, and threats of personal violence are a sufficient cause for divorce within the meaning of our statute, and that actual personal violence need not be shown, cited *Freeman v. Freeman,* 31 Wis. 235, 248–50; *Pillar v. Pillar,* 22 id. 658; *Wheeler v. Wheeler,* 53 Iowa, 511; *Warner v. Warner,* 54 Mich. 492; *Berryman v. Berryman,* 59 id. 605; *Whitmore v. Whitmore,* 49 id. 417; *Sackrider v. Sackrider,* 60 Iowa, 397; *Friend v. Friend,* 53 Mich. 543; *Kelly v. Kelly,* 18 Nev. 49; *Carpenter v. Carpenter,* 30 Kan. 712; *Avery v. Avery,* 33 id. 1; *Eygarth v. Eygarth,* 16 Pac. Rep. (Ore.), 650; *Sylvis v. Sylvis,* 17 id. (Col.), 912; *Palmer v. Palmer,* 45 Mich. 150; *Whitacre v. Whitacre,* 31 N. W. Rep. (Mich.), 327; *Williams v. Williams,* 67 Tex. 198; *Wagner v. Wagner,* 34 Minn. 441; *Lyle v. Lyle,* 86 Tenn. 372.

For the respondent there was a brief by *Winans & Hyzer,* and oral argument by *John Winans.*

LYON, J. The action is for a divorce brought by the plaintiff against the defendant, her husband. The alleged grounds for the divorce are cruel and inhuman treatment and habitual drunkenness. This appeal is taken by the plaintiff from a judgment of the circuit court denying the divorce. The question to be determined is whether either of the alleged grounds is established by the proofs.

The principal witnesses who testified on behalf of the plaintiff are herself and three adult children of the parties, two daughters and a son. These are the only surviving children of the marriage. The parties were married in 1856, and have resided in Rock county ever since. The testimony of the plaintiff and of the three children of the parties is to the effect that the defendant is, and has been for several years past, an habitual drunkard, and that when intoxicated he is violent, profane, and grossly indecent in his language and conduct; that at numerous times during the past few years he has called his wife a bitch and a whore, accusing her, without any apparent grounds therefor, of having had illicit sexual intercourse with several men, using at the same time very profane language, and has also many times in her presence applied the same vile epithets to their daughters; that during those years he has frequently threatened to take the life of his wife; that once, when intoxicated, he was so violent that his wife was compelled to leave their room, going to the room of their daughters, where he followed her, broke open the door, and brandished a butcher-knife, threatening to kill her, and asking her to kill him with it; that on one occasion a drunken fellow was stopping at their house, the wife was in bed upstairs, and he told the fellow to go up there, and used language which conveyed to his wife and children the idea that he desired him to go to bed with her, saying that the old woman was good enough for him; one of the daughters met the fellow at the top of the stairs, and compelled him

to return; that a short time before she left her husband.
which was in July, 1885, he pointed a pistol at their son, in
her presence, and menaced him with death; that on several occasions he pushed her about in anger, handling her
roughly, the last time shortly before she left him; in short,
that his conduct towards his wife was so outrageously
brutal and inhuman that it became impossible for her
longer to live with him as his wife.

The foregoing is but an outline of the testimony of the
wife and children, but the statement is sufficient to show
the manner in which, as they testified, he habitually treated
her. Some other testimony was given on the trial by o_her
witnesses in behalf of the plaintiff, which tends to corroborate some of the statements of herself and children. It is
not necessary to state here this corroborating testimony.

If the testimony of the plaintiff and the three children of
the parties is true, it proves a case of cruel and inhuman
treatment of the plaintiff by her husband, within the meaning of the statute. R. S. sec. 2356, subd. 5. This is so
within the somewhat restricted rule of *Johnson v. Johnson*,
4 Wis. 135; for surely the conduct of the defendant, as testified to by his wife and children, rendered it unsafe and
improper for his wife to live and cohabit with him. This
is the test of the statutory offense laid down in that case.
A broader rule (and in my opinion the better rule) on the
subject is laid down in *Freeman v. Freeman*, 31 Wis. 235,
by Dixon, C. J. It is there said: "Everybody knows that
the conduct of the husband towards the wife may be such,
even without any personal violence, actual or threatened,
as to render her marriage state intolerable, and, from mere
mental suffering and physical debility so produced, to make
it utterly impossible for her to perform the duties which
are expected of a wife, and which otherwise she would be
able and anxious to perform." In more homely language
it has been said elsewhere that there are many ways by

Crichton vs. Crichton.

which a cruel and brutal husband may break his wife's heart and make her life a burden to her, without breaking her head or committing any actual personal violence upon her. The turpitude of the husband and the anguish of the wife may be as great in one case as in the other; and so the statute makes it ground for a divorce whether the cruel and inhuman treatment be practiced by using personal violence or *by any other means*. The same testimony, if true, also makes a case of habitual drunkenness.

The defendant testified in his own behalf and denied most of the statements relating to his abuse of his wife and his drunkenness, testified to by her and their children. He also introduced some corroborating testimony of a general character, to the effect that the witnesses, who were his neighbors, had not seen him intoxicated many times, and were not cognizant of the alleged ill treatment of his wife. Yet there is much in the testimony of the defendant's witnesses, and some statements in his own, which tend to some extent to corroborate the testimony of the plaintiff and her witnesses. Indeed, the drift of the testimony of defendant's witnesses is to palliate his conduct and soften the plaintiff's grievances, rather than to controvert the statements of herself and children.

And here it may be observed that the members of defendant's family had much better means than other persons had of knowing the relations between the parties and the defendant's conduct towards his wife. Cruelty to a wife is, no doubt, usually practiced in the privacy of home, where no outside witnesses are present; frequently by husbands whose manners in their intercourse with the public are gentle and unexceptionable. He can crush the very life out of a helpless and confiding wife, but shrinks from appearing before the world in his true character. This is the moral cowardice of brutality, and is usually accompanied by physical cowardice as well.

The plaintiff and her children testified to a plain, straight-forward history of the married life of the parties, and to numerous instances of wrong and outrage on the part of the defendant towards his wife, running through a series of years, until she left him in July, 1885, and there is no material discrepancy in their statements. A perusal of this testimony leaves a strong conviction upon our minds that it is true, and a careful examination of the testimony of the defendant and his witnesses fails to shake that conviction. If we assume that the parties are equally credible, and hence that the testimony of the defendant offsets that of the plaintiff, and also that the corroborating testimony on each side balances that on the other side (which assumptions are very favorable to the defendant), we have the unimpeached testimony of the three children in support of the allegations of cruelty and habitual drunkenness on the part of the defendant. It is quite true that the learned circuit judge had the advantage of seeing those witnesses and hearing them testify, but we cannot conceive how this fact can possibly justify a total disregard of the testimony of the children. Our conclusion is that there is a clear and satisfactory preponderance of evidence in favor of the plaintiff, and that the findings of fact upon which the judgment rests, and the judgment, should not be upheld. We are always reluctant to disturb a judgment based on mere propositions of fact, but in this case we feel compelled to do so.

It appeared on the trial that some six or seven years before the trial the plaintiff left the defendant because of his cruelty and abuse, but that after a short absence, at his urgent solicitation and promises to do better, she returned to their home. In view of this fact, something was said on the argument about a condonation of all previous wrongs on his part. Condonation is not absolute, but only conditional, forgiveness. "It is subject to the implied condition

Crichton vs. Crichton.

that the injury shall not be repeated and that the other party shall thereafter be treated with conjugal kindness." *Phillips v. Phillips*, 27 Wis. 252. After condonation, former injuries will be revived by subsequent similar misconduct, although of a slighter nature. In the present case, the misconduct of the defendant after his wife returned to him was even greater and worse than before she left him. Hence, in determining the question of divorce, the court should consider all of the cruel and inhuman acts of the defendant established by the proofs, as well those committed before she returned to him as afterwards.

We cannot on this appeal consider the questions of allowances, alimony, or division of estate. These must first be determined by the circuit court.

The judgment of the circuit court must be reversed. The defendant must be charged with the taxable costs in this court. The cause will be remanded with directions to the circuit court to grant a divorce from the bonds of matrimony and to direct the payment by the defendant to the plaintiff of proper allowances, including reasonable attorney's fees for taking this appeal and arguing the same in this court; also of reasonable alimony, to be fixed by the court, or, in lieu of alimony, a division of the defendant's estate between the parties, in the discretion of the court.

By the Court.— Ordered accordingly.

TUCKER, Appellant, vs. LOVEJOY, Respondent.

November 13 — December 4, 1888.

Limitation of actions: Pleading: When cause of action accrued.

A complaint alleging that between September 1 and December 1, 1878, the plaintiff rendered services for the defendant which were reasonably worth $4,000, "which sum became due some time in September, 1884," is *held*, on demurrer, to show that the cause of action accrued as early as December 1, 1878. The allegation that the sum became due in 1884 is a mere conclusion of law, unsupported by the facts stated, and must be disregarded.

APPEAL from the Circuit Court for *Rock* County.

The following statement of the case was prepared by Mr. Justice TAYLOR as a part of the opinion:

This is an appeal from an order of the circuit court sustaining a demurrer to the plaintiff's complaint. The following is a copy of the complaint so far as is necessary to determine the question whether the demurrer was well taken: "And now comes the plaintiff above named, by Henry L. Buxton, his attorney, and complains and alleges (1) that between the 1st day of September, 1873, and the 1st day of December, 1873, this plaintiff and one Eric McArthur, and their agents and servants, rendered services for the defendant, at his request, in finding, surveying, making estimates of, and entering in the lists of unsold lands in the land offices of the United States of America situated at Wausau, Wisconsin, and Menasha, Wisconsin, and the land office of the state of Wisconsin situated at Madison, Wisconsin, the lands which are more particularly described and set forth in the schedule hereto attached, marked 'Exhibit A,' and made a part of this complaint; (2) that the defendant promised to pay the plaintiff and the said McArthur what the said services were reasonably worth; that this plaintiff was to receive one half of said amount,

---

Tucker vs. Lovejoy.

---

and the said McArthur one half thereof; (3) that said services were reasonably worth the sum of $4,000, which sum became due some time in the month of September, 1884, but on what particular day in said month this plaintiff is unable to state."

The remainder of the complaint consists of allegations as to the assignment of the interest of Eric McArthur in the alleged claim to the plaintiff, and of notice of such assignment given to the defendant before the commencement of this action, and prayer for judgment.

The defendant demurred upon two grounds: (1) That the complaint does not state facts sufficient to constitute a cause of action: (2) that the action was not commenced within the time limited by law, and the said defendant refers to subd. 3, sec. 4222, and sec. 4227, R. S., which he claims limit the plaintiff's right to sue. The demurrer was sustained by the circuit court, and from the order sustaining the same the plaintiff appeals to this court.

For the appellant the cause was submitted on the brief of *Henry L. Buxton.* The facts in this case are almost identical with those in the case of *Tucker v. Grover,* 60 Wis. 240, and the complaint was framed after the complaint in that case. The complaint alleges that in September, 1884, the plaintiff demanded payment of the sum which the services were worth. "Before that time the claim rested in the void contract which the defendant refused to carry out, and in an interest in the land he had verbally agreed to convey, and it became a money demand only when the defendant refused to so convey and the plaintiff made a demand for the money." *Tucker v. Grover,* 60 Wis. 244, and cases cited.

For the respondent there was a brief by *Wm. Ruger,* attorney, and *John Winans,* of counsel, and oral argument by *Mr. Ruger.*

TAYLOR, J.   The demurrer was sustained by the court below because it appears on the face of the complaint that the cause of action stated in the complaint accrued more than six years before the commencement of the action.   It is claimed by the learned counsel for the respondent that it appears on the face of the complaint that the cause of action stated in the complaint accrued as early as the 1st day of December, 1873, and it also appears on the face of said complaint that the action was not commenced until after the 8th day of May, 1884, eleven years after the same accrued.   We think that, considering the facts alleged in the complaint, the contention of the learned counsel for the respondent is sustained, and the demurrer was well taken. The legal conclusion deduced from the facts stated is that the plaintiff was entitled to pay for his services when they were fully performed, in the absence of any agreement fixing the day of payment at some other time, and no demand was necessary in order to maintain an action for the value of such services.   *Dill v. Wareham*, 7 Met. 438, 448; *Earle v. Bickford*, 6 Allen, 549, 551; *Sturgis v. Preston*, 134 Mass. 372.

But it is alleged by the learned counsel that the last allegation above quoted, viz., "that said services were reasonably worth the sum of $4,000, which sum became due some time in September, 1884, but on what particular day in said month this plaintiff is unable to say," is a sufficient allegation to rebut the legal conclusion which follows the previous allegations of fact.   We think the contention of the counsel for the respondent, that this is simply an allegation of a conclusion of law, and not of fact, must be sustained.   It is the statement of facts in a complaint which constitutes the cause of action, and when those statements fail to show a cause of action they cannot be helped out by alleging a conclusion of law.   The complaint having stated facts which show that his demand was due in December, 1873, these facts cannot be neutralized simply by an allegation that his demand was not due until several years thereafter. Suppose the plaintiff's action had been upon a promissory note which was alleged to have been made December 1, 1873, and became due by its terms on the 1st day of January, 1874, and the action had been commenced January 1, 1884, could the plaintiff have avoided a demurrer to the complaint that the statute of limitations had barred his claim, by inserting a general allegation that the money on the note became due on January 1, 1880? We think it very clear he could not. To avoid the statute he would have to allege facts showing that some other contract had been made which had postponed the payment of the note to some other time than that stated in the note itself.

Upon demurrer, the general allegation of a conclusion of law must be wholly disregarded. This is the rule as established by this court in the following cases, cited by the counsel for respondent: *Babb v. Mackey*, 10 Wis. 371, 376; *Howell v. Howell*, 15 Wis. 55, 61; *Franklin v. Kirby*, 25 Wis. 501; *Teetshorn v. Hull*, 30 Wis. 162, 167; *Hazleton v. Union Bank*, 32 Wis. 34, 43; *Lutheran Evangelical Church v. Gristgau*, 34 Wis. 328, 334; *Butler v. Kirby*, 53 Wis. 188, 192; *Forcy v. Leonard*, 63 Wis. 353, 360; *Pratt v. Lincoln Co.* 61 Wis. 62, 66; *State v. Egerer*, 55 Wis. 527, 529; *Feiten v. Milwaukee*, 47 Wis. 494, 497; *Lawrence v. Janesville*, 46 Wis. 364–371; *Eaton v. Gillet*, 17 Wis. 435; *Baxter v. State*, 17 Wis. 588, 589.

The demurrer was properly sustained.

By the Court.— The order of the circuit court is affirmed, and the cause is remanded for further proceedings.

SEVERSON and another, Appellants, vs. PORTER, Garnishee, etc., Respondent.

November 13 — December 4, 1888.

Voluntary assignment: Partnership doing business in names of individual partners: Fraud: Reservations of homesteads and personal property as exempt.

1. The business of a copartnership may be transacted without the use of a firm name, and it may be agreed that the names of the individual partners or any one or more of them shall be used and bind the firm.
2. A voluntary assignment by a firm doing business in the names of the individual partners, treating all their property as firm property and all debts as firm debts, is not fraudulent as to creditors although they did not know of the copartnership.
3. The reservation of the homesteads of partners in an assignment by the firm does not render such assignment void.
4. In an assignment by a firm a reservation to each partner of personal property (specifically described in the inventory) claimed to be exempt from execution, and which had, by prior agreement, been allotted to each in severalty and actually separated from the partnership assets, does not invalidate the assignment.

APPEAL from the Circuit Court for *Rock* County.

Garnishment. The principal action was brought against Joseph K. P. Porter. The garnishee, *Isaac G. Porter*, is the assignee named in a voluntary assignment executed by Joseph K. P. Porter, William B. Porter, and Joseph B. Porter, as partners, for the benefit of their creditors. The garnishee answered denying all liability as such. The plaintiffs took issue upon such answer. Upon the trial the circuit court found the facts in substance as follows:

In 1869 Joseph K. P. Porter, who then owned and occupied a farm of about 317 acres in section 5 of the town of Porter, Rock county, took his son William B. Porter into partnership with him, and the two carried on the business of farming on said premises until 1879, when they took into the partnership Joseph B. Porter, another son of said Joseph K. P. Porter. The firm then engaged in the general business of farming and tobacco growing, which they carried on until January 22, 1887, when the assignment above mentioned was made. This business was conducted without any partnership or firm name, but "the names of any one or more of said members of said partnership were used and signed as and for the name of the firm, and bound and made liable the said firm and all the three members thereof as partners." Joseph B. Porter, when he became a member of the firm, was admitted therein as an equal partner and became joint owner of all the partnership property equally with the other two.

From the times respectively when the two firms above mentioned were formed, all the debts owing by the firm and the members thereof, in whatever name contracted, were the debts of the firm. The firm last formed became liable for the payment of all such debts, and all of the personal property owned by the partners became the property of the firm and continued to be the property thereof until the execution of the assignment, January.22, 1887, except as hereinafter mentioned.

The title to the land above mentioned was in Joseph K. P. Porter, and he was the owner thereof until the assignment was executed. Prior to 1879 such land was subject to the incumbrance of a mortgage for $6,200, and the firm made payments to apply on the interest on said mortgage during the continuance of the partnership.

In October, 1883, the firm purchased about 320 acres of land in sections 8 and 16 in said town of Porter, the title being taken in the name of William B. Porter and Joseph B. Porter. The purchase price of said land was not found by the court, but it was found that the firm paid in cash $300, gave a note for $700 signed by all the members of the firm in their individual names and by one T. C. Rich-

ardson as accommodation maker, and that the balance of
the purchase money was secured by mortgage of the premises. After such purchase the business of the firm was
carried on upon both farms, and upon other lands leased
by it.

In January, 1887, the firm became financially embarrassed and unable to pay its debts. The members of the
firm then divided among themselves the personal property,
stocks, and farming implements owned by the firm, " to a
sufficient extent so that each owned in severalty sufficient
of said property to make up the amount of exemptions
allowed by law for each of said partners; " and thereafter,
on January 22, 1887, they executed to *Isaac G. Porter*,
the garnishee herein, the general assignment in question.

This action was commenced in April, 1887, upon notes
given in 1885 and 1886 for the balance of an account due
the plaintiffs for lumber sold and delivered. The said account was opened in 1871 against Joseph K. P. Porter, and
had continued to run in that name down to the time the
notes were given. After the formation of the partnership
in 1879, William B. Porter and Joseph B. Porter had each
got lumber from the plaintiffs, which was charged in the
account against their father, and had made divers payments
on said account. The notes, though signed by Joseph K. P.
Porter individually, were really obligations of the firm, the
lumber having been purchased and used in the business of
the firm. The plaintiffs did not know that the Porters
were in partnership, and had never inquired as to how they
were doing business.

After the assignment was made, each of the partners
claimed and retained the personal property exempt from
sale on execution selected as aforesaid; Joseph K. P. Porter
claimed as a homestead from the farm first above mentioned
forty acres of land upon which he had resided with his
family for many years; and William B. Porter, with the

consent of the other partners, selected a homestead from the farm second above mentioned consisting of forty acres upon which, prior to and at the time of the assignment, he had been residing with his family. At the time said second-mentioned farm was purchased by the firm, in October, 1883, there was owing to the plaintiffs on their account about $600. The inventory filed by the assignors contained a description of all the property assigned, and also of the homesteads and the personal property which the assignors intended to reserve.

The court further found that the assignment was made in good faith and without any intent to defraud or hinder or delay creditors.

As conclusions of law from the foregoing facts the court found, in substance, that the assignment was valid; that the garnishee was not liable as such to the plaintiffs; and that the partners were entitled to the exemptions of personal property and to the homesteads selected by them. From the judgment entered accordingly in favor of the garnishee the defendants appealed.

John M. Whitehead, for the appellants, contended, *inter alia*, that the separate property of J. K. P. Porter must be applied primarily to the payment of his separate debts. *Lord v. Devendorf*, 54 Wis. 491, 495; *McNair v. Rewey*, 62 id. 167, 171. Being in debt, J. K. P. Porter could not give his property to his sons to the injury of his creditors. Upon the same principle that persons not partners *inter se* are held to render themselves liable as such by holding themselves out to be partners, it will be held that where the members of a firm have allowed one of their number to appear as the owner of or having full power of disposition over the property owned by the firm, an innocent third party thereby led into dealings with such apparent owner has the same rights as if the latter were really the owner of such property. By the assignment J. K. P. Porter has given a preference to the creditors of a firm, alleged to have been composed of himself and his two sons, over his individual creditors; and the assignment is therefore void. Laws of 1883, ch. 349; *Keith v. Armstrong*, 65 Wis. 225, 228; 2 Bates on Partn. sec. 825. The real estate purchased in October, 1883, was purchased with partnership funds for partnership purposes, and must be treated as partnership property. *Bird v. Morrison*, 12 Wis. 138, 153; *Fowler v. Bailey*, 14 id. 125, 129; 1 Bates on Partn. sec. 281; *Fairchild v. Fairchild*, 64 N. Y. 471, 477. The real estate belonging to the partnership must be treated as mere personalty and not subject to the usual incidents of real estate. *Paige v. Paige*, 71 Iowa, 318; *Mallory v. Russell*, id. 63; *Page v. Thomas*, 43 Ohio St. 38; *Shanks v. Klein*, 104 U. S. 18; *Collumb v. Read*, 24 N. Y. 505; 1 Bates on Partn. sec. 290. W. B. Porter was not entitled to select a homestead from the partnership real estate. *In re Sauthoff*, 16 Nat. B. Reg. 181; *Phipps v. Sedgwick*, 95 U. S. 3; *Edwards v. Entwisle*, 2 Mackey (D. C.), 43; *Bishop v. Hubbard*, 23 Cal. 514; 1 Bates on Partn. secs. 564, 566.

I. C. Sloan, for the respondent, argued, among other things, that as all of the property of the assignors was assigned, if they claimed more as exempt than the law allows them that was a question to be determined by the circuit court in exercising the power conferred upon it by ch. 80, R. S., in supervising the proceedings of the assignee. Plaintiffs have mistaken their remedy in attempting to garnish the assignee. If all the property of the assignors passed by the assignment, then the assignee held it upon trusts declared, and he was not subject to garnishment as having any property belonging to the assignors. Whether W. B. Porter was entitled to a homestead in the farm conveyed to him and his brother in 1883, was a question to be decided by the circuit court upon a petition by the creditors for an order directing the assignee to sell that portion of the farm claimed as such homestead. Whether W. B. Porter could claim such homestead or not depends very largely upon the intention with which that land was purchased.

COLE, C. J. If the assignment in this case is valid, the judgment of the circuit court discharging the garnishee must be affirmed. The assignment transferred to the assignee all the property of the assignors of every kind. It is objected that the assignment was made with the intent to hinder and defraud creditors, but there is an entire absence of testimony to support such an assumption. On the contrary, the evidence shows beyond all doubt that the assignors acted in the utmost good faith in making the assignment, and did what they deemed was best for their creditors. They treated all the property as partnership property, and considered all debts contracted in the management of the business as the debts of the company. The testimony is clear, positive, and uncontradicted that the father, Joseph K. P. Porter, in 1869, entered into a partnership with his son William B. to carry on a general business of farming and raising tobacco. They conducted this business until 1879, when Joseph B., the other son of Joseph K. P., became a member of the firm, and joint owner of all the partnership property, and equally liable for all the debts of the old firm. And it was understood and agreed among themselves that all the old debts and subsequent debts, whether contracted in the name of one or two or all of the partners, should bind the copartnership and be deemed partnership liabilities. Unless we disregard all the evidence in the case, these facts must be deemed conclusively established. The object of Joseph K. P. Porter in entering into this partnership was, as he testifies, to aid his sons, to give them a "good chance" to acquire property; consequently, all the personal property owned by him, or the money contributed by his sons to the business, was treated as the property of the firm. It appears that the business was conducted and carried on with-

out any firm name, and that the names of any one or more
of the members were signed as and for the firm, and represented it. This was the intention of the parties, and there
was no legal objection to the business being conducted in
that manner; for if, by agreement among themselves, the
individual names of the partners, or any one of them, was
to be used and bind the firm, the obligations would be good
against the copartnership. In this case it appears that notes
were sometimes signed by each partner, or by two of them,
or by one alone; but still the intention was to contract a
firm debt. They could, doubtless, adopt any name, and
agree that it should represent the firm in its business transactions. This is a familiar and well-settled principle of the
law of partnership. See Parsons on Partn. 124 *et seq.* Says
this author: "When parties agree to transact business
jointly, or under an agreement to share in the profits, the
name or firm which they use is arbitrary and conventional.
They may use the name of both, or of one of them alone,
or any distinct designation by which all will be included
and bound as if their names were used."

We do not perceive any legal objection to the assignment. It is said there are reserved in the instrument certain exemptions in favor of the assignors, and that this
renders the assignment void. We think this position
untenable. As we have observed, all the property of the
assignors, of every kind and nature, is expressly transferred
and set over to the assignee for the payment of debts, "except such as is exempt from levy and sale under an execution by the laws of the state, the same being more fully
and particularly enumerated and described in the inventory." In the inventory of assets certain personal property
is specified as that claimed by the individual assignors as
and for their exemptions. There are also homestead exemptions specified, which are reserved as and for a homestead
by Joseph K. P. Porter and William B. Porter.

It has been decided in a number of cases that such a

reservation in an assignment of partnership property did not render the assignment void. *First Nat. Bank v. Hackett,* 61 Wis. 336; *Bates v. Simmons,* 62 Wis. 69; *McNair v. Rewey,* 62 Wis. 167; *First Nat. Bank v. Baker,* 68 Wis. 442; *German Bank v. Peterson,* 69 Wis. 561; *Cribben v. Ellis,* 69 Wis. 337. So far as the homestead is concerned, that is secured to the debtor by the statute, and a clause reserving what the debtor could not assign without the consent of his wife would surely not invalidate the instrument. See *Batten v. Smith,* 62 Wis. 92. But the court held that each of the assignors was entitled to the exemption of the personal property respectively selected by him. This decision was based upon a finding, which is fully sustained by the evidence, that in the forepart of January, 1887, and before the assignment was made, the partners divided the personal property of the firm to a sufficient extent, so that each owned in severalty an amount equal to the exemption allowed him by law. This will bring the case within the decision in *O'Gorman v. Fink,* 57 Wis. 649, where it is held that one partner with the consent of the others may claim a separate exemption out of partnership property where there has been a severance of such joint property. At all events, it is quite clear the reservation would not avoid the assignment; and we see no good reason for denying each partner his statutory exemption under the circumstances. The firm property was actually selected and separated from the partnership assets before the assignment was in fact made. The fact that such exempt property was included in the inventory, as it was, should not be deemed a waiver of the exemption, nor does it afford any reason for holding the assignment void. If the assignors have claimed and taken personal property of greater value than the law allows each to hold, the court could direct the assignee to recover the excess and apply it in payment of debts. The statute gives the court ample power to make all necessary orders for the execution of the trust. Sec. 1693, R. S. Whatever property is not exempt, or which the firm owned, or any member of it was interested in, was expressly assigned for the payment of the creditors of the assignors. If there should be any question in the case as between the creditors of the individual members and the creditors of the firm, as suggested by the respondent's counsel, it would be competent for the court to marshal the assets and apply them in an equitable order by paying partnership debts out of partnership assets, and individual debts out of private or separate property. But we think the proof shows clearly that all the assets and all the creditors are assets and creditors of the firm.

It is said that Joseph K. P. Porter had no right to give his property to his sons to the injury of his individual creditors. We fail to find any evidence in the case that he has done so.

It seems unnecessary to remark that, if the parties dealing with the firm were ignorant of the fact that a copartnership existed between Joseph K. P. Porter and his sons, this cannot affect the assignment, nor change the rights of the creditors. The evidence shows that the assignee was not liable as garnishee to the plaintiffs in this action, and there was no error in giving judgment in his favor.

By the Court.— The judgment of the circuit court is affirmed.

WILL OF O'HAGAN.

November 13 — December 4, 1888.

WILLS: *Attestation in presence of testator: Presumption from signatures: Findings of fact: Specificness.*

1. The signatures of witnesses to a will, following an attesting clause stating that they signed in the presence of the testator, raises a strong presumption of that fact, which will be overcome only by

clear and satisfactory proof to the contrary. So *held* in a case where the witnesses, while verifying their signatures, had no recollection of attesting the will.

2. A finding by the trial court that the will was executed by the testator in the city of B. on the day it bears date, and was at the same time subscribed by the attesting witnesses in his presence, is sufficiently specific, and it was unnecessary to find at what place in the city the testator executed and the witnesses subscribed the instrument, or whether the testator could and did leave his house on the day of its date.

APPEAL from the Circuit Court for *Rock* County.

The case is stated in the opinion.

Cornelius Buckley, for the appellant, to the point that the attestation clause at best raised a mere presumption of the due execution of the will, and that there should be positive evidence of that fact, cited *Swett v. Boardman*, 1 Mass. 258; *Dewey v. Dewey*, 1 Met. 349; *Hogan v. Grosvenor*, 10 id. 54; *Butler v. Benson*, 1 Barb. 527, 534–5; *Abbey v. Christy*, 49 id. 276; *In re Will of Van Geison*, 47 Hun, 5; *Downie's Will*, 42 Wis. 66.

For the respondent there was a brief by *J. G. Wickhem*, and oral argument by *B. M. Malone*.

LYON, J. *Daniel Riordan*, the respondent in this appeal, presented to the county court, for probate, an instrument in writing purporting to be the last will and testament of Peter O'Hagan, deceased, in which he devised and bequeathed all of his estate, real and personal, to his wife, Letitia O'Hagan. The instrument purports on its face to have been executed in the form required by the statute, and was attested in due form by J. A. Sherwood and P. Johnson. Probate of the instrument was opposed by the appellant, *Joseph A. O'Hagan*, a son of the testator by a former wife. The county court admitted the instrument to probate as such last will. The appellant, *Joseph A. O'Hagan*, thereupon appealed to the circuit court. After a hearing in that court, the order of the county court was affirmed. The contestant, *Joseph A. O'Hagan*, appeals to this court from the judgment of affirmance rendered by the circuit court.

The only question raised on this appeal going to the merits of the controversy is, Did the attesting witnesses to the will subscribe the same as such in the presence of the testator, as required by statute? R. S. sec. 2282.

The will is in the handwriting of E. P. King, Esq., of Beloit, in which city the testator resided when the same was executed. It bears date September 12, 1881. There is no question but that it was signed by the testator and by the two persons whose names appear thereon as attesting witnesses. It is understood that Mr. King died before the testator. After the signature of the testator, and before those of the attesting witnesses, is the following certificate: "The above instrument, consisting of one sheet, was on the day of the date thereof signed, published, and declared by the said testator to be his last will and testament in the presence of us who have signed our names at his request as witnesses in his presence and in presence of each other." Both the attesting witnesses were examined as witnesses on the hearing in the circuit court, and each disclaimed any recollection of attesting the instrument, yet each verified his signature thereto. The substance of the testimony of each of them is contained in that of the witness Sherwood, as follows: "I have no recollection of signing that instrument; not the least. I don't remember signing it. All I know is that it is my signature."

The theory of the defendant is that at the date of the will,— September 12, 1881,— the testator was sick and unable to leave his house; and, because both of the attesting witnesses testified that they had never been in his house, they could not have been present when he executed the will, inasmuch as it must necessarily have been executed at his house. The testimony tending to show that the testator was seriously ill at the time is very inconclusive and unsatisfactory, depending, as it does, mainly upon the recollection of the witnesses of what transpired on a specific day six years before they were called to testify. Besides, they fail to disclose any facts or circumstances which would have a tendency to impress the precise date upon their recollections. The testimony of the appellant himself is a fair specimen of that of the other witnesses on the same subject. He had testified to having been at the testator's house, September 15, 1881, and that the testator was then very ill. When interrogated as to his means of knowing the precise date, he said: "I am able to say that it was the 15th that I was at my father's, because I was building a house at the time. I have the papers to show." No papers were produced. The testimony tending to prove that the testator was able to go to Mr. King's office in Beloit on September 12th, is fully as strong and convincing as the testimony to the contrary. It is deemed unnecessary to state the testimony more fully.

In the case of *Will of Jenkins*, 43 Wis. 610, and *Will of Meurer*, 44 Wis. 392, it was held that, to authorize the probate of an instrument propounded as a will, it is not absolutely necessary that the attesting witnesses testify to all the facts essential to a valid execution of the will. In the *Jenkins Case* one of the attesting witnesses testified to the absence of at least one of those essential facts, yet it was held that such testimony did not necessarily defeat the probate of the will. In *Will of Lewis*, 51 Wis., 101, the rule of those cases was reasserted; and again in *Allen v. Griffin*, 69 Wis. 529.

In the *Lewis Case* the contention was that the attestation was made before the testator signed the instrument. One of the attesting witnesses in effect so testified. In the opinion it was said: "The instrument is attested as a will

in due and usual form. Such attestation is of itself not
only *prima facie* evidence that the instrument was properly
executed, but it raises a strong presumption that it was so
executed. Had the witnesses deceased before the probate
of the instrument, mere proof that the attesting signatures
were their handwriting would have established the will.
And the rule would be the same although the signatures of
the witnesses were not preceded by any attesting clause or
certificate. To defeat probate, the strong presumption of
regularity thus appearing upon the face of the instrument
must be overcome by proof. *Remsen v. Brinckerhoff*, 26
Wend. 325; *Ela v. Edwards*, 16 Gray, 91; 1 Greenl. Ev.
§ 126; *Burling v. Paterson*, 9 Car. & P. 570. In view of
this presumption, and considering also the infirmity of
human memory, it seems most reasonable that a will purporting on its face to be legally executed should not be defeated on any doubtful or inconclusive parol proof that it
was not legally executed. The opposite rule would greatly
imperil the testamentary right; for under such a rule almost
any will might be defeated by the dishonesty or imperfect
memories of the attesting witnesses. Hence, in the present case, if the fact that the witnesses subscribed the instrument before the testator defeats the probate thereof as
a will of the testator, the fact should not be found, against
the presumption of regularity, without very clear and convincing proof."

A similar question was presented in *Allen v. Griffin*. In
that case the proofs of irregular attestation were as strong
as they are here. In the opinion by Mr. Justice TAYLOR it
is said: "To reject the probate of a will upon such evidence as was offered in this case, on the ground that it does
not conclusively appear that the witness signed as such
after the signature of the alleged testatrix, would jeopar-
dize the probate of very many honest wills. We think, in
the absence of clear proof that the witness or witnesses

signed before the signing of the testator, it should be presumed that the testator signed first."

The learned counsel for the appellant in his brief asserts quite positively that the rule laid down in the *Lewis Will Case* is but a mere *obiter dictum*. We must assure the counsel that in our opinion he is mistaken. But, however that may be, we must apply the rule to this case, and it certainly is not *obiter dictum* here. We find in this case no such clear and satisfactory proof that the will was attested in the absence of the testator as will justify the reversal of the finding that it was attested in his presence, or which would support a contrary finding had one been made. In other words, the presumption arising from the attestation and the attesting clause to the effect that it was subscribed by the witnesses in the presence of the testator, is not overcome by proof. Hence the instrument was properly probated as the last will and testament of Peter O'Hagan.

Exceptions are preserved in the record to the rulings of the court admitting certain testimony against the objections of the appellant, and rejecting certain other testimony upon objections by the respondent. Without stating these in detail, it is sufficient to say of them that if all the testimony so objected to by appellant had been rejected, and all the testimony thus ruled out had been received, the result would not have been changed.

On the hearing in the circuit court, the appellant submitted several questions of fact, and requested the court to find thereon. The substance of these questions is, At what place in the city of Beloit did the testator execute, and the attesting witnesses subscribe, the instrument? Was the testator able to leave his house, September 12, 1881, and did he do so? We think no such specific findings were necessary. The circuit judge found that the instrument was executed by the testator in the city of Beloit on the day it bears date, and was at the same time subscribed by the at-

testing witnesses in his presence.   The finding is sufficiently
specific.

By the Court.— The judgment of the circuit court is affirmed.   The appellant must pay the costs of this appeal.

A motion by the appellant that the judgment be modified by allowing the costs of the appellant in this court to
be paid out of the estate. was denied January 29, 1889.

———

THOMPSON, Appellant, vs. THOMPSON, Respondent.

November 14 — December 4, 1888.

*Divorce: Final division of estate: Allowance to husband: Modification
of judgment: Jurisdiction:* Res adjudicata.

1. A judgment of divorce giving to the plaintiff wife all the property,
   real and personal, and confirming in her the title to the homestead
   (the title to which had been taken in her name although the husband had bought and paid for it). makes a final division and distribution of the estate of the husband, within the meaning of sec.
   2364, R. S., although it also directs that the plaintiff pay to the
 . defendant the sum of $42 per year until further order, and that
   the same be a lien upon the homestead. [Whether the court had
   power to make such allowance to the husband, the divorce having
   been granted on the ground of his drunkenness and cruelty, not
   determined.]

2. A modification of such judgment after the term and more than one
   year after its rendition, requiring the plaintiff to pay an additional
   $600 to the defendant and to give a mortgage of the homestead to
   secure such payment, is without jurisdiction and void. And although such modification is afterwards vacated and then again
   re-established, it does not become *res adjudicata*, but may be set
   aside at any time.

APPEAL from the Circuit Court for *Dodge* County.
The facts are sufficiently stated in the opinion.
For the appellant there was a brief by *Lander & Lander*
and *W. G. Coles*, and oral argument by *H. W. Lander*.

G. W. Stephens, for the respondent, contended, *inter alia*, that the provision made in the original judgment for the plaintiff is alimony to her, which is subject to modification and revision at any time by the court. *Blake v. Blake*, 68 Wis. 303; *Coad v. Coad*, 41 id. 23; *Thomas v. Thomas*, id. 229; *Williams v. Williams*, 29 id. 517. The fact that, by the original judgment, the plaintiff was ordered to pay the defendant $42 annually *until further order*, shows that there was no final division and distribution of the estate. This $42 was the annual interest on $600 which the court found the defendant was entitled to in the real estate, and the $42 was made a lien on the real estate.

ORTON, J. The plaintiff commenced suit against the defendant for divorce, charging him in her complaint with being an habitual drunkard and with cruel and inhuman treatment, and the court found the defendant guilty of the acts as charged and alleged in the plaintiff's complaint; and at the September term of the court, 1884, on the 24th day of January, 1885, ordered and adjudged that the marriage between the plaintiff and defendant be dissolved, and the parties and each of them freed from the obligations thereof. It seems that the defendant purchased and paid for a certain forty acres of land, and caused the conveyance thereof to be made to the said plaintiff, and they occupied the same as a homestead. The court further ordered and adjudged that the said plaintiff retain possession of all the property, both real and personal, except the wearing apparel of the defendant, and the title of the real estate confirmed. It was further ordered and adjudged that the plaintiff pay to the defendant the sum of $42 a year, and that the same be a lien upon the real estate, etc., until the further order of the court. About the 15th day of July, 1887, G. W. Stephens, Esq., filed a petition on behalf of the defendant to modify the above judgment; and the court on the 29th

day of July, 1887, modified said judgment as follows: The
above finding is repeated; and the court further found that
the interest of the defendant in the said forty acres of land
is $684, and interest at seven per cent. per annum on the
$600 from the 2d day of January, 1887. The $84 in the
finding is supposed to be two years' interest on $600 em-
,braced in the first judgment and remaining unpaid. Then
the court repeats the original judgment of divorce, and the
judgment that the plaintiff retain possession of all the property, real and personal; and adjudged that the defendant
have an interest in said land of $684, and that it be a lien
thereon; and that said land be chargeable therewith, and
that the plaintiff, within thirty days, execute a mortgage
on the same to said Stephens, as trustee, to secure the same,—
the $84 as due, and the $600 to be payable seven years
from January 2, 1887; the interest payable annually. In
case the plaintiff neglects or refuses to execute said mortgage within thirty days, then it is ordered and adjudged
that the sheriff sell said land upon giving public notice,
and make a deed to the purchaser, and from the proceeds
thereof pay said $684 and interest, and the balance to the
plaintiff, and that the plaintiff pay said Stephens $10 within
thirty days as the costs of the motion. On the 15th day of
October, 1887, on motion of the plaintiff, the above modification of the original judgment was vacated and set aside;
and on the 21st day of October, 1887, this last order was
vacated, and the modification re-established. Then on the
8th day of May, 1888, the plaintiff moved to vacate and set
aside the above modified judgment of July 29, 1887, and
all proceedings since the original judgment dated January
24, 1885. From the order denying said motion this appeal
is taken.

This, to say the least, is a strange record. We only know
from the brief of the respondent's counsel that the court
dismissed the order to show cause, which constituted the

motion of the appellant to set aside and cancel the modified judgment, on the ground that the matter was *res adjudicata*. It is proper to say that this modification, made more than two, years and after several terms of the court after the term at which the original judgment was entered, did not change it so far as the divorce itself was concerned, although the plaintiff is favored with a new finding that the facts of habitual drunkenness and cruel and inhuman treatment were established by the evidence, and a new judgment of divorce and of assignment to the plaintiff of all the property, both real and personal, and of the confirmation to her of the real estate, is repeated and re-entered. That judgment, in these respects at least, ought to be strong and conclusive enough to stand and be final. There can be no question but that the part of the original judgment which gives to the plaintiff all the property, both real and personal, and confirms in her the title to the forty-acre homestead, is a *final* division and distribution of the estate, both real and personal, authorized by sec. 2364, R. S. That statute makes such a judgment final, and it is final to the extent, at least, that any change or modification of it is beyond the jurisdiction of the court after the term or one year, like other final judgments. *Barker v. Dayton*, 28 Wis. 367; *Bacon v. Bacon*, 43 Wis. 197. It was therefore a question of jurisdiction raised by the motion, and always open for the consideration of the court. The court had no jurisdiction at the time to so modify said judgment, and such modification was void for that reason, and it may be shown at any time, and the objection for that reason cannot be waived. *Rape v. Heaton*, 9 Wis. 328; *Falkner v. Guild*, 10 Wis. 563; *Sayles v. Davis*, 20 Wis. 302; *Damp v. Dane*, 29 Wis. 419. The motion was therefore not too late, and the matter was not *res adjudicata*. What the allowance of $42 a year to the defendant to be paid by the plaintiff was for we are not advised, for there was no finding in relation to it. It was certainly not as *alimony*, for there is no such thing as alimony to the husband, at least by our statute. That allowance or that part of the judgment, if it can be called such, was properly made subject to "*the further order of the court*," and the amount could therefore be reduced or discontinued, but not increased, at any time. It is made a lien upon the land. Whether the court had power to make such an allowance to the defendant husband, after granting the plaintiff wife a divorce on the ground of habitual drunkenness and cruel and inhuman treatment, is not a question before us on this appeal, but it would seem to be at least questionable. But there can be no question but that the court had no power to incumber the land decreed to the plaintiff by the original judgment, by an additional $600 to be paid by the plaintiff, or require her to mortgage the land to secure it or the $42 in arrears; for this most materially affects her title and was beyond the jurisdiction of the court, as we have seen. The order, therefore, modifying said judgment was void, and the court ought to have granted the motion to vacate and set aside the same.

By the Court.— The order of the circuit court is reversed, and the cause remanded with direction to vacate, set aside, and cancel the said order dated July 29, 1887, and all proceedings subsequent to the original judgment dated January 24, 1885.

MORSE, Respondent, vs. STOCKMAN, Appellant.

November 14 — December 4, 1888.

EVIDENCE: DEEDS. *(1) Probate of will: Death of testator: Final decree. (2) Sheriff's deed. (3) Description in deed: Certainty.*

1. The final judgment or decree of a county court, construing a will, assigning the real estate of which the testator died seized, and settling his estate, recited, among other things, that the wife of the testator had died since his decease. *Held*, in an action of ejectment affecting a part of the real estate devised,. that it sufficiently appears from such a decree that the testator and his widow had previously died, and that the will had been admitted to probate.

2. Under sec. 4154, R. S., a sheriff's deed of land is presumptive evidence that the title, estate, or interest which it purports to convey, of every person whom it purports to affect, passed to and vested in the grantee, without proof of the judgment upon which the execution issued by virtue of which the sheriff sold the land.

3. A deed purporting to convey "the southeast *corner*" of a certain quarter-section of land, and "the southwest *fractional part* of the north half" of another quarter-section, without more definite description as to dimensions, quantity, or location, is void for uncertainty.

APPEAL from the Circuit Court for *Waukesha* County.

The following statement of the case was prepared by Mr. Justice CASSODAY:

It appears from the record that December 27, 1880, John M. Stockman executed his will, whereby, among other things, he, by the fourth clause thereof, devised the real estate in question to his wife, "Louisa, to her use during her life, and after her decease to" his two sons, "Charles and Ralph, during their lives, and to their heirs, share and share alike," with a power of sale in the widow; that March 18, 1881, John M. Stockman died, leaving, among other property, the lands in question; that said will was admitted to probate, and said estate settled; that January 13, 1883, the county court adjudged that the said widow, Louisa, had died since the death of the testator; that in so far as said fourth clause of the will devised said lands to the heirs of said Charles and Ralph, the same was in violation of the statute, and void; that said lands passed by virtue of said devise to Charles and Ralph; that said real estate was thereby assigned to said Charles Stockman and Ralph Stockman, the heirs at law and devisees of said testator.

The plaintiff claims title to the *undivided one-half of said lands*, and brings this action of ejectment to recover the possession thereof, under and by virtue of three several sheriff's deeds, each dated June 3, 1884, upon a sale made March 3, 1883, upon an execution issued out of the circuit court for Waukesha county, January 12, 1883, against the property of the defendant therein, the said Charles Stockman, and to cause the amount therein specified to be made of the real estate which he had March 13, 1882, or at any time afterwards, in whose hands soever the same might be. It appears that by virtue of said writ, levy, seizure, and sale the said share of said Charles in said several pieces of land were each and all sold and conveyed to the plaintiff herein March 3, 1883, by said several sheriff's deeds; that each of said deeds was in the usual form, duly witnessed, acknowledged, and recorded June 3, 1884; that said lands were all in township No. 5 north, of range No. 18 east; and the several pieces were otherwise described in said respective deeds, substantially as follows, to wit: The *first piece* is described as "commencing at the S. E. corner of section 34; thence north, 10 degrees west, 94 rods, to the bank of the lake, allowing 6 degrees for variation of needle; thence in a northeasterly direction along the bank of said lake to the meander post on the east line of said section 34 and on the south side of the said lake, known as meander post No. 9, in said township; thence south on the east line of said section, 156 rods, to the place of beginning,— containing 9⅝ acres, more or less." The second piece is described as "the E. $\frac{1}{4}$ of the S. W. fractional $\frac{1}{4}$ of the N. W. $\frac{1}{4}$ of section number 35," excepting therefrom the following pieces of land: "A piece of land commencing at the S. E. corner of the S. W. $\frac{1}{4}$ of the N. W. $\frac{1}{4}$ of said section 35, thence running north 56 36-100 rods, thence west 24 rods, thence south 56 36-100 rods, thence east 24 rods, to the place of beginning,— containing 8 45-100 acres." Also excepting a piece of land described as "commencing at the N. W. corner of the S. W. $\frac{1}{4}$ of the N. W. $\frac{1}{4}$ of said section 35; thence south, on section line, 16 rods; thence east 49 rods; thence south, 10 degrees east, 8 rods; thence east 29 83-100 rods, to the east line of the said forty-acre lot; thence north 23 64-100 rods to the N. E. corner of said lot; thence west 80 rods, to the place of beginning,— containing 9 62-100 acres, more or less." The third piece is described as "the N. $\frac{1}{2}$ of the S. W. $\frac{1}{4}$ of section 35, excepting therefrom the following pieces of land, to wit: Commencing at the center of said section 35; thence east 20 rods to the center line of the Milwaukee & Janesville Territorial road; thence south, 38$\frac{1}{2}$ degrees west, along the center line of said road, 96 rods; thence north, 44 degrees west, 92 rods; thence north 10 rods, to the quarter-section line; thence east on said quarter-section line 104 rods, to the place of beginning,— containing 30 acres, more or less." Also excepting "all that part of the N. $\frac{1}{2}$ of the S. W. $\frac{1}{4}$ of said section 35, bounded on the east line by the east line of said quarter-section, on the south by the south line of said quarter-section, on the west by the one-eighth section line, and on the N. W. by the Mukwonago & Janesville road, containing about 45 acres, more or less."

The defendant, *Ralph R. Stockman*, is not the Ralph Stockman named in the will, but the son of said Charles Stockman, and claims title to said lands solely by virtue of a quitclaim deed dated, signed, witnessed, acknowledged, and recorded October 3, 1881. The description in that deed as to any of the lands above described, it is said, was held void for uncertainty by the trial court, and that court accordingly directed a verdict in favor of the plaintiff for the said equal undivided one-half of the lands described. From the judgment entered thereon the defendant appeals.

For the appellant there was a brief by *Carney & Ryan,* attorneys, and *Winkler, Flanders, Smith, Bottum & Vilas,* of counsel, and oral argument by *C. H. Van Alstine.* They contended, *inter alia,* that there was no evidence on the part of the plaintiff, except as contained in the order of distribution, that the will of John M. Stockman was ever proved or allowed by any court; and unless it was so proved and allowed as required by law it is ineffectual to vest any title whatever. R. S. sec. 2294; *Bridge v. Ward,* 35 Wis. 687. The final decree speaks of a will, and the county court gave construction to one part of a will, declaring such part void; but it is nowhere shown that the will referred to on the final order was proved and allowed in the county court. The best evidence of that fact is the certificate required by law to be annexed to the will by the county judge. See R. S. secs. 2296, 3793. The plaintiff also failed to prove a valid subsisting judgment upon which the executions were issued and by virtue of which the sheriff sold and conveyed the lands. The sheriff's deed is presumptive evidence of only the facts recited there. R. S. sec. 4154. The sheriff's deeds in this case do not recite any judgment.

E. W. Chafin, for the respondent, argued, among other things, that the final order of distribution, by its own terms, presupposes the will referred to and due administration under it, of which administration the final order purports to be the conclusion. Under sec. 4154, R. S., the sheriff's deed is presumptive evidence that it passes the title of the judgment debtor.

CASSODAY, J. It sufficiently appears from the judgment and decree of the county court, entered January 13, 1883, that John M. Stockman and his widow had previously died, and that the will above mentioned had been admitted to probate. It is claimed that the several sheriff's deeds were improperly admitted in evidence by reason of their not being accompanied by the several judgment rolls in which the several executions were issued upon which the sales to the plaintiff were made. But the statute required such deeds, as well as the records thereof, to be received in evidence, " without any proof whatever of the previous proceedings, as presumptive evidence of the facts therein stated, *and that the title*, estate, or interest in the land therein described, which such conveyance purports to convey, of every person whom it purports to affect, *passed to and vested in the grantee therein* at the date thereof, or at such *previous date* as such conveyance purports to fix for that purpose." Sec. 4154, R. S.; *Hoffman v. Wheelock*, 62 Wis. 438. Manifestly the sheriff's deeds were *prima facie* evidence that all the title, estate, and interest which Charles Stockman had in the lands at the date fixed in the deeds for that purpose passed to and vested in the plaintiff by virtue of such deeds. The date so fixed therein is March 13, 1882. Besides, the attachment proceedings were put in evidence by the defendant, and it appears from them that such lands were attached at the date last mentioned in the suits in which the executions were issued.

The only remaining question is whether such title to any of the lands in question had previously passed from Charles Stockman to this defendant by virtue of the quitclaim deed of October 3, 1881, or whether that deed as to those lands was void for uncertainty. The first piece above mentioned, of 9⅘ acres, is described in the sheriff's deed as being in the " S. E. quarter of section 34." The only description in the quitclaim deed of any land in that quarter-section is " the

southeast *corner* of the southeast quarter of section 34."
Manifestly that describes nothing. Counsel speak of a
practical construction by previous location in fact, as in
Messer v. Oestreich, 52 Wis. 690; but there can be no such
construction where there is nothing to locate except a corner without dimensions. The second piece described in the
statement of facts is " the E. ½ of the S. W. fractional ¼ of
the N. W. ¼ of section 35," excepting therefrom one piece
described, of 8 45-100 acres, and another piece, including
other lands, of 9 62-100 acres. The only land in that quarter-section described in the quitclaim deed is " the W. ½ of
the S. W. ¼ of the N. W. ¼ of section 35," which of course
does not include any of the lands thus conveyed by such
second description. The third piece described in the statement of facts is the " N. ½ of the S. W. ¼ of section 35," excepting therefrom one piece, including other lands, of 30
acres, and another piece, made up mostly of other lands, of
45 acres. The only lands in that quarter-section described
in the quitclaim deed are " the S. ½ of the S. W. ¼," and the
" S. W. *fractional part* of the N. ½ of the S. W. ¼ of section
35." Of course, the first of these two descriptions does not
include any of the land thus conveyed by such third description, as it is on the other half of the quarter-section.
While the words, " the southwest *fractional part* of the
north half of southwest quarter . . . of section 35,"
ostenblsiy relate to the north half of that quarter-section,
yet the attempt to convey a " fractional part" thereof,
without any dimension, quantity, or location, is too indefinite, standing alone, to attach to any particular piece of
land, and is therefore void for uncertainty. We find no
evidence of any fact or circumstance in the case to aid such
attempted description. It follows that the verdict was
properly directed for the plaintiff.

By the Court.— The judgment of the circuit court is
affirmed.

Barney vs. The City of Hartford.

BARNEY, Respondent, vs. THE CITY OF HARTFORD, Appellant.

November 14 — December 4, 1888.

PLEADING. *(1) Injury from defective sidewalk: Description of defect. (2, 3) Motion to make definite and certain: Bill of particulars: Appeal.*

1. In an action for injuries sustained by reason of a defective sidewalk, a general allegation that the walk was defective or out of repair at the place named, or at most briefly stating in what the defect consisted, is sufficient without describing the defect in detail.

2. A complaint may be sufficiently definite and certain as to the nature and amount of damages without stating all that the defendant would be entitled to have stated in a bill of particulars.

3. The real object of a motion was to have a complaint made more definite and certain, but it also asked that the plaintiff be required to furnish a bill of particulars as to his loss. It being held that the complaint was sufficiently definite and certain, an order denying the motion is affirmed without prejudice to the right to ask for a bill of particulars.

APPEAL from the Circuit Court for *Washington* County.

Action to recover damages for injuries alleged to have been sustained by reason of a defective sidewalk in one of the public streets of the defendant city.

The complaint alleges (folios 6–9 of the printed case) that the sidewalk at a certain place was out of repair and defective in this, to wit: "That said sidewalk, at and about the place above specified, consisted of several wooden planks or boards which were laid lengthwise east and west, and adjoining boards laid north and south; that said boards or planks running east and west were laid upon wooden sleepers or stringers, one at each end thereof, and one near the middle thereof; that the inside board or plank, the board there nearest the fence along said walk on the south side thereof, was not nailed or fastened to any of said stringers, except insecurely at the middle of said board, but was loose at the ends; that said board or plank was so short that it did not rest, as to its ends, upon the stringers or sleepers, and was in nowise fastened at the ends, and that said board was several inches from the ground; that when one of the ends of said board was stepped upon the other end was lifted up several inches from the adjoining boards and from those running at right angles thereto on the east end thereof, leaving a dangerous space and trap in said walk; that said board was also warped, and said ends thereof were somewhat above the level of the adjoining boards; that said board was easily displaced; that the said stringers or sleepers laid to support said board were old, rotten, unsubstantial, and·insufficient, and would not hold nails or spikes, and that said board was decayed at its ends,— which defects and insufficiencies were of such a degree that said sidewalk at said place was unfit, unsafe, and dangerous to travel and step upon by persons using due care."

The complaint further alleges that the plaintiff, while walking along the sidewalk at the place in question, without knowledge of the danger and without negligence on his part, "was caught by his right foot and ankle, and was tripped by said board at said defective part of said walk, to wit, the east end of said particular plank or board, while said board and portion of said walk were in such condition, and while the end of said board was raised and sprung from the adjoining boards unbeknown to the plaintiff, and was thereby thrown and his said foot and ankle and leg were severely wrenched and bruised, and his said ankle severely sprained," etc.

The complaint further alleges that by reason of said fall and injuries the plaintiff was made dangerously sick, sore, lamed, and crippled, and was confined to his bed for several months, being deprived entirely of the use of his right leg, and suffering great pain, and that he is still unable to walk except with the aid of crutches, and will for a long time be so unable; that he was compelled to and did incur a large expense in attempting to be cured of said injuries, and still will be subjected to expense in properly treating the same; that at the time of the accident he was enjoying a large, lucrative, and profitable business as a dentist; that by reason of said fall and injuries he was for more than three months entirely unable to be at his place of business or give it any attention whatever, and he is now, and will be for a long time, unable to attend properly to his usual and necessary business, and that he has sustained, and will continue to sustain, great pecuniary loss thereby; that he has been obliged at great expense to hire help to aid him in his business, so that the same would not be totally destroyed, and that he will still be obliged to hire such help for a long time to come. It is further alleged that the plaintiff's ankle joint has been permanently injured.

The defendant obtained an order that the plaintiff show cause why the complaint "should not be made more definite and certain by stating particularly the amount paid out and expended by said plaintiff in attempting to be cured of his injuries, and by stating for what particular thing, service, or object the said expense was incurred, and by also stating particularly the amounts and elements of his alleged pecuniary loss to his business, and by also stating the amount actually paid out by him for help to aid him in his said business, and the nature and kind of said help, and to whom the same was paid; and why he should not be required to furnish the defendant a bill of particulars thereof; and why said complaint should not also be made definite as to the particular condition of said walk which caused the alleged injury, and how and in what manner the alleged defect caused said injury."

Upon the hearing of the order to show cause the court

denied the motion, and from the order entered accordingly the defendant appealed.

H. W. Sawyer, for the appellant.

H. K. Butterfield, for the respondent.

COLE, C. J. The complaint in this case, as a pleading, may be obnoxious to the objection of being unnecessarily prolix, but there is surely no ground for saying that it is not definite and certain in describing the defect in the walk which caused the injury. In folios 6, 7, 8, and 9 of the complaint the condition of the sidewalk is minutely described, and it is stated in what the defect or insufficiency consisted. It was unnecessary to go into so much detail in describing the defect. A general allegation that the walk was defective and out of repair at the place named, or at most stating briefly in what the defect consisted, would have been sufficient. A party is not required to set forth the evidence in his pleading, but to give a concise statement of the facts which constitute the cause of action, without unnecessary repetition. This is the requirement of the statute. Sec. 2646, R. S. The act of negligence complained of was, of course, the failure of the defendant city to keep the sidewalk in a reasonably safe and proper condition for persons walking over it. It is certainly true that the defendant was entitled to be informed as to what negligence it was claimed produced the injury, and it was so informed with great particularity. It is not necessary to quote the allegations of the complaint which describe the condition of the walk and its defects. An examination of them will suffice to show that they are sufficiently definite and certain in that regard.

But it is said the complaint is uncertain as to the nature or amount of damages, or pecuniary loss in his business, which the plaintiff sustained by his injury; but upon that point the complaint is not open to any objection. The defendant might have obtained a bill of particulars as to these items of damages, or might have examined the plaintiff about them, if it had desired to do so. It is true, in the rule to show cause it is asked, among other things, that the plaintiff show cause why he should not furnish a bill of particulars as to his loss; yet this seems to have been a very subordinate part of the relief demanded by the rule. The real object of the rule seems to have been to have the complaint made more definite and certain as to the defects and condition of the sidewalk, and that it should state with more particularity the amount paid out and expended by the plaintiff in attempting to be cured of his injuries, and the service or object for which such expense was incurred; also in stating the items of his pecuniary loss. As we have said, we think the complaint was sufficiently definite and certain upon all these points; but, had the defendant simply asked for a bill of particulars, the court would doubtless have ordered the plaintiff to furnish it. Under the circumstances, we think the rule to show cause was properly discharged.

By the Court.— The order of the circuit court is affirmed, without prejudice to the defendant's right to ask for a bill of particulars if it is deemed necessary for the defense. The cause is remanded to the circuit court for further proceedings according to law.

CAMPBELL, Respondent, vs. THE AMERICAN FIRE INSURANCE
COMPANY OF PHILADELPHIA, Appellant.

November 14 — December 4, 1888.

*Insurance against fire: Oral contract to insure: Neglect of agent to
write policy: Proofs of loss. Failure to disclose facts affecting
risk.*

1. The agent of an insurance company agreed orally with the plaintiff
   to write a policy insuring certain property to the amount of $500,
   for six months from a certain time, for an agreed premium, but
   said that the company might be unwilling to carry the risk after
   he had reported it. He did not write any policy or report the risk
   to the company. *Held,* that, although the premium was not in
   fact paid, there was a valid contract to insure, upon which, in case
   of a loss during the six months, the plaintiff might recover from
   the company the value of the property destroyed not exceeding the
   $500.
2. The plaintiff having given the company notice of the loss, it is no
   defense to the action that he did not make proofs of loss in the
   manner which the policy, had one been issued according to the
   agreement, would have required, especially where the defendant
   has denied all liability on the ground that it never insured or
   agreed to insure the property.
3. The agent not having questioned the plaintiff as to what the building contained besides the property to be insured, it is no defense
   that it contained other property which increased the risk, unless
   the plaintiff fraudulently concealed that fact.

APPEAL from the Circuit Court for *Rock* County.

Action upon a contract for insurance against fire. The
facts are stated in the opinion. At the close of the testimony the trial court directed the jury to find a verdict for
the plaintiff. From the judgment entered on the verdict
so found the defendant appealed.

For the appellant there was a brief by *Winans & Hyzer,*
attorneys, and *M. H. Beach,* of counsel, and oral argument
by *E. M. Hyzer* and *M. H. Beach.* They contended, *inter
alia,* that there was no valid agreement to insure, no con-

tract *in præsenti.* It was expressly stated by Mr. Sprague, the agent, that he could not make such a contract, and that he did not know whether or not the company would make it. No premium for the insurance was paid at the time, and no time was fixed for its payment, and no agreement was made about its payment, the amount only being mentioned. See *Taylor v. Phœnix Ins. Co.* 47 Wis. 365. A right of action might exist against the agent for negligence; but it cannot be said that there was a contract of insurance between plaintiff and defendant simply and solely because the agent neglected to report an application, when he had not even pretended to make a contract and had expressly told the plaintiff that he could not and did not make such a contract. *Fleming v. Hartford F. Ins. Co.* 42 Wis. 616–621. This action is prematurely brought. If the parol agreement to insure is valid, the policy would be the consummation of it, and its conditions, provisions, and requirements must be complied with strictly to enable the assured to recover. The claim is not payable under the terms of the policy until sixty days after satisfactory proofs of loss are received by the company.

For the respondent there was a brief by *Fethers, Jeffris & Fifield,* and oral argument by *M. G. Jeffris.*

TAYLOR, J. The respondent brought this action against the appellant to recover the value of a quantity of hay owned by him, and which had been destroyed by fire on the 18th day of July, 1887. The facts stated in the complaint, and established by the evidence on the trial of the action, and upon which the respondent claims the right to recover of the appellant the value of the hay so destroyed, are substantially as follows: The respondent alleges in his complaint that one Burr Sprague was an agent of said insurance company, residing at the village of Brodhead in this state, and was duly authorized by said company to make contracts of insurance against loss by fire on behalf of said company, and issue the policies of said company therefor. The complaint then contains the following allegations: "That on and prior to the 2d day of July, A. D. 1887, this plaintiff was the owner of and in possession of a large quantity of baled hay, of the value of about $1,200, which said hay was situated, located, and stored upon lands within the village of Brodhead, Green county, Wisconsin, in a tobacco shed owned by one J. B. Kirkpatrick and in possession of Jacob Bush, situated in block 206 in said village of Brodhead. That said hay was owned by and in possession of the plaintiff herein. That said hay was on the 2d day of July, 1887, and on the 18th day of July, 1887, and just before and at the time of the fire hereinafter mentioned, of the value of about $1,200; that on the 2d day of July, 1887, this plaintiff made an agreement with the above-named defendant, through its agent, the said Burr Sprague, for the insurance of said hay by said defendant against loss or damage by fire to an amount not exceeding $500, for the sum of $3 premium, said insurance to run for a period of six months from the 4th day of July, A. D. 1887, at twelve o'clock noon, to the 4th day of January, A. D. 1888, at twelve o'clock noon, upon the hay above described; that this plaintiff, in consideration of said insurance, agreed to and did pay the said defendant $3 premium on such insurance; that on the 2d day of July the said defendant, by its agent, Burr Sprague, agreed to and with this plaintiff that the said defendant would write a policy of insurance on said hay so as to protect said plaintiff from loss or damage thereon to an amount not exceeding $500, which said insurance and policy was to take effect and be in force for six months from on and after the 4th day of July, A. D. 1887, at twelve o'clock noon; that the policy so agreed to be written was never delivered to this plaintiff, and this plaintiff is in-

formed and believes that the same was never written by the
said defendant or its agent; that on or about the 19th day
of July this plaintiff demanded of the said defendant and
its said agent said policy so agreed to be written; that he
was then informed by said Burr Sprague that no policy had
been written; that on the 18th day of July, A. D. 1887, the
said hay was totally destroyed by fire and rendered value-
less." The complaint further alleges that the plaintiff had
procured no other insurance upon said hay previous to its
destruction by fire as stated; that he notified the appellant
company of the destruction of said hay by fire, and demanded pay for the value of said hay so destroyed, not exceeding $500, and that the appellant refused to pay for the
same or any part thereof.

The answer denies that the agent, Burr Sprague, had authority to make the contract of insurance set forth in the
complaint; denies having knowledge sufficient even to form
a belief as to whether the plaintiff was the owner of the
hay described in the complaint, or as to whether such hay
was destroyed by fire as alleged in the complaint, and requires plaintiff to make proofs of said facts; denies making
any agreement to insure said hay for any sum or for any
length of time, for the premium of $3 or any other premium;
denies that plaintiff agreed to pay said $3 or any other sum
for such insurance; denies that any policy was written or
agreed to be written on said hay as alleged by the plaintiff.
The answer then admits the receiving of a notice of the
loss, but claims that the same was not a sufficient notice.
The answer then sets up the form of the policy the company would have issued if one had been issued in conformity to the claim made by the plaintiff, and sets up that
by the terms of such policy no action could be maintained
against the company for any loss thereunder until sixty
days after proofs of loss had been given to the company as
required by said policy; and alleges that this suit is pre-

maturely brought. The answer also sets out at length the conditions of their policies in regard to proofs of loss, and alleges that the plaintiff has failed to make proofs of loss as required by such policies, and for that reason cannot recover in this action. The answer also sets up other conditions of the policies of said company in regard to surveys and representations and statements made by the insured in regard to the insured property, and alleges that the plaintiff, in violation of the said terms and conditions, concealed from the defendant company and its agent certain facts as to what other property there was in the building in which the hay was situated at the time he applied for insurance thereon as stated in his complaint; and alleges that the other property in said building greatly increased the risk and danger from fire; and alleges that by reason of this concealment the contract for insurance alleged to have been made with the agent of the company, if so made in fact, was rendered null and void.

On the trial, it was clearly established by the evidence of Burr Sprague that he was the agent of the defendant, and had full authority to take risks against fire for said company, and issue their policies covering such risks. And no contention is made on the hearing of this appeal that such agent could not have bound the company by issuing a policy of insurance upon the hay in question.

The evidence in regard to the contract of insurance is the evidence of the plaintiff and of said agent Sprague. The plaintiff testified as follows: "I saw Mr. Sprague about that hay on the 2d day of July, 1887, about 5 o'clock P. M. He was sitting on a dry-goods box in front of Terry's store. I had a conversation with him about that hay. I said 'Sprague, I have got a little baled hay that I want to get insured.' He says, 'Where is your hay?' I told him it was in Jake Bush's tobacco shed. He said, 'How far is that shed from his house?' I told him the shed was in the northeast corner of the block, and his house was in the northwest corner,— just across, opposite. He says, 'How much have you got, and how much insurance do you want on it?' I said $500. He said, 'I can write you in the *American Fire Insurance Company*, the same that your ice-house was insured in;' or he first asked, 'How long do you want it?' I told him two or three months, and he says, 'You better have it for six months. It will cost you no more for six months than it will for two or three months.' 'Well,' says I, 'all right.' Says he, 'I will write you the risk for $3.' He says, 'Really, the rates would be only $2.50, but I cannot write a policy for less than $3.' I says, 'That is all right; that was cheaper than I expected to get it.' I told him I was fearful about the 4th of July. It was so dry that it might get on fire. 'Oh,' said he, 'I will have the policy take effect on the 4th day of July at noon.'" The 3d of July was on Sunday.

Sprague's testimony on the same subject is as follows: "On July 2, 1887, *Mr. Campbell* told me he wished some insurance on some hay he had,— an amount of hay on which he wished insurance. I asked him as to the condition of the hay, whether it was loose hay or baled hay, and he said it was all baled hay. I asked him where it was. He said it was in the Bush barn, on what is known as the 'Bush block;' and I asked him how much he had there, and he said $800 or $1,000 worth, somewhere along there. I asked him how much insurance he wanted. He said he wanted $500 insurance. I asked him if he pressed hay there in the barn. He said, 'No;' he pressed it away from there, and stored it there. I asked him if there was any loose hay in the barn — unpressed hay. He said, 'No.' I then asked him if he knew the distance between that barn and the house, and particularly whether it was more than 100 feet. I said to *Mr. Campbell* that insurance companies did not like to take insurance on barns or property in barns, except private barns in connection with dwellings, and I did not known whether the company would carry it,—the company that I had. He asked me the rate, and I asked him how long he wanted to insure. He said six months. I told him that the rate for a private barn in connection with a dwelling was the same as a dwelling,— one per cent. for three years, or one half per cent. for one year; that this was worth more, and I would fix the rate at one half per cent. for half a year, or $2.50 for $500; and then I added that companies did not like to have a policy written for less than $3, and I would have to charge him $3 any way. He asked me if I would write it for that. *I said I would*, but I doubted whether the company would carry it, *but I would write it and report it;* and the company was also named. I recollect that I said to him that perhaps the *American* of Philadelphia, having his other risks, he being a patron of the company, might carry it for him. My recollection is that I said to him it was a kind of risk not desirable, and I did not know whether the company would carry it *after it was written and reported*. He had insurance in the same company at the time. I did not write any policy, or make any entries of this in my register. I didn't report it to the company till after the fire. . . . This conversation was on Saturday after the usual business hours,— after I had closed my office."

This is all the evidence given on either side in regard to the contract, and it appears to us to be conclusive upon the question whether a contract to insure was made. The plaintiff testifies that there was an agreement to write the policy for $500 for six months, to take effect from 12 o'clock noon on the 4th day of July, for a premium to be paid by him of $3. The agent of the defendant testifies to the same thing, except he does not say when it was to take effect; but he does say that he agreed to write the policy for six months for the agreed premium of $3, but is silent as to when it was to take effect; so that the only evidence on that point is the uncontradicted evidence of the plaintiff that it was to take effect at noon of July 4, 1887. The proof that the hay to be insured was destroyed by fire on the 18th of July, 1887, is not questioned, nor is there any question made as to the value of the hay destroyed. Neither is there any dispute but that the plaintiff demanded the policy after the fire, and the defendant refused to deliver it; nor that he notified the company of his loss and demanded payment before he commenced this action. The contention of the counsel for the appellant, that the evidence of the agent of the company contradicts the evidence of the plaintiff in any material point, is not sustained by the record. He admits that he agreed to issue the policy, but claims that he suggested to the plaintiff that the company might be unwilling to carry the risk after he reported it to the company. He never did report it to the company, and the company did not refuse to carry the risk before the loss occurred.

Under this evidence it is clear that if the agent had issued the policy as he admits he agreed to, the company would have been bound by it until it gave notice that it elected to cancel the same, and if no notice that it chose to cancel the same had been given before a loss it would be too late to affect the liability of the company to the plaintiff. All the evidence on the subject of the contract being before the court, and there being no material contradiction as to what the facts were, it seems to us that the learned circuit judge was correct in directing a verdict for the plaintiff upon that question. That the evidence established a contract to insure as claimed by the plaintiff, although the premium was not paid, is settled by the decision of this court in the case of *King v. Hekla F. Ins. Co.* 58 Wis. 508, and the case at bar is distinguished from the case of *Taylor v. Phœnix Ins. Co.* 47 Wis. 365, exactly as the case in 58

Wis. is distinguished.   This case and the case in 58 Wis.
are cases where the plaintiff bases his action upon the
breach of a contract to insure, and the case of *Taylor v.
Phœnix Ins. Co.* was an action upon a policy of insurance,
as though issued and in force, although a policy had not in
fact been issued.

That a person may maintain an action to recover damages for the breach of a contract to insure, is well established by the authorities, and the damages in such a case is
the sum which the policy was to insure, if the property to
be insured, and which was destroyed by fire during the time
of the life of the policy as it was agreed to be issued, was
of the value to be insured by the policy.   Upon this question there is no dispute.   If the company is liable at all it
is liable for the $500.   What was said by this court in the
case of *King v. Hekla F. Ins. Co., supra,* is strictly applicable to the facts in this case, and the ruling in that case is
supported by the elementary writers upon the subject of insurance, as well as by the authorities.   *King v. Hekla F.
Ins. Co., supra; Northwestern Iron Co. v. Ætna Ins. Co.*
26 Wis. 78; *Scott v. Home Ins. Co.* 53 Wis. 238; *Strohn v.
Hartford F. Ins. Co.* 37 Wis. 625; *Mechler v. Phœnix Ins.
Co.* 38 Wis. 665; *Fleming v. Hartford F. Ins. Co.* 42 Wis.
616; *Rockwell v. Hartford F. Ins. Co.* 4 Abb. Pr. 179; *Tay-
lor v. Phœnix Ins. Co.* 47 Wis. 365; *Carpenter v. Mut. S.
Ins. Co.* 4 Sandf. Ch. 408; *Perkins v. Washington Ins. Co.*
4 Cow. 645; *Kelly v. Commonwealth Ins. Co.* 10 Bosw. 82;
Lightbody v. North American Ins. Co. 23 Wend. 18, 24;
Ellis v. Albany City F. Ins. Co. 50 N. Y. 402, 405; *Com-
mercial M. M. Ins. Co. v. Union M. Ins. Co.* 19 How. 321;
Trustees v. Brooklyn F. Ins. Co. 19 N. Y. 305; 1 Wood on
Ins. § 11, and cases cited in note 7; *Bails v. St. Joseph F.
& M. Ins. Co.* 73 Mo. 37!, 387.

It is also objected by the learned counsel for the appellant that there was no valid contract to insure, because the

premium was not in fact paid. This objection was overruled by this court in *King v. Hekla F. Ins. Co., supra.* It is very clear this is no valid objection to the contract. The evidence shows that the premium was agreed upon, and that there was an implied promise on the part of the plaintiff to pay the same. A promise to pay by one party is always held to be a sufficient consideration to sustain a promise to do some act by the other party, and, as was said in the case above quoted, in order to relieve itself from its promise to issue the policy, it should have issued and tendered it and demanded the premium, or it should have notified the plaintiff that he must pay the premium before the policy would be issued. Nothing of the kind was done in this case.

The offer of the company to show on the trial that the plaintiff did not disclose the fact that the barn contained some other property than the hay insured, was properly rejected upon two grounds: *First,* it is not alleged in the answer that there was a fraudulent concealment of the facts sought to be proved; and, *second,* the fact that these things were in the barn would not avoid the contract to insure, as no inquiry was made by the agent in regard to them at the time of making the contract, although he did question the plaintiff in regard to the situation of the barn. Not having questioned the plaintiff as to what the barn contained, he cannot now claim that it contained other property which increased the hazard of insurance, unless he can show that the plaintiff concealed the facts fraudulently; and there is, as stated above, no such allegation in the answer. See *Dunbar v. Phenix Ins. Co.* 72 Wis. 492.

The objection that the plaintiff did not make proofs of loss as required by the policies issued by the company, and as would have been required by the policy had one been issued according to the agreement, is no defense to the action upon the contract to issue a policy and a refusal by the defendant. This point was expressly decided against the contention of the company in *Baile v. St Joseph F. & M. Ins. Co.* 73 Mo. 371. In that case the court say: "The company cannot be allowed to say to the plaintiffs: 'If we had issued you a policy it would have to contain a certain condition, and, as you have not complied with that condition, which the policy we would have issued would have contained, therefore you cannot recover.' This is certainly a most remarkable defense to interpose." See, also, upon this subject, *Eureka Ins. Co. v. Robinson,* 56 Pa. St. 266, 267. The defendant company had notice of the loss sustained by the plaintiff, and although the notice was not given in the particular form required by their policies it was sufficient to entitle the plaintiff to maintain his action for a breach of the contract to issue a policy.

We think no further proofs of loss were required for the further reason that the company denied all liability on the ground that it never had agreed to insure, and in fact never had insured, the plaintiff's property in any way. This court, as well as all other courts, hold that when the insurer denies all liability for the loss on the ground that there has been no insurance, or that the policy, if one has been issued, is void on the ground of fraud or otherwise, then the company cannot insist upon a strict compliance with the terms of the policy as to the manner of making proofs of loss. See *King v. Hekla F. Ins. Co.* 58 Wis. 508; *McBride v. Republic F. Ins. Co.* 30 Wis. 562, 568; *Parker v. Amazon Ins. Co.* 34 Wis. 363; *Harriman v. Queen Ins. Co.* 49 Wis. 71, 82.

We find no error in the record.

By the Court.— The judgment of the circuit court is affirmed.

KILLOPS, Respondent,. vs. STEPHENS and others, Appellants.

November 15 — December 4, 1888.

(1) Payment: Conflict of testimony: Appeal. (2) Mortgages: Fore-closure:' Attorney's fees: Excessive allowance: Remission.

1. The testimony of the parties being in direct conflict as to whether a certain payment was made upon a mortgage debt, and there being no other evidence on the subject, this court will not disturb the finding of the referee and trial court disallowing such payment.
2. In a judgment of foreclosure the court allowed as attorney's fees a sum greater than that stipulated in the mortgage, but before appeal the plaintiff remitted the excess, giving notice thereof to the defendants. *Held*, that the error was cured.

APPEAL from the Circuit Court for *Waukesha* County. The case is stated in the opinion.

For the appellants there was a brief by *Sumner & Tullar*, and oral argument by *D. S. Tullar*.

David W. Small, for the respondent.

LYON, J. The action is to foreclose a mortgage on real estate, executed by the defendant *Stephens* to one Cook, and by him assigned to the plaintiff. The case was here on a former appeal from a judgment dismissing the complaint. The judgment was reversed for error, and the cause remanded with directions to the circuit court to state an account of payments upon the mortgage debt, and authorizing the court to re-refer the cause, and to allow the introduction of further testimony. [66 Wis. 571.] An order of reference was accordingly made, further testimony taken, and the referee stated an account showing that there was due the plaintiff on the mortgage debt, at the date of the report, $260.34. The court confirmed the findings of the referee, and gave judgment of foreclosure accordingly. The defendants appeal from the judgment.

1. On the trial the defendants introduced testimony tend-

ing to show that on February 25, 1877, the defendant
Stephens paid the plaintiff, on account of the mortgage
debt, the sum of $200. The plaintiff testified that no such
payment was made. The referee failed to allow the payment, and the court denied a motion by the defendants to
modify the report by allowing the payment. The only
error going to the merits, assigned on this appeal, is the
refusal of the court to allow such alleged payment.

The payment is not evidenced by any receipt, indorsement, or other writing, and the only testimony on the subject is that of the plaintiff and the defendant *Stephens*.
Their testimony is in direct conflict, and fails to disclose
any fact or circumstance, bearing upon the question as to
whether such payment was or was not made, which gives
any greater force to the testimony of one party over that
of the other. The burden of proof was upon the defendants, and the circuit court was of the opinion that the testimony tending to show that the payment was made did not
preponderate over that tending to prove the contrary.
Under well-settled rules this court cannot, in such a case,
disturb the finding of the trial court.

2. The mortgage contained a stipulation for $30 solicitor's
fees over and above taxable costs, and the original order for
judgment directed that the plaintiff recover that sum. Before the judgment was entered the court made an *ex parte*
order allowing the plaintiff $100 solicitor's fees over and
above taxable costs, and that sum was included in the judgment. As a matter of course, this was error. But before
this appeal was taken the plaintiff filed with the clerk of the
court a remission of all such fees in excess of $30, and gave
the attorneys for the defendants written notice that he had
done so. On the authority of *Duffy v. Hickey*, 68 Wis. 380,
it must be held that such remission and notice thereof cured
the error in the judgment. It was claimed by counsel for
defendants that in the *Duffy Case* the remission was made

before judgment, and he argued that this fact distinguishes that case from the present one. We are of the opinion, however, that it is immaterial whether the proceeding is had before or after judgment. We think no good reason can be given for making a distinction between the two cases.

No other error having been assigned, the judgment of the circuit court must be affirmed on this appeal. Of course, this judgment does not affect the appeal of the plaintiff now pending.

It is understood that, since the argument, the plaintiff has deceased. The judgment herein will, therefore, be entered as of the day the appeal was argued, to wit, November 15, 1888.

By the Court.—Judgment affirmed.

LITTLEJOHN, Respondent, vs. TURNER and another, Executors, etc., Appellants.

November 15 — December 4, 1888.

VOLUNTARY ASSIGNMENT. *(1) Waiver of irregularities by filing claim. (2, 3) Sale of assigned property free from incumbrances: Jurisdiction: Collateral attack upon order.*

1. In the absence of fraud a creditor who files his claim in the manner prescribed by law thereby waives all objections to the regularity of the assignment and to the title of the assignee to the assets.
2. The court may, under sec. 1693, R. S., in a proper case, authorize the assignee to sell the assigned property free from all incumbrances.
3. One who had notice of the application for an order authorizing the sale of the assigned property free from incumbrances, but failed to appear and object, or, if he did object, has taken no steps to have the order set aside or reversed, cannot attack it in a collateral proceeding, except for fraud.

APPEAL from the Circuit Court for *Waukesha* County.

The following statement of the case was prepared by Mr. Justice TAYLOR as a part of the opinion:

The plaintiff brought this action in the circuit court, for the purpose of perpetually enjoining the sale of certain real estate, owned by him, upon an execution issued upon a judgment in favor of the defendants' testator, Elijah Gove, deceased, against one Benjamin Boorman, and to have the court adjudge that such judgment was not a lien upon said real estate.

The facts in the case, as claimed by the defendants, are substantially as follows: On May 5, 1883, Benjamin Boorman was indebted to said Elijah Gove $900 on two promissory notes then due. On that day said Gove commenced an action against said Boorman upon said notes, in the circuit court of Waukesha county. In said action, an attachment was issued, and upon such attachment the real estate now claimed to be owned by the plaintiff in this action was lawfully attached. On May 31, 1883, judgment was duly entered in said action, in favor of said Gove, for the sum of $1,011.46. In 1884, the said plaintiff, Gove, died; and the appellants, *Turner* and *R. L. Gove*,— the executors of the last will of said deceased,— were substituted as plaintiffs in said action; and on the 8th of January, 1885, execution was issued upon said judgment and placed in the hands of the sheriff of said county of Waukesha, who advertised the property so attached in said action for sale to satisfy such judgment. The foregoing facts, showing the claim of the defendants, *Turner* and *Gove*, as executors, etc., against the property in question, are not disputed, and are verities in the case.

The facts upon which the plaintiff, *Littlejohn*, relies to defeat this claim of said executors, are substantially as follows:

On the 4th day of May, 1883, the said Benjamin Boorman conveyed the real estate, which was attached in the action of said Gove on the 5th of May, 1883, to one Chester A. Blodgett, in trust, to sell the same and pay off certain liens then existing on the same, and, after paying said liens, if there was any surplus, to distribute the same equally among the other creditors of said Boorman. On the 19th of May, 1883, the said Benjamin Boorman made a volun· tary assignment of all his property, both real and personal, including the real estate mentioned and described in said trust deed, to said Chester A. Blodgett as assignee; and under this assignment the said assignee took possession of all the property of said Boorman, including the real estate in question in this action. The proper schedules of cred- itors and assets were made by the said assignee under said assignment. In the schedules of assets, the real estate in question in this case was included; and the debt due to said Elijah Gove was included in the schedule of the liabil- ities of the assignor. On the 15th of August, 1883, the said Elijah Gove, by his agent and attorney, Eugene S. Turner, filed proofs of the claim of said Gove against said Boorman with the clerk of the circuit court of Waukesha county, in said assignment proceedings. The proofs of this claim show the nature of the indebtedness, and state the fact that judgment had been recovered on said claim by said E. Gove against said Boorman on the 31st day of May, 1883, in the circuit court of said Waukesha county, stating the amount of the judgment, including the costs; but such proofs of claim made no mention of the fact that the real estate of the defendant Boorman had been attached in such action, or that said Gove claimed any lien, by attachment or other- wise, upon any of the property, real or personal, which had been assigned by said Boorman to his assignee, Blodgett.

On the 18th day of December, the said Chester A. Blodgett, as assignee of the estate of the said Boorman, presented to the circuit court of Waukesha county a peti-

tion setting forth the fact that said Boorman had made a
voluntary assignment of all his property to him for the
benefit of all his creditors; that he had duly accepted the
trusts of such assignment; that among the property of said
Boorman so assigned to him was the real estate in controversy in this action; and that in the discharge of his duties
as assignee he had executed a written contract with the
said *N. M. Littlejohn*, to sell him the property known as the
Saratoga Flouring-Mills, with the water power thereunto
belonging, and particularly describing the same, for the
sum of $17,000 in cash or the equivalent. This flouring-
mill property is the property in controversy in this action.

The petition then sets forth that the assignee has made
diligent and honest endeavors to sell said property, for
nearly seven months; and has endeavored to find a purchaser for said property at the sum of $25,000,— the value
fixed upon said property in the inventory of assets mentioned in said assignment proceedings; and sets forth particularly the means he has resorted to, to find a purchaser
for said property; that he has been unable to find a purchaser
at the price of $25,000; that the highest offer he has re-
ceived for said property,— other than the offer of $17,000
made by said *Littlejohn*,— is $15,000. The petition then
alleges that $17,000 is the highest sum that can be ob-
tained therefor, and in his opinion is the full value of said
property. The petition also sets up the fact that said property is mortgaged to the Waukesha National Bank for the
sum of $15,000, which said mortgage was due and unpaid,
and that in order to prevent a threatened foreclosure of said
mortgage the said assignee had, on October 15, 1883, paid
the interest due thereon to said mortgagee, amounting to
the sum of $462.94; that said payment of interest was
made out of the net profits made by the petitioner in running said mill, as assignee; and asks the court to approve
of such payment. The following is the prayer of the peti-

tion: "Wherefore, your petitioner submits the matter of said sale of said property to this court; and prays that, upon the considerations aforesaid, the said court may confirm said sale and authorize, by its order and decree in said matter to be made, your petitioner to make and execute a conveyance of said property in accordance with the terms of said contract so made as aforesaid with said *N. M. Littlejohn*, and, out of the consideration therefor, to pay and discharge all mortgages and uncontested liens and incumbrances against said property, retaining the residue therefor — if any — to be disposed of according to law; and for such other and further relief as in the premises may be just and proper."

Upon filing this petition, the following order was made by the court:

"CIRCUIT COURT, WAUKESHA COUNTY, STATE OF WISCONSIN.
"*In the Matter of the Voluntary Assignment of Benjamin Boorman, of Waukesha, in Said County.*

"On reading and filing of the petition of Chester A. Blodgett, the assignee of the above-named Benjamin Boorman, in this matter, representing among other things that it is advisable that said assignee be authorized to sell and convey certain real estate of the assets of said assignor, to wit, 'the Saratoga Flouring-Mills,' so-called, in the village of Waukesha in said county, with the water power thereto belonging and with which said mills are being operated; that the said real estate was appraised in the inventory of the assets of said Boorman at the sum of $25,000; that the said assignee is offered the sum of $17,000 for the said real estate, and has entered into a contract with *N. M. Littlejohn* to convey the same to him for said sum of $17,000 if this court shall approve of such conveyance,— therefore, it is hereby ordered, on the application of said assignee, that the said petition be heard before this court, at the court-house in said county, on the 26th day of December, instant, at four o'clock in the afternoon of that day, or as soon thereafter as the parties can be heard; and it is further ordered that notice of the time and place of such hearing be made known to all the creditors of said Benjamin Boorman, by mailing to each such creditor, addressed to his post-office address, a copy of this order.

"A. Scott Sloan, Judge.

"*Dated, December 18, 1883.*"

Proof of the service of this order as required therein was made by the affidavit of Andrew J. Frame, which affidavit was filed in said court. On the day fixed for the hearing of said order to show cause the court made the following order: " On reading and filing the above and foregoing petition, and on motion of Alex. Cook, attorney for the assignee, it is ordered that the said assignee of Benjamin Boorman accept the offer of *N. M. Littlejohn* to purchase the property, as stated in the foregoing petition, for the sum of $17,000 in money, free and clear of all incumbrances. And it is further ordered that, on the payment of said sum, the said assignee execute, acknowledge, and deliver to said *N. M. Littlejohn,* his heirs or assignee, any and all deeds and writings necessary and proper to carry out the said offer; and upon the payment of the said sum of $17,000 and the execution and delivery of all necessary papers, writings, deeds, or conveyances, the said assignee forthwith and immediately deliver to said *N. M. Littlejohn* the possession and control of all the property referred to in the contract, heretofore referred to in the foregoing petition, and hereby ordered to be sold; and on the terms and conditions of said contract with said *N. M. Littlejohn* being fully carried out, the said sale shall in all things be fully confirmed; and out of the proceeds of the said sale the assignee is directed, *first,* to pay the taxes now payable on said mill property, and to pay to said Waukesha National Bank the sum due to it for the principal and interest and insurance paid, including said sum of $462.94 interest, paid by him October 1, 1883, and all other uncontested liens upon said property; *second*, to retain in his hands a sufficient sum — if the same shall be sufficient — to pay the costs and expenses of the execution of his trust as such assignee to this time; *third*, to dispose of the balance (if any) according to law, the interest of the creditors of said Benjamin Boorman. *December 27, 1883.* A. SCOTT SLOAN, Judge."

After the making of this order, the assignee conveyed, by his deed, the property in question in this action to the said *N. M. Littlejohn;* and in said deed he made the following covenant: " And the said party of the first part, as such assignee and trustee as aforesaid, does, on behalf of said Benjamin Boorman, and of the creditors of said Boorman, and of himself as such assignee and trustee as aforesaid, covenant, grant, bargain, and agree to and with the party of the second part, his heirs and assigns, that, at the time of the ensealing and delivery of these presents, he is well seized of the premises above described, as such assignee and trustee as aforesaid, and that he has good right and lawful authority to make, execute, and deliver this conveyance, by the order and determination of the circuit court in and for said county of Waukesha in that behalf duly made and entered of record in said court."

None of the foregoing facts were disputed by the defendants, except the alleged fact that the deceased, Elijah Gove, had notice of the application made by the assignee to sell the property in question. Upon this question, the learned circuit judge found that he had notice of such proceedings; and, although the fact is disputed by the defendants, we think the finding is supported by the evidence. The circuit court, upon the trial of this action, found all the facts above stated, and, in addition thereto, found that the sum of $17,000 was a full and fair value and consideration for the property sold; and that at the time of such sale the uncontested liens upon such property which were prior to the lien of the appellants upon the attachment in the case of Gove against Boorman, amounted to the sum of $17,500 or thereabouts; and that the assignee procured the satisfaction and discharge of all said liens for the said sum of $17,000, and that the said $17,000 was applied to the satisfaction of said claims with the approval of said court. The said court also finds that, immediately after the conveyance to him by said assignee, the said *N. M. Littlejohn* entered into the possession of said premises, and had, in good faith, made permanent improvements upon said property of the value of over $22,000.

And, as conclusions of law, the court finds as follows: "*First*. That the sale and conveyance of the premises described in the complaint and known as the 'Saratoga Flouring-Mill Property,' by the assignee, under the order of the court, 'free and clear of all incumbrances,' passed the title thereto to the plaintiff, divested of any lien the defendants or either of them had by virtue of the said judgment. *Second*. That a sale of said premises under said judgment as threatened, and the filing of a certificate thereof, would create a cloud on plaintiff's title. *Third*. That the plaintiff is entitled to the judgment of this court, establishing his claim to said premises against the claim of the defendants or either of them, and restraining the sale thereof. *Fourth*. That the plaintiff is entitled to the judgment of the court that the defendants, or each of them, be enjoined and restricted from making any sale of said premises under or by virtue of said judgment or execution against Benjamin Boorman. *Fifth*. That the plaintiff's claim to said premises be established against any claim of the defendants or either of them, and they be forever barred against having or claiming any right or title to the said premises adverse to plaintiff. *Sixth*. That the plaintiff is entitled to a judgment against the defendants for his costs and disbursements therein. Judgment is therefore ordered for the plaintiff accordingly."

From the judgment entered upon these findings, the defendants appeal to this court.

For the appellants there was a brief by *Eugene S. & W. J. Turner*, attorneys, and *Harvey G. Turner*, of counsel, and a supplemental brief by *W. J. Turner*, and the cause was argued orally by *W. J. Turner* and *Eugene S. Turner*.

For the respondent there was a brief by *Weeks & Steele*, and oral argument by *T. D. Weeks*.

TAYLOR, J.   The learned counsel for the appellants claim, first, that the assignment is void because one of the sureties to the bond of the assignee was a practicing attorney in the courts of this state.

We think the undisputed evidence in the case shows that the appellants are not in a position to contest the validity of the assignment in this action. It seems to us very clear that Elijah Gove, in his life-time, presented his claim against the assignee, in the assignment proceedings, in the manner required to entitle himself to any dividends which might arise from the assets in the hands of the assignee; and by doing so he admits the regularity of the assignment and the right of the assignee to the assets of the assignor. This, we think, is well settled by the authorities cited below. In determining this question against the claim of the counsel for the appellants, we do not intend to decide that, by presenting and proving his claim, without referring to or reserving, in such presentation and proofs, his alleged lien upon the assigned property or any part thereof, he thereby waives such lien. All we decide is that, having come in under the assignment proceeding in such a way as to entitle himself to share in the dividends arising from the assets in the hands of the assignee, he waives all objection to the title of the assignee to such assets. *Ansonia B. & C. Co. v. Babbitt,*

74 N. Y. 395; *Cavanagh v. Morrow,* 67 How. Pr. 242; *May v. Wannemacher,* 111 Mass. 202; *Pierce v. O'Brien,* 129 Mass. 314; *Jones v. Tilton,* 139 Mass. 418; Burrill on Assignm. (5th ed.), 438, 465, 466.

In the case at bar there is no claim that the assignment is void on account of fraud in fact, but simply that it is void because a sufficient bond was not given as required by the statute. The objection to the proceedings is a technical one, and has little real merit. The objection could have been as easily ascertained by the defendant before he filed his claim as it could afterwards; and there is no evidence given in the action, or any allegation, that the defect which is now claimed to invalidate the bond and consequently the assignment, was not known to the creditor, Elijah Gove, when he filed his claim in the assignment proceedings. He must be held, therefore, to have filed his proofs of claim, with knowledge of the fact upon which his representatives now seek to invalidate the assignment, and so, by all the authorities, waives the irregularity.

Some of the authorities above cited, and many others not cited, seem to hold that, by filing proofs of his claim without making any reference to his lien upon the assigned property or in any way claiming to reserve to himself his rights by virtue thereof, the creditor also waives his lien; but, as we think the judgment in this case is right and should be affirmed,— even if it be admitted that the appellants had a valid lien upon the real estate in question when the order made by the circuit court upon the petition of the assignee, authorizing him to sell the property discharged of such lien to the respondent, was made,— we do not determine that question.

The real question in this case is, in our estimation, whether the circuit court has jurisdiction to entertain the petition of the assignee and to decide upon the same. If the court had jurisdiction to act upon the petition, under the law, then the decision of the circuit court binds all parties to the proceedings; and, whether the order was rightly or wrongly made, it binds all parties until the same is reversed or otherwise set aside. Its validity cannot be questioned in a collateral action. Upon this question, we understand the learned counsel for the appellants contend, in the first place, that the circuit court had no jurisdiction over the subject matter of the petition; and, second, if the court had jurisdiction, the appellants are not bound by the order of the court, because the deceased creditor, whom they represent, was not a party to the proceeding and had no notice thereof. The question of notice was found against the appellants by the court, and, as we have said above, upon sufficient evidence. There are, therefore, but two questions to consider: (1) Had the court jurisdiction of the subject matter of the petition? and (2) Was the creditor, whom the appellants represent, a party to such proceeding?

Upon the question of jurisdiction, sec. 1693, R. S., reads as follows: "The circuit court, or the judge thereof in vacation, shall have supervision of the proceedings in all voluntary assignments made under the provisions of this chapter, and may make all necessary orders for the execution of the same." This section is the first section of ch. 80 of the Revised Statutes, and that chapter regulates the proceedings in cases of voluntary assignments. It is not denied but that the assignment in question was made under the provisions of said chapter. Under the provisions of the section above quoted it is clear that the circuit court of the county in which the assignment proceedings are taken has some power over such proceedings, and may make all necessary orders for their execution.

It may be urged that there is no necessity for the court to make any order in regard to the sale of the property in the hands of the assignee, because he has the power to sell conferred upon him by the assignment, and it is his duty, under the assignment, to make sale of all the assigned property within a reasonable time and for the best price he can obtain for the same; and, as he only acquires, by the assignment, the rights of the assignor, he has no power to sell the property, except subject to such liens as the assignor has created or suffered to be placed thereon. This argument is plausible, and, as a general rule, it is a correct statement of the law. We think, however, courts of equity have the power, under certain circumstances which seem to render it necessary, to change the rule, and give the power to the trustee to sell the property free of the incumbrances, and transfer the lien of the incumbrances to the proceeds of the sale instead of to the property itself. This power has been recognized in sales upon foreclosure of mortgages, and also in sales made by receivers. *In re Bennett*, 12 N. B. R. 257; *Hackensack Water Co. v. De Kay*, 36 N. J. Eq. 548, 553; *Walling v. Miller*, 108 N. Y. 173, 177; *Wiswall v. Sumpson*, 14 How. 52, 65-67; *Albany City Bank v. Schermerhorn*, 10 Paige, 263; *Noe v. Gibson*, 7 Paige, 513. Such sales are also recognized, by the statutes of this state, in the settlement of the estates of deceased persons. And in the state of Pennsylvania, where the statute does not confer upon the courts any other special or general powers over the proceedings in voluntary assignment, there is a statute giving the power to certain courts to order the sale of incumbered property, held by the assignee, freed from the incumbrances. See 1 Brightly, Purd. Dig. 119, and Pub. Laws 1876. We think the petition to the circuit court, by the assignee, presented facts which called upon the court to determine the question whether a sale should be made of the property in question freed from the incumbrances. Had the purchase price been as large or larger than the incumbrances thereon, there can be no doubt but that the sale would have been rightly ordered. In that case, the incumbrancers having been paid off out of the proceeds, they could not have complained; and, if the sale was a judicious one and for the full value of the property, the general creditors could not complain. Upon the face of the proceedings in this case, it does not appear that any one objected to the order made by the court. All the other incumbrancers acquiesced in the sale; and, for anything appearing to the contrary in the record, the defendants in this case also acquiesced. The creditor whom they represent had notice of the application for the order and, it seems, failed to appear and object to the order; or, if he did appear and object, he has failed to take any steps to have the order set aside or reversed. In such case, the court having jurisdiction to act upon the application, the order made thereon cannot be impeached in a collateral action, except for fraud. If irregular or erroneous merely, the proceedings to set it aside must be taken in the case in which it was made. There is no claim made in the case at bar that the action of the assignee in obtaining the order of sale was fraudulent in fact; it must, therefore, stand until set aside or reversed upon appeal or otherwise. High on Receivers (2d ed.), 159, sec. 196; *Libby v. Rosekrans*, 55 Barb. 219; *Hackley v. Draper*, 60 N. Y. 88. We think that under the statute the circuit court had jurisdiction to act upon the petition of the assignee, and that the order made by said court is final and conclusive upon all the parties to said proceedings; and, the respondent having purchased the property in good faith, he is entitled to hold the same freed from the lien of the judgment of the said appellants; and that the judgment in this case, perpetually enjoining the sale of said property on said judgment, should be affirmed.

By the Court.—The judgment of the circuit court is affirmed.

BLACK and another, Respondents, vs. HURLBUT, Administrator, etc., Appellant.

November 16 — December 4, 1888.

(1) Practice: Setting aside judgment after the term. (2) Estates of decedents: Liability of administrator for money stolen.

1. Under sec. 2832, R. S., the circuit court may, at a subsequent term within one year, relieve a party from a judgment against him through his surprise or excusable neglect.
2. An administrator who retains money of the estate in his hands long after the time limited by law for the settlement of the estate, is liable for it if stolen.

APPEAL from the Circuit Court for *Waukesha* County. The case is stated in the opinion. The affidavit therein referred to, upon which the respondents based their motion to set aside the decision of the circuit court reversing the order of the county court, and to reinstate the appeal in the circuit court, was made by one of the respondents' attorneys, and was to the effect that the said attorneys, a Milwaukee firm, requested the clerk of the circuit court by letter, when they sent the notice of trial to him to be filed, "to notify them when the appeal was liable to be reached, in time for one of them to go to Waukesha and attend the trial for said respondents; that the clerk answered their said letter to the effect that the notice of trial had been received and filed, and making no objection to notifying them when the case was liable to be reached, as requested; that this correspondence was had a short time before the commencement of the term; that the affiant's firm depended upon the clerk to notify them as aforesaid, and that they did not receive from him any notice or information whatever relative to said appeal during said term, which was not formally adjourned until the latter part of July." The affidavit then continues as follows:

"Affiant is informed and believes that the clerk of this court was prevented from notifying the respondents' attorneys when said appeal was liable to be reached, by the assurance of said administrator, given in open court, that the matter of said appeal was about to be settled and that consequently said appeal would not be for trial, until the very last day of the term, when the said administrator called up said appeal and, in the absence of the attorneys for the respondents or any of them, and after it was too late to notify them so that they could be present, demanded a reversal of the order and judgment of the county court appealed from, under some rule or practice of this court, and that an order or direction to that effect was then verbally announced by Hon. A. Scott Sloan, the presiding judge of this court; that said Judge Sloan, being afterwards advised of the foregoing facts, refused to sign a written order for the reversal of said order and judgment appealed from, and the matter now rests upon said verbal order or direction, and the memorandum thereof, if any was made by the clerk in his minutes.

" Affiant further saith that he has been informed and verily believes that some proposition looking to a settlement was made to the respondent *John Black*, and by him peremptorily rejected, and that no proposal of settlement was ever made to the respondent *Christian Baumann* or his attorneys.

" Affiant further saith that this appeal has been regularly noticed for trial at the August special term of this court, 1886, and that nothing stands in the way of such trial except the foregoing proceedings." . . .

For the appellant there was a brief by *Edwin Hurlbut*, in person, and *C. H. Van Alstine*, of counsel, and oral argument by *Mr. Van Alstine*. They contended, *inter alia*, that the court had no power to open or set aside its judgment after the term, except the power given by statute. The case made fails to show excusable neglect to be present when the appeal was reached for trial. No excuse for relief under sec. 2832, R. S., was shown, and the granting of the motion for a new trial was an abuse of the discretion vested in the court by that section. To the point that an administrator is bound to employ only such prudence and diligence in the care and management of the estate or property as in general men of discretion and intelligence employ in their own like affairs, they cited *Williams v. Williams*, 55 Wis. 304; *McCabe v. Fowler*, 84 N. Y. 314, 318; *Fudge v. Durn*, 51 Mo. 264; *Whitney v. Peddicord*, 63 Ill. 249; *Noble v. Jones*, 35 Tex. 692; *Finlay v. Merriman*, 39 id. 56; *Thompson v. Brown*, 4 Johns. Ch. 619; *Furman v. Coe*, 1 Caines' Cases, 96, 106; *State ex rel. Townshend v. Meagher*, 44 Mo. 356; *Stevens v. Gage*, 55 N. H. 175; *Carpenter v. Carpenter*, 12 R. I. 544; *Job v. Job*, 23 Eng. Rep. 164; *Litchfield v. White*, 7 N. Y. 444; 2 Story's Eq. Jur. sec. 1272.

For the respondents there was a brief by *Rietbrock & Halsey*, and oral argument by *L. W. Halsey*. They argued, among other things, that the granting or denying the motion to reinstate the appeal was a matter within the sound discretion of the circuit court, and it requires a strong case for this court to overrule an order of this kind. *McLaren v. Kehlor*, 22 Wis. 300; *Seymour v. Chippewa Co.* 40 id. 62; *Lampson v. Bowen*, 41 id. 484; *Kalckhoff v. Zoehrlaut*, 43 id. 373; *McKnight v. Livingston*, 46 id. 356; *Whitney v. Karner*, 44 id. 563. The loss complained of could not have occurred if the administrator had settled the estate within the time required by law. 1 Perry on Trusts, secs. 407, 443–446; *Williams v. Williams*, 55 Wis. 304; R. S. secs. 3849, 3850. If the assets were lost or stolen, it was through the negligence of the administrator, and he is liable. *Cornwell v. Dick*, 8 Hun, 122; *Chambersburg S. F. Association's Appeal*, 76 Pa. St. 203; *Litchfield v. White*, 7 N. Y. 438;

AUGUST TERM, 1888.   129

Black and another vs. Hurlbut, Adm'r, etc.

Sheerin v. Public Adm'r, 2 Redf. 421; *Whitney v. Peddicord*, 63 Ill. 249; *Carpenter v. Carpenter*, 12 R. I. 544. An executor or administrator is bound to bring to the management and closing of an estate the same care and diligence which a prudent man would exercise under like circumstances. The liability of the administrator for the loss of the estate is not wholly dependent on the question of whether he acted in good faith. *Spaulding v. Wakefield's Estate*, 53 Vt. 660; *Re Macdonald*, 4 Redf. 321; *Wood v. Myrick*, 17 Minn. 408; *Knott v. Cottee*, 16 Beav. 80; *State ex rel. Townshend v. Meagher*, 44 Mo. 356; *Fudge v. Durn*, 51 id. 264; *Tracy v. Wood*, 3 Mason, 132; *Doorman v. Jenkins*, 2 A. & E. 256; Shearm. & Redf. on Neg. sec. 21. The burden of showing care was upon the administrator. *Darling v. Younker*, 37 Ohio St. 487, 41 Am. Rep. 532; Ewell's Evans' Agency, 327.

ORTON, J. The appellant was appointed administrator with the will annexed of the estate of Dennis Ryan, deceased, March 15, 1870. The county court, upon the application of the respondents as creditors of said estate, on September 5, 1882, made an order requiring the appellant to file an itemized account of his receipts and disbursements as such administrator, on or before the 19th day of said month, and he filed said account April 30, 1883, and the respondents filed their objections to the same February 12, 1884. The appellant afterwards filed his final account as follows: Debit: Personal property claimed by the widow, $61.50; received from sale of pine timber (from certain pine lands in Waupaca county), $800, making $861.50. Credit: Property claimed by widow, $61.50; cash paid to widow, $190; cash as expense of last sickness, $56.50; cash paid as expense of administration, $123.19; making in all $431.19; leaving a balance in his hands of $430.31. With said account the appellant filed a petition stating, in short, that one George B. Farner, between October, 1871, and November, 1873, stole $600 of the funds of said estate, and that he used due care to protect it, and prayed that he might be credited with the loss thereof in his account.   On March 11. 1884, the county court disallowed said claim, and declared the appellant chargeable with the balance of. said estate of $430.31, and on December 6, 1884, ordered and directed him to pay to the respondents, as creditors of said estate, said amount by a *pro rata* dividend to each of $68.84. From this last order an appeal was taken to the circuit court. At the May term [1886] of said court the appeal was reached for trial, and, no one appearing for the respondents, the court orally reversed the order of the county court, but no judgment was entered to that effect.   At the subsequent term the court set aside such decision, and reinstated said appeal, and finally, after trial and on hearing the evidence, affirmed the order or judgment of the county court, and from such judgment this appeal is taken.

The first point made by the learned counsel of the appellant is that the circuit court could not set aside its first decision at a subsequent term.   It might be a sufficient answer that no judgment was entered, and the decision only was announced, but the court had ample power by the statute (sec. 2832, R. S.) to relieve the respondents from such decision, on account of their excusable neglect and surprise, which were shown by affidavit. *McLaren v. Kehlor*, 22 Wis. 300; *Seymour v. Chippewa Co.* 40 Wis. 62; *Lampson v. Bowen*, 41 Wis. 484; *Whitney v. Karner*, 44 Wis. 563; *McKnight v. Livingston*, 46 Wis. 356.

The only other question is on the merits.   The circuit court must have found that the appellant did not use due care to protect said moneys from loss by theft, for we will not assume, in the absence of any written findings of the particular facts, that the court found that the money was not stolen.   It is unnecessary to review the evidence, which consisted entirely of the testimony of the appellant; for one fact which appears in the record is sufficient to charge the appellant with the loss, and that is that the moneys ought to have been paid to the creditors of the estate long before the time when it is claimed they were stolen. That neglect is not excused or palliated. It was inexcusable negligence that he retained the money in his custody where it could be stolen. If the estate had been settled and the money paid out to the creditors within the time required by law, the loss would not have occurred. Secs. 3849, 3850, R. S.; 1 Perry on Trusts, §§ 407, 443; *Williams v. Williams,* 55 Wis. 304; and other authorities cited in the brief of respondents' counsel.

By the Court.— The judgment of the circuit court is affirmed.

Guth, Respondent, vs. Lubach, Appellant.

November 16 — December 4, 1888.

(1, 2) Practice: Frivolous demurrer: Motion for judgment: Order to strike out: Costs as condition of answering. (3) Slander: Meaning of words: "Use."

1. A motion for judgment on the pleadings on the ground that a demurrer is frivolous is, in substance and legal effect, a motion to strike out the demurrer.

2. Under sec. 2681, R. S., upon striking out a frivolous demurrer, the court may make the payment of costs a condition of the privilege of pleading over, although costs were not asked for in the notice of the motion to strike out.

3. The words, "My father-in-law [the plaintiff] has *used* my wife for eleven years. The children are not mine; they are from him," are capable of the meaning, ascribed to them in innuendoes, that the plaintiff had been guilty of the crimes of incest and adultery.

APPEAL from the Circuit Court for *Washington* County.

The following statement of the case was prepared by Mr. Justice CASSODAY:

This is an action of slander. The amended complaint contains two counts, in each of which it is alleged, in effect, that the plaintiff is fifty-five years of age, and has been married to and lived with his present wife at Kewaskum, Wisconsin, ever since January 4, 1851; that he and his said wife have had sixteen children, six of whom are dead, including one daughter named Lizzie who was born February 5, 1853, and died October 6, 1870; that they have ten children still living, including Nicholas Guth, Jr., hereinafter mentioned, and Katherine, who was born September 6, 1856, and who, several years ago, was married to and is now the wife of the defendant; that said Katherine has several children still living as the fruit of her marriage with the defendant; that November 7, 1887, at said Kewaskum, the defendant falsely and maliciously spoke and published of and concerning the plaintiff, in the presence and hearing of divers good and worthy citizens of this state and neighbors of the plaintiff, who understood the German language and the effect and meaning of said words, the false, malicious, and defamatory words in the German language (which are given in German, with appropriate innuendoes), and a correct, literal, and exact translation into English is therein alleged, with a repetition of such innuendoes, as follows, to wit: "My father-in-law [the said plaintiff meaning] has used my wife [the defendant's wife and daughter of said plaintiff meaning] for eleven years [thereby meaning that said plaintiff had been guilty of the crimes of incest and adultery with said defendant's wife, who is a daughter of said plaintiff, as aforesaid meaning]. The children [the said defendant's said children meaning] are not mine [the said defendant's meaning]; they [the said defendant's children meaning] are from him [the said plaintiff meaning]." There are also the usual allegations to the effect that said words were understood by the persons in whose presence and hearing they were spoken, as charging the plaintiff with being guilty of the crimes of incest and adultery with the defendant's said wife.

The second count substantially repeats the facts above mentioned, and also alleges, in effect, that November 7, 1887, at said Kewaskum, the defendant, in a certain other discourse, then and there had with said Nicholas Guth, Jr., son of the plaintiff, in the presence and hearing of said Nicholas Guth, Jr., and other good and worthy citizens and neighbors of the plaintiff, falsely and maliciously spoke of and concerning the plaintiff the false, malicious, scandalous, and defamatory words, which, with innuendoes, were alleged therein to be as follows, to wit: "*Your father* [the said plaintiff meaning] *has been using my wife* [the said defendant's wife aforesaid meaning] *for the last eleven years* [thereby meaning that said plaintiff had been guilty of the crimes of incest and adultery with the said wife of said defendant, who is a daughter of said plaintiff, as aforesaid meaning]. Your *sister that has been dead so many years* [meaning the plaintiff's daughter Lizzie, who died as aforesaid], *your father* [the plaintiff meaning] used her [the said daughter meaning] *from the time she* [the said plaintiff's daughter meaning] was eleven years old until the time of her [the said plaintiff's daughter Lizzie meaning] death [thereby meaning that said plaintiff had been guilty of the crime of incest with said daughter, the said Lizzie, now dead]." That said words were understood by the said Nicholas, Jr., and others, as charging the plaintiff to have been guilty of the crimes of incest and adultery with the defendant's wife, and incest with said Lizzie during her life. The complaint prayed $10,000 damages, and costs.

The defendant demurred to each of said counts separately, on the ground that the same did not state facts sufficient to

constitute a cause of action. Thereupon the plaintiff moved
the court for judgment on the pleadings in the action, on
the ground that said demurrer to said complaint was frivolous. Upon the hearing of that motion, it was, in effect,
ordered by the court that the demurrer be, and the same
was thereby, overruled and stricken out as frivolous, and
that the plaintiff have judgment against the defendant as
demanded in the complaint, but with leave to the defendant to answer within twenty days, on payment of $10 costs
to the plaintiff and the clerk's fees. From that order the
defendant appeals.

The cause was submitted for the appellant on the brief
of *Barney & Kuechenmeister*, and for the respondent on
that of *Paul A. Weil*.

For the appellant it was contended, *inter alia*, that under
sec. 2681, R. S., a motion for judgment on account of the
alleged frivolousness of a demurrer was not proper without a previous motion to strike out the demurrer; and
upon the hearing of such motion it was an irregularity to
enter an order striking out the demurrer. Under the same
statute in New York it has been held to be error to allow
costs upon a motion when not prayed for in the notice of
motion. 4 Wait's Pr. 596; *Northrop v. Van Dusen*, 5 How.
Pr. 134; *Saratoga & W. R. Co. v. McCoy*, 9 How. Pr. 341.
Words in themselves not actionable cannot be rendered so
by an innuendo, without a prefatory averment of extrin-
sic facts which made them slanderous. The innuendo cannot aver a fact or change the natural meaning of words.
Frank v. Dunning, 38 Wis. 270, 273; *Weil v. Schmidt*, 28
id. 137, 140; *Hayes v. Mitchell*, 7 Blackf. 117; *Miles v. Van-
horn*, 17 Ind. 245, 79 Am. Dec. 477. Language alleged to
have been spoken, and unmodified by a statement of ex-
trinsic facts, will be interpreted in its ordinary sense as it
would be usually understood by the hearers. Townshend
on Slander, secs. 133, 142; 1 Starkie on Slander, 44. See,

also, *Holt v. Scholefield*, 6 Term, 691; *Patterson v. Edwards*,
7 Ill. 720; *Brown v. Brown*, 14 Me. 317; *Foster v. Browning*, Cro. Jac. 688, pl. 2; *Johnson v. Hedge*, 6 U. C. Q. B.
337; *McCuen v. Ludlum*, 17 N. J. Law, 12; *Hillhouse v.
Peck*, 2 Stew. & P. (Ala.), 395. There is no statement, except the innuendo, that the word "used" was employed by
the defendant in any other than its natural sense.

CASSODAY, J. If a demurrer be frivolous, the court, or
the presiding judge thereof, may, upon motion, strike out
such pleading, and thereupon either order judgment in favor
of the adverse party or in his discretion allow the party
interposing the same to plead over within a limited time on
such terms as may be just. Sec. 2681, R. S.; subd. 20,
sec. 2, ch. 194, Laws of 1879. We are clearly of the
opinion that the motion for judgment on the ground that
the demurrer was frivolous, was in substance and legal
effect a motion to strike out the demurrer. This is the
logic of the rule long since adopted by this court, to the
effect that an order to strike out a demurrer, with leave to
plead over on the usual terms, is, in substance, an order
overruling the demurrer, and hence would not be reversed
unless the demurrer was in fact well taken. *Hoffman v.
Wheelock*, 62 Wis. 435; *Straka v. Lander*, 60 Wis. 115;
Lerdall v. Charter Oak L. Ins. Co. 51 Wis. 430. Manifestly
it was so regarded by the learned trial judge. Hence the
order *overruling* the demurrer, as well as striking it out.

Complaint is made because the order allows costs upon
the motion when none were asked in the notice of motion.
But we do not understand the order as imposing costs upon
the defendant. In the exercise of the discretion vested in
the trial judge by the statute cited, he simply gave the defendant the privilege of answering within the time named
upon the payment of such costs and fees. The statute cited
authorizes the granting of such privilege "on such terms as

may be just." Of course he was not bound to so answer, and hence not bound to pay such costs. He was only bound to pay in case he availed himself of the privilege thereby granted.

The principal question for determination is whether the words alleged to have been spoken in the respective counts are capable of indicating the criminal conduct charged. Undoubtedly such words are to be construed in the plain and popular sense in which they were naturally understood by those who heard them. *Campbell v. Campbell*, 54 Wis. 90; *Bradley v. Cramer*, 59 Wis. 309; *Ellsworth v. Hayes*, 71 Wis. 434. We agree with counsel to the effect that it is not the office of an innuendo to enlarge the meaning of the alleged slanderous words, but merely to point out their application to the facts previously alleged. *Ibid.* It is for the court to determine whether the words employed are capable of the meaning ascribed to them by the innuendoes, and for the jury to determine whether such meaning is truly ascribed to them. *Ibid.* It is contended by the counsel for the defendant that the language employed, charging the plaintiff with having " used " the defendant's wife, were incapable of the criminal meaning ascribed to them in the innuendoes and charged in the complaint; and that no such meaning or definition can be found anywhere. The learned counsel seems to have momentarily forgotten such use of the word in the enumeration of particular sins by Paul, where he speaks of the change of " the natural *use* into that which is against nature; " and, again, of " the men leaving the natural *use*," etc. Romans, ch. 1, verses 26, 27. Besides, the language alleged in the first count to have been employed is fairly capable of meaning, as stated in the innuendoes, that the defendant disclaimed the paternity of the children which were ostensibly his, and asserted that they were from the plaintiff. We are forced to conclude that the words alleged to have been employed in the respective counts are capable of the criminal meaning ascribed to them by the innuendoes.

By the Court.— The order of the circuit court is affirmed.

Schwalbach, Appellant, vs. The Chicago, Milwaukee & St. Paul Railway Company, Respondent.

November 16 — December 4, 1888.

(1) Adverse possession of land as against grantee. (2, 3) Deed absolute in form: Evidence to establish condition. (4) Costs: Bill of exceptions.

1. The continued occupancy or possession of land by one who has conveyed it, or by persons claiming under him subsequent to the conveyance, will be presumed to have been in subordination to the title of the grantee; and to rebut such presumption there must be shown some clear, unequivocal act which would amount to an open denial of the grantee's title.
2. Conversations, had after the date of an absolute deed to a railroad company, with persons connected in some way with such company, but not shown to have had authority to speak for or bind it, are not admissible in evidence to prove that the grant was upon condition that a depot should be built on the premises.
3. Nor is a writing, drawn up at the instance of the grantor after the date of the deed, and stating that the deed was made upon that condition, admissible to prove such fact, where such writing was never signed by or on behalf of the company and there is no evidence that the company ever admitted that the real facts were stated therein.
4. Under sec. 2921, R. S., fees for drafting a bill of exceptions used on appeal to this court may be taxed as costs in the trial court.

APPEAL from the Circuit Court for *Washington* County.

Ejectment. The cause was before this court on a former appeal, when a judgment in favor of the plaintiff was reversed. 69 Wis. 292. Upon the second trial the court directed a verdict in favor of the defendant; and from the

judgment entered thereon the plaintiff appeals. The facts
will sufficiently appear from the report of the former appeal and from the opinion herein.

For the appellant the cause was submitted on the brief
of *P. & T. O'Meara.* They contended, *inter alia*, that
Exhibit 2 (referred to in the opinion) should have been admitted in evidence, and that it showed the possession of
Witlin to have been adverse. *Watson v. Gregg,* 36 Am.
Dec. 176. It was competent as tending to prove a forfeiture of the defendant's title by breach of condition subsequent. *Horner v. C., M. & St. P. R. R. Co.* 38 Wis. 165;
Messer v. Oestreich, 52 id. 684. It was for the jury and not
for the court to determine, in a case like this, whether there
had been a disseizin and adverse holding. *McPherson v.
Featherstone,* 37 Wis. 632; *Macklot v. Dubreuil,* 43 Am. Dec.
550; *Beverly v. Burke,* 54 id. 356; *Bartlett v. Secor,* 56 Wis.
520. Costs should not be taxed in the circuit court for a
bill of exceptions prepared exclusively for the purpose of
appeal to the supreme court. Such costs are included in
the gross sum allowed as attorney's fees in the supreme
court. The bills of exceptions mentioned in sec. 2921, R. S.,
include only those prepared by the direction of the circuit
judge, under the provisious of sec. 2879, to be *used in the
circuit court* on the hearing of motions for a new trial.

For the respondent there was a brief by *John W. Cary,*
attorney, and *H. H. Field,* of counsel, and oral argument
by *Mr. Field.*

COLE, C. J. After the evidence on both sides had been
received in this case, on motion therefor the trial court directed a verdict in favor of the defendant. The question
is, Was this error? It is claimed, on the part of the appellant, that the case should have been submitted to the jury
on the question of adverse possession. If there was any
evidence which tended to prove that the plaintiff or those

from whom he derived title had been in the possession of
the disputed strip, holding the same adversely to the defendant, for the requisite period, then the direction of the
court was erroneous. The inquiry is, Was there any such
evidence? The testimony given to prove adverse possession
was substantially the same as that before the court on the
former appeal. 69 Wis. 292. The head-note in that case
will give a sufficient answer to much of the argument now
made to establish the position that there was evidence of
adverse possession which should have been submitted to
the jury. It is as follows:

" The continued occupation of land by one who has conveyed the same to another is presumptively not adverse,
but in subordination to the title of his grantee. He is
estopped by his deed from claiming that it is adverse. In
order to destroy such presumption and hold by adverse
possession as against the title under the first deed, a person
claiming under a junior deed, given by the same grantor
while he still remained in possession of the land, must dis-
seize the rightful owner, either by ousting him from an
actual possession, or by taking such open and notorious
possession when the land is unoccupied that the owner must
be presumed to know that he holds adversely; and he
must show by clear and positive proof a continuance of such
adverse possession for the time prescribed by statute. A
covenant in a deed of land, for a quiet and peaceable possession by the grantee, runs with the land, and binds any
one to whom the same grantor subsequently conveys the
same land; and the possession of such second grantee must
be held to be in subordination to the title of the first
grantee. The recording of a deed is constructive notice of
its existence and contents to all subsequent purchasers of
the land, and renders them subject to whatever covenants
therein run with the land."

This is a full and complete answer to any argument that

the possession was adverse, founded upon the fact of the continued occupancy and cultivation of the disputed strip by Witlin, the common source of title, and by all deriving title from him subsequent to his deed to the railroad company. No inference that there had been a disseizin of the company can be made from such mere occupancy or possession, but there must be some further proof of ouster or claim of title hostile to the title of the true owner; otherwise, the presumption is such possession is subservient to the legal title; and any subsequent grantee, in order to destroy this presumption, must show an ouster of the rightful owner before the statute will begin to run in his favor. There was no evidence of any such ouster in the case, and there is an entire absence of all proof of any act or declaration which would tend to show adverse possession of the strip, either by the Schindlers or by the father of the plaintiff. The possession of the Schindlers was precisely of the same character as that of their grantor, Witlin, after his deed to the railroad company, and which, under the statute, must be deemed to have been in subordination to the legal title. *Schwalbach* took his deed, in 1866, in the same manner, and went into possession charged with notice of the title of the railroad company; and he did nothing — made no claim — which would amount to an ouster of the company.

There was evidence offered and rejected, including Exhibit 2, which it is said tended to show a claim of title and hostile possession by Witlin after his deed to the company. It is said that his deed to the company was upon the condition that a depot should be built upon the premises conveyed. The deed contains no such condition, but merely states that the strip conveyed is "for the uses and purposes of the railroad company." But it was sought to show that there was an agreement restricting the use of the strip, and a condition that upon failure to so use it the land should

AUGUST TERM, 1888. 141

Schwalbach vs. The Chicago, Milwaukee & St. Paul R. Co.

revert to the grantor. Now, assuming for the purposes of the case, without deciding the question, that it was compe· tent to prove by parol that the deed was given upon such a condition, still we find nothing in the proposed evidence which tends to show there was such a condition annexed to the grant, and that Witlin entered into the possession of the strip for a breach of the condition. To prove the al· leged condition, it was proposed to give in evidence certain conversations which the witness Huegin had with persons connected in some way with the railroad company, after the date of the deed executed by Witlin to it. It does not appear that these conversations were had with any officer or agent of the company who had authority to speak for it in the matter or to bind it by any business proposition. It is too plain for argument that it was not error to exclude such idle and unauthorized conversations as evidence in the case. Exhibit 2 was a writing, it appears, drawn up at the instance of Witlin a few days after the date of his deed to the company, which in effect stated that such deed was made upon the condition, and that the strip was conveyed for the only use, purpose, and occupation as a station for the company, and for no other use or occupation whatever; and, in the event that the company failed to so use and oc· cupy the land for a railroad station, the deed should be void, and the grantor should have the right to re-enter and take possession of the premises conveyed. This writing was never signed by the railroad company, or by any one in its behalf, and there is no evidence that it ever admitted that the strip was conveyed upon any such condition. It was therefore rightly excluded on that ground. There surely should be some evidence that the company admitted, at least, that the writing set forth the facts truly as to the alleged condition, and that the conveyance would have stated such condition had it expressed the full agreement of the parties. But no such admission was shown,— not a word or fact proven that would warrant the inference that the company ever admitted that the writing set forth the real facts as to the condition; so it is very obvious that it was not error to reject the writing as evidence for any purpose.

We conclude our remarks by saying that we find nothing in the evidence which tends to prove a disseizin of the company, or which will warrant the assumption that there was any possession by any party, adverse and hostile to its title. In order to show an ouster of the company, and gain title for himself, there should be some clear, unequivocal act by some one deriving title under the junior deed from Witlin, which would amount to an open denial of the title of the company. The facts proven to show adverse possession are no stronger than they were in the former case, when it was said there was an absence in the record of any evidence of disseizin of the company.

There was no error in taxing as costs the fees for drafting the bill of exceptions used on the former appeal. Sec. 2921, R. S., authorizes the taxation of such fees.

It follows from these views that the judgment of the circuit court must be affirmed.

By the Court.— Judgment affirmed.

JACOBSON, Appellant, vs. LANDOLT, Respondent.

November 16 — December 4, 1888.

Partnership: Dissolution: Intervention by attachment creditor: Vacating appointment of receiver.

One who has attached partnership property in the hands of a receiver appointed in an action for dissolution of the partnership may intervene in such action for the purpose of asserting his claim under the attachment, and may attack the validity of the appointment of the receiver by a petition setting forth the facts, upon which an issue may be made and determined. He cannot, however, attack such appointment in a summary proceeding by motion.

APPEALS from the Circuit Court for *Ozaukee* County. The respondent, *William H. Landolt*, commenced an action against one James W. Vail, on January 16, 1888, alleging in his complaint that the plaintiff and defendant were copartners, doing business as bankers at the city of Port Washington, in this state, under the firm name of James W. Vail & Co.; that they both desired a dissolution of such copartnership; that there were large assets belonging thereto, and a large number of creditors of the firm; and that the interests of all concerned required the appointment of a receiver of such assets, to be administered under the direction of the court. On the same day Vail signed an instrument in writing, as follows: "I hereby appear in the above-entitled action and consent to the appointment of a receiver therein." Also on the same day a receiver of the partnership assets was appointed by a court commissioner, and qualified as such by giving a bond as directed by the commissioner.

Subsequently the appellant, *Neils Jacobson*, gave notice of a motion to be heard March 6, 1888, for leave to intervene in the action, and to vacate the order appointing a receiver therein. The grounds for such motion were that on the 17th day of January, the day after the receiver was appointed, *Jacobson*, who was a creditor of the alleged partners, commenced an action against them, and sued out a writ of attachment therein, which was duly levied upon certain property of the debtors then in the hands of the receiver; that no action was in fact commenced by *Landolt* against Vail, because the summons had not been served upon him and he had made no effectual appearance in the action; that *Landolt* and Vail were not partners; that the action, if one was commenced, was collusive and fraudulent; that the commissioner had no authority to appoint a receiver; and that the complaint states no adequate cause for the appointment of a receiver. The motion was brought to a hearing at the time appointed therefor, upon affidavits and certain depositions taken under Circuit Court Rule XI. Pending the hearing of the motion, and on March 7, 1888, the circuit court made an order *ex parte* in the partnership suit, as follows: "The defendant having appeared in the above-entitled action on the 16th day of January, 1888, and having failed to answer or demur to the plaintiff's complaint, and it appearing that said copartnership is insolvent, and a large number of creditors having filed claims for a *pro rata* distribution of the assets in the hands of the receiver, and also that certain creditors claim liens upon or special rights in the property in the hands of the receiver of this court, on motion of Jenkins, Winkler & Smith, plaintiff's attorneys, it is ordered that all persons who have filed, or who may file, claims against said James W. Vail & Co., on their claiming an equal distribution of the assets in the hands of the receiver, be admitted as parties for the purposes of their respective claims, and that all persons who claim to have any liens upon or special rights in any property in the hands of the receiver, and may desire to do so, may present their respective claims to this court by petition duly verified, serving a copy of the petition on the attorneys for the receiver; that the receiver have leave within twenty days to answer the same, and the same may thereupon be heard in this court, or as the court shall direct. It is further ordered that the receiver heretofore appointed be and he is hereby authorized to bring suit within this state, or other states, for the purpose of recovering any demands due or assets belonging to said firm of James W. Vail & Co." The court afterwards denied the motion of *Jacobson* for leave to intervene and to vacate the order appointing a receiver. This order is dated March 28, 1888. The first appeal herein is by *Jacobson* from such order.

On May 4, 1888, *Jacobson* made a motion that he be admitted as a party to the partnership action, and that the order of March 7, 1888, be vacated and set aside. On May 8, 1888, the court made an order denying such motion. From such last-mentioned order *Jacobson* also appeals.

W. J. Turner and *W. H. Timlin,* for the appellant.

For the respondent there were briefs by *Winkler, Flanders, Smith, Bottum & Vilas,* and oral argument by *H. C. Sloan.*

LYON, J. The rules of law upon which these appeals must be determined are not difficult, and may be very briefly stated. The appellant, *Jacobson,* who claims a special lien upon a portion of the copartnership property in the hands of the receiver, has the right to intervene in the partnership action for the purpose of asserting such lien. But inasmuch as the property came into the hands of the receiver before he levied his attachment upon it, in order to successfully assert his claim and lien thereupon it seems necessary that he should obtain a vacation of the order appointing the receiver. Hence he is entitled in some appropriate proceeding to attack the validity of such appointment. But a summary proceeding by motion is not the appropriate method of making such attack. This can only properly be done upon the petition of the party interested, setting forth the facts upon which he relies to obtain a vacation of the appointment. To such a petition the receiver, who is the officer of the court and represents all parties adversely interested, may interpose an answer, and take issue upon any of the facts stated in the petition. The issue thus made is to be determined in the regular course of judicial procedure by a trial thereof and a determination of the material facts involved. The order of March 7, 1888, provides that "all persons who claim to have any liens upon or special rights in any property in the hands of the receiver, and may desire to do so, may present their respective claims to this court by petition duly verified, serving a copy of the petition on the attorneys for the receiver; that the receiver have leave within twenty days to answer the same, and the same may thereupon be heard in this court, or as the court shall direct." This order gives *Jacobson*, as well as all others similarly situated, the right to intervene in the partnership action, and to litigate therein any and all questions affecting his right to a paramount lien upon the property attached by him. It is scarcely necessary to add that nothing in the orders appealed from is *res adjudicata* upon any of the questions thus put in issue by the petition and answer.

Both of the orders appealed from were made after the order of March 7, 1888, and they deny the right of *Jacobson* to intervene. These orders while in force may be, and probably are, a modification of the order of March 7th, operating to except *Jacobson* from that order and bar his right to intervene in the action. For this reason that part of each of those orders which denies leave to *Jacobson* to intervene in the partnership action is erroneous.

For the reasons above stated, that portion of the order of March 28, 1888, first appealed from, which denies the motion to vacate the order appointing a receiver, was properly denied. That portion of the order of May 8th, from which the second appeal was taken, which denies the motion to vacate the order of March 7th, must also be affirmed, because the appellant could not be heard to make the motion before leave was granted him to intervene in the action, and because, in the condition the action then was, the order appears to have been a proper one and regularly made.

Our conclusions are therefore that so much of each of the orders appealed from as denies to *Jacobson* the right to intervene in the partnership action must be reversed, and the residue of each of such orders must be affirmed. Each party must pay his own costs.

By the Court.— Ordered accordingly.

STUTZ, Respondent, vs. THE CHICAGO & NORTHWESTERN RAILWAY COMPANY, Appellant.

November 16 — December 4, 1888.

DAMAGES: RAILROADS: EVIDENCE. *(1) Personal injuries: Fright. (2) Extent of injuries: Married woman: Inability to perform work. (3) Future suffering. (4) Excessive damages: Appeal. (5) Cross-examination: Immaterial error.*

1. The car in which the plaintiff was riding on defendant's railroad having stopped, in the night time, several hundred feet distant from the platform of the depot at her destination, she was directed by the conductor to leave the train at that place, and was compelled to walk up along a side track in which there was an open culvert or cattle-guard. Not knowing of such culvert she fell into it, in the darkness, and was injured. While she was trying to extricate herself, those in charge of the train switched some cars towards her on the side track, greatly frightening her. The conductor knew of the culvert in the track along which the plaintiff would be compelled to walk, and that cars would be switched upon such track. *Held*, that in assessing the plaintiff's damages the jury might consider the fright to which she was subjected by reason of the wrongful act of the conductor.

2. In an action by a married woman to recover for personal injuries, evidence that by reason thereof she was unable to perform her work as she had previously done is admissible to show the extent of her injuries, the jury being instructed that she could not recover for loss of time.

3. Where there is evidence tending to show that the plaintiff had not, at the time of the trial, fully recovered from her injuries, it is not error to instruct the jury that "she is entitled to recover for any further physical suffering which you may find from the evidence is reasonably certain to result from the injury complained of."

4. The trial court having refused to set aside a verdict for the reason that the damages were excessive, this court will not interfere on that ground unless it is apparent from the evidence that the jury were actuated by passion or prejudice.

5. An error in permitting a witness to be questioned on cross examination as to matters not inquired of on the direct examination, and to be contradicted afterwards as to such matters by the party so

questioning him, will not work a reversal where the matters so inquired about were merely collateral and it is not apparent that the error could have had any influence with the jury upon the issues of fact found by them.

APPEAL from the County Court of *Dodge* County.

The following statement of the case was prepared by Mr. Justice TAYLOR as a part of the opinion:

This is an action for personal injury to the plaintiff, alleged to have been caused by the negligence of the railway company. The material facts in the case are as follows: On the evening of the 4th of March, 1886, the respondent and a Mrs. Kreuziger took passage, in the caboose of a freight train, from Juneau to Minnesota Junction. The junction is north of Juneau. When the train drew near to the junction, it stopped so that the caboose in which the plaintiff and her companion were riding stopped several hundred feet south of the depot platform. The night was dark, and the evidence tended to show, and the jury found, that the conductor of the train told the plaintiff and her companion that they must leave the car at that place; and, by leaving the car at that place, it was necessary for them to alight on the right-hand side of the car, and walk up along a side track of the said road several hundred feet to reach the highway which they would take in going to their homes. This fact was well known to the conductor; and it was also well known to him that where the side track crossed said highway there was an open culvert across the track. Of this the plaintiff had no knowledge. The side track was raised above the surface of the ground, and was the only way for reaching the highway from the place where they left the car. The plaintiff had some bundles in her hands, and when she got off the train proceeded up the side track, and fell into the culvert and injured her knee. While in the cattle-guard, and struggling to extricate herself, the men in charge of the train switched some cars on the side track. She noticed the fact that cars were being placed on the side track, and became greatly excited and frightened by their approach. The cars, however, did not come nearer than 100 feet of the cattle-guard, and the plaintiff extricated herself and proceeded on her way home. For the injury resulting to her by being wrongfully directed to leave the car, and falling into the culvert, the plaintiff claims damages, alleging that the defendant company was negligent in directing her to leave the cars at the place mentioned.

Upon the trial in the county court, the jury found the material issues in favor of the plaintiff, and assessed her damages at $1,000. From the judgment entered on the verdict the defendant appeals.

For the appellant there was a brief by *Winkler, Flanders, Smith, Bottum & Vilas*, and oral argument by *C. H. Van Alstine*. They contended, *inter alia*, that mental suffering disconnected with the injury to the person is not an element of damage, and in the absence of malice, insult, and inhumanity, the mental suffering which may be considered is that only which is connected with, that is, arises from or grows out of, some hurt, wound, bruise, or other like bodily injury. *Indianapolis & St. L. R. Co. v. Stables*, 62 Ill. 313, 320; *Johnson v. Wells*, 6 Nev. 224; *Quigley v. C. P. R. Co.* 11 id. 350; *Canning v. Williamstown*, 1 Cush. 452; *Salina v. Trosper*, 27 Kan. 544, 564; *Wyman v. Leavitt*, 71 Me. 227; *Bovee v. Danville*, 53 Vt. 183, 190; *Keyes v. M. & St. L. R. Co.* 36 Minn. 290, 293; *Blakeney v. W. U. Tel. Co.* 22 Cent. L. J. 147; *Victorian Railway Comm'rs v. Coultas*, L. R. 13 App. Cas. 222; *Goodno v. Oshkosh*, 28 Wis. 304; *Stewart v. Ripon*, 38 id. 587; *Sheel v. Appleton*, 49 id. 129. The instruction that plaintiff was entitled to recover for any future pain she might suffer was erroneous because, at the most, the evidence tended to show that she might *possibly* suffer pain in her knee in the future. *White v. M. C. R. Co.* 61 Wis. 536, 541; *Strohm v. N. Y., L. E. & W. R. Co.* 96 N. Y. 305; *Ohio & M. R. Co. v. Cosby,* 22 Reporter, 497.

E. P. Smith and *J. E. Malone,* for the respondent, to the point that the plaintiff's mental suffering might be taken into consideration in assessing her damages, cited, besides cases cited in the opinion, *McKinley v. C. & N. W. R. Co.* 44 Iowa, 320; *Quigley v. C. P. R. Co.* 11 Nev. 369; Shearm. & Redf. on Neg. sec. 606*b; Masters v. Warren,* 27 Conn. 293; Sedgw. on Dam. (3d ed.), 632, note; *Ransom v. N. Y. & E. R. Co.* 15 N. Y. 418; *Blake v. Midland R. Co.* 18 Q. B. 93; *McGlinchy v. F. & C. Co.* 14 Atl. Rep. (Me.), 14; *Craker v. C. & N. W. R. Co.* 36 Wis. 657; *Smith v. P., Ft. W. & C. R. Co.* 23 Ohio St. 19.

TAYLOR, J. Upon the facts of the case as found by the jury there is no contention on the part of the learned counsel for the appellant that the plaintiff was not entitled to a verdict for some amount of damages. The errors relied upon for a reversal of the judgment are exceptions taken to the admission of evidence, to the instructions of the court to the jury, and a refusal to give an instruction requested by the appellant.

It is insisted that it was error to permit the plaintiff to give the following evidence: "How long were you in there?" (meaning the culvert.) "Oh, I could not tell,— I was so full of fright; at last, I helped myself out." "What were you frightened about?" Objected to; overruled; exception. *Answer.* "I was afraid the cars were switching back on me." "How did you go home?" *A.* "Full of fright." It is claimed by the learned counsel for the appellant that the plaintiff is not entitled to recover damages on account of the fright which she experienced by reason of the backing of the cars towards her upon the side track, and that the refusal of the court to so charge was error.

Upon the subject of damages, the trial judge instructed the jury as follows: "She is entitled to such amount of damages as, in your judgment, will compensate her for all the physical injuries directly resulting from the negligence complained of, *as well as the mental suffering resulting therefrom.* This does not include punitory damages, but does include such pain and suffering of body and mind as you find from the evidence she has suffered from the negli· gence of the defendant and without her fault, and which is directly the result of such negligence. . . . If you find the plaintiff is entitled to recover, say, from all the evidence, how much will compensate her for all the injuries sustained, the pain and suffering caused by the negligence complained of, if you so find; if you find it was the direct result thereof," etc. "The plaintiff, if she is entitled to recover, is entitled to full compensatory damages for *all the direct physical injury, as well as the mental suffering you may find from the evidence resulted from the injury caused by the negligence complained of.*" "By compensatory damages we mean such damages as, in your judgment, will be a reasonable compensation to the plaintiff for all the pains and suffering, in the past, resulting *from the accident,* and, also, any future suffering therefrom, which from the evidence you may find is reasonably certain to result from said injury." These instructions were separately excepted to by the appellant. The appellant also requested the judge to instruct the jury as follows: "The plaintiff is not entitled to recover any damages on account of any fright which she experienced on account of the cars backing down towards her upon the side track." This instruction was refused, and the appellant excepted.

It is argued by the learned counsel for the appellant that

the authorities are quite uniform in holding that no action can be maintained.for mere negligence on the part of the defendant, unaccompanied by insult, oppression, or indignity, which causes fright or other mental emotion only, and which does not result in injury to the person or the health of the plaintiff. And he therefore insists that it was error to allow the plaintiff to testify that she was frightened by the approach of the backing cars when she was in the culvert and struggling to extricate herself therefrom; and he also insists that the perils and dangers of the situation in which she was placed by the negligent act of the defendant cannot be considered in awarding her damages. We agree with the general proposition of the learned counsel that for a mere negligent act only compensatory damages can be recovered, and that such compensatory damages ordinarily include only damages for such mental suffering as arises from the personal injury received; and we may admit, for the purposes of this case, that when the only ground of action against the defendant is fright caused by the negligence of the defendant, which is not followed by any injury to the person or the health of the plaintiff and in no other way affects her rights of person or property, no action can be maintained. We are of the opinion, however, that in this case and others of like character,— where the cause of action is not grounded upon mere fright or terror, but upon the wrongful act of the defendant in putting her off the car in a place of danger, in the night-time,— in measuring the plaintiff's injury it is not only competent, but it becomes essential, to determine the extent of plaintiff's injury, that all the surroundings of the wrongful act of the defendant should be taken into consideration in order to render a just verdict. Certainly, it cannot be urged, with any show of authority or reason, that the same damages should be awarded to a plaintiff who is wrongfully put off a car in a terrible storm, several miles from any place of shelter, as should be awarded to one who is wrongfully put off at a station in a town or city, where he can readily get shelter and protection; nor that the same damages should be awarded to the person who is wrongfully put off the cars in the middle of a high bridge, in the night-time, where trains are constantly passing, and the person who is so put off at a pleasant station at midday. In all cases of this kind, the actual surroundings which accompany the wrongful acts are, and should always be, considered in estimating damages. This case does not present the question of the right to recover for mere mental suffer. ing, independent of bodily or physical injury. Under the rule contended for by the learned counsel for the appellant, it would be equally improper to show that it was a dark night when she was directed to leave the car, and that she was compelled to walk along a raised side track, on which cars were being switched, and which she was compelled to traverse in order to reach the highway leading to her home, as to show that she was frightened when struggling to escape from the culvert into which she had fallen, for fear of being run over by the approaching cars. Without stating that fact, the jury would have the right, in estimating her damages, to consider all the attendant dangers which surrounded and threatened her.

It is not pretended but that the agent of the company had full knowledge of all the dangers which surrounded the plaintiff, when he directed her to leave the cars. The company cannot, therefore, say that these dangers were too remote, and that the terrorizing effect which they might have was one which could not have been anticipated by it. As before said, the conductor, who directed the plaintiff to leave the car when and where she did, knew that cars would be backed upon the side track which he compelled her to travel upon; he knew the night was dark, and might reasonably be held to have known that the backing of cars upon that track while plaintiff was on it would be a cause of alarm to her, whether she had fallen into the cattle-guard or not. The backing of the cars on the track was intimately connected with the wrongful act of the conductor; in a certain sense, it was a part of the *res gestæ*,— as much so as the darkness, the raised side track, and the open culvert into which she fell. That the evidence was admissible, and proper to be considered by the jury, is, w think, supported by principle and authority. *Chicago d A. R. Co. v. Flagg*, 43 Ill. 364, 367. In this case the plaint iff was expelled from the car in the night-time, but on th trial gave evidence of no actual personal injury. On af firming the judgment, the court say: "It is also urged that as the conductor acted in good faith and without violenc or insult, and there is no proof of actual damage to th plaintiff, the verdict should have been for only nominal damages. The verdict was for $100. It was dark when this affair occurred; and the plaintiff was lame, and had two bundles that seemed to be heavy. In order to reach the station or village he had to pass over a covered railway bridge, which spanned a stream, and which had to be crosse by means of a plank or foot-path about three feet wide, lai down upon the timbers. The only light came from belo and from the ends of the bridge. For a stranger, laden wit bundles, to be compelled to walk through a dark railwa bridge on a narrow path, uncertain as to when a train ma come, and liable to be crushed if one does come, is certainl not a desirable experience. The jury had a right to tak these things into consideration," etc.

In *Seger v. Barkhamsted*, 22 Conn. 290, which was a action against the town to recover damages for maintair ing a defective bridge, the trial judge instructed the jur that, if they found for the plaintiff, they had a right to cor sider all the circumstances of danger and peril attendin the accident. To this instruction exception was taken; and on appeal the supreme court held the instruction right, and made the following remarks in regard to it: "That the plaintiff is entitled to be compensated for his personal injury there is, of course, no question; and that principle is sufficient to vindicate the charge on this point. Such actual injury is not confined to wounds and bruises upon his body, but extends to his mental suffering. His mind is no less a part of his person than his body; and the sufferings of the former are oftentimes more acute, and also more lasting, than those of the latter. . . . The dismay and consequent shock to the feelings which is produced by the danger attending a personal injury, not only aggravate it but are frequently so appalling as to suspend the reason and disable a person from warding it off; and to say that it does not enter into the character and extent of the actual injury and form a part of it, would be 'an affront to common sense.'" See, also, *Woolery v. L., N. A. & C. R. Co.* 107 Ind. 381; *Meagher v. Driscoll*, 99 Mass. 281; *Canning v. Williamstown*, 1 Cush. 451.

It must be remembered that in this case and in all others of a similar character the ground upon which the defendant is held liable for any damages is the wrongful act of the agent of the company in directing the plaintiff to leave the cars at the time and place designated, and not the fact that after leaving the cars the plaintiff fell into the cattleguard and was injured. That fact was only an aggravation of her damages she would have been entitled to recover had she received no personal injury; and in fixing the amount of the damages the plaintiff ought to recover it seems but reasonable and just that all the circumstances of peril and danger which surrounded her at the time she was unlawfully directed to leave the cars must be considered, and that it was not error to direct the jury that in assessing the damages they might consider the fright which the plaintiff was subjected to by the unlawful act of the conductor. This case does not fall within the rule, if there be such a rule, that no recovery can be had for merely putting a person in peril, when no personal injury results therefrom. The cases in which that rule has been laid down were all cases in which it was held that the defendant had not done any act which constituted a cause of action; and it does not apply to a case when the defendant has done that which constitutes a cause of action in favor of the plaintiff, and when the peril and fright are circumstances surrounding and attending the wrongful act of the defendant. We think the evidence objected to was properly admitted, and that there was no error in the instructions of the trial judge upon that question. The exceptions taken to the instructions given to the jury upon the question of damages were not insisted upon, on the argument, or assigned as error.

The fourth and fifth errors alleged relate to the cross-examination of the witness Askew, who was called for the defendant. While we think the court should not have permitted the witness to be questioned on his cross-examination as to any matter not inquired of by the defendant on the direct, or, if permitted to do so, the court should not have allowed the plaintiff to contradict his answers, we are of the opinion that this examination, upon a collateral matter, was not so material to the real questions at issue as to justify this court in reversing the judgment for such error on the part of the trial judge. It is not apparent that such error could have had any influence with the jury upon the issues of fact found by them on the trial.

The sixth alleged error is clearly not an error. It was clearly competent for the plaintiff to show by her evidence that the injury to her person was of such a character as to render her unable to perform her work after the injury as she had been able to do before. Although such evidence would be proper and competent in an action by the husband to recover for loss of service, it was also competent in this case as tending to show the extent of her injuries. The jury were instructed that she could not recover in this action "for loss of time."

It is also alleged that it was error to instruct the jury as follows: "She is entitled to recover for any further physical suffering which you may find from the evidence is reasonably certain to result from the injury complained of." It is said there was no evidence upon which to found an instruction of this kind. We think the record shows that there was evidence tending to show that the plaintiff had not, at the time of the trial, fully recovered from her injuries. There was sufficient evidence upon which to base the instruction.

The eighth error alleged as to the instruction given by the court becomes immaterial, as the jury found, in effect, that the conductor directed her to leave the cars at the place where she did leave them.

It is urged that the verdict is excessive and should have been set aside for that reason. The trial court having refused to interfere on that ground, this court will not set aside the verdict for that reason, unless it is clearly apparent from the evidence that the jury was actuated by passion or prejudice. We do not think the evidence discloses any such reason for reversing the judgment in the case.

By the Court. — The judgment of the county court is affirmed.

KREUZIGER, Respondent, vs. THE CHICAGO & NORTHWESTERN RAILWAY COMPANY, Appellant.

November 17 — December 4, 1888.

PRACTICE: EVIDENCE. *(1) Medical books: Waiver of objection: Reversal of judgment. (2) Personal injuries: Condition of plaintiff's family. (3) Opinion of expert based on conflicting evidence. (4) Negligence: Proximate cause: Special verdict.*

1. Evidence as to the statements of medical books or authors is inadmissible, but its admission may not work a reversal where both parties introduced and had the benefit of it and the question of its competency was not raised in the trial court by proper and specific objections.
2. In an action to recover for personal injuries, evidence that the plaintiff has a child of tender years is inadmissible.
3. An expert witness should not be permitted to give an opinion based upon contradictory testimony of other witnesses.
4. In an action to recover for personal injuries, it being a disputed question whether the injuries were the proximate result of the negligence complained of or of some independent and intervening cause for which the defendant was not responsible, it was error to refuse to submit that question to the jury for a special finding.

APPEAL from the County Court of *Dodge* County.

Action to recover damages for injuries to the person of the plaintiff, alleged to have been caused by the wrongful acts and negligence of the defendant's servants. The facts will sufficiently appear from the opinion. There was a special verdict finding the facts in favor of the plaintiff and assessing her damages at $1,700. From the judgment entered thereon the defendant appeals.

For the appellant there was a brief by *Winkler, Flanders, Smith, Bottum & Vilas,* of counsel, and oral argument by *C. H. Van Alstine.*

E. P. Smith and *J. E. Malone,* for the respondent.

ORTON, J. The facts of this case are mainly the same as in the previous case of *Stutz v. C. & N. W. R. Co., ante,*

p. 147, and they will be more fully stated in that case, and the errors assigned which are common to both cases will be there considered. The facts are in short as follows: The plaintiff and a lady friend, Mrs. Stutz, entered the caboose of one of the company's freight trains, at Juneau, in this state, to ride to Minnesota Junction, about three miles north. The train stopped a considerable distance south of the depot at the junction, and they were informed by the conductor that they must get out. At that place there was a side track extending north to a point opposite the depot, and under it, at the highway on which the plaintiff lived and to which she must go to reach her home, was a culvert or cattle-guard, with open spaces between the ties. The plaintiff and her friend, who were the only passengers, got out of the caboose as ordered, and walked north on the side track with the intention of reaching the highway and proceeding to their homes thereon. About the time they started the side track was unoccupied, and a part of the train was uncoupled and proceeded north, past the station, and then backed down south on the side track towards them as they were so walking thereon, but stopped 300 feet north of the culvert. The plaintiff and her friend, however, discovered that the cars were approaching towards them, and walked fast, so as to reach the highway in advance of them, and while so walking they both fell into the culvert, which was not observed in the dark. They were both much injured, and the plaintiff suffered epileptic fits as the result of the fright caused by the apprehension of the cars coming upon them before they could get out.

1. It is assigned as error that Dr. Halleck, as a medical witness for the plaintiff, was asked: "Do not all the authors, so far as you have read, and those of standing in the profession, lay it down among other causes of epilepsy, lay down fright and mental excitement as predisposing causes of epilepsy?" This was objected to on the ground of its

being leading and incompetent, by the counsel for the defendant, and said objection was overruled by the court, and exception taken. Dr. Shimonick, another witness for the plaintiff, was asked, "What are the causes of epilepsy?" and he answered: "Well, there are a great many causes. Among the great many causes laid down by the authors, is mental shock, excitement, mental overwork, fright, terror, shocks of all descriptions." The defendant's counsel moved to strike out that answer, and the motion was denied, and exception taken. The witness was then asked: "Now, will you give me the names, doctor, of some of the professional authors who treat on this subject of epilepsy, recognized by the profession, with which you are acquainted?" To this question the defendant's counsel objected generally, and the objection was overruled, and exception taken, and the witness answered: "Hamilton is one of the recognized authors in this country, Naegel of Germany, and Hammond of New York." The witness was then asked: "These authors that you have mentioned,— what do they say with regard to this disease being produced by fright or terror or shock?" The witness answered: "They place mental excitement from grief or agony or terror as one of the causes of epilepsy."

These questions and answers relating to medical books and authors were clearly improper, and the ruling erroneous. *Stilling v. Thorp*, 54 Wis. 528; *Boyle v. State*, 57 Wis. 472; *Soquet v. State*, 72 Wis. 659. There was very much of this kind of testimony of these and other medical witnesses admitted after general objection. But we are disposed to hold that this error, so often repeated, is not sufficient ground for reversal of the judgment, for two reasons: (1) The objection to this evidence was waived by the defendant, by having first introduced it, and by having had the benefit of the same kind of evidence, obtained on cross-examination of the plaintiff's witnesses. (2) The attention

of the court, or of the opposite counsel, does not seem to
have been called to this particular ground of its incompetency.   On the first cross-examination of the first medical witness, Dr. Halleck, the counsel of the appellant called
out the testimony that "he had to go a good deal by *authorities;* the *books* claim that it will;" and again, "I think
some *authorities* claim that about forty per cent. of patients
utter a cry."   The learned counsel asked: "Tell me what
books you are speaking of.   *Let us have the authorities.*"
The instances are numerous where this kind of testimony
was obtained by the defendant without objection, before
the question was raised, if raised at all, by objection.   The
counsel of the plaintiff first introduced this kind of evidence without objection, such as "I think the authorities
give hereditary causes oftener than any other."   "Authors
claim as a rule," etc.   Then, after such cross-examination,
when the witness is being re-examined by the plaintiff's
counsel, the counsel of the defendant made his first and
only objection as to its *competency;* and that was clearly
proper, for it was cross-examination as to matter called
out by the defendant.   In all other instances, the objection
was only general.   When Dr. Senn, a witness of the defendant, was cross-examined, he testified: "It would be
an exciting cause, and as such it would be enumerated in
the *books;*" and yet this was not objected to.   When he
was examined in chief he testified that "he had made no
special study of epilepsy," but said: "I think that *modern
science* recognizes two distinct causes."   This would seem to
be sufficient to justify holding that the defendant waived
all objection to this kind of testimony.   The principal part
of the medical evidence to this real point in controversy, on
both sides, appears to have been obtained from the *books* and
authorities.   It would be invidious and unfair to hold that
the plaintiff's part of this common error ought to reverse
her judgment.   The only time, as we have seen, that the

objection was made on the ground of *incompetency*, was when the evidence was strictly proper on cross-examination. The error is such a bold and flagrant one, by very late decisions of this court, it would seem as if the court would not have allowed it, and the plaintiff's counsel would not have asked or permitted it, if their attention had been called to the very point of *medical books*, or it might have been understood that objection to it had been waived by the defendant. The probability is now, since special attention is called to it, that this error will not occur again in this case.

2. The plaintiff, as a witness, was asked by her counsel, "Have you a family?" and she answered: "One living, and one dead." "How old is the child that you now have living?" and she answered: "He is seven years, will be eight in July." Exception was taken by the defendant's counsel to overruling objection to these questions. This was error. Upon the question of damages for the negligent killing or injuring a child, evidence as to the family and condition of its parents is admissible. *Johnson v. C. & N. W. R. Co.* 64 Wis. 425. From the admission of such evidence in this case, it might very naturally occur to the jury that the plaintiff would be entitled to greater damages on account of the support and dependence of her child. But in such a case the admission of such evidence was highly improper, and we cannot say that it did not affect the amount of the verdict. *Pennsylvania Co. v. Roy*, 102 U. S. 451; *Chicago v. O'Brennan*, 65 Ill. 160; *Pittsburg, Ft. W. & C. R. Co. v. Powers*, 74 Ill. 343.

3. Dr. Halleck testified that he heard the testimony of the plaintiff, *and the other evidence in the case*, and he was then asked by the plaintiff's counsel: "From *said evidence*, and that of the plaintiff, and your examination of her as her physician, were the subsequent attacks of the same nature as the attack described by the plaintiff?" and he an-

swered: "Yes, sir." Dr. Shimonick testified that "he made examination of the plaintiff ten days or two weeks ago, and heard the witnesses [evidence] relative to her condition after the accident, which was given yesterday, and of Dr. Halleck." He was asked: "From that evidence and that knowledge, and your own personal examination, what in your opinion was the difficulty which followed the accident?" and he answered:- "Epilepsy, I think." He was asked: "From the testimony upon this subject given in the case, in your opinion, is there reasonable cause for believing that she will not recover from this disorder?" These questions were all severally objected to by the defendant's counsel, and the objection overruled, and exception taken. On cross-examination, Dr. Shimonick testified that he examined the plaintiff about ten days or two weeks ago (about one year and a half after the accident); that he questioned her with regard to her condition; that he understood the trial was to take place; that he made *no personal examination* of her, so when he speaks of certain opinions resulting from the examination he is speaking simply from what she tells him and what her mother told him. The defendant's counsel thereupon moved that the above testimony given by Dr. Shimonick be stricken out. The motion was denied, and exception taken.

The above questions and testimony were clearly improper. The other evidence besides that of the plaintiff, upon which an opinion was asked, was in relation to her symptoms and appearance at different times, testified to by several different witnesses, in which they did not agree in all particulars. This was sufficient as to the opinion asked of Dr. Halleck. And as to the questions put to Dr. Shimonick, and his evidence which the court was asked to strike out, they were not only based upon the testimony of other witnesses which was to some extent contradictory, but upon what the plaintiff and her mother told him one year and a half after the accident. Such testimony is grossly incompetent and unsafe by all authorities and by common reason. It is singular that in such a case the only proper method of examination by hypothetical questions was most studiously avoided. These several rulings were erroneous. *Bennett v. State*, 57 Wis. 81; *Quinn v. Higgins*, 63 Wis. 669; *Gates v. Fleischer*, 67 Wis. 508; *Heald v. Thing*, 45 Me. 392.

4. The defendant's counsel asked the court to submit to the jury, as a special finding, the following question: "Did the plaintiff fall into the cattle-guard in and during an attempt to extricate Mrs. Stutz therefrom?" The court refused, and exception was taken. We think the court erred by such refusal. There was some evidence tending to show that the plaintiff fell into the cattle-guard by trying to help Mrs. Stutz out of it. Mrs. Stutz testified that, as she took a scream, the plaintiff tried to help, and then she tumbled in. W. H. Askew testified that the plaintiff told him that "Mrs. Stutz slipped into the culvert, and that she assisted her to get out; that she slipped down in doing so, and bruised her side slightly." This evidence makes a disputed or litigated question of the manner in which the plaintiff fell into the culvert, and whether the plaintiff fell in and received her injury as the direct and proximate result of the negligence complained of, or of some independent and intervening cause for which the company was not responsible. *Lewis v. F. & P. M. R. Co.* 54 Mich. 55. It is true the plaintiff denied that she ever said so to the witness Askew; and Mrs. Stutz testified afterwards that she did not know how the plaintiff fell into the cattle-guard, but still there was evidence enough to make a disputed fact, and a very important one.

For these errors the judgment will have to be reversed, and a new trial had.

By the Court.— The judgment of the county court is reversed, and the cause remanded for a new trial.

ALLARD and another, Respondents, vs. THE CHICAGO &
NORTHWESTERN RAILWAY COMPANY, Appellant.

November 17 — December 4, 1888.

*Railroads: Negligence: Fire set by engine: Evidence of other fires set
by other engines.*

In an action for the negligent burning of a building alleged to have
been fired by sparks from a locomotive, the testimony of defendant's inspector that the screen on the engine was the same as on
the defendant's other engines does not entitle the plaintiff to show
in rebuttal that other fires had been set by the other engines.

APPEAL from the County Court of *Dodge* County.

The following statement of the case was prepared by Mr.
Justice CASSODAY:

September 11, 1886, the plaintiffs owned a cheese factory
and creamery in the city of Juneau, situated on the east
side of the defendant's track, and eighty-five and one-half
feet therefrom. It is alleged in the complaint that on that
day the defendant ran "a locomotive attached to a freight
train of the defendant on the said line of railway, . . .
so negligently and carelessly . . . that sparks from the
smoke-stack of said locomotive escaped, communicated to
and set fire to" said factory, and in consequence thereof
the same was burned and destroyed, with the contents
thereof; that said locomotive was not then and there
equipped with a sufficient spark-arrester, screen, or device
to prevent the escape of fire therefrom; that such imperfect
construction and negligent management and operation
caused such burning and destruction, to the damage of the
plaintiffs. The answer consisted of admissions, denials, and
allegations.

At the close of the trial the jury returned a special verdict to the effect (1) that the engine was furnished with the
usual and ordinary appliances to prevent the escape of
sparks from the smoke-stack at the time the plaintiff's build-

ings were burned; (2) but that such appliances were not in good condition to prevent the escape of sparks from the smoke-stack; (3) that the engine in question at that time was not operated in the usual and ordinary manner; (4) that the defendant was guilty of negligence in the equipment of the engine in question with respect to the escape of sparks from the smoke-stack at the time of such burning; (5) that the defendant was guilty of negligence with respect to the operation of the engine at the time in question; (6) that said building was set on fire from a spark escaping from the smoke-stack of the engine in question; (7) that the value of the property destroyed was $3,000; (8) that they found for the plaintiffs and assessed their damages at $3,000. From the judgment entered upon said special verdict in favor of the plaintiffs for said sum as damages, and the costs, the defendant appeals.

For the appellant there was a brief by *Winkler, Flanders, Smith, Bottum & Vilas*, of counsel, and oral argument by *C. H. Van Alstine*. To the point that it was error to admit the evidence as to the setting of other fires by other engines, they cited *Gibbons v. W. V. R. Co.* 58 Wis. 335; *Bloor v. Delafield*, 69 id. 273; *Phillips v. Willow*, 70 id. 6; *Collins v. N. Y. C. & H. R. R. Co.* 109 N. Y. 243.

J. E. Malone, for the respondents, contended, *inter alia*, that in *Gibbons v. W. V. R. Co.* 58 Wis. 335, it was held that "testimony showing that some of the company's locomotives had previously or subsequently scattered fire is not admissible, *unless it is also shown that the locomotive which caused the fire was one of them or was similar in construction, state of repair, or management.*" In *Ross v. B. & W. R. Co.* 6 Allen, 87, it is held that such evidence "was rendered relevant and material by the ground taken in defense," and "on the same ground evidence concerning the emission of sparks from similar engines used on other roads was admissible."

CASSODAY, J. The freight train in question reached Juneau from the south, September 11, 1886, about 10.45 A. M., and left on its way north about 11 A. M. During the time it remained at that station the engine was engaged in switching. The wind at the time was blowing very strong from the west, or, rather, a little south of west. The buildings burned were situated about eighty-five feet east of the track. The machinery in the buildings was propelled by steam, but was stopped and the fire allowed to die down about 10 o'clock, or soon after, that morning. On leaving the building, a little before 12 o'clock, there appears to have been no fire inside. The fire was first discovered on the outside of the highest part of the westerly side of the roof a few minutes after 12 o'clock, and just before the arrival of another train from the north, at 12.09.

Prior to the time when the plaintiffs rested, the only evidence on their part tending to prove that sparks from any of the defendant's locomotives set the fire in question was circumstantial, and related entirely to the engine of the freight train as charged in the complaint. That engine appears to have been inspected on the 9th, and again on the 14th, of September, 1886; and the netting, which had been patched, was taken out and replaced by a new netting, September 16, 1886. The defendant's inspector of boilers and smoke-stacks was allowed, against objections by the plaintiffs, to testify in effect that, so far as his knowledge extended, the screen used on that engine was the same, so far as the netting was concerned, as on all the engines on the road; that there had been no finer screens on the road since he had been such inspector. To rebut such evidence, the plaintiffs were allowed, against the defendant's objections, to prove in effect that during the summer of 1886 and 1887 fires were frequently seen to start up along the defendant's railway between Minnesota and Burnett Junctions, just after the passage of trains, when there was no other known possible cause for such fires; and particularly by two freight trains,— the one going north, and the other south, between 11 and 12 o'clock each day; that such fires would burn grass and fences along such railway; and that the defendant would rebuild such fences when so burned. We are forced to the conclusion that the admission of such testimony on the part of the plaintiffs was error, and prejudicial to the defendant. The reasons for such ruling have been so recently and so fully given by Mr. Justice Orton as to require no repetition here. *Gibbons v. W. V. R. Co.* 58 Wis. 335. The mere proof that the screen or netting in the smoke-stack of the engine in question was the same as on other engines did not open the door for the admission of evidence tending to prove that other engines, on other occasions and under other circumstances, set such other fires. Especially is this so since the defendant did not prove or attempt to prove that such screens or netting on such other locomotives did not emit sparks sufficient in size and quantity to set such fires.

Other exceptions are urged which will probably be obviated upon a retrial, and hence need not be considered here. Particularly is this so in regard to the remarks of counsel to which objection was taken.

By the Court.— The judgment of the county court is reversed, and the cause is remanded for a new trial.

See note to this case in 40 N. W. Rep. 685.— REP.

WIGHTMAN, Respondent, vs. THE CHICAGO & NORTHWESTERN RAILWAY COMPANY, Appellant.

November 17 — December 4, 1888.

(1) Practice: Special verdict: Inconsistent findings: Directing jury to consult further: Polling the jury. (2, 3) Railroads: Round-trip tickets: Accidental separation of parts: Wrongful ejection of passenger: Damages.

1. Where the findings of a special verdict upon the subject of damages are inconsistent and manifestly made under a misapprehension of the instructions, the court may decline to receive the verdict and, after explaining the instructions previously given, direct the jury to retire for further consultation; and a request that the jury be polled before they so retire may be denied.

2. A round-trip railroad ticket, punctured for separation into two parts, and having on the "going" part the words "Not good for passage," and, on a line therewith, on the "returning" part the words "if detached," is nevertheless good for passage where the parts have become separated by accident, if both parts are in good faith presented to the conductor on the outward trip.

3. A verdict for $299.54 damages for injury to the feelings of a passenger wrongfully ejected from a railroad train and called a liar by the conductor, is *held* not excessive.

APPEAL from the Circuit Court for *Juneau* County.

The following statement of the case was prepared by Mr. Justice CASSODAY:

It appears from the pleadings, and is admitted, that April 15, 1886, the plaintiff purchased of the defendant at its depot in Elroy, and paid for, what is known as a "round-trip ticket" from Elroy to Wonewoc and return; that one half of said ticket was white, and upon that half were the words and figures: "R. T.— Going. Elroy to Wonewoc, 9–8–86, 2563. Not good for passage;" and the other half of the ticket was red, and upon that were the words and figures: "2563, C. & N. W. R'y. R. T.— Returning. Wonewoc to Elroy. W. A. Thrall, Gen'l Ticket Agt. if detached."

The words "Not good for passage" were on a line with the words "if detached." It is also conceded that July 26, 1886, the plaintiff, at Elroy, boarded one of the defendant's way freight trains with a caboose attached for passengers to ride in, then on its way southerly through Wonewoc; that, after said train started from Elroy with the plaintiff on board, the conductor in charge demanded fare of the plaintiff, who thereupon tendered the conductor the ticket mentioned, which the conductor refused to receive; that upon the plaintiff's refusal to pay fare the conductor stopped the train and caused the same to be run back to Elroy station, where the plaintiff was compelled to leave the train. This action is for damages by reason of such expulsion. The following rules of the defendant, in force at the time of the occurrence, are in evidence: "Rule 46. Passengers must not be ejected from the cars for any cause except at a station. Use no unnecessary force. Rule 47. Wood or construction trains must in no case carry passengers. *Freight trains must not carry passengers without tickets.*" The evidence is in conflict as to whether the plaintiff presented to the conductor the red half of the ticket, as well as the white half, when he first demanded fare, or not until after the train was stopped; and also as to some of the facts and circumstances attending such refusal of the conductor to receive the ticket, the refusal of the plaintiff to pay fare, and the ejecting of the plaintiff from the train.

At the close of the trial the jury returned a special verdict, to the effect (1) that the plaintiff had "the round-trip ticket from Elroy to Wonewoc and return given in evidence, No. 2563," on July 26, 1886, and above described; (2) that the plaintiff on that day entered the caboose of the defendant's freight train, which carried passengers, at Elroy, for the purpose of being carried therein from Elroy to Wonewoc on said ticket; (3, 4) that said ticket was broken apart and separated at the place where punctured for the purpose of separation, before it was offered to the conductor for passage, (5, 6) but not by or with any carelessness or negligence of or on the part of the plaintiff; (7) that when the conductor first came to the plaintiff to collect his fare the plaintiff produced and exhibited to him both the going and returning part of said ticket, (8) and not the going part only; (9) that the plaintiff did not omit to produce and exhibit to the conductor both parts of said ticket until after the conductor had stopped the train to back up to Elroy; (10) that the plaintiff left the train by order of the conductor; (11) that the conductor refused to carry the plaintiff on said ticket, because it was not a good and valid ticket, (12) through an unintentional mistake on his part as to its validity; (13) that the plaintiff still holds said ticket, and both parts thereof, without having offered to return them to the defendant; (14) that the conductor called the plaintiff a liar before the plaintiff called him a liar; (15) that the plaintiff's damages are assessed at $300; (16) that in estimating such damages they gave him $299.54 for injury to his feelings. Thereupon the court ordered judgment for the plaintiff upon said special verdict for the sum of $299.60, being the amount of damages assessed by the jury, less the sum of forty cents paid for the ticket, for which the court held that the plaintiff was not entitled to recover in this action. From the judgment entered thereupon accordingly the defendant appeals.

For the appellant there was a brief by *Winkler, Flanders, Smith, Bottum & Vilas,* and oral argument by *C. H. Van Alstine.* They contended, *inter alia,* that the company had the right to make proper rules and regulations respecting the use of the round-trip tickets which the statute required it to sell at a lower rate than that which it might charge for one-way tickets. The rule of which plain notice was given in the words "Not good for passage if detached,"

was a reasonable one, and was essential to prevent the abuse
of such tickets. The ticket could be kept intact without
inconvenience. Rules which frequently occasion much an-
noyance and inconvenience have been declared reasonable:
Requiring passengers to pay a greater sum for fare if paid
on the cars than when paid at the depot. *Toledo, W. & W.
R. Co. v. Wright*, 68 Ind. 586; *Railroad Co. v. Skillman*, 39
Ohio St. 444; *Swan v. M. & L. R. Co.* 132 Mass. 116. Requiring all passengers on freight trains to provide themselves with freight-train tickets containing a stipulation
whereby they waived all damages for injuries occurring
through ordinary negligence. *Arnold v. I. C. R. Co.* 83 Ill.
273, 276-7. Prohibiting conductors of freight trains from
carrying passengers who have not previously procured a
specified kind of ticket. *Falkner v. O. & M. R. Co.* 55
Ind. 369. Requiring conductors to eject passengers who
are without tickets, although they tender the fare. *Lane
v. E. T., V. & G. R. Co.* 5 'Lea (Tenn.), 124. Requiring
passengers to procure from the conductor stop-over tickets
if they desire to stop over at intermediate stations and then
resume their journey. *Yorton v. M., L. S. & W. R. Co.* 54
Wis. 234. Providing that through trains shall not stop at
certain stations. *Plott v. C. & N. W. R. Co.* 63 Wis. 511.
But the question of reasonableness of regulation does not
arise here, because the words " Not good for passage if detached " were a part of the contract between the parties.
Rawitzky v. L. & N. R. Co. 31 Am. & Eng. R. Cas. 131, 132;
Norfolk & W. R. Co. v. Wysor, 26 id. 234; *Boston & M. R.
Co. v. Chipman*, 146 Mass. 107; *De Lucas v. N. O. & C. R.
Co.* 38 La. Ann. 930.

The refusal to permit the defendant to poll the jury was
error for which the verdict should be set aside. *Smith v.
State*, 51 Wis. 620; *Webster v. McKinster*, 1 Pin. 644; *State
v. Austin*, 6 Wis. 205; *Ruthbauer v. State*, 22 id. 468; *Labar
v. Koplin*, 4 N. Y. 547. The request that the jury be polled

was made at the proper time. *Fox v. Smith*, 3 Cow. 24; *Crotty v. Wyatt*, 3 Bradw. 388; *Warner v. N. Y. C. R. Co.* 52 N. Y. 440.

Assuming that the ticket presented was valid, there was reasonable ground for dispute as to its validity, and the respondent, though able to purchase tickets, absolutely refused to do so. Under these circumstances he was not entitled to damages for wounded feelings. *Gibson v. E. T., V. & G. R. Co.* 30 Fed. Rep. 904; *Hall v. M. & C. R. Co.* 15 id. 57. If he was entitled to such damages, the amount awarded was clearly excessive. *Hughes v. Western R. Co.* 61 Ga. 131; *Pearson v. Duane*, 4 Wall. 605; *Quigley v. C. P. R. Co.* 5 Sawy. 107; *Tarbell v. C. P. R. Co.* 34 Cal. 616.

For the respondent there was a brief by *F. S. Veeder, Duane Mowry*, and *B. C. Smith*, and oral argument by *Mr. Veeder*.

CASSODAY, J. When the jury first announced their verdict, the answer to the fifteenth question was $300, and the answer to the sixteenth question was, in effect, nothing, instead of the amounts above stated. The court thereupon intimated to the jury that such findings were inconsistent with themselves; that the jury had failed to observe the instructions of the court; that by reason thereof they were at liberty to go to their room for further consultation; that if they meant to answer as they had indicated, then, when they came in, they should say so. Thereupon the counsel for the defendant asked to have the jury polled, to see if that was in fact their verdict; but the court declined, for the time being, to receive such verdict, until the jury should go to their room for consultation. The court thereupon indicated the nature of some of the instructions which had previously been given to them; that no opinion had been intimated to them as to whether they should find anything for injury to feelings or not; that that question was left entirely to them. The defendant's counsel thereupon requested the court to receive and record such verdict, which was refused, and the jury thereupon retired for further consultation. Upon returning into court they answered the fifteenth question, forty-six cents, and the sixteenth, §300; and thereupon the court, for the same reasons, again refused to receive said verdict, and ordered the jury to again retire for further consultation, which they did; and thereupon they again returned into court with the verdict complete and substantially as found in the above statement of facts; and the same was thereupon received by the court and entered of record. The jury had been told in the general charge, in effect, that if they found for the plaintiff and that he was entitled to damages for injury to his feelings, then in answering the fifteenth question they should state the total amount of damages allowed,— as for loss of time, which should be "simply nominal,— six cents," and damages for injury to his feelings, and the amount he paid for the ticket, in one general sum; and then, in answer to the sixteenth question, that they should "state what damages," if any, " he suffered for injury to his feelings." It is manifest that the jury misapprehended these instructions until their last consultation. The learned trial judge scrupulously avoided anything like dictation as to whether the jury should find in favor of the one party or the other upon any of those items, but merely insisted upon having the questions submitted determined by the jury with a correct understanding of the instructions which had been given to them on that subject. Such action was manifestly within the province of the court. *Fick v. Mulholland*, 48 Wis. 419; *State ex rel. White Oak Springs v. Clementson*, 69 Wis. 628; *McMahan v. McMahan*, 53 Am. Dec. 482; *State v. Overton*, 61 Am. Dec. 671; The Work of the Advocate, 676, and cases there cited. The request to poll the jury was before the verdict was thus perfected, and hence, as a peremptory right, was premature.

The several findings of the jury are all supported by the evidence. A railway company may, undoubtedly, make reasonable regulations for the safe and orderly conduct of its business, and to protect itself against impositions. *Plott v. C. & N. W. R. Co.* 63 Wis. 511; *Mosher v. St. L., I. M. & S. R. Co.* 127 U. S. 390; 2 Am. & Eng. Ency. Law, 759. But this does not authorize such company, under the guise of regulations, to abridge or impair a passenger's statutory or legal rights. The statute required the defendant, upon application "at its ticket station" in Elroy, and payment of the price, to sell to the plaintiff "round-trip tickets, good for first-class passengers" from that station to Wonewoc and return. Sec. 1803, R. S. It stands confessed that the defendant did so sell and deliver to the plaintiff the ticket in question upon such application, payment, and purchase. It is, moreover, confessed that such ticket, in the condition it was at the time of purchase, entitled the plaintiff at the time and place he did to board the train in question and ride thereon to Wonewoc, and thereafter to return therefrom to Elroy by any train stopping at those stations and carrying such first-class passengers. The only defense to this action for expelling the plaintiff from the train is the fact, as found by the jury, that the white portion of the ticket was broken apart and separated from the red portion, without any carelessness or negligence of or on the part of the plaintiff, at the place where punctured for that purpose, before it was offered to the conductor for passage. But the respective parts of the ticket were numbered alike, and each contained the letters "R. T.,"— the one having thereon, "Going. Elroy to Wonewoc;" and the other, "Returning. Wonewoc to Elroy." The jury, moreover, found that both parts of the ticket were produced by the plaintiff and ex-

hibited to the conductor when he first came to the plaintiff
to collect his fare, and that the plaintiff still held both
parts of the ticket. Manifestly the two parts of the ticket
belonged together and had formerly been attached to each
other. The plaintiff appears to have been unable to account for their separation, except that he had carried the
ticket in his pocket for some months. The ticket was
"punctured for the purpose of separation;" and, of course,
with the expectation that it would be separated when first
used. It is claimed, however, that the words "Not good for
passage," on the going part of the ticket, and the words "if
detached," on the returning part of the ticket, were, together,
in effect, a stipulation that the ticket should be deemed
forfeited if such parts should be separated *by any other
person than the conductor*. But such are not the words of
the contract, and if such is to be deemed its legal effect
then it is because such stipulation is to be implied from the
words employed. Had the going part of the ticket *alone*
been presented to the conductor, there might have been
some force in the argument; for to allow that part *alone* to
be used, unaccompanied by the other part, would have the
effect to convert this "round-trip ticket" into two separate
single-trip tickets, to be used promiscuously. That would
permit the returning part to be used before the going part,
and hence give to the holder a right not secured by the
statute. The words "Not good for passage — if detached"
would seem to have been so placed upon the ticket to prevent imposition by a separation of the parts and the use of
each as a single-trip ticket. But where such parts of the
ticket become separated by such inadvertence, and are then
in good faith both presented together and at the same time
to the same conducter on the going trip, the purpose of
such words would seem to be as fully attained as though
the two parts of the ticket had not previously been separated. In other words, the presentation to the conductor

Wightman vs. The Chicago & Northwestern R. Co.

of the two parts of the ticket, under the circumstances found, is the same, in legal effect, as though such parts had not been detached when so presented.

It is to be remembered that the ticket was the mere evidence of the contract of carriage, and that such evidence consisted of two parts designed for separation. To imply such forfeiture of the contract from such mere inadvertent separation, under the circumstances found, when no word, letter, or figure on either part of the ticket was thereby obliterated, and when no perceivable injury to the defendant could result therefrom, would be to destroy a statutory right upon the merest technicality and in the absence of a clearly expressed stipulation to that effect. Even a strict literalism is not to be so rigidly enforced as to defeat the manifest purpose of a contract under a statute. Whether a different rule should prevail where the passenger wilfully, and against the protest of the conductor, separates the coupons or parts of a ticket, as in some of the cases cited, need not be here considered.

It follows that, upon the facts found, we must hold the defendant liable. Upon the whole record, and the repeated rulings of this court, we cannot say that the damages are excessive.

By the Court.— The judgment of the circuit court is affirmed.

See note to this case in 40 N. W. Rep. 693.— REP.

KOENIGS, Respondent, vs. JUNG and another, Appellants.

November 8 — December 22, 1888.

(1) Boundaries: Line of street: Evidence: Actual location. (2) Ease-
ment: Prescriptive right to maintain vault: Ownership of surface.
(3) Appeal: Bill of exceptions. (4) Trespass: Damages.

1. A finding of the jury fixing the line of a street is *held* to be sustained by evidence that the street was originally located on such
line more than thirty years ago and has been maintained thereon
ever since, although a recent survey tends to show that another
line is the true one.
2. One who by prescription acquires the right to maintain a vault or
cellar under another's land does not thereby acquire any right to
the surface over such vault.
3. The refusal of the trial court to submit certain questions or give
certain instructions to the jury will not be reviewed on appeal unless such questions and instructions, the rulings thereon, and the
exceptions to such rulings are made part of the record by the bill
of exceptions. Merely filing them with the clerk is insufficient.
4. Defendants having committed a wanton and oppressive trespass by
entering plaintiff's close early on a Sunday morning, with a large
force of men, and pushing their work of digging up the soil with
offensive haste, against the plaintiff's protest, a verdict for $250
damages is *held* not excessive.

APPEAL from the Circuit Court for *Milwaukee* County.
The facts will sufficiently appear from the opinion.

The cause was submitted for the appellants on the brief
of *J. C. Ludwig,* and for the respondent on that of *Stark*
& Sutherland.

To the point that defendants' prescriptive right to maintain a vault under plaintiff's lot gave them no right to
claim the lot above it or to exclude plaintiff from its possession, counsel for the respondent cited 1 Washb. Real
Prop. (3d ed.), 12; 3 id. 338–40; *Caldwell v. Fulton,* 31 Pa.
St. 475, 72 Am. Dec. 760, and note; *Hartwell v. Camman,*
10 N. J. Eq. 128, 64 Am. Dec. 448, and note; *McClintock*
v. Bryden, 63 Am. Dec. 100; *Riddle v. Brown,* 56 id. 202;

Mott v. Palmer, 1 N. Y. 570; *United States v. Castillero*, 2 Black, 168; *Thorn v. Wilson*, 110 Ind. 325; Tiedeman on Real Prop. sec. 621.

COLE, C. J.   This is an action for a trespass on real estate.   The plaintiff claims to own and to be in possession of the east 122 feet of the south half of lot 1, in block 131, of the First ward of the city of Milwaukee.   The lot is claimed to have an east frontage of 30 feet on Milwaukee street, and to extend west at a uniform width from the west line of said street, 122 feet.   The *gravamen* of the complaint is that the defendants — who own premises on the north and west — wrongfully entered upon the west end of the plaintiff's lot, took down fences and improvements, dug up the soil, and proceeded to erect a building which extended upon and covered a narrow strip of about 2½ feet wide of the plaintiff's lot.   There was much testimony given on both sides as to the ownership and possession of the disputed strip.   The jury found, in answer to questions submitted by the trial court, that the plaintiff owned by deed of conveyance and had been in the continuous possession of this disputed strip for more than thirty years, except as to a cellar which had been dug into the west end of the lot, which was some twelve feet under the surface and had been in possession or occupation of the defendants for twenty years.

The first error assigned is that there was no testimony to support this finding of the jury.   We think there is abundant evidence in the case to sustain it.   The controversy doubtless had its origin in a disagreement as to the actual line of Milwaukee street on the east of the premises.   To support the plaintiff's claim as to its true line, it was proven, or testimony was given tending to show, that there was an actual location of the block, lots, and adjacent streets by the official engineers of the city in 1854, and the

actual grading and improvement of Milwaukee street at
that time; its maintenance by the city ever since, which
would be most cogent and satisfactory evidence that the
actual location of the street, as then made, was the correct
one. The city engineers would be less likely to make a
mistake as to lines and boundaries of a public street, when
original stakes and monuments could be found, than any
survey made more than thirty years afterwards. Besides,
evidence of the continued use and occupation or recognition
of the limits of the street by the public and city authorities
would be almost conclusive in determining the true line
thereof. The observations made by Mr. Justice ORTON in
Racine v. J. I. Case Plow Co. 56 Wis. 539, are very perti-
nent and applicable to the testimony in this case. He says:
" The early settlers who first buy and build upon the lots
[in a city] do not attempt to ascertain their lines by a computation of measurements of all the other lots and blocks
by the figures on the plat, or stated in the certificate of
survey, or the courses and distances marked thereon, or by
a resurvey from the starting point of the first one. But
they consult the stakes and other monuments and land-
marks, either natural or artificial, fixed and placed at the
time of the original survey, if any, and such is generally
the case, and such is the method adopted by those who buy
and build afterwards if such land-marks still exist; and
afterwards, and after such monuments or land-marks have
been destroyed or removed, such lines are ascertained by
constructions of a permanent character, which were built
according to such original monuments; and finally, as time
goes on, long usage, prescription, antiquity, and reputation
may be the only means of determining the true lines and
boundaries; and these methods, in this order, are to be pre-
ferred " to any other evidence. It would be most unreasonable to assume that the city engineers in 1854 did not
correctly locate Milwaukee street when it was graded and

improved. It has been used and recognized by the city authorities as a public street as at present located, and has not been changed since that time. Expensive and permanent buildings have been built upon it on both sides from time to time. From these and other facts the jury were fully warranted in finding that the true and correct boundaries of the plaintiff's lot were as he claimed them to be, and that under his conveyance he owned the strip in question. This inference might well be made from the testimony, even as against stronger conflicting evidence than any that was given on the trial.

The next error assigned is that the answer to the second and third questions submitted to the jury is not full and complete, and does not dispose of the issues of fact included in said questions, arising upon the evidence, and is contrary to the law and evidence. These questions were, in substance, as to which party, plaintiff or defendants, had possession of the whole or part of the disputed strip when the alleged trespass was committed; and if there had been an actual separate possession of different parts thereof by the plaintiff and defendants and their respective grantors, then what portions had been so possessed, and the manner in which such possession was respectively taken and held. The jury found that the plaintiff had been in possession of the whole of his lot under his deed for a period of thirty years or more; that the defendants had been in possession of the lower cellar for the same period, which cellar was some twelve feet under the surface of the strip. It appears that there was quite a sharp slope on the west end of the plaintiff's lot; that a vault or cellar had been constructed by the defendants and their grantors into the slope, extending beneath the disputed strip. This cellar, though originally built without the knowledge or consent of the plaintiff, yet, as it did not interfere with the use and enjoyment of his lot, he took no steps to have removed. The

question arising upon these facts is, How were the plaintiff's rights in the strip affected by the construction and use
of the vault or cellar upon it? Did it operate to divest
him of the right to the soil or surface in any way? The
plaintiff's counsel claims that it did not; that, at most, the
defendants, as occupants of the vault or cellar, acquired by
prescription only an easement in the land analogous to the
right to maintain a conduit for water or a sewer under the
surface of another's land. The defendants' occupation of this
vault was not inconsistent and did not interfere with plaintiff's use or enjoyment of his lot over the vault, and their prescriptive right to maintain such vault gave them no right
to the lot above it, or to exclude the plaintiff from its possession. It is quite plain that one person may have an
easement in another's land, and that a double ownership or
possession may exist, as where one person owns land, and
another has a right of way over it, or the right to maintain
a pipe for conducting water through it, or the right to mine
under the soil and the like. In such cases, one person
owns and enjoys the surface, while another enjoys the easement, or works the mine under the soil, and these interests
may be distinct and not conflict with each other. So it
may be true, as the jury found, that the defendants had acquired the right to maintain their cellar or vault on the
plaintiff's lot, but this would not give them the right to
interfere with the surface over the vault, or to disturb him
in the use of the soil above. They have no general property in the lot, nor the proprietary interest in the real estate
itself. Their right is limited to the use and enjoyment of
the easement which they have acquired. The authorities
cited by the plaintiff's counsel clearly sustain these views,
if such elementary law needs authority to support it. The
second and third questions, therefore, submitted the testimony as to this double ownership and possession of this
disputed strip. The jury fairly answered the issues in re-

gard to them. The verdict is full and complete, and is based upon sufficient evidence. There is no inconsistency in the verdict, nor anything strange or anomalous in the legal relation of the parties. The plaintiff owns the whole strip, but the defendants, by adverse possession, have acquired the right to maintain the lower cellar upon it as they have occupied it for twenty years, but nothing further than this.

The third and fourth errors assigned are the refusal of the court to submit certain questions asked by the defendants, and to give certain instructions asked on their part. As to these alleged errors, it is sufficient to say they are not before us for review. The bill of exceptions does not contain the questions nor the instructions asked by the defendants. They should have been incorporated in the bill of exceptions in order that this court might consider them. Filing these questions and instructions with the clerk did not make them a part of the record so that this court could entertain them. They should have been embraced in the bill of exceptions, together with the rulings of the court upon them and the exceptions taken to such rulings; otherwise they will not be considered. The practice on this subject has long been settled (*Reid v. Case*, 14 Wis. 429; *Cord v. Southwell*, 15 Wis. 211), and numerous decisions have affirmed the same rule.

There is the further point that the damages awarded were excessive. The jury gave $250 damages, which doubtless included some smart money. The charge of the learned circuit court upon the question of damages is quite full, and submits the case fairly upon the evidence. Among other things, the jury were told that they could only award the plaintiff actual compensatory damages unless the trespass was a wanton and wilful one; that, in determining what the actual damages were, they should not consider the value of the property, but were limited to such damages as from the evidence they should find would compensate the plaintiff for the injury sustained; and, if he had sustained substantial damages,— that is, damages more than nominal,— exemplary damages might be given, providing the defendants had been guilty of wanton and malicious conduct. This is the tenor of the charge, which is too lengthy to be quoted entire. There was certainly proof of actual damages. The plaintiff's counsel justly says that the trespass was a most wanton, high-handed, and oppressive one, and this language is not too strong to characterize the defendants' acts, when the time, manner, and circumstances attending the trespass are considered. The defendants entered upon the plaintiff's close at an early hour of a Sunday morning, with a large force of men, and pushed their work of digging up the soil with offensive haste, against the protest of the plaintiff and in wanton disregard of his rights. We are not prepared to say that the damages are excessive, in view of their wrongful acts.

By the Court.— The judgment of the circuit court is affirmed.

THE HARRISON MACHINE WORKS, Respondent, vs. HOSIG, Appellant.

December 4 — December 22, 1888.

PRACTICE: ATTACHMENT: APPEAL. *(1) Denial of motion: Error in copy served of order to show cause. (2) Dismissal of action: Assessment of defendant's damages: Request. (3) Appealable orders: Several appeals: Costs.*

1. In the copy served of an order to "show cause why an order should not be entered dismissing the action," etc., the word *dismissing* had a pen-mark drawn through it. *Held*, that the motion should not have been denied merely for that reason.

The Harrison Machine Works vs. Hosig.

2. Where an action in which the defendant's goods have been attached
is dismissed, he is entitled upon request (under sec. 2747, R. S.) to
have a jury impaneled to assess his damages by reason of the taking of his property, although no request to that effect was contained in his motion to dismiss.

8. In an action in which the defendant's goods had been attached the
plaintiff failed to file security for costs as required. The court
made an order denying defendant's motion to dismiss the action
and for judgment for his damages, etc., but afterwards made a
second order dismissing the action but denying defendant's motion
for judgment for his damages, etc., and also a third order dismissing the action and denying defendant's motion and request for
judgment in his favor and to have a jury impaneled to assess his
damages, etc. The defendant took one appeal from the first and
third orders, and a separate appeal from the second order. *Held*,
that each of the several orders was appealable, but, as all might
have been embraced in one appeal, costs will be allowed to the appellant on one appeal only.

APPEALS from the County Court of *Dodge* County.

The following statement of the case was prepared by
Mr. Justice CASSODAY:

This action was commenced in the county court of Dodge
county by the service of summons and complaint, and personal property of the defendant to the amount of $690 was
attached, August 23, 1887. An answer was served October
5, 1887. Upon an affidavit showing that the plaintiff was
a corporation organized under the laws of Illinois, and on
October 25, 1887, the court ordered the plaintiff to file security for costs in the sum of $500 within twenty days after
the service of a copy of that order on the plaintiff's attorney, and that all proceedings on the part of the plaintiff
therein be stayed until such security be filed. Such copy
was so served November 1, 1887. November 17, 1887, the
plaintiff obtained an order from the trial court extending
its time to file such security twenty days. December 17,
1887, the plaintiff obtained another order extending such
time for twenty days longer. Upon an affidavit showing
such facts, and that the time for filing such security had ex-

pired, the trial court ordered the plaintiff to show cause, January 30, 1888, "why an order should not be entered *dismissing* said action, and why the defendant should not have judgment for his damages, costs, and disbursements." Upon the hearing of that motion, it was made to appear that in the copy served of such order to show cause the word "dismissing"—above in italics—had a pen drawn through it; and the said court thereupon, and on January 30, 1888, "ordered that said motion be, and the same hereby is, denied, with ten dollars costs of this motion." This is one of the orders appealed from, and for convenience will be designated as "Order No. 1."

Upon a new affidavit showing the facts above stated, the defendant obtained an order for the plaintiff to show cause, February 7, 1888, "why an order should not be entered herein dismissing said action, and why the defendant should not have judgment for his damages, costs, and disbursements." Upon the hearing of this last order to show cause, an affidavit was read, to the effect that order No. 1 was entered as aforesaid without leave to renew such motion; and thereupon, and on said February 7, 1888, the said trial court, at the instance of the defendant, in effect, "ordered that said action be, and the same is hereby, dismissed," but therein denied the defendant's motion and request to have judgment in his favor and to have a jury impaneled to assess the damages he had sustained by reason of such taking and detention of his said property on such attachment. This order, so made February 7, 1888, will, for convenience herein, be designated as "Order No. 3."

On the said February 7, 1888, and upon the hearing of the said last-named order to show cause, the said trial court also, at the instance of the plaintiff, in effect, separately "ordered that the said motion to dismiss said action be, and the same hereby is, granted; and that said motion for judgment for defendant's damages, costs, and disbursements be, and hereby is, denied; and said cause is hereby dismissed without damages, costs, or disbursements." This last order will for convenience herein be designated as "Order No. 2."

February 27, 1888, the defendant appealed from the whole of said order No. 1; and also, in the same notice, from that part of said order No. 3 in effect refusing to enter judgment for said defendant and in effect refusing to impanel a jury at his request to assess his damages by reason of such taking and detention of his said goods on such attachment. May 10, 1888, the defendant separately appealed from that part of said order No. 2 in effect refusing the defendant's motion for damages, costs, and disbursements, and dismissing said action without damages, costs, and disbursements.

Motions to dismiss the appeals were made by the respondent and argued on behalf of the respective parties, and the appeals were subsequently argued on their merits.

For the appellant there was a brief by *J. E. Malone*, attorney, and *J. J. Dick* of counsel, and oral argument by *J. J. Dick*.

H. W. Sawyer, for the respondent, contended, *inter alia*, that the appeal from order No. 2 should be dismissed because, although it was duly entered and of force when the appeal was taken from the other two orders, the defendant did not embrace it in that appeal, as he might have done under ch. 49, Laws of 1883. The word *may* in that act should be construed as *must*. *Harrington v. Smith*, 28 Wis. 59; *Ryegate v. Wardsboro*, 30 Vt. 746. Otherwise the appellant may take separate appeals from several orders, and if he succeeds will recover costs in each case, and the court has no discretion in the matter. R. S. sec. 2949. But if all are included in one appeal the costs are within the discretion of the court. Sec. 2, ch. 49, Laws of 1883. Order No. 3 was not appealable because (1) order No. 2 dismissed the action and disposed of all questions in the case. (2) It was

entered at appellant's request and purely in his interests,
without plaintiff's knowledge. *Volenti non fit injuria.*
Rogers v. Hœnig, 46 Wis. 361. (3) The appeal from this
order is from that part thereof " refusing to enter judgment
for said defendant, and refusing to impanel a jury at the
request of the defendant *after said action had been dismissed.*" This was covered by the appeal from order No.
2. Where two appeals are taken to obtain relief which can
be obtained in one, one will be dismissed. *Groner v. Hield,*
22 Wis. 205; *Hopkins v. Hopkins,* 39 id. 166; *Wis. River
L. Co. v. Plumer,* 49 id. 668.

CASSODAY, J. The plaintiff is a corporation organized
under the laws of Illinois. It is therefore a foreign corporation, within the meaning of our statute. Sec. 2943,
R. S. In such a case, the defendant may require such plaintiff to file security for costs. *Ibid.* The defendant did
make proof by affidavit of such fact entitling him to such
security, and the trial court thereupon ordered the same,
as required by statute. Sec. 2945, R. S. The plaintiff
failed to file such security as thus required, notwithstanding the time for doing so had twice been extended. There
was no appeal from that order, and we must therefore assume it was properly made, even if the security was given
as required on the attachment proceedings. Sec. 2932,
R. S. The plaintiff having failed to file such undertaking
as thus required, the defendant thereupon became entitled,
upon motion, to have the plaintiff's action dismissed by the
court. Sec. 2946, R. S. January 30, 1888, the defendant
moved the court, upon an affidavit showing such default,
for an order dismissing the action, and for judgment for
damages, costs, and disbursements. That motion was
wholly denied, with costs, by order No. 1, appealed from.
It is said that that motion was denied by reason of a pen-
mark having been drawn through the word " dismissing "

in the copy served of the order to show cause. Such
ground for refusal would seem to be too finical for the
practical proceedings in courts of justice, where special regard is supposed to be had to the substance of things rather
than mere verbal expressions. The purpose of the motion
would seem to have been sufficiently manifest, and it
should have been granted, at least to the extent of dismissing the action.

To that extent the same motion, on being renewed February 7, 1888, was in effect granted. It appears that on
the decision of that motion the attorney of each party
drew up an order and induced the court to sign the same.
The substance of each of those orders is stated above, and
there respectively designated as Order No. 2 and Order
No. 3. But each of those orders granted the defendant's
motion so far as to dismiss the action; and of course costs
and disbursements would naturally follow as an incident,
but were not allowed. Upon such dismissal of the action
it became the duty of the court, on the request of the defendant, to impanel a jury to assess such damages, if any,
as he had sustained by reason of the taking and detention
of the property attached, or by reason of any injury
thereto, in order to have such damages included in the
judgment to be entered. Sec. 2747, R. S. It would seem
that the defendant had no other remedy. *Ashland Co. v.
Stahl*, 48 Wis. 593. Order No. 3 recites the issuance of the
attachment, the sheriff's return showing the seizure and
holding of the property attached, the defendant's request
to have such jury impaneled to assess such damages, and
his motion for judgment. There seems to be no substantial reason for denying such request. The statute cited
secured such assessment to the defendant as a matter of
right upon the showing made. So the defendant was entitled to his motion for judgment of dismissal with costs
and disbursements, and for such damages, if any, as should

be so assessed. Such judgment would be entered after the assessment; or before, leaving a blank for such damages when so assessed. It is true such order to show cause upon which orders Nos. 2 and 3 were made contains no request for such impaneling of a jury, but, when the court announced its decision in favor of dismissal, the defendant became entitled to the impaneling of such jury upon simple request, which appears to have been made. It is true that in each of the orders to show cause the defendant moves for "judgment for his damages" as a part of such motion, and the same was denied in orders Nos. 1 and 2, respectively. The defendant was not entitled to judgment for such damages as a part of such motion, but only upon their being assessed by such jury as incident to such dismissal.

The defendant has taken an appeal from said orders Nos. 1 and 3 in one notice and undertaking, and a separate appeal from said order No. 2. We think each of these several orders was appealable. Sec. 3069, R. S. Each was made in an action and affected a substantial right, within the meaning of the statute. *Ibid.* The mere taking of the one did not waive the right to take the other. But since the act to simplify appeals authorizes a party to embrace two or more orders in one notice of appeal and one undertaking, it is obviously not the policy of the statute to allow him to increase his costs by bringing separate appeals. Sec. 3052, R. S.; ch. 49, Laws of 1883. Especially is this so where, as here, all the orders relate substantially to the same proceeding. The case must therefore be treated the same as though all three orders were embraced in the first appeal.

By the Court.— The motions to dismiss the appeals are denied, with $10 costs. Order No. 1 is wholly reversed. Order No. 2 is reversed in so far as it denied the defendant's motion for judgment with costs and disbursements, and in so far as it may be implied therefrom that the defendant is to have no damages in any event. Order No. 3 is reversed in so far as it denied the defendant's request to have a jury impaneled to assess such damages, and in so far as it refused the defendant's motion for judgment with costs and disbursements. In so far as orders Nos. 2 and 3, respectively, dismiss the action, the same are affirmed. The defendant is only allowed such costs in this action, in this court, as are taxable on the first appeal. Sec. 2, ch. 49, Laws of 1883. The cause is remanded for further proceedings according to law.

KELLY, Respondent, vs. SMITH and wife, Appellants.

December 5 — December 22, 1888.

Equity: Cancellation of deed: Incapacity of grantor: Fraud: Inadequate consideration.

A judgment setting aside a conveyance of land from the plaintiff to the defendants is affirmed, the evidence being *held* to sustain the findings of the trial court that the plaintiff was a woman about seventy-five years old and unable, by reason of ignorance and mental weakness, to make a sale of her land or to comprehend the effect of such a sale, and that the defendants, upon whose counsel and advice she was accustomed to depend, took advantage of her ignorance and weakness of mind to obtain such conveyance for a grossly inadequate consideration.

APPEAL from the Circuit Court for *Waukesha* County. Action for the cancellation of a conveyance of land. The facts are stated in the opinion.

John M. Whitehead, for the appellants.

For the respondent there was a brief by *Dunwiddie & Goldin,* attorneys, and *John Winans,* of counsel, and the cause was argued orally by *B. F. Dunwiddie* and *John Winans.*

ORTON, J. The plaintiff, at the time of the trial, was about seventy-five years old. She is the widow of James Kelly, deceased, who died where she now lives, in Rock county, about eighteen years ago. She was born in Ireland, and married when about eighteen years of age, and had seven children, all of whom died there, together with her husband; and she then came to Canada, and there married the said James Kelly, and lived there about seven years, and then, with her husband, came to her present place of residence in Rock county, where the father of the defendant *Collin Smith* built for them a house on his own land, about three fourths of a mile from where she now lives. In a short time James purchased the twenty acres of land in question, and had it deeded to himself and the plaintiff, and the house they occupied on the land of Smith was by him moved on the same, and they occupied it together until James died as aforesaid. Since then the plaintiff has lived in the same alone, and managed her small farm, mostly by renting it for cash and in shares at the rate of about $75 per year. She seems to have been a woman of rather low natural capacity, and extremely ignorant and un-cultivated. She has resided where she now lives about thirty years, and is well known to all of her near neighbors, many of whom have at different times rendered her much assistance in the management of her business. She has no relatives in this country, and had no children by her last husband. Upon the death of her husband she became sole owner of the land and property, which had been her only means of support, and has occupied the house all the time since her husband's death, except about three years after his death. The land was of the value of $800, and it is not known by others whether she has any money or means be-

Kelly vs. Smith and wife.

yond this little farm and her household goods. On the question of her capacity or ability to do her own business and to sell her property, the findings of the circuit court are as follows:

"That the plaintiff is upwards of seventy-five years old, and is a person of great ignorance and mental weakness, being unable to read or write or count, and cannot tell the time of day by a time-piece, and does not know her age. That she is unable to count money of any kind, and, whenever she makes sales of such little produce as her land yields, has to depend entirely on others to compute the amount due her, and to tell her when she has received her full due, and to count the money with which she pays for such purchases as her necessities require. That she is entirely ignorant of all business forms and matters, and is unable to tell the name and comprehend the legal effect or character of any legal paper from hearing it read, and is wholly incompetent to do or understand any business transactions beyond the purchase of a few necessaries such as she is accustomed to buy, and to look after the sale and disposition of the produce of her little farm, and even in these matters she has to depend on the assistance and honesty of those with whom she deals, and is easily imposed upon and cheated. That she has always been accustomed to advise with her friends and neighbors, and especially with the defendants above named, about all her small matters, and to depend upon and act entirely upon their counsel and advice. That she is and was at the time of the execution of the conveyance hereinafter mentioned, by reason of her ignorance and mental weakness, incompetent to make a sale or disposition of her real estate, or to understand or comprehend the effect of any disposition thereof beyond the mere rental to which she had been accustomed."

It was further found, in substance, that the defendants, husband and wife, had long lived near the plaintiff, and knew well her mental weakness, ignorance, and incapacity, and that the plaintiff had been accustomed to rely upon their advice and counsel, and they exercised a controlling influence upon her, and they were very friendly and confidential in their relations.

There was evidence to sustain these findings, although, upon the question of the plaintiff's incapacity and inability to do business for herself, there was considerable conflict of the evidence. In such case we would not be warranted in disturbing the findings of the court, and, although they were excepted to by the learned counsel of the appellants, we shall have to accept the facts so found as true, in disposing of the case.

It was further found that on the 12th day of June, 1885, the defendants, *Collin Smith* and *Carrie B. Smith*, his wife, procured a deed of the said premises to be executed to them; that the only consideration of said conveyance was an agreement on the part of the defendants to pay the plaintiff annually, during her life, on the 1st day of September of each year, commencing September 1, 1885, the sum of $65, and to furnish her fire-wood in sufficient quantity for her use during her life, amounting in all to not more than $75 per year, which was the value of the rental of said premises; that no provision whatever was made for the plaintiff in case of sickness or in case the $75 per year was not sufficient for her necessities, or for her burial after her death, or for any care or attention which the plaintiff might need by reason of her old age, sickness, or helplessness; that the plaintiff had no advice or counsel except that of the defendants; that the legal effect and character of the conveyance were not explained, understood, or known to her, or comprehended by her, and that she supposed and understood at the time, and until some time afterwards, that she was merely renting her premises to the defendants; that the defendants took advantage of the plaintiff's misunderstanding, ignorance, and weakness of mind to wrongfully obtain said conveyance, and they have not as yet performed their agreement or paid anything thereon, except to deliver a small quantity of wood, which the plaintiff refused to accept.

This is a suit in equity to have said conveyance declared fraudulent and void, and canceled, and such was the judgment from which this appeal is taken.

The learned counsel of the appellants contends that the findings are not supported by the evidence. We have already said that the findings in respect to the plaintiff's incompetency and want of ability to make the contract or conveyance are supported by evidence, and so we may say of all the other material findings. This is all there is of this case. The testimony of some of the plaintiff's neighbors supports the findings literally as to her ignorance, incapacity, and dependence. It would be useless to refer to the evidence in any other than in this general way. The case rests solely on questions of fact, and neither party has cited any authorities, and none are necessary in the case made by the findings of the court. The facts found make a very strong case for the relief asked. The incapacity of the plaintiff to make a disposition of her property, by mental weakness and dense ignorance, is intensified by her age. To her the consideration of this sale is grossly inadequate to provide for her future wants, through helplessness, sickness, and death, and the property is of sufficient value for such purposes. The defendants, according to the evidence, used undue influence to induce her to dispose of her property in this way, or did not make her understand the legal effect of the paper she signed. The advice of their brother, an attorney at law, to give the property back to her, ought to have been followed by the defendants.

By the Court.— The judgment of the circuit court is affirmed.

See note to this case in 41 N. W. Rep. 69.— REP.

THE HORICON SHOOTING CLUB, Appellant, vs. GORSLINE, Respondent.

December 5 — December 22, 1888.

APPEAL. *(1) Order striking cause from calendar. (2) Order not shown by record.*

1. An order striking a cause from the calendar because prematurely noticed for trial, amounts merely to a continuance over the term, and is not appealable.
2. An appeal will not lie from an order which the record does not show was actually made.

APPEAL from the County Court of *Dodge* County.

Action for a trespass to land. The facts affecting this appeal will sufficiently appear from the opinion.

For the appellant the cause was submitted on the brief of *C. S. Matteson.*

For the respondent there was a brief by *S. J. Morse,* attorney, and *James J. Dick,* of counsel, and oral argument by *Mr. Dick.*

BY THE COURT. This appeal is from two alleged orders, one striking the cause from the calendar for the reason that it was prematurely noticed for trial; and the other refusing to change the place of trial on affidavit of the prejudice of the judge. The defendant moves to dismiss the appeal. We think the motion should be granted. The first order amounts only to a continuance of the cause over the term. Such an order does not affect the merits of the action, but is a mere matter of practice or procedure, and is not appealable. *McLeod v. Bertschy,* 30 Wis. 324. As to the alleged order refusing to change the place of trial, the record fails to show that any such order was made. The printed case contains what purports to be a remark of the judge to the effect that the application for such change was not properly made for want of notice thereof to the opposite party, but such observation was never embodied in an order. Hence there is nothing to appeal from.

Appeal dismissed.

=====

BEERY, Appellant, vs. THE CHICAGO & NORTHWESTERN RAILWAY COMPANY, Respondent.

December 5 — December 22, 1888.

(1) Appeal: Evidence: Immaterial error. (2, 3) Negligence: Cause of accident: Speed of railroad train: Instructions to jury: Degree of proof. (4) New trial: Newly discovered evidence.

1. In an action for personal injuries alleged to have been caused by negligence the trial court permitted the defendant to cross-examine the plaintiff as to incumbrances upon his property, the object being to show that he was pecuniarily embarrassed and was simulating or aggravating the character and extent of his injuries. The jury having found that there was no actionable negligence, it is *held* that the above ruling, even if erroneous, could not have prejudiced the plaintiff.

2. An accident to a railroad train was caused by the breaking of the side-rods of the engine. The speed at which the train was running was not unlawful or unusual, and it was not shown that it would tend to contribute to such breakage. *Held*, that it was not error to instruct the jury that the speed of the train had no connection with the accident and could not be considered on the question of negligence.

3. An instruction that the jury should feel " reasonably certain " as to what they should find to be the cause of an accident, is *held* not erroneous.

4. To support a motion for a new trial on the ground of newly discovered evidence that the breaking of the side-rods on defendant's engine was the result of negligence, the plaintiff filed affidavits of two section men that on the day after the accident they picked up pieces of the strap or iron frame which held the brasses of the side-rod in place, and now have such pieces in their possession. The

plaintiff's own affidavit stated that he had examined such pieces since the trial, and that one of them plainly showed that it had been cracked for some time before the final break. Plaintiff's description of this piece was adopted in the affidavits of the section men, but in none of the affidavits was there any attempt to describe the appearance of the piece when it was picked up, but only its appearance after it had been lying about exposed to the air and dirt for several months. *Held*, that it was not error to refuse to grant the new trial, the appearance of the piece after such exposure not warranting any inference that there was an old crack therein at the time of the accident.

APPEAL from the Circuit Court for *Sauk* County.

Action to recover damages for personal injuries, alleged to have been caused by defendant's negligence. The facts will sufficiently appear from the opinion. The jury found a special verdict to the effect that the defendant was not guilty of any negligence with respect to the condition of the engine in question. A motion for a new trial was denied, and from the judgment entered on the verdict in favor of the defendant the plaintiff appeals.

G. Stevens, for the appellant.

For the respondent there was a brief by *Winkler, Flanders, Smith, Bottum & Vilas*, and oral argument by *E. P. Vilas*.

Cole, C. J. This is an action to recover damages for injuries sustained by the plaintiff while a passenger upon a freight train on the defendant's road. While riding on the freight train between Reedsburg and La Valle the plaintiff, who was in the caboose, discovered that the engine was pounding and tearing up the track, and saw that the cars were jumping and moving in an unusual manner, saw the conductor, who was at the time on top of the train, get down and jump off, and, judging from appearances that there would be a general wreck of the train, deemed it safe to jump from the train, and avoid being caught in the crash, and thereby sustained the injury of which he complains. It appeared that the side-rods of the engine broke, and aside from the fact that the accident happened, and the presumption of negligence arising therefrom, the only evidence of negligence on the part of the defendant attempted to be shown was that the breaking of the side-rods was caused by some defect in the pins or fastenings where the connection with the driving-wheels was made, or that these parts were not kept properly oiled.

During the cross-examination of the plaintiff as a witness, after he had testified as to the circumstances of the accident, his injury, etc., and that he was the owner of a flouring-mill, he was asked by the defendant's counsel what amount of mechanics' liens were on the mill in August, 1887. This was objected to, but the court overruled the objection, and the witness answered. The first error assigned is this ruling of the court. It is said that the question had no bearing whatever upon the issue of negligence, which was the issue in the case. This is true. The object of the question doubtless was to show that the plaintiff was pecuniarily embarrassed, and was simulating or aggravating the character and extent of his injuries. But this ruling could not have prejudiced the plaintiff in any way, even if erroneous, because the jury found that no actionable negligence was proven. The question of damages was not, therefore, reached.

Two exceptions taken to the charge of the court are relied on as error here. The court charged that the speed of the train was not unlawful, and had no connection with the accident, and could not be considered on the question of negligence. It clearly appeared that the speed of the train was not unusual, and we fail to perceive how it could have contributed to the breaking of the fastenings of the side-rods of the engine. It is said such speed would or might have much to do with the heating of the brasses which constitute a part of the side-rods, if these brasses were not kept properly oiled, because it would greatly increase the friction of those parts. It was not shown what really caused the breakage of the side-rods, or that the rate at which the train was moving would tend to contribute to such breakage. The cause of the breakage of the side-rods rests in conjecture. The evidence does not explain it, or connect it with the speed of the train. It is quite as reasonable to assume that it was pure accident, against which no degree of care or vigilance could guard, as to attribute it to any other cause. It is more probable the proximate cause of the breaking was a sudden strain upon or cramping of these parts while the train was moving. It is a matter of common knowledge that at best the heavy and complicated machinery used upon railroads is liable to break by inequalities in the track, or a sudden strain, or from some other cause, where the greatest care and skill have been exercised in its construction and use. The learned circuit court left it to the jury to determine whether the breakage was an accident for which nobody could account and no one was responsible, or whether it was produced by the negligence of the engineer in not taking due care of the engine. But upon the evidence there was no ground for predicating negligence on the speed of the train.

The other exception is based upon the language of the court that the jury must feel *reasonably certain*, not only that the engine or the part in question had not been properly oiled and cared for, but they should feel *reasonably certain* that it affected the pins that broke so as to cause the dropping of the bars in question. The court added that in civil cases the jury did not arrive at conclusions beyond a reasonable doubt, but they should feel reasonably certain that what they find is true. It is said that this charge required the plaintiff to make out his case by something more than the mere preponderance of proof, and nearly approached the rule for the reformation of a written instrument, where the proof is required to be clear and most satisfactory. We do not think this is the meaning of the charge. The jury were merely told that they must be satisfied that their finding was in accord with the weight of testimony; in other words, that the preponderance of the evidence must convince their judgments of the truth of the fact found. This is all the charge means, not that the evidence to establish a fact must be clear and most satisfactory. We do not think there was anything misleading in the charge upon this point.

The only other error to be noticed is the refusal of the court to grant a new trial on the ground of newly discovered evidence. The material part of the newly discovered evidence is contained in the affidavit of the plaintiff, who states that, after the trial, he learned from Courtier and Webster, section men of the defendant, that "each picked up a piece of the strap or iron frame which surrounds the brasses and holds them in place, and which is bolted to the side-rod, and then had them in their possession; that the piece so picked up by and in the possession of Webster, which the plaintiff had seen and carefully examined, is broken off squarely at the edge of the square hole made to receive the key by which the brasses were tightened up and held firmly in place, both pieces being broken in the same place; that the piece of said strap or frame so picked up by and in the possession of the said Webster plainly shows that the iron on one side of said square hole had been cracked about half way off, and the other side also cracked, but not quite so much, for some time before the final break. It also shows plainly that the brasses had been loose, so as to play back and forth, for a long time." The plaintiff, of course, is speaking of the appearance of these pieces of iron at the time he examined them. The affidavits of both Courtier and Webster were used in support of the motion, in which each states that the next day after the accident he was present where it occurred, and then "picked up a piece of the strap or iron frame which holds the brasses of the side-rod of the locomotive in place, and took the same away and retained it in his possession, intending to have it made into an iron wedge; that said piece, with its cracks, marks of wear, and other defects, is correctly described in the affidavit of the" plaintiff, the language of which said affidavit, so far as relates to a description of said piece of said iron strap or frame and its said imperfections and defects, is hereby adopted and made part of each affidavit.

Now it will be noticed that neither of these persons attempts to describe, or does describe, the appearance of the broken piece at the time it was picked up, when it was possible to see whether there was an old crack in the piece or not. The plaintiff did not see the pieces until several months after the accident, when it was impossible to tell from existing marks whether there was an old crack in them when broken or not. These pieces had been lying about exposed to the air and dirt, and would naturally present the same appearance where broken. This is common experience. No safe or proper inference could be drawn from such appearance at that time as to the existence of an old crack in them. Courtier and Webster say they adopt the language of the plaintiff so far as relates to the piece of strap, but refrain from describing the appearance of the piece when found and when an old crack could have been seen if it existed. As bearing upon the question of negligence it would be material and important could it be shown that such a crack in the iron fastening existed at the time of the accident. There would then be ground for holding that the agents of the company should have discovered the defect in the machinery, and repaired it. But to prove the appearance of these pieces of iron and of the marks upon them after the lapse of some months, when the pieces had been exposed, would not warrant any inference that there was an old crack to be seen in them at the time of the accident. So really the newly discovered evidence does not tend to prove any fact material to the issue of negligence. It is too vague and uncertain to base any conclusion upon. We therefore think that the circuit court did not err in refusing to grant a new trial on the ground of newly discovered evidence.

By the Court.— The judgment of the circuit court is affirmed.

GILLETT, Appellant, vs. THE LIVERPOOL & LONDON & GLOBE INSURANCE COMPANY, Respondent.

December 5 — December 22, 1888.

Insurance against fire: Estoppel: Retention of policy without objection: Avoidance of policy by other insurance: Mortgagor and mortgagee.

A mortgage provided that if the mortgagors failed to insure the property the mortgagee might insure the same, the expense thereof being added to the mortgage debt. The mortgagee applied to the defendant company for insurance on the property to secure his interest therein. The defendant issued the policy in suit, insuring the *mortgagors* against loss, but providing that the loss, if any, should be payable to the mortgagee as his interest should appear. The policy also provided that it should be void if the assured obtained other insurance on the property or any part thereof without consent, etc. This policy was delivered to the mortgagee, who paid the premium, and retained the policy without objection for nearly a year before the property was burned. *Held:*

(1) The mortgagee was bound by the stipulations of the policy.

(2) Subsequent insurance upon the property, obtained by and insuring the interest of *one* of the mortgagors, avoided the policy.

APPEAL from the Circuit Court for *Marathon* County. Action on a policy of insurance.

Plaintiff held a mortgage on certain real estate of M. A. York & Co., a firm consisting of Mrs. M. A. York and her husband, Solomon. The mortgage was given by that firm to secure an indebtedness of $2,000, which still remains unpaid. The principal value of the mortgaged premises was in a saw-mill situated thereon, and certain machinery and fixtures therein. This mortgage contained a covenant by the mortgagors to keep the buildings on the mortgaged premises insured for at least $2,500, and to assign the policies to the plaintiff as collateral security for the mortgage debt, and, in default thereof, the plaintiff was authorized to effect such insurance, the costs and expenses of which to be added to and become a part of the mortgage debt. The mortgagors having failed to obtain such insurance, the plaintiff, on September 7, 1883, procured from the defendant company the policy in suit. This policy insures M. A. York & Co. against loss of the insured property or damage thereto by fire, for one year, in the sum of $1,000. It contains a stipulation that the same shall be void "if the insured shall have, or shall hereafter make, any other insurance on the property hereby insured, or any part thereof, without the consent of this company written hereon." It permits $2,000 total concurrent insurance, and provides that "loss, if any, under this policy, payable to *J. D. Gillett, Esq.,* as his interest may appear."

In March, 1884, Mrs. York, without the consent of the defendant company, procured further insurance on substantially the same property, in several other insurance companies, amounting in the aggregate to $4,000. August 16, 1884, the insured property was destroyed by fire. In November, 1884, plaintiff furnished defendant company with proofs of loss, in which such insurance of $4,000, obtained by Mrs. York, is stated. The defendant refused to pay the insurance written in the policy, and the plaintiff brought this action to recover it.

The foregoing facts are conclusively established by the pleadings and the testimony on the trial, to which further reference is made in the opinion. The circuit judge directed the jury to return a verdict for the defendant, which they accordingly did. A motion for a new trial was denied, and judgment entered for the defendant pursuant to the verdict. The plaintiff appeals from the judgment.

The cause was submitted for the appellant on the brief of *Silverthorn, Hurley, Ryan & Jones,* and for the respondent on that of *Cate, Jones & Sanborn.*

For the appellant it was contended, *inter alia,* that the policy in question insured only the mortgagee's interest in the property. On the face of the policy he was a party to the contract, and having applied only for insurance on his own interest, and having paid the premium, and the policy having been delivered to him alone, he was the owner of the policy and the real party in interest. The insertion in the policy of the names of the mortgagors amounted to nothing because they did not apply for the policy, or pay for it, and it was not delivered to them. The amount of the insurance was less than the mortgagee's interest, and so could not cover any interest of the mortgagors. The policy is to be distinguished from one making the loss, if any, payable to a third party, without the words "as his interest may appear." Cases cited upon policies not containing those words are not in point. See *Pitney v. Glen's Falls Ins. Co.* 65 N. Y. 6; *Dakin v. Liverpool, L. & G. Ins. Co.* 77 id. 601; *Union Trust Co. v. Whiton,* 97 id. 178; *Richmond v. Niagara F. Ins. Co.* 79 id. 237; *Westchester F. Ins. Co. v. Foster,* 90 Ill. 121; *Appleton Iron Co. v. British Am. Ass. Co.* 46 Wis. 23. The mortgagee being the assured party, the provision against other insurance being taken by the assured could be violated only by the *mortgagee himself* taking other insurance in excess of that authorized by the policy. A policy containing a provision making it void in case of other insurance is not avoided unless such other assurance is (1) valid; (2) upon the same identical property; (3) upon the same identical interest in the property; (4) issued to the same identical person or for his benefit. 2 Wood on Ins. ch. 11, secs. 372–377.

Two insurances effected on the same property are held not to avoid a policy prohibiting other insurance: (1) Where one policy is taken by the mortgagor and the other by the mortgagee. *Acer v. Merchants' Ins. Co.* 57 Barb. 68; *Westchester F. Ins. Co. v. Foster*, 90 Ill. 121; *Nichols v. Fayette Ins. Co.* 1 Allen, 63; *Woodbury, S. B. & B. A. v. Charter Oak F. & M. Ins. Co.* 31 Conn. 517; *Fox v. Phenix F. Ins. Co.* 52 Me. 333; *Norwich F. Ins. Co. v. Boomer*, 52 Ill. 442; *Titus v. Glens Falls Ins. Co.* 81 N. Y. 410; *Doran v. Franklin F. Ins. Co.* 86 id. 635; *Sauvey v. Isolated Risk & F. F. Ins. Co.* 44 Up. Can. Q. B. 523; *Guest v. New Hampshire Ins. Co.* 33 N. W. Rep. (Mich.), 31; *Carpenter v. Continental Ins. Co.* 61 Mich. 635; *City F. C. S. Bank v. Penn. F. Ins. Co.* 122 Mass. 165. (2) Where one policy is taken by the vendee of land under a contract of sale, and the other by the vendor. *Burbank v. Rockingham M. F. Ins. Co.* 24 N. H. 550; *Ætna F. Ins. Co. v. Tyler*, 16 Wend. 385; *Acer v. Merchants' Ins. Co.* 57 Barb. 68; *Mutual Safety Ins. Co. v. Hone*, 2 N. Y. 235; *Sprague v. Holland P. Ins. Co.* 69 id. 128. (3) When one of the policies does not cover all of the property covered by the other. *Boatman's F. & M. Ins. Co. v. Hocking*, 8 Atl. Rep. (Pa.), 417; *Sloat v. Royal Ins. Co.* 49 Pa. St. 14; *Baltimore F. Ins. Co. v. Loney*, 20 Md. 20; *Sunderlin v. Ætna Ins. Co.* 18 Hun, 522; *Parsons v. Queen Ins. Co.* 29 Up. Can. C. P. 188; *Illinois M. F. Ins. Co. v. Fix*, 53 Ill. 151. (4) Insurances effected by the owner and by an attaching creditor or other person interested. *Marigny v. Home M. Ins. Co.* 13 La. Ann. 338; *Gilchrist v. Gore Dist. M. F. Ins. Co.* 34 Up. Can. Q. B. 15; *Kelly v.*

Liverpool & L. & G. Ins. Co. 2 Han. (N. B.), 266. (5) By consignor and consignee on same property. *Williams v. Cresent M. Ins. Co.* 15 La. Ann. 651. (6) By the owner and his creditor. *National Ins. Co. v. Trudell*, Ramsay's App. Cas. (Low. Can.), 366. (7) Insurance for different parties having interests in the property. *Bates v. Commercial Ins. Co.* 1 Cin. Sup. Ct. Rep. 523; *Roos v. Merchants' M. Ins. Co.* 27 La. Ann. 409.

The policy in suit could not be avoided by subsequent insurance on the interest of *one* member of the firm of M. A. York & Co. 2 Wood on Ins. sec. 377; *Lowell Mfg. Co. v. Safeguard F. Ins. Co.* 88 N. Y. 591; *Irving v. Excelsior F. Ins. Co.* 1 Bosw. 507; *Manhattan Ins. Co. v. Webster*, 59 Pa. St. 227; *Converse v. Citizens' M. Ins. Co.* 10 Cush. 37; *Phœnix Ins. Co. v. Hamilton*, 14 Wall. 504; *Warren v. Davenport F. Ins. Co.* 31 Iowa, 464; *Harris v. Ohio Ins. Co.* 5 Ohio, 467.

LYON, J. To strengthen his security for the mortgage debt by an insurance upon the mortgaged property, two methods were open to the plaintiff. He might have taken a policy directly to himself, insuring his mortgage interest alone, if he could find an insurer willing to issue such a policy; or he could obtain a policy running to the mortgagors, stipulating that the loss, if any, should be paid to him as his interest should appear. Perhaps such a policy would not be an insurance of the mortgage interest, as such, but probably would cover such interest. Either mode would protect the plaintiff's security under his mortgage, but with this difference: had the policy run to himself alone, insuring only his mortgage interest, it would not be defeated by an unauthorized insurance upon the same property, obtained by the mortgagors, while a policy running to the mortgagors, insuring the property generally (as in the present case), would be defeated by such unauthorized insurance.

The plaintiff did not stipulate with the agent of the defendant company, Mr. Huntington, for a policy to himself,
insuring only his mortgage interest. The only testimony
on the subject was given by the plaintiff himself, and is as
follows: "I applied to Mr. Huntington for the insurance
on this property after the mortgage was executed. I received this policy upon the application." In answer to the
question by his own counsel, "At the time when you applied to Mr. Huntington for this insurance did you state to
him what interest you had in the property?" he further
testified: "I think I did tell him that I had a mortgage on
the property, and wanted to insure my interest in it." He
further testified that he paid the premium for such insurance. Thus, it is undisputed that the plaintiff applied
for an insurance upon the mortgaged property to secure
his interest therein under his mortgage, without any agreement or reservation as to its form or the stipulations it
should contain. The agent issued the policy in suit upon
such application, which gives the plaintiff the security he
desired. The plaintiff accepted it as a compliance with his
application, and held it nearly a year before the property
was burned, without making any objection that it did not
comply with the original parol contract for the insurance.
We think it too late for the plaintiff to be now heard to allege that the policy does not contain the terms of the contract of insurance which the parties made, even did the
testimony tend to show (which it does not) that a parol
agreement was in fact made to the effect that the policy
should issue to the plaintiff, insuring his mortgage interest
alone.

Much weight is given in the argument of counsel for the
plaintiff to the fact that the plaintiff paid the premium for
the insurance. But this fact must be considered in connection with the covenant in the mortgage that the mortgagors should insure the property, and, failing to do so,

Gillett vs. The Liverpool & London & Globe Ins. Co.

that the plaintiff might insure the same, and that the expense thereof should be added to and constitute a part of
the mortgage debt. So, when the plaintiff says he paid
the premium for the insurance, the effect of his testimony
is that he thereby increased the mortgage debt by the sum
so paid. Moreover, the above covenant clearly contem-
plates an insurance of the mortgagors' interest in the property, which could only be effected by a policy running to
them. The covenant is ample authority to the plaintiff to
insure the property in their names.

Having thus determined that the plaintiff is bound by
the stipulations in the policy in suit, it necessarily results
that the obtaining by the mortgagors of any unauthorized insurance on the same property invalidates the policy, under the stipulation therein against additional insurance without the consent of the defendant company. Has
this stipulation been violated? Mrs. York, one of the owners of the property, obtained policies in her name alone
in March, 1884, on substantially the same property, for
$4,000, without the consent or knowledge of the defendant
company. Nothing appears adverse to the validity of such
additional insurance. The policy in suit permitted concurrent insurance to the amount of $2,000 only. Had this
insurance been effected by M. A. York & Co., it would
doubtless have defeated the policy. It may be conceded
that these policies for $4,000 insure only the interest of
Mrs. York in the insured property, which, presumably, is
one half thereof.

It is maintained by counsel for plaintiff that, because the
policies were obtained by and issued to Mrs. York alone,
the $4,000 insurance is not a breach of the stipulation
against other insurance. The rule invoked to support this
proposition is thus laid down in 2 Wood on Ins. sec. 377:
"In order to amount to other insurance, the interests covered by the policies must be identical." We think such

interests are identical in the present case. The policy in
suit insures the interest of Mrs. York in the insured property, and the additional policies issued to her insure the
same interest. We find no established rule that because
Solomon York's interest in the property was insured by the
policy in suit, and not by the $4,000 policies, the latter pol-
icies do not constitute double insurance. In *Continental
Ins. Co. v. Hulman*, 92 Ill. 145, it was held that an unauthorized insurance by the wife was a breach of a stipulation
against other insurance in a former policy on the same
property, issued to her and her husband. Such we think
the law. Several distinctions between the Illinois case and
the one under consideration are noted by counsel, some of
which are real and some are not, but we think these do not
affect the applicability of the rule there laid down, to this
case.

The case of *Westchester F. Ins. Co. v. Foster*, 90 Ill. 121,
is relied upon as holding a different rule. The case is this:
Foster held a mortgage on certain property, executed by
B. He obtained an insurance upon the property, paid the
premium, and, without the knowledge or authority of B.,
took a policy in their joint names; the policy containing
the usual stipulation as regards other insurance. B. had
obtained another insurance in violation of the stipulation.
The court held that, under the circumstances, the insurance
was solely for F.'s benefit, and that the policy was not invalidated by such act of B. The difference between the
two cases is, the policy in the Illinois case ran to Foster, the
mortgagee, and in legal effect, as the court held, to him
alone, while here the policy runs to the mortgagors alone.
This difference is radical and controlling, and calls for the
application in this case of a different rule of law.

Another case much relied upon by counsel for the plaintiff may properly be noticed in this connection. It is that
of *Pitney v. Glen's Falls Ins. Co.* 65 N. Y. 6. Norman and

George N. Pitney were joint owners of the insured property, which was a quantity of wool. Norman obtained a policy in his own name. Afterwards he told the agent that he had forgotten to mention the interest of George and his intention to have that interest insured. The agent attempted to accomplish that purpose by inserting in the policy these words: "In case of loss, if any, one half payable to George N. Pitney, as his interest may appear." Under these circumstances, it was held that the interest of George N. in the wool was covered by the policy. That case does not hold that a breach of a covenant against further insurance would not have resulted, had either of the owners of the wool insured his interest therein in his own name without the consent of the company. Hence the case is not in point here. That case was decided by a bare majority of the commission of appeals; LOTT, C. C., and EARL, C., dissenting. We should hesitate to indorse all the doctrines there asserted without further examination.

We conclude that the policy in suit was invalidated by the unauthorized insurance obtained by Mrs. York, and hence that the court properly directed a verdict for the defendant.

By the Court.— The judgment of the circuit court is affirmed.

THE STATE EX REL. BURNETT COUNTY vs. HARSHAW, State Treasurer.

December 5 — December 22, 1888.

Counties: Division: Apportionment of debt: Subrogation.

By ch. 155, Laws of 1878, and ch. 197, Laws of 1879, Burnett county was authorized to borrow from the trust funds of the state, $20,000, to be used in aiding the construction of a railroad, and to be repaid, with interest, in fifteen annual instalments. Until the whole amount should be repaid the railroad company was required to pay annually into the state treasury, in lieu of all license fees, a sum equal to five per cent of its gross earnings, which sum was to be applied upon the indebtedness of the county. By ch. 172, Laws of 1883, Washburn county was formed out of part of the territory of Burnett, and, pursuant to that act, the existing debt was apportioned, and new certificates of indebtedness issued to the state by the respective counties. No provision was made by the act for the application of the sums paid into the treasury by the railroad. *Held*, that such sums should be applied upon the certificates of the two counties, ratably and in proportion to the amount of the indebtedness assumed by each.

MANDAMUS to compel the state treasurer to appl certain moneys paid into the state treasury by the St. loud, Grantsburg & Ashland Railway Company, upon th cer tificate of indebtedness issued by the relator pursua t to sec. 9, ch. 172, Laws of 1883. The respondent moved to quash the alternative writ. It appearing that *Washb rn* county might be or become interested in the application f said moneys, the relator was required to notify said coun and make it a party to the proceedings. Said county o *Washburn* thereupon appeared and filed an answer or re turn to the alternative writ, to which return a demurrer wa. interposed. Other facts are stated in the opinion.

For the relator there was a brief by *I. Grettum* and *I. C. Sloan*, and oral argument by *Mr. Sloan*. They contended that on the erection of a new county from territory of an old one the legislature may apportion the existing debts as it thinks proper, and the legislative discretion is not subject to judicial revision. *Depere v. Bellevue*, 31 Wis. 120; *Laramie Co. v. Albany Co.* 92 U. S. 307–315; *Mt. Pleasant v. Beckwith*, 100 id. 514; Dillon on Mun. Corp. sec. 187. It is clear from the language of sec. 9, ch. 172, Laws of 1883, that the intention was to have *Washburn* county borrow from any source the money necessary to pay the part of the debt apportioned to it, leaving *Burnett* county to pay the residue and to have the benefit of the five per cent. to be paid by the railway company. The railroad is wholly within *Burnett* county, and no part of it in *Washburn.*

For the respondent the cause was submitted on the brief of *L. K. Luse*, Assistant Attorney General.

COLE, C. J. The motion to quash the alternative writ, and the demurrer to the return made by *Washburn* county, involve substantially the same questions of law, and were argued together. Both the motion and the demurrer can therefore be conveniently disposed of in one opinion. The facts upon which the questions of law arise are these, in brief:

By ch. 155, Laws of 1878, and ch. 197, Laws of 1879, the commissioners of the school and university lands were authorized to loan, and the board of supervisors of *Burnett* county was authorized to borrow, from the trust funds of the state, $20,000, to be used in aiding the construction of a certain railroad. The county executed to the state certificates of indebtedness bearing interest at the rate of seven per cent., the interest and one fifteenth of the principal to be paid annually until the whole loan was paid. In consideration of the use of this money for the purpose named, the railroad company was required to make report of its gross earnings for each preceding year, and to pay into the state treasury, at the time named, for fifteen years, a sum equal to five per cent. of such gross earnings, which was in lieu of all license fees; and it was made the duty of the state treasurer, upon the receipt of said five per cent. each year, to at once indorse the amount upon the certificates of the county, so long as any certificate should remain unpaid. When the loan made by the commissioners was fully paid and discharged, the railroad company was required to pay to the state the amount exacted from other railroad companies for license fees.

By ch. 172, Laws of 1883, the legislature divided the

county of *Burnett*, and organized the county of *Washburn* from territory theretofore embraced in the former county. By the ninth section of the act it was provided that each county should be the absolute owner of all county property situated within its boundaries. The indebtedness of *Burnett* county was to be apportioned between the two counties according to the assessed valuation of property at the last assessment. Provision was made for the collection and return of the taxes of 1883. The law authorized the new county of *Washburn* and *Burnett*, after the former indebtedness of *Burnett* had been apportioned, to borrow from the trust funds of the state, on terms satisfactory to the commissioners, sufficient money to take up and cancel the indebtedness of *Burnett* county to the state, and each county gave the state its certificate of indebtedness for the amount thus borrowed.

It appears that on the settlement and adjustment of the indebtedness of *Burnett* county by the officers of the two counties the sum of $4,139.45 was apportioned to *Burnett* county, and $10,774.01 was apportioned to *Washburn* county on the basis of settlement. There has been paid into the state treasury by the railroad company, pursuant to the acts above referred to, the sum of $1,061.02. The point in controversy is, Should *Burnett* county be credited that entire sum on its indebtedness to the state, or should it be applied on the certificates of each county ratably, according to its indebtedness? *Washburn* county insists and claims that upon the facts it is entitled to its proportionate share of the amount, and the question is, Is this contention right?

It would certainly seem but just and equitable to apportion the amount between the two counties according to the portion of the debt which each assumed and became liable to pay on the settlement between them. This five per cent. of the gross earnings paid by the railroad company into the state treasury was manifestly intended to aid *Burnett* county in paying its debt to the state. This fund was in the nature of a security provided for the benefit of that county. There can be no doubt, we think, of the correctness of this proposition, in view of the legislation upon the subject. The county had originally made the loan from the state, presumably for the benefit of the railroad company, and by the arrangement the company was to aid in discharging this debt. Now, on the division, both counties have become liable for the payment of the debt to the state, or of certain portions of it. Why, then, should not each have the benefit of this railroad fund in the proportion which each has assumed to pay? It is a familiar doctrine in equity that a person secondarily liable for a debt which he has paid is substituted to the place of the creditor, and is entitled to the benefit of all the securities possessed by the creditor, and may make use of all remedies to enforce them as the creditor himself could do. This is subrogation, or the substitution of one person in place of another as creditor. The principle may well be applied here for the benefit of *Washburn* county. To make the matter still more plain, suppose the railroad company had given a mortgage for the benefit of *Burnett* county and to aid that county in paying its debt to the state. Can there be a doubt that on the division of the debt between the two counties the security would pass so that each county would be entitled to its proportionate share of it? It seems to us perfectly clear that a court would give each county the benefit of the security in the case supposed; and if we regard the railroad fund in the nature of a security, as we must do, the case stands upon the same footing precisely as though a mortgage had been originally given by the railroad company.

The learned counsel for the relator says: " The law is well settled that on the organization of a new county out of the territory of the old one, in the absence of a provision apportioning the existing debts between the two, the old county remains liable for all the debts at the time of the division." This is doubtless a correct statement of the law as to the division of towns and counties. The legislature, however, in the present case, saw fit to apportion the existing debt of *Burnett* county between it and the new county, and determined the portion which each should pay. The indebtedness was to be apportioned between the two counties according to the assessed valuation of property at the assessment of 1882. There can be no doubt but *Washburn* county was bound and became liable on the division to pay its share of the debt which *Burnett* county owed the state. It has assumed the obligation, and now seeks to have its equitable share of a common fund which is in the nature of a security for that debt. Its claim rests upon reasonable and equitable grounds. It is true, the legislature did not expressly provide that the new county should have the benefit of this five per cent. fund paid by the railroad company into the state treasury, but it is a fair and legitimate inference, from the legislation considered together, that such was the intention; for the railroad company is required to make payment of five per cent. of its gross earnings for the preceding year, so long as any bond or certificate of indebtedness remains unpaid. The substituted bonds or certificates given by the two counties under the law of 1883, take the place of the certificates originally given by *Burnett* county. Now, it is apparent, if the contention of the relator's counsel is sound, that the portion of the debt to the state assumed by *Burnett* county may be paid long before the new county has discharged its portion of the debt. So, according to this view, the railroad company would be relieved from paying this five per cent. of its gross earnings, though a considerable portion of the debt assumed by *Washburn* county had not been discharged. We are confident the legislature did not contemplate such a result, and that to so hold would be doing violence to the intent and spirit of the various acts passed upon this subject. It is perfectly plain the legislature intended the railroad company should pay five per cent. of its gross earnings into the state treasury each year, so long as any certificate or bond executed to the state by either *Burnett* or *Washburn* county remained unpaid; and it is the duty of the state treasurer, under these laws, to apply this fund ratably, and in proportion to the amount each county has assumed. and become liable to pay upon its certificate or bond, until the entire debt of the state is paid.

It follows from these views that the motion to quash the alternative writ is granted, and the demurrer to the return of *Washburn* county is overruled.

By the Court.— Ordered accordingly.

Heath and another, Respondents, vs. Solles and another, Appellants.

December 6 — December 22, 1888.

Liens: Materials furnished to one for improvements on land of another.

Under sec. 8314, R. S., as amended by ch. 349, Laws of 1885, one who furnishes materials for a house which a husband is building on his wife's land with her knowledge and consent, may have a lien therefor upon such land although it was understood that the husband should pay the entire cost of the house.

APPEAL from the Circuit Court for *Juneau* County.

The facts are sufficiently stated in the opinion.

For the appellants there was a brief by *Turner & Barney,* and oral argument by *H. W. Barney.* They cited

Lauer v. Bandow, 43 Wis. 556, 561; *Engfer v. Roemer*, 71 id. 11; *Smith v. Gill*, 37 Minn. 455; *Jones v. Walker*, 63 N. Y. 612; *Fullerton Lumber Co. v. Osborn*, 72 Iowa, 472; *Flannery v. Rohrmayer*, 46 Conn. 558; *Gilman v. Disbrow*, 45 id. 563.

For the respondents there was a brief by *Duane Mowry,* attorney, and *Winsor & Winsor*, of counsel, and oral argument by *F. Winsor*.

TAYLOR, J. This action was brought against *Edgar Solles* and *Susan Solles*, by the respondents, to obtain judgment against the appellant *Edgar Solles* for the value of a bill of lumber claimed to have been sold to him by the respondents, to be used, and which was in fact used, by him in constructing a dwelling-house upon the lands of the appellant *Susan Solles*, and to have the amount found due the respondents declared a lien upon the building and lands of said *Susan Solles*. *Susan Solles* was the wife of *Edgar Solles*. On the trial in the circuit court the respondents obtained a personal judgment against *Edgar Solles* for the amount of their claim, and the court adjudged the same a lien upon the lands of said *Susan Solles*, and directed the same to be sold for the payment of the judgment. Both the defendants appealed to this court. Since the appeal was taken the said *Susan Solles* died, and her administrator has been substituted as appellant in her place.

On the part of the appellants it is alleged as error that the judgment in favor of the respondents against the appellant *Edgar Solles* is not supported by the evidence. The controversy on this point is that the appellants claim that the materials sold by the respondents, and which were used in the construction of the dwelling-house in question, were sold to one Benz, and not to said *Solles*. The evidence clearly shows that as between *Edgar Solles* and Benz, the latter was bound to furnish and pay for all the materials and perform all the labor in the construction of said dwelling-house; and it is claimed that the evidence establishes the fact that the respondents knew that fact and sold the lumber and materials to the said Benz and not to the said *Edgar Solles*. An examination of the record shows that this claim on the part of the appellants was controverted on the trial by the respondents, and evidence was given on their part showing that the lumber and materials were sold to said *Edgar Solles* and not to said Benz, and that the credit was given by the respondents to said *Edgar Solles* and not to said Benz. This issue was fairly presented to the jury, and they found against the appellants and in favor of the respondents. We are satisfied that the evidence sustains the verdict upon that question, and the verdict and judgment ought not to be reversed because not sustained by evidence.

The appellants also allege as error that the court adjudged that the respondents were entitled to a lien upon the dwelling-house and the forty acres of land upon which it was erected, for the sum so found due to them from the appellant *Edgar Solles*. It is admitted that *Susan Solles*, the wife of *Edgar Solles*, owned the land on which the house was built; that she knew that it was being built by her husband on her land, at the time of its construction, and that she consented that it should be built on her land. She alleges that she consented that it should be built on her land under the following circumstances: Her husband, *Edgar Solles*, had received as pension money about $900, and he proposed to use that money in building a house on her land. He made a contract with one Benz, by which the said Benz was to furnish all the materials and do all the work in the construction of said dwelling-house on her land, the husband to furnish all the money to pay said Benz the amount to become due on his contract. And they claim that *Edgar Solles* has paid said Benz the full amount due on his said contract. The said *Susan Solles* claims and offered to show that she would not have consented to the building of the house on her land had not her husband agreed to pay all the bills. All offers on the part of the appellants to show that *Susan Solles* did not authorize any lumber or materials to be purchased on her account, or on the credit of her husband, and that she was ignorant of the fact that the lumber was so purchased, were excluded as immaterial. The circuit court held that the only material questions in the case were: *First*, whether in fact *Edgar Solles* purchased the lumber in question of the respondents and was indebted to them therefor; *second*, whether such lumber and materials were used in the construction of said dwelling-house on the premises of the said *Susan Solles; third*, whether said building was erected with the knowledge and consent of said *Susan; fourth*, the amount of the indebtedness; and, *fifth*, whether the respondents had filed a petition for a lien as required by statute. These were the only questions submitted to the jury, and they found in favor of the respondents upon all of them.

In view of the statutes upon the subject, we think the learned circuit judge was right in his view of the case. Previous to the enactment of ch. 349, Laws of 1885, this court had decided that under the statutes of this state relating to mechanics' and other liens, the interest of a person in real estate, not acquired after the lien attached, upon which a building or other improvement was erected or made, could not be sold to satisfy such lien unless the person so interested and owning the same was personally liable for the payment of the debt which was claimed to be a lien. This rule, however, did not apply to the lien of a subcontractor. See *Wheeler v. Hall*, 41 Wis. 447; *Lauer v. Bandow*, 43 Wis. 556; *Dewey v. Fifield*, 2 Wis. 82; *Rees v. Ludington*, 13 Wis. 277. 281. It had also been held by this court that a person having a lien under the statute upon a building which was so constructed as to become a part of the realty, could not enforce his lien against the building alone, and his lien failed entirely unless the person contracting the debt for the materials or work in the construction of the building had some interest in the lands upon which it was constructed which could be sold on execution against him. *Rees v. Ludington*, 13 Wis. 280; *Schmidt v. Gilson*, 14 Wis. 514; *McCoy v. Quick*, 30 Wis. 521, 529; *Rice v. Hall*, 41 Wis. 453; *Edleman v. Kidd*, 65 Wis. 18. In the statutes of 1878 a lien was given to a person furnishing machinery against the machinery itself, although the person to whom the machinery was sold had no interest in the realty to which it was attached, and authorized the lien claimant to remove the machinery from the premises to which it had been attached. See latter part of sec. 3314, R. S.; *Paige v. Peters*, 70 Wis. 178; *Wilkinson v. Hoffman*, 61 Wis. 637, 638; *Wilson v. Rudd*, 70 Wis. 98.

In 1885 the legislature amended the lien law by adding to said sec. 3314 the following: "And shall also attach to and be a lien upon the real property of any person on whose premises such improvements are made, such owner having knowledge thereof and consenting thereto." So that the section reads, after stating the kinds of buildings, structures, and improvements made upon real property, upon which, for the materials furnished or labor performed in the construction thereof, the persons so furnishing the materials or doing the work may have a lien, as follows: "Such lien shall be prior to any other lien which originates subsequent to the commencement of the construction, repair, removal, or work aforesaid, or upon such dwelling-house, building, machinery, bridge, wharf, or erection thereon, well, fountain, fence, water, lot, or land, *and shall also attach to and be a lien upon the real property of any person on whose premises such improvements are made, such owner having knowledge thereof and consenting thereto, and*

may be enforced as provided in this chapter." Ch. 349, Laws
of 1885, was amended by ch. 466, Laws of 1887, which declares that ch. 349, Laws of 1885, "shall not be construed
as giving a lien where the relation of landlord and tenant
exists, and shall be a lien only upon the piece or parcel of
land not exceeding forty acres or one acre respectively as
specified in section 3314 of the Revised Statutes and all the
acts amendatory thereof."

It is very evident that this statute of 1885 was intended
to change the law as theretofore existing in this state, as interpreted by the decisions of this court, by extending the
lien of the mechanics and others so as to extend to and
cover the interest of persons in the real estate upon which
the kind of improvements designated in said sec. 3314,
R. S., were made, other than the person or persons incurring
debts for making such improvements. Of the right of the
legislature to extend the lien as contemplated by said
amendment there can be no reasonable doubt. Nor can
there be any just cause of complaint by the owner of the
real estate upon which the improvement is made. He has
the whole benefit of the improvement made, and it is in
furtherance of justice and equity that his property, which
is presumed to have been enhanced in value by the labor or
materials furnished, should pay for them. The amendment
is supported on the same grounds that all other liens for
work or materials are supported.

The statute seems to us to admit of but one construction,
and that is the construction put upon it by the learned circuit
judge. If the owner permits a husband or wife, child, parent, or a stranger to erect a building on his or her land, with
his or her knowledge and consent, under the clear meaning
of the statute his or her interest in the real estate is charged
with a lien for the unpaid work or materials. We cannot
amend the statute or qualify its language by saying that
his or her interest in the land shall not be chargeable with

the lien when it was understood that the person making the improvement was to pay the entire cost thereof. Such a construction would destroy the object of the amendment, and embarrass, rather than aid, the mechanic's material·man and laborer. Under the statute, the only thing the lien claimant has to establish oñ the trial, when he claims a lien upon the real estate upon which a building is erected by some person other than the owner of the realty, is the fact that the owner knew that the building was being constructed on his or her premises, and that he or she consented to such construction.

There was no dispute as to these facts on the trial in the court below, and the other material issue, viz., whether the lumber was sold to *Edgar Solles* and not to Benz, was found against the appellants upon sufficient evidence.

By the Court.— The judgment of the circuit court is affirmed.

McDONOUGH, Respondent, vs. THE MILWAUKEE & NORTHERN RAILROAD COMPANY, Appellant.

December 6 — December 22, 1888.

Railroads: Fences: Killing of stock: Depot grounds: Court and jury.

At a certain point on defendant's railroad there was a station building, but for several years no agent had been kept there, and the building had been closed up and had gone to decay. Freight, if taken on at that place, was not billed until it arrived at the first station beyond. There was a side track there, where trains sometimes passed each other, and where the company received charcoal to be transported, but there were no grounds for a depot outside of the usual right of way. A cattle-guard had been put in about 850 feet south of the station building, and another about 721 feet north of it and about 850 feet north of the north end of the side track. Beyond these points the road was fenced. In an action for the killing of horses which, as the jury found, got upon the track near the north cattle-guard where the track was not fenced, the court, assuming that there were depot grounds where the station building was located, submitted to the jury the question whether the point at which the horses got upon the track was within the limits of such depot grounds, and the jury found that it was not. *Held*, that there was no error in thus submitting to the jury the question of the extent of the depot grounds, and that the evidence showing the foregoing facts, among others, justified the finding.

APPEAL from the Circuit Court for *Brown* County.

The case is sufficiently stated in the opinion. The defendant appeals from a judgment in favor of the plaintiff.

Alfred H. Bright, for the appellant, to the point that it is for the court and not for the jury to say whether, under the evidence, a particular locality is depot grounds or not, cited Pierce on Railroads, 30; *Illinois Cent. R. Co. v. Whalen,* 42 Ill. 396; *Chicago & G. T. R. Co. v. Campbell,* 47 Mich. 265; *Flint & P. M. R. Co. v. Lull,* 28 id. 511; *McGrath v. D. M. & M. R. Co.* 57 Mich. 555.

For the respondent there was a brief by *Huntington & Cady,* and oral argument by *H. J. Huntington.*

TAYLOR, J. This action was brought by the respondent to recover the value of a span of horses which had escaped from his inclosure and was killed upon the track of said appellant by a passing train. On the trial there was no dispute that the plaintiff's horses were killed by a train on the track of said company, as alleged in the complaint. There was no contention that the horses escaped from the plaintiff's inclosure by his negligence, nor as to the value of the horses. The plaintiff based his claim for damages against the company on the ground that the company had neglected to fence its line of road at the point where the horses got upon the tracks of said company, and that by reason of its failure so to fence its track as required by sec. 1810, R. S., as amended by ch. 193, Laws of 1881, the horses got upon the track, and in a short time thereafter were killed by a passing train of the company.

The only material controversy on the trial was whether the company was bound under the statute to fence its track at the place where the horses of the plaintiff got upon the line of defendant's road. The company contended that the place where they came upon the line of its road was a part of its "depot grounds," within the meaning of these words as used in the statute; and the plaintiff contended there were no "depot grounds" in the vicinity of the place where they got upon the track, and, if there were "depot grounds" in fact in that vicinity, the place where the horses went upon the track was not a part of such grounds, and was unfenced. On the part of the company it was contended that the horses got upon the line of its road very near where there was a flag station, and where its trains stopped to take on passengers when flagged or to let them off when desired. The evidence showed that there had at one time been a station-house at that point, and an agent of the company had been kept there, but for several years before the time in question the company kept no agent there, the station building had been closed up and had gone to decay; that no freight was shipped or delivered at that place in the ordinary way; that if freight was taken on the trains at that place it was not billed until it arrived at the first station beyond; that there was a side track there, where trains sometimes passed each other, and where the company received charcoal and transported it. The evidence also showed that there were no grounds for a depot at that place outside of the usual right of way, and that the company had put in cattle-guards south of the station building about 350 feet, and north of the building about 721 feet, and beyond these points north and south the road was fenced. The evidence also showed that at the time in question the cattle-guard south had been permitted to go to decay.

The company contended that the evidence showed there were "depot grounds" there within the meaning of the statute, and that the horses came upon the track in the immediate vicinity of the old station-house, and so came upon its track at a point where it was not required to fence by the statute. On the other hand, the plaintiff contended that the horses got on the track at a point more than 700 feet north of the station-house, and more than 350 feet north of the north end of the side track at that place; and he further claimed that the evidence did not show that there were any "depot grounds," within the meaning of the statute, at the place where the station-house stood.

The learned circuit judge seems to have come to the conclusion that the company had "depot grounds" at the place where the station-house was located, and he did not submit that question to the jury. He submitted the following questions: "(1) Did the plaintiff's horses, on the night they were killed, go upon defendant's railroad track at a point near the north cattle-guard? (2) If your answer to the first question be 'Yes,' then did said horses remain on said track until they were killed? (3) If you answer the first question, 'No,' then did the horses go upon defendant's track at or near the wagon track across the railroad track south of the depot building? (4) Was the point where the plaintiff's horses went onto the defendant's track last before they were killed, within the limits of defendant's depot grounds? (5) Did the engineer in charge of defendant's train which killed these horses, intentionally or wantonly run over and kill the horses? (6) What was the value of the horses when killed?" The jury answered the first and second questions, "Yes;" the third, fourth, and fifth questions, "No;" and fixed the value of the horses at $300. The jury found that the horses entered upon the track at the north cattle-guard, which was 354 feet north of the north end of the company's side track, and 721 feet north of the station building; and they have also found that the place where the horses got upon the track last before they were killed was not within the limits of the defendant's depot grounds.

It is claimed by the counsel for the appellants that if there were "depot grounds," within the meaning of the statutes, at the place mentioned, as the learned circuit judge seems to have held, then it was error to submit the question to the jury as to the extent of such grounds; and that the court should have held, as a question of law, that such grounds extended from the south to the north cattle-guard; claiming that the limits of the depot grounds had been designated by the company as the ground between such cattle-guards.

Upon all the other material questions in the case the court charged the jury favorably to the company. He charged the jury that if the horses went upon the track near the station-house, as claimed by the company, then the plaintiff could not recover, unless they found that they were wilfully and wantonly killed. An examination of the instructions of the learned circuit judge will show that upon every point he charged the jury most favorably to the defendant. He stated to them that if the horses got upon the track at one point, and then left the track and returned to it again, that the last entry upon the track was the only one they could consider; and, in effect, if they found that the horses first entered on the track at the north cattle-guard, and then went outside of the right of way, and came upon the track again at or near the station-house, the plaintiff could not recover,— a proposition which perhaps admits of some doubt. Under the instructions of the court and upon the evidence, the jury have expressly found that the horses got upon the track at the north cattle-guard, and continued along down the track, without departing therefrom, to the place where they were killed.

The only possible error that the defendant can complain of is that the jury were not justified in finding that the place near the north cattle-guard was not a part of the company's depot grounds at that point. Taking the view of the case that the trial court did, we think he was right in submitting, as a question of fact, to the jury the extent ·of the supposed depot grounds. See the following cases in this court: *Fowler v. Farmers' L. & T. Co.* 21 Wis. 77; *Blair v. M. & P. du C. R. Co.* 20 Wis. 254; *Dinwoodie v. C., M. & St. P. R. Co.* 70 Wis. 160, 164–5.

The jury having found, upon sufficient evidence, that the place where the horses entered upon the track was not a part of the depot grounds, and that the track was not fenced at that place, the legal liability of the company was established. *Bennett v. C. & N. W. R. Co.* 19 Wis. 145, 149, 150; *McCall v. Chamberlain,* 13 Wis. 637; *Brown v. M. & P. du C. R. Co.* 21 Wis. 39; *Antisdel v. C. & N. W. R. Co.* 26 Wis. 145; *Pritchard v. L. C. & M. R. Co.* 7 Wis. 232; *Lawrence v. M., L. S. & W. R. Co.* 42 Wis. 322. The jury having found that the horses entered upon the track at a place where the company was by law bound to build and maintain a fence, that it had neglected its duty in that respect, and that the horses, after entering upon the track at such point, remained on said track and were shortly thereafter killed by a passing train, a complete case is established against the company. These facts show with sufficient certainty that the want of a fence caused the injury. See cases above cited.

Upon the questions of law arising on the trial, we think the rulings and instructions of the trial judge were sufficiently favorable to the appellant, and, as said above, upon the questions of fact submitted to the jury their findings and verdict are sustained by the evidence.

By the Court.— The judgment of the circuit court is affirmed.

BRICKNER WOOLEN MILLS COMPANY, Respondent, vs. HENRY
and others, Appellants.

December 6 — December 22, 1888.

*Pleading: Joinder of causes of action: Law or equity? Prayer for re-
lief: Mills and mill dams.*

A complaint alleges that the defendants wrongfully, by means of
their dam and works on a river, prevent the water from coming
to plaintiff's two mills in such quantities and at such times as to
successfully run such mills. The facts as to each mill are stated
in a separate count, and it appears that the plaintiff's right to the
water as to one of his mills is as a riparian proprietor, and as to the
other is under a grant, from the grantor of one of the defendants,
of water from said defendant's dam. There is but one prayer for
relief which is, *first*, for damages; *second*, that "defendants' dam
and works and their operation thereof be declared a private nuisance" as to one of plaintiff's mills, and that "the same, or such
parts thereof as cause such injury, be abated, and that such relief
be granted by perpetual injunction or otherwise," as shall seem
proper; and *third*, that plaintiff's rights to water from defendants'
dam and also its rights to the water of the river, as riparian proprietor, be determined and protected, and the defendants enjoined
from interference therewith. *Held*, that the complaint does not
improperly join two causes of action. The prayer does not ask for
legal relief by the destruction or discontinuance of any part of the
dam or works, but merely that the defendants' acts to the plaintiff's injury shall cease.

APPEAL from the Circuit Court for *Sheboygan* County.
The case is stated in the opinion.

For the appellants there was a brief signed by *Quarles,
Spence & Dyer*, of counsel, and oral argument by *Charles
Quarles*. They contended, *inter alia*, that the court will determine *in limine* what the specific cause of action relied
upon in each count is, and in doing so will and must look
not only to the averments of the count but also to the
prayer for relief and to the general frame-work of the
pleading. *Kewaunee Co. v. Decker*, 30 Wis. 624–630; *Gil-*

lett v. Treganza, 13 id. 472; *Hammond v. Mich. State Bank,*
Walker Ch. 214. Applying the tests indicated, the complaint sets up two causes of action entirely diverse in scope
and object. The first count is for a private nuisance, under
sec. 3180, R. S.; the second is an action for partition of
water power under sec. 3149, R. S., as amended by ch. 203,
Laws of 1881. These actions are so different in their procedure and methods of trial that they cannot be joined in
one complaint.

For the respondent there was a brief by *Seaman & Williams,* and oral argument by *W. H. Seaman.*

ORTON, J. The defendants demurred to the complaint
on the ground that two causes of action were improperly
joined. This appeal is taken from the order overruling the
demurrer. The complaint is long, and minutely sets out
the interests of the parties in the subject matter; but for
the purpose of considering this one point the cause or
causes of action are very plain and simple and may be
stated in few words. *First.* The plaintiff, as a corporation,
is the owner of a dam and water power on the Sheboygan
river, at Sheboygan Falls, and woolen mills thereon, called
"Sheboygan Falls Woolen Mills," of great cost and value,
and in successful operation. The defendant *Henry* is the
owner of a dam and water power above on said river, and
a flouring mill thereon, and he and the other defendants,
who hold under him, conspired to hold back the waters of
said river, by means of their dam and works, from coming
down to the plaintiff's woolen mills in sufficient quantity
and at such business hours as to permit of their successful
operation, without right, unreasonably, and unnecessarily,
to the plaintiff's great and irreparable injury. *Second.* The
plaintiff owns, also, woolen mills abutting upon and extending into said river, above the others, and below the dam of
the defendants, called "Riverside Woolen Mills," and ob-

tained the right from the grantor of said *Henry* to have
the water of said river brought from the said dam of the
defendant *Henry*, by means of a trunk, to the said woolen
mills, in sufficient quantity and at proper times to run said
mills profitably and successfully; and this right the plaintiff has enjoyed uninterruptedly for thirty years, and until
the acts complained of.   The defendants conspired, also, to
prevent the waters of said river from coming down in said
trunk to the plaintiff's mill in sufficient quantity and at
such times as to successfully and profitably run the said
mills.   The defendants make a most unreasonable use of
the waters of said river, to the great detriment of the
plaintiff, and prevent it from enjoying its just share of the
same at said woolen mills.   The defendants have refused
to allow the plaintiff such just share of said water power
as said woolen mills are entitled to have.   In short, the defendants have conspired to take away from the plaintiff's
two woolen mills, by means of their dam, the share of said
river and water power to which they are entitled, to the
plaintiff's irreparable injury.   The plaintiff alleges that it has
no adequate remedy at law.

There is but one prayer, and that follows the second
cause of action.   The peculiar form of the prayer seems to
have caused the contention on the demurrer.   The prayer
is not an essential part of the complaint.   But the learned
counsel of the appellants contend that at least one cause
of action is at law, because the prayer is for an *abatement*
of the defendants' mill-dam as a *nuisance*, and for $6,000
damages.   It is true that the prayer asks " that defendants'
said dam and works and *their operation thereof* be declared
a private nuisance " as to said lower water power, etc., and
" that the same, or such parts thereof as cause such injury,
be *abated*."   This language is loose and inaccurate, but it
certainly does not mean that any part of the dam or works
shall be destroyed or discontinued, for the plaintiff is de-

pendent upon the dam for water power for the Riverside
Woolen Mills. The meaning clearly is that the defendants'
acts to the plaintiff's injury shall cease, and nothing more.
Then an injunction is asked against the continuance of such
acts, and that the plaintiff's rights to the water by said
trunk, or his share of the waters of the river, be ascertained and secured. The prayer is a proper one, and consistent, as we understand it, for the case in equity.

But is there really more than one cause of action in this
complaint? That the plaintiff is injured and damaged by
the acts of the defendants in respect to both woolen mills,
the parties being the same, would not seem to constitute
two causes of action, unless the plaintiff should choose to
divide the complaint into two counts and call them such.
The injury in respect to both mills is alike, and continuous.
The defendants prevent sufficient water to come to either
one of the woolen mills of the plaintiff, and the plaintiff
has already suffered damages thereby of $6,000, and the
future injury will be irreparable.

But, conceding that there may be two causes of action
stated in the complaint, that they are properly joined there
can be no question. It is too obvious for argument. It is
only the separate statement of the way or manner in which,
and the means by which, the plaintiff has been and will be
injured by the defendants in respect to the woolen mills.
The two causes of action are like such as are stated in respect to two different tracts of land or two articles of personal property of the plaintiff, affected about the same by
the wrongful acts of the defendant. That the plaintiff's
rights as to one of its mills are as a riparian proprietor, and
as to the other by grant from the grantor of the defendant
Henry, can make no difference. The injury in respect to
both is the same or very closely connected. A court of
equity, having otherwise jurisdiction of the case, can award
the damages as well as a court of law. There is nothing

complicated about the case or the question. *Douglas Co. v. Walbridge*, 38 Wis. 179; *Hurlbut v. Marshall*, 62 Wis. 590; *Leidersdorf v. Second Ward S. Bank*, 50 Wis. 406; *Childs v. Harris Mfg. Co.* 68 Wis. 231; *Patten Paper Co. v. Kaukauna W. P. Co.* 70 Wis. 659.

By the Court.— The order of the circuit court is affirmed, and the cause remanded for further proceedings according to law.

PATTEN, Respondent, vs. THE NORTHWESTERN LUMBER COMPANY, imp., Appellant.

December 6 — December 22, 1888.

Liens: Logs and timber: Supplies: Place of furnishing.

Under sec. 1, ch. 469, Laws of 1885, a lien is given where supplies are furnished to be used, and are in fact used, in the cutting, etc., of logs in any of the counties named; and the residence of the person furnishing the supplies, or the place where they are delivered to the person who uses them, is wholly immaterial.

APPEAL from the Circuit Court for *Taylor* County.
The case is stated in the opinion.

For the appellant there was a brief by *Griffin & Walmsley*, and oral argument by *H. B. Walmsley.* They contended, *inter alia*, (1) that the statute under which this lien claim is to be enforced is unconstitutional and void for failure to make any sufficient provision for the protection of the owner of the logs, giving him reasonable notice of the proceedings and opportunity to be heard. *Reilly v. Stephenson*, 62 Mich. 509; Jones on Liens, sec. 723. (2) The supplies in this case were furnished in Chippewa county and not in Taylor county, and therefore there is no lien, notwithstanding they were used in Taylor county and the cutting, etc., of the timber was done in that county.

For the respondent there was a brief by *Stafford & Connor*, and oral argument by *T. J. Connor*.

TAYLOR, J. This action was brought by the respondent to recover for the value of certain supplies sold to E. S. Craig, to be used by him, and which were used by him, in cutting, felling, hauling, and putting in the river a quantity of logs in the county of Taylor, in this state. In said action the logs so put in by said Craig, and in the cutting, hauling, and putting in of which said supplies were used, were attached, and the plaintiff claims a lien upon such logs for the amount of the supplies so furnished and used. The logs are properly described in the complaint. The appellant was made a defendant in the action, and claims to be the owner of the logs in question. The case was tried upon a stipulation admitting certain facts, and judgment was rendered in favor of the respondent, and his claim was declared a lien upon the logs in question, and the court directed them to be sold to satisfy the respondent's demand.

There is no dispute upon the facts in the case. It is admitted that the respondent sold the supplies in question to the said Craig for the purpose of being used in putting in said logs, and that they were in fact so used by him. There is no dispute as to the value of the supplies so sold and used, nor is there any dispute upon the question as to whether the goods sold by respondent to Craig, and used by him in getting out said logs, were "supplies" within the meaning of sec. 1, ch. 469, Laws of 1885. It is admitted that the cutting, hauling, and banking of the logs in question was all done in Taylor county, and that such supplies were used in said county in doing such work. It is also undisputed that the plaintiff sold and delivered such supplies to said Craig in the county of Chippewa, and not in the county of Taylor, and that the respondent resided and had his place of busines in Chippewa county at the time of such sale. It is also admitted that if the plaintiff was entitled to a lien upon the logs in question for the value of the supplies so sold to Craig, he had complied with the statute in filing the proper claim for a lien.

The contention of the learned counsel for the appellant is that the court erred in holding that the plaintiff had a lien upon the logs for the value of said supplies. The point made and urged upon this court' by the able argument of the learned counsel is that the statute only gives a lien when the supplies are sold and delivered to the person using them within the county in which they are used in getting out the logs, and, as it is admitted that these supplies were sold and delivered to Craig in the county of Chippewa, the plaintiff is not entitled to a lien under the statute.

In view of statutes of this state, passed from time to time, upon the subject of liens for supplies sold and furnished for getting out logs, timber, and other products of the forests in certain counties in this state, we are clearly of the opinion that ch. 469, Laws of 1885, under which the claim for lien in this case is made, should not receive the construction contended for by the learned counsel for the appellant. We think it is very clear that the lien is given to the person furnishing supplies for getting out logs, etc., in certain counties, upon the theory that as the supplies furnished and used by the men and teams in getting out the logs entered into and enhanced the value of the timber converted into logs by their use, it is equitable that the owner of the logs should see to it that the persons employed by them for getting out such logs should pay for them, and if he does not then the logs themselves should be charged with their payment; and that the residence of the party furnishing the supplies, or the place where they were delivered to the person or persons using them, was not in-

tended by the legislature to be material in determining the
question whether the party furnishing such supplies should
have a lien.   The legislature must be presumed to have intended to legislate for the benefit of all persons in the
state, unless the act itself clearly shows that there was an
intention to limit the benefits of the legislation to a particular class of persons, or to those residing and doing business in a particular locality.

It is admitted by the learned counsel for the appellant
that under the statutes upon this subject enacted previously
to ch. 469, Laws of 1885, the lien for supplies was not limited to persons selling and delivering the supplies within the
county in which they were used, and that the seller might
have his lien under the previous acts of the legislature, if he
proved that they were sold to be used, and were in fact
used, in getting out logs, etc., in any one of the counties
designated in the acts.   The acts of the legislature upon
this subject will be found as ch. 215, Laws of 1860; ch. 186,
Laws of 1861; ch. 154, Laws of 1862; ch. 517, Laws of
1865; ch. 66, Laws of 1866; ch. 100, Laws of 1867 (the last
chapter is the first act in this state giving a lien for supplies); ch. 120, Laws of 1870; ch. 139, Laws of 1873; ch.
267, Laws of 1874; ch. 372, Laws of 1876; ch. 95, Laws of
1877; sec. 3329, R. S. 1878; ch. 167, Laws of 1879; ch. 62,
Laws of 1880; ch. 330, Laws of 1881; ch. 273, Laws of
1882; ch. 319, Laws of 1882; ch. 469, Laws of 1885; ch.
530, Laws of 1887.   It will be seen by examination of the
above statutes that at first, and down to ch. 100, Laws of
1867, the lien was confined to labor and services performed
in getting out logs, etc.   In 1867, ch. 100 extended the lien
to "supplies furnished," and this lien for supplies existed
down to the enactment of ch. 330, Laws of 1881, which
abolished the lien for "supplies," and extended the lien for
labor and services to all the counties in the state.   Previous to the enactment of ch. 330, Laws of 1881, the lien

upon logs and lumber, both for labor and supplies, had been limited to a few counties in the state. This law of 1881, which abolished the lien for supplies and extended the lien for labor and services to all the counties in the state, remained the law until the enactment of ch. 469, Laws of 1885, which retained the lien for labor and services in getting out logs and timber in all the counties of the state, and revived the lien for supplies furnished for that purpose in certain counties specified; Taylor being one of the counties specified in which a lien for supplies should exist.

The learned counsel claims that because the language used in the old statutes giving the lien for supplies as well as for labor and services, viz., "any person furnishing labor, services, or supplies in the counties [naming them] shall have a lien," etc., is changed by naming the counties first, there is a change of meaning. We cannot think the legislature could have intended so radical a change of meaning by a mere change of the location of the names of the counties. We can see no real difference in the meaning of the language in the two sentences: "Any person furnishing supplies in cutting, hauling, . . . in the counties of Taylor, . . . shall have a lien," etc., and " In the counties of Taylor, . . . any person furnishing supplies in cutting, hauling, . . . shall have a lien," etc. There is a sufficient reason for the change of the phraseology in the new law of 1885. In the first section of the act the legislature retained the general lien for labor and services in all the counties as enacted in ch. 330, Laws of 1881, and restored the lien for supplies in a few counties named. In all the acts down to 1881, the lien was limited for all purposes to a few counties named. In the act of 1885, the general lien was provided for, as well as the limited lien, and this may well account for the change of phraseology, without any intent to change the rule of law as stated in the previous acts.

If the language used in sec. 1, ch. 469, Laws of 1885, is susceptible of the construction put upon it by the learned counsel for the appellant, it is also clearly susceptible of the construction contended for by the counsel for the respondent; and as the latter construction is in accord with the previous legislation upon the same subject, as well as in accord with just and equal legislation, we are of the opinion that the learned circuit judge was right in holding that the supplies were furnished by the respondent in the county of Taylor, within the meaning of the statute. What is material under the act is that the supplies are furnished to be used, and are in fact used, in cutting, felling, hauling, etc., logs in Taylor county; and the residence of the person furnishing the supplies, or the place where they are delivered to the person who uses them, is wholly immaterial. This construction of the statute seems to be in accord with the construction given to acts of a similar character by the courts of other states. *Gaty v. Casey,* 15 Ill. 189, 192; *Great Western Mfg. Co. v. Hunter,* 14 Neb. 452; *Atkins v. Little,* 17 Minn. 342, 356–7; *Greenwood v. Tennessee Mfg. Co.* 2 Swan, 130.

By the Court.— The judgment of the circuit court is affirmed.

LEINENKUGEL, Respondent, vs. KEHL and others, Appellants.

December 7 — December 22, 1888.

(1) Deeds: Attestation: Validity. (2) Action to quiet title: Parties: Joinder of causes of action.

1. A conveyance of land need not be witnessed in order to pass the legal title as between the parties.
2. In an action to quiet title to land and to have a certain deed declared valid, all persons claiming interests in the premises hostile to such deed and which would be affected by a judgment affirming its validity, may be made parties, although they claim separate parcels of the land: and there is no misjoinder of causes of action, although it is asked that the plaintiff's title under such deed be established as against the claims of all the defendants.

APPEAL from the Circuit Court for *Chippewa* County.

Action to have the plaintiff's·claim to certain lands established, and to have the defendants enjoined and debarred from asserting their adverse claims thereto. The complaint alleges that the plaintiff is the owner and in possession of said lands. The conveyances constituting the plaintiff's chain of title are then set forth. One of such conveyances is a quitclaim deed to the defendant *Mary Allen*, executed August 8, 1866, but not witnessed or acknowledged or recorded. The complaint shows that after the execution and delivery of such deed to said *Mary Allen*, she and her husband gave a mortgage of the premises; that such mortgage was foreclosed; and that the plaintiff holds the title under mesne conveyances from the purchaser at the foreclosure sale.

The complaint further shows that the defendants *Stanley* and *Kehl* claim to own portions of said lands under and by virtue of conveyances executed subsequent to said quitclaim deed of August 8, 1866, but by the same grantors, and that said defendants each well knew that his grantors had no interest or ownership in the land at the time their conveyances were executed. Other facts will sufficiently appear from the opinion.

The defendants each demurred separately to the complaint on the grounds that several causes of action are improperly joined and that it does not state facts sufficient to constitute a cause of action. From an order overruling the demurrers the defendants appeal.

For the appellants the cause was submitted on the brief of *Marshall & Jenkins*. They contended, *inter alia*, that a deed not sufficiently witnessed is inoperative to pass the legal title. *Doe v. Doe*, 37 N. H. 276. The law was the same at the time of the making of the deed, with reference to witnesses, as now. "All conveyances executed within this state of lands or any interest in lands therein, shall be

executed in the presence of two witnesses, who shall sub-
scribe their names to the same as such." R. S. sec. 2216.
A deed must be executed in the form and with those solemnities prescribed by the law where the land is situated,
in order to have any validity. 1 Nat. Law Review, 292–4;
Cantu v. Bennett, 39 Tex. 303; *Warrender v. Warrender,*
9 Bligh, 127–8; 2 Dwar. on Stat. 648; Story on Confl. of
Laws, sec. 351*d*, 364; 2 Wait's Act. & Def. 506; *Crane v.
Reeder,* 21 Mich. 26; 3 Washb. on Real Prop. (4th ed.), 238;
McLaughlin v. Randall, 66 Me. 226. Several causes of ac-
tion are improperly united. *Mrs. Allen's* claim is entirely
separate and distinct from the claim of her co-defendants.
The interest of each of the defendants is several and not
joint. See R. S. sec. 2647; Bliss on Code Pl. sec. 123;
Hubbell v. Lerch, 58 N. Y. 237; Pomeroy on Rem. sec. 483.

For the respondent there was a brief by *Hollon Richardson,* attorney, and *H. H. Hayden,* of counsel, and oral argument by *Mr. Richardson.* To the point that attestation
was not essential to the validity of a deed as between the
parties, they cited, besides cases cited in the opinion, 1
Devlin on Deeds, secs. 255, 464–5; *Dole v. Thurlow,* 12 Met.
157–166; *Kingsley v. Holbrook,* 45 N. H. 320; *Fitzhugh v.
Croghan,* 2 J. J. Marsh. 429; *Price v. Haynes,* 37 Mich.
489; *Ricks v. Reed,* 19 Cal. 551–576; *Hepburn v. Dubois,*
12 Pet. 375; *Morton v. Leland,* 27 Minn. 35.

COLE, C. J. We agree with the plaintiff's counsel that it
is immaterial on this appeal to inquire whether the action
was brought under sec. 3186, R. S., or under the general
powers of a court of equity to quiet title to real estate. In
either aspect the plaintiff would be entitled to the relief
asked if the evidence sustained the allegations of the complaint. The plaintiff alleges that at the commencement of
the action he was the owner in fee simple and was in possession of the real estate described; and this allegation

with proof of the necessary facts would make out a case under the statute. But the vital question in the case, and the one upon which the controversy turns, is whether the deed to *Mary Allen* of August 8, 1866, passed the legal title as between the parties. It appears that that deed was not witnessed nor acknowledged, though in due form and sufficient in other respects to convey the title to the grantee. The contention of the defendants is that a deed not prop- erly witnessed and acknowledged was inoperative to pass the title, even as between the parties thereto, under the statute then existing. Was, then, that deed valid?

This question is hardly an open one in this court. In *Myrick v. McMillan*, 13 Wis. 188, decided in 1860, it was held that an acknowledgment of a deed by the grantor was not essential to pass the legal title as between the parties to the instrument. It is true, the conveyance in that case was executed under the territorial statute of 1839. But there is no substantial difference between the territorial and state statute upon this subject, as an examination will show. The next case which involved the question is *Quin-ney v. Denney*, 18 Wis. 485. In that case we are confident that the deed under which the respondent claimed was neither witnessed nor acknowledged, though the report is not clear upon this point. The deed was executed in 1845, and the ruling in *Myrick v. McMillan* was followed. *McMahon v. McGraw*, 26 Wis. 614; *Gilbert v. Jess*, 31 Wis. 110; *McPherson v. Featherstone*, 37 Wis. 632,— presented the same question, and were determined the same way. In *Knight v. Leary*, 54 Wis. 460, it was held that the certifi- cate of the acknowledgment of a deed was no part of its execution; and this arose under ch. 86, R. S. 1858. *Hew-itt v. Week*, 59 Wis. 444-456, affirms this same principle. Attestation and acknowledgment are formalities required by the statute to entitle the deed to be recorded so as to operate as nótice to subsequent purchasers, but are not es-

sential to transfer the title as between the parties. The
reasons for this construction of the statute are stated in the
opinions, and need not be repeated. If the question were
res integra, we think the same construction should be
placed upon the statute. But to now hold, in view of our
decisions upon the subject, that a deed must be witnessed
and acknowledged to pass the title, would be revolutionary,
and might do much mischief. There can be no doubt that
the legislature may prescribe the form and solemnities to
be observed in a conveyance of real estate within its limits;
but the question always is, What requisites are made essential for that purpose in this state? That question will find
its answer in the decisions above cited, which we have no
purpose to disturb, for we think they are in accord with
the great weight of authority upon this subject. It is alleged in the complaint that the defendants and their grantors, who are or were interested in avoiding the deed to
Mary Allen, were not any of them purchasers in good faith
for a valuable consideration, so they would be affected by
the equities of the plaintiff under that deed though it were
not recorded.

The next point made by the demurrer is that several
causes of action had been improperly united. Each of the
defendants has or claims an interest in the premises hostile
to the deed just referred to. They have a common connection with the subject matter of the action, and they
ought to be joined, though they hold separate parcels of
land. Indeed, the controversy cannot well be determined
without they are before the court. Of course *Mary Allen*
is a proper party, as it is her deed which is asked to be decreed valid, because she claims a part of the premises under
another title adverse to that deed. The same is true of
Stanley and *Kehl*. Their interests would be vitally affected
by a judgment which should affirm the validity of that
deed. The defendants certainly have one common interest

touching that deed, and it would seem plain that they should be before the court before the plaintiff has the relief which he asks in respect to it. We think there is no misjoinder of causes of action, in view of the facts stated. Story's Eq. Pl. sec. 284 *et seq.; Hamlin v. Wright*, 23 Wis. 491.

It follows from these views that the order of the circuit court overruling the demurrer to the complaint must be affirmed, and the cause remanded for further proceedings according to law.

By the Court.— It is so ordered.

BEST, Respondent, vs. SINZ, Appellant.

December 7 — December 22, 1888.

(1) Parties: Joinder. (2) Written contracts: Parol testimony. (3) Evidence: Immaterial error. (4, 5) Instructions to jury: Compensation for collecting money.

1. Though two have joined in a power of attorney authorizing a third person to collect their respective shares on the distribution of an intestate estate, one may sue alone to recover his share so collected.

2. Parol testimony of a prior contract is not admissible to show that a power of attorney to collect money was in fact an absolute assignment of the claim to be collected.

3. An error in the admission of evidence to prove a fact as to which there was no controversy, is immaterial.

4. An instruction that " the idea that if you appoint an agent who is incompetent he can charge you two or three times the amount of the claim, if he chooses to make such expenses, is not tenable in the law," is not erroneous, there being evidence to which it is applicable.

5. The jury were repeatedly told that the defendant was entitled to reasonable compensation for collecting a claim, and that they must fix the same from all the testimony. The judge remarked that if he had charged ten per cent. this would be about the

amount expended for railroad fares in making the collection. The jury allowed the defendant ten per cent. *Held*, that the hypothetical allusion to that amount was not error prejudicial to the defendant.

APPEAL from the Circuit Court for *Milwaukee* County.

The plaintif was one of four heirs of a brother who died intestate in the state of Indiana. The estate of such deceased brother was settled in the proper court, and the plaintiff's share thereof, awarded to him by the court, was $97.23. Plaintiff and another heir gave the defendant a power of attorney, in the usual form, to collect their respective shares. The instrument is silent as to the compensation the defendant should receive for his services. He collected the money, but refused to pay over to the plaintiff his share thereof. The plaintiff brought this action in a justice's court to recover his share. The case was appealed to the county court, and afterwards the place of trial was changed to the circuit court.

The defendant answered in abatement the non-joinder as party of the heir who joined with the plaintiff in the power of attorney; and also in bar of the action that the contract between the parties in the suit was that the defendant should " keep the plaintiff and the other party so empowering to make said collection free and harmless of any and all expense accruing out of said collection, in consideration of which they waived and ceded any and all of their claim to said inheritance to this defendant. In pursuance of said agreement defendant undertook and went and collected the same at his own expense and time." The defendant answered, further, that his expenses in making the collection, including the value of the time spent therein, greatly exceeded the sum collected.

On the trial the circuit court found against the defendant on the plea in abatement, and also ruled out testimony offered by him to prove the special contract alleged in the answer, that the defendant was to have the whole sum collected by him. The jury were instructed that the plaintiff was entitled to a verdict for the amount collected for him by the defendant, less reasonable compensation for collecting the same. A further statement of the charge will be found in the opinion. The jury allowed the defendant ten per cent. on the amount collected as compensation for his services, and returned a verdict for the plaintiff for the balance of the $97.23, and interest thereon from the date the money was demanded of the defendant by plaintiff's attorney. A motion for a new trial was denied, and judgment rendered for the plaintiff pursuant to the verdict. The defendant appeals from the judgment.

For the appellant there was a brief by *Haring & Frost*, and oral argument by *E. W. Frost*.

For the respondent the cause was submitted on the brief of *J. C. Ludwig*.

LYON, J. I. The plea in abatement was properly overruled. The money sued for was awarded the plaintiff by the order of distribution made by the proper court, and belonged to him in severalty. The other heirs of his deceased brother had no interest in it, and he had no interest in the sums awarded them. It is immaterial that one of them joined with the plaintiff in the power of attorney. This fact only made the defendant the several agent of each to collect his distributive share of the estate, and created no joint interest in the money.

II. The contract alleged in the answer, to the effect that the defendant indemnified the heirs who executed the power of attorney against expenses, and was to retain all he collected, is, in substance and legal effect, an assignment of the claim to him. Had the indemnifying clause been omitted, thus leaving such heirs liable for the expenses of collection, which might exceed the sum collected, or had there been a failure to collect, there might be some doubt as to whether the alleged contract is anything more than a stipulation for compensation. In such case it might plausibly be said that the heirs retained an interest in having the claim collected at the least possible expense, and to that extent were interested in the claim itself. But the indemfying clause removes all doubt, for it divests the heirs who are alleged to be parties to it of all interest in the claims, and relieves them from all liability for expenses incurred in their collection. A contract respecting a chose in action which works such a result is an absolute assignment of such chose in action, no matter what may be the form of the contract.

The defendant offered parol testimony on the trial to show that such contract was made by the parties before the power of attorney was executed, and that the instrument was executed pursuant thereto. This was an offer to show by parol that the power of attorney is not what, on its face, it purports to be,—an instrument authorizing the defendant to collect money for the plaintiff, and by necessary implication binding him to pay it over to the plaintiff when collected,—but an absolute assignment to the defendant of the claim to be collected. The court excluded the testimony. The ruling was correct. The proposition was to substitute an entirely different contract for that contained in the power of attorney, by proof of conversations or parol stipulations between the parties occurring before the instrument was executed. The rule is elementary that this cannot properly be done. The authoritative adjudications on the question are all one way.

It is conceded that parol evidence would have been admissible to show what compensation the defendant should be allowed for his services in making the collection; the power of attorney being silent on that subject. Had there been a parol contract fixing his compensation, the defendant might have proved it, but it was not claimed that any such contract existed. Testimony was received to show the value of such services, and the jury allowed the defendant compensation *quantum meruit*. But, as we have seen, the contract alleged in the answer is not one for compensation for services, and the rules of evidence on the subject of compensation have no application thereto.

III. An unauthenticated statement of the judge of the Indiana court in which the estate of plaintiff's deceased brother was settled, was offered in evidence by the plaintiff, and received under objection. This evidence was introduced to show the sum distributed to plaintiff as his share of such estate. Clearly the evidence was incompetent. But it was harmless. Probably the answer does not put the amount awarded the plaintiff in issue, and the defendant practically admitted that the sum claimed is correctly stated in the complaint. The claim is $97.23, and he testified that there was due plaintiff out of the estate $96 or $97, which he collected. So there was really no controversy on the subject, and the error in admitting the statement is of no importance.

IV. Two errors are assigned on the charge, to wit: (1) The court said to the jury: "The idea that if you appoint an agent who is incompetent he can charge you two or three times the amount of the claim, if he chooses to make such expenses, is not tenable in the law." We do not discover any bad law in this remark. It was probably called out by the fact that in his original answer the defendant alleged that he had expended in time, labor and money, to collect the sums due the heirs out of their deceased brother's estate, $682. By an amendment he afterwards tolled this sum down to $244. He also gave testimony that he incurred large expenses. Surely this remark of the court was not entirely inapplicable to the case. (2) Speaking on the subject of compensation, the court said: "If he had

charged ten per cent. upon these collections, the amount of
the plaintiff's share would be $9.72, and, the four shares
being added together, ten per cent. upon the aggregate
would make $38.88, which is about the amount of his rail-
road fare, as he estimates it himself at eighteen or nineteen
dollars each trip. You will have to decide, gentlemen of
the jury, upon the evidence, what reasonable compensation
he ought to have for the collection of this money." The
charge does not lay down any basis for determining such
reasonable compensation, and the court was not asked to
do so. A mere hypothetical allusion is made to ten per
cent. commission, but the jury were not instructed that it
was the proper or only basis on which to estimate compensation. On the contrary, by telling the jury that such ten
per cent. would only pay defendant's railroad fare, we
infer that the judge thought it was scarcely adequate compensation. But, however that may be, the jury were told
several times that the defendant was entitled to reasonable
compensation, and the whole testimony was before them
from which to fix the amount thereof.

These observations dispose of all of the errors alleged for
a reversal of the judgment which are deemed worthy of
consideration, adversely to the defendant.

By the Court.— The judgment of the circuit court is affirmed.

HERMANN, Plaintiff in error, vs. THE STATE, Defendant in
error.

December 8 — December 22, 1888.

Criminal law: Evidence: Age of girl: Scienter.

1. The testimony of the mother as to the age of her child is the best
evidence.
2. The defendant having, a few weeks before the trial, suffered a girl
less than sixteen years old to resort to her premises for an unlawful

purpose, and the question being whether she knew at the time that such girl was under the age of twenty-one, it was not error to allow the jury to determine that question from the girl's personal appearance, or from view only.

ERROR to the Municipal Court of *Milwaukee* County. The facts are sufficiently stated in the opinion.

For the plaintiff in error the cause was submitted on the brief of *J. C. McKenney*.

For the defendant in error there was a brief by the *Attorney General* and *L. K. Luse*, Assistant Attorney General, and oral argument by *Mr. Luse*.

ORTON, J. The information is under sec. 4, ch. 214, Laws of 1887. which provides that "any person, being the owner of any premises or having or assisting in the management or control thereof, who induces or knowingly suffers any girl under the age of twenty-one years to resort to or be in or upon the premises for the purpose of being unlawfully and carnally known by any person or persons, shall be punished by imprisonment in the state prison not exceeding three years nor less than one year." The information charges both that the defendant " *did induce and knowingly suffer* one Bertha Priess to resort to and be in or upon the premises," etc. The defendant was convicted and sentenced, after a motion by her counsel to discharge her for want of evidence that she knew that Bertha Priess was under the age of twenty-one years when she so suffered her to resort to or be in or upon her premises for such purpose.

Ottillie Priess, the mother of Bertha, as a witness, was asked by the district attorney, "What is the age of Bertha?" This was objected to by the defendant's counsel, and the witness stated that she had or kept a baptismal certificate. It was contended that such family record was the best evidence of her age. We have no statute that makes such

record evidence, and sec. 4160, R. S., makes the registration
of births in the register's office only *presumptive* evidence
thereof.   In both cases, the evidence would be merely hearsay or secondary, at best.   It certainly could not supersede
the testimony of the mother of the exact age of her child.
No evidence could possibly be better or more reliable.

The court, by proper instructions, allowed the jury to
determine the question whether the defendant *knew* that
Bertha was under the age of twenty-one years when she so
suffered her to resort to her premises for such purposes,
from her personal appearance, or from view only, and this
was excepted to.   The mother had testified that Bertha
was born on the 13th day of March, 1872.   The information was filed February 14, 1888, and charged the offense
with having been committed on the 10th day of January
previously; and the trial was had about the 17th day of
February, so that Bertha, at the time, was under the age
of sixteen years.   Where, as in this case, the girl is so far
under the age of twenty-one years, and just above the age
of childhood and puberty, a woman of experience in the
observation of girls would most certainly know that she was
under the age of twenty-one years.   There are appearances
of development and maturity, or of their absence, which
such a woman, or any woman, could not mistake.   Sixteen
is the first stage and tender age of womanhood.   I know of
no good reason why the personal appearance of this young
girl, on view in presence of the jury, was not very satisfactory evidence that the defendant knew that she was under
the age of twenty-one years.   In cases where the girl is
much nearer the age of twenty-one, such evidence would
be more unreliable, as a matter of course.   Each case must
be tried upon its own facts.   Our statute, even in criminal
cases, sanctions evidence obtained by view.   If the subject
of the *scienter* in this case had been that Bertha was a *girl*,
as well as under the age of twenty-one years, and the ques-

tion had been whether the defendant knew her to be a girl, her appearance alone would be satisfactory, without question. The evidence in this case, in a degree, is very much of the same character. The learned attorney general has furnished the court with authorities which sanction this kind of evidence. The cases of *State v. Arnold*, 13 Ired. Law, 184, and *State v. McNair*, 93 N. C. 628, are much in point. The following cases are authority by analogy: *Garvin v. State*, 52 Miss. 207; *Warlick v. White*, 76 N. C. 175; *People v. Gonzales*, 35 N. Y. 49; *People v. Muller*, 32 Hun, 209; *King v. N. Y. C. & H. R. R. Co.* 72 N. Y. 607; *Gaunt v. State*, 38 Alb. L. J. 103, 14 Atl. Rep. 600; *Clark v. Bradstreet*, 38 Alb. L. J. 287, 15 Atl. Rep. 56.

The record makes the court say, in instructing the jury, that "this girl is so near the age of twenty-one years, and her size is such, it would seem to make out a case similar to the one I have suggested." This must be a mistake in the record, or else it was a slip of the tongue or of the pen, or something is left out explanatory of it. But, as it is, it is favorable to the defendant, and she cannot complain.

By the Court.— The judgment of the municipal court is affirmed.

Sires, Plaintiff in error, vs. The State, Defendant in error.

December 8 — December 22, 1888.

Criminal Law: Excise Laws. *(1) Pleading: Sale of liquor " not to be drank on the premises:" Quantity. (2) Appeal from J. P.: Informal undertaking: Judgment: Surety: Writ of error.*

1. A complaint under secs. 1, 4, ch. 296, Laws of 1885, charging the defendant with selling intoxicating liquors "*not to be drank on the premises,* without having obtained a license or permit therefor," is sufficient, although the quantity sold is not stated.

2. On appeal from a justice's court in a prosecution for selling liquor without a license, the accused gave an undertaking, with surety,

in the form used in civil cases, and not as required by secs. 4714, 4717, R. S. In the circuit court he was again found guilty, and judgment was entered that he pay a fine of $50 and costs, and that in default of payment he be committed to the county jail until the fine and costs should be paid, his imprisonment, however, not to exceed six months. It was further ordered that the state have judgment against the accused and his surety for the amount of the fine and costs. A writ of error was sued out by the accused alone. *Held:*

(1) The judgment against the accused was not in excess of the authority given by the statute.

(2) Any supposed grievance of the surety cannot be considered.

ERROR to the Circuit Court for *Jackson* County.

The following statement of the case was prepared by Mr. Justice CASSODAY:

It appears from the record that January 21, 1886, the accused was arrested in the town of Alma, in Jackson county, upon a warrant issued on that day by a justice of the peace in said town, reciting the complaint, which was on oath, to the effect that said accused did January 20, 1886, at said town, " unlawfully sell, and for the purpose of evading the law give away, spirituous, malt, ardent, intoxicating liquors and drinks, *not to be drank on the premises, without having obtained a license or permit therefor;*" that, upon being brought before said justice, the said accused was tried and found guilty, and fined $50 and costs of suit, and committed until paid; that thereupon said accused appealed to the circuit court, giving an undertaking thereon; that upon a retrial in the circuit court, September 29, 1887, the said accused was found guilty by the jury, and judgment thereupon entered accordingly for such fine and costs, and that in default of the payment thereof he was to be committed to jail for a term not exceeding six months; and it was therein further ordered that the state have judgment to recover from said accused and his surety the sum of $147.63, being the amount of such fine and costs. To review that judgment the accused has sued out a writ of error.

Carl C. Pope, for the plaintiff in error, contended, *inter alia*, that no undertaking on appeal having been given as required by the statute (sec. 4714, R. S.) the appearance of the accused in the circuit court was purely voluntary, and no judgment could be rendered against the surety on the undertaking given. No other or further judgment could properly be rendered against the accused or the accused and his surety than for the penalty specified in sec. 4, ch. 296, Laws of 1885. The judgment in this case is double — against the accused under said section last mentioned, and against the accused and his surety under sec. 4717, R. S. This is clearly unauthorized.

L. K. Luse, Assistant Attorney General, for the defendant in error. The complaint is sufficient. *Allen v. State*, 5 Wis. 329; *State v. Downer*, 21 id. 274; *State v. Tall*, 56 id. 577. The accused is in no way prejudiced by the judgment upon the undertaking against his surety. The judgment against the accused would be just as effectual if no undertaking had ever been given. The surety has not appealed to this court, and must be presumed to be satisfied with the judgment. *Williams v. Starr*, 5 Wis. 534–547; *Palmer v. Yager*, 20 id. 97; *Kopmeier v. Larkin*, 47 id. 598; 4 Wait's Pr. 234; *Montgomery Co. Bank v. Albany City Bank*, 7 N. Y. 459. The judgment, though single in form, is in legal effect separate as to the accused and the surety. *State v. Brady*, 62 Wis. 129.

CASSODAY, J. There is no bill of exceptions. This being so, we are necessarily limited to the inquiry whether the complaint, of which the substance is stated above, charges the accused with the offense of selling intoxicating liquors without a license, under the statutes. Secs. 1, 4, ch. 296, Laws of 1885.[1] The complaint is silent as to the quantity

---

[1] Sec. 1, ch. 296, Laws of 1885, provides that town boards, etc., may grant licenses "for the sale in quantities of less than one gallon of

of such liquors sold or given away. The able counsel for the accused very plausibly argues that the complaint does not allege any want of a license to sell or give away such liquors "to be drank on the premises," but only the want of any such license or permit to sell or give away such liquors "not to be drank on the premises." He therefore insists that as a matter of fact, and for aught that appears in this complaint, the accused did have such license at the time to sell such liquors in quantities less than a gallon, "to be drank on the premises," and that such license gave him the absolute right to sell or give away such limited quantity, even though he knew at the time that such purchaser or donee did not intend to drink, and did not drink, the same until after he had taken it away from the premises; otherwise it is suggested that such sales in such limited quantities "not to be drank on the premises," would be unauthorized by any licensee except pharmacists, under sec. 2, ch. 296, Laws of 1885, and sec. 1, ch. 404, Laws of 1887. Assuming, for the purposes of this case, such to be the true construction of the complaint and the statute, and hence that the words of the statute, "to be drank on the premises," are used in connection with the license for the sale in such smaller quantities merely in contradistinction to the license for such sale in such larger quantities "not to be drank on the premises," then it necessarily follows that the allega-

strong, spirituous, malt, ardent, or intoxicating liquors, to be drank on the premises; and in like manner may grant licenses for the sale, in any quantity, of such liquors, not to be drank on the premises," etc. Sec. 4 provides that if any person shall sell or, for the purpose of evading any law of the state, give away any such liquors in any quantity whatever, without first having obtained a license or permit therefor, he shall, on conviction, be punished by a fine of not less than $50 nor more than $100, besides the costs of suit, or by imprisonment in the county jail not to exceed six months nor less than three months; and in case of punishment by fine such person shall, unless the fine and costs be paid forthwith, be committed to the county jail until such fine and costs are paid or until discharged by due course of law.— REP.

tion of the complaint in the words "without having obtained a license or permit therefor," does negative the having of any such license to sell in such smaller quantities. In other words, under such construction, the allegations of the complaint are to the effect that the sale or gift was made "without having obtained a license or permit therefor," even though it consisted of the smaller quantity, and equally so if it consisted of the larger quantity.

The statute merely requires an information to charge the offense with such degree of certainty that the court may pronounce judgment upon a conviction according to the right of the case. Sec. 4658, R. S.; *Hintz v. State*, 58 Wis. 497; *State v. Boncher*, 59 Wis. 481. No judgment is to be reversed by reason of any defect or imperfection in matters of form which do not tend to the prejudice of the accused. Sec. 4659, R. S. Even in England, where the forms of criminal procedure are far more stringently enforced than here, it has been held, in effect, that an indictment so defective that it would have been quashed upon application before verdict, may nevertheless be cured after verdict. *Queen v. Stroulger*, 17 Q. B. Div. 327. The complaint in question was certainly good after verdict. The absence of any bill of exceptions is a confession that all the allegations of the complaint were sustained by the evidence. If the accused was in fact authorized to do what he did by virtue of any license, then it should have been made to appear by bill of exceptions.

Error is assigned because the bond given on appeal from the justice was in the form used in civil cases, and not as required by secs. 4714, 4717, R. S. But the accused could appeal, and the circuit court take jurisdiction, without any bond. His liability would be the same in any event. No supposed grievances of the surety alone can be considered on this writ of error by the accused alone. If the surety had well-founded grievances, the law gave him a remedy, not only in the trial court, but also in this court. *State v. Brady*, 62 Wis. 129. The judgment against the accused is not in excess of the authority given by the statute. Sec. 4, ch. 296, Laws of 1885.

By the Court.— The judgment of the circuit court is affirmed.

CASES DETERMINED

AT THE

January Term, 1889.

FADNESS and others, Respondents, vs. BRAUNBORG and others, Appellants.

December 7, 1888 — January 8, 1889.

Religious societies: Trusts and trustees: Deeds: Perpetuities: Corporations: Officers: Ouster: Equity: Perversion of trust: Dismissal of minister: Withdrawal from synod: Change of faith.

1. The fact that a religious society, to whose trustees land was conveyed in trust for the erection thereon of a church, had not been incorporated when the deed was delivered, did not invalidate the trust.

2. The deed in such case vested the legal title in the trustees, and upon the subsequent incorporation of the society such legal title became vested in the corporation, subject to the trust.

3. The designation of the beneficiaries of a trust as the *members* of a certain church is sufficiently definite and certain, under subd. 5, sec. 11, ch. 57, R. S. 1849 (subd. 5, sec. 2081, R. S.).

4. Although sec. 1, ch. 57, R. S. 1849 (sec. 2071, R. S.), declares that trusts, except as authorized and modified in that chapter, are abolished, this was not intended to prohibit the trusts expressly authorized by ch. 47, R. S. 1849 (sec. 2000, R. S.), relating to religious societies.

5. A conveyance of land to the trustees of a religious society and their successors in office forever, in trust for the erection thereon of a church building for the use of the members of the society, did not suspend the power of alienation, within the meaning of secs. 14, 15, ch. 56, R. S. 1849 (secs. 2038, 2039, R. S.), such trustees being "persons in being by whom an absolute fee in possession could be conveyed" in the manner prescribed by law.

6. A religious society incorporated under the laws of this state is a civil corporation, governed by the statutes and such rules of the common law as may be applicable. The trustees are *officers* of the corporation, and before an equitable action can be maintained by members of the society, some of whom claim to be the rightful trustees, to recover possession and control of the property by ousting those who have been in the continuous possession and control thereof claiming to be such trustees, and by enjoining them from acting as such, the plaintiffs who claim to be the trustees must have been peaceably admitted to such offices or have established their title thereto by some direct action or proceeding, as by *quo warranto.*

7. The dismissal of one minister and the employment of another is a matter pertaining to the temporalities of a church, and does not necessarily operate as a change of faith or doctrine. When done by the majority of a religious society in accordance with the statute and the constitution and by-laws of the society, it does not operate as a wrongful exclusion of the minority who adhere to the former minister.

8. Land was conveyed in trust for the erection thereon of a church building for the use of the members of a certain church " according to the rules of said church. and according to the rules of said church " which might thereafter " be adopted from time to time by their authorized synods." The synod to which the church was attached was a mere confederation of local self-governing churches, acting, so far as the local organization was concerned, merely as an advisory body. *Held,* that the mere withdrawal of the church from such synod was not a violation or perversion of the trust.

9. Land was conveyed to trustees in trust for the erection thereon of a church building "for the use of the members of the Norwegian Evangelical Church of St. Paul's on Liberty Prairie, according to the rules of said church," etc. The grant was, presumably, made with reference to the articles of faith previously adopted by said church. The church was subsequently incorporated, the certificate of incorporation simply giving the name of the church. *Held,* that the trustees and officers of the corporation could not lawfully devote the church building to purposes other than those specified in the grant.

10. It is not the province of courts of equity to determine mere questions of faith, doctrine, or schism, not necessarily involved in the enforcement of an ascertained trust. To call for equitable interference there must be such a real and substantial departure from the designated faith or doctrine as will be in contravention of such trust.

11. Where the adoption of certain articles of faith by the majority of a
religious society is claimed by the minority to be such a departure
from the faith referred to in a trust deed as to result in a perversion of the use of the property granted, the fact that such minority
remained united with the majority for more than two years after
the adoption of such articles, constitutes an additional reason why,
in the absence of a clearly established violation of the trust, a
court of equity should not interfere. And the fact that before
suit was brought the majority repealed such articles and substantially reaffirmed those previously adopted, is still another reason
why the action should not be maintained.

APPEAL from the Circuit Court for *Dane* County.

The following statement of the case was prepared by Mr.
Justice CASSODAY:

It appears from the undisputed evidence or the findings
of the court, in effect, that prior to May 20, 1852, there was
an organized society or congregation known as the Norwegian Evangelical Lutheran Church on Koshkonong Prairie, of which Rev. A. C. Preus, a regularly ordained minister,
was the regularly called pastor.   That prior to that date a
meeting of the representatives of the Norwegian Evangelical Lutherans of southern Wisconsin and northern Illinois
was held at Luther Valley, in Rock county, at which said
Koshkonong congregation was represented.   That at said
meeting a "Constitution of the Norwegian Evangelical Lutheran *Church* of America" was adopted, in January, 1851,
containing, among other things, the following provisions:

"Section 1.· The name of the church shall be 'The Norwegian Evangelical Lutheran *Church* of America.'   Sec. 2.
The doctrine of the church is the one revealed in the Holy
Word of God, in the baptismal covenant, and in the canon·
ical writings of the Old and New Testaments, interpreted
in accordance with the symbolical books and confessional
writings of the Church of Norway, which are: (1) The
Apostolic creed; (2) the Nicene creed; (3) the Athanasian
creed; (4) the unaltered articles of the Augsburg Confes-

sion, as delivered to Emperor Charles the Fifth at Augsburg, 1530; (5) the Smaller Catechism of Luther. Sec. 3. *This church* will not acknowledge or recognize any one as minister of the gospel unless he is duly examined, rightfully called, and according to the rules of the church ordained to the clerical office. Sec. 4. The ceremonies of the church, or the divine services, shall be conducted in conformity with the rituals of the Church of Norway and Denmark in 1685, together with the altar book in use in those kingdoms, but modified as the supreme goverment of the church shall from time to time more precisely determine. Sec. 5. The government of the church shall until further [ordered] be a synodical presbyterial, so that every year a synod is held, or a meeting of the church, which is the highest authority of the church. Sec. 6. The synod shall consist of the clergy of the church; that is, the superintendent and ministers who are united with the synod, and who preside over congregations whose doctrines and specific church rules are in harmony with those of the church, and representatives elected from every congregation united with the synod. [Note added to section 6.] *Congregations not connected with the synod*, but whose doctrine and church rules are in conformity with those of the church, *may send delegates*, with right to introduce resolutions directly, and upon submission to state reasons of the same. The synod may thereafter, in its own discretion, allow these delegates the privilege of participating in the discussion upon such resolutions. Sec. 7. The congregations connected with the synod shall send representatives upon the following basis: Every principal congregation shall send three representatives; every annexed congregation which has two hundred members, send two; and every annexed congregation which contains less than two hundred members, one representative. The representatives must be members of the congregations and have credentials from those congregations which they represent. Sec. 8. The synod shall· have power (1) to make general and special rules and resolutions in all religious and ecclesiastical matters; (2) to decide, without further appeal, upon all matters of the church; (3) to select a superintendent from among the clergy connected with the church; (4) to select from its members a church council, to consist of not less than two clerical and four lay members, which shall be proportionately the same if the number be increased." "Sec. 11. When a congregation *wishes to unite* with the church, such congregation shall send its petition to the superintendent, which petition shall be subscribed by the minister, if it has a minister, and the directors, In this petition it must expressly allege *that the congregation submit* to the constitution in force for the Norwegian Evangelical Lutheran Church of America, as well as its other rules and resolutions, *but to every individual congregation is reserved the right to have its own laws for its home management*, only that these be not in conflict with the constitution and resolutions of the church. Sec. 12. With exception of sections 2 and 3, which always shall continue unchanged and irrevocable, this constitution, or any part thereof whatever, can be changed."

That meeting and constitution were preliminary to the organization and establishment of a synod, as such constitution had first to be submitted to the several congregations, and their several actions thereon to be reported back to such general meeting, and then finally acted upon, which was not done until 1853, when such synod was organized and established. No other synod or conference of Lutherans bearing that name has ever been organized in the United States.

Prior to May 20, 1852, the members of said Koshkonong congregation living on Liberty Prairie in Dane county voluntarily separated from said Koshkonong congregation and organized themselves into the " Norwegian Evan-

gelical Lutheran Church of St. Paul's on Liberty Prairie,"
and the said Rev. A. C. Preus continued to serve the said
Koshkonong congregation and the said Liberty Prairie congregation, which were some five or six miles apart, until
1860.

May 20, 1852, Niels Severson and Regnal, his wife, being
such members of said Liberty Prairie congregation, in consideration of five cents to them in hand paid, did give,
grant, bargain, and sell, release, confirm, and convey unto
"Casper Krough, Lars Torgerson, Lars Davidson, Anfind
Asmundson, and Sjure Starkson, trustees in trust for the
uses and purposes" therein mentioned, "all the estate,
right, title, interest, property, claim, and demand whatsoever, either in law or in equity, which" the said grantors
had in and to the two and a half acres of land therein described, to have and to hold unto them, the said trustees,
"and their successors in office forever, *in trust* that they shall
erect and build thereon a house of worship for the use of the
members of the Norwegian Evangelical Church of St. Paul's
on Liberty Prairie, *according to the rules of said church*,
and according to the rules of said church which may be
adopted from *time to time* by their *authorized* synods or
conferences; and in further trust and confidence that, *as
often* as one or more of the trustees hereinbefore mentioned
shall die or cease to be a trustee according to the rules of
said church, *then* and in such case it shall be the duty of
the minister or preacher having charge of said church, or,
in case there is none, then one of the elders or deacons or
other church officers whatsoever *to call a meeting of the
voters* of said church as soon as conveniently may be *and
according to the statute* in such case made and provided, *and
the voters* at the meeting so called shall proceed to nominate or appoint one or more persons *to fill the place or
places* of him or them whose office or offices have been
vacated as aforesaid; provided, that the person or persons so

nominated or appointed shall be twenty-one years old; and
in order to keep up the number of five trustees forever."
The said trustees, as well as said grantors, had, prior to the
organization of said Liberty Prairie congregation, been
members of said Koshkonong congregation. Upon the execution and delivery of said deed, the said trustees accepted
said trust, and went into possession of said lot, and built
thereon, during the years 1852, 1853, and 1854, a meeting-
house or church edifice, which is still standing thereon, and
for the possession of which this action is brought.

Upon the organization and establishment of said synod
in 1853, the said Liberty Prairie congregation, in February,
1853, sent delegates thereto, and became a member thereof.
There were from time to time joint meetings of said Koshkonong and Liberty Prairie congregations and trustees
from 1853 to 1860 inclusive. At such joint trustees' meeting, December 28, 1854, it was determined that, " should at
any time one of these congregations prefer to form an independent parish [*sognekald*], and to call to themselves a
separate minister, then shall whichever of the congregations which withdraws from the present union be entitled,
after the parsonage has been assessed, to receive its share
of the value of the parsonage in proportion to the number
of families of the congregation."

February 22, 1858, the legislature of this state, by " An
act to incorporate the Norwegian Evangelical Lutheran
Synod of the State of Wisconsin," among other things, enacted that: " Sec. 2. The said synod shall have full power
and authority to make a constitution for the government
of its members, and also to make and provide such by-
laws, rules, ordinances, and regulations as may seem best
adapted to carry out the objects of the members thereof,
and to alter, amend, or repeal the same at such times and
in such manner as may be deemed proper and necessary in
order to promote the interests, proceedings, and affairs of

said synod, and also to determine the number of officers that are to represent said synod as trustees thereof: provided, that such by-laws, rules, ordinances, and regulations shall not be in violation of the constitution and laws of this state or of the United States." Ch. 28, P. & L. Laws of 1858. By ch. 274, Laws of 1878, the name of said last-named synod was changed to "The Synod for the Norwegian Evangelical Lutheran Church of America." The title to said last-mentioned act was changed to "The Synod for the Norwegian Evangelical Lutheran Church of America" by ch. 89, Laws of 1885.

Rev. A. C. Preus having determined soon to enter upon another field of ministry, the said Koshkonong and Liberty Prairie congregations respectively joined in a written "public and voluntary call," made September 15, 1858, to Rev. J. A. Otteson, "to occupy the field of labor made vacant by the resignation of Rev. Preus," which, among others, contained the conditions: "(1) That you shall proclaim unto us the Word of God in its purity, in accordance with the confession of the Lutheran Church. (2) That you shall, in every respect, carry out our church polity, not only as to doctrine, but also as to discipline and ritual. (3) . . . The congregation, on their part, bind themselves to receive the truth, howsoever it may be proclaimed, and to submit themselves to their pastor in all things that in accordance with God's Word and true church polity he may demand. . . . The use and benefit of the parsonage of ninety acres, the buildings and fences of which to be kept in repair by the pastor. . . . Should you, reverend pastor, or the church, at any time desire to rescind this call, then you, as well as the church, ought to be notified betimes, which is held to be one year in advance." "P. S. At a subsequent meeting of the church-wardens it was, at the request of Rev. Otteson, determined that the last section of the written call, to wit, 'Should you, reverend pastor,' etc., be expunged." Rev. Otteson accepted said call in 1860, and continued to serve said Liberty Prairie congregation, as well as the Koshkonong congregation, until terminated as hereinafter mentioned.

The court found "that by the discipline and rules of the Norwegian Evangelical Lutheran church the call of the minister is one for life, unless he be regularly deposed for false doctrine, immoral life, or neglect of duties, and cannot be terminated by the action of the congregation without the consent of the pastor." In 1861 the said synod declared that, "in regard to the internal arrangement and government of the individual congregations, the synod is only an advisory body. No resolution by the synod in such matters can therefore have binding force on the individual congregation unless it voluntarily accepts it, and if a congregation finds that it is in conflict with the Word of God, or that it is not beneficial to it under its peculiar circumstances, then it has the right not to follow the resolution. This should be announced to the church council, accompanied with the reasons therefor. If such announcement is not sent in within six months after the meeting of the synod, the resolution is regarded as accepted by the congregation." The court found, in effect, that September 8, 1862, the said society or congregation of Liberty Prairie was duly organized under the statutes providing for the organization of religious societies, and a certificate of such organization was duly recorded; and ever since that time, up to May 17, 1885, the said society consisting of both parties here represented and their respective associates, acted as one religious corporation. At a meeting of said synod, in 1865, it was declared that "now it is certainly so, that the congregation, if they desire, can give this right to the synod, and authorize it on its behalf to establish ceremonies. But the question is here, if it is beneficial that the congregation surrender their right and give to the synod a legislative power in such respects. All were agreed that the synod ought not to have any kind of *legislative authority*, but that it should only be an advisory body. This authority to determine the ceremonies, which, according to the old constitution, was placed in the hands of the synod, it had never made use of. This has already been acknowledged for a long time, that the constitution of the synod was antiquated, and that already, six years ago in a meeting of the synod on Coon Prairie, it was declared that the synod should not be a legislative one, but only an advisory body." At a meeting of said synod in 1867 it was declared that "if the grace of God is not in the means of grace, we must obtain it somewhere else by means of our own labor, and it is impossible in that way to obtain any firm assurance and divine certainty. We must form the same opinion as regards the reform doctrine concerning election, according to which God has from eternity, without regard to the faith or the want of faith in men, predestinated some unto eternal life and others unto eternal death,— a doctrine which is well calculated to lead men either into security or into despair."

In 1876 the said synod· adopted a new constitution, of which the following extracts may have some bearing upon the questions considered:

"Chapter 1. *Name, Confession, and Liturgy.* Sec. 1. The ecclesiastical organization heretofore called the 'Norwegian Evangelical Lutheran Church of America' hereby adopts the name and title of the 'Synod of the Norwegian Evangelical Lutheran Church of America.' Sec. 2. The only source and rule of the faith and teaching of the synod is God's Holy Word, revealed in the canonical books of the Old and New Testaments. Sec. 3. The synod adopts as its confession of faith the symbolical books or confessional writings of the Norwegian Lutheran Church, for the reason that these writings give a pure and unadulterated exposition of the doctrine contained of the Word of God. These confessional writings are the following: The three ancient creeds, to wit, the Apostolic, the Nicene, and the Athanasian creeds; the unadulterated Augsburg Confession; Luther's Smaller Catechism. NOTE.— The only reason that the remaining symbols of the Lutheran Church are not enumerated among the symbolical books of our synod is, that hitherto they are not generally known in our congregations. Sec. 4. In order that uniformity of liturgical rights may be preserved, the synod advises the congregations to retain the Norwegian ritual of the year 1685, and the altar book of the year 1688.

"Chapter 2. *Composition and Subdivisions of the Synod, and Admission to its Membership.* Sec. 1. The synod is composed of the congregations that have united by adopting this constitution. Sec. 2. Standing members of the synod, who, as to their official position, are always under the supervision of the synod, are (*a*) pastors who serve congregations connected with the synod, and who are themselves members of the synod; (*b*) members of the church council. Sec. 3. As standing members of the synod may further be admitted (*a*) teachers of the educational institutions of the synod; (*b*) ministers of the Lutheran congregations which are not connected with the synod; (*c*) permanently located teachers of parochial schools of Lutheran congregations connected with the synod or otherwise. . . . Sec. 5. When a congregation desires admission into the synod, such congregation shall send an application for admission to the president of the district to which, by reason of its location, it should naturally belong. Together with such application shall be submitted a copy of the constitution and by-laws of such congregation, as evidence that the faith, confession, and polity of the congregation are truly Evangelical Lutheran; also a duly attested declaration that the constitution of the synod has been adopted

at a public meeting of the congregation. These documents
shall be laid before the district synod, which then acts upon
the application. Sec. 6. Any person desiring admission as
a standing member of the synod shall send an application
for admission to the president of the district in which he
resides, together with a declaration that he gives his un-
qualified assent to the doctrine and confession of the synod,
and accepts the constitution. If the applicant be a minister, he shall, before admission, also prove that he has been
properly examined and regularly called and ordained a
minister of the gospel. Such application, and the documents thereto pertaining, shall be laid before the district
synod, which then acts upon the application."

" Chapter 4. *The Object and General Interest of the Synod.*
The synod shall watch over the unity and purity of doctrine
and promotion of godliness, and hence (*a*) at synod meetings,
as well as at district meetings, take up for consideration
chiefly such doctrinal questions the discussion of which shall
be especially needful; take cognizance of and warn against
sects, errors, and sins, as also anti-Christian tendencies of
the times; (*b*) watch over the official conduct of standing
members, and also the religious condition of the congregations; (*c*) seek to settle religious controversies, and to give
advice and opinions on church questions; (*d*) establish and
control educational institutions for the training of pastors
and teachers, and promote home and foreign missions;
(*e*) further the use and spreading of the Holy Scriptures, of
other orthodox school-books, hymn-books, and devotional
literature; (*f*) collect and manage funds for the support of
the educational institutions of the synod, and for the de-
frayment of the current expenses of the synod.

" Chapter 5. *Business Sphere of the Different Meetings.*
Sec. 1. The district synods shall labor for the attainment of
the common objects, and shall . . . (*b*) admit into the synod
congregations and standing members within the bounds of

the district; (c) when circumstances require it, temporarily supend a congregation or a standing member from their privileges in the synod, and if, despite repeated warning, they wilfully persist in false doctrine or ungodly life, finally sever their connection with the synod, provided the case be not appealed to the synod meeting. . . . Sec. 4. Doctrinal questions and matters of conscience cannot be decided by majorities of votes, but only by the Word of God and the symbolical books of our church. Sec. 5. If not otherwise provided in this constitution, and if not otherwise determined in particular cases by the meeting concerned, all other matters are decided in the above-mentioned meetings by a plurality of votes, and in case the votes are equally divided the vote of the chairman decides the matter. Sec. 6. In respect to the *individual congregations* the above-named meetings *are merely advisory bodies.* Hence, if a congregation be of the opinion that a resolution conflicts with the Word of God, or finds that it is not conducive to the good of the congregation under its particular circumstances, the congregation should report the fact to the president of the meeting concerned, stating the reasons therefor. If no such report is sent in within six months after the publication of such resolution, the resolution shall be considered adopted by the congregation."

"Chapter 9. *Amendments of the Constitution.* With the exception of chapter 1, sections 2 and 3, and chapter 2, section 6, the contents of which shall not be altered, this constitution may be amended," etc.

In 1882 and 1883 a schism arose in the Liberty Prairie congregation respecting the doctrine of election. After a considerable controversy, Rev. Otteson, as pastor, February 10, 1883, and at the request of fifty-one members of the congregation, gave notice of a meeting to be held in Februrary, 1883, "for the consideration of the doctrine of the election of grace, or so much as the meeting may determine, and to see if we then, by the grace of God, can agree to retain the doctrines taught us in childhood, and as explained to us by our old fathers." At the meeting of the Liberty Prairie congregation, so called, the said church, on or about February 26, 1883, by a large majority of those present, adopted, as its "Articles of Faith," the following, to wit: "(1) The revealed gospel teaches us that God will not surely promise nor give to any sinner eternal life unless he participates in the merits and righteousness of Jesus Christ through faith in him. (2) The election to eternal life is that decree of God in his eternal plan of salvation by which he has determined what sinners alone he would glorify and save, and thus separated these elect from the others, who remain in perdition. (3) In this, his fixed election of certain sinners, in preference to others, to eternal glory and bliss, has God been governed by his purpose of grace,— whosoever believes shall be saved; that is, God elected and destined certain sinners, in preference to others, to eternal glory and salvation, according as he foresaw what sinners, in time, would accept of the proffered grace, believe in Christ, and persevere to the end in such belief. (See Pontoppidan, Sand. til. Gudf., Quest. 548.) The congregation rejects as false doctrine, when there is taught (1) that participation in the merits of Christ through faith in him is not determining for the will of God concerning the sure salvation of certain sinners in preference to others, but that this participation in the benefits of Christ shall belong only to the way, manner, order, and means by which God in time will execute his eternal decree to save those sinners whom he unconditionally elected to glory; (2) that the election to eternal glory and salvation in heaven shall not be dependent on nor conditioned by any means of the foreknowledge of God about what, in time, sinners should believe in Christ and by such belief partake of his merit; (3) that the election to eternal life has been made with regard to certain individual sinners, considered only as they, with the rest of the children of Adam, are still in the general corruption and perdition, and that God, in regard to these individual sinners, in preference to all others, shall have made this decree: Such and such shall and must be saved, I will myself provide for; that this, my decree, shall not be annihilated; (4) that God, in the election, shall have predestined certain individual sinners out of the whole and alike damned multitude, both to the end (the glory) and to the way (all the necessary means and blessings necessary to salvation), without the foreseen faith, casting the balance in this election to glory."

April 29, 1884, a resolution was unanimously adopted by the Liberty Prairie congregation to the effect that a call should be extended to Rev. O. M. Saevig, and that Rev. Otteson continue to serve the congregation for another year, and then voluntarily resign. Said resolution was acceded to by said Rev. Otteson at the time. The court found that such adoption of that resolution was "not intended as final, but as steps in the direction of harmonizing differences, which failed." At a regularly called meeting of the Liberty Prairie congregation, December 15, 1884, 143 voters were present, of whom 66 voted for the candidate of the plaintiffs' party, and 77 for the candidate of the defendants' party, but, as no one received a majority of two thirds, it was not regarded as a determination of the question.

It also appears that at a regularly called meeting of the Liberty Prairie congregation, March 4, 1885, two of the defendants, *Braunborg* and *Hendrickson*, were elected trustees without opposition. Up to that time there had always been five trustees of said Liberty Prairie congregation, and there continued to be five thereafter, including the two thus elected. At said meeting the Rev. Otteson, having refused to sign the articles of faith so adopted by

the congregation as aforesaid, and having expressed an un-
willingness to resign at the end of the year, a vote was
taken as to whether he should be retained by the congregation or discharged, and the result was that 56 voted to
have him remain and 87 voted for his discharge. Thereupon it was moved and carried that said Rev. Otteson be
declared discharged as such pastor, and also that nobody
should officiate as pastor without the permission of the
board of trustees, to which the minority protested to the
effect that the promise of Rev. Otteson to resign had been
upon conditions of compromise not fulfilled, and that they
would hold to their old minister and seek to maintain the
congregation in its usual form. March 19, 1885, it was
unanimously resolved by said defendant trustees "that we
permit our late pastor, Otteson, to use the church until the
29th of April, 1885," and that a meeting of the congregation be called for May 1, 1885. The church officers notified
Rev. Otteson that he could have the loan of the church for
confirmation, May 17, 1885, and for communion, May 20,
1885, but the said trustees refused to allow said Rev. Otteson to preach in or act as the pastor of said congregation
after May 17, 1885, but thereafter called and employed
Rev. G. G. Krostue as such minister and pastor. Said
Krostue was a regularly ordained minister of the Norwegian Lutheran Church. The defendants, *Henry Braunborg, Christian Hendrickson, Torge G. Thompson, Elling
Johnson*, and *Ole H. Fimrite* were severally elected trustees
by a majority of said congregation at the regular times and
place for electing the trustees thereof, and claim to be the
regular successors of the trustees named in said deed, and
that the defendant *Charles Schoyen* is the acting church-
warden, and that said defendants — trustees, and warden —
have had the exclusive control and management of said
church edifice ever since May 17, 1885, as in effect found by
the court. Since that time the said majority have contin-

ued to occupy said church edifice as a place of worship, with said Rev. Krostue as their minister.

After May 17, 1885, a portion of said minority of said congregation who so favored the retention of said Rev. Otteson separated from said congregation, and worshiped in private houses, halls, and school-houses, with said Rev. Otteson as their pastor. At the time of the annual meeting of said congregation, to wit, March 3, 1886, and in pursuance of notice, such portion of said minority met, and unanimously resolved to recognize said majority which so continued to occupy said church edifice as having withdrawn from the rightful Liberty Prairie congregation, who were therefore declared suspended. Thereupon, and on the same day, the said portion of said minority resolved to proceed' to elect five trustees, and thereupon voted for the same, each receiving twenty-seven votes, and that among the persons so elected such trustees were four of the above plaintiffs, to wit, *Fadness, Smithback, Brichtson,* and *Jargo,* and the plaintiff *Birge* was at the same time elected as church-warden by said portion of said minority. Said portion of said minority then directed such trustees to ask for the books of the congregation, and, if denied, to take copies. The other trustee so elected was Lars Huseboe. March 2, 1887, the said *Jargo* and Huseboe were re-elected such trustees for the term of three years.

Said majority of said congregation at their annual meeting, March 2, 1887, elected the defendants *Johnson* and *Fimrite* in place of Roe and Carstad, and re-elected *Schoyen* church-warden. At the same meeting said majority adopted the following constitution:

" *Constitution adopted March 2, 1887.* This congregation acknowledges the sacred Word of God, revealed in the canonical books of the Old and New Testament, as the only source and precept of faith, doctrine, and conduct. Sec. 3. The congregation confesses belief in the symbolical

books or the confessional writings of the Norwegian Lutheran Church, because they give a pure and unadulterated
exposition of the doctrine contained in the Word of God.
These confessional writings are: (1) The Apostles' creed;
(2) the Nicene creed; (3) the Athanasian creed; (4) Luther's
Smaller Catechism; (5) the Unadulterated Confession of
Augsburg, or that confession or creed which was delivered
to Charles V. at the diet of Augsburg in the year 1530.
The divine services in the congregation shall be performed
in conformity with the Norwegian Church ritual of 1685
and the ritual of 1688; these, however, so modified as the
corporation may find that the circumstances require. All
former precepts or regulations, of what name whatsoever,
adopted by this corporation, and which conflict with this
constitution, are hereby repealed."

'This constitution had been in force since the day and
year last aforesaid. At the time of adopting said last-
named constitution the said majority also unanimously
adopted the following declaration: "As grounds for withdrawal, the congregation adduce in particular the unjust
treatment allotted to it during the last synodical meeting
of the eastern district, when the synodical meeting refused
to admit the legally elected representative of the congregation, which refusal the congregation must consider as a
real, if not formal, expulsion. Unanimously adopted."

June 4, 1887, the "Eastern District Synod," in session at
Stoughton, passed a resolution to the effect that the synod
recognizes the West Koshkonong and Liberty congregations that were being served by Rev. Otteson as being the
rightful congregations in connection with the synod.

March 12, 1887, this action was commenced by said
trustees and officers so elected by said portion of said minority of the congregation and others of like interests,
against the trustees and officers so elected by said majority
of the congregation, to have the plaintiffs adjudged to be

the rightful and lawful congregation and entitled to the possession and control of said church property, and hold the same for the use and occupation of the plaintiffs and the exclusion of all others; and that the defendants be adjudged to have no right, title, or interest in said church property, nor right to manage or control the same or interfere therewith, and that they be perpetually enjoined from doing so. Upon such facts the court concluded, in effect, that the defendants had violated and perverted the trust created and prescribed in said deed, and were not the owners or entitled to the use of the church property; that the plaintiffs were the lawful and rightful congregation, and entitled to the exclusive use, possession, and control of the property described in the deed, and the whole thereof; and that the plaintiffs were the rightful and lawful trustees and officers of said congregation. Thereupon judgment was entered that the plaintiffs are the lawful and rightful congregation, and entitled to the exclusive use, possession, and control of all the property belonging thereto; that the defendants, and each of them, their associates, servants, and agents, etc., be perpetually enjoined from in any manner taking or retaining possession of, interfering with, assuming control of, or exercising any authority over, any property of said church, and from holding the keys of, or locking or unlocking, said church edifice, and that they deliver up said keys to the plaintiffs; that the plaintiff trustees are the lawful and rightful trustees, and the regular successors of the trustees named in said deed, and as such have the right to the exclusive possession, control, and custody of said church edifice and premises, and of all of the property of the congregation, to hold the same for the use of the plaintiffs. From such judgment the defendants appeal.

Pinney & Sanborn, attorneys, and *J. M. Olin*, of counsel, for the appellants, contended, *inter alia*, that the judgment is erroneous because it includes valuable property not covered by the action. The trust embraced in the trust deed is void under our statutes because it undertook to create a perpetuity unauthorized by law, not being within two lives in being at its execution. Every conveyance of lands to religious corporations creates a perpetuity, and necessarily implies a trust although none be expressed. *Gram v. Prussia E. E. L. G. Society*, 36 N. Y. 161. All uses and trusts in real property are abolished except those saved by ch. 57, R. S. 1849. And the exception in favor of charitable corporations in the statutes of 1878 does not apply to churches. *Ruth v. Oberbrunner*, 40 Wis. 238; *De Wolf v. Lawson*, 61 id. 469; *Methodist Church v. Clark*, 37 Mich. 730, 739; *Little v. Willford*, 31 Minn. 173. By a voluntary incorporation under the statute, made by the unanimous vote of the society, any pre-existing religious trust is made subject to the statute, and beyond the control of anybody except a majority of the legal members of the society. *Robertson v. Bullions*, 11 N. Y. 243; *Petty v. Tooker*, 21 id. 267; *Gram v. Prussia E. E. L. G. Society*, 36 id. 161. Unless there is a very plain and palpable abuse of a religious trust a court of equity will not interfere. *Miller v. Gable*, 2 Denio, 492; *Watkins v. Wilcox*, 66 N. Y. 654; *Burrel v. Associate R. Church*, 44 Barb. 282; *Att'y Gen. ex rel. Abbot v. Dublin*, 38 N. H. 460; *Trustees v. St. Michael's E. Church*, 48 Pa. St. 20; *Watson v. Jones*, 13 Wall. 679; *Happy v. Morton*, 33 Ill. 398. The government of the Evangelical Lutheran Church in the United States is, in its essential features, congregational or independent. Each congregation is completely self-governing in character, not subject to the control of any synod, and not required to be in connection with any synod. Buck's Theolog. Dict. Appendix V, 471; 12 Am. Law Reg. 331, 332; *Lawson v. Kolbenson*, 61 Ill. 421; *Ehrenfeldt's Appeal*, 101 Pa. St. 186; *Fernstler v. Siebert*, 114 id. 200; *Heckman v. Mees*, 16 Ohio, 583; *Miller v. Gable*, 2 Denio, 492, *Burrel v. Associate R. Church*, 44

Barb. 282; *Watkins v. Wilcox*, 66 N. Y. 654; *Bartholomew v. Lutheran Cong.* 35 Ohio St. 567; *Presbyterian Cong. v. Johnston*, 1 Watts & S. 9; *Trustees v. St. Michael's E. Church*, 48 Pa. St. 20; *Rector v. Shivers*, 16 N. J. Eq. 453; *McGinnis v. Watson*, 41 Pa. St. 9. It is the settled doctrine of the English courts that it is the duty of the court to inquire and decide for itself both as to the nature and power of church judicatories, and as to which of the contending parties adheres to the true standard of faith in the church organization. *Watson v. Jones*, 13 Wall. 679, 727; *Att'y Gen. v. Pearson*, 3 Meriv. 353; *Craigdallie v. Aikman*, 2 Bligh, 529; *Galbraith v. Smith*, 15 Sc. Sess. Cas. 1st Ser. 808. The following cases in this country also hold to the rule that the decisions of the synods are not binding upon the courts where property rights are involved, but only in cases of membership, church discipline, etc. *Smith v. Nelson*, 18 Vt. 566; *Watson v. Avery*, 2 Bush, 332; *State ex rel. Watson v. Farris*, 45 Mo. 183; *Watson v. Garvin*, 54 id. 354; *Landis v. Campbell*, 79 id. 433; *Hendrickson v. Decow*, 1 N. J. Eq. 578; *Livingston v. Rector*, 45 N. J. Law, 230; *Gartin v. Penick*, 5 Bush, 110; *Harmon v. Dreher*, 1 Speer's Eq. 90; *Shannon v. Frost*, 3 B. Mon. 253; *Stack v. O'Hara*, 4 Leg. Gaz. (Pa.), 2; *Gordon v. Williams*, 3 id. 113.

For the respondents there was a brief by *Ollis & Helms*, attorneys, and *I. C. Sloan*, of counsel, and the cause was argued orally by *I. C. Sloan* and *John Ollis*. They cited *Watson v. Jones*, 13 Wall. 679; *Petty v. Tooker*, 21 N. Y. 272; *Gable v. Miller*, 10 Paige, 644; *Miller v. Gable*, 2 Denio, 492; Angell & Ames on Corp. sec. 38; High on Injunctions, sec. 305; *Att'y Gen. v. Welsh*, 4 Hare, 572; *Hale v. Everett*, 53 N. H. 9; *Roshi's Appeal*, 69 Pa. St. 462; *Kniskern v. Lutheran Churches*, 1 Sandf. Ch. 439; *Winebrenner v. Colder*, 43 Pa. St. 244; *McBride v. Porter*, 17 Iowa, 203.

CASSODAY, J. 1. The first question with which we are naturally confronted is whether the trust imposed by the deed of May 20, 1852, was valid under the statutes. At the time that deed was made Liberty Prairie congregation or church society had not yet been incorporated. In fact, it was not incorporated until September 8, 1862. The deed of the land was to five trustees named, and their successors in office for ever, for the uses and purposes therein mentioned. The deed required such trustees to erect and build upon the land thereby conveyed "a house of worship for the use of the *members* of the Norwegian Evangelical Church of St. Paul's on Liberty Prairie, according to the rules of said church and according to the rules of said church which " might thereafter " be adopted from time to time by their authorized synods or conferences; and in further trust and confidence that, as often as one or more of " such trustees should " die or cease to be a trustee according to the rules of said church, then and in such case " it was therein made the duty of the minister, preacher, elders, deacons, or other church officers " to call a meeting of the *voters* of said church, . . . *according to the statute in such case made and provided*, and the voters at the meeting so called " were therein required " to nominate or appoint one or more persons to fill " such vacancies. From the language quoted, it is manifest that the grantors in the deed contemplated that the church or society would soon be organized and incorporated under the statutes, and that trustees should from time to time be elected by the persons qualified by statute to vote for the same; otherwise the statutes would not have been thus expressly referred to therein. Under the repeated decisions of this court, we must hold that the *mere fact* that such church or religious society had not yet been incorporated at the time of the delivery of that deed in no way frustrated the trust thereby created, if such trust was otherwise valid. *In re Taylor Orphan Asylum*, 36 Wis. 534; *Dodge v. Williams*, 46 Wis. 100–102; *Gould v. Taylor Orphan Asylum*, 46 Wis. 106; *Webster v. Morris*, 66 Wis. 397.

It is true that the statutes in force at the time the deed was executed had abolished all "uses and trusts," except as therein authorized and modified. Sec. 1, ch. 57, R. S. 1849; sec. 1, ch. 84, R. S. 1858; sec. 2071, R. S. 1878. The same chapter provided that "express trusts may be created for any or either of the following purposes: . . . (5) For the beneficial interest of *any person or persons*, when such trust is fully expressed and clearly defined upon the face of the instrument creating it, subject to the limitations as to time prescribed in this title." Sec. 11, ch. 57, R. S. 1849; sec. 2081, R. S. 1878. According to the same statutes, it was provided that the word "person" might extend and be applied to bodies politic and corporate as well as to individuals. Subd. 12, sec. 1, ch. 4, R. S. 1849; ch. 5, R. S. 1858; sec. 4971, R. S. 1878. But by the deed the trust here created was "for the use of the *members*" of the church. Such designation of the beneficiaries as a class was sufficiently definite and certain to answer the requirement of the statute quoted. *Webster v. Morris*, 66 Wis. 381; *Heermans v. Schmaltz*, 7 Fed. Rep. 566. Although the chapter on religious societies is not included in the same title as the chapter so abolishing other trusts, yet no one can reasonably claim that the latter chapter was ever intended to prohibit what was expressly authorized by the former. At the time of the making of the deed the statutes expressly authorized the trustees of such religious societies "to take charge of the estate and property belonging thereto, and to transact all affairs relative to the temporalities thereof," and to "take into their possession and custody all the temporalities of such church, congregation, or society, whether the same may have been given, granted, or devised, directly *or indirectly*, to such church, congregation, or society, *or to any other person or persons for their use.*" Secs. 1, 6, ch. 47, R. S. 1849; secs. 1, 7, ch. 66, R. S. 1858. So the next section of the same chapter provided that "such trustees may also, in their corporate name, . . . recover and hold . . . all churches, buildings, burying-places, and all the estate and appurtenances belonging to such church, congregation, or society, in whatsoever manner the same may have been acquired, or in whose hands soever the same may be held, as fully and amply as if the right and title thereto had been originally vested in the said trustees." So another section of the same statute provided that "all lands, tenements, and hereditaments that have been *or may hereafter* be lawfully conveyed by devise, gift, grant, purchase, or otherwise, *to any persons as trustees, in trust for the use* of any religious society organized, *or which may hereafter be organized*, within this state, either for a meeting-house, burying-ground, or for the residence of a preacher, *shall descend*, with the improvements, in *perpetual succession to*, and shall be held by, such trustees, in trust for such society." Sec. 21, ch. 47, R. S. 1849; sec. 23, ch. 66, R. S. 1858; sec. 2000, R. S. 1878. Such trust thus authorized, and such descent of trust property in such perpetual succession, cannot be regarded as a suspension of "the absolute power of alienation for a longer period" than prescribed by the statute then in force. Secs. 14, 15, ch. 56, R. S. 1849; ch. 83, R. S. 1858; secs. 2038, 2039, R. S. 1878. This is so because, within the meaning of those sections, such trustees were "persons in being by whom an absolute fee in possession" could be conveyed through the agency of the circuit court, as prescribed in the statute then in force. Sec. 18, ch. 47, R. S. 1849; sec. 19, ch. 66, R. S. 1858. Now, the trustees of such religious societies may lease, mortgage, sell, and otherwise dispose of real estate in the manner provided by their by-laws. Sec. 1992, R. S. 1878.

It is true that such deed did not expressly authorize a disposition of the land conveyed, nor did it expressly restrict
such alienation. Presumably, such conveyance was made
with reference to such powers of the trustees and the courts
over the property under the statutes. We must hold that
the trust imposed by the deed was valid under the statutes
then in force. It follows that that deed put the legal title
to the land conveyed in the trustees named therein, and
their successors, for the uses and purposes therein mentioned.

2. So there would seem to be no doubt that upon the incorporation of the society, September 8, 1862, the legal
title to such church property became vested in the corporation under the statutes cited, and as amended by ch.
337, Laws of 1860, and ch. 103, 169, Laws of 1862; and
hence such property thereby became subjected to the exclusive control and management of the trustees of said
society legally elected under the statutes, and their successors in office, in trust however for such uses and purposes
of said church or society. There is no claim that trustees
were not regularly elected annually by the united society
under the statutes from September 8, 1862, to and including the election of the defendants *Braunborg* and *Hendrickson*, March 4, 1885. There appears to have been no opposition to such election of these two trustees. It is claimed on
the part of the plaintiffs, and the court has partially, in
effect, found, that the defendants, having a majority of the
trustees on their side, May 17, 1885, caused the said church
edifice to be closed against the said Rev. Otteson, as pastor
of said congregation, and that such exclusion, and the
adoption of the articles of faith, February 26, 1883, and
the withdrawal of the majority of said society from the
synod, March 2, 1887, operated as a forfeiture of all right
of the defendants to act as trustees or officers of said society; and that said majority thereby forfeited all right

and title to and use of all the. property of the society.
There is no pretense, however, that the large majority of
the society represented by the defendants did not meet at
the regular times and places appointed for the annual meeting of said society in March, 1886 and 1887, respectively,
and elect trustees in place of those whose terms of office
then expired.   There is, moreover, no claim that any of the
trustees thus regularly elected are among the plaintiffs
named in this action. . By reason of these things, it is, in
effect, claimed that the minority who had adhered to said
Rev. Otteson, and with him separated from such majority
in the spring of 1885, at the time for holding the annual
meeting of the society, March 3, 1886, rightfully assembled
together and elected five trustees in place of those so
elected by the majority, and that the five so elected by the
minority, and their successors in office, are among the
plaintiffs; and that at the time for holding the annual
meeting of the society, March 2, 1887, such minority assembled and elected two trustees in place of two elected by
them the year before.

3. The question therefore recurs whether, by reason of
such supposed forfeiture, the plaintiffs,— trustees and officers thus elected by such minority,— in behalf of themselves
and those acting with them, can, by this bill in equity, oust
the defendants,— trustees and officers thus elected by such
majority,— and install themselves in their places, as in effect
adjudged by the trial court.   As indicated, the deed contemplated the early incorporation of the society under the
general statutes then in force, and entitled "Of Religious
Societies," above cited.   It was not so incorporated until
September 8, 1862.   Whatever doubt may have prevailed
prior to the enactment of ch. 337, Laws of 1860, there can
be no doubt since that the male persons of lawful age,
forming such society, were the persons who "became incorporated," and thereby acquired the right to "possess,

have, hold, and enjoy all the rights, privileges, and franchises incident to such corporations." Id. sec. 1. The language therein prescribed for the certificate is: "We, . . . whose names are hereunto subscribed, have agreed, and by these presents do agree, to become incorporated into a religious society," etc. *Ibid.* Upon the recording of such certificate, the same chapter declared that "the *persons named therein* shall be deemed and regarded in law *as corporators, and they and their associates* are hereby declared to be *a body corporate and politic*, with perpetual succession, by the name and style designated in such certificate, and by such name and style shall be competent to contract and be contracted with, . . . to purchase, have, hold, and enjoy property, both real and personal, and to sell, dispose of, and convey the same." Id. sec. 4. Since that time the statutes have continued to recognize the male members of such society of lawful age as the body incorporated. Ch. 411, Laws of 1876; ch. 91, R. S. 1878. The statute also provides that such corporation "shall possess the powers and privileges granted" by the "General Provisions Relating to Corporations" (ch. 85, R. S.), "so far as the same are applicable or necessary to accomplish its purposes." Sec. 1991, R. S. By the very act of becoming incorporated, the several members of the society, and their then officiating minister, one and all, subjected themselves to the several provisions of the statutes applicable thereto, and thereafter became severally bound by such statutes and the subsequent amendments thereof. Such statutes fixed the qualifications of voters and the manner of electing trustees, or prescribed the method of fixing the same. Secs. 1-3, ch. 66, R. S. 1858; secs. 1990–1993, R. S. Such trustees are designated as officers in the statute, where it is said that they shall "hold *their offices* until others are chosen." Sec. 1993, R. S. So, as observed, the powers and authority of the trustees over the property and affairs of the corporation are prescribed by statute. Manifestly, the relation of such trustees to the society is not that of private trustees to the *cestui-que-trusts*, but rather that of managing officers of a corporation to the corporators thereof. Such religious corporation is in no sense an ecclesiastical corporation, although it may be connected with an ecclesiastical body. On the contrary, it is a civil corporation, governed by the statutes and such rules of the common law as may be applicable. Such being the relation of the trustees and corporators, the more precise question suggested is whether it was competent for a small minority of such corporators, having a real or supposed grievance, to separate themselves from the others, and go through the form of disfranchising all other corporators, and then elect trustees and officers in place of those who had been regularly elected by the majority under the statutes, and then oust such majority trustees of the powers and authority given them by statute, and install themselves in their places. In other words, Is it the province of a court of equity, in an action like this, to perpetually enjoin, and in effect oust, the regularly elected trustees and officers of such corporation from exercising the powers and authority given them by statute, and install in their places those who confessedly never were elected such trustees or officers in the manner or by the voters prescribed by or under the statute? In *Kniskern v. Lutheran Churches*, 1 Sandf. Ch. 439, 564, the learned assistant vice-chancellor, assuming that the relation between the trustees of such religious corporation and the corporators was similar to that of private trustees and their *cestui-que-trusts*, removed the defendant trustees elected by the majority from office, and declared such offices vacant, and *ordered the appointment* of new trustees, and decreed that the one plaintiff trustee was entitle to the possession and control of the church property. But that decision has since been repeatedly, in effect, overruled in the same state, wherein the statutes were similar to ours. *Robertson v. Bullions*, 11 N. Y. 243, 271; *Petty v. Tooker*, 21 N. Y. 267, affirming *S. C.* 29 Barb. 256; *Gram v. Prussia E. E. L. G. Society*, 36 N. Y. 161; *North Baptist Church v. Parker*, 36 Barb. 171; *Burrel v. Associate Reformed Church*, 44 Barb. 282.

The views expressed above are fully supported by the reasoning of both opinions in *Robertson v. Bullions, supra.* It is there, among other things, in effect held that a religious corporation, under the statutes of that state, consisted of the members of the society who were themselves the corporators, and not merely of the trustees; that such trustees could not take a trust for the sole benefit of members of the church, as distinguished from other members of the congregation, nor for the benefit of any portion of the corporators to the exclusion of others, since no trust was authorized by the statute except for the use and benefit of the whole society; and that courts of equity, by virtue of their general jurisdiction over trusts, had no power to remove such trustees or officers who derive their offices directly from the statutes; nor had such courts power to prescribe qualifications for electors of such trustees, other than those prescribed by the statute. 11 N. Y. 265, 266, 271, 272. The other cases above cited from New York are of a similar import. From these authorities. and others to be cited, as well as reason, it follows, as a logical sequence, that before such corporators can recover the possession and control of church property *by virtue of being the rightful trustees* of such corporation, against those who have remained in continuous possession and control, claiming to be such rightful trustees, they must have been peaceably admitted to the offices of such trustees, or have established their title thereto by some direct proceeding or action brought for that purpose. *Ibid.; Lawson v. Kolbenson*, 61 Ill. 406; *Miller v. English*, 21 N. J. Law, 317; *People ex*

rel. Stewart v. Young Men's F. M. T. A. B. Society, 41
Mich. 67; *Trustees v. Bly*, 73 N. Y. 323. It is true that the
chapter of our statutes expressly giving to the courts "su-
pervisory power over corporations," and authority "to
annul corporations," does not extend to "religious corporations." Sec. 3251, R. S. The remedy directly given by
statute against persons who usurp, intrude into, or unlawfully hold or exercise, any public office, civil or mili-
tary, or any franchise, within this state, or any office in a
corporation created by the authority of this state, or when
any such officer has done or suffered some act which operates as a forfeiture of his office, is by *quo warranto*. Sec. 3466,
R. S. The trustees of such incorporation are obviously
officers thereof, within the meaning of the statutes. We
must hold that in so far as the judgment undertakes to oust
the defendants of their offices, and install the plaintiffs or
any of them in their places, or to restrain the defendants
or any of them from exercising powers given to them as
officers of the corporation by the statutes, the same is without authority of law, and hence cannot be sustained.

4. So, of course, we must hold that, in so far as the judgment assumes to cover the parsonage and other property
not covered by the action nor involved in the issues, it is
without authority. While these considerations necessarily
work a reversal of the judgment, they do not dispose of the
action.

5. It does not follow from anything thus far said in this
opinion that the plaintiffs, as corporators, have no rights
which the defendants are bound to respect. On the contrary, as already intimated, the rights of the several corporators are given by statute and hence are necessarily the
same. We may, therefore, properly inquire whether there
has been any such exclusion of the plaintiffs from the
church edifice or the meetings of the society, or any such
perversion of the use of that edifice, as to call for equitable

interference.   One branch of the argument is, in effect, that by the discipline and rules of the Norwegian Evangelical Lutheran Church the call of the minister is for life, and that such relation is indissoluble, except for false doctrine, immoral life, neglect of duty, or mutual consent; and hence that the vote of the majority of the corporators to discharge Rev. Otteson, March 4, 1885, and the exclusion of him from the church as pastor after May 17, 1885, was in effect the wrongful exclusion of all who adhered to him as such pastor, including the plaintiffs and the balance of the minority who acted with them.   Certainly the deed of trust makes no express reference to any such indissoluble relationship.   If it is to be inferred from the language therein employed, then it must be from the part declaring that the house of worship was to be " for the use of the members " of the church on Liberty Prairie, and "according to the rules of said church, and according to the rules of said church " which might thereafter "be adopted from time to time by their *authorized* synods or conferences."   We are referred to no rule of that church fixing such indissoluble relationship.   That church did not become a member of the synod until February, 1853.   The constitution of the synod at that time reserved " to every individual congregation . . . the right to have its own laws for its home management," provided they did not conflict with the constitution and resolutions thereof.   The call of the church to the Rev. Otteson, September 15, 1858, expressly stipulated that either he or the church might at any time rescind such call upon giving one year's notice.   That was subsequently expunged by the wardens.   But nothing seems to have been agreed upon indicating that such call was for life, nor that such relationship was indissoluble.   But, however that may be, yet when Rev. Otteson and the society united in procuring the incorporation of the society under the statutes in 1862, their relationship thereby became fixed.   At that time the

trustees seem to have had the power to employ the minister, but his salary or compensation was required to be
ascertained and fixed by a majority of the society entitled
to vote at the election of trustees. Sec. 18, ch. 66, R. S.
1858. This placed the matter of employing and discharging ministers substantially at the control of the majority of
the corporators, as the employment or continuance of a
minister would depend substantially on the amount of the
salary. 11 N. Y. 263, 264. The late Revision seems to
have left the matter to be regulated by the corporators and
trustees, under the constitution and by-laws of the society.
Sec. 1994, R. S.

Such dismissal and employment of a minister is, moreover, a matter of contract, and pertains to the temporalities
of the church, and does not necessarily operate as a change
of faith or doctrine. We must hold that it was competent
for a majority of the voters in the society to discharge
Rev. Otteson and employ another minister in his place;
and that such mere discharge of the one, and the employment of the other, did not operate in law as a perversion of
the trust, nor as an exclusion of the plaintiffs or any member of the society. *Hardin v. Baptist Church*, 51 Mich.
137; *Ehrenfeldt's Appeal*, 101 Pa. St. 186; *Smith v. Nelson*,
18 Vt. 511; *Sale v. First Regular Baptist Church*, 62 Iowa,
26, 49 Am. Rep. 136; *Landis v. Campbell*, 79 Mo. 433, 49
Am. Rep. 239.

6. The question remains whether there has been any
such perversion of the trust by reason of a departure from
doctrine and faith and a withdrawal from the synod as
calls for equitable interference. As indicated, the grant
was in trust "for the use of the members of the Norwegian
Evangelical Church of St. Paul's *on* Liberty Prairie, according to the rules of *said church*, and according to the rules
of said church" which might thereafter "be adopted from
time to time by their *authorized* synods or conferences."

Manifestly this language did not contemplate that such use of the church should be strictly in accordance with fixed and unalterable rules. On the contrary, it contemplated a living society, composed of thoughtful members who were not only to become incorporated under the statutes but capable of formulating such other rules for the church as might be adopted from time to time by their authorized synods or conferences. The synod or conference to which the society subsequently attached itself had not then been established, and the language employed was evidently in contemplation of its subsequent establishment and action by virtue of authority thereafter to be given by such church or society. The grant then is, in substance, for the use of the members of the church on Liberty Prairie, according to such rules as they had or might thereafter adopt for them-selves, or authorize such synod or conference to adopt for them. In other words, the deed, within certain limitations, contemplated a self-governing society and corporation. As already observed, the constitution of the synod to which it became attached in 1853, reserved "to every individual congregation . . . the right to have its own laws for its home management," provided they did not conflict with the constitution and resolutions thereof. This synod de-clared, in 1861, that "in regard to the internal arrange-ment and government of the individual congregations, the synod is only an advisory body. No resolution by the synod in such matters can, therefore, have binding force on the individual congregation, unless it voluntarily accepts it; and if a congregation finds that it is in conflict with the Word of God, or that it is not beneficial to it under its pe-culiar circumstances, then it has the right *not* to follow the resolution." In the articles of incorporation there is noth-ing indicating any particular faith, doctrine, or rule of action, unless it be the simple name of the "Norwegian Evangelical Lutheran Church of St. Paul's on Liberty

Prairie." This synod declared, in 1865, that "all were agreed that the synod ought not to have any kind of *legislative* authority, but that it should only be an *advisory body*. This authority to determine the ceremonies which, according to the old constitution, was placed in the hands of the synod, it had never made use of." The constitution of the synod adopted in 1876 declared that "the only source and rule of the faith and teaching of the synod is God's Holy Word, revealed in the canonical books of the Old and New Testaments. . . . The synod adopts as its confession of faith the symbolical books or confessional writings of the Norwegian Lutheran Church, for the reason that these writings give a pure and unadulterated exposition of the doctrine contained in the Word of God. These confessional writings are the following: The three ancient creeds, to wit, the Apostolic, the Nicene, and the Athanasian creed; the unadulterated Augsburg Confession; Luther's Smaller Catechism." This confessional is substantially the same as in the constitution of the synod in force in 1853. Such confession is therein declared to be unalterable. The congregations are therein *advised* to retain the Norwegian ritual of the year 1685, and the altar book of the year 1688. The constitution of 1876 provides for the admission of individual congregations into the synod by their adoption of the constitution of the synod, and submitting for its acceptance the constitution and by-laws of such congregation applying for such admission; and also their temporary suspension, and finally severance of connection, in case of persistent false doctrine or ungodly life. It is therein said that "the synod is composed of the congregations that have united by adopting this constitution." So it is declared therein that "doctrinal questions and matters of conscience cannot be decided by majorities of votes, but only by the Word of God and the symbolical books of our church. . . . If not otherwise provided in this constitution, and if not otherwise determined in particular cases by the meeting concerned, all other matters are decided in the . . . meetings by a plurality of votes. . . . *In respect to the individual congregations the above-named meetings are merely advisory bodies.*" Thus it appears that the congregations are not created or established by the synod, but that the synod is really nothing more than a conference of pastors, teachers, and members of the church council, as representatives of the respective congregations, who meet periodically for mutual benefit, counsel and advice. Obviously, the synod was not a union of the several local congregations as one church, with one head and one government, but rather a confederation of local self-governing churches, acting, so far as the local organization was concerned, merely as an advisory body. Such being the relation between the church on Liberty Prairie and the synod, no good reason is perceived, on principle or authority, why the mere withdrawal of such local church from the synod, March 2, 1887, was in violation of any of the rules of such church, or any rules of the synod authorized by the church. *Miller v. Gable*, 2 Denio, 492; *Trustees v. St. Michael's Ev. Church*, 48 Pa. St. 20; *Lawson v. Kolbenson*, 61 Ill. 407; *Petty v. Tooker*, 21 N. Y. 267; *Smith v. Nelson*, 18 Vt. 511. We must hold, therefore, that there was no such violation by such mere withdrawal. Since the church on Liberty Prairie was not, at the time of the commencement of this action, a merely subordinate branch of a general church organization having a general supervision or ultimate power of control over it, there seems to be no necessity for considering the numerous cases of that class cited by counsel.

7. But while the church on Liberty Prairie must be regarded as a self-governing corporation, owing no obedience or obligation to any higher ecclesiastical authority, it does not necessarily follow that the trustees and officers of the corporation, even with the sanction of the majority of the

corporators, can lawfully devote the church edifice to any
purpose they may see fit, regardless of the legal rights of
other corporators. Whether they can or not must depend
upon the terms of the grant and the law applicable. The
constitution of the synod, containing substantially the articles of faith quoted above, was adopted by the church on
Liberty Prairie as early as February, 1853. The language
of the deed induces us to infer that such local congregation,
.as a true Lutheran church, had previously adopted in substance the same articles of faith. The grant was made,
presumably, with reference to such articles of faith. The
statutes provide for "organizing a corporation in connection with a church of their own peculiar tenets to be associated therewith." Sec. 1990, R. S. The certificate may
specify that the signers "have organized themselves into a
religious society of the ——— church (sect, or denomination)," located at the place named. Sec. 1991, R. S. See,
also, ch. 284, Laws of 1880. Although the certificate of incorporation here simply gave the name of such church, yet
we are constrained to hold that the use of the church edifice
must be restricted to the purposes specified in the grant.

This brings us to the more delicate question, whether the
adoption by the majority of the specific articles of faith, February 26, 1883, given in full above, was a perversion of such
use. The substance of the affirmative portions of these
specific articles are to the effect that the election to eternal
life or salvation is only efficacious through the faith and
works of the recipient. The expert testimony tends to
prove, and it does prove, that such portions are educed
from the catechism authorized by the synod for general use
from Erick Pontoppidan, or "Truth Promoting Godliness,"
and are within the scope of the articles of faith contained
in the constitution of the synod above quoted. The negative
portions of such specific articles of faith reject as false,
when taught, certain doctrines in effect contrary to such

affirmative portions; and may indicate a spirit of intolerance towards those who seem to believe that such election is entirely independent of the volition of such recipient. We cannot say, however, from the testimony, that such negative portions of such specific articles are in conflict with the articles of faith contained in such constitutions. They may be inconsistent with certain portions of such articles of faith, but it is equally apparent that such portions are equally inconsistent with other portions of the same articles. It is not the province of courts of equity to determine mere questions of faith, doctrine, or schism, not necessarily involved in the enforcement of ascertained trusts. In fact, the doctrine here controverted seems to be too refined and subtle to be clearly comprehended even by learned theologians, much less by laymen. Courts deal with tangible rights, not with spiritual conceptions unless they are incidentally and necessarily involved in the determination of legal rights. Such trusts, when valid and so ascertained, must of course be enforced; but to call for equitable interference there must be such a real and substantial departure from the designated faith or doctrine as will be in contravention of such trust. *Miller v. Gable*, 2 Denio, 492; *Happy v. Morton*, 33 Ill. 398; *Lawson v. Kolbenson*, 61 Ill. 407; *Att'y Gen. ex rel. Abbot v. Dublin*, 38 N. H. 459; *Watson v. Jones*, 13 Wall. 723, 724; *Eggleston v. Doolittle*, 33 Conn. 396; *Keyser v. Stansifer*, 6 Ohio, 363. The specific articles here so adopted by the majority do not seem to constitute such radical departure as to be a diversion of the trust. Besides, the minority remained united with the majority under the ministration of the Rev. Otteson for more than two years after such adoption of such specific articles before their separation. Such acquiescence, of itself, is an additional reason why equity should not interfere, in the absence of such clearly established violation. *Hale v. Everett*, 53 N. H. 11; *Att'y Gen. ex rel. Abbot v. Dublin, supra.*

There is still another reason why this suit in equity should not be maintained for any such supposed departure from the faith or doctrine impliedly referred to in the deed, and that is the fact that ten days before the commencement of this action the said majority, represented by the defendants, unanimously adopted a constitution consisting, substantially, of the said articles of faith embodied in the constitutions of the synod, and containing a clause expressly repealing "*all former precepts or regulations," by whatsoever name, that had previously been "adopted" by said corporation and which were in conflict with the same. This would seem to be sufficient to remove all objections on the part of the minority to a reunion of the whole society. Such a consummation would seem to be in harmony with the injunction of Paul, "to walk worthy of the calling wherewith ye are called, with all lowliness and meekness, with long-suffering, forbearing one another in love; giving diligence to keep the unity of the Spirit in the bond of peace." Eph. iv. 1–3. It is to be hoped that such may be the result.

By the Court.— The judgment of the circuit court is reversed, and the cause is remanded with direction to dismiss the complaint.

Land, Log & Lumber Company and others, Respondents, vs. Brown and others, Appellants.

October 12, 1888 — January 29, 1889.

Constitutional law: Towns: Unincorporated villages: Taxation.

1. Ch. 292, Laws of 1883,— providing that "all powers relating to villages and conferred upon village boards by ch. 40, R. S., and all acts amendatory thereof, excepting those the exercise of which

Land, Log & Lumber Co. and others vs. Brown and others.

would conflict with the provisions of law relative to towns and town boards, are conferred upon towns and town boards of towns containing one or more unincorporated villages of not less than 1,000 inhabitants, and are made applicable to such villages, and may be exercised therein when directed by a resolution of the electors of the town," etc.,—is not void for uncertainty.

2. Said act does not incorporate the villages as separate municipalities, and is not in violation of sec. 3, art. XI, Const. The power given to the legislature to incorporate villages does not deprive it of power to legislate for their control and government before they are incorporated.

3. The fact that the law is applicable only to towns containing villages of a certain population does not render it a violation of sec. 23, art. IV, Const., providing that the legislature shall establish but one system of town and county government.

4. Nor is the act void under any rule of public policy which forbids the taxation of property for any purpose not benefiting it. It is for the legislature, not for the courts, to fix the limits of the taxing district.

APPEAL from the Circuit Court for *Oneida* County.

The case is sufficiently stated in the opinion.

For the appellants there was a brief by *Alban & Barnes*, and oral argument by *John Barnes*.

W. F. Bailey, for the respondents, contended, *inter alia*, that ch. 292, Laws of 1883, is in violation of sec. 3, art. XI, Const., which provides that "it shall be the duty of the legislature, and they are empowered, to provide for the organization of cities and incorporated villages," etc. If a community is in need of corporate functions, it is the duty of the legislature to incorporate it. It cannot grant corporate powers without corporation. The act is also in violation of the constitutional principle which prohibits unequal and partial legislation upon general subjects. *Durkee v. Janesville*, 28 Wis. 465; *People v. Salem*, 20 Mich. 473. It is also in violation of sec. 23, art. IV, of the constitution, which provides that "the legislature shall establish but one system of town and county government, which shall be as nearly uniform as practicable." *State ex rel. Peck v.*

Riordan, 24 Wis. 488; *State ex rel. Keenan v. Milwaukee Co.* 25 id. 346; *McRae v. Hogan,* 39 id. 529; *State ex rel. Walsh v. Dousman,* 28 id. 541. It also violates the provisions of sec. 13, art. I, of the constitution, which provides that "the property of no person shall be taken for public use without just compensation therefor." *Buell v. Ball,* 20 Iowa, 288; *Deiman v. Ft. Madison,* 30 id. 542; *Brooks v. Polk Co.* 52 id. 460; *Durant v. Kauffman,* 34 id. 194; *Smith v. Sherry,* 50 Wis. 216; *Borough of Little Meadows,* 35 Pa. St. 335.

The following opinion was filed November 8, 1888:

TAYLOR, J. This action was commenced by the said *Land, Log & Lumber Company* against the appellants to restrain said appellants, the board of supervisors of the town of *Pelican,* from allowing any bills or claims, either for the construction, maintenance, or operation of water-works in the village of Rhinelander, or in said town, and from allowing or auditing any bills for the payment of salaries or wages of any firemen, fire engineers, or other persons engaged in or about the operation of water-works in said village of Rhinelander; or from paying salaries or wages of any policeman or night-watch in said village or territory immediately adjacent thereto; and restraining the treasurer of said town of *Pelican* from paying a certain town order (described in the complaint) for the sum of $3,624.94, out of any funds of said town; and also from the payment of any orders by him, as such treasurer, for the payment of salaries or wages of water-works engineer, firemen, policeman, and night-watch; also restraining said board of supervisors and their successors in office from levying or assessing any taxes upon the property of the plaintiff or other tax-payers of said town for the purpose of paying, or to be used in the payment, for any work, labor, or material used or to be used in the construction of said water-works, or in the maintenance or operation of the same, or in the payment of wages or salaries "of engineer or firemen employed to operate the same, or for the wages or salaries of policemen or night-watch; and that the defendants *W. E. Brown*, *C. Faust*, and *G. H. Clark* be adjudged and decreed to pay and to deliver to the treasurer of the said town of. *Pelican* the amounts of the claims and bills which they, acting as a board of supervisors of said town, have illegally or fraudulently audited, and which have been paid for the purposes hereinbefore stated, being for the construction, maintenance, and operation of water-works, to the amount of $4,431; also the amount of bills and claims which they illegally and fraudulently allowed, and which have been paid to the subscribers for fire wells as herein stated, being the amount of $296.34; also the amount of bills and claims which they have illegally audited and allowed for the payment of salaries, and salaries or wages of policemen and night-watch, being for such last-mentioned purposes, to the amount of $430; and for such other order or relief or decree in the premises as may be proper and agreeable to equity; and that in the mean time, and until this action can be heard and determined, or until the further order of the court, the said board of supervisors and their successors in office, and the said treasurer and his successor or successors in office, and the town of *Pelican*, be temporarily enjoined and restrained from doing any of the acts hereinbefore prayed to be enjoined and restrained as a relief in this action, and for such other or further temporary order or relief as may be proper in the premises; and that the plaintiff may have and recover judgment for its costs and disbursements in this action."

A preliminary injunction was granted *ex parte*, as prayed for in the complaint. The defendants, upon answer and affidavits. moved to vacate such preliminary injunction. The motion was denied by the court, and from the order denying such motion the defendants appealed to this court.

The facts stated in the complaint and answer show that in the said town of *Pelican* there is quite a large village called Rhinelander, which is neither incorporated by special act nor by general law; that said town of *Pelican* is large in extent, containing 800 square miles; that most of the in-. habitants live in the village of Rhinelander; that the other parts of the town are thinly inhabited. It is further shown by the complaint and answer that at the town meeting held in said town of *Pelican*, in April, 1887, a resolution was adopted by the qualified electors of said town of *Pelican*, conferring on the town board of supervisors of said town all powers conferred on village boards by ch. 40, R. S. 1878, and the acts amendatory thereof, excepting those the exercise of which would conflict with the provisions of the law relative to towns and town boards. This resolution was passed under the authority of ch. 292, Laws of 1883. It is also alleged that at the time such resolution was adopted, the said village of Rhinelander contained more than 1,000 inhabitants. The answer then alleges that said town board, under the authority conferred on it by said resolution and said ch. 292, Laws of 1883, proceeded in a regular way to construct water-works in said village of Rhinelander; alleges that said water-works were greatly needed for the protection of the property in said village; and that in constructing, maintaining, and operating said water-works they expended a considerable sum of money, some of which has not been paid and is represented by the town order of $3,624.94, the payment of which is sought to be restrained by this action; and that it is necessary to expend other sums in order to maintain and operate said water-works, which are also sought to be restrained by the plaintiff. The answer also alleges that the maintenance of public peace and good order required the employment of police officers for said village, and that no more were employed than were necessary for the maintenance of the peace and good order in said village. All charges of fraud and corruption on the part of the defendants are denied.

The learned counsel for the respondent in his argument in this court insists that ch. 292, Laws of 1883, under which the defendants justify their action in erecting and maintaining water-works and other fire protections, is unconstitutional and void, and that their acts in employing policemen are also void, because the limits of the village were not fixed or designated before such policemen were appointed, as required by ch. 463, Laws of 1885. The answer, however, alleges that such policemen were duly appointed under the authority vested in said board of supervisors by ch. 19, Laws of 1881, as amended by ch. 463, Laws of 1885.

The only material question in the case, and that which has been argued by the counsel for the respective parties before this court, is the question of the constitutionality of ch. 292, Laws of 1883, and upon its construction, if it be held constitutional. It is contended by the learned counsel for the respondents: (1) That said chapter should be held void for uncertainty. (2) That if it be not void for uncertainty, and it must be construed as authorizing the town board in the exercise of their authority under said chapter to incur expenses which must be paid for by taxation of the entire taxable property of the town, then it should be held unconstitutional, as in violation of sec. 23, art. IV, of the constitution, as violating the uniformity of town government. (3) It is also argued by the learned counsel for the respondents that it is beyond the power of the legislature to direct a tax for village purposes to be levied and collected upon all the property in the town in which such village is situated.

The following is a copy of ch. 292, Laws of 1883: "All powers relating to villages and conferred upon village boards by the provisions of chapter 40 of the Revised Statutes and all acts amendatory thereof, excepting those the

exercise of which would conflict with the provisions of law
relative to towns and town boards, are hereby conferred
upon towns and town boards of towns containing one or
more unincorporated villages having each a population of
not less than one thousand inhabitants, and are made applicable to such unincorporated village or villages, and may be
exercised therein when directed by a resolution of the
qualified electors of the town at the last preceding annual
town meeting."

We are at loss to comprehend how this act can be declared void for uncertainty. At the time it was enacted it
was known that there were in different portions of the state
several large villages or collections of inhabitants in a
compact form, ordinarily called villages; that they were
portions of the towns in which they were situated, and composed a part of such towns, governed in all things by the
laws in regard to towns generally; and that such villages
had neglected or declined to incorporate as villages under
the general laws of this state in regard to the incorporation
of villages. It was also apparent to the legislature that
these villages, from the fact that they composed communities differing from the ordinary town communities, necessarily required the exercise of governmental powers in some
respects different from the ordinary township community,
especially in regard to police regulations, facilities for the
extinguishing of fires, and the care and improvement of
streets; and as they must remain an integral part of the
town in which they were situated until incorporated under
the general laws of the state, the legislature granted to the
boards of supervisors of the respective towns in which such
villages were situated the authority to exercise certain
powers in and over the inhabitants of such villages whenever the legal electors of the town in which any such village was situated should, at the annual town meeting, by
resolution duly adopted, require the board of supervisors

to assume and exercise the powers granted by said ch. 292, Laws of 1883, in respect to said villages.

It is clear that the act of 1883 does not undertake to incorporate such village as a separate municipality from the town, but simply enlarges the powers of the town board in which such village is situated for the purpose of meeting the necessities of the inhabitants of such village. The act is not void for uncertainty, as the powers granted to the town boards are defined by reference to the powers granted to village boards, and their powers are clearly defined in ch. 40, R. S. 1878, and the acts amendatory of such chapter. And the qualification that they shall not exercise any powers granted to a village board which are inconsistent or in conflict with the powers granted by law to town boards, is not in itself indefinite, however difficult it may be in certain cases to determine what powers of a village board would be inconsistent with the powers of a town board. It is the business of the courts to determine that question whenever a proper case arises, and not to declare the law unconstitutional because there may be doubts as to the exact extent of the powers granted in certain cases. We conclude that ch. 292, Laws of 1883, is not void for uncertainty, and also that it is not void for attempting to incorporate a village or villages by a special act.

As we have said above, the act of the town electors in conferring upon the town board certain powers in respect to such villages, under the provisions of said ch. 292, Laws of 1883, does not incorporate the village as a separate municipality. The village still remains a part of the town for all purposes of taxation and government. The act is certainly not void as violating sec. 3, art. XI, of the constitution. We are at a loss to see how an act of the legislature can be held as violating this section of the constitution, when the act does not purport to incorporate the village. It is not for the courts to say to the legislature, you must either incorporate these communities as villages or cities, or else you must not legislate in regard to their government. It is probable that the legislature might, in its discretion, enforce the incorporation of communities as cities or villages, under proper limitations; but this power does not deprive the legislature of the power to legislate for the control and government of such communities before it is deemed wise to incorporate them.

It is also argued that ch. 292, Laws of 1883, violates the provisions of sec. 23, art. IV, of the constitution, which provides that "the legislature shall establish but one system of town and county government." And we are informed that the learned circuit judge in sustaining the injunction in this case was of the opinion that the act was a violation of said sec. 23, art. IV. We think the learned circuit judge was mistaken in his opinion. Ch. 292, Laws of 1883, is an amendment of the laws concerning towns and the government thereof. Like many other laws of the state, it provides for the exercise of different powers by the boards of different towns, when there is anything in a town which calls for the exercise of such different or additional powers. The act is as general as any other general act. It provides for the exercise of the additional powers in all towns in which villages are situated having a given number of inhabitants. It is not subject to the criticism that, though general in form, it is special in fact, as it is a matter of public notoriety that there are and have been several towns in the state to which the act can be applied.

To hold that this section of the constitution requires the legislature to make all laws for the government of towns applicable to every town in the state, without any regard to the wealth, population, or other peculiarities of such towns, would be to hold a very large portion of the legislation on the subject of towns in this state unconstitutional and void. As instances of these laws, see sec. 1240, R. S., in regard to the assessment of highway taxes, and sec. 1320, in regard to building bridges. It is clear that the act in question is not a violation of the system of town government, but a part of the system, in order to adapt the system to the peculiar wants of certain towns in the state. The decisions of this court, cited by the learned counsel for the respondents, holding that certain laws énacted by the legislature were in violation of this section of the constitution, do not seem to us as applicable to the law in question in this case.

It is also argued by the learned counsel for the respondents that if the act must be construed as authorizing the town board to make expenditures in the village for waterworks, fire protection, or police regulations, then it should be declared void under some supposed rule of public policy which forbids the property of a person to be taxed when the purpose for which the taxes are levied and expended does not·benefit his property. As we have said above, the act of 1883 does not separate the village from the town, but simply confers authority upon the town board to exercise certain powers in respect to such village as a part of the town. The fact that money is raised by taxation upon all the taxable property of a town, to be expended for some improvement lawfully made in one corner of the town, and which, so far as any direct beneficial results are concerned, is confined to the immediate neighborhood of the place where the improvement is made, has never been held, in this state, a violation of any constitutional restriction or of any supposed public policy. If a rule for taxation should be adopted which limits the right of taxation for public improvements to such property only as it can be shown is directly benefited by such improvement, it would result in endless confusion and litigation, and render void very many acts for the government of towns and counties. The opening of very many highways, and the building of very many

bridges, by towns and counties, where the expenses of
opening such highways and building such bridges are made
charges upon all the property of a town or county, would
be unlawful. No matter how large the town, all expenditures for town government and for local improvements in
such town must be paid from taxes levied upon all the
property of the town, unless the legislature directs it to be
levied in some other way. It is for the legislature to fix
the limits of the taxing district, and not for the courts.
This court has repeatedly affirmed this rule. This court
has affirmed the validity of the law concerning the building
of bridges, which compels the whole county to contribute
to the building of a bridge in one town, and that without
regard to the question whether the bridge to be built would
be any direct benefit to any other town in the county. So
in regard to the highway taxes, this court held that highway taxes might be lawfully levied upon lands for the construction and repair of highways not within six miles of the
land taxed, and which in the then state of the town received
no possible direct benefit from the building and repair of
such roads. So with respect to school taxes levied upon
lands so far from the place where the schools in the town
were maintained that they would be of no practical use to
persons residing on the lands so taxed. So in regard to
local improvements in cities, this court holds that the district to be taxed for such improvements may be fixed, either
directly or indirectly, by the legislature; and that the justice or injustice of the limits of the taxing district, when
fixed by the legislature or some other authority authorized
by law to fix the same, cannot be questioned by the courts.
Teegarden v. Racine, 56 Wis. 545; *Dickson v. Racine*, 61
Wis. 545, 549; *T. B. Scott Lumber Co. v. Oneida Co.* 72 Wis.
158; *State ex rel. Baraboo v. Sauk Co.* 70 Wis. 485.

But if it were necessary that the court should be able to
find that the property of the plaintiff was directly or indi-

Land, Log & Lumber Co. and others vs. Brown and others.

rectly benefited by the expenditures made by the town in protecting the property of the village from destruction by fire, or in preserving peace and good order in said village, it would not be difficult to find that fact. Certainly every person resident in any town, or having any property therein, is interested in the peace and good order of all the people in said town, without any regard to their particular location; and when a considerable portion of the taxable property of said town is in imminent danger of destruction by fire, it would seem that all tax-payers in the town are to some extent interested in protecting the same from such destruction. Their burden of taxation is lightened by its preservation, and increased by its destruction. That the powers exercised by the town board in this case are such as are conferred upon village boards by ch. 40, R. S., is very clear (see subd. 10, 24, sec. 892, R. S.). and the powers so exercised by them do not appear to conflict with any of their powers as a town board.

As it is evident the injunction was granted in this case under the impression that ch. 292, Laws of 1883, was unconstitutional and void, and not because of an abuse of the powers granted by that act, we think it ought to have been dissolved on the motion of the appellants.

By the Court.— The order appealed from is reversed, and the cause is remanded with instructions to the circuit court to vacate the order granting the preliminary injunction, and for further proceedings according to law.

A motion for a rehearing was made by the respondent. In support of the motion there was a brief by *W. F. Bailey*, attorney, and *Stark & Sutherland*, of counsel. In opposition thereto there was a brief by *Alban & Barnes*. The motion was denied January 29, 1889.

See note to this case in 40 N. W. Rep. 482.— REP.

THE STATE EX REL. SMITH, Appellant, vs. GAYLORD, Village Clerk, etc., Respondent.

January 8 — January 29, 1889.

Taxation: Board of review: Jurisdiction: Waiver of notice of meeting: Certiorari: Review of evidence: Raising valuation of securities: Tax-payer's statement not conclusive.

1. The fact that proper notice was not given of a meeting of the board of review does not affect its jurisdiction to hear and decide cases in which the parties interested are present and are fully heard without making any objection on the ground that the legal notice was not given.

2. The courts will not, on *certiorari*, examine and weigh the evidence upon which the board of review acted in raising valuations, if there was competent evidence before it to warrant its decision.

3. Under sec. 1061, R. S., the board of review has power, upon evidence taken before it, to raise or lower the valuation of any property on the assessment roll, including securities or credits as to which the tax-payer has made the statement required by sec. 1056.

APPEAL from the Circuit Court for *Walworth* County. The case is stated in the opinion.

For the appellant there were briefs signed by the relator in person and by *J. F. Lyon & Son*, of counsel, and the cause was argued orally by *J. F. Lyon* and *Jay F. Lyon.* 1. The board of review, on June 26, 1888, adjourned for more than one day, and no written notice thereof was posted on the outer door of the village clerk's office, stating to what time said meeting was adjourned, as required by ch. 74, Laws of 1881, amending sec. 1060, R. S. 2. The action of the board of review is not supported by the evidence. 3. The relator's statement under oath, having been duly made pursuant to the statute, conclusively determines the valuation and amount of his personal property for which the assessment should be made. *State ex rel. Ward v. Assessors*, 1 Wis. 345; *Matheson v. Mazomanie*, 20 id. 191; *White v. Appleton*, 22 id. 639; *Ketchum v. Mukwa*, 24 id.

303; *Wauwatosa v. Gunyon*, 25 id. 271; *Phillips v. Stevens Point*, id. 594; *Lawrence v. Janesville*, 46 id. 364. By sec. 1061, R. S., it is made the duty of the board of review to review and correct errors made by the assessor. They are also expressly authorized to raise or lower valuations *made by the assessor* — but not any other valuations. They are directly commanded by sec. 1056 to make the assessment of " item 15 " for the amount as determined by the tax-payer's sworn statement.

For the respondent there was a brief by *Dodge & Fish*, and oral argument by *J. E. Dodge.*

ORTON, J. This is a writ of *certiorari* to the respondent, as clerk of the village of Elkhorn, to bring before the court the proceedings of the board of review of said village in respect to the assessment of the personal property of the relator for the year 1888. The facts appearing from the petition and return are as follows:

The relator made out the usual verified statement of his taxable personal property for that year, by entering in the column headed " Valuation by owner," " Gold and silver watches, 1 in number, $50; " " Average amount of moneys in possession or on deposit during year, $200; " " Average amount of notes, bonds, mortgages and other securities for debts due, or to become due, for each and every month during the year ending May 1st, over and above the average amount of *bona fide* unconditional debts owing for each and every of said months, as determined under sec. 1056, R. S., $3,000; " " All other personal property not including above and not exempt, $300; " " Total value of all personal property, $3,500,"— and returned said statement so made out to George W. Wylie, the assessor of said district. The assessor entered in said statement, in the column headed " Valuation by assessor," opposite the $3,000 for notes, bonds, mortgages, etc., which in said statement is marked

"Item No. 15," $5,300, against the protest of the relator. The relator appeared before the board of review on the 25th day of June, 1888, and presented written objections against such increase of his assessment by the assessor, and asked that it be made in pursuance of his statement, on the ground that such statement was conclusive upon the assessor and upon the board of review; and appointed J. F. Lyon, Esq., to appear for him before said board in the matter. The board of review, upon the relator's said objections, and on the ground that said sworn statement was binding upon the assessor, restored the valuation of said item No. 15 to the amount fixed by the relator. At the same time the said George W. Wylie claimed before the board that said item was assessed too low, according to said statement of the relator, and that it ought to be raised and increased to be a fair and equal valuation thereof, and offered to prove the same before the board. Thereupon said Wylie was duly sworn, and testified as a witness before the board in respect to such valuation, and was interrogated in respect thereto, against the repeated objection of the relator; and testified, substantially, that he had examined the records of Walworth county, and found thereon mortgages to the relator from several persons in the aggregate of $5,300, and that the relator told him that there had been nothing paid on said mortgages; that he asked the relator if he owed any debts, and he said he owed some debts when he left the state of New York forty years ago; and, when asked by the board if the relator made a statement of any debts the year before, the witness answered that he did not. Thereupon the board demanded of the relator that he be sworn and testify as to the value of his personal property, and he refused so to do, insisting that his said statement was conclusive as to the value of the property, as item No. 15. Thereupon the said attorney of the relator (the relator himself being present) was heard upon the question of the valuation of item No. 15, and presented to the board a brief thereon. The matter was then laid over for consideration, with the understanding that said J. F. Lyon, Esq., the attorney of the relator, should be notified of the taking of further testimony, and the board adjourned to 9:30 A. M. of the following day, June 26, 1888. At that time said attorney of the relator was further heard on the question, and requested the board to adjourn to some future time for further consideration thereof, and the board did adjourn to 9 o'clock A. M. of July 6, 1888, with the knowledge of said attorney. Notices of said adjournment were posted in three of the public places in said village. On said day the board again met, the said attorney being present, and had an opportunity and was requested to offer further testimony and to be further heard on the question, but he declined so to do. The board remained in session the whole day for such purpose, and late in the day decided to raise the valuation of item No. 15 in said statement to $5,300, and fixed the same at that amount.

On this record the circuit court affirmed the decision of the board of review.

I have been thus particular in stating the facts appearing of record, for a proper understanding of the first two points made by the learned counsel of the appellant: (1) That the notices required by the statute were not given of the meetings of the board; and (2) that the action of the board was not supported by evidence.

1. As to the first point, it may be said, in brief, that inasmuch as the statute has imposed the duty of posting the notices upon the clerk, and not upon the board, and the board are required to meet for a review of the assessments as a public and imperative duty, any neglect of the clerk in such particular would not affect the legality of their meeting for such purpose, or their jurisdiction to hear and decide cases in which parties interested have had act-

ual notice, or submit their assessments to a review by the
board by consent. Sec. 1060, R. S. The only object of such
notices is to apprise those interested of the time and place
of the meetings of the board, so that they may be heard
touching their own assessment. That others or all of those
assessed besides himself have not had due notice is immaterial to him, if he has had actual notice, and appeared, and
contested the raising of the valuation of his personal property as item No. 15, and been fully heard in the matter.
All the rights in the law he had, he has exercised and enjoyed, and he has no right to complain, on behalf of others,
that they had no notice. These are elementary propositions. But in this case the appellant waived constructive
notice by being all the time present and participating in
the proceedings, and by being heard fully in the matter,
without any objection or reservation on account of a want
of the proper legal notices, or of any other irregularity.
The meetings of the board were held and the arguments
made at his request or with his full knowledge. But the
question has been substantially so decided by this court.
Cramer v. Stone, 38 Wis. 259; *McIntyre v. White Creek*, 43
Wis. 620; *State ex rel. Smith v. Cooper*, 59 Wis. 666. The
boad, therefore, had jurisdiction, and that is the main question on the writ of *certiorari*.

2. In such a case, we may not examine and weigh the
testimony as to its preponderance, if there was competent
evidence before the board to warrant the decision. *State
ex rel. Moreland v. Whitford*, 54 Wis. 150; *Persons v. Bur-
dick*, 6 Wis. 63; *Dexter v. Cole*, 6 Wis. 319; *State ex rel.
Smith v. Cooper, supra*. The assessor and witness Wylie found
mortgages of record to the relator of the amount stated,
of $5,300. The relator was informed of that fact, and asked
if anything had been paid thereon, and he said there had
not, and tacitly admitted that he owned and held the same;
and he was asked to be sworn and to testify on the subject,

and he refused. This evidence is very nearly conclusive that he owned these securities. As to a deduction of his debts, if he had any, he was asked, and stated that he "left some debts in New York forty years ago." That is all he said about it. He did not claim that he owed any debts whatever during the year 1888, and the year before he claimed to owe no debts to be deducted from his assessments. This evidence was quite sufficient to justify the action of the board.

3. The main question presented is whether the sworn statement of the relator was conclusive upon the board of review, as to the item No. 15, of notes, bonds, mortgages, etc. Such statement may be conclusive, so far as the assessor is concerned, by force of the language at the end of sec. 1056, R. S.: "And the average amount of such year, so determined [by the sworn statement], shall be *assessed* for taxation." But that question is not in the case, for the board ignored the action of the assessor in raising item No. 15 to $5,300, and set the amount back to $3,000, as fixed in the statement, and predicated their action upon the statement alone. If this action of the board and this construction of the law were erroneous, the relator was not injured by it, and has no right to complain. Whether the statement was conclusive upon the board of review is another and different question. If the assessor is bound to take the statement as to item No. 15, and adopt its valuation as his own, he is certainly required to so enter it upon the assessment roll; for his assessment roll must be complete, and as such passes before the board of review and the boards of equalization, and, when so adjusted, becomes the tax roll on which the taxes are collected. By sec. 1036, R. S., the term "personal property" shall mean and include (besides other things) "all debts due from solvent debtors, whether on account, note, contract, bond, mortgage or other security, or whether such debts are due or to become due."

By sec. 1040, all "personal property" (which includes such securities) is assessed in the district where the owner resides. By sec. 1044, the assessor must place upon the assessment roll, opposite the name of any person, "all the personal property" owned by himself, wife, etc. By sec. 1050, every assessor shall ascertain and set down in separate columns the number and value of certain articles named, and, under subd. 10, the value of all other "personal property, except such as is by law exempt." From these provisions it is quite clear that the assessment roll must contain all the personal property of a person, and its valuation by the assessor, whether such valuation shall have been ascertained by the assessor independent of or in accordance with the sworn statement of such person. The valuation of it on the roll is his valuation of it. By sec. 1056, *to determine* the amount of notes, bonds, mortgages, etc., the person to be assessed shall be required to make a statement thereof under oath, etc. The assessor *determines* the valuation in such case by such statement, and it becomes his valuation by this evidence, the same as the valuation of other personal property by the examination of such person under oath.

We now approach understandingly the jurisdiction, powers, and duties of the board of review, as prescribed in sec. 1061, R. S. By that section, "the board shall, under their official oaths, carefully review and examine said roll and . *statement*, and all valuations of real and personal property, and *bank stock*, and shall correct any errors," etc. The bank stock is first valued by the president, cashier, or other officer in charge, in a statement required by the assessor, according to sec. 1051, and may be revalued by the assessor, according to sec. 1057. The statement above referred to is evidently that statement. The board, therefore, reviews and examines the assessment roll of the valuation of bank stock, and the valuation in the statement of the officer of the bank. "They shall correct any errors," etc. "*For that purpose* they are hereby required to hear and examine any person or persons upon oath who shall appear before them, in relation to the assessment of *any property* on said roll, or in relation to any property omitted therein, and, if it appear that any property has been valued by the assessor too high or too low, they shall increase or lessen the same, to the true valuation, according to the rules for valuing property prescribed in this chapter."

It is very clear that the review and examination here spoken of is not for the mere purpose of correcting errors in the assessment roll, as contended by the learned counsel of the appellant, but it is also for the purpose of lowering or raising the valuation of any property on the assessment roll according to the testimony of those who shall appear before them. "They shall determine the correct value of any bank stock which has been valued in his statement thereof by an officer of the bank at one price and by the assessor at a different price." "Any person who thinks the aggregate valuation of his personal property by the assessor too high, may appear and state to the board under oath the true aggregate valuation of *all personal property* upon which he is liable to taxation," etc. This certainly includes the *securities* as well as articles of personal property and bank stock, for it is the aggregate of the whole. "The board of review shall, when satisfied *from the evidence* taken that the assessor's valuation is too high or too low, lower or raise the same accordingly, whether the person assessed appear before them or not." The assessor's valuation is that which is on the assessment roll; for the assessor has to append to the roll his affidavit "that the valuation of personal property and bank stock in said roll is as fixed by [him] [unless changed by the board of review]; that each and every valuation of the property made by [him] is the just and equitable value thereof, as [he] verily believes."

It is the assessor's assessment roll and his valuation, in the meaning of the language of this section, irrespective of the statements made of bank stock or securities. This is the plain and obvious meaning of the language, taken in connection with the other provisions above alluded to. In this view, there is the fullest authority, jurisdiction, and power of the board to review the entire assessment roll, to correct errors therein, and to raise or lower the valuation of the personal property therein assessed.

The only restriction upon the power of the board is that, in raising or lowering the valuation of the personal property of any person on the assessment roll, or as made by the assessor, which is the same thing, the board must act and so decide on *evidence taken before them.* There is no exception of any class or kind of personal property in the statute, and no exception can therefore be made by judicial interpretation. It is very clear that the legislature did not intend to except from the review and correction by the board of review that important and valuable kind of personal property known as securities or credits. It is in that form that taxable property can be most easily concealed and protected from taxation. It is the common form and method of evading taxation. Some of the greatest capitalists and wealthiest persons of the state have but little, if any, visible property subject to taxation, and their property consists almost exclusively in money, notes, bonds, mortgages, and other securities, concealed from the assessor, and only known to themselves. They make the statement under oath of an average amount of valuation of such money and securities, deducting their average indebtedness. Is that final? If it is, then the statute is a very convenient and impenetrable shield against just and equal taxation. The board can correct or raise the valuation of all other kinds of personal property by evidence. Why not of this most valuable kind? It is said that the dishonest tax-payer can be prosecuted for perjury, if his average valuation is too low. It may be answered that such a conviction would not equalize the assessment, or relieve the honest tax-payer from bearing more than his just share of the burthen of taxation, while the convict is forever exempt. To convict would require evidence, and the board of review could obtain that evidence as readily.

But the language of the statute is clear enough to evince such an intention of the legislature without argument. The cases cited by the learned counsel of the appellant are not applicable to the statute now in force and above considered. The case of *State ex rel. Smith v. Cooper*, 59 Wis. 666, was one in which the statement to the assessor was not made by the tax-payer, and the board of review raised the valuation of his average securities upon evidence similar to that taken in this case, and this court held that the board acted within its powers in doing so. In *Shove v. Manitowoc*, 57 Wis. 5, the statement to the assessor was made on oath, and the average value of this class of property stated therein. The board of review raised such valuation to a much larger amount, but did it arbitrarily and without evidence. In construing this section of the statute, Mr. Justice CASSODAY says: "Thus it appears that the board of review were authorized to increase or lessen the assessment only upon being 'satisfied from the evidence taken' that it was too high or too low." But the action of the board was held unlawful only because it was not based on evidence taken. To that extent it is authority in this case. It may be that this particular point was not contested, but it is an opinion on the construction of the statute as to the power of the board to raise the average valuation of this class of personal property above what it was valued in the statement under oath of the tax-payer.

It follows that the board of review had the power to

raise the average valuation of the securities of the relator, and did so on sufficient evidence.

By the Court.— The judgment of the circuit court is affirmed.

THE STATE EX REL. DWINNELL, Appellant, vs. GAYLORD, Village Clerk, etc., Respondent.

January 8 — January 29, 1889.

TAXATION. *(1) Village of Elkhorn: Board of review how constituted. (2) Excusing assessor from voting. (3) Taxable property: Notes, mortgages, etc., in another state.*

1. By statute the inhabitants of the town of Elkhorn were incorporated as the village of Elkhorn, and it was provided that the elective officers of the village (including three supervisors, one assessor, and one clerk) should severally have and exercise all the powers and perform all the duties " prescribed by statute in reference to said several designated officers in the several towns of this state." At that time assessors were the only officers authorized to review assessments, but subsequently boards of review were provided for, which (under sec. 1060, R. S., as amended by ch. 74, Laws of 1881) consisted in towns of the supervisors, clerk, and assessors, and in villages in which taxes were assessed and collected independently consisted of the president, clerk, and assessors. *Held,* that it was the intention of the act incorporating the village of Elkhorn that the officers of such village should have the powers and perform the duties then prescribed by statute in reference to similar officers in towns, and also such powers and duties as should at any time subsequently be prescribed in reference to such *town officers;* and hence that the board of review in that village should be constituted as such boards are constituted in towns, and not as they are constituted in other villages.

2. A quorum being present and voting, the fact that an assessor was excused from voting does not invalidate the action of a board of review.

8. Moneys, and notes secured by mortgages of land in another state, in the hands of an agent in that state to be loaned, collected, and reloaned, but belonging to a resident of this state, are "property in this state" (sec. 1034, R. S.) and taxable here.

APPEAL from the Circuit Court for *Walworth* County. The following statement of the case was prepared by Mr. Justice CASSODAY:

It appears from the record, in effect, that June 18, 1888, the relator, *George W. Dwinnell*, made out the usual statement of his personal property subject to taxation in the village of Elkhorn in Walworth county, and presented the same to, and verified the same before, George W. Wylie, one of the assessors of said village, wherein he placed in the column headed "Valuation by Owner," and opposite the following words and figures, to wit: "15. Average amount of notes, bonds, mortgages, and other securities for debts due or to become due, for each and every month during the year ending May 1, over and above the average amount of *bona fide* unconditional debts owing for each and every of said months, as determined under sec. 1056, R. S.,"— the sum of "$5,000." Thereupon said assessor placed opposite the same words and figures, and in the column headed "Valuation by Assessor," the sum of "$19,000;" and in the next column, headed "Remarks," the following: "$14,000 added by me for moneys out of the state. GEORGE W. WYLIE, Assessor."

June 26, 1888, the matter of said assessment came before the board of review of said village, legally in session, with all the members of the board present, consisting of John Matheson, Esq., chairman of the board of supervisors; F. W. Isham and H. C. Norris, supervisors; George W. Wylie, assessor of said village; and the said *Charles C. Gaylord*, the clerk of said village,— under and by virtue of ch. 153, P. & L. Laws of 1857, and ch. 133, P. & L. Laws of 1858. Said relator then and there appeared in person and by his attorney before said board, and objected to such increase of valuation to the amount of $14,000 by the assessor as being wholly unauthorized by law, for the reason that such statement under oath was conclusive; and for the further reason that such increase was unauthorized by the facts; and thereupon offered said sworn statement in evidence. Said assessor thereupon claimed that said $5,000 was too low, and should be increased, and offered to support the same by proofs; and thereupon the board took testimony, and in effect proved that *Dwinnell* admitted that he had and owned $19,000 as such average amount of such property; that he had it in the hands of his son-in-law in Nebraska as broker or agent; that he was not assessed thereon in Nebraska for the previous year, and did not know whether he had been in 1888; that if that property was assessable in Elkhorn at all, then the $19,000 was not too high. Said relator, *Dwinnell*, was thereupon sworn, but did not deny such admissions, but gave evidence tending to show that they were true. He also testified, in effect, that he had passed the money into the hands of said son-in-law, to loan, collect, and reloan for him, and gave him the power of attorney to do his business, and discharge mortgages, to loan, collect, and reloan; that such moneys were sent to said son-in-law to invest, and were in notes held by said agent, whom he paid for looking after such securities and moneys; that he regarded himself as a resident and tax-payer of said village. Thereupon, and at the request of the attorney for the relator, and with his knowledge and consent, the said board adjourned to July 6, 1888, to consider and inform themselves upon their legal duty; and due notice thereof was posted on the town hall, at the post-office, on the Park Hotel, and on the Nickel Plate Hotel, respectively, but no notice thereof was posted on the outer door of the village clerk's office. Verbal notice thereof was given to said relator and his said attorney.

Said board again convened July 6, 1888, at the appointed hour, with the said attorney of the relator present, and he was invited by said board to offer further testimony or be heard further on the matter if he wished. The board took some further testimony with his consent, sufficiently stated above. Thereupon said board of review, by unanimous vote (with the exception of said Wylie, the assessor and a witness, who was excused from voting), did decide and fix the amount and valuation of the relator's personal property so described at the sum and amount of $19,000. Thereupon said judgment and proceedings before said board of review were taken to and before the circuit court for Walworth county upon a common-law writ of *certiorari;* and, upon the hearing of said matter by and before said court, it was found by the said court, in effect, that said proceedings of said board were within its jurisdiction, and were regular, and that the said decision of said board was supported both by the law and the sworn testimony and the evidence given before said board; and it was thereupon ordered, adjudged, and decreed by said court that said action of said board in said matter be and was thereby affirmed, and that the same should stand as of full force, with costs. From that judgment of the circuit court the relator appeals.

For the appellant there was a brief signed by *J. F. Lyon & Son*, and the cause was argued orally by *J. F. Lyon* and *Jay F. Lyon*. They contended, *inter alia*, that money, notes, etc., in the hands of an agent in another state to loan, collect in, and reloan, as a permanent business, the agent having full control and management of them, and which are taxable in that other state, are not taxable here. Taxation and protection are reciprocal; and the owner of such property receives no benefit in respect thereto from the laws of this state. *Redmond v. Comm'rs*, 87 N. C. 122; *Mayor v. Baldwin*, 57 Ala. 61, 68; Cooley on Taxation (1st ed.), 14, note 4; *People v. Gardner*, 51 Barb. 358; *Wilkey v. Pekin*, 19 Ill. 160; *Wilcox v. Ellis*, 14 Kan. 588, 603; *Fisher v. Rush Co.* 19 id. 414; *People ex rel. Hoyt v. Comm'rs*, 23 N. Y. 224, 226; *Hutchinson v. Board*, 66 Iowa, 35. In accordance with this principle the state of Nebraska holds the property in question taxable there. *Finch v. York Co.* 19 Neb. 50. And this has been held constitutional. *Tappan v. Merchants' Bank*, 19 Wall. 491, 502. The *situs* of personal property for the purpose of taxation does not follow the domicile of the owner. *Albany v. Meekin*, 3 Ind. 481, 56 Am. Dec. 522; *Alvany v. Powell*, 2 Jones Eq. 51; Burroughs on Taxation, ch. 4; 1 Desty on Taxation, 59, 64; Welty on Assessments, sec. 43; *People ex rel. Hoyt v. Comm'rs*, 23 N. Y. 224; *Fisher v. Rush Co.* 19 Kan. 414; *People v. Niles*, 35 Cal. 282, 285; *St. Louis v. Wiggins Ferry Co.* 40 Mo. 580, 586, 589; *Taylor v. St. Louis Co. Ct.* 47 id. 594, 601; *Curtis v. Ward*, 58 id. 295; *State ex rel. Dunnica v. Howard Co. Ct.* 69 id. 454. That the *situs* in a case like this is at the domicile of the agent, see, also, *Catlin v. Hull*, 21 Vt. 152; *Bullock v. Guilford*, 59 id. 516, 519; *People ex rel. Westbrook v. Trustees*, 48 N. Y. 390; *Culbertson v. Comm'rs*, 52 Ind. 361, 366; *Herron v. Keeran*, 59 id. 472; *Foresman v. Byrns*, 68 id. 247; *Goldgart v. People*, 106 Ill. 25; *People v. Home Ins. Co.* 29 Cal. 534; *In re Jefferson*, 35 Minn. 215; 1 Desty on Taxation, 57; Welty on Assessments, sec. 45; 56 Am. Dec. 530. That the *situs* is not at the domicile of the principal, see, further, *People ex rel. Pacific S. M. Co. v. Comm'rs*, 5 Hun, 200, 64 N. Y. 541; *People v. Comm'rs*, 4 Hun, 595; *People v. Smith*, 88 N. Y. 576; *Hunter v. Board*, 33 Iowa, 376, 379; Browne on Assessment, 408.

Under sec. 1, ch. 133, P. & L. Laws of 1858, it was the intention of the legislature that the officers of the village of Elkhorn should have the same powers and duties and be subject to the same liabilities that similarly designated town officers *at that time* had and were subject to; but that

The State ex rel. Dwinnell vs. Gaylord.

such powers, duties, and liabilities would be modified not by the modification of the powers, duties, and liabilities of similarly designated town officers, but by amendments relating directly to village officers. The provisions relating to villages govern, therefore, as to the composition of the board of review of the village of Elkhorn, and such board should consist of the chairman of the board of supervisors, the village clerk, the assessor, and no others. In this case, in increasing the valuation, the board was composed of but two members, and allowed two outsiders to participate in their proceedings and act with them.

For the respondent there was a brief by *Dodge & Fish*, and oral argument by *J. E. Dodge*. They argued, among other things, that the question is not whether Nebraska can in some form lay a tax which must be paid by the relator on account of having made investments there, but simply whether the valuable property consisting in the ultimate right to receive payment, vested in the person of the relator, has its *situs* in Wisconsin so as to be "property within this state." That it has its *situs* here is declared by the courts of substantially every state in the Union, excepting perhaps New York and Kansas. *State Tax on Foreign-held Bonds*, 15 Wall. 317; *Kirtland v. Hotchkiss*, 42 Conn. 426; *San Francisco v. Mackey*, 22 Fed. Rep. 602; *Bullock v. Guilford*, 59 Vt. 516; *Mayor v. Hussey*, 67 Md. 112; *Worthington v. Sebastian*, 25 Ohio St. 8; *Bradley v. Bauder*, 36 id. 28; *Grant v. Jones*, 39 id. 506; *Kellogg v. Winnebago Co.* 42 Wis. 97; *Johnston v. Oshkosh*, 65 id. 473; *Comm. v. Am. Dredging Co.* 15 Atl. Rep. (Pa.), 443.

CASSODAY, J. Some of the questions presented in this case were also involved in *State ex rel. Smith v. Gaylord*, *ante*, p. 306, and are fully considered in the opinion of Mr. Justice ORTON filed herewith. In this case, therefore, we will confine ourselves to questions not there considered.

1. It is claimed that the board of review was illegally constituted; that the two supervisors, Isham and Norris, acted as members of such board without authority of law; that as the assessor, Wylie, was excused from voting, the action of the board complained of was only by two legally constituted members. Sec. 1, ch. 153, P. & L. Laws of 1857, as amended by sec. 1, ch. 133, P. & L. Laws of 1858, provided that "the inhabitants of the district of country included in the limits and boundaries of the town now known as the 'Town of Elkhorn,' in the county of Walworth, are hereby created a body corporate and politic, by the name and style of 'The Village of Elkhorn,' . . and shall be competent to have and exercise all the rights, and be subject to all the liabilities and duties, appertaining to a municipal corporation, and shall have and exercise all the rights and be subject to all the liabilities of the inhabitants of the several towns in this state. . . . The elective officers of said corporation shall be three supervisors, one of whom shall be designated as chairman, one assessor, one clerk, one treasurer, one superintendent of schools, four justices of the peace, and two constables, who shall be elected at the same time and in the same manner, *and shall severally have and exercise all the powers*, and be subject to and perform *all the duties* and liabilities, prescribed by statute in reference to said several designated officers in the several towns of this state. . . ." At that time "each assessor" was to appear at a time and place named, "for the purpose of reviewing his assessment," and was to "continue such review from day to day so long as" should be necessary for that purpose. Sec. 32, ch. 18, R. S. 1858. Such assessor at the time, therefore, was the only officer authorized to review such assessment. But the act so incorporating the inhabitants of the whole town of Elkhorn into such village clearly intended by the language quoted, not only that the several elective officers therein named

should have and exercise the same powers and duties then prescribed by statute in reference to said several designated officers in the several towns, but also such as might at any time subsequently be prescribed by statute in reference thereto in the several towns; in other words, that said village should at all times thereafter, with respect to the powers and duties of such elective officers therein named, stand on the same footing as such several designated officers in the several towns. Any other construction would create endless confusion, when the manifest purpose was to prevent any confusion. The result is that the statutes respecting such boards of review are applicable to the village of Elkhorn.

The statute provides and for a long time has provided that "*the supervisors, clerk, and assessors of each town,* the mayor, clerk, and assessors of each city, the president, clerk, and assessors of each village in which taxes are assessed and collected independently of the town, shall constitute a board of review for such town, city, or village. . . . A majority shall constitute a quorum." Sec. 1060, R. S., and ch. 74, Laws of 1881. Elkhorn, obviously, is not a village in which taxes are assessed and collected independently of the town, but one which in many respects is on the same footing as a town, but with increased or enlarged municipal powers. It has no president in name, but the chairman of the board of supervisors exercises corresponding powers. It follows that the board of review in question was legally constituted. The mere fact that the assessor was excused from voting is of no significance.

2. It is strenuously urged that the moneys, notes, and mortgages in the hands of the relator's agent in Nebraska were not taxable in Elkhorn, where he resided. An able brief is presented, and numerous authorities are cited in support of such contention. We do not feel called upon to analyze and harmonize the numerous cases cited. Counsel

is undoubtedly correct in claiming that taxes are only to be levied upon such property as the legislature may prescribe. Sec. 1, art. VIII, Const. The question, therefore, is whether moneys, notes, or notes secured by mortgages on lands in another state, owned by a resident of this state, but in the hands of an agent in such other state for the purpose of being loaned, collected, and reloaned, are among the classes of property prescribed for taxation in the taxing district of such owner's residence. Taxes must be levied upon all property in this state except such as is exempted therefrom. Sec. 1034, R. S. The classes of property so exempted are enumerated in sec. 1038, R. S. None of the property here in question is enumerated in that section. The term "personal property," as used in the "title" of the Revised Statutes on "Taxation," must "be construed to mean and include . . . *all debts due from solvent debtors, whether on account, note, contract, bond, mortgage, or other security, or whether such debts are due or to become due.*" Sec. 1036. All personal property must be assessed in the assessment district where the owner resides, except as otherwise provided by statute. Sec. 1040, R. S., and ch. 354, Laws of 1883. No statute provides for the assessment of the classes of property in question in any other than the district of the owner's residence. The owner of personal property is to include in his statement thereof, under oath, "the average amount of such money, notes, bonds, mortgages or other securities *owned or* held by him," etc. Sec. 1056, R. S. No exception is made as to the residence of the debtor, or the location or possession of the evidence of such indebtedness. The substance of it is that if such resident of this state *owns* such moneys, notes, bonds, mortgages, or other securities, then he is required to list them for taxation, if they are taxable under the statutes. Whether they are taxable or not depends upon whether such credits are property within this state. The statutes expressly declare them to be property.

The question, therefore, narrows down to this: whether such credits, belonging to such resident, are property *in this state*, within the meaning of the statute. It must be conceded that the taxing laws of the state have no extraterritorial operation. Such notes and mortgages. however, are mere evidences of indebtedness. The destruction of such evidences does not necessarily extinguish the debts. They are merely choses or things in action. Such mere credits have no other *situs* than the domicile of the owner, unless made so by statute. As observed by counsel for the village, in the case of such intangible species of property the thing that is valuable is "*the right of the creditor to receive* property or money" and to enforce such right by action in court. When, as here, there is an absence of any statute prescribing a different rule, and an absence of any evidence of any injustice by reason of double taxation, we must hold, under our statutes cited, that, for the purposes of taxation, a debt has its *situs* at the residence of the creditor, and may be taxed there. This ruling is certainly supported by the great weight of authority. *State v. Darcy*, 16 Atl. Rep. (N. J.), 160; *Comm. v. American Dredging Co.* 15 Atl. Rep. (Pa.), 443; *Worthington v. Sebastian*, 25 Ohio St. 1; *Bradley v. Bauder*, 36 Ohio St. 28; *Kirtland v. Hotchkiss*, 100 U. S. 491; and the numerous cases cited by Mr. Freeman in 56 Am. Dec. 527–530. As will there appear, in some states exceptions are made where such evidences of debt are held in another state in such a way as to acquire a *situs* there. Such cases are urged upon us with much force by the learned counsel for the relator, but we decline to follow them; and, besides, the evidence does not squarely bring the case within the rulings of some of those cases.

3. The evidence seems to be sufficient to sustain the action of the board of review.

By the Court.— The judgment of the circuit court is affirmed.

NILAND, Respondent, vs. MURPHY, Appellant.

January 8 — January 29, 1889.

Statute of frauds: Oral contract for sale of land: Acceptance of deed:
Refusal to pay price: Measure of damages: Evidence.

1. Where a conveyance has been executed and accepted in pursuance
   of an oral contract for the sale of land, an action may be maintained for a breach of the promise to pay the contract price.
   The statute of frauds does not apply to such an executed agreement.
2. The measure of damages in such case is the amount promised to
   be paid, and interest. And though it was not all due presently at
   the time of the sale, yet the whole amount may be recovered
   where it is all due before the trial and the grantee has from the
   outset refused to execute the notes and mortgage which he agreed
   to give for the deferred payments.
3. Evidence of the value of the land is properly excluded in such a
   case, the value having been fixed in the deed.
4. Evidence that after receiving a deed the grantee directed a sale of
   the premises, shows an acceptance of the deed.

APPEAL from the Circuit Court for *Milwaukee* County.
Action to recover the sum of $6,000, being the purchase
price of land conveyed to the defendant pursuant to an
oral contract of sale. The defendant purchased the land
of the plaintiff's agent, McDermott, at Ashland on March
25, 1887, and under his instructions a deed, together with
drafts of notes and a mortgage to be given for deferred payments, was sent to him at Milwaukee on the day of sale,
upon the receipt of which he was to forward to McDermott
his draft for $1,500, and execute and return the notes and
mortgage. The defendant received the deed, notes, and
mortgage at Milwaukee on March 29. After the receipt of
the deed, and on the same day, he telegraphed to McDermott: "Sell those lots to-day, if possible, at two hundred
to two fifty. I go up to-night;" and on the following day
he telegraphed: "Could not leave last night. If not al-

ready sold, sell to-day at best you can over cost." On March 31 the defendant went to Ashland and told McDermott that he would not accept the deed, and left it in McDermott's office, though the latter refused to receive it. The court found that the defendant accepted the deed, and that the plaintiff was entitled to recover the purchase price. From a judgment entered accordingly the defendant appeals.

For the appellant there were briefs by *Finches, Lynde & Miller*, attorneys, and *E. P. Smith*, of counsel, and oral argument by *Mr. Smith*. They contended, *inter alia*, that no recovery could be had in this action because it was brought for the breach of an alleged parol contract, absolutely void in not complying with the requirements of sec. 2304, R. S. *Brandeis v. Neustadtl*, 13 Wis. 142; *Popp v. Swanke*, 68 id. 364, 368; *Clarke v. Lincoln L. Co.* 59 Wis. 665; *Hooker v. Knab*, 26 id. 511. It cannot be said that the deed takes the place of and evidences the contract. It contains none of the stipulations, part and parcel of the alleged contract, nothing as to the manner and time of payment, nothing as to the securities to be given. *Thomas v. Sowards*, 25 Wis. 631–6; *Campbell v. Thomas*, 42 id. 441; *Popp v. Swanke*, 68 id. 364. There was no delivery or acceptance of the deed, and therefore defendant had a right to repose upon the statute and repudiate the transaction. *Miller v. Pelletier*, 4 Edw. Ch. 106; *Brandeis v. Neustadtl*, 13 Wis. 158; *Little v. Needham*, 39 Mich. 147; *Cooper v. Jackson*, 4 Wis. 547, 551; *Fonda v. Sage*, 46 Barb. 109. If there had been a delivery and acceptance of the deed, and a consequent transfer of title, there could be no recovery of damages pursuant to the contract, because "it cannot for any purpose be considered as ever having had an existence." *Brandeis v. Neustadtl, supra;* 2 Pomeroy's Eq. Jur. sec. 964. It cannot be said that the contract to pay might rest in parol and be separated from that to convey — that one was legal and the other illegal,— for the contract to pay would be without consideration if the contract to convey were void. *Little v. Needham*, 39 Mich. 149; *Griswold v. Messenger*, 6 Pick. 517; *Flint v. Sheldon*, 13 Mass. 448. If there had been an oral promise to pay money *presently* in consideration of land sold and conveyed, an action would lie to enforce the same. *Basford v. Pearson*, 9 Allen, 390. But a parol contract containing other terms than for the immediate payment of the entire purchase money, cannot be shown. If the deed had been delivered and accepted the grantor might recover, on proper pleadings, what the land was reasonably worth. But in that case evidence as to the value of the land must be admitted.

For the respondent there was a brief by *Jos. W. Hiner*, attorney, and *Quarles, Spence & Dyer*, of counsel, and oral argument by *T. W. Spence*. To the point that the action could be maintained, they cited *Alger v. Scoville*, 1 Gray, 394; *Trowbridge v. Wetherbee*, 11 Allen, 364; *Bowen v. Bell*, 20 Johns. 338; *Pomeroy v. Winship*, 12 Mass. 514–523; *Brackett v. Evans*, 1 Cush. 79–82; *Linscott v. McIntire*, 15 Me. 203; *Thayer v. Viles*, 23 Vt. 494; *Wolfe v. Hauver*, 1 Gill, 84; *Thomas v. Dickinson*, 12 N. Y. 364; *Michael v. Foil*, 100 N. C. 178; *Holland v. Hoyt*, 14 Mich. 242; *Green v. Batson*, 71 Wis. 57–58. The measure of damages is the stipulated price and interest. 3 Parsons on Cont. (7th ed.), 208–210; *Goodpaster v. Porter*, 11 Iowa, 161; *Shawhan v. Van Nest*, 25 Ohio St. 490; *Van Valkenburg v. Croffut*, 15 Hun, 147; *Thomas v. Dickinson*, 12 N. Y. 364; *Haskell v. Hunter*, 23 Mich. 305; *Chapman v. Ingram*, 30 Wis. 290; *Crawford v. Earl*, 38 Wis. 312; *Taft v. Wildman*, 15 Ohio, 123; *Evans v. C. & R. I. R. Co.* 26 Ill. 189; *Saladin v. Mitchell*, 45 id. 79; *Old Colony R. Corp. v. Evans*, 6 Gray, 34.

COLE, C. J. To our minds the proof is perfectly conclusive that the defendant accepted the deed which was sent
to him at Milwaukee pursuant to the understanding at the
time of the purchase at Ashland. He requested the agents
of the plaintiff to send the deed by mail to him there, when
he agreed to remit the $1,500 and execute the notes and
mortgage for the deferred payments. The evidence shows
that the deed was sent and was accepted. These facts, we
think, are proven by the most satisfactory testimony. The
court below so found, and no other inference could be made
from the admitted facts. The counsel for the defendant
insists that the deed was not accepted, but that the purchase was repudiated by his client. This position we deem
untenable. It appears that after the deed came to hand
the defendant sent the telegrams which were offered in
evidence to the McDermotts, directing them to sell the lots.
These dispatches are inconsistent with any other theory
than that the defendant had fully accepted the deed, and
considered the property his own. Otherwise he would not
have assumed the right, as he did, to dispose of it. So in
this case we must hold that the defendant accepted the
deed and became the owner of the lots. The case will be
decided upon that assumption.

The suit is brought to recover the consideration agreed
to be paid for the real estate. It is objected that the action cannot be maintained, because the contract was for
the sale of lands, and, not being in writing, was within the
statute of frauds. But when, in pursuance of a verbal contract, a conveyance has been executed and accepted, an action may be maintained for a breach of the promise to pay
the contract price. The statute does not apply to such an
executed agreement. *Bowen v. Bell*, 20 Johns. 338; *Remington v. Palmer*, 62 N. Y. 31; *Hodges v. Green*, 28 Vt. 358;
King v. Smith, 33 Vt. 22; *Weld v. Nichols*, 17 Pick. 538;
Page v. Monks, 5 Gray, 492; *Preble v. Baldwin*, 6 Cush. 550;

Worden v. Sharp, 56 Ill. 104; *Wetherbee v. Potter*, 99 Mass. 354. If some of the stipulations in the contract are within the statute and others are not, and those which are within it have been performed, an action lies on the other stipula· tions, if they are separate. Browne on Stat. of Frauds, §§ 116, 117. The learned counsel for the defendant says that, even if there had been a delivery and acceptance of the deed so as to pass the title, still there could be no recovery of the consideration, because the contract was void. The above authorities, and others to the same effect, which might be cited, shows that this position is unsound. Says Browne, in the sections above cited: " When so much of a contract as would bring it within the statute of frauds has been executed, all the remaining stipulations become valid and enforceable, and the parties to the contract re· gain all the rights of action they would have had at common law. Thus when, in pursuance of a verbal contract, a conveyance or lease of land is executed or goods are sold and delivered, an action may be maintained for the breach of the promise to pay the price or of any of the other stipulations of the contract: provided, of course, they be not such stipulations as the statute requires to be in writing." There is nothing in the decisions of this court in conflict with this view of the law. In *Brandeis v. Neustadtl*, 13 Wis. 142, there was a parol executory contract for the sale of lands where a part of the purchase money was paid. Dixon, C. J., held that the purchaser, after a demand for the repayment by the seller of the money paid, and after the refusal by him to repay, might maintain an action to recover such money paid. In *Campbell v. Thomas*, 42 Wis. 437, there had been no such complete performance of the verbal agreement to sell as would take the case out of the statute. That case is plainly distinguishable from the one at bar, where there has been an acceptance of the deed by the vendee, and a parol agreement for the sale has been fully executed. "The statute of frauds has no application to an executed agreement, and is no defense in an action brought to recover the money which the party is bound by the contract to pay." *Remington v. Palmer*, 62 N. Y. 31. In *Liddle v. Needham*, 39 Mich. 147, there had been no acceptance of the deed by the father, and the court would not imply a promise on his part to pay for the land which had been deeded to his son. The case may be good law, but it certainly does not conflict with the views which we have expressed. Here an undertaking to pay must surely be implied from an acceptance of the conveyance. *Vilas v. Dickinson*, 13 Wis. 488.

But it is further insisted that there could be no recovery for the full amount named as the purchase price, because the money was not all due presently when the sale was made. The money, however, was all due before the action was tried, and the defendant had from the outset refused to execute the notes and mortgage which he agreed to give. Upon the facts, we think the plaintiff was entitled to recover the amount of money which the defendant had agreed to pay; that is to say, the consideration specified in the deed. The measure of damages for the breach of a promise was the amount promised to be paid, and interest. *Tripp v. Bishop*, 56 Pa. St. 424, and cases cited by plaintiff's counsel on his brief. These authorities show that it was not error to exclude proof of the value of the land, because the parties themselves, by agreement, had fixed such value in the deed. Nor was there any error in admitting the evidence as to the contents of the deed which had been lost.

Upon the whole case we think the judgment of the circuit court was correct, and must be affirmed.

By the Court.— Judgment affirmed.

See notes to this case in 41 N. W. Rep. 835, 836.— REP.

THE CONTINENTAL NATIONAL BANK OF CHICAGO, Respondent, vs. McGEOCH, imp., Appellant. ·
THE CONTINENTAL NATIONAL BANK OF CHICAGO, Respondent, vs. WELLS, imp., Appellant.

January 9 — January 29, 1889.

NEGOTIABLE INSTRUMENTS. *(1) Liability of indorsers: Statutes of another state: Judicial notice: Demurrer. (2) Uncertainty in amount and time of payment: Collateral securities.*

1. In an action against the indorsers of an instrument for the payment of money, made and payable in another state, the court will not, on demurrer, take judicial notice of laws of that state relating to the liability of indorsers, which have not been pleaded.

2. A written instrument for the payment of a specified sum of money at a time specified, is rendered non-negotiable by an alternative contract therein that the payee may sell the collateral securities mentioned therein, and, if these decline in value, may sell them before the money for which the instrument was given would otherwise become due, in which case the proceeds of the sale, less the expenses thereof, shall be applied in payment or part payment of the debt, and if a deficiency remains the amount thereof shall become due forthwith.

APPEALS from the Circuit Court for *Milwaukee* County.

These are separate appeals by the defendants *Daniel Wells, Jr.*, and *Peter McGeoch*, from orders striking out the separate demurrer of each to the complaint as frivolous. Both appeals present precisely the same questions.

The causes of action stated in the complaint are balances alleged to be due the plaintiff on four instruments in writing for the payment of money, to each of which all of the defendants are parties. The complaint contains a separate count on each. The first count is upon the following instrument:

"$150,000. CHICAGO, ILL., May 10, 1883.

"Ninety days after date we promise to pay *The Continental National Bank of Chicago*, or order, one hundred and fifty thousand dollars, at the banking-house of said bank, value received, with interest at the rate of eight per cent. per annum after maturity, having deposited with said bank, as collateral security, warehouse receipts for provisions, which said security, or any part thereof, we hereby give the said bank, or its president or cashier, authority to sell, on the maturity of this note, or at any time thereafter, or before, in the event of said security depreciating in value, at public or private sale, at their discretion, without advertising the same or giving us any notice, and to apply so much of the proceeds thereof to the payment of this note as may be necessary to pay the same with all interest due thereon, and also to the payment of all expenses attending the sale of said collateral security; and in case the proceeds of the sale of said collateral security shall not cover the principal, interest, and expenses, we promise to pay the deficiency forthwith after such sale, with interest at eight per cent. per annum. And it is hereby agreed and understood that if recourse is had to said collaterals, any excess of collaterals upon this note shall be applicable to any other note or claim held by said bank against us; and in case of any exchange of, or addition to, the collaterals above named, the provisions of this note shall extend to such new or additional collaterals."

This instrument is signed by McGeoch, Everingham & Co. as makers, and indorsed by the defendant *Daniel Wells, Jr.* All of the defendants except *Wells* were members of the above firm.

The second count is upon an instrument of the same date and in the same form, for $100,000, signed by the defendant J. H. Peacock as maker, and indorsed by the defendants *Daniel Wells, Jr.,* and McGeoch, Everingham & Co. The third count is upon an instrument for $150,000, dated June 1, 1883, payable in sixty days after date. Otherwise it is in the same form as in the first and second counts. This last instrument is signed by the defendant *Peter McGeoch*, as maker, and indorsed by the defendants *Daniel Wells, Jr.*, and McGeoch, Everingham & Co. The fourth count is upon an instrument for the payment of $100,000, and is of the date and in the form of that contained in the third count. It is signed by the defendant *Daniel Wells, Jr.*, as maker, and indorsed by McGeoch, Everingham & Co.

The complaint alleges that all these instruments were made for the purpose of procuring credit thereon, and were indorsed as above before the same were discounted by the plaintiff. Judgment is demanded for about $26,000 and interest.

Each of the defendants *Wells* and *McGeoch* demurred separately to each count in the complaint on the ground that it fails to state a cause of action, and to the whole complaint because several causes of action are improperly united. The court, on motion of the plaintiff, struck out both demurrers as frivolous, with leave to the respective defendants to interpose answers. These appeals are from the orders striking out the demurrers.

For the appellant *Wells* there was a brief by *Wells, Brigham & Upham*, attorneys, and *J. T. Fish*, of counsel, and oral argument by *J. R. Brigham*. They contended, *inter alia*, that the contract in the notes providing for the sale of the collateral security did not destroy their negotiability. 1 Daniel on Neg. Inst. sec. 52; *Towne v. Rice*, 122 Mass. 67; *Haynes v. Beckman*, 6 La. Ann. 224; *Nat. Bank v. Gary*, 18 S. C. 282; *Arnold v. Rock River V. U. R. Co.* 5 Duer, 207; *Kirk v. Dodge Co. M. Ins. Co.* 39 Wis. 138; *Ward v. Perrigo*, 33 id. 143; *Hodges v. Shuler*, 22 N. Y. 114; *Perry v. Bigelow*, 128 Mass. 129. Though the effect of the stipulations is to make the note become due earlier than the day fixed, in the event of the sale of the collaterals, that does not deprive the note of its negotiability. *Walker v. Woolen*, 54 Ind. 164; *Palmer v. Hummer*, 10

Kan. 464; *Ernst v. Steckman*, 74 Pa. St. 13; *Cota v. Buck*, 7 Met. 589. Notes payable " on or before " a fixed day are negotiable. *Mattison v. Marks*, 31 Mich. 421; *Manufacturers' Nat. Bank v. Newell*, 71 Wis. 309.

For the respondent there was a brief by *Van Dyke & Van Dyke*, and oral argument by *G. D. Van Dyke*. They argued, among other things, that uncertainty of amount or time or fact of payment renders an instrument non-negotiable, which but for such uncertainty would be negotiable. *First Nat. Bank v. Larsen*, 60 Wis. 206, 212, 216; *Morgan v. Edwards*, 53 id. 599; *Smith v. Marland*, 59 Iowa, .645; *Chandler v. Cary*, 31 N. W. Rep. (Mich.), 309, and note; *Cook v. Satterlee*, 6 Cow. 108; *Haskell v. Lambert*, 16 Gray, 592; *Costelo v. Crowell*, 127 Mass. 293. As to uncertainty of time of payment, see *First Nat. Bank v. Bynum*, 84 N. C. 24; *Brooks v. Hargreaves*, 21 Mich. 254; *Miller v. Biddle*, 1 Ames Cas. on Bills & Notes, 76; *Smith v. Van Blarcum*, 45 Mich. 371. As to uncertainty of the fact of payment, see *Haskell v. Lambert*, 16 Gray, 592.

LYON, J. Under the rule which has prevailed in this court since the decision of the case of *Diggle v. Boulden*, 48 Wis. 477, if the demurrers to the complaint were not well taken the orders striking them out must be affirmed.

It will be observed that the complaint contains no averments of demand and notice to charge the indorsers of the several instruments in suit as such, but that the indorsers of such instruments are charged as primarily liable for the payment thereof. If the instruments are negotiable promissory notes, the omission of such averments renders the complaint demurrable as to the indorsers, for without such demand and notice they are not liable on the instruments. If the instruments are not negotiable, inasmuch as the indorsements were made before they were negotiated, the indorsers are liable as original promisors, and no such demand and notice were necessary to charge them as such. *Houghton v. Ely*, 26 Wis. 181; *Gorman v. Ketchum*, 33 Wis. 427; *Parry v. Spikes*, 49 Wis. 384.

It was said in the argument by counsel for the plaintiff that under the laws of the state of Illinois, where these instruments were made and dated and where they are payable, the indorsers are mere guarantors, whether the instruments are negotiable or not, and are liable thereon without any proceedings to charge them as indorsers. The proposition, if correct, is not available here, because the laws of Illinois in that behalf are not pleaded, and on demurrer we cannot know judicially what they are. Could we indulge in any presumption on the subject, it would be that the law-merchant prevails in that state, and certainly, under the law-merchant, demand and notice are necessary to charge the indorser of negotiable paper. Hence the controlling question for determination is, Are the instruments in suit negotiable? That is to say, are they promissory notes, within the law-merchant?

Each of these instruments contains two contracts in the alternative. One is a contract by the defendant signing the instrument to pay the plaintiff or order a specified sum of money at a time specified therein. Were this all there is of the instrument, the same would be negotiable. See *Morgan v. Edwards*, 53 Wis. 599, for an authoritative definition of a promissory note. The alternative contract is that the plaintiff might sell the collateral securities mentioned therein, and, if these declined in value, it might sell the same before the money for which the instruments were given would otherwise become due, in which case the proceeds of the sale, less the expenses thereof, should be applied in payment or part payment of the debts, and if a deficiency remained the amount thereof should become due forthwith. Had the collateral declined in value the next day after the plaintiff discounted any of the instruments in suit, we cannot doubt the plaintiff was authorized to sell them at once, and could have maintained an action upon the instrument immediately thereafter for any deficiency remaining unpaid upon the instrument.

Counsel for appellants submitted an ingenious argument to the effect that, although in the contingency mentioned the plaintiff was authorized to sell the collaterals before the money for which the instruments in suit were given was due, yet it was not authorized to apply the net proceeds of such sale in payment thereof until the money became due by the other terms of the instruments, and hence such instruments contained no agreement to pay any portion of the debt until the same thus became due. We cannot accept the argument as sound. The plain, unambiguous language of the contract is that, in such case, the contract of the defendants was "to pay the deficiency forthwith after such sale." So, had the collateral been sold the next day after the instruments were executed, and a deficiency remained after applying the proceeds of such sale, by the terms of the contract the deficiency became due and payable at once. There seems no room here for any different construction of the language employed. Thus we find that such alternative contract introduces two elements of uncertainty in the instruments, to wit, in the sum payable in case any sum becomes due before the time first specified in the instrument, and in the time when the same shall so become due. These elements of uncertainty thus introduced into the instruments, particularly the one first mentioned, destroy their negotiability. *Morgan v. Edwards*, 53 Wis. 599; *First Nat. Bank v. Larsen*, 60 Wis. 206; *Cushman v. Haynes*, 20 Pick. 132; 2 Am. & Eng. Ency. Law, 329. It is further argued that, inasmuch as the instruments do not draw interest from date, presumably the interest thereon to the time they became due was retained by plaintiff when it discounted them, and, because the contract provides for

the payment of interest on any deficiency, the above construction thereof might require the defendants to pay
double interest on the same debt; and it is claimed that a
construction must be erroneous which leads to such a result.
It is a sufficient answer to this position that no method is
given for computing the amount of such deficiency, and a
correct computation thereof would exclude double interest.

It is probable that, had no authority been given to sell
the collaterals before the debt became due, there would
still remain an element of uncertainty in the instruments
fatal to their negotiability. The authorities just cited seem
to support this view. Thus in the work last cited it is said
that a promise to pay a fixed sum, subject to deductions
from some cause stated in writing, is uncertain, and therefore not negotiable. In *Cushman v. Haynes* it was held
(SHAW, C. J., delivering the opinion) that an acceptance by
a consignee of goods for $1,000, "or what might be due
after deducting all advances and expenses," is not negotiable, and such is the doctrine of this court as laid down in
Morgan v. Edwards, and *First Nat. Bank v. Larsen, supra.*

It must be held that none of the instruments in suit are
negotiable, and hence the action is well brought thereon
against the indorsers as original promisors. It necessarily
follows that the objection that causes of action are improperly joined is not well taken. Indeed, that ground of demurrer is rested upon the hypothesis that the complaint
states no cause of action against the indorsers. The hypothesis being negatived, the objection fails.

By the Court.— Both orders appealed from are affirmed.

See note to this case in 41 N. W. Rep. 409.— REP.

POTTER, Respondent, vs. VAN NORMAN, Appellant.

January 9 — January 29, 1889.

PLEADING. *(1) Striking out demurrer as frivolous: When order reversed. (2) Money had and received: Action, tort or contract?
Conversion.*

1. The rule that an order striking out as frivolous a demurrer to the
   complaint and allowing the defendant to answer upon the usual
   terms will not be reversed unless the demurrer was well taken,
   adhered to.
2. A complaint shows that property was consigned in the name of one
   H. to the defendant to be sold, but that H. was not the owner or
   entitled to the proceeds thereof, and that the plaintiff was entitled
   to such proceeds; that the defendant sold the property for $824.15
   above all expenses; that before receiving or selling said property
   the defendant had full notice of plaintiff's right to the proceeds or
   value thereof, and plaintiff duly demanded of him such value before the receipt or sale thereof by the defendant, but, notwithstanding this, the defendant unlawfully converted to his own use
   the aforesaid value of the property, to wit, $824.15, and refused
   and still refuses to pay or account to the plaintiff therefor, though
   due demand has been made. Judgment is demanded for said
   sum of $824.15, with interest from the date of the sale. *Held:*
   (1) The facts stated are sufficient to entitle the plaintiff to recover.
   (2) The action is upon contract for money had and received.
   The allegation of a conversion does not, in view of the other allegations, render it a tort action.

APPEAL from the Circuit Court for *Milwaukee* County.
The case is sufficiently stated in the opinion.

For the appellant there was a brief by *Winkler, Flanders, Smith, Bottum & Vilas*, and oral argument by *H. C.
Sloan*. They contended, *inter alia*, that the right of the
plaintiff to all the proceeds of the shipment was dependent upon his contract with Thayer. He had himself but
a partial interest in the hogs, the extent of which is not
shown. But he has no rights under the contract with

Thayer because he violated that contract by his agreement to sell to Harris. By the terms of the contract with Thayer the plaintiff was to receive the *net proceeds* upon a sale by the commission merchant and no other sum. He was, in effect, a mere agent to receive the amount realized upon *this* sale, and had no authority to otherwise dispose of the hogs. It also appears that, prior to the receipt or sale of the hogs, the defendant had notice of the plaintiff's *rights in and to the proceeds*, so that, according to the complaint, the defendant had notice of the existence of the contract; and as the hogs were actually shipped in the name of Harris, defendant knew that plaintiff had not fulfilled his contract with Thayer and hence was not entitled to the proceeds. Defendant was therefore not obliged to make payment until instructed by Thayer so to do; and until so instructed was not liable to an action. *Cooley v. Betts*, 24 Wend. 203; *Halden v. Crafts*, 4 E. D. Smith, 490; *Brink v. Dolsen*, 8 Barb. 337. Defendant was a sub-agent of Thayer, and liable to him. Mechem's Agency, sec. 524. The complaint alleges that before suit Thayer assigned to the plaintiff his interest in the hogs and his claim against the defendant, but it does not allege that the plaintiff notified the defendant of such assignment. *Webber v. Roddis*, 22 Wis. 61.

Counsel also urged the reconsideration of the rule making no substantial distinction between striking out a demurrer as frivolous and overruling it on argument. The rule abrogates rights conferred upon parties by secs. 2845–2847, R. S. These sections treat a demurrer as an issue which is to be placed upon the calendar for trial, in the same manner as other issues, at a term of court. But under the rule in question the party whose pleading is demurred to may safely force a hearing at any time, even though he knows the demurrer is not frivolous.

For the respondent there was a brief signed by *Van Dyke*

& *Van Dyke*, attorneys, and *H. T. Reed*, of counsel, and oral argument by *G. D. Van Dyke*.

TAYLOR, J. This is an appeal from an order of the circuit court of Milwaukee county, striking out a demurrer of the defendant to the complaint of the plaintiff as frivolous, on motion of the plaintiff. The order striking out the demurrer allows the defendant to answer the complaint within twenty days from the date of the order on the payment of $10 costs.

Upon an appeal from such order this court has repeatedly held that the order of the circuit court will not be reversed unless it appears that the demurrer was well taken. The question whether it was frivolous or not will not be considered by this court. See *Hoffman v. Wheelock*, 62 Wis. 434, and cases cited in the opinion in that case.

Was the demurrer well taken? We think this question was decided rightly by the court below. The complaint substantially alleges that on the 10th day of January, 1888, the plaintiff and one Thayer were in possession of and the owners of a lot of live hogs at Cresco, in the state of Iowa; that about that time the plaintiff, with the assent and knowledge of his co-owner, delivered the hogs to the Chicago, Milwaukee & St. Paul Railway Company at Cresco, and with the assent of said Thayer the said hogs were consigned in the name of the plaintiff alone, to be transported and delivered by said railway company to the defendant, a commission merchant at Milwaukee, Wisconsin, to be sold by said defendant for the plaintiff, and to account to the plaintiff for the net proceeds or value thereof. The complaint then states that after the property had been shipped and consigned as above stated, but before the same started on its way to Milwaukee, the plaintiff made a verbal agreement with one Harris, whereby plaintiff was to sell to said Harris said hogs, on the payment to him of the cost thereof, to wit, $900, and $25 more, the whole to be paid to plaintiff from the proceeds of said hogs as soon as sold; that the plaintiff was to be and remain the full and absolute owner of said property, and the title and right of possession thereof was to remain in him, until he was so paid; and it was also agreed that the hogs were to go forward to Milwaukee in the name of the plaintiff as consignor, as already consigned, and that Harris would be entitled to receive from the proceeds thereof only the excess of their actual cost and $25; and that no part of said sum has ever been paid to the plaintiff.

The complaint then alleges that after the making of the agreement with Harris, he (Harris), without the knowledge and consent of the plaintiff or Thayer, induced the clerk of said railway company to change the shipment thereof, so that the same would go forward in the name of said Harris as consignor, and the shipment was so changed, and the hogs were forwarded to said defendant in the name of Harris as consignor; that the defendant received the hogs on or about the 10th of January, 1888, and sold the same, and received upon such sale the sum of $824.15, above all expenses of sale and transportation. The complaint further alleges that before the receipt of said hogs by the defendant, and before the sale thereof by him, the defendant had full notice of plaintiff's ownership of and rights in and to the proceeds or value thereof, and plaintiff duly demanded of him such value before the receipt or sale thereof by the defendant, but, notwithstanding this, said defendant unlawfully, and without the plaintiff's, or plaintiff's and said Thayer's, consent, converted to his own use the value of said hogs, viz., the sum of $824.15, and refused, and still refuses, to pay or account to plaintiff, or to plaintiff and Thayer, therefor, though due demand has been made on him by plaintiff so to do.

The complaint then sets out that the defendant refuses

to pay over the money to plaintiff because he claims that Harris was indebted to him on account, prior to the shipment of said hogs to him in the name of Harris, in a sum equal to or greater than the value of said hogs; and that he has passed to the credit of said Harris the value of said hogs. The complaint further alleges that the indebtedness of Harris to defendant, if any existed, was not incurred in any way by reason of the shipment of said hogs in the name of the said Harris, and that defendant has suffered no damage or incurred any risk in any way in consequence of such shipment, and that he passed to the credit of Harris the proceeds of such stock after full notice of plaintiff's right in and to the same.

The complaint then alleges an assignment from Thayer to the plaintiff of all his interest in the hogs, and all his interest in or claim against said defendant for the value of said property or damages for its conversion as aforesaid.

It seems to us very clear that, upon the facts stated in the complaint, the plaintiff is entitled to recover from the defendant in some form of action the amount received by him on the sale of the hogs in question, less the expenses of transportation and sale. The facts stated being admitted, they clearly show that Harris had no claim to the possession of the hogs, or to the proceeds of their sale, unless they brought more than $925, and the facts alleged show they did not bring that amount. The facts stated also show that the defendant knew before he received the hogs on the consignment of them to him by Harris, that Harris did not own the hogs and was not entitled to the proceeds of the sale, and that the plaintiff was entitled to such proceeds. The facts stated also show that the defendant has denied the right of the plaintiff to such proceeds, and has on demand refused to pay them to the plaintiff, or to plaintiff and Thayer. These facts clearly show an indebtedness of the defendant to the plaintiff, which the plaintiff can recover in an action at law, either upon a general complaint for money had and received for the plaintiff's use, or upon a complaint alleging all the facts. See *Grannis v. Hooker*, 29 Wis. 65; *Wells v. Am. Exp. Co.* 49 Wis. 224, 230; *Graham v. C., M. & St. P. R. Co.* 53 Wis. 482.

But it is insisted by the learned counsel for the appellant that the complaint must be construed as stating an action in tort to recover for the conversion of the money received by the defendant on the sale of the hogs made by him as the agent of the plaintiff, and that, giving that construction to the complaint, it fails to state facts showing a tortious conversion of the proceeds of the sale by the defendant, and that the demurrer was therefore well taken. The only allegation in the complaint which can be construed as tending to show that the plaintiff may have intended to charge the defendant with a tort, and to proceed against him for the recovery of damages for such tort, is the following: After stating the facts showing that the plaintiff was entitled to the proceeds of the sale made by the defendant and that the defendant had notice of such fact, it is alleged that "the plaintiff demanded of him *such value* before the receipt or sale thereof by the defendant; but, notwithstanding this, said defendant has unlawfully, and without plaintiff's, or plaintiff's and said Thayer's, consent, converted to his own use *the aforesaid value* of said hogs, to wit, the sum of $824.15, and refused, and still refuses, to pay or account to plaintiff, or to plaintiff and said Thayer, therefor, though due demand has been made on him by the plaintiff so to do." The prayer for judgment is not for damages for the tortious conversion of the hogs or the proceeds thereof, but for the said sum of $824.15, with interest from January 10, 1888, and costs.

These allegations, we think, must be construed to mean that the defendant had the right to sell the hogs as he did,

Potter vs. Van Norman.

and that he committed no wrong in making such sale, and that it was the duty of defendant, upon such sale being made, to account to the plaintiff for *the value* of the hogs so sold, less expense of sale and transportation, and a refusal on the part of defendant to account for such *value* to the plaintiff after demand. It is quite doubtful, to say the least, whether these allegations would be sufficient to charge the defendant with the conversion of the identical money received on the sale of such hogs, or to charge that the identical money received on the sale was the money of the plaintiff, and in order to maintain an action for the conversion of the money received on the sale of the hogs it would be necessary to state facts showing that the money so received by the defendant was the money of the plaintiff. The mere statement that the defendant was liable to account to the plaintiff for the value for which the hogs were sold would hardly be construed to mean that the identical money received on the sale was the money of the plaintiff. The mere allegation that the defendant unlawfully converted the value of the said hogs to his own use is not sufficient to change the complaint from an action to recover upon contract as for money had and received to the plaintiff's use into an action of tort for the conversion of money in his hands belonging to the plaintiff, when all the other allegations of the complaint are consistent with a claim to recover upon an express or implied contract. This was so held by this court in the case of *Whereatt v. Ellis*, 58 Wis. 625, 627. It is said in that case that the allegation "that the defendant converted certain crops to his own use," in an action by the plaintiff to recover the value of a share of said crops alleged to belong to the plaintiff, did not change the action into one for tort, in view of the other matters which give character to the action.

We think this complaint should be construed as a complaint to recover from the defendant the value of the hogs of plaintiff lawfully sold by the defendant, and for which value the defendant was legally bound either by express or implied contract to pay to the plaintiff. The question does not, therefore, arise in this case whether a principal who intrusts his property to an agent to sell and account to him for the proceeds of the sale can maintain an action of tort against his agent for refusal to account for such proceeds, or, if a principal can maintain such action against his agent in any case, what facts he must state in his .complaint to make out a good cause of action; and we do not feel called upon to discuss these questions upon this appeal.

By the Court.— The order of the circuit court is affirmed, and the cause is remanded for further proceedings.

HANSEN and another, Respondents, vs. THE FLINT & PERE MARQUETTE RAILROAD COMPANY, Appellant.

January 9 — January 29, 1889.

CARRIERS. *(1) Liability of carrier for loss beyond its own lines: Special contract: Receipt. (2) Agency: Proof of authority to make contract.*

1. An agent of the defendant company gave a receipt for goods shipped in the following form: " Milwaukee ——— 188-. — Shipped by Roundy, Peckham & Co. the following articles, in good order, to be delivered in like good order, as addressed, without unnecessary delay.— Consigned to Hansen & Kirsh, Onekama, Mich." On the face of the receipt the agent stamped and wrote: " F. & P. M. R. R. Co.— Rec'd. Nov. 2, 1887.— By agent, P., Milwaukee." *Held.* that this imported a contract to carry the goods through to Onekama, and that defendant's liability did not cease on the delivery of the same, at the end of its line, to a connecting carrier.

2. .Express authority of the agent to make such contract need not be shown, he having acted as such agent in the proper place for receiving goods for the company, and having been in possession of

JANUARY TERM, 1889. 347

Hansen and another vs. The Flint & Pere Marquette R. Co.

the company's stamp to be used on such receipts, and the company having taken possession of the goods and caused them to be shipped, presumably with knowledge of the receipt.

APPEAL from the Circuit Court for *Milwaukee* County. The facts will sufficiently appear from the opinion.

Frank M. Hoyt, for the appellant, contended, *inter alia*, that by the great weight of American authority where a carrier receives goods for transportation beyond his own line he is not responsible for any loss occurring beyond his line unless there is a special contract or some usage of business which shows that such carrier takes the goods for the whole route. *Peet v. C. & N. W. R. Co.* 19 Wis. 118–124; *Nutting v. C. R. R. Co.* 1 Gray, 502; *Van Santvoord v. St. John*, 6 Hill, 157; *Converse v. Norwich & N. Y. Transp. Co.* 33 Conn. 166; 2 Am. & Eng. Ency. Law, 860 *et seq.;* Hutchinson on Carriers, sec. 145 *et seq.;* Lawson on Carriers, sec. 235 *et seq.* The mere receiving and giving a receipt for goods marked to a point beyond the carrier's line is not sufficient. *Hadd v. U. S. & C. Exp. Co.* 52 Vt. 335, 6 Am. & Eng. R. Cas. 443. It was error to exclude testimony showing that the foreman of the warehouse, who stamped the receipt, had no authority to make a contract for the defendant to points beyond its own line. *Grover & B. S. M. Co. v. M. P. R. Co.* 70 Mo. 672; 2 Am. & Eng. Ency. Law, 806, note 2.

For the respondents there was a brief by *Winkler, Flanders, Smith, Bottum & Vilas*, and oral argument by *E. P. Vilas.*

ORTON, J. The facts are substantially as follows: Roundy, Peckham & Co., merchants of the city of Milwaukee, on November 2, 1887, upon an order from *Hansen & Kirsh*, the respondents, of Onekama, Michigan, shipped to them by the appellant company a large bill of goods. Roundy, Peckham & Co. on that day sent the goods to the warehouse of the appellant by their drayman, and received in return the following receipt: "Original. — MILWAUKEE, ———, 188–. — Shipped by Roundy, Peckham & Co. the following articles, in good order, to be delivered in like good order, as addressed, without unnecessary delay.— Consigned to *Hansen & Kirsh*, Onekama, Mich.— Description of articles.— Weight." Here follows a list of the articles shipped, covering four sheets of paper, upon each of which is the same heading as above, and on the face of the receipt, and on each page or sheet, is stamped by the agent of the appellant company the following: "F. & P. M. R. R. Co.— Rec'd. Nov. 2nd, 1887.— By Agent — Milwaukee." On the face of the stamp is written the letter "P." The stamp was affixed to the receipt by a Mr. Pawlett, the agent of the appellant company, on that day, who wrote the letter "P." thereon as his initial letter, and the stamp used by him was the one customarily used by the agent for such purpose. A portion only of the goods arrived at Onekama, their destination, the remainder having been burned or damaged at Manistee, Michigan, by fire. The value of the goods so lost was $651.74, for which, and interest of $45.62, making a total of $697.36, the jury rendered a verdict for the plaintiffs by direction of the court, and from the judgment thereon this appeal is taken.

The contention of the learned counsel of the appellant is that the defendant was entitled to show that its route and line as a carrier extended no further than Manistee, Michigan, and that said goods were safely carried to that point, and deposited in a warehouse, and in a place set apart for the use of the captain and proprietor of a boat called "Adriene," which plied between Manistee and Onekama, who receipted for the goods, and was in the act of removing them and had removed a part onto his boat when the warehouse was totally destroyed by fire, and the goods not then removed were destroyed or injured without negligence of the defendant; and that the defendant was entitled to show further that Roundy, Peckham & Co. well understood that the custom was between the defendant's line and such connecting carrier that such connecting carrier had nothing to do with the defendant's line, and the circumstances connected with the giving of the receipt, and that the agent, Pawlett, had no authority to make a through bill of lading between Milwaukee and Onekama. This evidence was ruled out by the court, and proper exceptions taken. The admissibility of this evidence depends upon the legal character of the receipt as being a full and perfect contract to carry the goods through the entire route, or otherwise. If the receipt constitutes a through bill of lading of the goods from Milwaukee to Onekama, then it could not be contended that any parol evidence could be given to explain or vary it, and what is established by contract cannot be changed or affected by custom. The general usage of a railroad company in respect to forwarding goods marked for points beyond its terminus will be deemed to enter into its contract of transportation. *Hooper v. C. & N. W. R. Co.* 27 Wis. 81; *Wood v. M. & St. P. R. Co.* 27 Wis. 541. Nor could it be contended that the express authority of the agent must be proved when he acted as such in the proper place for receiving goods for the company, and was in possession of the company's stamp to be used on such receipts, and the company took possession of the goods and caused them to be shipped with knowledge of the receipt, which it must be presumed the company had before they were so shipped. No other proof of agency is necessary than that the agent's acts justify the party dealing with him in believing that he had authority. *Kasson v. Noltner*, 43 Wis. 646.

The sole question, therefore, is, Does the receipt import a full and complete contract to carry the goods to their destination, or such a contract that it was fully performed by a delivery of the goods to the connecting carrier? I

cannot well see how a receipt or bill of lading could be
drawn to make a through contract, if this receipt does not.
It has all the usual terms. The destination and the consignees at that place are named. The goods are "*shipped*"
by Roundy, Peckham & Co., "in good order, to be *delivered* in like good order, as *addressed*, without *unnecessary
delay*." The address is "*Hansen & Kirsh*, Onekama, Mich.,"
as the consignees. Outside of the stamp upon it, it is more
like a shipping bill or bill of lading than a mere receipt.
The goods are not received, but *shipped*, by Roundy, Peckham & Co. The stamp is marked "Rec'd. Nov. 2, 1887,
by agent, P., Milwaukee." All the apt words to make a
perfect through contract are used, and none omitted. Manistee as the destination is not mentioned, nor is it found in
the contract anywhere for any purpose, nor is it known
from the receipt or contract that there was any connecting
carrier on the route, or if so what one, by water from Manistee. The respondents took no responsibility of carriage
beyond Manistee, but the company assumed it and contracted for it. Even within the rule contended for by the
learned counsel of the appellant,— which is claimed to be
the general rule by the authorities,— "that where a carrier
receives goods for transportation beyond his own line he is
not responsible for any loss occurring beyond his line *unless there is a special contract* or some usage of business
*which shows that such carrier takes the goods for the whole
route*," the defendant was bound to carry the goods the
whole route; for there was a special contract to that effect,
as we have seen. In *Wahl v. Holt*, 26 Wis. 703, the bill of
lading, or "shipping receipt," as it is called in the opinion,
had the same apt words: "To be delivered in good order
and condition as when received, *as addressed* on the margin,
or to his or their consignees." On the margin was: "Account, C. Wahl, George F. Wilson, Providence, R. I." But
the receipt in that case had also, "Care A. T. Co., Buffalo,"

and, "By the Commercial Line of Propellers from Milwaukee to Buffalo." These words were held to mean only that
the line of propellers by which the goods were shipped *ran*
"from Milwaukee to Buffalo," and "were not intended to
define the points between which the Commercial Line had
undertaken to transport the goods;" and it was held that
the proprietor of the Commercial Line contracted to carry
the goods to Providence, R. I. In that case, as in this,
there was mixed land and water transportation by connecting lines. The shipping receipt or bill of lading in the
present case is more explicit, definite, and complete, as a
through contract, than that in the above case, and there is
no mention of an intermediate point at the termination of
the defendant's line, to break the continuity between Milwaukee and Onekama. It is very clear that that case rules
this, and is sufficient authority for holding that this is a
through contract, without citing other authorities. That
case as well as this is readily distinguishable from *Parmelee
v. Western Transp. Co.* 26 Wis. 439, as well as from all
other cases in which the end of the route was held to be an
intermediate point, or the end of the defendant's line. We
think that the court was warranted in directing a verdict
for the plaintiffs.

By the Court.— The judgment of the circuit court is affirmed.

IN RE MABBETT.

January 9 — January 29, 1889.

*Insolvency: Discharge: Failure to schedule portion of homestead not
exempt: Fraudulent conveyance: Intent: Court and jury.*

1. The homestead of an insolvent debtor was mortgaged for $10,000.
   It contained a narrow strip, valued at $637.50, in excess of one
   fourth of an acre. The title had been in his wife for nine years

before he applied for a discharge from his debts. *Held*, that the failure to include said strip in the inventory of his estate was not sufficient to bar a discharge.

2. Upon an application by an insolvent debtor for a discharge from his debts, the question whether a previous conveyance or mortgage of his property was made with intent to defraud his creditors is a question of fact and should be passed upon as such by the jury or court.

APPEAL from the Circuit Court for *Milwaukee* County.

The following statement of the case was prepared by Mr. Justice CASSODAY:

It appears from the record, in effect, that May 20, 1887, *Joseph S. Mabbett* filed his petition in the circuit court for a discharge from all his debts as an insolvent debtor, with the ordinary affidavit, under and in pursuance of ch. 179, R. S., and the several acts amendatory thereof; that he alleges generally and in detail that the petition and affidavit conformed in every respect to said statutes; that the schedules annexed showed a total indebtedness of $49,682.43; and property consisting only of household goods and furniture, household stores, wearing apparel, and ornaments of the person, valued at $1,700, and books, prints, and pictures, valued at $250 (all mortgaged to one Waldron, March 15, 1875, to secure a debt of $5,455.44, owing him from *Mabbett*), and no other personal property, and no real estate, choses in action, debts due, or moneys belonging to him. On the hearing of the order to show cause why such discharge should not be granted, certain of his creditors filed their objections, and specified for the grounds thereof that the petitioner had failed to schedule property not exempt; and thereupon the court ordered the trial of such issue. It appeared from the evidence that *Mabbett* had a homestead in the city of Milwaukee, April 15, 1878, consisting of a lot and a half; that on that day he deeded it, through a third person, to his wife; that April 25, 1878, he borrowed $10,000, and his wife gave a mortgage on such homestead to secure it; that the homestead contained 4¼ feet front, and 127 feet back, in excess of one fourth of an acre, valued at $637.50. At the close of the testimony the court withdrew the cause from the jury, and by order dismissed the petition. From that order the petitioner appeals.

For the appellant the cause was submitted on the brief of *Nath. Pereles & Sons.*

[No appearance for the respondents.]

CASSODAY, J. The objecting creditors have failed to argue the case or present any brief. It is therefore subject to reversal under the rule. There may be some reason for withdrawing the matter from the jury and dismissing the petition not apparent upon the record or which has not suggested itself to us. The mere failure, however, to inventory the portion of the homestead in excess of the exemption is not, as it seems to us, under the facts stated, sufficient to bar a discharge. It was only four and one-quarter feet front, and of the value of $637.50. There was a mortgage on the premises of $10,000, given nine years before the petition was filed. Assuming the mortgage to have been valid, then such strip, or the avails thereof, would necessarily have been first sold or applied on the mortgage debt. But the title of that had been in the petitioner's wife for more than nine years prior to the filing of such petition. We cannot say, as a matter of law, that the putting of the title in the wife, or the giving of the mortgage, or the giving of the previous mortgage on the household goods, was with intent to defraud creditors. If either was claimed to have been made with such intent, then the question of such intent should have been found by the jury or court. Sec. 2323, R. S. We do not think it can be said, as a matter of law, from the facts disclosed in the record, that the petitioner wilfully swore falsely in his affidavit filed, or upon his examination, within the meaning of

sec. 4302, R. S. Nor does it appear that he had done any
of the things therein enumerated as a bar to such discharge.[1]

By the Court.—The order of the circuit court is reversed,
and the cause is remanded for further proceedings according to law.

SANGER, Respondent, vs. GUENTHER, Garnishee, etc., Appellant.

January 10 — January 29, 1889.

*Debtor and creditor: Chattel mortgages: Delay in filing: Estoppel:
Garnishment: Failure to prove issuance of execution: Appeal.*

1. When the mortgagee of chattels delays the filing of his mortgage
   at the request of the mortgagor and in order that the credit of the
   latter may not be injured, he is estopped to assert such mortgage
   as against creditors who, after the execution of the mortgage and
   before its filing, gave credit to the mortgagor upon the faith that
   his property was unincumbered; and this is so although the mort-

---

[1] Sec. 2323, R. S., provides that the question of fraudulent intent, in
all cases arising under the provisions of title XXII, relating to "Fraudulent Conveyances and Contracts," shall be deemed a question of fact,
and not of law.

Sec. 4284 provides that an insolvent debtor applying for his discharge
shall annex to his petition and schedule an affidavit stating that the
account of his creditors and the inventory of his estate are in all respects just and true, and that he has not, at any time or in any manner
whatsoever, disposed of or made over any part of his estate for the
future benefit of himself or his family or in order to defraud any of his
creditors, etc.

Sec. 4302 provides that "every discharge granted to an insolvent
under this chapter shall be voidable in each of the following cases:
(1) If such insolvent shall wilfully have sworn falsely in his affidavit
annexed to his petition, or upon his examination, in relation to any
material fact concerning his estate or his debts, or to any other material
fact; . . . "— REP.

gagee had no actual intent to defraud any creditor. *Standard Paper Co. v. Guenther*, 67 Wis. 101, followed.

2. The fact that a creditor who took the note of the mortgagor before the mortgage was filed, required such note to be signed also by other persons, is not conclusive that he did not rely upon the property of the mortgagor ultimately to pay it.

3. The fact that the creditor permitted the mortgagee to take possession and dispose of the mortgaged property does not estop him from requiring the latter to account therefor.

4. An affidavit for garnishment stating that an execution has been issued on a judgment against the principal defendant and has not been returned, is sufficient to give the court jurisdiction over the proceeding; and where the fact that an execution had been issued was not contested in the trial court it cannot be objected, on appeal, that there was no proof of that fact.

APPEAL from the Superior Court of *Milwaukee* County.

Garnishment in aid of an execution issued on a judgment in favor of the plaintiff and against the Freie Presse Company, L. R. Roeder, and M. L. Roeder, upon a promissory note executed by them June 16, 1884. Said judgment was rendered March 26, 1885, and this proceeding by garnishment was instituted December 2, 1886. The garnishee denied all liability as such, and issue was taken on his answer. Upon the trial of such issue it appeared that on May 10, 1884, the Freie Presse Company had given a chattel mortgage upon its personal property to the garnishee; that such mortgage was not filed until November 12, 1884; and that on March 31, 1885, the garnishee took possession of the mortgaged property, and had sold portions thereof prior to the commencement of this proceeding. Other facts will appear from the opinion. The garnishee appeals from a judgment in favor of the plaintiff.

For the appellant there was a brief by *Frisby, Gilson & Elliott*, and oral argument by *F. L. Gilson*. They contended, *inter alia*, that the plaintiff is equitably estopped from questioning the title of the garnishee, by reason of his laches in delaying for twenty months to take any steps to collect his judgments, while the garnishee was expending time and money in disposing of the property. 2 Pomeroy's Eq. Jur. sec. 818; *Somersetshire C. C. Co. v. Harcourt*, 2 DeG. & J. 596; *Chapman v. Chapman*, 59 Pa. St. 214; Bigelow on Estoppel, 453, note 1; *Brooks v. Curtis*, 4 Lans. 283. The mortgage to the garnishee should be treated as though it had been executed on the day it was filed, November 12, 1884, and plaintiff can only defeat it by obtaining a lien prior to such filing. Jones on Chat. Mortg. 245; *Cameron v. Marvin*, 26 Kans. 612-627; *Overstreet v. Manning*, 67 Tex. 657; *Ransom v. Schmela*, 13 Neb. 73; *Hayman v. Jones*, 7 Hun, 238; *Kennedy v. Nat. Union Bank*, 23 id. 494; *Jones v. Graham*, 77 N. Y. 628.

For the respondent there was a brief by *Markham, Williams & Bright*, and oral argument by *A. H. Bright*.

COLE, C. J. The counsel for the respondent is fully justified in insisting that this case, in all its essential facts, is the same as *Standard Paper Co. v. Guenther*, 67 Wis. 101. The cases cannot be distinguished in principle. The findings of fact by the trial court abundantly sustain this view. The head-note in the *Standard Paper Case* correctly states the principle decided in the following language: "When the mortgagee of chattels delays the filing of his mortgage at the request of the mortgagor and in order that the credit of the latter may not be injured, he is estopped to assert such mortgage as against creditors who, after the execution of the mortgage and before its filing, gave credit to the mortgagor upon the faith that his property was unincumbered; and this is so although the mortgagee had no actual intent to defraud any creditor."

In this case the trial court found, in substance, that the note which is the basis of the judgment on which this garnishee process was issued was given on the 16th day of June, 1884, in consideration of the settlement and discontinuance by the plaintiff of a certain action then pending and being prosecuted by the plaintiff against the Freie Presse Company; that such note was received in settlement of that suit, and further credit extended to the Presse Company in good faith, upon the belief that the property of the Presse Company was unincumbered. The chattel mortgage was then in existence, but had been kept from the files of the proper office by the mortgagee and garnishee at the solicitation of the agents of the mortgagor, because it would hurt its credit and interfere with its business to have it placed upon record. The court also found that the plaintiff herein had no notice of the existence of this mortgage when he took the note, but relied upon the property of the Presse Company being unincumbered. That there is abundant testimony to sustain these findings cannot be successfully denied. Now, in the *Standard Paper Co. Case*, Mr. Justice TAYLOR in effect says that the withholding of the mortgage from the record by the mortgagee at the request of the mortgagor operates as a fraud upon the parties who deal with and give credit to the mortgagor upon the supposition that the property which he apparently owns is unincumbered; that, if the mortgagee is permitted to insist upon the validity of his mortgage as against those who have given credit under such circumstances, it amounts to a legal fraud, whether there is any actual intent on the part of the mortgagee to defraud a creditor or not. This undoubtedly would be the inevitable effect of such secret arrangements between the mortgagor and mortgagee about withholding from the record the chattel mortgage. It would in many cases operate as a fraud upon parties dealing with the mortgagor without notice of any such incumbrance upon his property.

It is said by the learned counsel for the garnishee that the plaintiff had notice of the existence of this mortgage, and did not rely upon the property of the Presse Company

being unincumbered when he settled the suit and took the
notes. But the plaintiff himself testified that he had no
notice of the chattel mortgage, and took the notes relying
on the property of the Presse Company being unincumbered. But the same counsel insists that the plaintiff, by
taking additional security, waived his right to rely upon the
property of the Presse Company. It does appear that the
Roeders signed the notes with the Presse Company at
the time of the settlement, but the plaintiff says he did not
regard them as responsible. There is certainly nothing in
the evidence which warrants the assumption that the plaintiff, when he received the notes, did not rely upon the
property of the Presse Company as means to pay them.
Notwithstanding the plaintiff required the Roeders to sign
the notes of the Presse Company, still it is a question of intent whether he did not in fact rely upon the property of
the company ultimately to pay them. He says, in effect,
that he did, and the trial court found that he did, and this
is conclusive upon the question.

But it is further claimed that the plaintiff is equitably
estopped from questioning the title of the garnishee by reason of his laches in delaying for twenty months to take any
steps to collect his judgment against the Presse Company
while the garnishee was expending time and money in disposing of the mortgaged property. It is true the plaintiff
permitted the garnishee to take possession of the mortgaged
property and dispose of it, but we cannot perceive how his
delay or silence should estop him from insisting upon his
rights. The garnishee is only bound to answer for property in his hands, belonging to the judgment debtor, which
should be applied to the payment of the latter's debt.
Upon the facts of this case the garnishee cannot hold the
property of the Presse Company under his chattel mortgage, as against the plaintiff. This is what we have already
intimated. Why should the plaintiff be estopped from

calling on him to account for the property in his hands or under his control to satisfy the plaintiff's demand? We perceive no ground for applying the doctrine of estoppel to the plaintiff upon the undisputed facts.

The affidavit for the garnishment was in aid of an execution under sec. 2753, R. S., as amended by ch. 286, Laws of 1885, and states that an execution had been issued on the judgment against the Presse Company which had not been returned. It is objected here, for the first time, that no proof was made of the issuing of the execution, and it is insisted that the proceeding should be dismissed for that reason. We think the objection comes too late. The fact that an execution had been issued was not contested in the court below, no question seems to have been made upon it where the proof could have been supplied and the objection obviated, and it ought not now to prevail. The statement in the affidavit that an execution had been issued which had not been returned was sufficient to sustain the jurisdiction of the court over the proceeding, and the plaintiff was not called upon to prove it unless the fact was contested or challenged in some proper manner in the trial court. It is unnecessary to remark that the filing of the mortgage in November, 1884, could not affect or defeat the plaintiff's rights which originated in the previous June, when he received his notes. The county court found, upon the evidence, that the garnishee had in his possession and under his control property, money, credits, and effects of the Presse Company, or the proceeds of the sale thereof, sufficient to pay the plaintiff's claim, and this accords with the facts proven. This disposes of all the material questions in the case.

By the Court. — The judgment of the superior court is affirmed.

THE TOWN OF WOODVILLE, Appellant, vs. THE TOWN OF HARRISON, Respondent.

January 10 — January 29, 1889.

Limitation of actions: Time of delivery of summons to sheriff: Alteration of return day: Evidence: Justices' courts.

1. No record evidence of the time when a summons issued by a justice of the peace was delivered to the sheriff for service being required by statute, such time may be proved by parol.
2. If after a summons issued by a justice of the peace is delivered to the sheriff for service the return day fixed therein is changed, such alteration makes another and entirely different process of it, which, in contemplation of law, the sheriff did not and could not receive until the alteration was made. And the fact and time of such alteration may be proved by parol.

APPEAL from the Circuit Court for *Calumet* County.

One Teiss and his family, having become a charge upon the plaintiff town for their support, were relieved by it. It is alleged that such paupers then had a legal settlement in the defendant town. On October 26, 1886, the supervisors of the former town served upon the supervisors of the latter notice of such relief, as prescribed by sec. 1513, R. S. On November 12, 1886, the latter supervisors served upon the former a denial in writing of the liability of the defendant town for the support of the persons thus relieved, pursuant to sec. 1514. The plaintiff town thereupon brought this action to recover $14.40, that being the amount thus expended by it for the relief of such alleged paupers. The entries in the docket of the justice before whom the action was brought show that the summons was issued February 10th, returnable February 23d, and was duly served by the sheriff February 16th, and by him returned to the justice February 21st, all in 1887.

The defendant town answered, among other things, that the action was not commenced within three months after

service of such denial; thus pleading the limitation contained in sec. 1514.   On the trial the sheriff who served the
summons testified that he thought it was delivered to him
for service February 11, 1887.   Certain questions were then
propounded to him by the defendant for the purpose of
showing, and the answers to which might have tended to
show, that when he received the summons, on February
11th, the return day written therein was February 22d
(which was a legal holiday), but after the 12th of that
month such return day was altered to the 23d.

The plaintiff recovered judgment for the sum claimed,
and thereupon the defendant took an appeal to the circuit
court.   The cause was tried in that court on the return of
the justice to such appeal, and the court reversed the judgment of the justice because of the rejection of such offered
testimony.   From such judgment of reversal the plaintiff
appeals to this court.

J. E. McMullen, for the appellant, to the point that parol
evidence was not admissible to contradict or vary the
docket of the justice, cited *Coffman v. Hampton,* 27 Am.
Dec. 511; *Clark v. M'Comman,* 7 Watts & S. 471; *Seibert
v. Kline,* 1 Pa. St. 43; *M'Lean v. Hugarin,* 13 Johns.
184; *Posson v. Brown,* 11 id. 166; *White v. Hawn,* 5 id. 351;
Brintnall v. Foster, 7 Wend. 103; *Healy v. Kneeland,* 48
Wis. 497; R. S. secs. 4142, 4143; *Zimmerman v. Zimmerman,* 15 Ill. 84.

For the respondent there was a brief by *Silas Bullard*
and *A. A. Nugent,* attorneys, and *Gabe Bouck,* of counsel,
and oral argument by *Mr. Bullard.*

Lyon, J.   If the action was not commenced on or before
February 12, 1887, it was barred by the limitation of sec.
1514, R. S.   It was not commenced until the summons was
delivered to the sheriff for service.   Sec. 4240.   The docket

of the justice does not show, and the statute does not require that it should show, when the summons was delivered to the sheriff. Neither does it require the sheriff to certify when he received it, and he did not so certify. Had he done so his certificate would, at most, be presumptive evidence only of the fact thus certified. Sec. 4241. Hence there is no record evidence of the time the summons was delivered to the sheriff for service, and the statute requires none. Hence the fact may properly be proved by parol. Doubtless the rule would be the same had the sheriff certified the date of service, or had such date been entered in the docket of the justice.

If a summons returnable February 22d was delivered to the sheriff on the 11th of that month, and the return day was subsequently altered to the 23d, the alteration made another and entirely different process of it, which, in contemplation of law, the sheriff did not and could not receive until the alteration was made, although he may have had in his possession from the 11th the paper which by the alteration became the summons in the action. If so altered, the fact and time of such alteration may in like manner and for the same reasons be proved by parol; for it is only one method of proving when he received the summons for service. The summons is in the record, and it shows unmistakably, on its face, that the return day originally written therein has been altered.

The cases which hold that the authorized entries in the docket of the justice import absolute verity have no application here. Had testimony been offered to show directly that the summons was not issued on the 10th, or was not made returnable on the 23d, or, perhaps, that it was not served on the 16th, those cases might be applicable; but the rejected testimony was not offered for any of these purposes, or to dispute any authorized record, but only to prove a fact resting in parol. It was therefore error to re-ject such testimony, and the error is vital in the case. Hence the circuit court properly reversed the judgment of the justice.

By the Court.— Judgment affirmed.

ZEMLOCK, Respondent, vs. THE UNITED STATES, Appellant.

January 11 — January 29, 1889.

Lands granted to aid in improvement of Fox and Wisconsin rivers: Sale by state: Right to flood without compensation.

1. The lands granted to this state by the act of Congress of August 8, 1846, to aid in the improvement of the Fox and Wisconsin rivers, were not granted merely as a location for the improvements, but to be sold and the proceeds used in making the improvements. And where such lands were sold by the state without any express reservation of the right to flood them, if necessary in making the improvements, without making compensation therefor, no such reservation can be implied from the mere fact that the lands were granted to the state to aid in making such improvements.
2. Nor is any such reservation created by the act of the legislature of August, 1848 (Laws of 1848, p. 58). Sec. 16 of that act, providing that when any lands appropriated by the board of public works to the use of such improvements shall *belong to the state* they shall be absolutely reserved to the state, refers to an ownership by the state at the time of the appropriation, and not to an ownership of which the state had lawfully divested itself prior to the taking of the lands by the board.

APPEAL from the Circuit Court for Winnebago County. The case is sufficiently stated in the opinion.

E. E. Chapin, for the appellant.

For the respondent the cause was submitted on the brief of *Hume & Hilton,* attorneys, and *Gabe Bouck,* of counsel.

TAYLOR, J. This is an appeal from the judgment of the circuit court of Winnebago county awarding damages against the appellant for overflowing and injuring the plaintiff's land, by reason of the maintenance by the appellant of the dam across the Fox river at Appleton in this state. The nature of the respondent's action, and the grounds upon which the liability of the appellant for the damages caused by the overflow of the respondent's lands is based, are stated at length in the case of *Jones v. U. S.* 48 Wis. 385.

The only alleged error in the proceedings in the circuit court which is urged by the learned counsel for the appellant arises upon a motion for a nonsuit made by the appellant at the close of the plaintiff's evidence, which motion was in the following language: "The defendant moved for nonsuit on the ground that the lands described in the petition were included in a grant made by the *United States* to the state of Wisconsin under an act of Congress approved August 8, 1846, to aid in the improvement of the Fox and Wisconsin rivers and to connect the same by canal, and were conveyed by said state of Wisconsin in accordance with and in pursuance of an act of the legislature of said state approved August 8, 1848, and the several acts supplemental thereto and amendatory thereof, by which said acts the said state reserved the right to flow said lands in the works of said improvement, and the plaintiff purchased the same subject to such reservation." This motion was renewed after all the evidence was presented by both parties, and the motion was denied in both cases, and appellant duly excepted.

The appellant also asked the court to instruct the jury as follows: "If the jury find from the evidence that the lands described in the petition were granted by the *United States* to the state of Wisconsin on the admission of such state into the Union, for the purpose of aiding in the improvement of the Fox and Wisconsin rivers, and that afterwards said lands became the property of the state of Wisconsin for the purposes contemplated by the act of Congress approved August 8, 1846, and that the lands described in the petition were transferred by the state of Wisconsin in pursuance of the act of the legislature approved August 8, 1848, to Jonathan Lincoln, from whom, by regular chain, plaintiff derived title, then the plaintiff cannot recover." To the refusal to give this instruction the appellant also duly excepted.

The motions and instructions asked raise the same questions. The contention of the learned counsel for the appellant is that, as the evidence clearly established the fact that the land owned by the respondent, on account of which he claims damages for its overflow by the maintenance of the dam by the appellant at Appleton, is a part of the lands granted to this state by the *United States* to aid in the improvement of the navigation of the Fox and Wisconsin rivers, the grantee of the state and those claiming under him hold said lands subject to the right of the state, its assignees and grantees, to flow such lands without making compensation therefor if it becomes necessary so to do in making improvements in the navigation of said rivers. This is the only question raised by the learned counsel for the appellant in this court. It is admitted that the maintenance of the dam at Appleton is necessary for the improvement of the navigation of the Fox river, and that it is maintained by the *United States* for that purpose, and also that this dam causes the overflow and damage to the plaintiff's lands. The only question is whether there was any express or implied reservation on the part of the state when the lands in question were granted to Jonathan Lincoln by the state, March 1, 1850, from whom the plaintiff derives title, to flow such lands in the future without making compensation therefor if it became necessary to do so in making improvements in the navigation of said Fox river. There is no claim that any reservation was made in the grant from the state to Lincoln in 1850. The proof shows that the grant was absolute and without any condition or reservation. The contention of the learned counsel for the appellant is that, notwithstanding the absolute nature of the grant, under the law of the state and considering the purposes for which the lands were granted by the *United States* to this state, there was an implied reservation that the state or those claiming under it might, if necessary to improve the navigation of the Fox river, flow said lands without making any compensation.

The argument of the learned counsel fails to convince us that there was any such reservation implied or expressed when the state granted the lands in question to the said Lincoln. The evidence does not show that the lands were flowed by reason of any works of improvement made by the state or its authorized agents at the time the lands were conveyed to the said Lincoln. If there was any reservation, it must arise out of the fact that the lands were granted to the state to aid the state in improving the navigation of said Fox river, or upon some law of the state in force at the time of the grant which created such reservation notwithstanding the terms of the grant. We are unable to see anything in the purposes for which the grant was made to the state upon which an implied reservation to flood the same without compensation can be founded. It is very clear that the lands were not granted to the state merely for the purpose of a location for the improvements, as lands might be granted for the location of a highway or other public improvement. On the other hand, it was the clear intention of the *United States* and of this state that the lands granted should be sold by this state, and the proceeds of such sale should be used in making the improvements contemplated. The power of sale on the part of the state was absolute, and, if exercised without any reservation, none can be implied from the mere fact that the purpose of the grant was to aid in making improvements in the navigation of the Fox river.

If we understand the argument of the learned counsel for the appellant, he does not rely upon the mere fact that the lands were granted to the state for the purpose of aiding in making the improvement, but he insists that the legislature of the state had, previous to the date of the grant to Jonathan Lincoln, passed a law making such reservation in all grants thereafter made. It may be admitted that the legislature might have passed an act in general terms reserving to the state, its grantees or agents, the right to flood any land thereafter granted by the state to any person or persons, by making improvements in the Fox and Wisconsin rivers, without making compensation for such flooding, and that such act would create a reservation of such right, notwithstanding the absolute terms of the grant itself. The only act of the legislature upon which the learned counsel relies as creating such reservation, is the act of August, 1848, which provides for the construction of improvements contemplated by the act of Congress in granting lands to the state for the improvement of the navigation of the Fox and Wisconsin rivers in this state. And secs. 15 and 16 of said act are the only ones on which the learned counsel relies as creating such reservation. See Laws of 1848, p. 58. Secs. 15 and 16 of said act read as follows:

"Sec. 15. In the construction of such improvements the said board shall have power to enter on, to take possession of, and use all lands, waters, and materials the appropriation of which for the use of such works of improvement shall in their judgment be necessary.

"Sec. 16. When any lands, waters, or materials appropriated by the board to the use of said improvements *shall belong to the state*, such lands, waters, or materials, and so much of the adjoining lands, waters, or materials as may be valuable for hydraulic or commercial purposes, shall be absolutely reserved to the state; and whenever a water-power shall be created by reason of any dam erected or other improvements made on any of said rivers, such water-power shall belong to the state, subject to future action of the legislature."

Among other things, this act provided for the creation of a "board of public works," with power to make improvements in said rivers. It also provided for a sale of the lands granted by Congress to the state for the purpose of aiding in making such improvements, fixing a minimum price at which the lands might be sold; also allowing pre-emption rights to settlers on said lands; and sec. 43 of the act provided that "whenever sales of any of said lands shall be made, either at public or private sale, in conformity with the provisions of this act, it shall be the duty of the governor of the state to grant to the purchaser, upon the certificate of the register, a patent for the lands so sold, which patent shall be under the seal of the state, and countersigned by the secretary of state, *and shall vest* in the purchaser, his heirs and assigns, an absolute estate in fee simple." Secs. 17, 18, 19, and 20 of said act provide for making compensation to those whose lands, materials, or waters are taken by the board of public works without their consent. This act was in force when the lands in question were granted to the said Lincoln, in March, 1850.

It is alleged in the petition in this case that the "board of public works," for the purpose of improving the navigation of Fox river, erected the dam in question, which causes the overflow of plaintiff's lands, in 1852. The answer to the petition alleges "that the dam referred to in said petition was erected for the purposes set forth in said petition, at the place mentioned and described in said petition; but says that the dam across that part of said Fox river leading from the waters of Little Lake Butte des Morts to Green Bay, described in said petition, was constructed and fully completed prior to 1850, and maintained by parties other than the defendant herein." Under the pleadings and evidence in this case it must be held that at the time the state granted these lands to the said Lincoln, neither the state nor the "board of public works" had in any way or manner entered upon, taken possession of, or used the lands in question for the purposes of such improvement. The *United States* does not, therefore, by its answer or proofs, bring itself within the language of said secs. 15 and 16 of said act of 1848.

It seems to us that said sec. 16 can only admit of one construction, so far as applicable to the question involved in this case. The language is: "When any lands," etc., "appropriated," etc., "shall belong to the state," etc. This language clearly refers to the ownership of the state at the time of the appropriation, and not to an ownership at any previous date, and of which ownership the state had lawfully divested itself previous to the time of the taking by the board of public works. If the construction contended for by the learned counsel for the appellant should be given to the act, it would subject all lands which the state had ever owned to this right of overflow by the works of said improvement without compensation, whether they were lands granted to the state to aid in the construction of such works, or for any other purpose, such as school lands. Had the legislature intended that the lands granted to the state to aid in the improvement should always be subject to be taken for that purpose without making compensation to the grantee of the state, it seems to us it would have used more definite language; and it would not have declared, as it did in sec. 43 of the act, that the grant of the state of any such lands "should vest in the grantee, his heirs and assigns, an absolute estate in fee simple."

It would probably have been a wise thing on the part of the state if in its conveyances of these lands bordering on the waters of Lake Winnebago and the Fox river and its tributaries it had reserved the right to overflow the same as far as necessary by the works of improvement, and it seems that in all grants made after 1850 such a reservation was in fact made.

We think the motion for a nonsuit was properly overruled, as well as the motion to instruct the jury as requested by the appellant. There being no other matter assigned as error, the judgment of the circuit court must be affirmed.

By the Court.— The judgment of the circuit court is affirmed.

FISHER, Respondent, vs. SCHURI and others, Appellants.

January 11 — January 29, 1889.

Pleading: Redundant matter: Appealable order: Action, tort or contract? Conspiracy: Joinder of causes of action: Motion to make definite and certain.

1. An order refusing to strike certain matter from a complaint as redundant or irrelevant is not appealable.
2. A complaint sets forth the employment of the plaintiff as a minister, under a written contract, by the officers of an unincorporated religious society, his salary. perquisites, etc., and alleges that the members of the society were satisfied with him and desired his continuance as such minister, but that the defendants (two of whom were trustees of the society, who signed the contract of employment and had control of the temporal affairs of the church), wrongfully *conspiring* and contriving together to injure the plaintiff and drive him from his position as such minister, did various

acts, which are fully set forth. Then follows a statement of plaintiff's damages by reason of such acts. *Held,* on motion to make more definite and certain, that the complaint is in tort for a conspiracy, and states but one cause of action.

APPEAL from the County Court of *Winnebago* County. The facts will sufficiently appear from the opinion.

The cause was submitted for the appellants on the brief of *Weisbrod, Harshaw & Nevitt,* and for the respondent on briefs by *Gary & Forward.*

ORTON, J. The defendants moved that the amended complaint be made more definite and certain as to which cause of action stated therein the plaintiff intends to rely on, or which they are bound to answer, and to strike out from said complaint the allegations in respect to the defendants having published in a newspaper in the city of Oshkosh a public notice to the members of said congregation not to pay the plaintiff their subscription to the funds and expenses to pay him his salary as the minister thereof, and the allegations of his damages on account thereof. The motion was denied, and the defendants appealed from said order.

That part of the order refusing to strike out of the amended complaint any matter as redundant or irrelevant is not appealable. *State ex rel. G. B. & M. R. Co. v. Jennings,* 56 Wis. 113; *Kewaunee Co. v. Decker,* 28 Wis. 669; *Noonan v. Orton,* 30 Wis. 609; *Freeman v. Engelmann Transp. Co.* 36 Wis. 571; *Carpenter v. Reynolds,* 58 Wis. 666.

The only respect in which the amended complaint is claimed to be indefinite and uncertain is "that it sets forth several causes of action in the same count, and likewise sets forth, or purports to set forth, causes of action against [the defendants] individually, and others against them as trustees." These grounds for the motion do not seem to imply

any indefiniteness or uncertainty. They seem to show that
the defendants at least assume to understand the complaint,
and they are certain that it sets forth several causes of action in the same count, and that some are against them individually and others against them as trustees. It is not
perceived how the complaint in these respects could be
made more definite and certain to the defendants, as they
understand it. These grounds would seem to be appropriate
to a demurrer. But we are disposed to think that the
learned counsel of the appellants do not understand the
complaint, and that to them at least it is indefinite and uncertain. In this view alone would it seem proper to consider the grounds of the motion.

The complaint is long, but perhaps no longer than necessary to set forth the material facts. The allegations are,
in substance, as follows:

(1) The plaintiff is an ordained minister of the Evangelical Reformed Church, and one of that kind of churches was
established at Oshkosh as a voluntary and unincorporated
society or association, and owned a church building and
parsonage, and had officers duly elected, and conducted
divine worship according to the rules of said church, under
the name of the Helvetia Evangelical Reformed Church.

(2) The president, secretary, and two trustees of said
church employed the plaintiff to be the settled minister
thereof, and entered into a written agreement with him to
the effect that he should preach to said church and congregation, and administer the rites thereof, for ten years from
December 1, 1882, to December 1, 1892, and have the use
of the parsonage, at a salary of $500 a year, and enjoy all
the emoluments appertaining to a minister of said church;
the salary to be raised by subscription, and to be increased
from time to time proportionably to the increase of the
membership of said church. That agreement is set out.
The plaintiff entered upon his employment, and fulfilled all

of his duties and his part of the contract, and the church increased in membership, and the trustees performed their part of the contract, and there was entire harmony and prosperity for two years, and the plaintiff received his perquisites for baptisms, confirmations, marriages, and funerals and other outside services as such minister of at least $500 per year.

(3) The members and congregation were satisfied and friendly with him, and desired his continuance in his ministry to them, and he was willing, offered, and desired to do so.

(4) The defendants *Conrad Schuri* and *J. M. Beglinger* were the trustees who signed said agreement and had control of the temporal affairs of the church; and the defendant *John Ryf* was a member of the church, and approved and consented to the same. These defendants, disregarding their duty and obligations to the plaintiff, " unlawfully, maliciously, and without any just cause or good reason, *conspiring, conniving,* and *contriving* to injure the plaintiff, and to break up his relations with the congregation as their minister, and to drive him from his position as minister of said congregation, and to deprive him of the support of said congregation, and to induce said congregation to refuse to support the plaintiff and to pay him the salary and the fees aforesaid, to which he is entitled under said contract, in the year 1885," etc. Then follows what the defendants did to injure the plaintiff. They influenced and prejudiced the members and congregation against him, so that they refused to call upon him to perform any services as their minister, and called upon other ministers for that purpose for which his customary fees were paid; and in June, 1885, the defendants, "*maliciously conspiring, conniving* and *contriving* together to injure the plaintiff, and drive him from his position as minister," and to break up the congregation and society, and thereby to prevent him

from receiving his salary and fees, and prevent them from paying his salary, and prevent him and the congregation from having access to and the use of said church building, "*unlawfully, maliciously,* and with *force,* for the purposes aforesaid, fastened and nailed up the doors and windows of said church building, and secured the same so that the plaintiff and said congregation were excluded therefrom, and continued to keep said building so closed, and refused to open the same, and have thereby prevented the plaintiff from performing his contract and having and receiving his fees as aforesaid."

(5) The defendants, after so preventing the plaintiff from performing religious services, and after so disorganizing, breaking up, and scattering said church and congregation, caused to be published in a newspaper in Oshkosh a public notice to the members of said congregation not to pay any part of their unpaid subscriptions for the funds and expenses of said society to the plaintiff, and advised and induced them not to do so.

(6) These several acts and influences of the defendants caused the plaintiff to be injured in the estimation of other religious societies and other churches of the same denomination, of which there are a large number in the United States. The plaintiff has been thereby damaged in the loss of his salary of $5,000; and in the loss of his fees and perquisites of $5,000; in his inability to get employment elsewhere, $6,000; and in his personal injury, anxiety of mind, reproach, contempt, ridicule, and disgrace, occasioned thereby, $4,000; and to his general damage of $20,000.

I have stated the substance of the complaint more at length that the scheme and theory of it may readily appear. The allegations in respect to the plaintiff's profession and situation and attitude towards the church and congregation and towards the defendants, and to his employment, salary, and perquisites, and to the written contract, as also to the official character of two of the defendants, as trustees, having control of the church building and property, are all merely matters of inducement before the main charges of injury. Then follows in strong and sufficient language the charge of *conspiracy* and malicious intent, and the acts done in carrying out the conspiracy, and the special and general damages. It is a very clear and easily understood complaint in tort for *conspiracy*, and stating but one cause of action. It will be found to be according to the usual form of the books. The defendant *Ryf*, who did not sign the contract of employment, assented to it, and was one of the conspirators. The complaint could not be made more definite and certain than it is.

By the Court.— The order of the county court is affirmed, and the cause remanded for further proceedings according to law.

SMITH, Respondent, vs. MORGAN and others, Appellants.

January 11 — January 29, 1889.

Logs and timber: Wrongful cutting: Measure of damages: Interest:
Offer of judgment: Costs.

1. Where, in an action for the wrongful cutting of timber, the plaintiff recovers as damages, under sec. 4269, R. S., the highest market value of such timber while in the possession of the defendants, he is not entitled to recover interest on such value.

2. In an action for the wrongful cutting of timber an offer of judgment under sec. 4269, R. S., is only available to the defendant to prevent further costs, in cases where "the jury find such cutting was by mistake." An offer of judgment under that section is not available under sec. 2789.

APPEAL from the Circuit Court for *Winnebago* County.

The following statement of the case was prepared by Mr. Justice CASSODAY:

This action was commenced January 8, 1884, and is for

damages for wrongfully cutting timber on lands of which the title was at the time in the state, but which was subsequently, and before the commencement of this action, acquired by the plaintiff. On the former appeal it was held, in effect, that the plaintiff was entitled to recover the highest market value of the logs so cut or the lumber made therefrom. *Smith v. Morgan,* 68 Wis. 358. Upon the cause being reversed and remanded, the plaintiff amended his complaint; whereupon the defendants admitted a certain amount of such cutting, but alleged it to have been done in good faith; served an affidavit on the plaintiff's attorneys, January 11, 1888, that the same was done by mistake, and offered to allow judgment to be taken therein against them for $1,000 and costs, which the plaintiff refused to accept.

Upon the trial of the cause the jury returned a special verdict, to the effect that (1) the defendants cut from said lands 68,924 feet of logs, board measure; (2) of which the stumpage value was $3 per 1,000 feet; (3) and the highest market value at Oshkosh, $11 per 1,000 feet; (4) and the highest market value per 1,000 feet of the lumber manufactured from said logs, while it remained in the possession of the defendants *R. T.* and *John R. Morgan,* was $14 per 1,000 feet; (5) that the said *Morgans* manufactured into lumber, of said logs, 62,032 feet, board measure. Upon the motion of the plaintiff's attorneys, judgment was ordered upon said special verdict to the effect that the plaintiff have and recover of the said defendants for said 62,032 feet of lumber at $14 per 1,000 feet, amounting to $868.44; also for 6,892 feet of logs at $11 per 1,000 feet, amounting to $75.81; *also for interest on said two sums,* respectively, from January 1, 1884, amounting to $310.18,— amounting, in all, to $1,244.43 damages; and the further sum of $310.58, costs and disbursements, making a total of $1,555.01. The defendants appeal from that part of said judgment which adjudges to the plaintiff interest to the amount of $310.18

on the damages found by the jury; and also from that part which allows costs to the plaintiff after January 11, 1888; and from that part which denies costs to the defendants after said last-mentioned date.

For the appellants there was a brief by *Jackson & Thompson*, and oral argument by *H. B. Jackson*.

For the respondent there was a brief by *Cate, Jones & Sanborn*, and oral argument by *D. Lloyd Jones.* They argued, among other things, that though sec. 4269, R. S., is in the nature of a penal statute, it is *not* a penal statute and does not inflict a penalty. It simply fixes a statutory rule of damages. *Arpin v. Burch*, 68 Wis. 619; *Koons v. C. & N. W. R. Co.* 23 Iowa, 493. This rule of damages has been applied to trespasses committed before its enactment, which could not be done if the statute were penal. *Brewster v. Carmichael*, 39 Wis. 456; *Webster v. Moe*, 35 id. 75. The same rule should apply as in an action for money had and received. In such case the plaintiff would be clearly entitled to interest. That interest is recoverable as damages in tort actions, see *Bonesteel v. Orvis*, 22 Wis. 525; *Arpin v. Burch*, 68 id. 619; *Chapman v. C. & N. W. R. Co.* 26 id. 295. Even if the statute inflicts a penalty, interest should be allowed after breach. *Clark v. Wilkinson*, 59 Wis. 543; Field on Damages, sec. 546, and note; *Wyman v. Robinson*, 73 Me. 384.

CASSODAY, J. The special verdict included the highest market value of the logs and lumber before the trial and while in the possession of the defendants. It did not include any interest on such value to the time of the rendition of the verdict. The trial court, however, after the rendition of such verdict, increased the amount of damages by adding to the amount of the verdict $310.18 as interest upon such highest market value to the time of such verdict. This is the principal error assigned. Prior to the statutes authorizing such damages, it was held by this court, in effect, that in an action by the land-owner to recover such damages he was limited to the highest market value of the stumpage at any time between the cutting and the commencement of the action. *Single v. Schneider*, 24 Wis. 299; *S. C.* 30 Wis. 570; *Webster v. Moe*, 35 Wis. 75; 3 Suth. Dam. 375, and cases cited in the note, 376–379. To such value interest might have been added. *Ingram v. Rankin*, 47 Wis. 406. Here the value of such stumpage was found to be only three dollars per thousand feet. This being so, under the common-law rule mentioned the plaintiff's damages for such cutting and conversion would have been limited to a little over $200. Under the statute, however, the plaintiff rightfully recovered a verdict for "the highest market value of such logs, timber, or lumber, in whatsoever place, shape, or condition, manufactured or unmanufactured, the same" may "have been, at any time before the trial, while in possession of the" defendants, which "highest market value," as found by the jury, amounted in the aggregate to $944.25. Of this amount some $700 must have been included by reason of the moneys expended and the labor performed in, about, and upon the timber by the defendants, but which they forfeited by reason of such wrongful cutting. Sec. 4269, R. S. To that extent, then, this statute is, in its nature, penal. *Wright v. E. E. Bolles Wooden Ware Co.* 50 Wis. 170; *Cotter v. Plumer*, 72 Wis. 479; *Fleming v. Sherry*, 72 Wis. 503. It is therefore to be strictly construed. This, in effect, has often been held. Being penal in its nature, and the damages found by the jury being largely such as were recoverable only by virtue of the statute, the plaintiff is necessarily confined to the rights thus given by the statute. The measure of damages thus given by statute cannot properly be extended beyond the letter of the statute. *Thomas v. Weed*, 14 Johns. 255. To hold that the plaintiff may not only recover such en-

larged damages, but that he may, in addition, also recover
other damages recoverable at common law, would be to reverse the ordinary rule of construing such statutes, and by
mere implication to extend the rights thus expressly given,
not only beyond the language of the statute, but also beyond the scope and purpose of the statute. We cannot
sanction such a departure.

Error is assigned because the court allowed the plaintiff
for costs after the offer of the defendants to allow judgment
for the amount stated. The plaintiff did not accept such
offer as prescribed in sec. 4269, R. S. This being so, the
affidavit of the defendants was necessarily, by the express
language of the statute, to be "deemed traversed." *Ibid.*
Upon the issue so formed the jury found in favor of the
plaintiff, "and also the true value of such logs, timber, or
lumber when so cut, as well as their highest market value,"
as therein provided. *Ibid.* Under that section of the statute, such offer to allow judgment is only available to the
defendant to prevent further costs in cases where "the *jury
find such cutting was by mistake, and* the sum, exclusive of
costs, for which judgment was so offered was not less than
the value of" the aggregate amount of the items therein
mentioned. Sec. 4269, R. S. Since the jury did not find
that such cutting was by mistake, it is manifest that such
offer was not available to prevent costs under that section.
But the offer of the defendants was made under that section, and that section specifically prescribes the method of
making such offer in a case like this, and hence the provisions of that section must prevail as to all matters and questions growing out of the subject matter of the chapter in
which it is found. *Subd. 14, sec. 4972, R. S. *Smith v. Todd*,
55 Wis. 464; *Carpenter v. Murphey*, 57 Wis. 546; *Druse v.
Horter*, 57 Wis. 646. The defendants, having sought to
prevent further costs by making an offer to allow judgment
as prescribed in sec. 4269, and failed, cannot now avail them-

selves of the benefit of the general provision of the statutes
on that subject found in sec. 2789, R. S.

By the Court. — That portion of the judgment of the circuit court allowing to the plaintiff $310.18 for interest, as
damages in addition to the findings of the jury, is reversed;
and the other portions of the judgment appealed from are
affirmed; and the cause is remanded for further proceedings according to law. The costs and disbursements in this
court are allowed in favor of the defendants, and against
the plaintiff.

HUGHES, Appellant, vs. THE CITY OF FOND DU LAC, Respondent.

January 11 — January 29, 1889.

*Municipal corporations: Defective streets: Nuisance created by city:
Notice of injury: Reasonable time: Charter construed.*

A provision in a city charter that no action against the city for injuries sustained by reason of any defect in any street shall be maintained unless written notice of the injury was given to the proper
officers within five days of the occurrence thereof, does not apply
where the injury was caused by a nuisance created by the positive
acts of the city's agents, such as leaving a large wooden roller in
the street. [*Quære*, whether the provision requiring notice to be
given within *five days* is not invalid, as fixing a time unreasonably
short.]

APPEAL from the County Court of *Winnebago* County.
The case is sufficiently stated in the opinion.

For the appellant there was a brief by *C. S. Matteson*,
attorney, and *Henry J. Gerpheide*, of counsel, and oral
argument by *Mr. Gerpheide.*

For the respondent the cause was submitted on the brief
of *P. H. Martin.* To the point that the time fixed within
which notice should be given was reasonable, he cited *Nich-*

olas v. Minneapolis, 30 Minn. 546. The provision of the Fond du Lac charter is taken from the Minneapolis charter construed in that case.

Cole, C. J. It appears from the complaint that while the plaintiff was driving with a horse and carriage, in the evening, along one of the public streets of the defendant city, his horse was frightened at a large wooden roller in the street, became unmanageable, partially overturned the carriage, and the plaintiff was thrown out upon the ground with violence, and greatly injured. This action is brought to recover damages for such injury. A demurrer to the complaint was sustained by the trial court on the ground that it states no cause of action. There is a section of the city charter which, as amended, provides that no action against the city on account of an injury received or damage sustained by means of any defect in the condition of any street shall be maintained unless the action shall be commenced within one year from the happening of the injury, nor unless notice in writing, signed by the party injured, shall have been given to the sidewalk superintendent of the city, or one of the aldermen of the ward in which such injury shall have occurred, within *five days* of the occurrence of such injury. Sec. 5, ch. 299, Laws of 1885. The complaint shows that within thirty days after the happening of the accident a written notice was given to the mayor and common council, stating the facts as to how and where the injury was sustained; but there is no averment that the five days notice was given, which is required by sec. 5, ch. 299. The complaint was doubtless held defective because it did not allege that such notice was given. The counsel for the defendant insists that the complaint is fatally defective for that reason, because, he says, the liability of the city is wholly statutory, and it was incumbent upon the plaintiff to show that he had complied with the requirements of the charter in that regard in order to maintain the action. In several actions against towns and cities for injuries suffered by reason of a defective highway or sidewalk, the giving of the prescribed notice has been held to be in the nature of a condition precedent to the right to sue for the damages. *Susenguth v. Runtoul*, 48 Wis. 334; *Benware v. Pine Valley*, 53 Wis. 527; *Wentworth v. Summit*, 60 Wis. 281. I should have great doubt about the validity of the provision requiring the notice to be *given within five days of the injury*, even if the liability of the city in the case was wholly statutory. The time fixed is unreasonably short, and in many cases could not be complied with. The injured person might be unconscious, or so seriously hurt that he could not state " the place where, and the time when, such injury was received, and the nature of the same," within that period; so that the remedy given is coupled with an impossible condition. Such a provision is unreasonable and unjust, and fairly obnoxious to all the objections taken to the enactments in *Durkee v. Janesville*, 28 Wis. 464, and *Hincks v. Milwaukee*, 46 Wis. 559. It is an arbitrary and unreasonable provision, which professes to give a remedy for an injury, but annexes to it a condition which in many cases cannot be complied with because the time fixed for serving the notice is so short.

But the facts in this case show that the city created a nuisance in the public street, and it is liable therefor upon the same principles as an individual would be for a similar act. It is a fair inference from the complaint that the roller — which was an unsightly object, naturally calculated to frighten horses — was put and left in the street by the agents and servants of the city. It is alleged that the roller belonged to the city, was used by it for the purpose of making its streets more compact, and was carelessly left where it obstructed a public street. At common law any act or obstruction which unnecessarily incommodes or impedes the lawful use of a highway by the public is a nuisance. Angell on Highw. sec. 223. In this case the city itself created the nuisance, as much as though it had dug a ditch in the street, or placed a pile of stone or any other obstruction in the highway, which made it dangerous to travelers; and why should it be exempted from liability to a party injured, on general principles? The injury was not caused by an act of non-feasance, but by malfeasance,— doing an act which was wholly wrongful. The injury was produced by its positive act as much as by its neglect. A municipal corporation is no more exempt from liability in case it creates a nuisance, either public or private, than an individual. SELDEN, J., in *Weet v. Trustees*, 16 N. Y. 161, 172. That was an action brought for an injury in falling into a hole beneath a platform which constituted an extension of the sidewalk. The court, after a most able and exhaustive discussion of the authorities, rested the liability of the village upon the ground that it constructed the platform in such a manner as to constitute it a public nuisance. Among other cases referred to was the case of *Mayor v. Furze*, 3 Hill, 612, and it was commented on as follows: "This case illustrates another distinction which is directly applicable to the case under consideration. The decision therein is not put exclusively upon the ground of the liability of the corporation for a mere non-feasance. The facts of the case show that the corporation had created a nuisance. They constructed the sewers, the obstruction of which produced the overflow upon the plaintiff's premises. The injury was produced as much by their positive act as by their neglect. Under such circumstances, a corporation, whatever may be its nature, is liable to the same extent and upon the same principles as an individual would be for a similar injury." And finally the court closes the opinion by saying that "it follows from the preceding reasoning that, if we regard the injury to the plaintiff as the result of mere neglect to keep the highways of the village in repair, the defendants would be responsible in this action for such neglect, upon the ground that their acceptance of the franchise granted by their charter raised an implied undertaking or contract on their part to perform that duty, which, upon the principles referred to, inures to the benefit of every individual interested in such performance. But it is unnecessary to revert to this doctrine to establish the responsibility of the defendants in this cause, for the reason that the injury to the plaintiff was not the result of a mere non-feasance on the part of the defendants, but was produced by their construction of the platform in question in such a manner as to constitute it a public nuisance."

The case before us comes fully within the doctrine of these authorities, which are applicable to the facts stated in the complaint; therefore sec. 5, ch. 299, Laws of 1885, does not apply. See, also, *Little v. Madison,* 42 Wis. 643; *Pettigrew v. Evansville,* 25 Wis. 223; *Weightman v. Washington,* 1 Black, 39; *Nebraska City v. Campbell,* 2 Black, 590; *Stetson v. Faxon,* 19 Pick. 147; *Comm. v. Rush,* 14 Pa. St. 186; Whart. Neg. §§ 262–264; Cooley on Const. Lim. 246 *et seq.*

It follows from these views that the order of the county court sustaining the demurrer to the complaint was erroneous and must be reversed.

By the Court.— Order reversed, and cause remanded for further proceedings.

BARRETT, Appellant, vs. STRADL, Respondent.

January 12 — January 29, 1889.

Ejectment: Recovery for improvements: Title under holder of life es-
tate: Adverse possession as against remainder-man: Presumption
that possession continues to be adverse: Improvements made after
notice of plaintiff's claim.

1. One entering into possession of land under a conveyance from the
holder of a life estate only, cannot hold adversely to the remainder-man during the continuance of the life estate.

2. But where the conveyance from the tenant for life purports to convey an estate in fee, and the grantor intended to convey the fee,
and the grantee supposed he was getting the fee, the possession of
the person entering under such conveyance becomes adverse to the
remainder-man immediately upon the death of such life tenant.

3. Findings that during a certain time a person had the exclusive possession of land, that he claimed to be the sole owner of the premises under and by virtue of a deed thereof to him, and that he
asserted his title founded on said deed in good faith, are *held*
equivalent to a finding that he was in possession holding adversely
under color of title asserted in good faith.

4. If the defendant in ejectment was at one time in possession of the
land, holding adversely to the plaintiff under color of title asserted
in good faith, and his possession continued down to the commencement of the action, it will be presumed to have continued to be
adverse, in the absence of any evidence showing a change in the
character of the possession in that respect.

5. Where the defendant in ejectment entered upon the possession of
the premises under color of title asserted in good faith, and has
held adversely to the plaintiff, he is entitled (under sec. 3096, R. S.)
to recover for improvements made by him, even though they were
made after he had notice of the plaintiff's claim.

APPEAL from the Circuit Court for *Manitowoc* County.
The following statement of the case was prepared by
Mr. Justice TAYLOR as a part of the opinion:

The appellant brought an action of ejectment in the circuit court to recover the undivided three-fifths of the W. ½
of the S. E. ¼ of section 5, town 20, range 22, in Manitowoc

county. The respondent answered the statute of limitations of ten years by adverse possession by himself and his grantors as a defense. He also set up a claim for improvements made on said lands by him during his adverse possession thereof; also a claim for the taxes paid by him on said lands during such possession.

On the trial of the action there was a special verdict, finding as follows: (1) That the plaintiff was, at the commencement of the action, the owner in fee of an undivided two-fifths of the lands described in the complaint. (2) That the plaintiff was entitled to the possession of such undivided two-fifths of said land. (3) That at the commencement of said action the defendant unlawfully withheld the possession of said two-fifths of said premises from the plaintiff. (4) Finds the value of the use of the premises described in the complaint, with all the improvements thereon, from the 5th of February, 1885, to the present time, $80 per year. (5) Finds the value of the use of said premises, as they were on the 5th of February, 1885, $30 per year. (6) That the value of the use of said premises, excluding the value of any permanent and valuable improvements made by the defendant and his grantor, Wenzel Kadlic, was $20 per year. (7) That the premises are worth at the present time $1,200 more than they would have been without the improvements made thereon by the defendant between the 5th of February, 1885, and the 20th of December, 1886. (8) Finds that the taxes paid on said lands in 1886 and 1887 were $56.71. The ninth finding is as follows: "Did the defendant in fact enter and take possession of the premises described in the complaint, under his deed from Wenzel Kadlic, claiming to be the sole and exclusive owner in fee of said premises, and asserting his said ownership under said deed in good faith?" This question was answered by the court in the affirmative. "(10) When did the defendant first have actual knowledge that the premises in ques-

tion belonged to the heirs of Catherine Barrett? *Answer.*
When the circuit court decided to that effect in this action.
(11) When did the defendant first have good reason to believe that the premises in question belonged to the heirs of
Catherine Barrett? *A.* At the county court in November,
1886. (12) Was the defendant in the sole and exclusive
possession of said premises from February 5, 1885, to the
commencement of this action on the 20th of December,
1886? *A.* (By consent) Yes. (13) Did the defendant during the time specified in the twelfth question claim to be
the sole and exclusive owner in fee of said premises under
and by virtue of his deed from Wenzel Kadlic? *A.* Yes.
(14) Did the defendant during the time specified in the
twelfth question assert his title founded on the deed from
Wenzel Kadlic to him, in good faith? *A.* Yes. (15) Did
the defendant subsequently to February 5, 1885, ever notify
the plaintiff that he disputed or denied plaintiff's title? *A.*
(By the court) No."

The plaintiff requested the court to submit to the jury
the following question: "During the period from February 5, 1885, until December 20, 1886, did the defendant
know, while making the improvements made by him during
that time, that his title to the premises in question was
contested by plaintiff claiming a superior title to them?"
The court refused the request, and the plaintiff excepted.

Upon the special verdict the defendant moved the court
to order judgment as follows, viz.: "That, together with
the judgment in plaintiff's favor for the recovery of an undivided two-fifths share, part, or interest of and in the
premises described in the amended complaint, and two fifths
of the rents and profits of said premises since February 5,
1885, as found by the jury, and as may be directed by the
court, with plaintiff's costs for the trial of that issue, the
further provision or judgment that the defendant do recover
of and from the plaintiff a two-fifths share or part of the

taxes specified in said verdict, together with two fifths of the $1,200 found by the jury as the value of defendant's improvements, besides all costs incurred by the defendant upon the trial of the issue as to taxes and improvements; that plaintiff's recovery for rents and profits and costs be set off against defendant's recovery for taxes, improvements, and costs; and that the defendant be adjudged to have a lien upon the plaintiff's interest in said premises to secure the payment of the balance that may be coming to the defendant for such taxes, improvements, and costs, over and above the offset aforesaid; and that said plaintiff pay to the defendant the amount of such balance, with interest at seven per cent. per annum from the date of said verdict, within three years, as a condition of execution for the possession of the premises recovered. The court entered judgment in accordance with the terms of said motion.

The plaintiff moved for judgment on the special verdict, rejecting the answers to the seventh and eighth questions, and also made a motion to set aside the special verdict and grant a new trial, " or to set aside so much of said verdict as, or that part thereof which, relates to the question of defendant's improvements, on the following grounds: (1) That the court erred in admitting evidence against plaintiff's objections; (2) that the court erred in rejecting evidence offered by plaintiff; (3) that the court erred in refusing to submit to the jury the questions, and each of them, which the plaintiff requested the court to submit in the special verdict; (4) that the court erred in directing the jury to find that the plaintiff was the owner and entitled to the possession of an undivided two-fifths of the premises, when the evidence showed he was the owner of an undivided three-fifths of said premises; (5) that the verdict of the jury is against the weight of evidence; (6) that the said verdict is contrary to law; (7) that the answer to question 11 of said verdict is inconsistent with the answer to question 14 thereof; (8) that the answer to question 10 of said verdict is unmeaning, and not responsive; (9) that the court erred in directing the answer to the ninth question, said answer being unsupported by any testimony in the case; (10) that the answer to question 7 is against the weight of evidence; (11) that the answer to question 10 is against the weight of evidence; (12) that the answer to question 11 is against the weight of evidence; (13) that the answers to questions 13 and 14 are, respectively, against the weight of evidence; (14) that the answers to questions 7, 10, and 11 show prejudice and partiality on the part of said jury in favor of the defendant."

It was stipulated by the parties to the action that the question of the defendant's claim for the payment of taxes and making improvements on the premises in question should be tried at the same time and by the same jury which was impaneled to try the right of the parties to the lands in question.

For the appellant the cause was submitted on briefs by *Ellis, Greene & Merrill.* They contended, *inter alia,* that the possession of land by a tenant for life cannot be adverse to the remainder-man; and if he sells and conveys to a third person by words purpórting to pass the absolute property, the possession of the purchaser is not, and cannot be, during the continuance of the life estate, adverse to the remainder-man. 1 Am. & Eng. Ency. Law, 237; R. S. sec. 2202; *Delancey v. Ganong,* 9 N. Y. 10; 1 Washb. on Real Prop. 126 (97), 118, 182; *Jackson v. Mancius,* 2 Wend. 357; *McCorry v. King's Heirs,* 39 Am. Dec. 165; Sedgw. & W. Trial of Title, 214; *Carpenter v. De Noon,* 29 Ohio St. 379; *Dennett v. Dennett,* 40 N. H. 505; *Keith v. Keith,* 80 Mo. 125; *Hanson v. Johnson,* 62 Md. 25; *Sands v. Hughes,* 53 N. Y. 287; *Pinckney v. Burrage,* 31 N. J. Law, 21; *Poor v. Larrabee,* 58 Me. 543; *Gernet v. Lynn,* 31 Pa. St. 94;

Henly v. Wilson, 77 N. C. 216; *Turman v. White's Heirs,*
14 B. Mon. 560; *Jones v. Billstein,* 28 Wis. 222; *Wiesner v.
Zaun,* 39 id. 189. Sec. 3096, R. S., gives claim for improvements to a person only "while holding adversely." Defendant's claim for improvements and taxes was, therefore,
limited to those made after February 5, 1885, when the life
estate of Patrick Barrett terminated. The same result follows from the doctrine that a tenant for life cannot charge
the remainder-man or reversioner with improvements or
ordinary taxes. 1 Washb. on Real Prop. 123 (95), 124 (96);
Phelan v. Boylan, 25 Wis. 679; *Curtis v. Fowler,* 33 N. W.
Rep. (Mich.), 804. The court also rightly ruled that there
could be no recovery for improvements made after the
commencement of the action, on December 20, 1886.
Welles v. Newson, 40 N. W. Rep. (Iowa), 105.

The verdict does not determine the issue whether the defendant held *adversely* between the dates above mentioned.
"Holding adversely" must mean something more than
holding "under color of title asserted in good faith," for
the statute requires it in addition. The phrase has a settled
legal meaning, viz., possession which, if continued the prescribed time, would give title under the statute of limitations. The essence of such possession is *hostility* to the
true owner. Sedgw. & W. Trial of Title, sec. 749; 1 Am.
& Eng. Ency. Law, 228; 3 Washb. on Real Prop. 134 (489);
Whiting v. Edmunds, 94 N. Y. 309; *Thompson v. Felton,*
54 Cal. 547; *Sparrow v. Hovey,* 44 Mich. 63; *Rung v.
Shoneberger,* 26 Am. Dec. 95; *Putnam Free School v.
Fischer,* 38 Me. 324; *Grant v. Fowler,* 39 N. H. 101; *Hodges
v. Eddy,* 38 Vt. 344. Possession begun in subserviency can
never become adverse to the true owner until surrender or
disclaimer, although a person has exclusive possession
under absolute conveyance from the first occupant, and
claims absolute title in good faith. *Whiting v. Edmunds,*
94 N. Y. 309; *Quinn v. Quinn,* 27 Wis. 168; *Wright v.*

Sperry, 25 id. 617; *Maxwell v. Hartman,* 50 id. 660; *Schwallback v. C., M. & St. P. R. Co.* 69 Wis. 298; *S. C.* 73 id. 137.

The defendant's possession after February 5, 1885, was not adverse, because he was then a tenant by sufferance. In New York it is held that if a person claiming under a tenant for life created by law holds over he is not a tenant by sufferance, but a trespasser, and his possession may be adverse. *Livingston v. Tanner,* 14 N. Y. 64; *Jackson v. Harsen,* 7 Cow. 323; *Sands v. Hughes,* 53 N. Y. 287. But, as appears in *Livingston v. Tanner,* a statute in that state makes such a person a trespasser. At common law he is a tenant by sufferance, and so under our statutes. Wood on Landl. & T. sec. 6; Platt on Leases, 97; *Miller v. Manwaring,* Cro. Car. 397; Com. Dig. ESTATE, 1; *Griffin v. Sheffield,* 38 Miss. 390; R. S. secs. 2180, 2183, 2186. Such a tenant cannot hold adversely until he surrenders possession or disclaims. Smith on Landl. & T. 31; Fawcett on Landl. & T. 49; *Austin v. Wilson,* 46 Iowa, 362; *Creigh's Heirs v. Henson,* 10 Grat. 231; *Whiting v. Edmunds,* 94 N. Y. 309.

One who has knowledge of an adverse claim cannot recover for improvements made after such knowledge. 1 Am. & Eng. Ency. Law, 294; *Witt v. Trustees,* 55 Wis. 376, 380; *Woodhull v. Rosenthal,* 61 N. Y. 382; *Gordon v. Tweedy,* 74 Ala. 232; Sedgw. & W. Trial of Title, sec. 694; *Green v. Biddle,* 8 Wheat. 1; *Canal Bank v. Hudson,* 111 U. S. 66; *Haslett v. Crain,* 85 Ill. 129; *Morrison v. Robinson,* 31 Pa. St. 456; *Hatchett v. Conner,* 30 Tex. 104; *Cole v. Johnson,* 53 Miss. 94; *Whitney v. Richardson,* 31 Vt. 300; *Henderson v. McPike,* 35 Mo. 255; *Bright v. Boyd,* 1 Story, 487; *Putnam v. Ritchie,* 6 Paige, 390; 2 Story's Eq. Jur. secs. 799a, 799b; *Dawson v. Grow,* 29 W. Va. 333; *Holmes v. McGee,* 64 Miss. 129; *Rennie v. Young,* 2 De G. & J. 136; *Dart v. Hercules,* 57 Ill. 446.

For the respondent there was a brief by *Nash & Nash,*

and oral argument by *L. J. Nash*. They argued, among other things, that the adverse possession referred to in sec. 3096, R. S., is not precisely the same thing as the adverse possession referred to in the statute of limitations; and one who holds actually a limited estate, but in good faith believes he is in possession under title in fee, may recover for improvements made during the continuance of the limited estate. *Plimpton v. Plimpton*, 12 Cush. 458; *Wales v. Coffin*, 100 Mass. 177; *Bedell v. Shaw*, 59 N. Y. 46. So, also, the "good faith" which will entitle one to protection as a *bona fide* purchaser of land without notice of another's rights, is not the same thing as the "good faith" which will entitle the same person to maintain his claim for improvements placed on the land. *Hadley v. Stewart*, 65 Wis. 481. It was error to rule as matter of law that defendant could recover nothing for improvements made after the commencement of the action. *Zwietusch v. Watkins*, 61 Wis. 615. The findings establish an adverse holding within the rule in *Stevens v. Brooks*, 24 Wis. 326; *Sydnor v. Palmer*, 29 id. 227; *Jackson v. Smith*, 13 Johns. 406; *Finn v. Wis. R. Land Co.* 72 Wis. 546.

TAYLOR, J. The material facts as to the title of the lands in question are as follows: Patrick Barrett, the father of plaintiff, became possessed of, and the owner in fee of, the the lands described in the complaint in 1856. In 1874 he conveyed by warranty deed to his son-in-law John Nash, and three days after the conveyance to Nash he (Nash) conveyed the same land to Catherine Barrett, the wife of said Patrick Barrett, and plaintiff's mother. The mother died intestate in June, 1875, while living on the premises, and without having conveyed the same. Patrick Barrett, the father and husband, also lived on the land with his wife, Catherine Barrett, at the time of her death, and continued to occupy said land after the death of his wife until

February 7, 1877, when he conveyed by warranty deed to one Wenzel Kadlic, for the consideration of $2,100, taking a mortgage in part payment for the sum of $1,600. Kadlic occupied the premises until the year 1880, and on April 19, 1880, he conveyed the land to the defendant by warranty deed, for the sum of $1,650, and as a part of this consideration the defendant assumed the payment of the $1,600 mortgage given by Kadlic to Barrett. Upon receiving this deed the defendant went into the immediate possession of the land, claiming to own the same, and he remained in possession up to the present time, making permanent improvements on the land, and has made payments on the $1,600 mortgage so as to reduce the amount of the same to $1,200 or less when this action was commenced. Patrick Barrett died on February 5, 1885.

These facts show that Patrick Barrett at the time he sold the premises to Kadlic had only a life estate in the same as a tenant by the curtesy of his wife, Catherine Barrett. There is no contention on the part of the defendant and respondent but that the plaintiff was the owner of the undivided two-fifths of the premises at the time this action was commenced, nor that the defendant withheld the possession from him as alleged in his complaint. The real controversy between the parties is whether the possession of the defendant was of such a character as to entitle him to recover for permanent improvements made by him on the lands, under sec. 3096, R. S. 1878. The part of the section applicable to the controversy in this case reads as follows: "In every case where a recovery shall be had of any land, on which the party in possession, or those under whom he claims, while holding adversely by color of title asserted in good faith, founded on descent or any written instrument, shall have made permanent and valuable improvements, or shall have paid taxes assessed, such party, for himself and for the benefit of those under whom he claims, shall be entitled to have from the plaintiff, his heirs or assigns, if he insist upon his recovery, the value of such improvements at the time the verdict or decision against him is given, and the amount paid for taxes, with interest from the date of the payment, to be assessed and recovered as hereinafter provided, and for the payment thereof shall have a lien on the real estate so recovered." Under this section the court below held that the defendant could only recover, in any event, for improvements made by the defendant on said lands, and for the taxes paid thereon, between the date of the death of Patrick Barrett and the date of the commencement of this action.

The principal contention of the learned counsel for the appellant is that the defendant cannot set up that he was in possession holding adversely by color of title asserted in good faith, because he entered and held by a conveyance from the grantee of Patrick Barrett, who had only a life estate in the premises, made during the life-time of said Barrett. The claim of the learned counsel is that one who enters upon the possession of real estate by deed from a person holding only a life estate in the premises cannot, so far, at least, as those entitled to the reversion are concerned, be in possession under claim of title, holding adversely to them, within the meaning of the statute. The learned circuit judge held with the counsel for the plaintiff so far as to hold that the possession of the defendant could not be adverse as against those owning the reversion during the life-time of the person owning the life estate, either for the purpose of establishing a title to the land by adverse possession, or for establishing a claim for improvements made on the land during the life of such person; and on the trial limited the defendant in his claim for improvements and taxes to such as were made and paid after the death of Barrett, the owner of the life estate, and before the commencement of plaintiff's action.

The contention of the learned counsel for the appellant, that a person entering into the possession of land under a conveyance from a person having only a life estate therein cannot hold adversely to the person entitled to the remainder, during the life-time of the person owning the life estate, so as to set the statute of limitations running against the remainder-man, is well settled by the authorities in other states, and is fully recognized by this court. See *Wiesner v. Zaun*, 39 Wis. 189. The reason of this rule is based upon the fact that the remainder-man cannot, during the life of the person holding the life estate, bring an action against the person in possession under such life tenant, to recover possession of the premises; and it would be absurd, therefore, to bar the right of the remainder-man by a possession which he has no right to object to, and to prevent which he has no remedy by action.

We think it is equally well settled that when a person enters under a deed from the person who holds the life estate, which on its face conveys an estate in fee, and when the grantor intends to convey the fee, and the grantee supposes he is getting a conveyance of the fee, the person entering under such deed holds *in fact* adversely to all the world, but he cannot avail himself of the rights of an adverse possession under the statute as against the remainder-man during the life of the owner of the life estate, but immediately upon the death of the person holding the life estate such possession, if continued, becomes adverse to the remainder-man. In the language of the court in *Sands v. Hughes*, 53 N. Y. 294: "There is no rule which prevents a hostile title being acquired, or an adverse possession being originated, during the running of an assessment lease (granting a limited estate), which possession would ripen into a title in twenty years after the end of the lease." See, also, *Christie v. Gage*, 71 N. Y. 193; *Millard v. McMullin*, 68 N. Y. 345; *Fleming v. Burnham*, 100 N. Y. 1, 8, 12; *Jackson v. Schoonmaker*, 4

Johns. 402; *Clarke v. Hughes*, 13 Barb. 147; *Miller v. Ew-ing*, 6 Cush. 34; *Jackson v. Harsen*, 7 Cow. 323, 327; *Ger-net v. Lynn*, 31 Pa. St. 94; 1 Am. & Eng. Ency. Law, 237, and cases cited in note 1, and 238, note 2. The rule estab-lished in the cases above cited was adopted by this court in the case of *Wiesner v. Zaun*, 39 Wis. 188, 203, 204. The reason of the latter rule is that immediately on the death of the life tenant the remainder-man may maintain an action to recover the possession from the person in possession claiming adversely.

The rule invoked by the counsel for the appellant, that a person entering under a tenant in possession, even though he take a deed in fee, cannot hold adversely to the landlord, does not apply to the case of a person entering under a deed from a person in possession owning a life estate. This rule only applies to the case where the person in possession holds the conventional relation of tenant to the owner of the fee, and not to the case of a person holding a life or other limited estate derived from some other source than from the owner of the reversion. On this point see *Saun-ders v. Hanes*, 44 N. Y. 365; *Christie v. Gage*, 71 N. Y. 193; *Jackson v. Harsen*, 7 Cow. 323, 326.

The above authorities clearly negative the claim made by the learned counsel for the appellant that the defendant produced no evidence on the trial which tended to show that he was in possession of the premises, holding them ad-versely to the claim of the plaintiff, at the time he made the improvements for which he claimed pay.

It is further urged by the learned counsel for the appellant that the special verdict is imperfect in not expressly find-ing that the defendant was in possession holding adversely to the plaintiff at the time the improvements were made. On the part of the respondent it is claimed that there was no request that such a finding should be included in the special verdict. It is also insisted that the findings num-

bered 12, 13, and 14 are equivalent to an express finding of
the fact that the defendant was in possession holding adversely to the claim of the plaintiff when the improvements
for which he was allowed were made. These findings, if
sustained by the evidence, show that during the time in
question the defendant had exclusive possession of the premises, that he claimed to be the sole owner thereof under and
by virtue of the deed to him from Kadlic, and that he asserted his title founded on said deed in good faith. We are
clearly of the opinion that these findings are equivalent to
an express finding that he was in possession, holding adversely under color of title asserted in good faith, when the
improvements were made.

The only other question bearing upon this point is
whether these findings are supported by the evidence. It
seems to us that the evidence is clear and undisputed that
the defendant, when he bought the land from Kadlic, believed he was getting a good title in fee to the premises.
He paid a full consideration for a perfect title in fee, and
he testifies that he paid a man to examine the title for him
previous to his purchase, and that such person reported to
him that the title was perfect, and the deed given and
taken was a deed purporting to convey the estate in fee.
After his purchase, and down to the death of the tenant for
life, his assertion of title was constant, as evidenced by his
possession and his continuing to pay upon the mortgage he
had assumed to pay as a part of the purchase price. There
certainly is no evidence which tends to show that he abandoned his claim of title under his deed from Kadlic, and all
the evidence shows that his possession continued under
claim and color of title under said deed after the death of
Barrett, the owner of the life estate. Such possession was
therefore adverse to the claim of the plaintiff after the
death of Barrett, by all the authorities.

It is further insisted by counsel for appellant that the

evidence shows conclusively that not long after the death
of Barrett the defendant became possessed of such facts regarding the defect of his own title and the validity of the
title of plaintiff, that he could not thereafter hold adversely
to the claim of the plaintiff, and consequently the improvements made were not recoverable under the statute. If the
evidence in the case shows, as it clearly does, that there
was a time when the defendant was in possession of the
land in question, holding adversely to the plaintiff under
color of title asserted in good faith, and such possession
continued down to the commencement of the action, it will
be presumed to have continued an adverse holding, unless
some evidence is produced which shows that the character
of the possession was changed to one recognizing the title
of the plaintiff. Whether there was such a change in the
relation of the defendant to plaintiff previous to his making
the improvements for which he recovered compensation
was a question of fact for the jury. After reading the evidence, we are not prepared to say that the claim of the
plaintiff is clearly established. The record would seem to
indicate that the case was tried on the part of the plaintiff
upon the theory that, if the defendant had at any time notice that the plaintiff claimed to own the land in controversy, no improvements made on the land after such notice
by the defendant could be made a charge against the plaintiff. This is clearly indicated by the request made by the
plaintiff to submit to the jury the following question: "During the period from February 5, 1885, until December 20,
1886, did the defendant know, while making the improvements made by him during that time, that his title to the
premises in question was contested or disputed by plaintiff
claiming a superior title to them?" This question was not
submitted, and under the decisions of this court it was an
immaterial question. See *Zwietusch v. Watkins*, 61 Wis. 615,
620. To defeat a claim for improvements under the statute,

when the evidence shows that the defendant entered under color of title asserted in good faith and has held adversely to the plaintiff, the evidence must show that the adverse possession is no longer asserted in good faith; that is, that the adverse possession has been interrupted in some way, either by abandonment or otherwise, so that the continued possession is no longer adverse to the real owner. That notice of claim of superior title by the plaintiff, or the commencement of an action to recover the premises, does not in itself interrupt the adverse possession of the defendant or change his attitude in regard to his adverse claim, is fully sustained by the decisions of courts outside of this state, as well as by the decisions of this court in the case of *Zwietusch v. Watkins*, 61 Wis. 615. *Workman v. Guthrie*, 29 Pa. St. 495, 513; *Moore v. Greene*, 19 How. 71; *Langford v. Poppe*, 56 Cal. 73, 76; *Jackson v. Haviland*, 13 Johns. 229, 234; *Kennedy's Heirs v. Reynolds*, 27 Ala. 364; *Ferguson v. Bartholomew*, 67 Mo. 212. Upon this point of notice of an adverse claim as affecting the good faith of the party claiming to hold adversely, see, also, *Warren v. Putnam*, 68 Wis. 481, 483; *Fleming v. Sherry*, 72 Wis. 503, 507, 508.

It is the entry upon the possession under the color of title asserted in good faith which creates the possession which entitles the possessor to recover for his improvements; and it is unnecessary that the person making the entry should believe that his title was superior to every other title to the property at the time of making his entry, in order to make his possession adverse; nor does a subsequently acquired knowledge that there is a better title in some other person necessarily change the nature of his possession from an adverse possession to a possession subordinate to the true title. In order to change the nature of the possession, there must not only be a knowledge that there is a better title, but there must be an express or implied yielding to such superior title. 1 Am. & Eng. Ency. Law, 277, 279, 292; *Doth-*

ard v. Denson, 72 Ala. 541, 545; *McCagg v. Heacock,* 42 Ill. 157; *Rawson v. Fox,* 65 Ill. 200; *Russell v. Mandell,* 73 Ill. 136, 137; *Smith v. Ferguson,* 91 Ill. 304, 311; *Stubblefield v. Borders,* 92 Ill. 279; *Ewing v. Burnet,* 11 Pet. 41; *Wright v. Mattison,* 18 How. 50, 57; *Pillow v. Roberts,* 13 How. 472. The cases cited by the learned counsel for the appellant, which hold that the defendant cannot recover for improvements made after he has knowledge of an adverse claim, were cases arising under statutes differing from ours. This is especially so with cases in Illinois. See 1 Starr & C. Ann. Stats. Ill. 994. The Illinois statute expressly provides that the defendant shall not recover for improvements made after notice of the claim of the real owner, and it also defines what shall constitute such notice. It must be admitted that what would constitute an adverse possession so as to set the statute running in favor of the possessor against the real owner, under sec. 4211, R. S., might not be sufficient to constitute such an adverse possession as would entitle the possessor to recover for improvements, under sec. 3096, R. S. Under sec. 4211, an entry under color of title, claiming title exclusive of any other right, is all that is required. Under sec. 3096, the possessor must hold by color of title asserted in good faith. It seems to us very clear, from all the evidence in the case, that the defendant took possession of said lands by color of title, and that he asserted that title in good faith, and that such claim and assertion of title was not abandoned by the defendant before this action was commenced, and, if we are to believe he verified his answer believing it to be true, he asserted such title after the commencement of this action.

It is urged by the counsel for the appellant that the evidence clearly shows that the defendant had, before making the improvements on the land for which he has recovered, abandoned his adverse holding and recognized the ownership and title of the plaintiff. The jury have found against this claim, and upon the whole evidence we cannot say the finding of the jury on this point is wholly unsupported by the evidence.

It is also urged that the jury assessed the improvements at a sum greatly in excess of their real value to the farm. We can only say that the verdict is sustained by the evidence introduced by the defendant, and, the circuit judge having refused to set aside the verdict on that ground, we do not feel authorized to reverse the judgment for that cause.

By the Court.— The judgment of the circuit court is affirmed.

MARSHALL, Appellant, vs. PINKHAM, Respondent.

January 12 — January 29, 1889.

Res adjudicata.

In an action to restrain the preparation and sale of an imitation of plaintiff's medicine, and for damages, the plaintiff's husband was joined with her, and she claimed to derive her right to the medicine from another as the inventor. *Held*, that a judgment against her in that action is conclusive and binding upon her in a subsequent suit by her alone in the same court against the same defendant, in which she alleges that she is the inventor, but in which the matters involved are otherwise the same.

APPEAL from the Circuit Court for *Fond du Lac* County. The facts are sufficiently stated in the opinion. The plaintiff appeals from a judgment dismissing the complaint with costs.

C. K. Pier, for the appellant.

For the respondent there was a brief by *Sutherland & Sutherland*, and oral argument by *D. D. Sutherland*.

ORTON, J. The complaint is in substance and in brief as follows: The plaintiff has for several years manufactured, advertised, and offered for sale, and sold at retail and whole-sale, a valuable medicine known as "Marshall's Rheumatic Oil," labeled and wrapped with her own proper label, device, and trade-mark, exclusively invented, originated, and adopted by her; that the merits of the medicine had become known and recognized, and it had a large sale in Wisconsin and elsewhere, and was a source of great profit to her; and that the defendant, well knowing the same, wrongfully prepared a compound inferior to hers, but in imitation of it, and offered for sale and sold the same in the territory aforesaid, put up in similar packages with an imitation of her said wrapper, label, and trade-mark, to deceive the public and injure her in the loss of sales and reputation of her superior article. The plaintiff prays for past damages and an injunction.

The substance, and in brief, of the answer is that the defendant made and makes a compound known and labeled as "Marshall's Rheumatic Oil," "Marshall's Rheumatic Liniment," "Marshall's Rheumatic Oil Liniment," and "Marshall's Liniment," and that he had a right to manufacture, label, and sell the same in that way, and that the plaintiff had not the exclusive right to manufacture, label, and sell the article she claims she manufactured and sold as her own original invention and discovery, nor the exclusive right to her wrapper, label, or trade-mark; and he denies that he has infringed the same. The answer further sets forth, substantially, that the plaintiff brought suit in the same court against the defendant for the same subject matter and with the same prayer for relief, being solely interested therein, and having nominally joined with her her husband, Charles H. Marshall, as plaintiff, which resulted in a similar judgment for the defendant, which was affirmed in this court as *Marshall v. Pinkham*, 52 Wis. 572, which is claimed as *res adjudicata*, or as an estoppel of this action.

The only difference in the form of the two actions is that in the former the plaintiff claimed the right to said medicine, derived from one Samuel Marshall, the original, inventor thereof; and in this, that she is the original inventor and discoverer thereof; and in the former she joined with her her husband, and in this she sues alone. In this case the findings of the court and conclusions of law are substantially like those in the former case, upon the evidence; and on examination of the evidence we think the findings are sustained by it in all particulars. Besides the findings in the case as an original one, the circuit court found that the subject matter and matters in controversy are the same as in the former case; and, as a conclusion of law, that the decision and judgment in the former case were upon the merits and points directly involved in this case, and are binding upon the parties to this action, and are final and *res adjudicata*. We have no question but that this finding and conclusion of law are sustained by the evidence and the record in the former suit. In the former case in this court the statement of facts is very full and complete, and very difficult on such a mass of evidence, and the opinion of Mr. Justice CASSODAY is very full, critical, and exhaustive of the facts and law, and this groundless and expensive controversy ought to have ended with that case. We shall not countenance such a needless and unlawful repetition and renewal of the same matters in controversy by incumbering the reports with an opinion in this case of greater length than absolutely necessary to identify it.

By the Court.— The judgment of the circuit court is affirmed.

STEPHENSON, Respondent, vs. DUNCAN, Appellant.

January 14— January 29, 1889.

Master and servant: Dangerous employment: Assumption of risk:
Promise by master to remove danger: Continuance in service after
reasonable time for performance.

1. The risk from an uncovered saw projecting over its frame and
partly across a narrow passage-way along which a servant in a
mill is obliged to go in the performance of his duties, being apparent, is assumed by the servant in accepting and remaining in
the service.

2. A servant having the right to abandon the service because it is dangerous may refrain for a reasonable time from so doing in consequence of assurances by the master that the danger shall be
removed, and will not be held to have thereby assumed the risk.
But if he continues in the service for a time longer than it is reasonable to allow for the performance of the master's promise he will
be deemed to have waived his objection and assumed the risk.

APPEAL from the Circuit Court for *Taylor* County.

Action to recover damages for personal injuries alleged
to have resulted from the defendant's negligence in not
providing a proper and safe covering for a saw in his shingle-mill, in which the plaintiff was employed, and in not
providing a safe and proper passage-way by such saw, and
in allowing the saw to project over its frame and partly
over the passage-way along which the plaintiff was obliged
to pass in the performance of his duties. Other allegations
of the complaint will sufficiently appear from the opinion.
The defendant appeals from an order overruling a general
demurrer to the complaint.

The cause was submitted for the appellant on the brief
of *Cate, Jones & Sanborn,* and for the respondent on that of
Schweppe & Foster.

To the point that the promise of a master to remedy a
defect of which he has been notified by a workman is binding upon him, and that if he fails to remedy it he is liable

for damages caused thereby after the expiration of the time within which it could have been remedied, counsel for respondent cited Shearm. & Redf. on Neg. 126, and note; *Parody v. C., M. & St. P. R. Co.* 15 Fed. Rep. 205; *Laning v. N. Y. C. R. Co.* 49 N. Y. 521; *Steen v. St. P. & D. R. Co.* 37 Minn. 310; *Greene v. M. & St. L. R. Co.* 31 id. 248.

COLE, C. J.   When the plaintiff entered upon his employment of operating the machinery and shingle-mill owned by the defendant, the unsafe condition of such shingle-mill, the fact that the saw was not covered, and that it projected over its frame partly across the narrow passage-way along which he was obliged to go in tightening and loosening the belt, were all matters presumably within his knowledge. The condition of the passage-way and the relation of the saw to it, if unsafe and dangerous, would be seen and comprehended by a person of common intelligence, and the plaintiff assumed the risk incident to the service when he undertook the employment.   Under such circumstances, the plaintiff could not maintain the action for the injury he sustained because the defendant failed to provide safe machinery and did not cover the saw with a substantial covering nor provide a safe passage-way in place of the defective one; for, as we have said, he must be held to have assumed the risk by accepting and remaining in the service with knowledge of the existing defects in the machinery. The rule of law upon this subject has been laid down by this court in the following language: "It is well settled that the master may conduct his business in his own way, although another method might be less hazardous; and the servant takes the risk of the more hazardous method as well, if he knows the danger attending the business in the manner in which it is conducted.   Hence, if a servant, knowing the hazards of his employment as the business is conducted, is injured while employed in such business, he cannot maintain an action against the master for such injury merely because he may be able to show that there was a safer mode in which the business might have been conducted, and that had it been conducted in that mode he would not have been injured." *Naylor v. C. & N. W. R. Co.* 53 Wis. 661; *Hobbs v. Stauer*, 62 Wis. 108. These decisions are all we deem it necessary to cite in reply to the argument that, as between master and servant, it is the duty of the former to provide suitable means and appliances to enable the servant to do his work as safely as the hazards incident to the employment will permit. This is undoubtedly the general rule, but it cannot apply here, for the reason that the plaintiff must be deemed to have entered upon the employment with full knowledge of the existing defects; therefore he assumed the risk. The fact that the saw was not covered, that the passage-way was narrow and dangerous, would be seen at a glance.

But probably the liability of the defendant was not intended to be rested upon the ground that the machinery used was not originally in a safe condition, for it is further alleged in the complaint that about ten days prior to the accident the plaintiff informed the defendant of the defective and dangerous condition of the shingle-mill, saw, and passage-way, and requested the defendant to repair the same, and to provide a suitable and safe passage-way, and to cover the saw, notifying the defendant, at the same time, that he would not remain and work the shingle-mill unless the same were put in a safe condition at once; that the defendant then promised and agreed to repair the mill, cover the saw, and put the passage-way in a safe condition, and by these promises induced the plaintiff to remain in his employment about the shingle-mill until he was hurt. If the complaint had stopped here, it might be held to state a cause of action, for it would then state a cause of action within the rule laid down and approved by courts of the highest authority, which hold that where the servant, having the right to abandon the service because it is dangerous, refrains from doing so in consequence of assurances by the master that the danger shall be removed, such assurances remove all ground for holding that the servant by continuing in the employment engages to assume the risk. This doctrine is laid down in *Hough v. Railway Co.* 100 U. S. 213, in a very elaborate and learned opinion by Mr. Justice HARLAN, where the law is fully discussed, and many authorities cited. The doctrine certainly rests upon rational grounds, and is amply supported by writers upon the law of negligence, as a reference to the above opinion will show. It follows that it was the clear duty of the defendant to remove the danger or repair the defect in the passage-way, and negligence will not be imputed to the plaintiff if he continued his employment for a reasonable time to allow the defendant to remove the defects.

The real question in each case is whether the master, under all the circumstances, had a right to believe and did believe that the servant waived his objection to the defect in the materials provided for the work, and assumed the risk, exempting the master from liability. "This is a question of fact, not of law; and it must be left to the jury, at least if not entirely free from doubt. There can be no doubt that, where a master has expressly promised to repair a defect, the servant can recover for an injury caused thereby within such a period of time after the promise as would be reasonably allowed for its performance, and, as we think, for an injury suffered within any period which would not preclude all reasonable expectation that the promise might be kept." 1 Shearm. & Redf. on Neg. (4th ed.), § 215. It appears that the plaintiff remained in his employment after the defendant promised to make the saw and passage-way safe, and was then injured by slipping and falling upon the saw while going through the passage-way to tighten the belt. As a matter of law, we could not say this period was so long that it precluded all reasonable expectation that the defendant would make good his promise. The defendant would have a reasonable time to remove the defects, and the plaintiff should not be held to waive his objections to the machinery or assume any risk in respect to it while relying upon the defendant's promise to make it safe. But if the plaintiff did continue his employment for an unreasonable time after the defendant could have removed the defects, he would then be deemed to have waived his objections and assumed the risk of operating the machinery in the unsafe and dangerous condition in which it was. The difficulty with the complaint is that it is alleged that *the plaintiff* — obviously meaning the defendant — had ample time and opportunity, and was abundantly able, to repair and put in a safe condition the machinery and apparatus between the time the plaintiff informed him of its defects, and the time when the plaintiff was injured, but neglected and failed to do so, as was his duty, for the protection of the plaintiff. This allegation fairly implies that the plaintiff continued his employment beyond the period of time within which he might reasonably expect the defendant would keep his promise and put the machinery in proper condition. We must therefore hold the complaint defective, because it does not allege or show that the plaintiff was injured within such a time after the defendant's promise as it would be reasonable to allow for its performance under the circumstances; for if the plaintiff continued in the employment longer than there were reasonable grounds for expecting the defendant would remove the defects, and was then injured, he would assume the risk of the dangerous condition of the machinery as when he entered upon the service.

We hold the complaint fatally defective because it does

not appear that the plaintiff was injured while he had a reasonable expectation that the defendant would keep his promise. The demurrer to the complaint should have been sustained for this reason.

By the Court.— The order of the circuit court is reversed, and the cause is remanded for further proceedings according to law.

See note to this case in 41 N. W. Rep. 337.— REP.

St. CROIX LAND & LUMBER COMPANY, Appellant, vs. RITCHIE, Respondent.

January 14 — January 29, 1889.

REGISTRY OF DEEDS. *(1) Clerical errors: Tax deeds. (2) Index: Omission of description of land: Recording at length. (3) Presumption as to time of recording.*

1. The registry of a conveyance of land is not invalidated by a mere clerical error in transcribing the instrument, not affecting the sense or obscuring its meaning. So *held,* where in copying upon the record a tax deed in the statutory form, the word *is* was omitted from the formula "as the fact is," where it occurs the second time in such deed.

2. The omission from the general index of the description of the land affected by the instrument entered therein for record, is cured by correctly recording the instrument at length in the proper record book, and from the time the instrument is so recorded at length the registry is valid and effectual.

3. Nothing appearing to the contrary, the presumption is that a conveyance was recorded at length on the day it was received for record in the register's office.

APPEAL from the Circuit Court for *Taylor* County.

The action is replevin, brought to recover the possession of a quantity of pine saw-logs cut by the defendant between January 1 and March 1, 1888, upon certain lands alleged

to belong to the plaintiff company, and by him removed
therefrom. The complaint alleges that the entry by defendant upon such lands, the cutting and removal of the
logs, and the subsequent detention thereof by the defendant, were unlawful and wrongful. The answer denies
plaintiff's title to the land; alleges that the logs were so cut
and removed by the defendant under a license from the
real owners of the land; that the plaintiff's only claim of
title is under a certain void tax deed, and that the three
years statute of limitation has run against such deed. It is
not alleged in the complaint, nor was it proved upon the
trial, that the plaintiff was ever in the actual possession of
the land from which the logs were taken. Such land seems
to have always been vacant and unoccupied.

The cause was tried by the court, a jury having been
waived. To prove its right to recover the logs, the plaintiff put in evidence a tax deed of such land, dated August
20, 1880, executed in due form to Taylor county pursuant
to a sale of the land in 1876 for nonpayment of taxes
thereon, with the certificate of the proper register of deeds
thereon showing that such tax deed was received for record
on the day it bears date. Also the entries in the general
index and the index of grantees, which the register is required by statute (R. S. secs. 759, 760) to make and keep,
and the record at large of such tax deed in the volume and
on the page indicated in such indexes. It was stipulated
by the parties that the plaintiff had acquired all the title
which Taylor county took under the tax deed; also that in
May, 1882, sufficient money was deposited by the defendant with the proper county clerk to redeem the land in
question from the tax sale thereof in 1876, which sale is the
basis of the tax deed to Taylor county.

The form of such tax deed is a literal compliance with
the statute prescribing the same. R. S. sec. 1178. But in
copying the deed upon the record the register omitted the

word "is" from the formula "as the fact is," where the same last occurs in the tax deed, recording only the words, "as the fact." The entries in the general index comply with the statute requirements in that behalf (R. S. sec. 759), except there is no entry under the head, "Description of Land."

On the foregoing facts the circuit court held that the plaintiff could not recover, and judgment was entered dismissing the complaint with costs. The plaintiff appeals from the judgment.

For the appellant there was a brief by *Clapp & Macartney*, of counsel, and oral argument by *N. H. Clapp.* The omission of the word *is* in the record of the deed *in extenso* was an immaterial clerical error, not affecting the record. Wade on Notice, secs. 152–3, 162, 170; *Wyatt v. Barwell*, 19 Ves. Jr. 435; *Ince v. Everard*, 6 Term, 545; *Partridge v. Smith*, 2 Biss. 183; *Lybrand v. Haney*, 31 Wis. 233; *Austin v. Holt*, 32 id. 489; *Scheiber v. Kaehler*, 49 id. 303; *Bulger v. Moore*, 67 id. 430. The indexing of the deed was sufficient. *Oconto Co. v. Jerrard*, 46 Wis. 317; *Jones v. Berkshire*, 15 Iowa, 248; *Barney v. Little*, id. 527; *Calvin v. Bowman*, 10 id. 529; *White v. Hampton*, 13 id. 260; *Bostwick v. Powers*, 12 id. 456; *American Emigrant Co. v. Call*, 22 Fed. Rep. 765–7; *Disque v. Wright*, 49 Iowa, 541; *Sinclair v. Slawson*, 44 Mich. 123.

W. F. Bailey, for the respondent.

The following opinion was filed January 29, 1889:

LYON, J. The plaintiff company never having had the actual possession of the land upon which the logs in controversy were cut by the defendant, it became essential to its right of action to show, by proof of other facts, that it was entitled to the possession of the logs. The plaintiff attempted to show this by proof that it was the owner in fee of the land and hence was in constructive possession thereof (the same being vacant) and entitled to the possession of the logs wrongfully taken therefrom. But such proofs show that its title was derived exclusively from the tax deed of the land to Taylor county. Such deed did not confer upon the grantee therein, or upon the plaintiff, who is the grantee of Taylor county, the constructive possession of the land or the right to the possession of the logs wrongfully taken therefrom, or bar the right of redemption from the tax sale, unless the same was properly recorded. *Hewitt v. Week,* 59 Wis. 444; *Semple v. Whorton,* 68 Wis. 626; *Fleming v. Sherry,* 72 Wis. 503.

Was there an effectual recording of the tax deed? Certainly there was, unless the omission of the word "is" in copying the deed upon the record, or the omission of the description of the land from the entries of the deed for record in the general index, invalidates the record. In all other respects the record is faultless.

1. We are not aware of any rule of law which invalidates a registry because of a mere clerical error in transcribing an instrument, not affecting the sense or obscuring its meaning. Such a rule would be intolerable, for it would unsettle titles by making their validity depend upon the absolute accuracy of the registration and record of conveyances,— a degree of perfection to which records made by the average register of deeds have not yet attained.

The formula "as the fact is" occurs twice in the tax deed to Taylor county, as it does in the statutory form of such deeds. R. S. sec. 1178. As first employed, the whole formula is recorded correctly. But in recording it when it is repeated in the deed the word "is" was dropped out, and only the words "as the fact" spread upon the record. Giving to the phrase all the importance claimed for it, still we can but think the omission quite inconsequential and harmless. It is a mere ellipsis of a word,— not authorized, perhaps, by the strict rules of rhetoric, but yet one which does not change or obscure the meaning of the phrase. Especially is this so in view of the fact that the phrase appears fully in an earlier portion of the record of the tax deed. One reading such record first finds the full formula "as the fact is," then he finds it again shorn of its verb, yet manifestly inserted and used for the same purpose as the full formula. He knows also that the statute calls for the omitted verb. No person of average intelligence could possibly be misled by the omission, or find the least difficulty in supplying the missing verb. Without it, the phrase asserts the truth of certain recitals of fact in the deed, and does no more with the verb expressed. We hold the omission to be a mere clerical error, not affecting the identity of the instrument recorded or the validity of the record, and which would not have affected the validity of the tax deed had it occurred therein.

The case of *Hilgers v. Quinney*, 51 Wis. 62, establishes no other or different rule. In that case a tax deed was held invalid for substantial defects in the affidavit of the treasurer of posting notices of the tax sale. We had there no question, as we have here, of the effect of a mere clerical omission not affecting the sense of the instrument.

2. The omission to enter a description of the land under the appropriate head in the general index is cured by the transcribing of the deed at length, containing such description, in the proper record. This case is not distinguishable in principle from that of *Oconto Co. v. Jerrard*, 46 Wis. 317, where it was held that the omission in the general index of the description of the land conveyed by the deed was cured by correctly transcribing the deed at large on the record, and that, when so transcribed, there was a valid registry of the instrument. In that case there was a special reference in the index to the volume and page of such record, while here there is no such special reference. But the index in the present case shows, under the appropriate head,

the volume and page where the deed is recorded. We discover no difference in principle in the two cases. A person examining either index is referred to the place where the record at large may be found, and neither contains any ininformation not found in the other. We think *Oconto Co. v. Jerrard* rules this case as to the effect of such omission in the general index. *Pringle v. Dunn*, 37 Wis. 449, substantially holds the same rule. The rule thus adopted by this court has remained in force for several years, and doubtless many titles have been approved and estates purchased and sold on the faith of it. To repudiate the rule at this late day would be a violation of the judicial maxim *stare decisis*. We must, therefore, adhere to it.

The learned counsel for the defendant relies upon the cases of *Shove v. Larsen*, 22 Wis. 142; *Hay v. Hill*, 24 Wis. 235; and *Lombard v. Culbertson*, 59 Wis. 437, as holding a different rule. *Shove v. Larsen* decides that a correct description of the land in the index cures a mistake in the description in the record at large of the deed. *Hay v. Hill* is to the effect that where the index, although correct, bears upon its face evidence that it was made after the land affected by it had been conveyed to another, the last grantee was not chargeable with constructive notice, when he took his conveyance, of the deed thus indexed afterwards. *Lombard v. Culbertson* holds that the transcribing of an instrument at length upon the record, concerning which instrument there are no entries whatever in the index, is not a valid registry thereof. Although language may be found in some of the opinions in these cases which seems to favor the contention of counsel, yet we think it quite obvious that neither of the cases conflicts with the rule of *Oconto Co. v. Jerrard*, which is here approved and followed. The precise proposition here decided is that the omission from the general index of the description of the land affected by the instrument entered therein for record, is cured by correctly

St. Croix Land & Lumber Co. vs. Ritchie.

recording the instrument at length in the proper record book, and that from the time the instrument is so recorded at length the registration is valid and effectual. We do not determine the effect of a misdescription of the land in the general index, or of any other error or omission therein.

Nothing appearing to the contrary, the presumption is that the deed was recorded at length on the day it was received for record in the register's office. *Oconto Co. v. Jerrard, supra.*

Cases elsewhere, under statutes differing from ours, were cited by counsel in support of their respective views. These cases give us little aid. We must determine this case (and have done so) in the light of our own statutes and adjudications.

It results from the foregoing views that the tax deed under which the plaintiff claims was duly recorded August 20, 1880. Hence the attempted redemption in 1882 is inoperative, and the three-years statute of limitation had run in favor of such deed long before the logs in question were taken from the land by the defendant. The plaintiff was therefore the owner in fee and in constructive possession of the land when the logs were taken from it, and is entitled to recover such logs in this action.

By the Court.— The judgment of the circuit court is reversed, and the cause will be remanded with directions to render judgment for the plaintiff in accordance with this opinion.

The following opinion was filed March, 12, 1889:

By THE COURT. As stated in the opinion herein heretofore filed, the action is replevin for saw-logs. It was tried by the court (a jury having been waived), and resulted in a judgment dismissing the complaint. It is not there stated, but the fact is, the order for judgment was made on motion of the defendant at the close of plaintiff's testimony. The defendant introduced no testimony. The judgment is, therefore, in the nature of a judgment of nonsuit.

In the judgment of this court entered January 29, 1889, the circuit court was directed to render judgment for the plaintiff. This mandate is manifestly erroneous. It should be that a new trial be awarded. The clerk is directed to amend the judgment heretofore entered accordingly.

BENTLEY and others vs. THE STATE.

January 14 — January 29, 1889.

Building contracts: Sufficiency of plans and specifications: Warranty.

Ch. 252, Laws of 1882, authorizing the construction of two transverse wings to the capitol, provided for a board of commissioners who should procure " suitable and proper plans, drawings, and specifications for the construction " of said wings, and let the contract for their erection. It also authorized them to employ an " architect or superintendent to superintend the work on said building " as it progressed, and to certify to the board monthly estimates of all materials furnished and labor performed. Pursuant to such act the board procured plans, engaged an architect, and entered into a contract with the plaintiffs whereby all the materials were to be furnished and all the work done according to the plans and specifications furnished by the board, and under the direction and to the entire satisfaction of the architect. The contract further provided that the architect might vary from such plans, and that any doubt as to the quality of materials or workmanship, or as to allowances for extras, should be determined and adjusted solely by the architect. After the plaintiffs had in good faith constructed a large portion of one wing, and the materials and work had been approved by the architect, accepted by the board, and paid for by the state, the wing fell by reason of latent defects in the plans. At the special request of the state the plaintiffs restored the wing according to amended plans and specifications furnished by the board. *Held,* that the state warranted the sufficiency of the original plans, and was liable to the plaintiffs for the expense of restoring the portion of the building so destroyed.

ACTION against the state, commenced in the supreme court pursuant to ch. 139. R. S. The following statement of the case was prepared by Mr. Justice CASSODAY:

Ch. 252, Laws of 1882, went into effect March 31, 1882, and authorized the construction of two transverse wings to the state capitol,— one on the north, and the other on the south,— to be built by contractors according to the plans and specifications therein provided for, and under the superintendence of an architect or superintendent therein authorized; the bid or bids therefor not to exceed, in the aggregate, $100,000 payable in 1882, and $100,000 payable in 1883. The said act also required the board of commissioners therein authorized to procure suitable and proper plans, drawings, and specifications for the construction of said buildings, and, after the adoption of the same, to advertise for twenty days for sealed proposals for the erection of said buildings; and that the contract therefor should be let by such board to the best responsible bidder or bidders, to whom such contract was to be awarded, and with whom it should be made.

The complaint alleges, in effect, that May 25, 1882, the said board of commissioners, having been fully appointed and duly organized, caused notice to be given that until June 15, 1882, at 10 o'clock A. M., sealed proposals in the form of a contract, for which blanks were furnished by said board, would be received by them for the construction of said two wings, designed by D. R. Jones, architect, and stating that plans and specifications therefor would be on exhibition at the office of said Jones, in Madison, after May 25, 1882; that the plaintiffs made a bid for such construction of said two wings in accordance with the blank contract furnished to them by said board; that when such proposals were opened, June 15, 1882, it was found that the lowest bid exceeded the amount of the appropriation therefor, and hence was not accepted; that prior to that time

said board had employed said Jones as such architect and
superintendent, and had given him the general charge and
control of the same and of the letting of the contract; that
said Jones then and there twice successively changed said
plans and specifications, so as to make said wings cheaper
than originally designed, and said board requested the
plaintiffs and others to again bid on the same according to
such altered plans; that, while the plaintiffs were required
to enter into a contract for the doing of the whole work, it
was well understood that large portions of the material
were to be furnished by subcontractors, who made their
bids therefor, and who were then and there present and
modified their bids according to such altered plans and
specifications; that among other things there was to go
into said building a large quantity of cast-iron work, minutely described in said specifications, which was to be made
and furnished by a subcontractor; that one James Fyfe, of
Portage, Wisconsin, did then and there figure and bid on
such work, and make the lowest bid for the same; that
these plaintiffs did not know said James Fyfe, but said
Jones, who knew him, told the plaintiffs that he was reliable, and requested these plaintiffs to accept his bid for such
cast-iron work, and they did so at his request, requiring
said Fyfe to furnish the same according to the said specifications and contract, by which all the material furnished
was subject to the approval of said Jones, the superintendent of the building; that these plaintiffs did thereupon
make the bid of said James Fyfe for cast-iron work the
basis of their calculation, and bid for the whole work, and
that upon their final bid so made after the said several
modifications of said plans and specifications the contract
was let to them, and that they then, with the approval of
said Jones, let the cast-iron work to said James Fyfe; that,
omitting the formal parts, the plaintiffs, as parties of the
first part, and the state of Wisconsin, as party of the second

part, June 16, 1882, made, entered into, and executed the
following

"CONTRACT.

"That the said party of the first part hereby agrees to
furnish all the materials and perform all the work required
to erect and complete the building of two transverse wings to
the present state capitol at Madison, in the state of Wisconsin, and to do everything necessary and required to be done
in, to, and about said building, according to the plans and
specifications made for the same by D. R. Jones, architect;
which plans and specifications are signed by the said Jones
and dated May 25, A. D. 1882, and which were twice revised by the said Jones, architect, and Henry Koch, consulting architect, on the 15th day of June, 1882, and after
such revision were adopted by the said commissioners. All
the work shall be executed in a thorough, complete, and
most workmanlike manner, and agreeably to such directions as may be given from time to time by said D. R.
Jones, architect and superintendent (or such persons as may
be employed by the party of the second part to superintend
the work), and to such superintendent's full and entire satisfaction, without reference thereon to any other person.

"If any alteration should hereafter be made by order of
the party of the second part or their superintendent, which
they may deem necessary, varying from the plans and specifications as revised as aforesaid, either by adding thereto
or diminishing therefrom or otherwise however, such alterations shall not vacate the contract hereby entered into, but
the value thereof shall be ascertained by said superintendent and added to or deducted from the sum of money hereinafter mentioned as the case may be; nor shall such
alterations, either in addition, diminution, or otherwise,
supersede the condition for the completion of the whole of
the work at the time herein expressed, but the party of the
first part shall, if such alterations of whatever sort require

it, increase the number of his workmen so that the same,
as well as the work contained in the plans and specifications
as so revised as aforesaid, shall be completely finished and
so delivered up to the party of the second part, clean and
in good order for use, by the 1st day of January, A. D. 1884;
and the said party of the first part shall have all wood,
flooring, and joists, and roof timber, necessary for the building, piled in the city of Madison, outside of the capitol
grounds, before the 1st day of November next (1882), all
flooring to be covered from the weather; and shall also
have all doors, sash, inside and outside finishing lumber,
prepared in readiness for putting up before the 1st day of
April next,— it being the intention to thus secure better
seasoned wood.

" If any doubt or doubts should arise as to the quality of
materials being used, or of the workmanship, during the
execution of the work, or as to estimating allowances for
extra material or work (should any occur), or making out
the accounts as to such extras, or other work for which the
party of the first part may think he has a claim over and
above the sum hereinafter mentioned, the admission or allowance for such materials or work, or of any such claim
or claims, shall be judged of, determined, and adjusted,
solely by the superintendent; it being the intention of the
parties to this contract that all such work of every kind
that may be necessary for completely finishing the work
proposed, or for the rectification of any failure from whatever cause arising, and the well maintaining, sustaining,
and supporting the whole work, as well as alterations and
additions, should such be made, so that the whole may remain sound and firm, are implied in the aforesaid specifications as so revised as aforesaid, although the same may not
therein be specifically expressed; and it is hereby agreed
that on this, as well as on all other matters of difference, no
reference to any other person than the superintendent is to

be allowed or admitted, and his determination shall be final and conclusive.

" The masonry to the bottom of the water-table, but no further than to the top of the principal or first story, shall be laid on or before the 10th day of November, 1882, and securely protected from injury by the weather, during the season of frost, by a covering of plank, and said masonry shall also be well banked with earth to protect it from water.

" If the party of the first part should neglect or refuse to carry on the work with such dispatch as shall be thought necessary by the superintendent to complete the same by the time hereinbefore mentioned, or should neglect or refuse to furnish such materials for or to do the work as by the superintendent directed, it shall be lawful for the party of the second part, or their superintendent, to employ such other person or persons as said party of the second part shall think fit or necessary to furnish such unprovided materials, or to finish any of the unfinished work, after having given notice in writing to the party of the first part, three days before employing such person or persons; said notice to be left at the shop, counting-house, or usual place of abode of the party of the first part, or delivered to the foreman on the work; and the bill or bills of any artificer that may be so employed, or for materials furnished, and all expenses incidental thereto, shall be deducted out of any money that may be due or to become due on this contract, and owing to the party of the first part, or any part thereof, as the case may be; and in case of a deficiency the party of the first part and his sureties shall be held liable therefor; and the said superintendent is hereby empowered to have any material which he may reject removed from the premises forthwith, to secure its non-usage.

" No part of the work covered by this contract is to be

relct or subcontracted without the consent in writing of the party of the second part.

"In consideration of the faithful performance by the party of the first part, as above stated, the party of the second part agrees to pay the party of the first part, on the certificate of the superintendent, as follows, viz.:   In all, the gross sum of $188,370, to be paid in manner as follows, to wit: Eighty five per cent. of the proportionate value of the work done, monthly, as the work progresses, on the estimates of the superintendent; and the remaining fifteen per cent., together with all other sums, if any, due on this contract, shall be paid on the completion and acceptance of the entire work as herein contracted for, or as soon thereafter as the said commissioners are satisfied that said work is completed and are assured against the existence of any mechanic's lien on said building: provided, however, that no materials shall be estimated or paid for until upon the grounds and suitable to be used in the permanent construction of the building, except for such materials as are herein required to be piled in the city of Madison outside of the capitol grounds."

The complaint further alleges "that by the contract and specifications said D. R. Jones was given complete control and superintendence over said building, and made the sole judge of all materials furnished and labor done.   And the plaintiffs further show that they proceeded to perform their said contract according to the plans and specifications, and under the directions of said D. R. Jones; that they had reason to believe, and did believe, that said building had been properly planned by said Jones, the architect and agent of the state of Wisconsin, and proceeded with said building in good faith; that by the 8th day of November, A. D. 1883, these plaintiffs had a very large portion of said two wings completed, and had placed therein a large quan-

tity of cast-iron material furnished by said James Fyfe,
which had been approved and accepted by said D. R. Jones
on behalf of the state of Wisconsin; that on said day one
of said two wings broke down and fell, destroying a very
large amount of material, and the fruits of a very large
amount of labor bestowed thereon by these plaintiffs; that
all of the material and work so destroyed and lost had been
by said architect, prior to the falling of said building,
approved and accepted, and had been accepted by said
board of commissioners, and paid for by said state upon
the certificates of said architect.

"And these plaintiffs allege, upon information and belief,
that said wing broke down and fell by reason and in consequence of defects in the plans and specifications so prepared by said D. R. Jones, and in accordance with which
the same was required to be constructed; that said plans
and specifications were especially defective in respect to
such cast-iron work, among other particulars, in failing to
provide a proper plan for the construction of the same, with
respect to bearings and supports for columns and girders,
and in failing to provide for proper plates for certain piers
and parts of corridor walls upon which iron columns supporting great weights were to and did rest; that said plans
and specifications required that such plates should be one
inch in thickness, and of the size of the bases of the columns,
which was in all cases less than twelve inches square;
whereas these plaintiffs, upon their present information and
belief, allege that said plates for said piers and parts of corridor walls should have been two feet square, and more
than one inch in thickness; that said plans and specifications also provided that lines of iron girders, extending
from end to end of said south wing, should be placed upon
the caps of the lower tiers of columns for the support of
other tiers of columns, lines of girders, floors, and other
heavy portions of said building above; that the upper and

lower surfaces of such lines of girders were required to be of the width of about eight inches, and each comprised several lengths,—each length consisting of two iron girders or joists, bolted together side by side; that such lines of girders were required to be so placed upon the caps of the lower tiers of columns that the ends of each of such lengths should have its bearing and support upon the cap of one of such columns, except in cases where the ends of such lines of girders extended into walls, in which cases they were to be and were anchored to such walls; that such iron plates of the size aforesaid were required to be placed upon the upper surfaces of such lines of girders, over the columns beneath, and over the joints where the ends of such lengths came together as aforesaid, and the bases of the next tier of columns above were to be and were placed on these iron plates; that it was further required by said plans and specifications that the ends of such lengths, composing these lines of girders, should be connected and fastened together where they rested on the caps of columns as aforesaid by means of iron straps bolted to the ends of each of such lengths. And these plaintiffs, upon their present information and belief, allege that by reason of the contraction and expansion of such lines of girders, and of the impracticability of obtaining unchangeable and perfect bearings for the support of the bases of such columns in the manner aforesaid, such plan of construction, arranging, and adjusting such columns, plates, and girders was defective and insufficient.

"And these plaintiffs allege that they did not at the time of the construction of said building, and before the fall thereof, know that said plans and specifications were defective and insufficient in any respect, but that they relied upon the same as being in all respects sufficient, and upon the skill and judgment of said architect, and put in said plates, columns, girders, and other iron-work as constructed by said

Fyfe, approved and accepted by said Jones, and as required by said plans and specifications. And these plaintiffs, upon information and belief, allege that by reason of the defects and insufficiencies aforestated, and without fault or negligence on the part of these plaintiffs, the said south wing broke down and fell as aforestated; that said plans and specifications were defective and insufficient in other respects.

"And these plaintiffs allege that after such breaking down and fall of said building other architects were employed by the state of Wisconsin, and thereupon extensive amendments to the plans and specifications were made on behalf of the state of Wisconsin, both for the north wing and the said south wing, whereby the same were greatly strengthened, and at large additional cost and expense, and that alterations were then made and said building finished by these plaintiffs, at the special request of the state of Wisconsin, in accordance with such new amended plans and specifications; that such work was done under the direction of said board of commissioners; that in doing the same these plaintiffs were obliged to expend, and did expend, the sum of $22,038.20 for labor and materials in restoring so much of said south wing as had been finished and was destroyed by said fall, which had occurred in consequence of the carelessness and want of skill of the architect, the agent of the state of Wisconsin as aforesaid, and without fault on the part of these plaintiffs; that said building was completed by these plaintiffs, and accepted by the state of Wisconsin, by the 29th day of November, 1884, and that said state has paid these plaintiffs for the same, except, however, for the cost and expense of restoring said south wing as aforesaid; that said architect unreasonably, and without just cause, refused to give these plaintiffs his certificate covering the work done and materials furnished by plaintiffs in rectifying such failure and restoring that portion of said south wing which was destroyed by the fall thereof as aforesaid; that the plaintiffs have a just claim for the same, with interest from the 29th day of November, 1884; that they applied to the legislature of the state at the session of 1885, and again at the session of 1887, for the allowance and payment of the same, but the legislature refused to allow the same.

"Wherefore said plaintiffs bring this action against the state of Wisconsin, pursuant to the statute in such case made and provided, and demand judgment against the state for said sum of $22,038.20, with interest from the 29th day of November, 1884, and costs."

The complaint also stated, in effect, that the plaintiffs, deeming themselves aggrieved by the refusal of the legislature to allow their just claim against the state as aforesaid, pursuant to the statute in such case made and provided bring this their complaint against the state of Wisconsin, and allege as above set forth.

To such complaint the state demurred on the ground that said complaint did not state facts sufficient to constitute a cause of action.

For the plaintiffs there was a brief by *Wm. Ruger* and *F. C. Winkler,* and the cause was argued orally by *J. G. Flanders* and *Wm. Ruger.* They cited Bishop on Cont. secs. 246, 253, 1410–17, 1424; Wood's Master & Serv. secs. 155, 277, 282, 318, 321; *Kellogg Bridge Co. v. Hamilton,* 110 U. S. 108; *Clark v. Pope,* 70 Ill. 128; *Louisville, E. & St. L. R. Co. v. Donnegan,* 111 Ind. 179; *Seymour v. Long Dock Co.* 20 N. J. Eq. 396; *Schwartz v. Gilmore,* 45 Ill. 455; *Daegling v. Gilmore,* 49 id. 248; *Bonnet v. Glattfeldt,* 120 Ill. 166; *Horner v. Nicholson,* 56 Mo. 220; *People v. Stephens,* 71 N. Y. 527, 549–51; *Craker v. C. & N. W. R. Co.* 36 Wis. 669–74; Dillon on Mun. Corp. (3d ed.), secs. 459–60, 479, 938–9; *Grand Rapids & B. C. R. Co. v. Van Dusen,* 29 Mich. 431, 440–1; *Cleary v. Sohier,* 120 Mass. 210;

Haynes v. Second Baptist Church, 88 Mo. 285; *Hollis v. Chapman,* 36 Tex. 1; *Cook v. McCabe,* 53 Wis. 250; *Rawson v. Clark,* 70 Ill. 656; *Niblow v. Binsse,* 1 Keyes, 476; *Kingsley v. Brooklyn,* 78 N. Y. 200, 216; *Whelan v. Ansonia Clock Co.* 97 id. 293; *Rudd v. Bell,* 55 Wis. 563; *Burke v. Dunbar,* 128 Mass. 499; *Sinnott v. Mullin,* 82 Pa. St. 333.

The *Attorney General* and *L. K. Luse,* Assistant Attorney General, for the state, cited Lloyd on Building Cont. 88, 183, 186, 194; Roscoe's Building Cases, 50; Emden on Building Cont. 79, 138; *Thorn v. Mayor,* 45 L. J. 488; *Scrivener v. Pask,* L. R., 1 C. P. 715; *Sinnott v. Mullin,* 82 Pa. St. 333; *Cannon v. Wildman,* 28 Conn. 473; *Clark v. Pope,* 70 Ill. 133; *Schwartz v. Saunders,* 46 id. 22; *School Trustees v. Bennett,* 27 N. J. Law, 513; *Sherman v. Bates,* 15 Neb. 18; *Loundsbury v. Eastwick,* 3 Phila. 371; *Bond v. Newark,* 19 N. J. Eq. 376–82; *Glacius v. Black,* 50 N. Y. 145–50; *Green v. State,* 8 Ohio, 314; *Adlard v. Muldoon,* 45 Ill. 193; *Pack v. New York,* 8 N. Y. 222; *Barry v. St. Louis,* 17 Mo. 121; *Painter v. Pittsburg,* 46 Pa. St. 213; *Corbin v. American Mills,* 27 Conn. 278; *Railroad Co. v. Hanning,* 15 Wall. 656.

CASSODAY, J. The only question raised by the demurrer is whether the complaint above set forth states facts sufficient to constitute a cause of action upon contract. The contract was only to be let after the state, through its board of commissioners, had procured and adopted "suitable and proper plans, drawings, and specifications" for the construction of the two wings of the capitol. Sec. 3, ch. 252, Laws of 1882. Such commissioners were expressly " authorized to employ an architect or superintendent *to superintend the work on said building as it progressed,*" and for which he was to receive from the state such compensation as the commissioners should determine. Id. sec. 4. Such architect was thereby required, at the close of each month, to

make out estimates in detail of all materials furnished and
labor performed during said month, and duly certify the
same to the board, who, after having examined, approved,
and recorded the same, and after deducting fifteen per
cent. of the total amount, to be retained until the completion of the contract, were to certify to the correctness
thereof, when the same was to be paid by the state. Id.
sec. 5. It appears that such commissioners were duly appointed and organized as a board, and employed such
architect on or before May 25, 1882. It also appears that
on or before that date the state, through such board and
architect, did undertake to procure and adopt such "suitable and proper plans, drawings, and specifications;" and
thereupon gave the requisite notice of receiving sealed proposals in the form of a blank contract furnished by them
for the construction of such wings according to such plans
and specifications; and that it became necessary twice to
modify and alter such plans and specifications in order to
secure any bids for such construction within the appropriation; and that the contract was awarded to the plaintiffs.

The contract is given above. It appears that it required
all the materials to be furnished and all the work to be
done according to such plans and specifications, and agreeably to such directions as might be given from time to time
by such architect, and to his full and entire satisfaction;
that it expressly authorized the state or its architect to
vary from such plans and specifications, either by adding
thereto or diminishing therefrom or otherwise, and the
value of such alterations were to be ascertained by him
and to be added or deducted from the contract price named
therein as the case might be; that such alterations and additions, as well as the work contained in the plans and
specifications, were to be completed January 1, 1884; that
any doubt or doubts as to the quality of materials being
used or the workmanship thereon, or as to estimating allow-

ances for extra materials or work, or for the rectification of any failure from whatever cause arising, the same was to be judged of, determined, and adjusted solely by such architect, and such determination was to be final and conclusive. From the whole contract it seems to have been the duty of such architect, from time to time, as the work progressed, to inspect and approve or disapprove all material and workmanship as it went into the buildings; and the plaintiffs were bound by his determinations, and required to follow his directions. In other words, the contract gave such architect complete control and superintendence over such construction, and made him the sole judge of all materials furnished and labor performed. He was, moreover, thereby authorized and empowered to modify, change, and alter such plans and specifications as he might from time to time deem expedient; and the plaintiffs had no alternative, under the contract, except to follow his directions and conform to such modified, changed, and altered plans and specifications, but with the right to additional compensation for any and all extra materials and work required by such modifications, changes, and alterations.

Under the pleadings, we must assume that the plaintiffs proceeded in good faith to perform their said contract according to such plans and specifications, and under the direction of the architect, and without any knowledge of any defects or inefficiency; that on November 8, 1883, they had a very large portion of said two wings completed, and had placed therein a large quantity of cast-iron materials, furnished by a contractor selected by said architect, and which cast-iron materials had been approved and accepted by the architect on behalf of the state; that by reason and in consequence of defects in such plans and specifications, and without any fault or negligence of the plaintiffs, and on November 8, 1883, the south wing broke down and fell,

destroying a very large amount of material and the fruits
of a very large amount of labor bestowed thereon by the
plaintiffs; that all the material and work so destroyed and
lost had previously been approved and accepted by the
architect, and been accepted by the board of commissioners, and paid for by the state upon the certificates of
the architect; that thereupon other architects were employed by the state, and extensive amendments to such
plans and specifications were thereupon made on behalf of
the state, both for the north and south wings, whereby the
same were greatly strengthened, and at large additional
cost and expense; that such alterations were then made
and the buildings finished by the plaintiffs, at the special
request of the state, in accordance with such new amended
plans and specifications; that such work was done by the
plaintiffs under the direction of said board and said architect; that in doing the same they were obliged to expend,
and did expend, $22,038.20 for labor and materials in restor-
ing so much of said south wing as had been finished and
was destroyed by such fall; that the building was completed by the plaintiffs and accepted by the state, November 29, 1884; that the state has paid for the same, except
the amount last stated; that the architect unreasonably and
without just cause refused to certify the work done and
materials furnished in rectifying such failures and restoring
such south wing.

Under such a contract, and upon such facts, it is strenuously urged upon the part of the state that the plaintiffs
were bound to furnish all the materials and perform the
necessary work to restore the south wing, according to such
new or modified and altered plans and specifications, to the
point and in the condition where it was when it fell, at
their own cost and expense. In other words, the contention is that the plaintiffs assumed the risk of the sufficiency
and efficiency of the plans and specifications, and the ma-

terials and workmanship thus exacted, approved, accepted, and paid for by the state; and hence must suffer and make good the loss occasioned by such defects. Under the contract, it is very manifest that, had the plaintiffs departed from such plans and specifications and refused to follow the directions of the architect, there could have been no recovery for the building of the south wing, even had they in the first instance built it as they were finally directed by the architect to do. On the contrary, they could only recover by furnishing materials and doing the work according to such plans, specifications, and directions, as they allege they did. The fall was not the result of inevitable accident, as in several of the cases cited by counsel. According to the allegations of the complaint, it was in consequence of inefficient and defective plans and specifications therein mentioned. According to such allegations, we must infer that there was in such agency of the state a lack of learning, experience, skill, and judgment to draw adequate and efficient plans and specifications for a building of that magnitude. But, as observed, the state, through its own chosen agency, undertook to furnish, for the guidance of the plaintiffs, "suitable and proper plans, drawings, and specifications for the construction" of such buildings, and then bound the plaintiffs to build according to them unless otherwise directed by its architect. Under the allegations of the complaint, we must assume that such inefficiency and defects were not patent to an ordinary mechanic, but were, as to the plaintiffs, latent. It is nevertheless contended that, if it were possible by means of temporary supports to have completed the buildings according to such plans and specifications, then the plaintiffs were bound to so complete them, unless sooner stopped through the agency of the state, even though they would have been worthless when so completed; and that since they were not so stopped, and the buildings were not so completed according to such original plans and specifications, the plaintiffs were bound to suffer the loss and make the same good by restoration. In other words that, under the act authorizing the structures and the contract, the state was not bound to make good and was not responsible for the inefficiency and defects of what it thus undertook through its agency to furnish; but that the plaintiffs were bound to make good what they thus undertook to furnish and perform, notwithstanding the failure of such conditions precedent on the part of the state.

The case most relied upon in support of such contention is *Thorn v. Mayor*, L. R. 1 App. Cas. 120, affirming *S. C.* 44 L. J. Exch. 62. The facts in that case were to the effect that the city of London desired to remove an existing bridge over the Thames at Blackfriars, and erect a new one in its place. Accordingly its engineer prepared plans of such intended new bridge, and specifications of the works to be executed. The specifications stated, in effect, that the accuracy of the drawings of the existing bridge was not guarantied; that the city should not be liable for any extra work in removing more than indicated in the drawings; that the contractors were to take out their own quantities, and satisfy themselves as to the nature of the ground through which the foundations were to be carried; that no surveyor was authorized to act for the city, and that no information given was guarantied; that piers were to be put in by means of wrought-iron caissons, as shown on the drawings; that the contractors were to assume all risks and responsibility in the sinking of such caissons, and to employ their own divers or other efficient means for removing and overcoming any obstacles or difficulties that might arise in the execution of the work; that the quality of the concrete was put under the control and direction of the engineer; that extra or varied work was to be certified, accounted, and paid for at prices named. Thorn, having taken the contract, entered upon the works according to such plans and specifications. After a while it transpired that such caissons were not sufficiently strong to resist the tide-waters, and accordingly it became necessary to alter the plans for shutting out the water while putting in the piers. This occasioned the loss of material and work, and necessitated extra material and work, and a considerable delay. The ordinary method at the time of shutting out such water was by means of coffer-dams. The city voluntarily paid the contract price, *and also voluntarily paid for the cost of the extra work rendered necessary by such alteration of the plans, but refused to pay for the contractor's loss of time and labor occasioned by the attempt to execute the original plans,* and the action was brought to recover what the city thus refused to pay. The question presented was whether there was any implied warranty on the part of the city that such caissons would prove efficient to shut off the water while building the piers. Each of the two courts cited above held that there was no such warranty, and hence that the city was not liable.

The value of such decisions as authority, however, is somewhat impaired by reason of the uncertainty as to the precise grounds upon which they were based. This grows out of the fact, so common among English decisions, especially of the present day, of rendering numerous opinions in the same case. Thus, in that case, there were five different opinions rendered in the Exchequer Chamber, and four in the House of Lords. Each of these opinions puts such decision upon grounds differing more or less from some if not all the others. The conclusions of each court, therefore, are to be found in the general average. The prevailing opinions in each of those courts seem to go on the theory that the contract was for the building of the bridge on piers; and that although the contract referred to the plans, etc., in which the caissons were specifically described, yet that the caissons were merely an unusual mode of doing the work, which was likened to the scaffolding in building a house; and that in no event was there any express or implied warranty as to the efficiency of such caissons; that in the absence of any such warranty, and upon the facts stated, the plaintiff could not recover in that form of action, even if he could in some other form. Some of the opinions seem to go upon the theory that the contractor assumed the risk of the efficiency of the plans and specifications, while others seem to go upon the theory that, when the caissons proved themselves inefficient, the plaintiff was at liberty to decline further work under the contract, but that as he continued the work in the absence of any such warranty he was without remedy,— especially in that form of action. All the opinions seem to agree that the case, as brought and presented, necessarily turned upon the presence or absence of such a warranty or undertaking on the part of the city, which was found not to exist.

The facts of that case distinguish it from the one at bar in several particulars. In that case the caissons so specified were not included in the thing contracted for, but were only referred to in the specifications as a means to be employed in the construction of the piers. Here the defects and inefficiency were in parts of the structure contracted for. In that case the city's engineer only had control and direction as to a small portion of the work, in which the caissons were not included, but the construction was almost wholly under the control and supervision of the contractor and his engineer and employees. Here, as indicated, the state's architect was to inspect, approve, and accept the materials and workmanship as they went into the building, and did so accordingly, with full power to modify and alter plans and specifications. In that case the defective parts were never accepted by the city. Here they were inspected, accepted, approved, and paid for by the state. In that case the agency of the city, as to the defective parts, terminated with the drawing of the plans and specifications. Here the agency of the state continued, with the absolute right of control and supervision, during the entire execution of the works. In that case the contract expressly disclaimed any guaranty, risk, or responsibility as to several particulars, including the sinking of such caissons, and in removing and overcoming any obstacles or difficulties arising in the execution of the works. Here there is no such disclaimer on the part of the state, but a general assumption of the right to determine all questions relating to the material and workmanship. In that case the stipulation respecting compensation for extras seems to have been more limited than here. The cases may fairly be regarded as distinguishable in their facts. Certainly we are unwilling to apply the rules there announced by some members of the court to the facts here admitted by the demurrer. According to such facts, the state undertook to furnish suitable plans and specifications, and required the plaintiffs to conform thereto, and assumed control and supervision of the execution thereof, and thereby took the risk of their efficiency. What was thus done, or omitted to be done, by the architect, must be deemed to have been done or omitted by the state. Moreover, we must hold, notwithstanding the English case cited, that the language of the contract is such as to fairly imply an undertaking on the part of the state that such architect had sufficient learning, experience, skill, and judgment to properly perform the work thus required of him, and that such plans, drawings, and specifications were suitable and efficient for the purpose designed. There seems to be no lack of able adjudications in support of such conclusions. *Clark v. Pope*, 70 Ill. 128; *Daegling v. Gilmore*, 49 Ill. 248; *Schwartz v. Saunders*, 46 Ill. 18; *Seymour v. Long Dock Co.* 20 N. J. Eq. 396; *Sinnott v. Mullin*, 82 Pa. St. 333; *Smith v. B., C. & M. R. Co.* 36 N. H. 459; *Grand Rapids & B. C. R. Co. v. Van Dusen,* 29 Mich. 431; *Burke v. Dunbar,* 128 Mass. 499; *Kellogg Bridge Co. v. Hamilton,* 110 U. S. 108. The case is not unlike in principle to a class of decisions frequently made by this and other courts, and recently sanctioned by the House of Lords, to the effect that where goods or machinery are ordered for particular use, to the knowledge of the manufacturer or vendor, there is an implied undertaking or warranty on his part that they will be fit for such use in the ordinary manner, and that in case of failure by reason of latent defects not discoverable by ordinary diligence upon inspection, such manufacturer or vendor is liable. *Drummond v. Van Ingen,* L. R. 12 App. Cas. 284.

By the Court.— The demurrer to the complaint is overruled, with leave to answer within twenty days.

ROBINSON, Appellant, vs. ROHR and others, imp., Respondents.

November 10, 1888 — February 19, 1889.

Municipal corporations: Officers: Negligence: Individual liability.

The board of street commissioners of a city, disregarding the requirement of the charter that all work for the city should be let by contract, resolved that the work of repairing and reconstructing a bridge should be done by themselves under the supervision of their committee and a superintendent appointed by them. *Held,* that for injuries to a person, caused by the negligence of the employees of the board engaged in doing the work in pursuance of such resolution, the street commissioners were liable individually, and the city was not liable.

APPEAL from the Circuit Court for *Jefferson* County.

Action to recover damages for personal injuries alleged to have been caused by the negligence of the defendants and their employees. The seven defendants who answered the complaint constituted the board of street commissioners of the city of Watertown. The city was made a defendant, but did not answer or appear in the action. The facts are sufficiently stated in the opinion. The plaintiff appeals from a judgment in favor of all the defendants except the city.

Harlow Pease, for the appellant.

For the respondents there was a brief by *Gregory, Bird & Gregory* and *Charles H. Gardner*, and oral argument by *Geo. W. Bird.* 1. The respondents were the senior aldermen, and as such constituted the board of street commissioners of the city of Watertown (ch. 204, P. & L. Laws of 1871), a legislative body having all the powers of the common council except the power to levy taxes (ch. 46, Laws of 1879), and served without pay. They did nothing respecting the repair or construction of the bridge except at meetings of this body duly held, and then only to vote upon motions or resolutions regularly brought before such meetings, upon which it was their duty to vote. That duty was a legislative duty, for the performance of which, however negligent, erroneous, or improper, no individual can maintain an action against the officers personally. Cooley on Torts, 376; *Baker v. State*, 27 Ind. 485; *Walker v. Hallock*, 32 id. 239; 2 Thomp. on Neg. 817. 2. The duty to vote and act upon such motions and resolutions was also a duty which they owed to the public at large and not to any individual, and therefore no liability to individual suits could result from the negligent, improper, or erroneous performance of it. Cooley on Torts, 379; Wharton on Neg. sec. 284; Shearm. & Redf. on Neg. (3d ed.), secs. 166, 167, 176, 177; *Kahl v. Love*, 37 N. J. Law, 5; *Hall v. Smith*, 2 Bing. 156. The respondents having authority to act upon the general subject matter of the repair and reconstruction

of the bridge, even if they proceeded illegally in the execution of that authority, in that they neglected to let the
work by contract, such neglect does not render them liable
in this action. The charter provision requiring the work
to be let by contract being simply for the protection of the
public, a failure to comply with it can be taken advantage
of only by the public. *East River G. L. Co. v. Donnelly*,
93 N. Y. 557; *Oconto v. C. & N. W. R. Co.* 44 Wis. 231.
3. The respondents, as such board, having authority to act
on the subject, and having acted in good faith with an
honest view to obtain for the public a lawful benefit, are
not liable even though they failed to exercise their authority in the specific manner directed by statute. *Squiers v.
Neenah*, 24 Wis. 588; *Hamilton v. Fond du Lac*, 40 id. 47; ·
Smith v. Gould, 61 id. 31; *Alvord v. Barrett*, 16 id. 175.
4. Public officers are answerable for their own personal
malfeasances and misfeasances only, and not for those of
their employees or agents; and this rule applies to every
kind of public agency. Shearm. & Redf. on Neg. sec. 177,
and note 2. 5. The respondents, as public officers, were
charged with a duty which could not be performed without
the aid of others; and in such case the doctrine of *respondeat superior* does not apply so as to make them liable for
the negligence of the persons employed, even though the
officers did not follow the statute strictly in the exercise of
their authority. *Bailey v. Mayor*, 3 Hill, 531; *Martin v.
Mayor*, 1 id. 550; *Donovan v. McAlpin*, 85 N. Y. 185;
Fitzpatrick v. Slocum, 89 id. 359.

The following opinion was filed December 4, 1888:

ORTON, J.   The above defendant, *William Rohr*, and six
others are charged in the complaint as follows: They were
constructing and repairing stone piers and abutments
under the Main-Street bridge over the Rock river, in the

city of Watertown, and there was standing in an upright
position on said bridge a large and heavy hoisting-machine,
known as a derrick, which was placed there by them, and
before that day had been used by them in repairing and
constructing said piers and abutments. The plaintiff was
walking along upon that portion of the bridge which was
set apart for persons traveling on foot, and through the
carelessness and negligence of the defendants, their agents,
servants, and employees, said derrick was allowed to fall
across and upon said bridge, and upon the plaintiff, while
she was walking along as a traveler on said highway
bridge, and without fault on her part; whereby she was
greatly hurt, bruised, and injured.

The defendants by answer admit that the piers and abutments of said bridge were being constructed and repaired,
but deny that *they* were constructing or repairing the same,
and deny that it was through their fault or that of their
agents, servants, or employees, that the derrick fell upon
the plaintiff, and that she was greatly injured thereby, or
that she received any injuries by reason of their negligence
or that of their agents, servants, and employees, and deny
that the plaintiff was without fault, and aver that her own
negligence contributed to her injury. They allege that
said bridge had been out of repair for some time, and
needed repair and reconstruction; and that as the board of
street commissioners of said city, in its collective and legislative capacity, *they had duly let the work of repairing and
constructing said piers and abutments to competent persons to
do that work*, and the said persons were then engaged in
the due prosecution of said work, exercising due and proper
caution in operating the said derrick.

The facts in respect to said mason-work on the piers and
abutments, stated in respondents' brief and proved on the
trial, were as follows: The clerk of the city was directed
by the defendants, in accordance with the requirement of

sec. 3 of subch. 9 of the city charter[1] in respect to all such work, to advertise for proposals for doing the mason-work and furnishing materials for the bridge according to the plans and specifications adopted by them as the board of street commissioners, to be received up to a certain date; and on that day the proposal of one Charles Baxter for doing said work and furnishing materials was accepted by them, and they directed a contract to be entered into with him according to said proposal, and that the said work be let to him, he being the lowest bidder for the same. But before any contract was entered into with him, and before, as they ascertained, he had acquired any rights in the same, by resolution of the defendants as such board the whole matter was left open and undisposed of for their future action. Their committee, to whom the matter had been referred, reported plans and specifications of said mason-work and materials, and recommended that said work and furnishing materials be done by themselves, under the supervision of their committee on streets and bridges, and that a superintendent be appointed, and said resolution was accordingly adopted by them. In this manner the work upon said bridge commenced and was carried on by the defendants through their superintendent and other persons employed by them, and under the supervision of their committee, up to the time the plaintiff was injured by the falling of the derrick by the negligence of their servants. No contract was ever let to any one to do said work or to furnish materials for the same, but the defendants did the work, instead of a contractor obtained according to the requirement of the charter as the lowest bidder for the same.

---

[1] Ch. 233, Laws of 1865. Sec. 3, subch. 9, is as follows: "All work for the city or either ward thereof shall be let by contract to the lowest responsible bidder, and due notice shall be given of the time and place of letting such contract."— REP.

On these facts the circuit court directed a verdict for the
defendants, except the city of Watertown.

It will be seen that the facts proved do not support the
answer as to letting the work to other persons. It may be
said here that all the authorities cited by the learned counsel of the respondents have application only to the case
made by the answer, and in no respect to that made by the
facts proved. The same elementary authorities cited by
them make the very distinction which here exists between
the answer and the proofs. The board of street commissioners, when they determined upon the work and adopted
the plans and specifications of it, acted as public officers,
exercising judicial and legislative power, and they are not
amenable to any one except the public for any errors, negligence, or mere misfeasance in the matters within their
jurisdiction. In this case they are not charged with any
dereliction in these respects. But when, after adopting the
plans and specifications, they undertake to carry them out
practically and do the work themselves, and employ agents
and servants to execute the plans and specifications man-
ually, then, if they are acting as officers at all, they are
merely *ministerial* officers, and not judicial or legislative,
and, according to the same authorities, are liable to third
persons for their negligence or misfeasance, or, as the authorities say, as public officers they acted *in a ministerial
capacity,* and are therefore liable. Cooley on Torts, 339–
376. If, as public officers, they owe only a duty to the
public and are not liable to persons, yet, if they so act as to
owe a duty to individuals, then their negligence therein is
an individual wrong which may be redressed by private
action. In this case the defendants owed a duty to the
traveling public, and to the plaintiff while traveling over
the bridge, to look out for her personal safety, while they
were managing the work through their servants. This is
not a public, but a private, duty, which they must discharge

properly or be liable to those injured by their negligence. As public officers, acting for the public alone, they are exempt from personal liability. The doctrine of *respondeat superior* does not apply to such. But if, as the authors say, they engage in some special employment, and their duties are of a more private character, and concern individuals as well as the public, they are amenable to private actions. Whart. Neg. § 284; Shearm. & Redf. Neg. §§ 166, 167. This distinction is plainly marked and easily applied. The authorities cited by the learned counsel of the respondents apply only to the first class, and therefore are not applicable to this case; such as *Squiers v. Neenah*, 24 Wis. 588; *Hurley v. Texas*, 20 Wis. 637; *Hamilton v. Fond du Lac*, 40 Wis. 47; *Smith v. Gould*, 61 Wis. 31. Special attention is called to *Alvord v. Barrett*, 16 Wis. 175, as illustrating the rule contended for by the learned counsel. But in that case the court said: "If the town clerk had been guilty of any *neglect of duty or misconduct*, whereby the appellant had sustained damages, the case would have been different." So in *Harris v. Baker*, 4 Maule & S. 27, the trustees for lighting streets were not liable to a person injured by falling over a heap of dust deposited in the highway, because, the court said: "They were too far removed from the cause of it." But suppose the trustees had deposited the heap in the highway, wrongfully or negligently, they would not then have been too far removed from the cause of the injury. In *New Clyde S. Co. v. River Clyde Trustees*, Hay, Dec. 79, 14 Scot. Jur. 586, it is conceded that the remedy would be against the persons who committed the wrong. The defendants rejected the contractor, who would have been liable for such an injury, and took his place to do the work, and thereby assumed the liabilities of a contractor to those injured by the negligence of their servants. The board *planned* the ditch, and are not liable for their *plan*; but if the commissioners dug the ditch, and negligently left it unguarded, and a person falls into it in the dark, are they not liable? By personally and practically undertaking to do the work through servants of their own employment, they are brought into contact and relation with the traveling public and the plaintiff, and assume corresponding duties and obligations.

This is sufficient as to the principle which governs this case, treating the defendants as officers as well as operatives. In such case it follows as of course, if *they* are liable, the *city* is not so; and that cases in which it is held that the municipality is not liable for such a personal injury caused by negligence or wrong, are authorities that the persons or officers who did the wrong or were guilty of the negligence are liable. In *Wallace v. Menasha*, 48 Wis. 79, the city treasurer sold the property of one person for the tax of another. It was held that the city was not liable for such a tort. His acting *colore officii* made no difference. In that case the doctrine and distinction as above stated, together with the above and other authorities, are fully and ably reviewed by Mr. Justice LYON, and it is a case in point with this, in principle. In *Uren v. Walsh*, 57 Wis. 98, it was held that the defendants were liable to personal action for unlawfully tearing down a fence to open a highway, and it made no difference that they pretended to act as public officers. This class of cases is distinguished from the cases cited by the learned counsel of the respondents, by the chief justice in an able review of the doctrine. It was a personal wrong for which the town was not liable, and is distinguished from those cases where the municipality is held liable because in such cases it directed the act, or ratified it, or it was within its general powers. In that class of cases the damages are the natural and proximate consequence of the illegal act, and not the result, as in this and similar cases, of some incidental and independent act of negligence or of wrong, not necessary to the work, and committed while doing it, to the injury of third persons. For such an act of negligence or of wrong as that complained of the municipality was never held liable. The city of Watertown had nothing to do with it, never authorized or ratified it, and it was not within its general powers or for its benefit. The city might as well be held liable for an assault and battery committed by these commissioners while prosecuting this work. But treating the defendants as officers and lawfully doing the work, they would be liable, and the city would not be. A city is not liable for injuries or damages caused by the neglect of its officers in the performance of their duties *(Schultz v. Milwaukee,* 49 Wis. 254); or for their misfeasance or malfeasance, or omission to perform their duties, or for negligence in its performance *(Little v. Madison,* 49 Wis. 605). When an officer of a corporation performs an illegal act resulting in an injury to another, he is liable. *Peck v. Cooper,* 112 Ill. 192. Whenever a person sued sets up a defense that he was an officer of the government acting under color of law, it plainly devolves upon him to show that the law which he invokes authorized the *particular act* in question to be done, and that he acted in good faith. *Tweed's Case,* 16 Wall. 504. But where the issue is negligence, motives or good faith are immaterial. *Hover v. Barkhoof,* 44 N. Y. 113. Where an officer injures another while performing *ministerial* duties, he is liable. *Mills v. Brooklyn,* 32 N. Y. 489. For a personal injury caused by the negligence of several persons they are severally or jointly liable. *Creed v. Hartmann,* 29 N. Y. 591; *Peoria v. Simpson,* 110 Ill. 294; *Wright v. Compton,* 53 Ind. 337; *State ex rel. Reynolds v. Babcock,* 42 Wis. 138. These general propositions are indisputable, and with the authorities are taken from the brief of the learned counsel of the appellant. We conclude, therefore, that the plaintiff had a right to recover against the defendants, except the city of Watertown, and that the court erred in directing a verdict in their favor.

By the Court.—The judgment of the circuit court is reversed, and the cause remanded for a new trial.

A motion for a rehearing was denied February 19, 1889.

WILL OF ABRAM EHLE.
ESTATE OF JAMES A. EHLE.

January 29 — February 19, 1889.

Wills: Construction: Limitation of general devise by subsequent clause: Insufficient description of land: Survivorship: Evidence: Burden of proof: Descent.

1. A testator devised "all of [his] real estate" to his son J. for life, remainder to J.'s three infant children in fee. The will then states that "the land so devised consists of 160 acres" in the town of G., and directs that upon the death of J. it shall be divided into three portions by lines running from north to south, each portion containing 53⅓ acres, and that the western third, embracing the buildings, shall belong to A., one of said children, and the other two thirds shall belong to the other two children respectively. The testator died seized of 260 acres of land in a compact form, 240 rods in length and 173⅓ rods in width. *Held:*

    (1) Even if there was a sufficient description of the 160 acres to be divided, the devise of *all* the testator's real estate was not limited to that amount by the later clause of the will. The 100 acres not to be divided would go to the infant devisees as tenants in common.

    (2) It being impossible to determine from the will the exact location of the 160 acres to be divided, the direction as to division is void for uncertainty.

2. The testator, his son J., and the wife and three infant children of the latter perished in a fire which consumed the testator's house. The evidence (fully stated in the opinion), showing the arrangement of the house, the probable origin of the fire, the location of

the bodies when found, etc., is *held* to sustain the findings of the circuit court that the testator died first and that J. died before his wife or either of the three children. The title to the testator's real estate therefore vested, under the will, in the three children, and its descent must be traced from them. If the mother survived them, the land descended to her and, upon her death, to her parents, under subd. 2, sec. 2270. R. S.; but if the children, or any of them, survived their mother the land descended to their next of kin (in this case their mother's parents aforesaid) under subd. 4 of that section. The personal estate of J. also passed to and through his widow and children.

8. In such case those claiming the real estate by descent from J., on the ground that it descended to him from his children, had the burden of showing that he survived such children. But those claiming the personal property of J. under and through his widow and children had the burden of showing that they or some of them survived him.

APPEALS from the Circuit Court for *Sheboygan* County.

The following statement of the case was prepared by Mr. Justice CASSODAY:

August 31, 1881, Abram Ehle made his last will and testament, the essential portions of which to be here considered are as follows:

"I give and devise to my wife, Susan Ehle, all of my real estate for the term of her natural life, with reversion at her death to my son James for the term of his natural life, and at his death said real estate shall revert to and become the property of his three children, namely Abram T., Flora, and Mary, absolutely. The land so devised consists of 160 acres, all in Greenbush, county of Sheboygan; and at decease of my son James shall be divided into three (3) portions, by lines running from north to south, each embracing fifty-three and one-third acres, or thereabouts; but the western third, of fifty-three and one-third acres, embracing the residence and farm buildings, shall become the property of my grandson aforesaid, Abram T., the other two thirds, respectively, becoming the property of my two

grandchildren, Flora and Mary, respectively; it being understood, and my will, that Flora, aforesaid, shall possess
the east third, and Mary, her sister, the middle third; . .
provided, also, that in case of the death of either of the
three (3) grandchildren, reversioners above specified, who
shall die before arriving at his or her legal majority, then
the reversion to that individual minor shall be divided and
become the property of the other two beneficiaries in equal
proportion, and in case of the death of a second reversioner
the survivor shall take the whole. Also I will and direct
that my gold-headed cane shall be the property of my son
James for the term of his natural life, with reversion at
his decease to my grandson, Abram T., aforesaid. Then I
give and bequeath to my son, James Ehle, all the goods and
chattels in my possession, absolutely."

April 20, 1885, Susan Ehle, mentioned in the will, died.
The said Abram Ehle, and the said James A. Ehle, mentioned in said will, and his three infant children, to wit,
Abram T., Flora, and Mary, mentioned in said will, and
their mother, Helen Ehle, the wife of the said James, were
each and all burned to death on the morning of February
16, 1886, at the house of said Abram Ehle, in which they
all resided, in the town of Greenbush, Sheboygan county.
Thereupon said will was admitted to probate in the county
court of that county.

From the judgment and assignment of said estates, entered in said matters respectively in said county court, the
blood relatives and heirs at law of said Abram and James
appealed to the circuit court; and thereupon the jury
was waived therein, and the cause was tried by said circuit court; and, upon the trial thereof therein, the court
found, in relation to the estate of said Abram, in addition to
the facts stated, in effect, that said Abram survived his
wife, Susan, mentioned in the will; that said James was
the only child of said Abram; that said infants, Flora,

Abram T., and Mary, were the only children of said James and grandchildren of said Abram; that said Helen was the mother of said infant children, and the wife of said James; that, of the persons above named at said burning, the said Abram died first in order of time, and the said James next, and the said infant children, with their said mother, died last; that *John W.* and *Caroline Taylor* are the maternal grandparents and only heirs at law surviving said three infant children; that said *John W. Taylor* is the only duly qualified administrator of the estates of said three infant children; that by said will the said Abram bequeathed and devised all of his estate to said three infant children, subject to the life interest therein in favor of their said father, the said James.

As conclusions of law therefrom, the court found, in relation to said Abram's estate, in effect, that under said will all of the estate of said Abram vested in said three infant children, in their life-time, as devisees and legatees; that, by the death of all of said infant children all of such estate vested in said *John W.* and *Caroline Taylor* as heirs at law of said infant children, and in said *John W. Taylor* as administrator of the estates of said grandchildren; that the judgment and order of the county court therein, assigning all of the real estate left by said Abram to the said *John W.* and *Caroline Taylor* as heirs at law of said infant children, and all of the residue of the personal property left by said Abram to the said *John W. Taylor* as administrator of the estates of said infant children, be, and the same was thereby, affirmed; that the costs of the respective parties be taxed therein, and constitute a charge upon said estate, and be paid out of the same; and ordered judgment accordingly. From the judgment entered thereon accordingly the blood heirs of said Abram and the said James, respectively, have appealed.

In addition to the facts stated, the court, in relation to

JANUARY TERM, 1889. 449

Will of Abram Ehle.   Estate of James A. Ehle.

the estate of said James, found, in effect, that said infant children and their mother all survived the said James; that all of the estate left by said James upon his death vested in said infant children, in their life-time, as his heirs at law; that by the death of said infant children, and by the appointment of said *John W. Taylor* as administrator of their estates, all of the residue of said estate of said James A. vested in said *John W. Taylor* as such administrator; that the judgment and order of the county court entered therein, assigning all of such residue, after paying all expenses of administration, to said *John W. Taylor* as administrator, be, and the same was thereby, affirmed; that the costs of the respective parties therein be taxed therein, and be and constitute a charge upon said estate, and be paid therefrom; and ordered judgment accordingly. From the judgment entered thereon accordingly the blood heirs of said James have appealed.

Geo. P. Knowles, for the appellants, to the point that where there is an irreconcilable repugnancy between two clauses of a will the latter clause must prevail as being the latest expression of the testator's intention, cited *Heidlebaugh v. Wagner*, 72 Iowa, 601; *Vaughan v. Cator*, 85 Tenn. 302; *Baker and Wheeler's Appeal*, 115 Pa. St. 590; *Christy v. Badger*, 72 Iowa, 581; *Hoppock v. Tucker*, 59 N. Y. 202; *Van Nostrand v. Moore*, 52 id. 12; *Freeman v. Coit*, 96 id. 63; *Pratt v. Rice*, 7 Cush. 209.

For the respondents there was a brief by *Seaman & Williams*, and oral argument by *W. H. Seaman*.

CASSODAY, J. The testator, Abram Ehle, died seized of 260 acres of land, consisting of six forties, and a narrow strip of twenty acres on the west side thereof, all in compact form, and being 240 rods in length, north and south, and 173½ rods in width, east and west.

1. It is claimed that the will only covers 160 acres of

such lands; and that as to the other 100 acres the testator died intestate; and hence that the same, upon the death of Abram, descended to James; and then, upon his survival of his wife and children, and his death, descended to his heirs at law, who in that event would have been the same as the heirs at law of Abram. The determination of the question may have some bearing upon the burden of proof in connection with the more important question of survivorship which will be considered hereafter. Undoubtedly the learned counsel for the appellants is correct in claiming "that the plain intent of the testator, as evinced by the language of his will, must prevail." It is moreover true that such intention must be collected from the whole will; that in construing it the different parts are to be examined and compared, with the view of ascertaining such intention as evinced by the whole will and not as may appear from some particular part when taken alone. *Baddeley v. Leppingwell*, 3 Burrows, 1542; *Will of Rowse*, Lofft, 99; *Lane v. Vick*, 3 How. 472; *Hopkins v. Glunt*, 111 Pa. St. 290. By the first clause of the will the testator disposed of "*all*" of his real estate to his three grandchildren "*absolutely*," subject, however, to the two intervening life estates, — one of which had been extinguished by the death of Susan Ehle prior to the death of the testator. Standing alone, the language of that clause of the will would be too plain for construction. But it is claimed that such clause is immediately followed by another, which is either repugnant to the first, or necessarily restricts its meaning to a particular 160 acres. If such is the plain meaning of that clause, then it must prevail over the first clause, in accordance with a rule well understood and supported by authorities cited by counsel. The clause referred to is to the effect that "the land so devised consists of 160 acres," to "be divided into three portions, by lines running from north to south, each embracing fifty-three and one-third acres or thereabouts," with " the residence and buildings " on the western third. Assuming, for the present, that the description of such 160 acres is sufficiently definite and certain to be located, still we would not be justified in holding that the second clause is repugnant to the first. On the contrary, the second clause, upon such assumption, merely devised such 160 acres in three equal specific parts to the respective grandchildren, leaving the other 100 acres to go to them as tenants in common. This is in harmony with the rule that where the whole will indicates nothing to the contrary a devise by words of general description is not to be cut down or limited by a subsequent attempt at a particular description. *Freeman v. Coit*, 96 N. Y. 68; Schouler on Wills, § 475. So it is in harmony with the rule that no presumption of an intent to die intestate as to any part of the estate is to be indulged, when the words of the will, fairly construed, are such as to carry the whole. *Raudenbach's Appeal*, 87 Pa. St. 51; *Ferry's Appeal*, 102 Pa. St. 207; *Given v. Hilton*, 95 U. S. 591; Schouler on Wills, § 490.

2. But we are not prepared to hold that the description of the 160 acres, attempted in the second clause of the will, is sufficiently definite and certain to be supported. True, it is to be divided by north and south lines into three equal parts, and the western third is to embrace the residence and farm buildings. Neither the length nor the breadth of such parts, however, are given. They may be the whole length of the farm,— 240 rods,— or less than 148 rods, or at any point between those distances. Of course, the width would increase as the length diminished. If we understood counsel correctly as to the location of the buildings, and we assume that the lengths of such strips were calculated to extend the whole length of the farm, then it is very plain that the west line of such 160 acres might be the west line of the whole farm, or the 160 acres might be moved gradually eastward, until such west

line struck such residence or farm buildings; and yet the western third would all the time answer the calls of such description. The same would be true, in a more limited sense, in case such strips only extended to the quarter line, or any point between that line and the south line of the farm. Thus it appears that the farm embraced an infinite number of 160-acre tracts, each of which would answer all the calls of the description given. We must hold that such attempted description of 160 acres is void for uncertainty.

3. This brings us to the important question of fact, whether the testator, Abram Ehle, and his son, James A. Ehle, or either of them, survived all three of the infant children. The determination of the question depends upon inferences and conclusions to be drawn from facts and circumstances in evidence and which are substantially undisputed, and the rules of law applicable as to the burden of proof. To enable us the better to educe such inferences and conclusions in the light of the legal principles applicable, it seems to be necessary to briefly state the situation on the night of this horrible disaster.

The house consumed was a wooden structure, and had been built about thirty-three years. The main part was two stories high, thirty-four feet long and twenty-four feet wide, with a cellar under the whole, and the front end facing the north. In the west third of this main part there was a front and back hall leading from the front door south to the kitchen in an addition or extension. Near the front door, and opposite the foot of the stairway leading above, was a door leading eastward into the front room, which was about eighteen feet long and sixteen feet wide. Immediately south of this front room was the family room, of about sixteen feet square, with two beds in it, in which James and his wife and three children slept. One of the beds in that room stood in the southwest corner, and was usually occupied by Helen and her two little girls. The other bed stood near it, and was usually occupied by James and his little boy. The heads of both beds were against the south wall of that room. On the north side of that room, and near the middle, was a chimney, running from the bottom of the cellar through the top of the roof. On the east side of this chimney was a door between this room and the front room. Near the chimney was a stove, with a zinc or iron sheet under it, and the pipe going into the east side of the chimney, in which fire was kept when the weather was very cold. There was also a stove in the cellar, with a pipe running into the chimney below, in which fire was sometimes kept in very cold weather. In the hall, and on the projected line of the partition between the front room and the family room, was a door between the front and back halls above mentioned. On the east side of the south end of this back hall was a door leading south into the kitchen. This kitchen comprised the north two-thirds of a one-story addition to, or extension of, the main building; being thirty feet long north and south, and twenty feet wide east and west, and the west line of which was on the west line of the main building projected south. In the south third of this extension there were two bedrooms,— the one on the east being occupied by a Mrs. Kinney, with a door from it opening into the kitchen, and the one on the west by the young man mentioned below, with a door from it opening into the kitchen, and a window on the west side of it looking into the wood-shed. This wood-shed extended along the whole west side of the extension mentioned, and about five or six feet further north along the west side of the main building. At the southwest corner of this back hall there was a window looking into this wood-shed.

On either side of the main building there was a wing extending north to within two or three feet of the front of the main building. The west of these wings was eighteen feet wide east and west, and twenty-six feet long north and south, occupied by Abram, who was at the time nearly eighty-two years of age. On the north end of that room there were two windows and a door, and one window on the west side. In the northwest corner of this room was a bureau upon which a kerosene lamp was kept burning all night. On the east side of the room, and a foot or two south of the partition line between the front and family rooms and the front and back halls projected, there was a stove in which wood fires were kept all night. The pipe from this stove passed up and through the partition into the back hall, and from thence through the partition into the family room, and from thence into the chimney described. This stove seems to have been an old one, and occasionally when the fire would fall down the door would fly open and coals come out upon the floor. A little south of the stove there was a door leading from this room occupied by Abram into the back hall, and across that hall in a southeasterly direction was a door leading into the room at the foot of the bed usually occupied by Helen and her two little girls. These doors were frequently left open, so that James and his wife might answer the calls of Abram, who was in poor health, and quite feeble, and required considerable attention. Helen was quite active and nervous, and easily awakened. James had a phlegmatic temperament, and it was at times difficult to wake him up. In very cold weather it was difficult to keep Abram warm, and consequently at such times his fire required much attention, and the door between his room and the back hall was usually kept shut. This was done by James or Helen, but the more frequently by Helen, as she was awakened more easily.

The old gentleman slept in a bed in the southwest corner of his room, with the head to the west. On the back or south side of his bed was a window looking out into the wood-shed.   At the foot of his bed was a door leading from his room into the wood-shed, but which was kept closed in cold weather.   In the southeast corner of his room, and next to the back hall, and just by the side of the window from the back hall into the wood-shed, there was a closet in which the old gentleman kept some of his clothing, medicine, pain-killer, liquors, and other things.   There was no door to this closet, but calico curtains were hung up in front of it. .. He kept a candle therein, with snuffers, and matches to light it.   The old gentleman was in the habit of going to this closet, and lighting the candle, and getting medicines or liquors in the night.   After the fire his body was found in the ruins beneath where this closet was, with a candlestick and snuffers near.

No one escaped from the burning house except the young man.   He had been to a neighbor's the evening before, and returned about half past ten.   There was at that time a light in the old gentleman's room, but none in the kitchen. All had apparently gone to bed.   He came through the wood-shed into the kitchen, and locked the kitchen door. Without striking any light, he passed from the kitchen into his bedroom at the southwest corner of the kitchen, and shut the door, and went to bed with his shirt, drawers, and stockings on.   After sleeping for some hours, he was awakened by the barking of the dog in the wood-shed.   He first noticed smoke in the room.   He jumped up, opened the door into the kitchen, and saw red light and flames therein. The flames from the kitchen struck him in the face, and burned his hair.   At the same time he heard the cry of James from the more remote portion of the kitchen directly in front of him, but did not see him, and neither saw nor heard any one else.   He jumped back, and then through the window, without lifting it, into the woodshed.   He reached back through the window for his trunk, just beneath, but the fire was so intense as to compel him to desist.

It was very cold — ten or twelve degrees below zero. He
had nothing on but the night-clothes mentioned. He could
see through the window back of the old gentleman's bed
that his room was all on fire. The west side of the kitchen
and on the south side of the old gentleman's room was on
fire. The fire was then, as it appeared to him, strongest
in the window opening into the wood-shed from the back
hall, and in that corner between the old gentleman's room
and the kitchen. As he went from the wood-shed around
the west side of the house to the front, he saw that fire had
broken through and was coming out of the west window of
the old gentleman's room and then going up toward the
top of the house. The front part of the main building was
all on fire, and the main part was burning stronger than
the west wing. The wind was blowing hard from the
northwest — a little more from the west than the north.
He then went to the barn, and saw that the roof of the
main part south of the chimney was all on fire and crack-
ing. He then went to Rosenthal's, about eighty rods distant. He got there about 4 o'clock in the morning. After
the fire the bodies of Helen and her three little children
were found together in the ruins near the window, beneath
the southeast corner of their family sleeping room. The
body of Mrs. Kinney was in the ruins near the window,
beneath the northeast corner of the kitchen. The body of
James was found in the ruins beneath a point about six
feet south of the door leading from the back hall into the
kitchen, and near the east wall of the stairway leading
from the kitchen to the cellar under the main building;
and at or near such body were found the remains of his
watch that he was in the habit of carrying in his vest-pocket,
marking time at about 20 minutes of 3, his knife that he
was in the habit of carrying in his pants-pocket, and the
buckles from his suspenders and overshoes. Perhaps the
buckles from the overshoes might be otherwise accounted

for, but the other things pretty clearly indicate that James was dressed at the time of his death. It is stipulated as a fact in the case, in effect, that death would result quicker from excessive heat than from smoke.

The facts and circumstances thus summarily given induce the conviction that the fire originated in the room occupied by the old gentleman, either by the falling of coals from his stove, or more probably by the curtains taking fire from the lighted candle in his hand, while helping himself to medicine or liquor in the closet. The fact that his body was found in the ruins beneath this closet is a very strong circumstance in favor of this latter supposition. Besides, the young man asserts, in effect, that the fire in that corner — in the back hall, between that closet and the kitchen — seemed to be the strongest when he first went out into the wood-shed; that the old gentleman's room was full of fire and that the windows had broken through, and that the wind was blowing very strong from the northwest. Assuming that the fire thus originated in the old gentleman's room, such a wind would naturally blow it through his door, into the back hall, and from thence through the door into the kitchen, which was substantially the condition of things disclosed by the evidence upon such first discovery. So it would naturally blow from the back hall through the door into the family sleeping-room. But had the fire originated in the family room, with the wind blowing hard from the northwest, as it did, the fire would naturally have been more advanced and intense in that part of the house, and less advanced and intense in the vicinity of the old gentleman's room and closet, the back hall, and the part of the kitchen adjoining, than appeared upon such first discovery. The inevitable conclusion from all the evidence is that the fire originated in the old gentleman's room, and that he expired before any other person in the house. Such was, in effect, the finding of the trial court.

4. This being so, it necessarily follows, as already indicated, that immediately upon his death the title to the real estate, under the will, became vested in the three infant children absolutely, subject only to the life estate of their father, James. And it follows, as a necessary corollary to this proposition, that those who claim any part of such real estate by descent from such children (subd. 2, sec. 2270, R. S.) under James, have the burden of proving that he survived the death of each and all of those children. *Newell v. Nichols*, 75 N. Y. 78; *Fuller v. Linzee*, 135 Mass. 468. The case certainly presents no preponderance of evidence in favor of such survivorship of James. In the absence of such preponderance of evidence, we are compelled to hold that such life estate of James became extinguished by his death prior to the death of all of the three children, and that upon the death of all three of them the lands descended to their mother, if living; and then, in that case, upon her death, which must have immediately followed, to her parents, *John W.* and *Caroline Taylor*, under subd. 2, sec. 2270, R. S.; but in case said children or any of them survived their mother, then said lands descended to their " next of kin, in equal degree," under subd. 4 of the same section. *Estate of Kirkendall*, 43 Wis. 167; *Ryan v. Andrews*, 21 Mich. 229. As both paternal grandparents had previously died, it is obvious that such " next of kin " were their maternal grandparents, to wit, the said *John W.* and *Caroline Taylor*. *Ibid.* Such maternal grandparents were next of kin to said infant children in the second degree, whereas their next of kin on their father's side were in a much more remote degree. 2 Bl. Comm. 203. Such were, in effect, the conclusions of the trial court.

5. The succession to the personal estate of which Abram Ehle died seized is a more difficult and delicate question. By the will he bequeathed such personal estate to his son James absolutely. James, therefore, died seized of such

personal estate, as well as any property owned by him in his own right. Under the statutes, all of the property of which he so died seized, on his death descended to such of his children and widow as might be living at the time of his death. Secs. 2270, 3935, R. S. If none of them survived him, however, then the same descended " to his next of kin, in equal degree," as prescribed in those sections; for in that event he would " have no lawful issue, widow, father, mother, brother, nor sister." Subd. 4, sec. 2270, R. S. The burden, therefore, of proving that the widow and children, or some of them, survived James, rested upon those claiming under and through such widow and children. *Newell v. Nichols*, 75 N. Y. 78; *Fuller v. Linzee*, 135 Mass. 468. The learned counsel for the appellants strenuously insists, not only that there is no preponderance of evidence in favor of such survivorship, but that such preponderance is really the other way. The evidence most relied upon in support of this contention is the fact that at the time the young man opened his door into the kitchen, and the flames struck him in the face, he heard the cry of James in the flames some ten or twelve feet in front of him; but he did not see him, and heard no other person then, nor at all. Had James at the time been in the family room with his wife and children, and perished there with them, and his voice had been recognized as emanating from that room, without hearing any other utterance, then there would have been much force in the argument. The case most relied upon in support of such contention was, in principle, similar to the case just supposed. *Pell v. Ball*, 1 Cheves Eq. 99. But that adjudication, as well as the weight of the authorities and reason, is to the effect that where the death of two or more persons results from a common disaster *the case must be determined upon its own peculiar facts and circumstances, whenever the evidence is sufficient to support a finding of such survivorship;* but in the absence of any such evidence the question of such survivorship must necessarily be regarded as unascertainable, and hence, in such case, the rights of property must be determined as if death occurred to all at the same moment of time. *Newell v. Nichols,* 75 N. Y. 78; *Wing v. Angrave,* 8 H. L. Cas. 183; *Russell v. Hallett,* 23 Kan. 276; 3 Whart. & S. Med. Jur. § 734; *Coye v. Leach,* 41 Am. Dec. 523–525, notes; *Rhodes v. Rhodes,* L. R. 36 Ch. Div. 586, cited in *Whiteley v. Equitable L. A. Society,* 72 Wis. 176.

We are therefore called upon to inquire whether there is any evidence to support the finding that the children and their mother survived the death of James. If the cry of James was evidence that he survived any one, aside from his father, there would be more plausibility in saying it was Mrs. Kinney, as both of their bodies were found beneath the ruins of the same room. Her bedroom was more remote from the place of the origin of the fire than any one in the house. The young man was manifestly in no more danger in his room than she was in hers, if as much. But he heard no cry from her, notwithstanding the door of her room was but a few feet from his. At the time he looked into the kitchen the fire in the northwest corner of that room, where the body of James was found, must have been much more intense than near her bedroom, or in the northeast corner of the kitchen, where her body was found. This being so, we would naturally suppose that she would have made some outcry at the time the young man looked into the kitchen, if she was then in that room. From her situation, and all the circumstances, it may fairly be inferred that she became suffocated without much exclamation, or else that she did not leave her room until after the young man had escaped into the woodshed, and when the circumstances were more unfavorable to his hearing such cry from her or any of the remaining victims.

But there are other circumstances strongly against the

contention of the appellants. It is established by uncontradicted evidence that James was enveloped by intense flames at the time of the utterance of the cry, and hence he must have expired within a few seconds thereafter. There is no evidence as to whether the door leading from the back hall into the room occupied by the children and their mother was open so as to admit the fire prior to such cry, unless it be inferred from the fact that James is supposed to have slept in his bed that night as usual, and must have passed out into the back hall before being enveloped in flames. He manifestly had his pants and vest on when he expired. Whether he put them on just before leaving his sleeping-room, or had worn them all night in consequence of the severity of the cold, which necessitated more frequent attention to his father's fires, is a mere matter of conjecture. So, whether he shut the door when he passed out of his sleeping-room, or left it open, or whether the fire had got into that back hall before he passed into it, or whether the door between his father's room and that back hall was open or shut when he passed from his sleeping-room into that hall, are mere matters of conjecture. It may be fairly inferred that at the time he left his sleeping-room there was no fire in it or visible from it; otherwise he would have attempted to rescue his wife and children. So it may be fairly inferred that he left that room either in answer to a recognized cry or to supply a supposed want of his father, and that the fire entered the back hall after he got into it, either by his opening the door into his father's room or in some other way. The only other hypothesis is that he had been absent from his sleeping-room for some little time before the fire.

Another circumstance tends to prove that the fire did not penetrate the family sleeping-room until some time after James had left it, and that is the fact that his wife succeeded in taking the three children from their beds to a

point near their east window, where they were manifestly
overtaken by the flames, or suffocated by the smoke, and expired together.   The direct evidence, therefore, establishes
the fact that James uttered the cry under circumstances
which made death certain to him within a few seconds;
whereas, there is no evidence that at that same moment of
time the flames had penetrated the family sleeping-room,—
much less that at that same moment death was equally imminent to the children and their mother.   It is not the case
of death to several from the same direct operating cause,
as an explosion; nor yet the case of several burning to
death in the same room, or in the same building, in the
absence of all evidence tending to show the situation of
the victims and the place of the origin and the progress of
the fire.   On the contrary the death of the several victims
resulted from a succession of causes.   The probable location of the several members of the household is established
beyond controversy.   The building covered quite a large
space of ground.   That the fire originated in the northwest
wing of the building, and took the life of the old gentleman
as its first victim, is ascertained to a moral certainty.   That
the fire was gradually pushed from that room towards the
southeast corner of the southern extension of the house by
a very strong wind from the northwest is pretty clearly
established.   That such progress was more or less obstructed
by partition walls, ceilings, and doors is equally certain.
That such fire naturally, and therefore probably, first advanced from the old gentleman's room into the back hall
seems to be morally certain.   That James first met the fire
in that hall, or at or near the door between it and the
kitchen, seems to be an inevitable conclusion from all the
evidence.   That the children and their mother were not
reached by the fire until a subsequent stage in its progress
seems probable from the construction of the building and
the direction of the wind; and there is no affirmative evi-

dence to overcome such probability. Such being the evidence, we are forced to the conclusion that the finding of the court, to the effect that the three children and their mother all survived the death of James A. Ehle, is sustained by the evidence.

By the Court.— Each and both of the judgments of the circuit court are affirmed. In pursuance of the stipulation of the parties on file, the costs and disbursements of both parties herein are ordered to be paid out of the estates in the hands of the administrator.

FAIRFIELD, Appellant, vs. BARRETTE, Respondent.

January 30 — February 19, 1889.

Boundaries: Acquiescence: Adverse possession: Evidence: Appeal: Immaterial errors: Instructions to jury.

1. Plaintiff owns the east half, and defendant the west half, of a quarter section. While the premises were occupied by their respective grantors, the plaintiff's grantor had objected that the fence between the tracts was too far east, and had procured a survey, which, however, showed that the true division line was still further east; whereupon he had importuned the defendant's grantor to allow the fence to be rebuilt on the old line, and the latter had finally consented to do so "for the present." The fence had been rebuilt accordingly, and had remained on the old line without further question for more than twenty years, when the plaintiff, being dissatisfied because the fence was too near his house, asked the defendant to join him in having a new survey made. The defendant declined to do so, and the plaintiff himself procured a new survey, which substantially agreed with the former one, showing the true line to be east of the fence. Thereupon the defendant, with the consent and by the direction of the plaintiff, proceeded to build a fence upon the line fixed by the surveys. The plaintiff afterwards brought suit to recover possession of the strip between the old fence and the new one. *Held*, that the possession of such strip by the plaintiff and his grantor had not been

adverse to the defendant and his grantor, and that the line of the old fence had not been established as the division line by agreement or acquiescence.

2. Evidence as to how the old fence would agree with the fence on the division line of a corresponding quarter section to the north, owned by a third person, was immaterial.

3. Where the trial court would have been justified in directing a verdict for the defendant, the plaintiff was not injured by omissions in the instructions given or by the refusal to give others.

APPEAL from the Circuit Court for *Crawford* County. Ejectment. The facts are stated in the opinion.

For the appellant there was a brief by *Fuller & Ward*, and oral argument by *C. S. Fuller*. To the point that it was error not to instruct the jury that an agreement as to the boundary line might be inferred from the circumstances and the actions of the parties, they cited *Pickett v. Nelson*, 71 Wis. 546, and cases there cited.

Wm. H. Evans, for the respondent.

ORTON, J. The plaintiff owns the east half of the northwest quarter of section 10, town 6, range 6 W., and the defendant the west half, which extend south to a highway which crosses said quarter section, by an irregular and somewhat of a circular line, near the south end. The plaintiff's dwelling-house and other buildings stand on the north side of this highway, and on the east side of and very near the north and south division line of said quarter. Nearly thirty years ago there was a division fence standing near the supposed north and south line of said quarter, which was replaced by one Thomas A. Savage, who then owned the west half of said quarter, and said fence so remained, and the plaintiff and his grantors occupied, cultivated, and improved the east half thereof up to said fence. A short time before this suit was brought the defendant built a fence on what he claimed was the true line between his half of said quarter and that of the plaintiff, commenc-

ing at the south end a few feet east of the old fence, with
an increasing distance from it as it extended north, and
thereby took possession of the strip of land between where
the old fence stood and the new fence. This suit in ejectment was brought by the plaintiff to obtain the possession
of this strip of land, and on the trial the plaintiff relied
upon an adverse possession of it by him and his grantors
of over twenty years for his title. The jury rendered a
verdict for the defendant, and the plaintiff has appealed
from the judgment entered upon such verdict.

The testimony established substantially the following
facts: From March, 1857, to August, 1859, the east half of
said quarter was owned by one Chester A. Pease, and from
July, 1855, to July, 1869, the west half belonged to the
said Thomas A. Savage. Some time about 1859 the said
Pease was dissatisfied with the location of the old line fence,
for the reason, probably, that it came too near his dwelling-house and other buildings, and requested the said Savage to join him in having a new survey made of the division
line, so as to have the fence removed to it, and for some
time Savage declined to do so and was willing to rebuild
the old fence where it had been; but finally Pease employed the county surveyor, Judge Brunson, to survey said
line, and paid him for his services. This newly surveyed
line was so far east that it came too near Pease's house,
and he was evidently disappointed, and importuned Savage
to consent to have the fence rebuilt on the old line. Savage was satisfied with the survey, but, as he testified, Pease
" whined " about it and wanted him to rebuild where the
old fence stood for his own convenience, and he finally consented to do so, as he testified, "*for the present*," and so it
was rebuilt and remained as aforesaid. That limitation or
reservation, "*for the present*," is presumed to have continued, and to give color to any consent or acquiescence on
the part of the defendant, and to the holding of the plaint-

iff. The plaintiff, or some of his grantors, set out an orchard and vines and gooseberry bushes, and it was occasionally cultivated up to or near said fence. There is no evidence of any question being raised after that about the fence or the line until a short time before this suit, when the plaintiff first questioned the location of it.

There seems to have been a close similarity and analogy between the circumstances attending the rebuilding of the old fence by Savage and the building of the new fence by the defendant. The plaintiff was dissatisfied with the old fence for the reason that it was too near his house and other buildings, and requested the defendant to join him in having the line resurveyed. The defendant declined to do so, and it was postponed by the plaintiff saying: "We'll let it go this year, and next year we'll survey it." About two years afterwards the defendant was about to rebuild the old fence where it had been. The plaintiff still insisted on a new survey of the line, and finally employed a surveyor by the name of Appleby to survey the line. The line he fixed was about the same one fixed by Judge Brunson. When the defendant was about to put up the new fence on the new line, the plaintiff said: "All right, that is where it should be," and pointed to a post he had fixed as the starting-point,—and said: "That post is right on the corner, and that is the post to start from." After the defendant commenced putting up the fence, the plaintiff was present, and pointed out the new line, and sent for stakes and put them along on it where the fence should be built. When the apple trees, vines, and gooseberry bushes were about to be disturbed by the new fence, the plaintiff said that "they were not of any account, and to cut them down." He said that the new line was correct, for the surveyor had run it twice, to be sure of it. When the defendant told him that he would put the fence on the new line, the plaintiff said: "Yes; that is where it must be put." "We got it surveyed

for that, and we will have it on that line." "That is where
it has got to be." The line ran over the top of the plaintiff's
root-house, and he said: "I guess I'll have to set a post on
the top of it. Yes; I guess I'll have to,"— and it was so run
so as not to make a jog in the fence. Two years before this
the plaintiff claimed that the old fence was not on the line,
and that it ought to be rebuilt on the true line. It is proper
to say that the plaintiff, as a witness, denied these statements; but the testimony of the defendant was corroborated in most respects in relation to them by the witness
Brandes, who was employed by him to put up the fence,
and the jury were warranted in finding them true.

It is very clear from the testimony that the plaintiff not
only consented, but *specially directed* the defendant to build
the fence on the line fixed by the Appleby survey, which he
procured to be made. The old line where the fence stood
so long was disputed by the plaintiff's intermediate grantor,
Pease, when the grantor of the defendant, Savage, rebuilt
the fence, and was again disputed by the plaintiff himself;
and two surveys which substantially agreed were procured
by the plaintiff and his grantor, and such new line was recognized by them as the true division line of the quarter.
The testimony in respect to such surveys was admitted without objection, and the jury had the right to find that the
line fixed by them is the true one, and that the parties respectively owned the land by virtue of their title papers on
each side of that line. At least, the plaintiff is estopped
from denying it. It may properly be assumed that the
plaintiff had always been dissatisfied with the old line for
the same reason that moved him to have the line resurveyed, for nothing had transpired to change his opinion.
These facts show anything rather than an adverse possession by the plaintiff and his grantors, or the establishment
of a division line by agreement or acquiescence; for it was
disputed by the plaintiff or a former owner every time the

old fence was to be rebuilt, and a resurvey was demanded
by them to ascertain the true line. The facts are utterly
inconsistent with adverse possession of this strip of land by
the plaintiff or his grantors. The rule is that evidence of
adverse possession must be strictly construed, and every
presumption is in favor of the true owner, and that the
plaintiff entered under his deed, and that his possession is
only co-extensive with his title, and restricted to the premises granted by his deed. *Graeven v. Dieves*, 68 Wis. 321;
Sydnor v. Palmer, 29 Wis. 252. There must be ignorance
of the true line, and an agreement, express or implied, to
adopt a certain line as the true one, and a peaceable and
continued occupancy up to such line, without adverse claim
by the adjoining owner or with his consent or acquiescence,
for twenty years, to establish a boundary line by adverse
possession. *Bader v. Zeise*, 44 Wis. 96; *Gove v. White*, 23
Wis. 282; *Tobey v. Secor*, 60 Wis. 310. These elements of
an adverse possession in view, the building of a fence on
such line, or the making of other improvements with relation to such line, may be evidence of such practical establishment of a boundary line between adjacent owners.
Warner v. Fountain, 28 Wis. 405. There has not only been
no agreement, express or implied, to make the old fence the
true line, but such line has been disputed by the plaintiff
and a former owner, and there has been no acquiescence in
such boundary. Whenever the question has arisen between
the plaintiff and defendant or their grantors as to the true
line, the plaintiff and the former owner of the east half of
said quarter have not only not acquiesced in the line where
the old fence stood or consented to it, but have claimed and
insisted that such was not the true line, and that the fence
should be removed or rebuilt on the true line, to be fixed by
a resurvey. In view of such facts, the title of the plaintiff
as well as of the defendant must be referred to their deeds,
and their possession restricted by them.

But aside from the want of the least evidence of an adverse possession, or of acquiescence in the line where the old fence stood, there is abundant evidence of *estoppel* of the plaintiff and the former owners from making the claim that the true line was where the old fence stood, which is inconsistent with the plaintiff's present claim that such is the true line. The plaintiff "should now be bound by the state of facts which he formerly induced the defendant to act upon." Bigelow on Frauds, 438; *Vilas v. Mason*, 25 Wis. 310; *Perry v. Williams*, 39 Wis. 339; *Zielke v. Morgan*, 50 Wis. 560. This is a very striking case of inconsistent claims, and of "blowing hot and cold." The plaintiff had the line surveyed, and induced and directed the defendant to build the fence upon it at considerable cost, insisting that such was the true line, and he would have the fence nowhere else, and then, in a short time thereafter, claiming in this action that he had no right to build the fence there, and that by doing so he was wrongfully dispossessing the plaintiff of this strip of land, which he owns, if at all, by virtue of a claim he has always disputed and repudiated.

The plaintiff does not claim title by deed or by the true line, but alone by adverse possession. According to the evidence, he has been holding such possession wrongfully, and by sufferance, and subordinate to the title of the defendant. It would seem that when the plaintiff had procured a resurvey to ascertain the true division line and the place where to rebuild the division fence between him and the defendant, and that when Pease, the former owner, procured a survey to ascertain the same facts as between him and Savage, the former owner of the defendant's half of the quarter, and that when such surveys were substantially alike as to the true line, and were proved by testimony not objected to by either party, *that* line ought to be accepted as the true line. But we will not so decide, for the whole case seems to have rested upon the plaintiff's proof or want of proof of title by adverse possession, and if the plaintiff fails in such proof the verdict will stand as to the right of possession of the strip of land in controversy as between the parties. The plaintiff must stand or fall upon his own title, and, having failed to show any such adverse possession of the strip of land in controversy, the motion for a new trial on the ground that the verdict was contrary to the law and evidence was properly overruled.

The only other grounds of such motion, made the subject of argument in this court, are that the testimony as to how the old fence would agree with the fence on the division line of a corresponding quarter section north, owned by one Ward, was improperly rejected, and that certain instructions of the court, that there should be an "agreement" between the adjacent owners that a certain line should be the boundary on which to predicate adverse possession, were improper. The testimony rejected was certainly quite immaterial, for where Ward built his fence could not affect the question of adverse possession, or of the true division line between these parties. The only possible objection to the instructions is that the court did not say that such an agreement might be implied or inferred from circumstances and the intention of the parties. The court did not say that such an agreement must be an express one. But it is a sufficient answer to the objections of the appellant to the instructions given, and the exceptions to the court's refusal to give certain instructions, that the facts rendered them all immaterial. There was no evidence of any agreement, express or implied, and there was no holding in good faith, and no adverse possession, against which a mere consent of the plaintiff to have the fence built on another line could not prevail. The plaintiff was not injured by the instructions given, or by the refusal to give those asked by the appellant, and would not have been injured if the court had instructed the jury to find for the defendant.

By the Court.— The judgment of the circuit court is affirmed.

THE UNITED STATES EXPRESS COMPANY, Respondent, vs. JENKINS, Appellant.

January 30 — February 19, 1889.

(1) Deposition taken in another action: Stipulation: Second trial. (2) Special verdict: When request to be made. (3, 4) Stolen property: Recovery from receiver: Preponderance of evidence sufficient: Defendant's refusal to testify.

1. A stipulation that a deposition taken in another action may be read and used upon the trial of the action in which such stipulation is made, gives the right to have it read and used upon a second trial of the latter action.
2. Where the request for a special verdict is not made until after the commencement of the argument to the jury, it is not error to refuse it.
3. In an action to recover money which the defendant has been convicted of receiving knowing that it had been stolen from the plaintiff, the latter may recover upon a preponderance of the evidence. It is not necessary in the civil action to show any guilt on the part of the defendant.
4. If, in such civil action, the defendant declines to explain how he came by the money which it is alleged belonged to the plaintiff, that fact, though not evidence that the money was the plaintiff's, may nevertheless be considered by the jury as corroborating the plaintiff's evidence.

APPEAL from the Circuit Court for *Crawford* County.

Action to recover money had and received. The cause was before this court on a former appeal, and is reported in 64 Wis. 542. When the case was called for the second trial, at the November term, 1886, the plaintiff applied for a continuance because of the absence of certain witnesses whose testimony was material to his defense. The affidavit upon which such application was based did not specifically state that the defendant had been advised by his counsel that he had a valid and substantial defense to the action in whole or in part; nor did it state that the witnesses in question were not absent by defendant's consent, connivance, or procurement. The circuit court denied the application. Other facts will sufficiently appear from the opinion.

John D. Wilson, for the appellant.

T. J. Brooks, for the respondent.

TAYLOR, J. This is an action to recover for money had and received by the defendant for the use of the plaintiff. The answer was a general denial. On the trial in the circuit court the plaintiff recovered, and from the judgment entered in his favor the defendant appeals to this court.

The learned counsel for the appellant alleges the following as errors occurring on the trial in the court below: (1) That the court erred in refusing to grant a continuance of the action on the application of the defendant; (2) that the court erred in permitting the deposition of John Day to be read in evidence against the objection of the defendant; (3) that the court erred in refusing to direct a special verdict by the jury; (4) errors in the instructions of the learned circuit judge to the jury.

There was some contention upon the argument that the evidence fails to support the verdict. We think there is no ground for this contention. The action was brought to recover from the defendant the same money which he had been convicted of receiving knowing the same to have been stolen from the plaintiff. There is no claim but that the evidence in this action made as strong a case against the defendant as the case of the state against the defendant. In the case of *State v. Jenkins*, upon writ of error, it was strongly pressed upon this court that the conviction of the defendant was not sustained by the evidence, and after a careful consideration of that case this court came to the conclusion that the evidence sustained the conviction, and refused to set aside the verdict and grant a new trial. See *Jenkins v. State*, 62 Wis. 49. If the evidence was sufficient to sustain a conviction in the criminal case, there can be no question as to its sufficiency to sustain the verdict in this case.

That the court refused to grant a continuance of the action upon the application of the defendant was a matter very much in the discretion of the trial court, and we find nothing in the case to show that the court abused its discretion in this matter. The affidavit upon which the continuance was asked did not conform to the requirements of the rules of court in such cases.

1. It is urged that it was error to permit the deposition of John Day to be read in evidence. This deposition was read in evidence under the following stipulation of the parties to the action:

" *United States Express Co. vs. Joseph Jenkins.*

" *Cynthia Jenkins vs. J. B. Davis et al.*

" It is hereby stipulated and agreed by and between the parties in both the above-entitled actions, by their respective attorneys, that the evidence and testimony of the following named witnesses, to wit: R. Pike, Chas. A. Miller, Daniel Clark, A. J. Pipkin, Morris Carroll, H. McReynolds, M. McSpaden, J. W. Sanger, G. Guentzel, J. McGlaughlin, A. Dexter, A. Alderman, R. Spiegelberg, Wm. Nauert, James Kerr, S. Bartholemew, J. Sidler, and John Day,— given on the trial of the *State of Wisconsin vs. Joseph Jenkins*, tried at the February term, 1884, of the circuit court of Grant county,— be read in evidence in the trials of above-entitled actions, from the reporter's minutes of said testimony as taken on said trial of *State v. Jenkins*, and that the same be read and used upon the trial of such actions as evidence in said actions; and it is further stipulated and agreed that the testimony of said witnesses, as given at said trial of *State v. Jenkins,* is what they would swear to if present at the trial of said actions, and the same is to be subject to any proper objections as to competency, materiality, or otherwise; and those cases not to be taken up before Thursday, 29th inst.

"Thomas & Fuller and Brooks & Dutcher, Attorneys for U. S. Ex. Co. and the Sheriff.

"Bushnell & Watkins and Alex. Provis, Attorneys for Joseph & Cynthia Jenkins.

"*Dated May 10th, 1884.*"

This deposition was read on a previous trial of this action, in which a verdict was obtained by the defendant, which was reversed on appeal by this court, and a new trial directed. See 64 Wis. 542. It is contended by the learned counsel for the defendant that the stipulation only authorized the reading of said testimony or deposition on the former trial, and does not give the right to have it read on the new trial ordered by this court. We are of the opinion that the stipulation is broad enough to permit the reading of the evidence in any trial of the action which is necessary to determine the rights of the parties in said action.

2. The statute giving the right to a party to demand a special verdict in any case, requires that such demand must be made "at or before the close of the testimony and before any argument to the jury is made or waived." See sec. 2858, R. S. In this case the demand for a special verdict was not made until after the testimony in the case was closed, and after the plaintiff had commenced his argument to the jury. The demand came too late to make it the duty of the court to direct a special verdict, and it was in the discretion of the judge whether he would grant it or not. There was no error, therefore, in not granting the

request for a special verdict. *Lockhart v. Fessenich*, 58 Wis. 588.

3. Exceptions are taken to nearly all the instructions given by the learned judge to the jury. After reading the instructions as they are found in the record, we find nothing to which exception can be justly taken. There are, in fact, but two which seem to be relied upon as erroneous in this court. The first is that it was error to charge the jury in this case that "the plaintiff must recover upon the preponderance of the testimony. It is not necessary that you should be convinced beyond a reasonable doubt," etc. It is claimed by the learned counsel for the defendant that, in order to entitle the plaintiff to recover in this action, it is necessary to convict the defendant of a crime, and that therefore the rule as to the sufficiency of evidence in criminal cases should be applied to this case. There are two answers to this proposition: (1) The rule contended for by the learned counsel for the appellant has been repudiated by this court (see *Washington Union Ins. Co. v. Wilson*, 7 Wis. 169; *Wright v. Hardy*, 22 Wis. 348; *Blaeser v. Milwaukee M. M. Ins. Co.* 37 Wis. 37; *Hartwig v. C. & N. W. R. Co.* 49 Wis. 358; *Whitney v. Clifford*, 57 Wis. 156); and (2) the plaintiff might recover in this action without showing any guilt on the part of the defendant. The action is for money had and received for plaintiff's use, and all it would be necessary to prove on the part of the plaintiff to establish its right to the money in the hands of the defendant would be that the money found in his possession was the money of the plaintiff, that it had not come to the hands of the defendant by the assent of the plaintiff, either express or implied, and that the money had been demanded of the defendant.

It is also objected that the court commented to the jury upon the fact that the defendant, although in court and having the right under the law to testify in the action in his own behalf and explain, if he could, how the money in question came into his possession, declined so to do; and stated to the jury that they might consider that fact in coming to a conclusion as to the ownership of the money in question. This being a civil action, the statute rule in criminal cases does not govern the case, and the rules of law applicable to civil cases must apply. When the case which the evidence of the plaintiff tends to establish is such that if not in reality the truth of the matter, and the evidence to disprove it is in the power of the defendant to produce in court, his neglect or refusal to produce it is to be taken as a circumstance against him. It is a kind of suppression of evidence which courts have always disapproved. See 2 Whart. Ev. (2d ed.), §§ 1266–1268, and cases cited in notes. In *Brown v. Schock*, 77 Pa. St. 471, where the question to be tried was the identity of the plaintiff, his refusal or neglect to appear in person in the court was held to be a circumstance which might be considered against him. So the refusal to produce documents which are in the possession of the opposite party and have been called for and parol evidence of the contents given, if there be doubt as to the interpretation of the contracts upon such parol evidence, the interpretation most unfavorable to the party suppressing the evidence will be adopted. See *Cooper v. Gibbons*, 3 Campb. 363; *Crisp v. Anderson*, 1 Starkie, 35; *Hanson v. Eustace's Lessee*, 2 How. 653; *Clifton v. U. S.* 4 How. 242; *Barber v. Lyon*, 22 Barb. 622; *Cross v. Bell*, 34 N. H. 83; *Life & F. Ins. Co. v. Mechanic F. Ins. Co.* 7 Wend. 31. There is a strong presumption that the defendant must have known when and of whom he obtained the money in question, and he could have explained that matter to the jury by his own testimony. He was not bound to do that, but if he failed to do it he left himself subject to the suspicion that he could not explain it in a way to defeat the contention of the plaintiff upon the subject. His declining to explain how he came by the money is not evidence that the money was the money of the plaintiff, but, in the language of this court in the case of *Hinton v. Wells*, 45 Wis. 272, "it is a fact to be taken into consideration as corroborating the evidence of the plaintiff." We think the remarks of the learned judge upon this subject were sufficiently guarded, within the rules of law applicable to questions of a similar nature.

We think the case was fairly tried, and submitted to the jury upon instructions to which there can be no reasonable objections.

By the Court.— The judgment of the circuit court is affirmed.

REISER, Respondent, vs. STAUER and another, Appellants.

January 30 — February 19, 1889.

Contracts: Instructions to jury.

1. The plaintiff agreed to take entire charge of all engines, boilers, and pumps in the defendants' saw-mill, to keep them in good repair and running order, and to keep in repair "all other machinery located and situated in said saw-mill," for a certain sum for one year. During the year the plaintiff superintended the digging of a well and the putting in of a pump, water-pipes, and hydrants in the mill-yard, constituting a system of water-works for the protection of the property against fire. In an action to recover extra compensation therefor, it is *held* that the contract did not in terms cover such work, and, there being evidence tending to show an implied contract that plaintiff should be paid therefor, a verdict in his favor will not be disturbed.

2. There being evidence of declarations of the plaintiff that he considered the work as embraced in his contract, a charge that if, at the time it was being done, plaintiff assumed that it came within the contract and that it was his right and duty to superintend it under

the contract, and defendants understood that he was doing the
work as part of his duty under the contract, he could not recover,
was sufficiently favorable to the defendants.

APPEAL from the Circuit Court for *Crawford* County.

Action to recover $633.75 for work, labor, and services
of the plaintiff in superintending the building of a well,
laying water-pipes, and setting hydrants, and other work
and labor in connection with the same on the mill premises
of the defendants, and also for machinery and materials
sold, furnished, and delivered by the plaintiff to the defendants at their said mill premises. The defendants owned
and operated a saw-mill in the city of Prairie du Chien,
and the plaintiff owned and operated a machine shop and
foundry in the same city.

The answer alleges that all the work, labor, and services
performed and materials furnished by the plaintiff were
performed and furnished under a written contract whereby
it was provided that the plaintiff, in consideration of $1,400,
for the period of one year, "agrees to take entire charge
and control of all engines and boilers and pumps, and see
that said engines and boilers and pumps are properly and
satisfactorily run and operated to the said *Stauer & Daubenberger;* and also agrees to keep said engines and boilers and pumps in good repair and in running order; said
engines and boilers and pumps are located and situated
in the saw-mill of *Stauer & Daubenberger* at Prairie du
Chien, Wisconsin. The said *Christian Reiser* further
agrees, in consideration of said sum of $1,400, to keep in
repair and to repair all other machinery located and situated in said saw-mill during the time herein specified." The
answer also alleges full payment for all labor performed
and materials furnished under said contract.

It appeared that the well, water-pipes, and hydrants
mentioned in the complaint constituted a system of water-
works in the defendants' mill-yard for the protection of the

property against fire, and that such water-works were constructed during the year covered by the written contract set forth in the answer. No special employment of the plaintiff to superintend such construction was shown. Other facts will sufficiently appear from the opinion. The plaintiff had a verdict for $399.80, and from the judgment entered thereon the defendants appeal.

T. J. Brooks, for the appellants.

For the respondent there was a brief by *Fuller & Ward,* and oral argument by *C. S. Fuller.*

Cole, C. J. The appellants claim that the judgment in this case should be reversed, (1) because the verdict is contrary to the evidence, and (2) for errors in the charge of the court.

There is ample testimony to support the verdict, as an examination of the bill of exceptions will show. It well may be, as counsel claims, that the finding is against what appears to be the weight of testimony. But the jury had the right to weigh the evidence, and to credit the plaintiff's testimony as against the conflicting evidence; and that testimony tended to prove that there was an implied contract that he should be paid for his labor in digging the well, putting in the pump, and constructing the water-works. It is said the plaintiff had entered into a written contract by which he was bound to perform these services for a stipulated salary. By the written contract he agreed to take entire charge and control of all engines, boilers, and pumps, and to see that such engines, boilers, and pumps were properly and satisfactorily run and operated; also to keep said engines, boilers, and pumps in good repair and running order,— said engines, boilers, and pumps being located and situated in the mill of the defendants at Prairie du Chien. This was the precise service which, by the contract, he had undertaken to perform. Nothing is said in the contract about digging a well, putting in a pump, or constructing a system of water-works to be used for the protection of the property in case of fire. It is inconceivable how so important a matter should have been entirely omitted from the contract if the parties really intended that the plaintiff should superintend and take charge of these works for the salary he was to receive. For, as we have said, the contract is plain, and distinctly specifies the service the plaintiff had to perform.

But it is said the contract should be read in the light of surrounding circumstances, and that the acts and declarations of the parties themselves should have controlling weight in its construction. In this case such evidence was admitted not for the purpose of construing the contract, which the court below held to be perfectly intelligible in its meaning, but as bearing upon the question whether there was an implied contract that the plaintiff should be paid for his services in putting in the water-works. We think the court was entirely right in holding that the putting in of the water-works to protect the property from fire was not a service within the letter and intent of the contract as written, and it certainly is not.

There was evidence of declarations of the plaintiff that he considered this work as embraced in his contract. But upon that point the court directed the jury, if they should find from all the circumstances that, at the time this work was being done, the plaintiff assumed that it was work which came within the contract, that it was work he had the right to superintend and which it was his duty to superintend by virtue of his general employment under the contract, and that the defendants also so understood that he was doing that work as a part of his duty under the contract,— there could be no recovery. It seems to us that this was as favorable to the defendants' contention as the law would allow. The written contract being definite, plain, and unambiguous in its terms; the matter of taking charge of or of putting in a system of water-works not even being mentioned in it; the plaintiff's work being clearly specified to be to take charge of and control and keep in repair all engines, pumps, and machinery located or situated in defendants' mill at Prairie du Chien,— clearly defines and specifies the duty the plaintiff was to perform. It is true he had entered into a contract to do certain things for a year for a stated salary. But, as the counsel on the other side justly observes, the contract did not call for the personal service of the plaintiff in the sense that his time belonged to the defendants. He might, as he did in fact do, employ others to run the engines and keep the machinery in repair; and so long as this business was properly attended to, to the satisfaction of the defendants, the contract was kept and performed on his part. If, in addition to the specified service, the plaintiff superintended the construction of the water-works under a reasonable expectation that he was to be paid for that work what it was worth, and if the defendants had reasonable grounds to believe, while the water-works were being constructed, that it was outside of the contract and that the plaintiff expected to be paid for it, having accepted the work they are liable to him for just compensation.

The circumstances from which the law will imply a contract were quite fully stated by the court in its charge, and the whole case seems to have been fairly submitted upon the evidence. We perceive no error in the charge of which the defendants can complain, and the judgment of the circuit court must therefore be affirmed.

By the Court.— Judgment affirmed.

MORRIS, Respondent, vs. PECK, imp., Appellant.

January 30 — February 19, 1889.

*(1) Mortgages: Non-negotiable note: Assignment: Pleading. (2) Fore-
closure: Judgment: Error in computation of amount due. (3)
Judgment: Special term: Authentication: Appeal.*

1. In an action to foreclose a mortgage securing a non-negotiable note
   or contract for the payment of money, an allegation that the
   plaintiff paid the mortgagee the whole amount due thereon (stating time, place, and amount), " for and in consideration of which"
   the mortgagee "then and there sold, assigned, and delivered to
   said plaintiff all her right, title, and interest in and to said contract and mortgage and the amount due thereon," sufficiently
   avers the transfer of the securities to the plaintiff, and shows his
   ownership thereof and his right to maintain the action.

2. In an action to foreclose a mortgage the defendant appeared and
   had due notice of the application for judgment. By a mistake in
   computation the amount which the referee reported to be due after
   deducting payments, and which was inserted in the judgment,
   was slightly too large. *Held,* that the defendant must have called
   the attention of the trial court to the error, or at least have demanded that the plaintiff remit the excess, before such error will
   be available to him on appeal. *Zwickey v. Haney,* 63 Wis. 464,
   distinguished.

3. Where in an action in the circuit court for one county judgment is
   rendered at a special term of that court held in another county, the
   want of proper authentication of the judgment by the clerk of the
   latter county (sec. 2428, R. S.) is not a jurisdictional defect, but, at
   most, a mere irregularity which will not be corrected on appeal
   unless an opportunity is first given to the circuit court to supply
   the alleged defect in the record.

APPEAL from the Circuit Court for *Richland* County.
The facts are stated in the opinion.

For the appellant the cause was submitted on briefs by
Michael Murphy.

For the respondent there was a brief by *Black & Burnham,* attorneys, and *F. J. Lamb,* of counsel, and oral argument by *Mr. Lamb.*

Lyon, J. This appeal is by the defendant *Nancy Peck* from a judgment for the foreclosure of a certain mortgage on real estate, executed by her and the defendant O. P. Peck to one Eva A. Rolfe, and by her alleged to have been assigned to the plaintiff. The appellant asks a reversal of the judgment on either of the three following grounds:

1. The appellant *Nancy Peck* interposed a general demurrer to the complaint, which was overruled by the court. The first error is assigned upon this ruling, and it is claimed that the demurrer should have been sustained. The complaint sets out an instrument for the payment of money, which, it is alleged, the mortgage in suit was given to secure. Such instrument is denominated in the complaint a contract in writing for the payment of money. It is doubtless a non-negotiable promissory note. The point of the demurrer is, the complaint does not show that the note was ever transferred to the plaintiff so as to enable him to maintain this action. The proposition is unfounded in fact. The complaint alleges that the plaintiff paid Eva A. Rolfe, the mortgagee, the whole amount due on such instrument and mortgage at her request (stating date, place, and amount), and that "for and in consideration of which the said Eva A. Rolfe then and there sold, assigned, and delivered to said plaintiff *Edward Morris* all her right, title, and interest in and to said contract and mortgage and the amount due thereon." This is an effectual averment of the transfer of the securities to the plaintiff, showing his ownership thereof and his right to maintain this action to foreclose the mortgage. Hence the demurrer was properly overruled — no other objection having been made to the complaint, which is in the usual form of complaints in such actions.

2. The action was brought in the circuit court of Richland county. The judgment purports to have been made

at a special term of that court held at the court house in
the county of Crawford, on the first day of the May term,
1888, which was a general term of the circuit court of the
latter county. Such term was also a special term of the circuit court of Richland county, and the judgment was properly rendered at such special term. The judgment is signed
by the judge, and was afterwards filed and recorded in the
circuit court for Richland county. It bears no signature
thereon, or other authentication thereof, by the clerk of
the circuit court of Crawford county. The want of such
authentication is assigned as error.

It may be the regular practice required that the judgment should have been authenticated by such clerk by filing the same, or in some other authorized manner, before
it was transmitted to Richland county. Such seems to be
the requirement of the statute. R. S. sec. 2428. But we
do not think the judgment should be reversed for such irregularity, if it be one. The appellant should have moved
the circuit court of Richland county to strike the judgment
from the files and records of the court, or for any other
appropriate relief because of such a want of authentication.
In such case it would have been proper for that court to
have returned the judgment to Crawford county for authentication — thus curing the irregularity and saving the .
expense and delay of an appeal to this court. The judgment bears the signature of the circuit judge, and was made
at an authorized special term of the court in which the action was pending. In such case, we do not think the want
of proper authentication is a jurisdictional defect, but that,
at most, it is a mere irregularity, which this court will not
correct on appeal unless an opportunity is first given the
circuit court to supply the alleged defect in the record.

8. Several payments having been made upon the mortgage debt, running through a period of over five years, the
court sent the securities to a referee for computation of the

amount due upon them, and the referee afterwards reported as so due the amount inserted in the judgment. It is now claimed that this amount is about eight dollars too large. This is probably true. Because of such excess the appellant claims a reversal of the judgment, and relies upon the case of *Zwickey v. Haney*, 63 Wis. 464, as authority therefor. In that case judgment was taken by default for interest on the mortgage debt for one year, over and above what was demanded in the complaint. For that reason a judgment of foreclosure was reversed. That case is clearly distinguishable from this. The judgment there included a demand not claimed in the complaint, and entirely outside the cause of action therein stated. Here the plaintiff has only recovered the specific debt, less payments, which he claimed to recover, the error consisting solely in a mistaken computation of the amount unpaid on the securities. Such computation was inside the limits designated in the complaint. Moreover, the judgment in that case was by default, while here the appellant appeared in the action and had due notice of the application for judgment. These differences take the case out of the rule of *Zwickey v. Haney*, and require the application of a different rule of practice. We hold, therefore, that the appellant should have called the attention of the circuit court, either by motion or otherwise, to such error in the computation, or at least should have demanded of the plaintiff that he remit the erroneous excess from the judgment, before the error can be available to him in this court on an appeal from the judgment. The record fails to show that he has done so.

For the foregoing reasons the judgment of the circuit court must be affirmed.

By the Court.— Judgment affirmed.

THE McCORMICK HARVESTING MACHINE COMPANY, Respondent, vs. HAMILTON and others, Appellants.

January 31 — February 19. 1889.

Mortgages: Homestead: Duress: Parent and child.

The evidence in this case is *held* (contrary to the finding of the trial court) to show that the mortgage sought to be foreclosed was executed, as to the homestead embraced therein, by the defendant wife under duress and undue influence exerted by means of threats that unless she so executed it the plaintiff would cause the imprisonment of her son for a crime of which the latter was not in fact guilty. The mortgage is therefore void as to such homestead.

APPEAL from the Circuit Court for *Richland* County. The facts are stated is the opinion.

For the appellants there was a brief by *L. H. Bancroft*, and oral argument by *Mr. Bancroft* and *H. W. Chynoweth*.

For the respondent there was a brief by *Eastland & Son*, and oral argument by *H. A. Eastland*.

The following opinion was filed February 19, 1889:

ORTON, J. This appeal is from the judgment of foreclosure of the following mortgage: By *Peter Hamilton* and *Bridget*, his wife, to the respondent company, on the south half of the northwest quarter of section 13, and the southeast quarter of the northeast quarter of section 14, town 10 N., range 1 W., to secure the payment of three notes given by *M. J.* and the said *Peter* and *Bridget Hamilton*, for $600, payable June 1, 1887; $600, payable June 1, 1888; and for $600, payable January 1, 1889,— dated November 20, 1885. The defendant *Bridget Hamilton* answered the complaint in the action by setting up substantially that the last above described forty acres was the homestead of herself and husband, *Peter Hamilton;* and that she was induced and unduly influenced to sign said mortgage, so far as said homestead was concerned, by duress and threats of imprisonment of her son, the said *M. J. Hamilton*, for the crime of embezzlement; and that said mortgage in respect to said homestead is therefore void. The circuit court found against her on that issue, and rendered judgment of foreclosure as to all the land described in said mortgage. An appeal was taken to this court from said judgment by both *M. J.* and *Bridget Hamilton*, but the case of *Bridget Hamilton* alone has been brought to the attention of the court.

The ground relied upon is that the judgment is against the law and evidence. By force of what we deem is a very strong preponderance of the evidence against it, we are compelled to differ with the learned circuit court in its finding on this issue. The general facts, and the testimony on the issue of duress, are as follows:

Some time in the year of 1881, *M. J. Hamilton*, the son of the said *Peter* and *Bridget Hamilton*, became the agent of the respondent company, at Richland Center in this state, to sell its machinery. Until May, 1885, an annual settlement had been made with him and his accounts adjusted. Before that time the said *M. J.* had been subject to occasional and temporary insanity, and about that time he had given evidence of a return of that malady, and was wild and reckless in his sales and business, and the company had been notified by his family that they must send an agent to look after their business in his hands. Accordingly, William Varco, the general agent of the company, came there and examined his affairs, and induced his brother John to be associated with him in business by their advertisement, but left *M. J.* ostensibly to continue in it. The agent Varco at the same time induced the father of *M. J.*, the said *Peter Hamilton*, to become his security for the business left in his hands. About the 18th day of November thereafter, his brother John notified the company that *M. J.* had again become insane, and had been taken to the insane hospital. The said Varco again came to look over his business and adjust his accounts. He found that *M. J.* owed the company about $1,200, and had in his hands about $600 worth of the company's property, consisting of various articles and notes received for machinery. He turned over this property to *M. J.*, and charged him with a deficiency to the company of $1,800, for which he demanded mortgage security of the father and mother, *Peter* and *Bridget Hamilton*, upon their whole farm, including their homestead. He charged *M. J.*, who had then returned, with being guilty of embezzlement. When asked by *M. J.* if he thought he could find him guilty of embezzlement in consequence of his having fallen short in his accounts he cited the case of a man who was found guilty of embezzlement under similar circumstances, and said if the mortgage was not given he would "crack his whip." The agent and witness Varco gave this version of that threat: "Finally I said, 'I am getting tired of this. If I cannot settle this, I will crack my whip.'" This threat evidently excited *M. J.* very much, and put him in great fear.

Varco had several interviews with the mother, *Bridget Hamilton*, and tried to induce her to sign the mortgage for the homestead, and she as persistently refused, but offered to sign the mortgage for the balance of the farm, and Varco refused to take such a mortgage. She testified as follows: "He wanted me to sign a mortgage on my homestead, or he would send my son to state prison for one year or ten. He said, if I did not give a mortgage, he would have to go to state prison one year or ten. He said, 'Don't you think more of your son than the *McCormick Company* does?' I said, 'I ought to.' He replied, 'Would you rather sign a mortgage on your homestead than to have your son go to state prison for a year or ten? . . . The *McCormick Company* knows the law and they will use it.' He said, if

JANUARY TERM, 1889.   489

The McCormick Harvesting Machine Co. vs. Hamilton and others.

I did not sign the mortgage he would commence proceedings at once, and send my son to the state prison. 'Would you not rather sign the mortgage than to have your son go to state prison?' When Mr. Varco first suggested taking the mortgage, I offered to sign a mortgage for all the land but the homestead forty, including twenty acres of wheat and some grass and corn; but he insisted he wanted all the farm, or send the boy to prison." On cross-examination she repeated that he said: "Your son must go to state prison unless you sign the mortgage. Don't you think more of your son than the *McCormick Company?*" She testified further: "I put my name on the mortgage entirely against my will, and I told them so then. I never would have signed for any other purpose but to keep my boy from state prison, and I believed, did I not sign it, they would send him to state prison. I did not do it willingly. I was forced to do it."

James Hamilton, brother to *M. J.*, testified as follows: "They were talking there all the evening. He [Varco] wanted her [his mother] to sign the mortgage. She told him she would not. He wanted to know of her if she did not think more of her son than the *McCormick Company* did. Then he told her he wanted to know why it was she would not sign the mortgage, and she told him that she did not think she had any reason to; that her son had not done anything, and that she did not owe anybody; and it seemed to me like he got mad, and he jumped up and said *he would crack his whip*, and started out of the office. I asked him, provided my mother did not sign that mortgage, what they wanted to do with my brother. He said they had one fellow *in* for three years on just such a case as that, and this was a good chance for another; but it was not him who would execute it; that it would be the company." This explains what Varco meant when he threatened that he would turn it over to the company. James told his mother this conversation, and he said to his mother: "For God's sake, if it is a case of embezzlement and they can imprison him, don't have him imprisoned for this place."

William Varco, the agent, testified as follows: Supposing a certain state of facts, he said: "And that, in my opinion, it would constitute embezzlement. *Mrs. Hamilton* asked me what would be the penalty if he was guilty of embezzlement. I told her that I did not know; that I understood it to be a penitentiary offense, but, as to the penalty, that would be with the court and jury." This language clearly means, that *it would be* with the court and jury to fix the penalty in the case of her son. He testified further: "She said, 'Would you send *Mike* to the penitentiary?' I said, 'No.' I asked this mortgage in a settlement of this business between ourselves, to stop litigation of any kind. She said she did not think that, in view of the amount of business he had done for the *McCormick Company*, that they would send him to the penitentiary. I said, of course I could not tell whether they would be disposed to or not, but if they could, without a superior power to prevent it, would you expect them to think more of your son than you? Finally I said: 'I am getting tired of this. If you cannot settle this, *I will crack my whip.*' I told *Mrs. Hamilton* I thought it would be better to settle up and avoid litigation. I supposed that, as a matter of course, if they did not settle up, they would commence some suit." When asked: "Did not you tell him [*M. J.*] that you thought he was liable for embezzlement?" he replied: "I told him I thought he was." He further testified "that he was not positive that *Mrs. Hamilton* did not say that it was entirely against her will and against every vein in her body that she signed the mortgage." When asked: "You say that you never stated to *Mrs. Hamilton* that it would go pretty hard with the boy if he did not sign the mortgage?" he replied: "I won't say any such thing. I rather think *it would* have gone hard with the boy. He would have had a lawsuit on his hands." When *Mrs. Hamilton* still insisted, as he testified, that if he was even' guilty of embezzlement he had done so much for the company that they would not prosecute him, he again said: "Do you think they would think more of your· boy than you do?" This testimony of Varco, the agent of the company, corroborates the testimony of *Mrs. Hamilton* in all essential particulars, and she is corroborated further by her sons in respect to his charging *M. J. Hamilton* with the crime of embezzlement, and one of them corroborates her testimony that this charge was brought to her knowledge before she signed the mortgage to induce her to sign it.

It is true that the finding of the circuit court in such a case, or in other cases, ought not to be disturbed by this court without a clear preponderance of the testimony against it, and that on the question of the credibility of the witnesses the trial court or the jury has superior advantages and better means of determining it than this court, having seen the witnesses and heard them testify, yet, when the testimony, as in this case, not only very strongly preponderates against the finding but is all one way against it, and the material facts stand admitted by the agent of the company who made the threats and was guilty of the duress, then the duty of this court is clear to find the facts otherwise and reverse the judgment. It is perfectly certain that *Bridget Hamilton* would never have signed the mortgage which included their homestead if Varco had not threatened that if she did not he would prosecute and imprison her son *M. J. Hamilton* for the crime of embezzlement, and that she signed it for no other consideration than to prevent his imprisonment for that pretended crime, notwithstanding she did not herself think that he was guilty of any crime whatever. She evidently feared that the power of the company and Varco might be sufficient to effect such a result. The evidence tends to show that, after having known for some time, while *M. J. Hamilton* was acting as the agent of the company, that he was subject to occasional and temporary insanity, and having kept a superintending control of his business, and brought him to frequent settlements,— most probably on that account,— this general agent of the company made an accounting of this young man's business when he was again suffering to some extent his terrible malady, and finding a balance of $1,200 against him, and turning over to him articles of personal property and notes valued at $600 which belonged to the company, compelling him to purchase them to swell his deficiency to the company, and after having exacted the security of his father, who owned a farm of 120 acres, so far as we know unincumbered, and after having been offered a mortgage on eighty acres of the land with twenty acres of wheat upon it, probably ample security for the $1,800, that he then threatened this unfortunate boy with a prosecution for embezzlement, which added the excitement of fear to his deranged intellect, and threatened his mother, whose love and sympathy for him were so great that she would become homeless rather than he should be sent to prison for such a crime. She believed that if she did not sign away their homestead he would be prosecuted and imprisoned for that crime. If Varco had not virtually admitted in his testimony that he did so threaten, the facts that he was so persistent to have the mortgage embrace the homestead, and refused to take it if it did not, and that she as persistently refused and delayed and was most earnestly unwilling to do so, and that she finally signed the mortgage very reluctantly, would naturally suggest the inquiry, What caused or induced her to do it? What other cause was there or could there have been, if it was not to keep her son from imprisonment for some pretended crime with which he had been threatened? She had no occasion to fear anything else. She could see no way by which they could pay the $1,800, and she expected if she signed the mortgage she would sooner or later be turned out of her homestead. The testimony of Varco alone, under such a most reasonable probability, is amply sufficient to establish the fact that he did so threaten her with the imprisonment of her son. *M. J. Hamilton* was not guilty of embezzlement, or of any crime, and Varco knew it. There is no testimony in this case that casts even a suspicion of crime upon him, and the presumption of the law is that he has been guilty of no crime.

In view of these facts, the law is well settled that the mortgage, so far as the homestead is concerned, is absolutely void. If these facts did not technically constitute *duress* of imprisonment, for which contracts will be set aside, *in equity* it is very clear that *Bridget Hamilton* was so put in fear and under terror by the repeated threats of Varco that they would imprison her son, and she was so unduly influenced and overpowered by them, that she did not sign away her homestead of her own free will, and such act should be declared void. *Fay v. Oatley*, 6 Wis. 42; *Bogie v. Bogie*, 37 Wis. 373; *Kuelkamp v. Hidding*, 31 Wis. 503; *Watkins v. Brant*, 46 Wis. 419; *Lefebvre v. Dutruit*, 51 Wis. 326; *Smith v. Smith*, 60 Wis. 329. "When one is under the influence of extreme terror, or of threats, or of apprehensions, short of duress, his acts may be avoided, for in cases of this sort he has no free will, but stands *in vinculis*." 1 Story, Eq. Jur. § 239. But the modern doctrine of *duress* is established where actual or *threatened* violence or restraint contrary to law compels one to enter into or discharge a contract. Bouv. Law Dict. "When there is a fear of imprisonment, excited by threats, it is *duress*." Will. Eq. Jur. 209. "Terrifying a woman by threats of prosecuting her husband for alleged embezzlement is such coercion as to avoid a transfer of her property thus obtained." *Ibid.; Richards v. Vanderpoel*, 1 Daly, 71. In *Eadie v. Slimmon*, 26 N. Y. 9, Slimmon went to the house of Eadie and charged him with embezzlement committed while he was in his employment, and demanded of his wife that she should assign to him a policy of insurance she held on her husband's life, or that her husband should be arrested at once and taken to prison. She became frantic with grief and terror, and finally assigned the policy. It was set aside. "A threat to procure the arrest and imprisonment of one's son under a false criminal charge, and reasonable ground to believe that such threat will be executed, probably constitute duress." *Schultz v. Culbertson*, 46 Wis. 313. In *Harris v. Carmody*, 131 Mass. 51, the father gave his note of $1,000, and, secured it by mortgage on his real estate, induced by the threat that his son would be prosecuted and imprisoned for the crime of forgery if he did not do so. It was held that the mortgage should be avoided. It is a maxim, "If a man menace me that he will imprison or hurt in body my father *or my child* except I make unto him an obligation, I shall avoid this duress as well as if the duress had been to mine own person." Bac. Max. 18; *McClintick v. Cummins*, 3 McLean, 158.

There seem to be very few cases where it is held that a contract or conveyance may be avoided by duress to one's child, but many cases by duress to one's husband or wife, and such seems to have been the limit by the older authorities. But natural affection is as strong towards one as towards the other, and the same moral obligation of mutual protection exists between them, and the threats of personal injury to the child would be as great an inducement or undue influence as to the husband or wife, and there is no possible reason for the exception. The maxim *persona conjuncta æquiparatur interesse proprio*, under which it has been so often held that duress to the wife is the same as to the hus-

The McCormick Harvesting Machine Co. vs. Hamilton and others.

band himself, may well embrace duress to a child to influence the parent. It is sufficient that the threat of imprisonment of the child produces such fear and terror of the parent as to overpower his will and coerce his assent against every mental power of resistance.

The contract is then void by every principle of equity. It is the worst species of fraud, because it attacks the weakest point of human nature, and appeals to natural affection. What will not a mother do to save her child from imprisonment for crime of which he is not guilty? We cannot but regard this case as one of the strongest that would be likely to occur. The homestead is sacred to the wife especially, and should not be taken away without her signature to the deed as an act of her own free will. She knew that her poor insane son was not guilty of any crime, but she did not know but that he might be arrested and imprisoned on the pretended charge of embezzlement, baseless as it was, and suffer great bodily as well as mental harm, and loss of reputation and character. She kept pressing upon Varco: You would not prosecute and imprison my son, would you? No; but what the company might do he could not say. But would you think the company thought more of your son than you do? He kept before her all the time the fear that the company would do so.

The circuit court ought to have found the issue that *Bridget Hamilton* signed the mortgage by threats, duress, and undue influence, so far as the homestead was concerned.

By the Court.—The judgment of the circuit court is reversed, and the cause remanded with direction to render judgment of foreclosure of the mortgage as to the first-described eighty acres only, and enter judgment as to the other or homestead forty acres that the mortgage be canceled, set aside, and held for naught, on the ground that it was procured as to said homestead by threats, duress, and undue influence.

The following opinion was filed February 27, 1889:

ORTON, J.   Since handing down the opinion in this case, my attention has been called to the fact that there was a mistake as to the southeast quarter of the northeast quarter of section 14, town 10 N., of range 1 W., being the homestead of the said *Peter Hamilton* and *Bridget Hamilton*, his wife, and that there was a mistake in this respect in the record and in the opinion and judgment of this court.   The opinion and judgment of this court is therefore hereby modified in this respect, so that it may have the effect to have the judgment of the circuit court declare the said mortgage void as to whatever homestead the said *Peter Hamilton* and *Bridget Hamilton*, his wife, or either of them, had and held in any part of the mortgaged premises, not exceeding forty acres, whatever its description may be.   The opinion and judgment in this respect will stand as so corrected, and the circuit court is ordered to render judgment according to this correction, unless the specific description of said homestead can be certainly ascertained, in which case such description should be inserted in the judgment declaring the mortgage void in respect to the same, and the judgment of foreclosure should be entered as to the balance or residue of the mortgaged premises, whatever its description may be by this correction.

REED and others, Respondents, vs. WILSON, Executrix, etc.,
Appellant.

January 31 — February 19, 1889.

Estates of decedents: Settlement of account of deceased executor.

Under the laws of this state (R. S. secs. 3258, 3800, 3933, 3934) the executor of a deceased executor cannot be compelled to render and settle the account of the latter. Under sec. 3934 such account may be settled by the county court upon the application of any person interested, but the moving party must furnish the proofs to enable the court to state and settle it.

APPEAL from the Circuit Court for *Iowa* County.

The following statement of the case was prepared by Mr. Justice TAYLOR as a part of the opinion:

The material facts in this case are the following:

January 10, 1874, John B. Terry died at Mineral Point in this state, testate. His will was duly admitted to probate, February 16, 1874. Alexander Wilson, and Caroline and Adaline Terry, sisters of the deceased, were appointed executors of said will, and gave bonds for the faithful discharge of their duties as such executors, and letters testamentary were issued to them February 16, 1874. *James Hutchinson* was the sole security on their official bond. The important provisions of the will are the following: *First.* The homestead of the testator is given to his two sisters, Caroline and Adaline, during their lives. *Second.* Legacies of $100 each are given to Mrs. Cartwright and Mrs. Sudduth, two nieces of deceased. A legacy of $200 is given to the Presbyterian Church at Mineral Point. The library of the testator is given to Frank Paddock. *Third.* All the residue of the estate, real and personal, is given to the executors in trust. They were to sell all his lands outside of Mineral Point, and his real and personal property, and convert the same into money, which they were to invest, and pay the interest arising therefrom to the said two sisters of the testator, Caroline and Adaline, during their lives. *Fourth.* Upon the death of the two sisters the homestead and all property and trust funds in the hands of the trustees were to be divided equally between the respondents, *Jane E. Reed*, a sister of the testator, *William V. Baker*, and *Caroline Terry, Jr.,*— now, by marriage, *Caroline Terry Kelsey*,— a nephew and niece of the testator.

Caroline and Adaline Terry both died before the death of Alexander Wilson. Alexander Wilson died March 5, 1888, testate. His will was duly admitted to probate June 1, 1888, and letters testamentary were issued to the appellant on the same day, she being named in the will as executrix. On the 13th of July, 1888, the respondent *Jane E. Reed* filed in the county court of Iowa county, in the matter of the estate of John B. Terry, deceased, a petition of which the following is a copy:

" The petition of *Jane E. Reed* respectfully shows to the court that John B. Terry died at Mineral Point in said Iowa county, about January 10, 1874, leaving a will which was admitted to probate in this court on February 16, 1874; that in and by said will Alexander Wilson, Caroline Terry, and Adaline Terry were appointed joint executors thereof, and they soon thereafter qualified as such, a bond being given as required by said will in the sum of $1,000, with one *James Hutchinson* as surety; that said executors have all since died, the said Alexander Wilson having died last, and being at the time of his death the sole surviving executor of said will, and a resident of Mineral Point, Wisconsin, and having had the principal care and management of the estate of said John B. Terry; that said Alexander Wilson died about March 5, 1888, leaving a will, in which his wife, *Frances H. Wilson*, was named executrix, which will was duly admitted to probate in this court on June 5, 1888, and letters testamentary thereon issued to the said *Frances H. Wilson*, who is now such executrix.

" And your petitioner further shows, on information and belief, that the said executrix of the will of said Alexander Wilson has in her possession or under her control all of the property, books of account, vouchers, deeds, receipts, papers, and memoranda appertaining to the estate of the said John B. Terry, which were in the possession or under the control of the said Alexander Wilson, previous to his death.

" That on May 1, 1888, letters of administration *de bonis non* with the will annexed, on the estate of said John B. Terry, were duly issued by this court to one *John H. Vivian*, of Mineral Point, Wisconsin, who is now acting as such administrator; that by his said will said John B. Terry left the income of his estate to his sisters, said Caroline Terry and Adaline Terry, for their lives, and after their death his residuary estate to your petitioner, his sister, *William V. Baker*, his nephew, and *Caroline Terry* (now *Caroline Terry Kelsey*), his niece, in equal distributive shares; that no person other than said residuary legatees, *Sarah F. Baker*, wife of the said *William V. Baker*, and said administrator *de bonis non*, is in any manner interested in the estate of said John B. Terry, save the interest which the said *James Hutchinson* may have as surety in the account of said Alexander Wilson as executor, and the settlement thereof.

" That no account of the administration of the estate of said John B. Terry was ever made or rendered, but said estate was by said Alexander Wilson, the last surviving executor thereof, left unsettled and not wholly administered at his death, and on information and belief your petitioner alleges that said Alexander Wilson as executor was, at the time of his death, indebted to the said estate of said John B. Terry to the amount of several thousand dollars.

" That said executrix of the estate of said Alexander

Wilson has not filed, or made, or rendered any account of the administration of the estate of said John B. Terry by the said Alexander Wilson, and has not settled the accounts of the said Alexander Wilson as sole surviving executor thereof, nor has *James Hutchinson*, the said bondsman, paid or offered to pay any sum whatever on account of his liability as surety on said bond.

"Wherefore your petitioner prays that the accounts of said Alexander Wilson as the last surviving executor of said estate of John B. Terry, deceased, may be settled by this court; and for an order directing the same, and citation to said executrix of the estate of said Alexander Wilson, ordering and requiring her to render and settle said accounts, and that personal notice thereof may be given to said *James Hutchinson*, and to all persons interested, as provided by law."

Upon the presentation of this petition the said county court made an order of which the following is a copy:

"In County Court, State of Wisconsin, Iowa County *In the Estate of John B. Terry, Deceased.* On application of *Jane E. Reed*, one of the legatees under the will of the said John B. Terry, for the settling of the account of Alexander Wilson, deceased, late sole surviving executor of the estate of said John B. Terry, it is ordered that said account be settled before this court at a special term thereof, to be held at the court house in the village of Dodgeville in said county, on the 2d day of August, 1888, at the opening of the court on that day, to wit, 9 o'clock A. M., or as soon thereafter as counsel can be heard. It is further ordered that a citation be issued to *Frances H. Wilson*, executrix of the will of said Alexander Wilson, to render and settle the account of the said Alexander Wilson as sole surviving executor of the said John B. Terry, and to do and perform such other things as may be required of her by this court in relation thereto, returnable at the same time and place.

It is further ordered that notice of the time and place of the settling of said account be given to *Frances H. Wilson*, executrix of the will of said Alexander Wilson, *James Hutchinson, John H. Vivian*, administrator *de bonis non* with the will annexed of the estate of said John B. Terry, *Jane E. Reed, William H. Baker, Caroline Terry Kelsey*, and *Sarah F. Baker*, being the only persons interested, by personal service of said notice at least twenty days before said 2d day of August, 1888. By the court, JOHN T. JONES, Judge.

Upon making this order, said county court issued a citation to the appellant, which, after reciting the matters alleged in the petition, concludes as follows: "Now, therefore, you are hereby cited and required to appear before our said court, at a special term thereof to be held at the court house in the village of Dodgeville in said Iowa county, on the 2d day of August, 1888, at the opening of court on that day, to wit, at 9 o'clock A. M., or as soon thereafter as counsel can be heard, to render and settle the account of the said Alexander Wilson as sole surviving executor of the estate of the said John B. Terry, and to do and perform such other things as may be required of you by this court in relation thereto."

The following notice was given by said county court to all the parties interested: "In County Court, State of Wisconsin, Iowa County. *In the Estate of John B. Terry, Deceased.* Notice is hereby given that at a special term of the Iowa county court, to be held in and for said county at the court house in the village of Dodgeville in said county, on the 2d day of August, 1888, at the opening of court on that day, to wit, at 9 o'clock A. M., or as soon thereafter as counsel can be heard, the following matter will be heard: The application of *Jane E. Reed*, one of the legatees under the will of the said John B. Terry, for the settling of the account of Alexander Wilson, deceased, late sole surviving

executor of the estate of said John B. Terry. And it is
further ordered that notice thereof be given to *Frances H.
Wilson*, executrix of the will of said Alexander Wilson,
James Hutchinson, John H. Vivian, administrator *de bonis
non* with the will annexed of the estate of said John B.
Terry, *Jane E. Reed, William V. Baker, Caroline Terry
Kelsey*, and *Sarah F. Baker*, the only persons interested,
by personal service of a copy of this order at least twenty
days before said 2d day of August."

On the day fixed in said notice the appellant appeared
specially to object to the jurisdiction of said county court
to issue said citation requiring her, as executrix, to account
with the Terry estate, and moved the court to vacate and
release her from further compliance therewith. This motion was overruled by the county court, and it was ordered
by said county court "that said *Frances H. Wilson*, executrix as aforesaid, do, on or before Wednesday the 8th of
August, 1888, at 9 o'clock A. M. of said day, render and
file in this court the final and complete account of the said
Alexander Wilson as executor of the last will of said John
B. Terry, deceased, from the time of his appointment as
said executor to the time of his death, and that the said account thus rendered be considered and settled by this court,
without further notice, on the said 8th day of August, 1888,
at 9 o'clock A. M. of said day, or as soon thereafter as
counsel can be heard; and it is further ordered that the
said *Frances H. Wilson*, executrix, and one H. D. Post,
who have been duly subpœnaed by the said petitioner, *Jane
E. Reed*, to attend before this court as witnesses at this
time with certain documents and papers in their possession,
particularly described in the subpœnas served upon them,
do appear without further subpœna or writ of this court
with the said books, papers, and documents so described in
said subpœnas, on the said 8th day of August, 1888, at 9
o'clock A. M., to give testimony in said matter."

From this order the executrix, *Mrs. Wilson*, appealed to
the circuit court of Iowa county.   Afterwards, and on the
28th day of September, 1888, the appeal was heard in the
said circuit court, and after such hearing the circuit court
made an order affirming the order of the county court, and
from this order of the circuit court *Frances H. Wilson*, as
executrix of the estate of Alexander Wilson, deceased, appeals to this court.

For the appellant there was a brief by *Orton & Osborn*,
and oral argument by *P. A. Orton*.

For the respondents there was a brief by *Spensley &
McIlhon* and *W. R. Spooner*, and oral argument by *Calvert
Spensley* and *W. R. Spooner*.   To the point that when a
representative dies, not having settled his sole account, a
final account should be rendered by his own executor or
administrator, they cited Schouler on Ex'rs, sec. 531; *Curtis v. Bailey*, 1 Pick. 198; *Perrin v. Lepper*, 40 N. W. Rep.
(Mich.), 859, 900; *Perrin v. Calhoun Circuit Judge*, 49
Mich. 342; *Ray v. Doughty*, 4 Blackf. 115; *Steen v. Steen*,
25 Miss. 534-5; *Nowell v. Nowell*, 2 Me. 75; *Gregy v. Gregg*,
15 N. H. 190; *Gale v. Luttrell*, 2 Eng. Ecc. 283.

TAYLOR, J.   The only question discussed upon the appeal
from said order was " whether the county court had authority, under the laws of this state, to compel the executrix of the deceased executor of the will of said Terry to
render and settle the account of her testator as executor of
the will of said Terry."   This question has not been heretofore passed upon by this court, and is a question not entirely free from doubt.

The rule of the English law that an executor of an executor is the executor of the first testator, and must execute
the will of the first testator, is abolished by statute in this
state.   See secs. 3258, 3800, R. S. 1878.   Sec. 3258 reads as
follows: "An executor of an executor shall have no au-

thority to commence or maintain any action or proceedin
relating to the estate, effects, or rights of the testator o
the first executor, or to take any charge or control thereo
as such executor." This section clearly prohibits the ex
ecutrix of Alexander Wilson from in any way intermeddlin
with the estate of the testator Terry, and from commen
ing any action or proceeding in relation to such estate
such executrix. So far the statute is very clear. Sec. 380(
R. S., provides for the appointment of an administrato
with the will annexed for the purpose of completing th
administration of the will of the testator Terry. Unde
these sections it appears to us that the executrix of the
estate of Alexander Wilson has no duty to perform in regard to the settlement of the estate of Terry merely by
reason of the fact that she is the executrix of her husband's
will. She is a stranger to the administration or execution
of the will of Terry, and can no more be called upon to
settle that estate than if she had not been named as executrix of the will of her husband. This has been so held by
the courts of New York, New Jersey, California, and Illinois, under similar provisions of law. *Schenck v. Schenck's
Ex'rs*, 3 N. J. Law, 562, 563, 565; *Dakin v. Demming*, 6
Paige, 95; *Bush v. Lindsey*, 44 Cal. 121; *Wetzler v. Fitch*,
52 Cal. 638; *In re Fithian*, 44 Hun, 457; *Tracey v. Hadden*,
78 Ill. 30. But these decisions do not in any way interfere
with the rights of those claiming an interest in the estate
of Terry to compel the executrix of Wilson, or to compel
his widow, irrespective of her representative capacity, to
make a disclosure upon oath of any money, property, or
effects belonging to the estate of Terry, which may have
come into her possession or under her control as executrix
of the estate of her husband or otherwise; and she may be
compelled by the county court, upon application of some
person interested in the estate of Terry, to make such disclosure in regard to such matters under the provisions of

sec. 3825, R. S. 1878. This was so decided in the case of
Perrin v. Calhoun Circuit Judge, 49 Mich. 342, 345. The
proceeding in the Michigan case was a proceeding under
sec. 4408, Comp. Laws, Mich., which section is literally the
same as our sec. 3825, R. S. of this state. The relief which
a party may have under said section is commented upon
by this court in *Saddington v. Hewitt,* 70 Wis. 240. Upon
the nature of the duties of the executrix, upon the law of
this state as it stood previous to the enactment of ch. 1,
Laws of 1870, now secs. 3933, 3934, R. S. 1878, and upon
authority, we think the county court had no authority to
compel the appellant, as executrix of her husband's estate,
to render an account and settle the business of her husband
as the executor of the estate of Terry.

It is claimed by the learned counsel for the respondents
that secs. 3933, 3934, R. S., confer this power upon the
county court. It is admitted that these sections give the
county court jurisdiction to settle the accounts of a deceased
executor, and it may be claimed that the enactment of
these sections clearly implied that the county court had
theretofore power to settle such account; but it is insisted
on the part of the learned counsel for the appellant that,
in the absence of any direction as to who shall render or
state the account or how the same shall be settled and adjusted, there is no power to compel the executor of a
deceased executor to render and settle such account. The
claim is that the party or parties desiring to have the account of the deceased executor settled and adjusted must
produce to the court the evidence from which the court
may state and settle the account, and, if the evidence or
any part of it necessary to state such account is in the possession or control of the executrix, it must be obtained from
her in the same manner as if it were in the hands or under
the control of any other stranger to the estate of Terry.
This argument is sustained to some extent by the language

of sec. 3933, R. S.   The language of the section is: " No
action shall be commenced upon the administration bond of
such deceased executor or administrator against the sureties
in such bond, or either of them, until such sureties, or one
of them, shall have an opportunity to apply for and have a
settlement of the administration accounts of such deceased
executor or administrator."   The delay in bringing action
on the bond is for the benefit of the sureties, and to allow
them time to settle the accounts of their principal in his
stead.   And sec. 3934 expressly confers power upon the
county court to settle the accounts of a deceased executor
or administrator *upon the application of the surety in the
bond, or of any other person interested in the settlement,* upon
notice given, etc.

The provisions of these sections do not pretend to cast
any duty upon the representative of a deceased executor or
administrator which did not theretofore rest upon him,
and, as we have said above, no such duty rests upon such
representative under any other provision of the statute.
We think the moving party must furnish the proofs to enable the court to state and settle the account.   He can
have all the knowledge which the representative has by
calling him or her as a witness, and by compelling the pro-
duction of all books, accounts, or other documentary evidence in the possession or control of the representative,
and can obtain a discovery of all property or effects belonging to the estate of Terry in the hands or under the control
of the executrix by a proceeding under sec. 3825, R. S.
The executrix is undoubtedly a party interested, within
the meaning of sec. 3934, R. S., as the settlement of such
account might establish a claim against the estate of her
testator, and as such she might apply to the county court
for a settlement of the accounts of her deceased husband.
And in such case she would have to furnish the proofs upon
which the accounts should be stated and settled.   But, if

she declines to make the application for a settlement, we are of the opinion that the county court cannot compel her to do so.

By the Court.— The order of the circuit court is reversed, and the cause is remanded to said court with instructions to enter an order reversing so much of the order of the county court appealed from as requires the said *Frances H. Wilson,* executrix, etc., to render and file in the said county court, on or before the 8th day of August, 1888, the final and complete account of the said Alexander Wilson as the executor of the last will of said John B. Terry, deceased, from the time of his appointment as such executor to the time of his death, and that the said account thus rendered be considered and settled by said court, without further notice, on the said 8th day of August, 1888, at 9 o'clock A. M. of said day, or as soon thereafter as counsel can be heard; and for further proceedings according to law.

JACKSON, Appellant, vs. THE NORTHWESTERN MUTUAL RELIEF ASSOCIATION, Respondent.

January 31 — February 19, 1889.

Life insurance: Mutual benefit company: Refusal to make assessment: Action at law or in equity: Damages.

By the terms of a contract of life insurance the company agreed to pay to the beneficiary, upon the death of the insured, " eighty per cent. of an assessment levied and collected therefor, not exceeding $4,000," etc. *Held,* that for a breach of such contract by neglect and refusal to make the assessment the beneficiary may maintain an action at law and, if it appears that such an assessment would have produced a substantial sum, may recover substantial damages.

APPEAL from the Circuit Court for *Iowa* County.

The following statement of the case was prepared by Mr. Justice CASSODAY:

The amended complaint alleges, in effect, the incorporation and existence of the defendant at the times named; its right to do a mutual life insurance business and issue the policy or certificate sued upon; the application of the plaintiff's wife to the defendant, March 19, 1886, for such policy upon her life, to the amount of $4,000, payable in case of death to the plaintiff; that said wife submitted to a medical examination by the defendant's physician, and thereupon her application was approved and accepted; and thereupon, and on March 23, 1886, the defendant issued and delivered to her thereon its policy for such insurance in the form of a certificate of membership executed in due form, the essential portions of which certificate to be considered on this demurrer are as follows: " That in consideration of the payment of an assessment not to exceed ninety cents on the maturity of the certificate of any other member at the office of the association, within thirty days after due notice thereof, the association, upon maturity of this certificate, and within sixty days after the proof and allowance of such claim, upon presentation hereof, will pay the above-named member, or, in case of death, the beneficiary, if living, otherwise the heirs of such member, a benefit, in case of: . . . *Second.* Maturity by death or by limitation on the 23d day of September, A. D. 1926, eighty per cent. of an assessment levied and collected therefor, not exceeding four thousand dollars, less any payment before made on account of disability, or any indebtedness due or accrued to the association from such member."

The said amended complaint further alleges: " That on the 13th day of February, 1888, at said Mineral Point, the said Cordelia Jackson died, and, on information and belief, this plaintiff alleges that the said Cordelia Jackson, during

her life-time, so kept, performed, and complied with all the
terms and conditions, and paid the assessments made and
demanded of her under the terms of said policy of insurance
or certificate of membership, by her to be kept and performed by the terms thereof, as to keep the same in full
force, validity, and effect up to the time of her death, and
that the same was in full force and effect when she died;
that on the 28th day of February, 1888, this plaintiff notified defendant of the death of said Cordelia Jackson, and
asked for blanks on which to make out formal proofs of her
death, but that said defendant refused to send or furnish
them to plaintiff; that on or about the 16th day of April,
1888, plaintiff served upon the defendant sworn proof of
the death of said Cordelia Jackson, presented said certificate, and filed with defendant a claim and demand for the
amount which the said defendant, under and in said policy
of insurance or certificate of membership number 2,939,
agreed to pay plaintiff in case of the death of the said Cordelia Jackson, and has often since made demands for said
amount; but that defendant has at all such times denied,
and now denies, any and all liability to plaintiff under or
on account of said policy of insurance or certificate of membership, and has always refused, and now refuses, to levy
an assessment upon the members of such association for the
use and benefit of plaintiff, as provided for in said policy of
insurance or certificate of membership, and has always refused, and still refuses, to pay to plaintiff any sum whatever
under or on account of the same.   Plaintiff shows, on information and belief, that at the time said Cordelia Jackson
died, eighty per cent. of an assessment upon the members
of said association, as provided for in said policy of insurance or certificate of membership, would have amounted to
at least four thousand dollars.   And plaintiff alleges and
claims on information and belief that, on the death of the

said Cordelia Jackson, said defendant became indebted to plaintiff under the terms, conditions, and provisions of said policy of insurance or certificate of membership in the sum of four thousand dollars. Plaintiff further shows that defendant has failed to comply with the agreements and undertakings by it made and assumed in and by said policy of insurance or certificate of membership, in that it has neglected and refused to make an assessment upon its members for the use and benefit of plaintiff, as provided for in said policy of insurance or certificate of membership, or to pay to plaintiff, on demand made as aforesaid, the whole or any part of the said sum it agreed to pay him on the death of said Cordelia Jackson. By reason of which premises above set forth plaintiff alleges that he has been damaged in the sum of four thousand dollars. Wherefore plaintiff demands judgment against the defendant in the sum of four thousand dollars, or for such other and further relief or judgment as he may be entitled to in the premises, together with his costs and disbursements herein."

To such amended complaint the defendant demurred on the ground that it did not state facts sufficient to constitute a cause of action. December 4, 1888, the court sustained such demurrer, and from the order sustaining the same the plaintiff appeals.

For the appellant there was a brief by *Spensley & McIlhon* and *H. W. Chynoweth*, and oral argument by *Calvert Spensley* and *H. W. Chynoweth*.

For the respondent there was a brief by *F. E. Parkinson*, attorney, and *Burr W. Jones*, of counsel, and oral argument by *Mr. Jones*. To the point that plaintiff's remedy was in equity and not at law, they cited *Smith v. Covenant Mut. Ben. Asso.* 24 Fed. Rep. 685; *Bailey v. Mut. Ben. Asso.* 71 Iowa, 689; *Newman v. Covenant Mut. Ben. Asso.* 72 id. 242; *Rainsbarger v. Union Mut. Aid Asso.* id. 191.

CASSODAY, J. This is an action at law to recover damages for an alleged breach of contract of insurance. There is no claim that the facts alleged do not constitute a binding contract of insurance, nor that they do not show a breach of such contract. The theory of the defendant is that, conceding the validity of the contract and the breach of it, yet that the plaintiff has mistaken his remedy by bringing his action at law instead of proceeding in equity to enforce the assessment mentioned in the contract. If such is the fact, then, under the earlier decisions of this court, and since adhered to, the question may be properly raised by demurrer.

The only question presented is, therefore, whether, upon the showing made, an action at law for damages by reason of the breach of contract alleged can be maintained. The question, it will be observed, is not as to the true amount or the true measure of damages, but only whether the plaintiff is entitled to substantial damages for such breach. There are certainly authorities to the effect that a bill in equity may be maintained to enforce payment of such certificates by compelling a specific performance of similar contracts through assessments as stipulated. *Covenant Mut. Ben. Asso. v. Sears*, 114 Ill. 108; *Smith v. Covenant Mut. Ben. Asso.* 24 Fed. Rep. 689; *Rainsbarger v. Union Mut. Aid Asso.* 72 Iowa, 191; *Tobin v. Western Mut. Aid Society*, 72 Iowa, 261. It has also been held that *mandamus* is not an appropriate remedy to compel such assessments. *Burland v. Northwestern Mut. Ben. Asso.* 47 Mich. 424; *Excelsior Mut. Aid Asso. v. Riddle*, 91 Ind. 84. The decided weight of authority, however, seems to be to the effect that an action at law to recover damages may be maintained upon such contract for a refusal or neglect to make such assessment. *Earnshaw v. Sun Mut. Aid Society*, 68 Md. 465; *Suppiger v. Covenant Mut. Ben. Asso.* 20 Bradw. 595; *Neskern v. Northwestern E. & L. Asso.* 30 Minn. 406; *Lued-*

ers' Ex'r v. Hartford L. & A. Ins. Co. 12 Fed. Rep. 465;
Kansas Protective Union v. Whitt, 36 Kan. 760; Kaw Valley L. Asso. v. Lemke, 19 Pac. Rep. (Kan.), 337; Freeman v.
National Ben. Society, 42 Hun, 252; Reynolds v. Equitable
Accident Asso. 1 N. Y. Supp. 738; Elkhart Mut. A., B. &
R. Asso. v. Houghton, 103 Ind. 286; Burland v. Northwestern Mut. Ben. Association, 47 Mich. 424; Bac. Ben. Soc.
§ 453. But to maintain such action at law, such breach
must be alleged and proved. Curtis v. Mut. Ben. Life Co.
48 Conn. 98; Taylor v. National T. Relief Union, 94 Mo. 35.
    The principal difference in these two classes of adjudica-
tions turns upon the question whether such recovery for
such breach of contract is limited to mere nominal damages, or extends to substantial damages. In some of these
cases which allow substantial damages the courts have gone
so far as to hold that the beneficiaries may recover the
maximum amount named in the contract, unless the defendant shows by pleadings and proof that such sum should
be reduced. But, as indicated in some of the other cases
cited, the recovery cannot exceed the amount stipulated in
the contract. We make no attempt to analyze the cases,
nor to point out any supposed fallacies. We agree with
that class of cases which hold, in effect, that, for a substantial breach of such contract, the beneficiary may recover
substantial damages in an action at law. As indicated in
Earnshaw v. Sun Mut. Aid Society, 68 Md. 465, there may
be some difficulty as to the true measure of damages and
the enforcement of the judgment in case of recovery. So
there may be difficulty in obtaining the requisite proof to
establish the plaintiff's claim. But these considerations are
not before us on this demurrer, which concedes the truth-
fulness of all the allegations of the complaint.
    The question is one of pleading upon contract. Under
the contract in question the plaintiff was entitled, upon the
death of his wife, to eighty per cent. of an assessment to

be thereupon levied and collected therefor, not exceeding $4,000, less any payment, etc. Upon such death it became the duty of the defendant under the contract to make such levy and collection. According to the allegations of the complaint, it not only neglected and refused to do so, but denied all liability. It is also alleged, in effect, and of course admitted by the demurrer, that eighty per cent. of such assessment " would have amounted to at least four thousand dollars." With this confession before us we cannot hold, as a matter of law, that the plaintiff has only sustained nominal damages by reason of such breach, merely because there may be a total or partial failure of proof, or that it may be difficult in advance of such levy and attempted collection of such assessment to ascertain the precise amount of damages which the plaintiff may be entitled to recover. Several of the authorities cited sustain these views. The breach of an agreement to make such levy and collection of such assessment seems to be somewhat similar to the breach of an agreement to insure, upon which actions at law have frequently been sustained.

By the Court.— The order of the circuit court is reversed, and the cause is remanded for further proceedings according to law.

GARVIN, Respondent, vs. GATES, Appellant.

February 1 — February 19, 1889.

(1) Contracts: Logs and logging: Court and jury. (2) Settlement: Instruction to jury. (3) Recoupment: Partial performance of contract. (4) Evidence: Conversations with third persons.

1. By the terms of a contract logs were to be delivered into a certain stream " in good driving water," and landed " so that they could be easily started through the dam in the spring." It appeared that at the point where the logs were landed the stream, at its or-

dinary stage, really had no good driving water, but that at times of high water logs could be run therefrom by means of the water set back from a flooding dam below; and the evidence tended to show that the logs might have been run down the stream had not the dam below been choked with other logs. *Held*, that it was not error to submit to the jury the question whether the logs were delivered in good driving water.

2. In an action for a balance alleged to be due upon an account stated. the plaintiff attempted to prove a settlement of all matters between the parties. The court charged the jury that if all matters were settled, and the defendant, knowing just how the plaintiff had performed the contract upon which his claim was based, had talked over that matter, and the parties agreed as to the amount due, then they were bound by the settlement: that no advantage could be taken, but the parties must have fully understood and agreed that any claim for a breach of the contract was included in the matters settled, otherwise such claim was still open and unadjusted. *Held*, sufficiently favorable to the defendant.

3. In an action upon a contract which the plaintiff had not fully performed and which the defendant had employed a third person to complete, the defendant may recoup what such completion was fairly worth, but not necessarily all he paid therefor.

4. A party may state his understanding of a conversation between him and a third person who has testified as to the same on behalf of the opposite party.

APPEAL from the Circuit Court for *Clark* County.

The complaint alleges, for a first cause of action, that on March 25, 1886, an account was stated between the parties and a balance of $369 was found to be due from the defendant to the plaintiff; that the defendant promised to pay said sum. but no part thereof has been paid. For a second cause of action it is alleged that the defendant is indebted to the plaintiff in the sum of $101.10 upon an account for goods, etc., sold and delivered, labor and services rendered, the use and hire of a team, and moneys paid for the defendant at his request, between March 25 and July 25, 1886. Judgment is demanded for said sums, with interest.

The answer, besides denying all allegations not admitted,

alleges that in November, 1885, the plaintiff agreed for a
stipulated compensation per thousand feet to cut, mark,
stamp, haul and deliver, during the ensuing winter, all the
pine timber on a certain quarter section of land, and "to
deliver the logs into Hay creek in good driving water, and
land them so they can be easily started through the dam in
the spring;" that in pursuance of such contract the plaintiff delivered into Hay creek a quantity of logs from such
quarter section; that on March 25, 1886, the parties had an
accounting by which it was ascertained that after allowing
to the plaintiff the stipulated compensation for all logs
which he claimed to have delivered according to the agreement, and deducting advances made by the defendant,
there remained a balance of $369 in favor of the plaintiff.
The answer then alleges that said accounting and settlement was to be final only in case the logs were delivered
in accordance with the agreement, and that it was procured
by the plaintiff by falsely representing that the logs had
been so delivered, the plaintiff then well knowing that he
had not delivered the logs in good driving water so that
they could be easily started through the dam, but the situation of the logs being then unknown to the defendant.
The answer then alleges that the defendant was put to great
expense in starting said logs through the dam in addition
to what he would have been had the logs been landed in
good driving water, to wit, in the sum of $300.

Further, by way of counterclaim, the answer alleges that
the plaintiff is indebted to the defendant in the sum of
$200 for the driving of about 200,000 feet of logs belonging
to the plaintiff, in the spring and summer of 1886. Judgment is demanded on the counterclaim for $131.

A reply admitted the making of the agreement set up in
the answer, and alleged that the logs of the plaintiff, driven
by the defendant, were not to be charged for by the defendant at a higher rate than fifty cents per thousand.

The evidence given on the trial, and the instructions to the jury, will sufficiently appear from the opinion. It seems to have been agreed by the parties on the trial that the amount found due to the plaintiff on the accounting was $309.43, and that the defendant was indebted to the plaintiff upon the second cause of action in the sum of $93.80. The jury found a verdict in favor of the plaintiff for $329.49. Whether the jury allowed the entire difference between this amount and the face of the plaintiff's claims with interest, for the driving of the plaintiff's logs by the defendant, or allowed something upon the defendant's claim for expenses incurred because the logs were not landed in good driving water, does not appear. The defendant appeals from the judgment entered on the verdict.

R. J. MacBride, for the appellant, contended, *inter alia*, that the court erred in charging that if what the defendant paid for having the logs hauled from above the beaver dam down the creek into good driving water was more than it was fairly worth, then the plaintiff would not be liable to account to him for the full amount paid, but only for what it was fairly worth. The true rule is that in such a case the defendant would be entitled to recover the *cost* of fulfilling and completing the plaintiff's contract. *Hinckley v. Beckwith*, 13 Wis. 31, 36; *Peters v. Whitney*, 23 Barb. 24; *Usher v. Hiatt*, 18 Kan. 195; *Masterton v. Mayor*, 7 Hill, 61; *Fox v. Harding*, 7 Cush. 516; 1 Sedgw. on Dam. (7th ed.), 459, note *a; Boyd v. Meighan*, 48 N. J. Law, 404.

For the respondent there was a brief by *James O'Neill* and *Geo. L. Jacques*, and oral argument by *Mr. O'Neill*.

COLE, C. J. The principal controversy in this case turns upon the question whether the plaintiff performed his contract by delivering the logs which he cut for the defendant into Hay creek in good driving water, landing them so that they could be easily started through the dam in the spring.

The defendant claims that he did not thus deliver them,
and that in consequence of the logs being delivered at a
wrong place he was put to great expense in getting them
to water where they could be floated down the stream.
The agreement is plain, and bound the plaintiff to " deliver
the logs into Hay creek in good driving water, and land
them so they can be easily started through the dam in the
spring." Was this condition kept and performed by the
plaintiff?

The contract should be construed in the light of the surrounding circumstances and the situation of the parties in respect to the subject matter about which they were contracting. This rule is familiar in the interpretation of contracts,
that the court should as far as possible put itself in the situation of the parties, and see how the terms of the instrument
affect the property or subject matter. 1 Greenl. Ev. § 287.
The evidence shows that the logs in question were delivered
or landed on Hay creek at an old beaver dam. This beaver
dam was a little distance above a flooding dam, constructed
to set back the water. The evidence is quite in accord and
conclusive that Hay creek, at the point where the logs were
landed, in its ordinary and usual stage of water really had
no good driving water for floating logs; but the water
which set back from the flooding dam at times of high
water was sufficient to enable logs to be run from that
point. The court below submitted the question to the jury
upon the evidence whether the plaintiff had performed his
contract by landing the logs at a place that lumbermen
would consider fairly good driving water, and where the
logs could be got at with fair facility in the season of ordinary driving water. It seems to us that this was peculiarly
a question of fact for the jury. But one of the main errors
relied on for a reversal of the judgment is this action of the
court in submitting the question whether the logs were
landed in good driving water. It is said the evidence was

all one way on that point, and that the court should have
determined as a matter of law that the logs were not landed
in good driving water within the meaning of the contract.
We cannot agree with counsel in that view of the matter.
The parties must be presumed to have contracted with
reference to the nature of Hay creek in its natural condition. And when the plaintiff landed the logs in the creek
as near the flooding dam as was necessary to enable them
to be run down the stream when the water was set back by
the dam in the spring as it usually was, he had performed
his contract.   There is considerable testimony that the logs
might have been run down the channel of the creek through
the beaver dam, had not the dam below been choked with
logs. So that the difficulty in getting the logs down the
stream was not because they were not landed in good driving water, but because the dam was filled with other logs,
which prevented these from being driven. We do not say
that this was the fact, but merely that there was evidence
tending to prove such a state of things, which it was proper
to submit to the jury with the other circumstances. So it
was impossible to say, as a matter of law, that the real ob-
stacle to running the logs was because they were not
landed, as the contract required, in good driving water; for
there certainly is evidence that they might have been driven
in the spring from where they were landed, if the dam below had been free from other logs. So that error cannot
be predicated upon the fact that the question was submitted
whether the plaintiff performed his contract by placing the
logs where they were put by him. If the logs were landed
where men in the lumber business, engaged in driving logs,
would consider there was good driving water in view of the
character of the stream and its surroundings, this was all
that was required by the contract.

Another error assigned is the ruling of the court in allowing the plaintiff to answer, under objection, the question

put to him, in substance, whether he knew the location of the beaver dam in the winter when he was putting in the logs. It is said it made no difference whether he knew or did not know of the existence of the beaver dam; that he was bound to deliver the logs in good driving water. The counsel on the other side say, in answer to this objection, that the question was not asked to excuse non-performance of the contract, but to explain a conversation that the witness Bailey had testified to, and to show that the plaintiff had not knowingly landed the logs at an improper place. It seems to us it was competent for the plaintiff to state his understanding of the conversation he had with Bailey, and which the latter had testified to.

The question asked the plaintiff on cross-examination, and ruled out, as to whether he had given the defendant a note for a yoke of oxen purchased in November, 1876, was clearly irrelevant, and properly excluded.

Some exceptions were taken to the charge of the court. In the complaint it was alleged that there was an accounting between the parties in March, 1886, and that a balance of $369 was found due from the defendant to the plaintiff. On the trial there was an effort made to prove a settlement of all matters between the parties. In regard to this account stated, the court, in effect, charged that if all matters were settled and the defendant, knowing just how the logs were landed, had talked over that matter, and the parties agreed as to the amount due, then they were bound by the settlement; that no advantage could be taken, but the parties must fully understand and agree that any claim for a breach of the contract was included in the matters settled, otherwise such claim was still open and unadjusted. This is really all the charge amounts to, and we can perceive nothing in it unfavorable to the defendant. The defendant claimed that he had paid $300 for hauling the logs from above the beaver dam down the creek into good driving

North vs. La Flesh and others.

water.   As to that claim the court charged that, if the defendant paid for this hauling more than it was reasonably
worth, the plaintiff would not be liable to account to him for
the full amount, but only for what the hauling was fairly
worth.   We do not perceive any valid objection to the rule
of damages thus laid down.   It seems to be founded in good
sense, and accords with principles of justice and equity.
Upon what principle could it be claimed that the defendant
was entitled to recover of the plaintiff more for the hauling
than it was fairly worth to do it?   It is not to be presumed
he would pay more than the service was reasonably worth,
but if he should see fit to do so he ought to bear the loss.
We think the charge is unobjectionable.

These remarks dispose of all the questions which we deem
it necessary to notice.

By the Court. — The judgment of the circuit court is affirmed.

NORTH, Appellant, vs. LA FLESH and others, Respondents.

February 1 — February 19, 1889.

LIENS.   *(1) Materials furnished to husband for improvements on wife's
land.   (2) Mingling lienable and non-lienable items in one account: Waiver of lien.   (3) Practice: Judgment.   (4) Application of payments.   (5-7) Pleading: Immaterial variances between
petition and complaint: Description of premises.*

1. Under sec. 3314, R. S., as amended by ch. 349, Laws of 1885, one
   who furnishes materials for a house which a husband is building
   on his wife's land with her knowledge and consent, may have a
   lien therefor upon such land, although the materials were purchased by the husband upon credit without the authority of his
   wife.   *Heath v. Solles, ante,* p. 217, followed.

2. The fact that such materials are charged in one continuous account
   with non-lienable goods sold to the husband, does not impair the
   right to a lien therefor, where the value of the lienable materials

can easily be ascertained from the account itself without a restatement thereof.

3. In such a case, in an action against both husband and wife, the
   plaintiff may have a judgment against the husband for the whole
   amount of his account, and a further judgment making a portion
   of that amount a lien upon the land of the wife.

4. In such a case the non-lienable items in the account against the
   husband included more than $280 which the plaintiff had advanced
   without charge, for the accommodation of the husband, to pay
   freights chargeable to the latter. Payments amounting to about
   $310 had been made on the general account, no application thereof
   being made by the parties. *Held*, that it was equitable to apply
   all such payments on the non-lienable items.

5. The fact that the petition for the lien states that the materials were
   sold to both the husband and the wife, while the complaint and
   the proofs show that they were sold to the husband alone, is immaterial. The petition might be amended at any time to correspond
   with the complaint and proofs.

6. So it is an immaterial variance that the petition states that the materials were used in the erection of a certain building on the land
   in question, while the complaint alleges that they were used in the
   erection of a house and barn thereon.

7. In the petition for a lien it is sufficient to describe the building for
   which the materials were furnished as " a certain building," if the
   land on which the building stands is accurately described.

APPEAL from the Circuit Court for *Clark* County.

This is an action on an account for goods, wares, and
merchandise alleged to have been sold and delivered by the
plaintiff to the defendant *Thomas J. La Flesh* between
May 18, 1886, and May 23, 1887, to the amount of $1,516.33,
and to enforce a lien upon a certain forty-acre lot of land
described in the complaint, for $466.80 of such amount. It
is alleged in the complaint that the defendant *Elizabeth
La Flesh*, who is the wife of the defendant *Thomas*, is the
owner of the land upon which the lien is sought to be enforced, and that a portion of said goods, wares, and merchandise, of the value of $466.80, consisted of building ma-
terials which were sold to be used, and were used, in the
erection of a house and barn upon such land, with the

knowledge and consent of the defendant *Elizabeth.* It is also alleged that the defendant *James H. Reddan* has or claims a lien upon the same land, but which lien, if any, is subsequent to that of the plaintiff.

A petition for a lien was filed, and this action commenced, within the times limited by the statute. R. S. sec. 3318. The sufficiency of the petition is considered in the opinion.

The defendants *La Flesh* answered separately, alleging, amongst other things, that the defendant *Thomas* purchased the materials in question upon his own credit and for his own use and benefit as principal contractor, and erected the building in question as such for his wife, and that the plaintiff is a subcontractor only to the defendant *Thomas.* Also that the defendant *Elizabeth* never authorized her husband or any other person to purchase such materials for her use, and did not know until this action was commenced that her husband had purchased the same on credit; and further, that he agreed to erect the building at his own expense. It is not denied that the buildings were erected with her knowledge and consent.

The cause was tried by the court (a jury having been waived), and thereafter the following findings of fact and conclusions of law were filed:

FINDINGS OF FACT.

"(1) That during all the time mentioned in the complaint the plaintiff was a hardware merchant and dealer in building materials at Neillsville, Clark county, Wisconsin. (2) That the defendant *Thomas J. La Flesh,* during all the time mentioned in the complaint and for a long time prior thereto, was a dealer in building materials, and a dealer in general merchandise, hardware, lumber, lath, shingles, etc., and had a general store in Clark county, Wisconsin. (3) That on and between the 18th day of May, 1886, and the 23d day of May, 1887, plaintiff sold and delivered to the defendant *Thomas J. La Flesh*, on his own personal credit and account, and as such merchant, goods, wares, and merchandise and building materials, and performed labor for him, and paid out and expended moneys for him, at his request, in all to the amount of $1,723.67. (4) That the defendant *Thomas J. La Flesh* paid thereon in money, shingles, groceries, etc., $310.21, leaving a balance due unpaid, on the 24th day of May, 1887, of $1,412.96. (5) That a further payment was made thereon, November 17, 1887, of $299.93, so that, after computing interest at seven per cent., there was due at the date of the trial of this action, March 15, 1888, $1,188.64. (6) That said merchandise was charged to said defendant *Thomas J. La Flesh*, on the books of the plaintiff, in the order in which they were purchased and in one continuous account, without reference to the use thereof in any particular building, and without reference to any rights to or claim for lien. (7) That the defendant *Elizabeth La Flesh* is the wife of *Thomas J. La Flesh*. (8) That the defendant *Thomas J. La Flesh* was not the agent of the defendant *Elizabeth La Flesh*, and had not authority from her to so act, and that he did not act as the agent of the defendant *Elizabeth La Flesh* in any of the matters claimed in this action. (9) That the defendant *Elizabeth La Flesh* was the owner of the lands described in the complaint all the time mentioned therein, and still is the owner thereof. That she constructed a building thereon, and knew that it was being constructed, and consented that it might be constructed thereon. (10) That the defendant *Elizabeth La Flesh* did not know and did not consent that any of the materials used thereon should be or had been purchased on credit, but believed that they were being paid for as used and purchased. (11) That the defendant *James H. Reddan* has a mortgage on said real estate of said *Elizabeth La Flesh*, which was executed to him August 4, 1887, for $5,000, by said defendant *Elizabeth La Flesh*, which is subsequent to the last date of goods furnished by the plaintiff to the defendant *Thomas J. La Flesh*. (12) That the plaintiff has no lien for any of the materials mentioned in the complaint on the property described in said complaint."

CONCLUSIONS OF LAW.

"(1) That the plaintiff is entitled to judgment against the defendant *Thomas J. La Flesh* for the sum of $1,188.64, without costs, and without judgment for a lien on the premises described in the complaint, or any part thereof. (2) That the defendants *Elizabeth La Flesh* and *James H. Reddan* are entitled to judgment against the plaintiff *Henry A. North*. Let judgment be entered accordingly, to be signed by the clerk."

Judgment was entered in accordance with the foregoing conclusions of law. The plaintiff appeals from such judgment.

James O'Neill, for the appellant.

For the respondents there was a brief by *R. F. Kountz*, attorney, and *R. J. MacBride*, of counsel, and oral argument by *Mr. MacBride*. They contended, *inter alia*, that a contract or agreement more specific than the mere purchase of the materials in the ordinary course of trade is necessary to entitle a party to a lien. It must be shown that the materials were furnished especially to be used in or about the building. *Cotes v. Shorey*, 8 Iowa, 416; *Jones v. Swan*, 21 id. 181; *Stockwell v. Carpenter*, 27 id. 119; *Hill v. Sloan*, 59 Ind. 186; *Miller v. Roseboom*, id. 345; *Hills v. Elliott*, 16 Serg. & R. 56; *Choteau v. Thompson*, 2 Ohio St. 114; *Rogers v. Currier*, 13 Gray, 129; *Hill v. Bishop*, 25 Ill. 349; *Fuller v. Nickerson*, 69 Me. 236; *Mehan v. Thompson*, 71 id. 492; *Weaver v. Sells*, 10 Kan. 609; *Delahay v. Goldie*, 17 id. 265; *Read v. Hull, etc.*, 1 Story, C. C. 250; *Phillips on Liens*, 212-214, sec. 122. No proper claim for a lien was filed. Sec. 3320, R. S., provides that such claim shall state *the name of the person against whom the demand is claimed.* The claim in this case states that the demand is for materials sold *Elizabeth La Flesh* and *Thomas J. La Flesh,* while the proof is that they were sold to *Thomas J. La Flesh* only. Not having complied with the statute, the plaintiff gained no lien. *Kelly v. Laws,* 109 Mass. 395; *Hoffman v. Walton,* 36 Mo. 613; *Hicks v. Murray,* 43 Cal. 515; *Mayes v. Ruffners,* 8 W. Va. 384; *Ward v. Black,* 7 Phila. 342; *McElwee v. Sandford,* 53 How. Pr. 89; *Hays v. Tryon,* 2 Miles (Pa.), 208. The claim for a lien is also defective in that it does not describe the property, as required by sec. 3320, R. S. It states merely that the materials were sold to be used and were used in the construction of "a certain building" on certain real estate, but does not state what kind of a building. In the complaint and on the trial the plaintiff claimed a lien on two buildings, a house and a barn; and the proof is that two buildings were built upon the place. A description of the property in the claim for a lien was essential. Phillips on Liens, secs. 176, 379; *Dewey v. Fifield,* 2 Wis. 73; *Dean v. Wheeler,* id. 224; *Short v. Ames,* 22 Weekly Notes of Cases, 354. The description should be such as would be sufficient in a conveyance. *Brown v. La Crosse C. G. L. & C. Co.* 16 Wis. 555; *Donnelly v. Libby,* 1 Sweeny (N. Y.), 259; *Lindley v. Cross,* 31 Ind. 109; *Runey v. Rea,* 7 Oreg. 130; *Williams v. Porter,* 51 Mo. 442; *Lemly v. La Grange 1. & S. Co.* 65 id. 545.

LYON, J. That portion of the judgment of the circuit court which denies the plaintiff a lien upon the land of *Mrs. La Flesh,* described in the complaint, rests mainly upon the sixth finding of fact, which is to the effect that all the merchandise sold by the plaintiff to the defendant *Thomas* was charged to the latter on the books of the plaintiff in the order of their purchase in one continuous account, without reference to the use thereof in any particular building, and without reference to any rights to or claim for a lien. In other words, that, considered in connection with other findings of fact, the transaction was a sale by one merchant to another in the usual course of business, without reference to use in any building or right to a lien.

If such finding of fact be sustained, the case is probably within the rule of *Esslinger v. Huebner*, 22 Wis. 632. In that case Mr. Justice PAINE, commenting upon a certain instruction given to the jury, said: " The plain meaning of this is that, although the lime was sold generally to F. W. Huebner on account, and without any reference to this or any other building, yet if he allowed any portion of it to be used in his wife's building, that would give the lien. This is not the law. How it might be in such a case if the purchaser used the material in his own building it is not necessary to inquire. But it seems clear that one who sells materials to another generally, without reference to any building, cannot follow them with a lien into the buildings of other parties to whom the purchaser may transfer them. And it would make no difference that they were used upon the separate property of the purchaser's wife." Whether the rule of that case is affected by subsequent legislation upon the subject of liens, and, if so, to what extent, need not be here determined, for the reason that we are satisfied that the evidence in the case does not support the sixth finding of fact. The evidence is almost conclusive that the plaintiff sold and delivered the materials in question to the defendant *Thomas* to be used in the erection of the buildings on his wife's land, and that they were in fact so used. Indeed, the only testimony to the contrary is the inference which might, perhaps, under some circumstances, be drawn from the fact that the plaintiff charged such materials in his books in the order of sales, with non-lienable goods. But notwithstanding his mode of book-keeping, the testimony of the plaintiff, the contractor who erected the buildings, and the agent or servant of the defendant *Thomas J. La Flesh* to whom a considerable portion of the materials in question was delivered, satisfies our minds that the finding in question is not sustained by the proofs.

The learned circuit judge filed a written opinion, in which he cited the case of *Esslinger v. Huebner*, and also that of *McMaster v. Merrick*, 41 Mich. 505, and seems to have rested the judgment mainly upon these cases. He quotes from the latter case the following: "It is also settled that one of the plainest cases of waiver is where privileged and unprivileged claims are mingled together in the same dealings, so that the lien is not kept ascertainable without re-stating and charging the accounts." We are inclined to think that this case led the circuit court into the error of giving undue influence to the fact that the plaintiff did not keep a separate account of the materials sold by him to *Thomas* to be used in the construction of the buildings. For this reason we will briefly review that case: There, as here, lienable and non-lienable items were charged in one general account. The transactions between the parties in respect to the lienable items related to work upon logs in sawing the same and drying and shipping the lumber, but, unlike this case, a large percentage of the account of the defendant (who did such work and claimed a lien therefor upon the lumber) had been paid by the plaintiff's assignor, and such payments had been applied by the mutual consent of both parties in payment of a general account. The case is somewhat involved in its facts, and a full statement of it will not be attempted. It is sufficient to say that the terms of the contract between the parties to the transactions there in question, and the course of dealing between them, rendered it impossible to ascertain from their accounts alone the amount for which the defendants should have a lien on the lumber. To ascertain such amount it was necessary to investigate those transactions and apportion payments. Of course this could not be done "without restating and charging the accounts." Because it could not, and because the right of the defendant to a lien was a very doubtful one, the Michigan court held that he had waived it. We make no controversy with that court in respect to the doctrine of that case. It is quite probable that we should rule the same way in a similar one. In this case, however, the value of the lienable materials is easily ascertainable from the account itself, and no restatement thereof is necessary for that purpose. The plaintiff is only required to show what materials charged therein were sold and delivered by him to be used in the construction of the buildings in question, and that must be shown in any case. That proof having been made, the amount of lienable charges in the account becomes a mere matter of computation,— not a cause for any restatement or recharging of the account. Hence the rule of the Michigan case has no application to the facts of this case.

On the same general subject counsel for defendants relies upon certain Iowa cases, and gives what purports to be a quotation from *Cotes v. Shorey*, 8 Iowa, 416, to support his position. We fail to find in the report of that case the language quoted. In that case the judgment refusing to enforce a lien was reversed because of the refusal of the trial court to instruct the jury as follows: "If the jury believe from the evidence that the plaintiff sold the materials charged in the account of the plaintiffs to the defendant for the purpose of erecting a house with the same, though the particular house was not then understood by the parties, and if the jury also believe that said materials, or any part thereof, were used by the defendant in erecting the house described in the plaintiffs' petition, the jury will find for the plaintiffs and establish their lien as prayed," etc. There is nothing in the case to interfere with the right to a lien here claimed. Moreover, the Iowa statute under which *Cotes v. Shorey* was decided provides that "every person *who by virtue of a contract with the owner* of a piece of land performs work or furnishes material *especially* for any building, and which material is used in the erection or reparation thereof," has a lien, etc. The language of our statute is: "Every person who, as principal contractor, performs any work or labor, or furnishes any materials, in or about the erection, construction, repairs, protection, or removal of any dwelling-house or other building, · . . . shall have a lien therefor," etc. There is a material difference in the two statutes, in that the Iowa statute makes a contract with the owner of the land that the materials are to be furnished especially for the building essential to the lien, while ours merely requires that they shall be furnished therefor, without reference to any contract or agreement except that implied from the sale and delivery of the materials to be so used. Hence, did the Iowa cases hold what it is claimed they do, they would afford us little aid in construing our statute.

It must be held that the sixth finding of fact is unsupported by the testimony; that the materials in question were sold by the plaintiff to be used in the construction of the buildings upon the land described in the complaint; and that, were the defendant *Thomas* the owner of such land, the plaintiff would be entitled to a lien thereon for the value of such materials.

Is he entitled to such lien as against *Mrs. La Flesh*, who was and is the owner of the land? This question is answered affirmatively by the judgment of this court in the case of *Heath v. Solles, ante,* p. 217. It is not denied that *Mrs. La Flesh* had knowledge that her husband was erecting the buildings upon her land, and consented thereto. Under the case last cited, nothing more is required to

charge her land with the lien. That is a stronger case
against the lien than is this, for the reason that the husband of Mrs. Solles expressly promised his wife to erect
the building at his own expense, which he failed to do.
Yet, because she knew that the improvement was being
made, and consented thereto, her property was charged
with the lien. The present case is ruled by that judgment.
Hence it must be held that the plaintiff is entitled to a lien
upon the forty acres of land upon which the buildings were
erected (the same not being within the limits of an incorporated city or village), although the materials were purchased by the defendant *Thomas* upon credit, without the
authority of his wife, who is the owner of the land. The
statute upon which that and the present case rests is sec.
3314, R. S., as amended by ch. 349, Laws of 1885. The
full discussion of the question under consideration in the
opinion in that case, prepared by Mr. Justice TAYLOR, renders it unnecessary to say anything more upon the subject.

The sum for which the lien should be allowed will now
be considered. The plaintiff alleged in his petition for a
lien that the value of the materials used in the erection of
the buildings was $483.56. In his complaint he only claims
$466.80. This discrepancy was caused by omitting certain
items in the account, which probably were not used in the
buildings. From the smaller sum should be deducted $18,
paid by *Mrs. La Flesh* for articles charged in the account,
but returned, and, after the filing of the petition, again
taken and used in the building. The court found that payments had been made on the general account to the amount
of $310.21. No appropriation of these payments has been
made by the parties, and the plaintiff seeks to apply them
to the non-lienable items in the general account, except
the $18 which we apply on the lienable items. It appeared
on the trial that over $280 of the plaintiff's account con-
sisted of advances made by the plaintiff to pay freights

chargeable to the defendant *Thomas*. The money was so advanced without charge, for the accommodation of said *Thomas*. In view of this fact, we think it entirely equitable to apply all the payments except the $18 above mentioned upon the account for cash advances and non-lienable goods. Hence the lien should be for $448.80, and interest thereon from the commencement of the action, which was August 3, 1887.

The court found the amount unpaid on the whole account on May 24, 1887, to be $1,412.96. In the fifth finding of fact, he found and allowed a further payment of $299.93, made November 17, 1887. This was several months after the action was commenced, and after issue joined therein. We are unable to find in the record any testimony relating to this alleged payment or any admission thereof. It was therefore improperly allowed. If such payment was in fact made, we think the circuit court may direct it to be allowed upon the judgment, because made after issue, and hence not covered by the pleadings in the action. We are also of the opinion that the interest should be computed from the commencement of the action.

Some minor objections to the regularity or sufficiency of the pleadings and proceedings in the circuit court were made by counsel for the defendants on the argument of this appeal. Some of these will now be briefly noticed. (1) It was objected that there was a variance between the petition for a lien and the complaint in that the petition charged the sale of the materials to both defendants *La Flesh*, while the complaint charged the sale to the defendant *Thomas* alone. This variance is quite immaterial. It can harm no one. The complaint states the fact as it was proved on the trial. And the petition is amendable at any time to make it correspond with the complaint and proofs. (2) The same remarks are applicable to another and similar objection, that the petition charges that the materials were used in the erection of a certain building on the land in question, while the complaint alleges that the same were used in the erection of a house and barn thereon. (3) It is said that the buildings are not sufficiently described. The description thereof is as definite as the statute which gives a lien for materials furnished in the erection of a dwelling-house or other building upon the land. R. S. sec. 3314. Both the petition for the lien and the complaint contain an accurate description of the land upon which the buildings were erected. That is sufficient. (4) Some criticism was made in the argument upon the practice by which judgment in the same action for one amount was rendered against the debtor, and a further judgment therein, making a portion of that amount a lien upon the land of another defendant. We perceive no valid objection to this practice. Certainly *Mrs. La Flesh* is not injured by it; and, inasmuch as the statute gives the defendant *Thomas* the right to a common-law trial by jury, we are equally unable to perceive that he has any valid ground for complaint. (5) Sec. 3324, R. S., gives the plaintiff the right to have his costs paid out of the proceeds of the sale of the property against which the lien is adjudged. Of course the defendant *Thomas* is liable for all the costs in the action.

It follows from what has been said that the judgment of the circuit court must be reversed, and the cause will be remanded with directions to that court to render judgment for the plaintiff in accordance with this opinion.

By the Court.— Ordered accordingly.

LOGAN and others, Respondents, vs. DIXON and others, Appellants.

February 1 — February 19, 1889.

Partnership: Estates of decedents: Claim for contribution: Limitation: Appeal.

1. The claim of surviving partners against the estate of a deceased partner for contribution for losses sustained by the firm is a contingent claim which does not become absolute until the business of the firm is settled, the assets converted, and the debts paid, and which (under sec. 3860, R. S.) need not be presented for allowance until it so becomes absolute. If, before such claim becomes absolute, the estate of the deceased partner has been settled and the assets distributed, the claim is not barred by sec. 3844, R. S., but the surviving partners may pursue their remedy against the heirs and distributees under ch. 141, R. S.

2. To establish a claim for contribution from the estate of a deceased partner, the state of the accounts of the several partners with the firm should be shown, as well as the fact that upon the closing up of the business there were losses which were paid by the surviving partners out of moneys not belonging to the firm. But where, in an action to enforce such contribution, it was admitted in the pleadings that each partner had an equal interest in the business, and the trial proceeded throughout on the implied understanding that neither partner had contributed more than his share to the capital stock and that if there were any losses upon the closing up of the business each was liable to contribute equally to pay the same, and the trial court was not requested to take proofs or make findings on that subject, and on appeal it is not claimed that the appellants would be in any way benefited by the taking of an account to show the *status* of each partner with the firm, a judgment rendered on the theory of the equal liability of the partners will not be reversed for the want of a formal finding on that subject.

APPEAL from the Circuit Court for *Waupaca* County.

The following statement of the case was prepared by Mr. Justice TAYLOR as a part of the opinion:

The material facts in this case are the following:

First. In January, 1877, one H. S. Dixon, then living,

and the plaintiffs, entered into a copartnership under the firm name and style of the New London Stave Company. That said copartnership was composed of the following named firms and persons, to wit, the firm of Logan & Co., composed of the plaintiffs *Thomas Logan* and *G. W. Spaulding;* the firm of Dickinson & Frayser, composed of the plaintiffs *C. E. Dickinson* and *Anthony Frayser;* and the other plaintiffs, *H. H. Paige, James Stimpson*, and *W. A. Sterling*, and the said H. S. Dixon, now deceased. That said firm of Logan & Co. composed one member of the firm called the "New London Stave Company," the firm of Dickinson & Frayser one member of said firm, and the said *Paige, Stimpson, Sterling*, and Dixon composed the other members of the New London Stave Company, each of said partners having an equal share in said business, and being entitled to an equal division of the profits, and equally accountable for the losses of said partnership.

Second. That the New London Stave Company continued to do business as a partnership composed of the members aforesaid until the 29th of April, 1881, when the copartnership was dissolved by the death of said H. S. Dixon.

Third. That said Dixon died intestate on said 29th day of April, 1881, in the county of Waupaca, and that on the petition of *Alice Dixon*, widow of said deceased, letters of administration on the estate of said Dixon were duly issued to one Parley Dickinson, on the 6th day of June, 1881.

Fourth. That at the time of his death the said Dixon left a widow, *Alice Dixon*, and four children, *Charles L. Dixon, Albert E. Dixon, Susan Dixon*, and *Fred Dixon*, who were the sole heirs of the said H. S. Dixon.

Fifth. That said Parley Dickinson duly qualified as such administrator, and afterwards such proceedings were had in said county court of Waupaca county that on the 22d day of May, 1882, a judgment or decree of said county court was made whereby all the estate of the said H. S.

Dixon, deceased, was distributed to the said defendants in this action as the next of kin and heirs at law of said H. S. Dixon, deceased, each receiving one fifth part thereof; and that the amount of personal property belonging to the estate of said Dixon so distributed to said widow, heirs, and next of kin amounted to the sum of $12,000 besides certain real estate described in the complaint herein.

Sixth. That the said plaintiffs, as the surviving partners of the firm known as the New London Stave Company, after the death of said H. S. Dixon, proceeded to close up the business of said firm; and that on or about the 15th day of October, 1885, the business of said firm was finally closed up and settled, and the debts of the same paid in full by said surviving partners; and that upon such settlement of the affairs of said firm the said surviving partners were compelled to pay, and did pay, to the creditors of said firm, who were such at the time of the death of the said H. S. Dixon, about the sum of $13,481.25 over and above the assets then belonging to the said firm.

All these facts were admitted by the answer, except the alleged facts stated as sixth in the above statement. Upon the trial, and, as we think, upon sufficient evidence, the court found the facts in favor of the plaintiffs substantially as stated in said sixth item above. This action was brought by the plaintiffs to recover of the distributees of the estate of said H. S. Dixon, deceased, the one-sixth part of the said sum of $13,481.25, under the provisions of secs. 3274–3286, R. S. There is no claim made but that the facts stated in the complaint in this action made out a good cause of action against said distributees of the estate of said H. S. Dixon, deceased, unless the claim of the plaintiffs was barred by sec. 3844, R. S.

Upon the trial in the court below judgment was rendered in favor of the plaintiffs against each of said defendants for the sum of $390.94 damages, and $57.83 costs; in all, the sum of $448.77. From this judgment the defendants appeal to this court.

For the appellants there was a brief signed by *Cate, Jones & Sunborn*, and oral argument by *D. Lloyd Jones*.

For the respondents there was a brief signed by *Gary & Forward*, of counsel, and oral argument by *George Gary*.

TAYLOR, J. Upon this appeal it is contended by the learned counsel for the appellants (1) that the claim of the surviving partners, if they have any, against the estate of the deceased partner, was a proper one to be presented to the county court for allowance in the settlement of the estate of the said H. S. Dixon, deceased, and, not having been presented to said court within the time limited by law, their right of action is barred; (2) that the circuit court has no jurisdiction of this action; (3) that the findings should have stated an account between each member of the firm, before it can be ascertained or adjudged how much the defendants ought to pay.

The learned circuit judge held that the first objection of the appellants was not well taken, because the county court had not made the proper order or given the proper notice to the creditors of H. S. Dixon, deceased, to present their claims for allowance, and so the statute relied upon was no bar to the plaintiff's action. Whether the learned circuit judge decided this question rightly, or not, we do not deem it necessary to determine on this appeal, as we are of the opinion that the plaintiffs could maintain their action if the county court had made the proper order and given the proper notices for limiting the time within which claims should be presented to said court against the estate.

It is very clear to our minds that the claim of the plaintiffs against the estate of H. S. Dixon, for contribution for the payment of the debts of said partnership, was a contingent claim of the surviving partners against said estate, and that such claim did not become absolute in favor of said survivors until they had settled and paid all the debts of said firm, and applied all the assets of said firm to the payment thereof; and if such contingent claim was one which might have been presented to the county court for adjustment (a question which we do not decide), still the plaintiffs were not bound under the law to present the same until it became absolute and ascertained by the settlement and payment of the debts and liabilities of said firm and the application of the assets of the firm to that purpose. The law is very plain that the surviving partners must wind up the affairs of the partnership. This proposition is not controverted. Pars. Partn. (3d ed.), 440; *Peters v. Davis*, 7 Mass. 257; *Evans v. Evans*, 9 Paige, 178; *Dyer v. Clark*, 5 Met. 562; *Miller v. Jones*, 39 Ill. 54; *Gleason v. White*, 34 Cal. 258. Until the affairs of the firm are wound up and all the debts paid, "neither partner has any remedy against or liability to the other for payment from one to the other of what may have been advanced or received" in said business. *Richardson v. Bank of England*, 4 Mylne & C. 172; *West v. Skip*, 1 Ves. Sr. 242; *Howard v. Priest*, 5 Met. 585. The representative of a deceased partner may, however, upon a proper showing apply to a court of equity for the appointment of a receiver and the settlement of the partnership business in that way. *Evans v. Evans*, 9 Paige, 178, 180; Pars. Partn. (3d ed.), 446. After the affairs of the partnership are closed up and all the debts paid, if there be a balance of assets they must be divided among the partners according to their respective interests in the partnership; and if the firm is insolvent, and some of the partners have paid more than their proportionate share towards the discharge of such debts, they may maintain an action for contribution against those members of the firm who have not paid their just proportion of such debts. *Gleason v. White*, 34 Cal. 258; 3 Pom. Eq. Jur. sec. 1416.

Under the foregoing rules of law applicable to the rights and liabilities of partners as between themselves, it is very clear that the surviving partners could not maintain any action or proceeding against the representative of the deceased partner for contribution for the losses sustained by the firm until after the business of the firm had been wound up and settled by the survivors, and, until that was done, their claim against the estate of the deceased partner was a purely contingent claim, not clearly ascertainable until the business of the firm was wound up and fully settled. The surviving partners hold the property of the firm in the character of trustees, for the settlement and payment of the debts of the firm, and for the purpose of distributing the surplus, if there be any, to the several members of the firm, and to the representative of the deceased member. Pars. Partn. (3d ed.), 443, and notes. If the firm be insolvent, the survivors assume the character of sureties for the deceased partner, if the creditors of the firm elect to proceed against them to collect their claims due from the partnership, and in the character of sureties for the deceased partner they can maintain no action against the estate of the deceased partner until they pay the debt of the firm. In any view of the case, the claim of the surviving partners against the estate of the deceased partner for contribution is a contingent claim within the meaning of the statute, and became absolute only when the business of the firm was finally settled, the assets converted, and the debts paid. This, we think, was fairly settled by this court in the case of *Ernst v. Nau*, 63 Wis. 134.

Having satisfactorily shown that the claim of the plaintiffs was a contingent claim against the estate of the deceased partner, the plaintiffs had an option either to present the claim against the estate as a contingent claim, under secs. 3858, 3859, R. S., or to delay until the claim became absolute by the settlement of the affairs of the firm, and then present the claim under sec. 3860, R. S., within one year after it shall become absolute. When a creditor presents a claim under sec. 3860, he can only be paid out of the assets of the deceased still remaining in the hands of the executor or administrator not then lawfully distributed or applied to the payment of other debts theretofore presented and allowed against the estate; and sec. 3861 provides that when, at the time such claim is presented under the provisions of sec. 3860, the executor or administrator shall not have sufficient assets to pay the whole of such claim, the creditor shall have the right to recover such part of his claim as there are not assets in the hands of the executor or administrator to pay, from the heirs, devisees, or legatees who shall have received sufficient real and personal property from the estate that was liable for the payment of the debts of the deceased.

The allegations in the complaint in this case show that the administrator of the estate of H. S. Dixon, under an order and decree of said county court of Waupaca county, duly settled his accounts as such administrator on the 22d day of May, 1882, and distributed to the widow and heirs at law of deceased all of said estate, and that the amount of the estate so distributed by order of said court was over $12,000, and that on the same day said administrator was discharged; and it is further alleged that said administrator has not now, and has not had since the date of said decree distributing said estate, any assets, estate, money, or property belonging to the said estate of said H. S. Dixon. These allegations are not denied in the answer. The complaint also alleges that the plaintiffs, as surviving partners of the said firm, fully completed the settlement of the affairs of the said copartnership on or about the 15th day of May, 1885, and that the claim of the plaintiffs against said H. S. Dixon, deceased, became absolute on that day. These allegations of the complaint are not denied by the answer, although the answer denies that they proceeded with due diligence to settle the affairs of said partnership; and there are other denials as to the amount of the debts owing by the firm, and the amount of debts paid by the surviving partners in the settlement of the business of said partnership. This action was commenced in November, 1885.

Holding, as we do, that the claim of the plaintiffs against the estate of H. S. Dixon was a contingent claim which could not have been adjusted or allowed by the county court until the surviving partners had settled and wound up the business of the firm, and which did not become absolute before the estate of Dixon had been settled and the assets distributed to the heirs and widow, it was not barred by sec. 3844, R. S., and the plaintiffs could properly pursue their remedy against the heirs and distributees of said deceased, under the provisions of ch. 141, R. S. This question was fully considered by this court in *Mann v. Everts*, 64 Wis. 372. In that case the chief justice says: "According to our view, the statute refers to a contingent claim or liability which can be established by proof, and the amount ascertained. Where a contingent liability exists, and the contingency happens so that the contingent liability becomes an absolute debt which may be proven by the creditor before the settlement of the estate has been closed and the property distributed, there the statute bars the claim if not presented to the commissioners or the county court within the time allowed." See, also, *Webster v. Estate of Lawson, post*, p. 561, in which an opinion is now filed; *McKeen v. Waldron*, 25 Minn. 466.

No argument has been made on the part of the appellants that the evidence does not support the findings of fact so far as such findings relate to the amount of losses which were sustained by the said New London Stave Company in carrying on and closing up said business. We must therefore consider that such findings are supported by the evidence. But it is insisted by the learned counsel for the appellant that it does not follow that because the losses were in fact the sum of about $12,000 the estate of the said deceased partner is liable to contribute to the amount of one sixth part of said losses, and that to determine the question as to how much each partner should pay of said losses an account of the partnership business must be stated as between the several partners, showing the state of the account of each several partner with the firm. It is insisted that upon such an accounting it might appear that the partnership was indebted to the estate of the deceased partner in a sum sufficient to balance the one-sixth part of said losses, and that in such case the estate of said deceased partner could not be compelled to contribute to the other partners for the amount of the losses of the firm. There is no doubt that, in order to make out a case for contribution from the estate of a deceased partner, the state of the accounts of the several partners with the firm ought to be shown, as well as the fact that there were losses incurred on the closing up of the whole business which were paid by the surviving partners out of the money not the property of the firm. This case, we think, proceeded upon the theory that there were six equal partners composing the firm. In fact, this is alleged in the complaint and admitted by the answer of the defendants. We think the trial proceeded also upon an implied understanding that neither partner had contributed more than his equal share of the capital stock of said firm, and that, if there were any losses upon the closing up of the business of the firm, each was liable to contribute equally in paying such losses. No evidence was given on the trial tending to show that any one partner had contributed more or less than his equal share. No exception was taken to the findings by the appellants because such findings did not show the state of the accounts between the separate partners and the firm, nor was there

any request made to the court, either to take proofs on that
question or to make findings in that respect. Nor is it
claimed by the learned counsel upon the argument of this
appeal that, if such an account were taken, it would be in
any way beneficial to their clients. Considering the admissions in the pleadings and the character of the evidence
in the case, the want of exceptions to the findings upon the
point now raised in this court, and in the absence of any
claim even that the appellants would be benefited by such
an accounting, we do not think the judgment should be set
aside for the want of a formal finding upon a subject which
would apparently be of no advantage to the appellants.

By the Court.— The judgment of the circuit court is affirmed.

Neeves, Appellant, vs. Eron, Respondent.
Neeves and others, Appellants, vs. Eron, Respondent.

February 2 — February 19, 1889.

Ejectment: Failure to pay for improvements: Judgment.

Under sec. 3098, R. S., if the plaintiff in ejectment fails to pay the
amount of the assessment for improvements and taxes within
three years from the date of the verdict assessing the same, he is
barred of his recovery whether the judgment so providing has
been entered or not; and if the judgment has not been entered
within such three years the plaintiff is not thereafter entitled to
have it entered, but the defendant may have it entered *nunc pro
tunc* and then declared absolute in his favor.

APPEALS from the Circuit Court for *Portage* County.
The facts are sufficiently stated in the opinion.

For the appellants there was a brief by *L. P. Powers,*
attorney, and *Bleekman, Tourtellotte & Bloomingdale,* of
counsel, and oral argument by *F. H. Bloomingdale.*

For the respondent there was a brief by *Cate, Jones &
Sanborn,* and oral argument by *D. Lloyd Jones.*

ORTON, J. These were actions of ejectment, tried at the November term, 1881. The findings in favor of the plaintiffs were filed January 6, 1882. The claim of the defendant for taxes and improvements was submitted to a jury in each case, November 22, 1882, and a verdict in one case rendered for $7.89, and in the other for $70.72. Nothing further was done in either case until August 30, 1887, when a motion was made by the plaintiffs in one case, and by the plaintiff in the other, for judgment in the actions for the plaintiffs upon the payment of said assessments. These motions were denied, and the plaintiffs appealed from said orders. The questions being alike in both cases, they were submitted together, and there will be but one opinion.

We think the question whether either or both of these orders was or were made at chambers, is more technical than substantial, and, the main question involved being important to the parties, we will not further consider it, but dispose of the main question in the case. This question depends upon the meaning or construction of secs. 3098, 3099, R. S. Those sections would seem to be very plain, and their meaning apparent. The preceding section provides for the trial of the claim for improvements and taxes by a jury, and the verdict is called "the amount assessed." Then sec. 3098 provides that, when the right to recover the same shall be established, and the amount thereof *assessed*, such *assessment*, with the costs of such issue, shall be set off against the sum awarded for costs and damages to the plaintiff in the action, "and, if there remain any excess, the judgment in such action shall provide that the plaintiff shall pay the amount thereof, with interest, . . . within three years from the date of such *assessment*, as a condition of *execution*, and shall have no claim for rents and profits while the same remains so unpaid after *assessment*, and that, in default of such payment, *he shall be deemed to have abandoned his claim of title to the premises in question*, and, together with all persons claiming under him, shall be *for-ever barred* of a recovery, and of claim of title, and the title to the premises in question shall be deemed absolutely vested *in the defendant;* . . . but that upon payment as aforesaid the plaintiff shall have *execution* for the premises recovered." Sec. 3099 provides that " at the expiration of the three years limited in any such judgment the court may make an order, . . . upon application, . . . after notice and upon satisfactory proof of the fact, *declaring* that the plaintiff has failed to make the payment, . . . and that the judgment has become absolute in favor of the defendant."

1. In such a case there is but one judgment to be entered, and that is the above *conditional* one; and upon payment of such assessment within "three years from the date of such assessment," according to the condition in said judgment, the plaintiff shall have *execution* for the premises recovered, that is, execution on such conditional judgment. That judgment has never been entered. It may now be entered, but it must be *nunc pro tunc,* for it could not otherwise contain that condition of payment within three years from the date of such assessment. The plaintiff should have entered up that judgment as soon as the assessment was made; or, if it was the duty of the defendant to have so entered it, upon his neglect he could have had it so entered. *Ballou v. C. & N. W. R. Co.* 53 Wis. 150. If the defendant neglected to tax his costs, he would forfeit them by ch. 202, Laws of 1882; and the subtraction of the setoff was a mere mathematical operation. The circuit court no doubt considered that the motions were for judgments at that date, and not of the date of the assessment, and therefore denied them.

2. The three years in which the plaintiff could pay the assessment has long since expired. The word " assessed " or " assessment " is too often repeated in these sections to

be misunderstood. It is the amount *assessed* by the jury for taxes and improvements, and the three years limitation is from the date of the same. It would now do the plaintiffs no good to have entered such conditional judgment, for that limitation has expired. The defendant is now entitled to have such judgments entered *nunc pro tunc*, and then proceed to have them declared absolute in his favor, under sec. 3099. The judgments ought to be entered, and the matter so closed of record. In any event, it is now quite immaterial to the plaintiffs whether they are entered at the date of the assessment or not, or whether they are now entered or not. The time in which he could pay the assessments was not dependent upon the entry of such judgments, but upon the date of such assessments, and that time has expired. He is now barred of his recovery, and the title has become absolutely vested in the defendant. There can be no other possible result, unfortunate as it may be to the plaintiffs. This is not the only case where a party may lose or forfeit his rights by his own negligence.

By the Court.— The orders of the circuit court denying the motions are affirmed.

Dunn, Respondent, vs. Estate of Fleming, Appellant.

February 2 — February 19, 1889.

Limitation of actions: Mutual account current: Instructions to jury.

The question whether the plaintiff's claim was " for the balance due upon a mutual and open account current " (sec. 4226, R. S.) and therefore not barred by the statute of limitations, is *held*, on defendant's appeal, to have been fairly submitted to the jury by instructions to the effect that such an account must contain credits as well as debits, that the burden of proof was upon the plaintiff, and that the jury must determine whether it was such an account and, if so, the amount due thereon.

APPEAL from the Circuit Court for *Portage* County.

The following statement of the case was prepared by Mr. Justice CASSODAY:

The deceased died in the spring of 1885. The plaintiff presented a claim against his estate to the county court purporting to be based upon an account of charges against the said John Fleming, commencing March 15, 1867, and ending with July, 1884, for sundry items of cash, labor, wheat, oats, team work, etc., amounting in the aggregate to $440.25; and also credits, commencing in 1870, and continuing from time to time until the year 1884, for sundry items of cash, team work, hay, hauling lumber and potatoes, cutting oats, wool, and $20 for land in 1871, amounting in the aggregate to $40.80, leaving a balance against the estate of $399.45. The claim was rejected by the county court. Thereupon the plaintiff appealed to the circuit court. Upon the trial in that court the jury returned a verdict in favor of the plaintiff and against said estate for $470.38. From the judgment entered thereon the administrator appeals.

For the appellant there was a brief by *Cate, Jones & Sanborn*, and oral argument by *D. Lloyd Jones*. They contended, *inter alia*, that the mutual and open account current referred to in the statute is defined to be " accounts which are made up of matters of setoff. There must be a mutual credit founded on a subsisting debt on the other side, or an express or an implied agreement for a setoff of mutual debts." Angell on Lim. sec. 149; *Hannan v. Engelmann*, 49 Wis. 278. It must show a system of mutual dealings and of reciprocal demands between the parties. *Fitzpatrick v. Estate of Phelan*, 58 Wis. 250. Mutual accounts imply entries by each party. *Baker v. Mitchell*, 59 Me. 223. There must be some connection between the items in the account. *Belles v. Belles*, 12 N. J. Law, 339. The account must be kept with the assent of both parties.

Hodge v. Manley, 60 Am. Dec. 253, 25 Vt. 210; *Green v. Caldcleugh,* 28 Am. Dec. 567, 1 Dev. and Bat. Law, 320. Under these rules the court below erred in refusing to instruct the jury that it must appear that each party makes charges against the other, and that it must appear that both plaintiff and Fleming consented that there should be an account and that the items, etc., should become a matter of account.

For the respondent the cause was submitted on the brief of *James O. Raymond* and *O. H. Lamoreux.*

CASSODAY, J. It is agreed on both sides that the only question for consideration is whether the claim presented was barred by the statute of limitations. Sec. 3841, R. S. This depends upon whether it is "to recover the balance due upon a mutual and open account current" within the meaning of the statute. Sec. 4226. If the claim constituted such an account, then the cause of action "accrued at the time of the last item proved in such account." *Ibid.* As to whether it was such an account, the court charged the jury as follows: "Now, an open, that is, unsettled, and mutual account current, is an account consisting of credits as well as debits, charges and credits, between the parties. An account in which A. charges B. with a number of items extending through a considerable time, but in which B. has no credits, is not a mutual account current between the parties." This instruction seems to be in harmony with the repeated rulings of this court. *Hannan v. Engelmann,* 49 Wis. 282; *Fitzpatrick v. Estate of Phelan,* 58 Wis. 254. The court also charged the jury that: "Upon the issue thus presented the burden is upon the plaintiff to convince you that there was such open, mutual account, and if there was, then to satisfy you of the balance due him, to entitle him to recover thereon. If you shall be satisfied that such open, mutual account existed, then the plaintiff can recover, if at all, such sum only as the evidence satisfies you was due him at the time of Mr. Fleming's death on account of transactions between the parties had within six years immediately preceding that event." These instructions put the burden of proof upon the plaintiff, and left it to the jury to find whether it was such an account and, if so, the amount due thereon. It seems to us that the question was fairly submitted to the jury, and that the evidence supports the finding that it was such an account.

These portions of the charge cover the principal exceptions relied upon. There are other exceptions to other portions of the charge, but as they are either involved in what has already been said, or are more favorable to the estate than to the plaintiff, it is unnecessary to specifically consider them.

By the Court.— The judgment of the circuit court is affirmed

GREEN and another, Appellants, vs. WALKER, Respondent.

February 2 — February 19, 1889.

(1) Evidence: Deposition taken on legal holiday. (2) Husband and wife: Agency: Estoppel.

1. Sec. 2576, R. S., as amended by ch. 142, Laws of 1885 (providing that no court shall be opened or transact any business on any legal holiday, unless it be for the purpose of instructing or discharging a jury, or of receiving a verdict and rendering a judgment thereon), does not render inadmissible in evidence a deposition taken in another state on a day made a legal holiday in this state.

2. Where a husband has charge of his wife's business which consists in dealing in horses, the fact that in looking after the horses he treats them as his own with her knowledge ought not to estop her from asserting her title to them as against his creditors.

APPEAL from the Circuit Court for *Portage* County. The facts are stated in the opinion.

For the appellants the cause was submitted on the brief of *James O. Raymond.*

For the respondent there was a brief by *Lamoreux & Park*, and oral argument by *B. B. Park.*

COLE, C. J. This is an action of replevin to recover the possession of a span of horses. The plaintiffs claim to own them as copartners. The defendant, as sheriff, justifies the taking and holding of the horses under an execution issued on a judgment against Simon Green, the husband of the plaintiff *Alice.* The real controversy, therefore, is, Was the property seized on the execution the property of the plaintiffs, or was it the property of the judgment debtor? The plaintiff *Alice*, in order to prove that she had been in business on her own account and had a separate estate, offered in evidence two depositions,— one of Albert Green, a brother-in-law; the other, of Mrs. Beers, her mother. These depositions were both taken,— the former in Michigan, the latter in Missouri,— on the 22d day of February, 1887. The depositions were objected to because taken on a legal holiday, and excluded on that ground. The depositions were clearly material to the issue, and their exclusion was doubtless prejudicial to the rights of *Mrs. Alice Green.* The question is, Were they properly excluded because taken on a day which is made a legal holiday in this state? We are clear that this question must receive a negative answer.

The statute relating to this subject is sec. 2576, R. S., as amended by ch. 142, Laws of 1885. That section provides, in effect, that no court shall be opened or transact any business on the first day of the week, or any legal holiday, unless it be for the purpose of instructing or discharging a jury, or of receiving a verdict and rendering a judgment thereon. The 22d day of February is made a legal holiday by sec. 2577. Now, if it be conceded — a point we do not decide — that the taking of a deposition in this state is a judicial act, which is prohibited, still it is plain our statute can have no extra-territorial effect. It could not prohibit the taking of a deposition in Michigan or Missouri, merely by making the day on which it was taken a legal holiday. The legislature might perhaps provide that no such deposition taken in another state should be used as evidence in the courts of this state. The legislature has not seen fit to do this, but has prohibited the courts, with certain exceptions, from transacting any business on a legal holiday. But this prohibition only relates to judicial acts, and does not apply to mere ministerial acts,— such as the issuing of a summons by a justice of the peace,— as this court has decided. *Weil v. Geier*, 61 Wis. 414. It would be a most liberal, not to say forced, construction of language to hold that the taking of a deposition by a notary public was the act of a court, or a judicial act in a legal sense. We have been referred to decisions holding promissory notes and other contracts made on Sunday void, but these cases afford little aid in solving the question before us. The case of *Wilson v. Bayley*, 42 N. J. Law, 132, does hold that a deposition taken upon a legal holiday upon notice to, but against the objection of, the opposing counsel, cannot be used. The question is not discussed at all, but the decision is placed upon the provisions of their statute in relation to legal holidays. That statute declares that no person shall be compelled to labor upon any legal holiday, and some stress seems to be placed upon this clause in the opinion. In *Rogers v. Brooks*, 30 Ark. 612, the court held that a deposition taken on the 4th of July was good, but we infer that that was not a legal holiday. The court says the statute did not prohibit the taking of depositions on the 4th day of July, and therefore refused to suppress the deposition.

We are not aware of any statute in this state which declares that a deposition taken in another state on a day which is made a legal holiday here, shall not be used as evidence in our courts. But the learned circuit court did not exclude the depositions on the ground that the taking them was a judicial act, but it thought that the policy of the law, or the purpose of it, was to exempt a citizen of the state from being called into court for any purpose on a legal holiday. The statute does not say that no person shall be required to attend to any business whatever on a legal holiday. If it did, it might be claimed with much reason that it would be a violation of the spirit of the law to require a citizen to go to another state to take a deposition on such a day. There is no law which prohibits a citizen from laboring or pursuing his worldly business on any day of the week except Sunday. On a secular day which is made a holiday the ordinary business of courts is suspended, and while the law does not require, its policy may favor, the appropriation of the day to rest and festivity. Still every man is left free to follow the dictates of his judgment and conscience in that regard. He may abstain from work or not. Says Mr. Justice GEIER, when speaking of a kindred question, in *Richardson v. Goddard*, 23 How. 44: "Public officers, school-boys, apprentices, clerks, and others who live on salaries or prefer pleasure to business, claim the privilege of holiday, while those who depend on their daily labor for their daily bread, and cannot afford to be idle, pursue their occupations as usual." We do not understand that the prohibition of the statute goes so far as to excuse a lawyer from disregarding a legal notice served on him on a holiday, or from attending to many things connected with his profession. However that may be, we see no ground for saying that the policy of the statute condemns the taking of a deposition in another state on a day which is made a legal holiday here, and that such deposition cannot be used as evidence in our courts. We therefore hold that the depositions in question were erroneously suppressed or excluded.

Some exceptions were taken to the charge, but it is not necessary to notice them at any length. We will only remark that the court stated the law rather strongly in that part of the charge where he says: "The plaintiffs are not estopped from asserting their title to the property in question by reason of their having at any time known, without warning him thereof, that Fowler was suing Simon Green upon a demand that might have been enforced by a suit against them, if such was the fact, unless the evidence satisfies you that the plaintiffs knowingly permitted Simon to so act with reference to their property, and deal with others in relation to it, as if he were the owner." One of the plaintiffs and a judgment debtor were husband and wife. On account of this relation, the husband, if he had charge of the wife's business, as he might lawfully, would necessarily have the possession of her property apparently, and would often deal with it as if he were the owner. The business of dealing in horses would require the services of a man to look after them. The husband might perform that service for the wife, and in so doing treat the horses as his own, with her knowledge; but that ought not to estop her from asserting her title to the property as against his creditors. But because the depositions were excluded the judgment of the circuit court is reversed, and a new trial ordered.

By the Court.— Ordered accordingly.

MARTIN, Respondent, vs. STEWART and another, Trustees, etc., Appellants.

February 2 — February 19, 1889.

Railroads: Fences: Killing of stock: Contributory negligence.

1. Under sec. 1810, R. S., as amended by ch. 193, Laws of 1881, if fences have been duly erected in good faith along the right of way of a railroad, although they are afterwards destroyed or become defective, an action for an injury alleged to have been caused by the lack of or defects in the fence will be defeated if it appears that the plaintiff was guilty of contributory negligence.

2. The plaintiff turned his colt into a pasture beside a railroad track, knowing that there was nothing to prevent the animal from going upon the track, and using no precaution to prevent it from doing so. The animal went upon the track and was killed by a passing locomotive. *Held*, that the plaintiff was guilty of contributory negligence. The fact that he had no other pasturage for the colt is of no importance.

APPEAL from the Circuit Court for *Portage* County.

This action is to recover the value of a colt belonging to the plaintiff, which was killed by a passing locomotive on the track of the railway operated by the defendants, by reason of their alleged negligence in failing to keep in repair and maintain a fence along their right of way contiguous to the plaintiff's land.

There is no general verdict in the case, but the jury found specially that the colt escaped from the plaintiff's pasture, and went therefrom upon the defendant's right of way; that the fence between such pasture and right of way was destroyed August 15, 1886; that the plaintiff turned his colt into the pasture September 2, 1886, knowing at the time that such fence had been so destroyed and had not been replaced, and kept the colt there until it was killed; that on said September 2d he talked with defendants' section foreman about repairing the fence, and the latter promised to repair it before September 10, 1886, but did not do so; that the colt was killed September 10, 1886, in the manner above stated, nearly opposite the defective fence; that the plaintiff had no other pasturage for the colt; and that the value of the animal when killed was $120. There was no finding on the question whether or not the plaintiff was guilty of negligence contributing to the death of the colt.

The defendants moved, at the proper times, for a nonsuit, for judgment on the special verdict, and for a new trial, all of which motions were denied by the court, and judgment for the plaintiff for $120 and costs was ordered and duly entered. The defendants appeal from the judgment.

For the appellants there was a brief by *D. S. Wegg* and *Howard Morris*, attorneys, and *Winkler, Flanders, Smith, Bottum & Vilas*, of counsel, and oral argument by *J. G. Flanders*.

For the respondent there was a brief by *Lamoreux & Park*, and oral argument by *B. B. Park*.

Lyon, J.   The learned counsel for the plaintiff submitted an ingenious argument to sustain the proposition that the liability of the defendants for the value of the colt killed upon their railway track by their locomotive was absolute, and that the question of the contributory negligence of the plaintiff is not in the case. We think this proposition is inaccurate. Sec. 1810, R. S., as amended by ch. 193, Laws of 1881, after charging railway companies with the duty of constructing fences and cattle-guards, provides that, " until such fences and cattle-guards shall be duly made, every railroad corporation owning or operating any such road shall be liable for all damages done to cattle, horses, or other domestic animals, or persons thereon, occasioned in any manner, in whole or in part, by the want of such fences or cattle-guards; but after such fences and cattle-guards shall have been in good faith constructed, such liability shall not extend to damages occasioned in part by contributory negligence, nor to defects existing without negligence on the part of the corporation or its agents."

This statute is plain and unambiguous, and admits of but one construction. Until fences are erected along the right of way, pursuant to the statute, the liability of the persons or company operating the railway for injuries occasioned in whole or in part by the want of such fences, is absolute; but after such fences are once in good faith constructed, although thereafter they are destroyed or become defective, an action for an injury alleged to be caused thereby will be defeated if it appear that the plaintiff was himself guilty of negligence which directly contributed to the injury. In the present case the right of way where the accident happened had once been fenced, and remained so fenced for several years, but the fence had been recently destroyed or injured by fire. Although the defendants were in default for not restoring it as soon as they should have done, there is no proof or claim that they did not intend to do so, or of any bad faith on their part. Hence the case comes within the latter clause of sec. 1810, which in effect prohibits a recovery if the negligence of the plaintiff contributed to the injury complained of. Such is the doctrine of the cases in this court cited by counsel for the defendants. These are *Jones v. S. & F. du L. R. Co.* 42 Wis. 306; *Lawrence v. M., L. S. & W. R. Co.* 42 Wis. 322; *Richardson v. C. & N. W. R. Co.* 56 Wis. 347; and *Carey v. C., M. & St. P. R. Co.* 61 Wis. 71. The complaint herein was framed in this view, for it alleges that "without the fault or negligence of the said plaintiff, but solely from the fault and negligence of said defendants, their employees and servants, by reason of their failure to properly repair and maintain their fence aforesaid," the colt escaped upon the right of way and was killed.

Although there is no direct finding upon the question, we do not hesitate to hold that the special verdict establishes conclusively that the plaintiff was guilty of negligence which contributed directly to the injury of which he complains.. He turned his colt into the pasture knowing that there was nothing to prevent it from going upon the railway track, and it does not appear that he used the slightest precaution to prevent the animal from so doing. Under the cases above cited, and many others decided by this court, this makes a perfectly clear case of contributory negligence on the part of the plaintiff, and defeats a recovery in the action. It is of no importance that the plaintiff had no other pasturage for his colt. This fact could not excuse his neglect, in the known presence of imminent danger to the animal, to use proper precautions to save it from injury. Moreover, the statute (sec. 1812) gives the plaintiff the right, upon proper notice, to rebuild or repair the fence (if the defendants fail to do so) at the expense of the defendants.

The evidence being conclusive that the plaintiff was guilty of negligence which contributed directly to the killing of his colt, the motion for a nonsuit should have been granted. But, that motion having been denied, the defendants' motion for judgment upon the special verdict should have been granted.

By the Court. — The judgment of the circuit court is reversed, and the cause will be remanded with directions to that court to render judgment for the defendants upon the special verdict.

HOULEHAN, Respondent, vs. RASSLER, Appellant.

February 2 — February 19, 1889.

(1) Appeal: Exceptions: Stipulation construed. (2) Execution: Exemption: "Purchase money."

1. A stipulation that the exceptions taken to the conclusions of law and order for judgment be taken as a part of the record and stand as and in lieu of a bill of exceptions, is *held* to be a waiver of the objection that the exceptions are not sufficiently specific, and to amount to a stipulation that such exceptions shall be effectual to raise the question whether the conclusions of law and order for judgment are warranted by the findings of fact.

2. Money loaned to be used in purchasing certain property, and actually so used by the borrower, is "purchase money" within the meaning of subd. 20, sec. 2982, R. S., and the property so purchased is not exempt from execution issued upon a judgment in an action by the lender to recover the money lent.

APPEAL from the Circuit Court for *Lincoln* County.

The case is sufficiently stated in the opinion.

Milo Woodbury, for the appellant, cited *Carey v. Boyle*, 53 Wis. 579–582; *Jones v. Parker*, 51 id. 218.

For the respondent the cause was submitted on the brief of *Pinney & Sanborn*, of counsel.

ORTON, J. This is an action of replevin brought by the plaintiff against the defendant for one black gelding horse and one set of double harness, valued at $140. The defendant was a constable, and levied an execution upon said property issued upon a judgment rendered by a justice of the peace against the plaintiff, in an action brought by J. C. Garland and F. S. Garland against him, for $70.34 and costs, and this was the taking complained of in the action. The action was finally tried in the circuit court without a jury, and the court found, in substance, that the said Garlands, under the firm name of J. C. Garland & Son, loaned to the plaintiff, *Houlehan*, "at his special instance and request, eighty dollars, to be used by said plaintiff in purchasing, and to enable him to purchase, a team of horses and their harness of one J. Murray; and that the said eighty dollars were used by said plaintiff in making said purchase, and were by him paid to said J. Murray as a part of the consideration for said horses and harness." And the court further found, in substance, that the said judgment in favor of J. C. Garland & Son and against said plaintiff for $70.34, was for the unpaid balance of the indebtedness incurred by making said loan of $80; that said defendant, as constable, levied the execution issued on said judgment on said horse and harness, and that said horse is one of the span of horses, and the harness was the set of double harness, so purchased by the plaintiff of said J. Murray, as aforesaid, and for which said property the said $80 were paid as a part of the consideration; and that at the time of said seizure and levy, and when the action was commenced, the plaintiff was the owner of the said two horses and their said harness only, of which one horse and the harness were so seized and levied upon as aforesaid.

On these findings of fact the court found substantially the following conclusions of law: (1) That said action of J. C. Garland & Son against the plaintiff was not brought for the recovery of the whole or *any part* of the *purchase money* of the property so seized and levied upon; (2) that said $80 so loaned to the plaintiff by J. C. Garland & Co., and so used by the plaintiff *in purchasing* said team of horses and said harness as aforesaid, were not a part of the "purchase money" of said property, within the meaning of subd. 20, sec. 2982, R. S.; and (3) that at the time of said levy and demand said property was exempt from seizure and sale on said execution.

On these findings of fact and conclusions of law, and other appropriate findings of fact and conclusions of law, the court rendered judgment for the plaintiff, from which this appeal is taken. It was stipulated that "the exceptions taken to the conclusions of law and order for judgment, duly filed by the defendant, be taken as a part of the record in this action, and stand as and in lieu of a bill of exceptions herein, the same as if the exceptions had been incorporated in a bill of exceptions duly settled and signed by the judge of the court."

It is objected by the learned counsel of the respondent that there being no exceptions to the findings of fact, and only a general exception " to each and all of the conclusions of law herein, and to the order of the court in this action directing judgment to be entered in favor of the plaintiff," the judgment ought to be affirmed. I suppose that means that there are no questions to be considered by this court. That might be so, so far as the conclusions of law are concerned, if it were not for the above stipulation. That means something. The exceptions "should be taken as a part of the record in this action." If they were not proper exceptions, they should not be taken as a part of the record. The stipulation is evidently a waiver of any objection to the form of the exceptions. It is true that the findings of fact are not excepted to, and of course they should not be, to raise the question whether they warrant or support the conclusions of law or order for judgment. They are taken as true and warranted by the evidence. We think the obvious meaning of the stipulation is that the exceptions taken should be effectual for some purpose, and there can be no other purpose except to raise the question whether the conclusions of law and order for judgment are supported by the findings of fact. The exception to the order for judgment is sufficient, because it is specific, and it is equally error if it is not sustained by the findings of fact. *Allerding v. Cross*, 15 Wis. 530; *Ludlow v. Gilman*, 18 Wis. 552. We will therefore treat the question as properly raised. The practice is a loose one, and ought not to be encour-

aged. A stipulation may answer in place of a bill of exceptions, if it can be understood. *Martin v. Fox & Wis. Imp.
Co.* 19 Wis. 552. But it ought to be plain and unambiguous.

The main question in this case is whether the property
levied upon by the defendant as constable was exempt.
We are compelled to differ with the learned circuit court
on that question, and to hold that the property was not
exempt. The statute is very plain and explicit, and is susceptible of but one meaning, and the facts found bring this
property clearly within its very terms. The plaintiffs in
the case in which the execution was issued "loaned to the
plaintiff, at his special instance and request, eighty dollars, *to be used by said plaintiff in purchasing, and to enable
him to purchase,* a team of horses and their harness of one
J. Murray; and that said eighty dollars *were used* by said
plaintiff *in making said purchase,* and were by him *paid to
said J. Murray as a part* of the *consideration* for said horses
and harness." I repeat these facts here, to show how
clearly they come within the very terms of the statute.
The statute is: "No property exempted by the provisions
of this section shall be exempt from execution issued upon
a judgment in an action brought by *any person* for the recovery of the whole *or any part* of the *purchase money* of
the same property." Subd. 20, sec. 2982, R. S. Was this
$80 any part of the *purchase money* of the property? It
was loaned to be used in *purchasing* the property, *and to
enable* the plaintiff *to purchase* it, and was actually used in
making the *purchase,* and *was paid* to Murray as a part of
the *consideration* of it. What other possible language could
be used that is stronger or more explicit to make that
money a part of the purchase money of the property? And
yet the contention is that it was not, and the court gave
that as a reason for the finding. The facts and the terms
of the statute are too plain to admit of argument. It is
contended that the one who loans the money should have

actually paid it to the person who sold the property. The statute does not say so. The learned counsel of the respondent claims that the evidence in the case shows that the money was not loaned for such purpose. But the evidence is not before us. The findings of fact by the court are alone to be considered, and they do not support the conclusions of law or order for judgment.

By the Court.— The judgment of the circuit court is reversed, and the cause remanded with direction to render judgment for the defendant.

WEBSTER, Respondent, vs. ESTATE OF LAWSON, Appellant.

February 4 — February 19, 1889.

Partnership: Accounting: Suretyship: Estates of decedents: Contingent claim: Parties: Limitation.

W. & L., as partners, holding mortgages on certain logs and lumber, took possession thereof and proceeded to manufacture and sell the same under an agreement with the mortgagors to apply the proceeds on the mortgage debts, the residue if any to be returned to such mortgagors. The value of the property largely exceeded the debts. L. assumed charge of the property and of the execution of the agreement with the mortgagors, one S. being employed by the firm to do the work. Without the knowledge of W., L. became a secret partner with S., and they together, fraudulently and to the injury of W., mismanaged the business of executing the agreement with the mortgagors, converting large quantities of the mortgaged property and its proceeds to their own use without accounting therefor to W. or the firm of W. & L. Afterwards the firm of W. & L. was dissolved, and in the division of assets the mortgages and mortgaged property were transferred to L., who took all the rights and assumed all the obligations, liabilities, and duties of the firm in respect thereto. L. having died, the mortgagors brought suit to compel W., as surviving partner, to account for the mortgaged property and its proceeds. The administrators of L. refused to assume the defense, and W. was compelled to defend the suit and afterwards to pay a judgment rendered against him therein. *Held:*

(1) After the mortgaged property and the rights and obligations pertaining thereto were transferred to L., the same ceased to be partnership property, and as between L. and W. the latter became a mere surety for the faithful performance by L. of the agreement with the mortgagors. The amount of the judgment which W. was compelled to pay by reason of L.'s failure to perform such agreement, is, therefore, a proper claim against the estate of L., without reference to other partnership matters. [Whether W. has a right to be reimbursed by said estate for his expenses incurred in defending the suit brought by the mortgagors, not determined.]

(2) The fact that S. may also be liable to W. by reason of his participation in the fraudulent mismanagement of the business as aforesaid, does not interfere with the right of W. to present his claim against the estate of L.

(3) Such claim of W. was a contingent claim which did not become absolute until he paid the judgment, and (under sec. 3860, R. S.) it might be presented at any time within one year after it so became absolute.

APPEAL from the Circuit Court for *Winnebago* County. This proceeding arises out of the judgment in *Clinton v. Webster*, 66 Wis. 322, and the transactions upon which such judgment is based. During the most of the time of such transactions *Webster*, the claimant and respondent herein, and Publius V. Lawson, since deceased, were partners. That action related to their copartnership business and affairs, and, Lawson having died in 1881, it was brought against *Webster* as surviving partner.

The transactions above mentioned were substantially as follows: In June, 1879, the firm of Clinton, Gillis & Co., which was then engaged in the manufacture and sale of lumber and in a general lumber and logging business at Clintonville in this state, executed to one Hay a chattel mortgage on a large quantity of logs, to secure the payment of a promissory note of the firm to Hay for $3,500. In August of the same year, Clinton, Gillis & Co. executed to Webster & Lawson another chattel mortgage on a large amount of logs, lumber, and other personal property, to secure the payment of four promissóry notes made by that firm to Webster & Lawson, amounting in the aggregate to $2,100. In October, 1879, or earlier, Webster & Lawson became the holders and owners of the note and mortgage so executed to Hay, on which $3,000 then remained unpaid. Thereupon, pursuant to an agreement between the two firms made October 10, 1879, Webster & Lawson took possession of the mortgaged property, and proceeded to work up the logs and sell the lumber and other mortgaged property, under a contract with Clinton, Gillis & Co. to apply the proceeds thereof in payment of the mortgage debts.

The action of *Clinton v. Webster* was brought to compel *Webster*, as surviving partner of the firm of Webster & Lawson, to account for such property and its proceeds. On such accounting it was found that the property and proceeds were sufficient to pay both mortgage debts in full, and $4,195.27 in addition thereto. On December 10, 1884, the circuit court rendered judgment against *Webster* for that sum, and for one half the aggregate costs. On appeal, this court on May 15, 1886, affirmed the judgment as to the $4,195.27, and directed the circuit court to insert in the judgment full costs in favor of Clinton, Gillis & Co. The judgment was modified accordingly, and thus became a judgment against *Webster* for $4,195.27, and for costs adjusted at $2,417.22; total, $6,612.49.

The present proceeding is a claim by *Webster*, filed May 11, 1887, in the proper county court, against the estate of his former partner, Lawson, for the amount of such judgment and interest, and for $5,000 expenses alleged to have been necessarily incurred by him in the defense of the action of Clinton, Gillis & Co.

In his complaint filed in support of such claims, *Webster* alleges substantially the facts above stated, and, further, that he was compelled to pay, and, on or about August 7,

1886, did pay, the judgment of Clinton, Gillis & Co. against
him, and the interest thereon from December 10, 1884, in
full; that he tendered the defense of that action to the administrators of the estate of Lawson, who refused to defend
the same; that he necessarily expended $5,000 in defending
the same; that the estate of Lawson remains unsettled;
and that the letters of administration therein remain in
force.

It is further alleged in the complaint, in substance, that
from the time Webster & Lawson took possession of the
mortgaged property, Lawson had the entire charge thereof
and of the manufacture and sale of the logs and lumber
and the disposition of all the mortgaged property. It is
then alleged that after Webster & Lawson had taken possession of the mortgaged property they made a contract
with one Stacy, in which the latter agreed for a stipulated
price to saw, sell, and ship the logs and timber, and Webster & Lawson agreed to pay him in addition the expenses
of raising certain sunken logs, should he raise the same.
That Stacy commenced sawing the logs, and selling and
shipping the lumber, rendering accounts thereof from time
to time to Webster & Lawson at Menasha, which was their
principal place of business, and such transactions were entered as reported on the books of the firm under the head
of "Clintonville Account," which was designed to be an
accurate account of all transactions affecting the mortgaged property.

The complaint then proceeds to allege and charge that in
January, 1880, Lawson, without the knowledge of *Webster*,
became a secret partner with Stacy in the business of executing such agreement, and that Lawson and Stacy & Lawson in the execution thereof were guilty of many acts of
fraud, greatly to the injury of *Webster*. It is charged that
they converted large quantities of the mortgaged property
and the proceeds thereof to their own use, without account-

ing therefor to *Webster* or the firm of Webster & Lawson at Menasha, where such account was kept; that they over-charged the wages of the men, the expenses of the business, and the cost of supplies; and that they rendered false ac-counts of their doings to *Webster* or Webster & Lawson, at Menasha. The acts of alleged fraud are stated in detail and at great length, but the foregoing is a sufficient sum-mary of them for the purposes of this appeal. It is claimed that the judgment in the case of Clinton, Gillis & Co., was the direct result of such frauds on the part of Lawson and Stacy & Lawson.

The tenth paragraph of the complaint, upon which the decision of the appeal herein is mainly rested, is as follows: "(10) That in the summer of 1880 this claimant became dis-satisfied with the management of said business at Clinton-ville, and became suspicious that lumber manufactured from said logs was being disposed of or disappearing without any account thereof being rendered to said Webster & Lawson, and that said 'Clintonville account,' and the reports and statements rendered by Stacy & Lawson, which were en-tered in said account, were incorrect; that said Lawson in-sisted and assured this claimant that they were correct and all right; that differences arose between them in relation thereto, and on the 1st day of November, A. D. 1880, the partnership between them was dissolved by agreement; that this claimant insisted that said Lawson should take the said 'Clintonville account' and said chattel mortgages, and assume the same and the rights and obligations of the firm of Webster & Lawson under the contracts of October 10, 1879, aforesaid, or that said Stacy or Stacy & Lawson should account to said Webster & Lawson fully for all of said logs, and for the lumber, for the sawing of which under said contracts they had charged Webster & Lawson; that it was agreed between them that in the division of the as-sets and property of said firm of Webster & Lawson the said Lawson would take said 'Clintonville account' as a part of said property and assets; that the understanding between them in relation thereto was that said Lawson should take all the rights and assume all the liabilities of the firm of Webster & Lawson growing out of the dealings and transactions between said firm of Webster & Lawson and Clinton, Gillis & Co., and of said contracts of October 10, 1879, and of all the dealings and transactions concerning said logs and lumber and property mentioned and included in the chattel mortgages aforesaid." It is alleged in the following paragraph that the "Clintonville account," when transferred to Lawson, showed there was due on the chattel mortgages $6,582.57, but that there was charged to Lawson therefor only $5,082.57, being a deduction of $1,500, and that such deduction was made upon the faith of Lawson's representation that the mortgaged property was insufficient to pay the whole amount of the mortgage debts.

After the complaint was filed in the county court, the administrators of the estate of Lawson moved in that court that the same be quashed and the claim dismissed for the following reasons: "(1) Because the claim involves only specific items of a general copartnership account, which cannot be settled except by a bill in equity to adjust all copartnership accounts. (2) Because the claim is not a contingent claim, and the time within which to file and present the same expired on or about the 12th day of July, 1883; wherefore the same is barred by lapse of time and the limitation by statute provided in such claims against the estates of deceased persons. (3) Because the claim of a partner against a deceased partner for fraud or negligence in copartnership business does not survive against the estate of a deceased partner. (4) Because the claim of the claimant *Webster* is a claim against the firm of Stacy & Lawson, composed of Wm. H. Stacy and Lawson, deceased, Wm. H. Stacy being alive and surviving; and the trial thereof requires the presence of said Stacy as a party. (5) Because the claim is barred by the general statute of limitations against actions, to wit, six years."

The county court denied the motion, and on appeal by the administrators the circuit court affirmed the order of the county court in that behalf. This appeal is by the administrators from the order or judgment of affirmance made by the circuit court.

For the appellant there was a brief by *Hooper & Hooper*, and oral argument by *Moses Hooper*.

For the respondent there was a brief by *Gary & Forward*, and oral argument by *George Gary*.

LYON, J. One of the principal grounds upon which the claim of *Webster* against the estate of Lawson, his former partner, is predicated, is stated in paragraph 10 of the complaint, which is set out at length in the foregoing statement of facts. Those allegations are, in substance, that in the division of the assets of the firm of Webster & Lawson on the dissolution of their copartnership, the "Clintonville account," so called, including the chattel mortgages, the demands against Clinton, Gillis & Co. thereby secured, the interest of Webster & Lawson in the mortgaged property and in all contracts and transactions growing out of the mortgages, and all the rights of the firm therein and thereunder, were transferred by the firm, or rather by the partners which constituted it (the firm having theretofore been dissolved), to Lawson, who thereupon assumed all obligations and liabilities of the firm in respect to the mortgaged property and the dealings therewith.

Under the above allegations, it is clear that *Webster* and Lawson segregated the property and rights thus transferred to Lawson, and the obligations and liabilities pertaining thereto or incurred on account thereof, from the balance of the partnership assets (if there were any other assets), and vested the whole title thereto and interest therein in Lawson. From thenceforth Lawson became and was primarily chargeable with all such obligations and liabilities, and *Webster* was merely his surety for the faithful performance of such obligations and the discharge of such liabilities. See *Gates v. Hughes*, 44 Wis. 332, and cases there cited. After such transfer to Lawson, the property and rights so transferred ceased to be partnership property, and could no longer have any place in an accounting of partnership affairs. The sum which Lawson agreed to pay therefor, and which was charged to him, would alone enter into such accounting, just as the money would enter into it had he paid cash therefor, or had the same been sold for cash to any other person.

In view of these considerations, we cannot doubt that, had Lawson lived, *Webster* could, after paying the Clinton judgment, have maintained an action against him on account thereof, without reference to other partnership transactions. Such is the doctrine of *Sprout v. Crowley*, 30 Wis. 187, and the cases there cited. If *Webster* could have maintained such an action had Lawson lived, certainly the cause of action may properly be interposed in the county court by *Webster* as a claim against Lawson's estate after his death.

There seems to be no necessity that Stacy be made a party to an action or proceeding upon such claim. No independent charge of liability on account thereof is made against him. All such charges are against Lawson or the firm of Stacy & Lawson. For the consequences of the mismanagement or fraud of that firm Lawson was responsible, and no valid reason is perceived why *Webster* may not hold his estate to such liability without proceeding against his partner, Stacy. *Webster* contracted with Lawson alone, and, after the transfer to him of the "Clintonville account," trusted to him alone properly to deal with

and dispose of the mortgaged property. If others partici-
pated in the alleged mismanagement of the property to
the injury of *Webster*, the latter may maintain actions
therefor against them, but this does not interfere with his
right to present his claim therefor in the county court
against the estate of Lawson, in which proceeding the other
wrong-doers cannot be joined. Joint as well as several
claims against the estate of a deceased joint debtor may be
presented to the county court, and there adjudicated. R. S.
sec. 3848.

The case made by the complaint, in the aspect in which
it is above considered, may be briefly summarized as follows: Before the dissolution of the firm of Webster & Lawson, it took possession of the mortgaged property, and
became chargeable with the duty of disposing of enough
of it to pay the debts secured by the mortgages, and returning to the mortgagors the residue of the property, or the
proceeds of such residue. The value of the property was
largely in excess of such debts. Lawson assumed the charge
of the property and the performance of such duties. While
in the execution thereof, and, as *Webster* believed, in the
proper execution thereof, the firm was dissolved, and the
interest thereof in the "Clintonville account," including
the mortgages, the debts they were given to secure, and
the mortgaged property, was duly transferred to Lawson,
who assumed all of the obligations, liabilities, and duties
pertaining thereto which Webster & Lawson owed Clinton,
Gillis & Co. As between *Webster* and Lawson, the former
was thereafter merely a surety for Lawson for the faithful
performance of his duties in the premises to Clinton, Gillis
& Co. Lawson failed to perform those duties, and the result of his failure was the judgment of Clinton, Gillis &
Co. against *Webster*, which could not have been recovered
had Lawson properly dealt with the mortgaged property.
The administrators of Lawson's estate refused to assume

the defense of the action of Clinton, Gillis & Co., and *Web-ster* was compelled to defend it at great expense, and after-wards to pay such judgment and interest thereon. Hence he was compelled to pay, and did pay, a large sum of money, which in justice and equity Lawson, were he alive, ought to repay, and against whom an action for money paid, laid out, and expended for his use by *Webster*, could be maintained. We cannot doubt that such cause of action is the proper subject matter of a claim against Lawson's es-tate, which the county court may adjudicate.

If the foregoing views are correct, they overrule all ob-jections interposed to the complaint on the merits, leaving only for determination the objection that the claim was not filed in the county court within the time limited by statute. Strictly, this objection is not available on this motion to quash and dismiss the claim and complaint. The motion is the equivalent of a general and special demurrer to the complaint. It is general, because it denies that a cause of action is stated therein; and special, because it asserts that the complaint shows on its face that some statute of limita-tion has run against the claim. The complaint does not state when the claim was filed in the county court, or the time allowed for the presentation of claims. Hence, it does not appear on its face that it is barred by the statute, and a special demurrer thereto on the ground that the statute had so run would necessarily be overruled. But it is stated in the printed case (perhaps it is conceded) that the time al-lowed by the county court for the presentation of claims against the estate of Lawson expired July 12, 1883, and that the claim herein was filed in that court May 11, 1887. We will dispose of the objection, therefore, on the theory that those facts are properly before the court.

It has already been observed that, as between *Webster* and Lawson, the former stood in the relation of surety for the latter, for the proper performance of the obligations which the firm of Webster & Lawson was under to Clinton, Gillis & Co. on account of the mortgaged property. The liability of Lawson to *Webster* was a contingent liability, and remained so until *Webster* actually paid money on account of his obligation to Clinton, Gillis & Co. On August 7, 1886, he paid the judgment which that firm recovered against him because of Lawson's failure to perform his obligations and discharge his liabilities. The claim of *Webster* then became absolute, and the statute gave him one year from that date to present it to the county court. R. S. sec. 3860. He so presented it May 11, 1887, which was within the year.

It was argued by the learned counsel for the administrators that the liability became absolute at an earlier date, and he cited cases elsewhere to sustain his position. We do not care to review those cases, for the reason that it was settled by this court in *Ernst v. Nau*, 63 Wis. 134, that the claim of a surety against a principal debtor remains contingent until the surety pays the debt; and that, if the debtor has deceased, sec. 3860 gives the surety the right to present his claim, which by such payment became absolute, to the county court for allowance within one year thereafter. That decision rules the present case, and further discussion is unnecessary. Of course there is nothing in the objection that the six years statute of limitation has run against this claim.

We conclude, therefore, that the county court properly denied the motion to quash the complaint and dismiss the claim, and that the circuit court properly affirmed the order of the county court in that behalf.

What the effect would be were that portion of paragraph 10 of the complaint omitted therefrom in which are alleged the transfer of the chattel mortgages, etc., to Lawson, and the assumption by him of all liabilities growing out of the transactions connected therewith, is not here determined. We must take the complaint as it is drawn, and decide this appeal upon the allegations it contains. It is sufficient that these make a case within the jurisdiction of the county court.

Only a single other averment in the complaint requires notice. It is alleged therein that a portion of the logs included in the chattel mortgages remained in Lawson's possession, undisposed of, at the time of his death, and that the same were converted to his own use by one of the administrators of Lawson's estate. Neither the value thereof nor the date of such conversion is stated. It may be doubtful whether the estate of Lawson is chargeable with the value of these logs. We are now inclined to think it is so chargeable. The legal title to the logs was in Lawson when alive, and after his death in his administrators. It would seem that the estate should be held for their value, and that the remedy of the administrators is against the party who so converted them. We leave this question undecided, however, until the circumstances are fully developed by the proofs. If the facts show that such value is not so chargeable, the same should be deducted from *Webster's* claim herein. We also withhold any ruling upon the question of *Webster's* right to be reimbursed for his expenses in his litigation with Clinton, Gillis & Co.

By the Court.— The judgment of the circuit court affirming the order of the county court is affirmed.

RAISBECK, Appellant, vs. ANTHONY and another, Respondents.

December 4, 1888 — March 12, 1889.

Mines and mining: License: Limitation of rights: New discovery.

1. By the terms of a mining license a range of mineral was not to be worked beyond a point 800 yards west of a certain fence. When it had been worked for nearly half of the distance the crevice

pinched out and became barred by a solid wall of rock. A shaft was then sunk about forty-five feet ahead, and by drifting from it a few rods in the same direction a crevice was struck in which mineral was again found. The crevice, before it reached the barrier, and after the barrier was passed, was of the same general character, and there was no change in its general direction or in the rock or the mineral found. *Held,* that the crevice west of the barrier was a continuation of the crevice or range east of it, and that there was no new discovery such as would give rights not limited by the terms of the original license.

2. The limitation on the right to work the range having been created by contract, the discoverers of the range and those claiming under them could be relieved therefrom only by contract; and the evidence (showing, among other things, that the land-owner told one of the owners of the range to go where he pleased upon the range and work it as he pleased) is *held* insufficient to show that the limitation was ever abrogated.

APPEAL from the Circuit Court for *La Fayette* County.

This is an action in equity brought by the plaintiff, who is the owner in fee of certain lands in which is a range of mineral, against the defendants, who claim under the discoverers of such range to be the owners thereof. A trial of the action resulted in a judgment for the defendants dismissing the complaint. The plaintiff appeals from such judgment.

The facts in the case, and the grounds upon which the judgment rests, are fully and clearly stated in the opinion of the circuit judge. Although somewhat lengthy, the case can best be stated by inserting here such opinion in full. It is as follows:

"This action was brought to perpetually restrain the defendants from working further ahead a certain range of mineral. This range is on the west half of the southeast quarter and the east half of the southwest quarter of section 21, town 2, range 1 east, in said county of La Fayette. When said range was discovered said land was owned by Robert Raisbeck, father of the plaintiff, and is now owned by the plaintiff as his devisee. Robert Raisbeck died in 1886. The plaintiff claims that the limit of the defendants to work this range is a point 300 yards west of a certain stone fence that bounds the public highway which passes over said land. The range has been worked to that point. The defendants were notified to not work beyond it, and as they persisted in doing so this action was commenced to perpetually restrain them and for damages, and a temporary injunction was granted restraining them from working the range beyond that point pending this action. The range bears zinc ore, and in that consists its principal value.

"John Anthony, Sr., under whom the defendants claim as heir and widow, and one Wallace Dixon, discovered this range or the crevice that led to it about the year 1872. Wallace Dixon died in the spring of 1887, and John Anthony, Sr., died June 19, 1886. After the range was struck it was worked for three or four years by John Anthony, Sr., and Wallace Dixon, the discoverers, alone. Afterwards the plaintiff and his father became interested in the range as part owners, and it is undisputed that in the year 1878 the range was owned by John Anthony, Sr., one of the discoverers, Robert Raisbeck, the owner of the land, and his son, this plaintiff. About the last-mentioned date Robert Raisbeck sold his interest in the range to John Dixon. This plaintiff, John Anthony, Sr., and John Dixon, owned and worked the range until the year 1881, when the latter sold his interest therein to his partners, and until the death of John Anthony, Sr., the range was owned by him and the plaintiff. After John Anthony, Sr.'s death, the range was, as stated above, owned by the defendant *John Anthony* as the heir of his father, subject to the interest therein of his mother, the defendant *Louisa Anthony*, as widow, and this plaintiff, and up to the time the injunction in this action was served it was worked by them and their servants. Since the range was discovered the rent upon all ores taken therefrom has been regularly paid to the owner of the fee.

"There is, as above stated, no question under the testimony that the plaintiff owned one half of the range as far as it had been worked, and the defendants the other half. The matter in dispute is whether the defendants have any right to work the range beyond the point to which the work upon it had been prosecuted when the injunction was served. The contention of the plaintiff is that his father, the land-owner, when he gave John Anthony, Sr., and Wallace Dixon the right to search for ores in his land, originally confined their right to follow westward any range or valuable discovery they might make to a certain stone fence that bounded a field to the west of the place where they began to mine, and that when, in following the range they discovered westerly, they reached this fence, they were only permitted to follow this range into said field under an agreement that their right to work it should be limited in that direction by a point 300 yards west of said fence. As the range has been worked to that point, there is no doubt that, if the discoverers were originally limited by Raisbeck, deceased, in their right to follow the range on his land, by said fence, and by subsequent agreement they were permitted to follow it 300 yards only beyond the fence, the defendants have no further right in it, and that the part of the range beyond that limit belongs solely to the plaintiff, the owner of the fee, unless since such agreement new rights have arisen. The range, at the time the injunction was served, was yielding valuable zinc ore, and seemed likely to continue to do so.

"The testimony is very meager upon the question of whether at the time John Anthony. Sr., and Wallace Dixon began to mine, about the year 1872, they were limited by Robert Raisbeck to follow any range they might discover.

The license or lease under which they began to mine was
verbal, as in those days was usually the case. All of the parties to it are dead, and all of the testimony bearing upon
the rights the two miners originally possessed is circumstantial, hearsay, or the recollection of witnesses of statements of the parties in interest in casual conversations had
years ago.   There is testimony tending to show that when,
in their progress in working the range, the discoverers
reached the fence, they, for a short time, did not prosecute
the work onward.   Whether because they were originally
limited, or because, as one witness who worked the mine
says, the range ' pitched down ' at that point into the water,
and it became necessary to stop work upon it and bring up
a drain to unwater it, it would be difficult for me, from the
testimony, to say positively; but my impression is that it
was not expected at the time of the license to mine, that a
range would be discovered that would run westerly beyond said fence, and that none of the parties had in contemplation such a discovery when the mining began.   I
am confirmed in this impression by the facts shown by the
testimony that, although at that time considerable mining
had been done on the land of the licensor east of the fence,
some of it within the yard surrounding his house, no range,
so far as the testimony shows, had been discovered that
ran into said field on the west.   It seems to me probable
that when the boundary of the field was reached, then
arose a question of right of the discoverers to proceed, and
that they did not prosecute the work until an understanding was arrived at.   What that understanding or agreement was it is impossible, from the testimony, to definitely
state.   It was oral.   It seems to have been the intention
to place it in writing.   A writing was drawn up, but it was
never executed.   What the contents of it was no one can
state.   I think, however, from all the testimony, it is a fair
conclusion that the discoverers proceeded with their work

in.the field upon the understanding that they were limited, in the distance they might follow the range into the field, to a point 300 yards west of the fence. As to whether that limit was absolute or contingent, I cannot, with satisfaction to myself, certainly determine. I base the conclusion that that was understood to be a limit upon the testimony of various witnesses as to what they had heard the parties in interest say. I must say, however, that I was never more impressed with the principle that testimony of this kind is inherently weak than I was upon this trial; for although I deduced. from it that it was agreed that there should be a limit, I could not but feel that the recollection of some of the witnesses could not be much relied upon. Take the witness Davidson, for instance,— the most positive witness upon this question that the plaintiff produced. No one who heard him could believe that much of what he testified regarding conversations took place as he detailed it, and I say this without any purpose to charge any wilful misrepresentation to him, but only to show the weakness, as testimony, of the statements of a witness of what he recollects of conversations had years before, in a casual manner, upon a subject in which he had no interest.

"The reason why a limit was named by the land-owner, Raisbeck, as a condition of permitting the discoverers to follow the range, is not to be determined from the testimony. There was nothing artificial or natural in the field which would indicate a reason why work should stop at the end of 300 yards. For aught there was in the field itself, the limit might as well have been 200 yards, or 400 yards, or its western boundary. It was claimed upon the argument that the limit, if there was one, was contingent upon whether the mine proved productive enough to yield a rent to the land-owner that would make it desirable to him to have mining continued, rather than to have it stopped and the surface of the ground upon the line of the range remain undisturbed. There is some testimony to support this claim, and in itself it does not seem to one raised in the mining region unreasonable, for it is a matter of common knowledge among those acquainted with the lead-mine region that farmers, who are willing to have an arable field or pasture dug up if ore is raised in quantities that will yield them a fair rent, will not permit their land to be dug over by miners who are endeavoring, by prospecting, to discover ores in paying quantity, upon the line even of a known crevice or range. If the limit was not thus contingent, the only plausible reason why a limit was stated is that Raisbeck, the land-owner, was willing, as a matter of favor, to give the discoverers the right to work the range that far because they had discovered it, and that when that limit was reached, no matter how valuable the ore might be or appear to be, beyond it he would then, as owner of the fee, exclude them from the range.

"Whatever might have been the exact agreement, the work was continued westwardly in the field. In the year 1878, the range, to use the miner's phrase, began to 'pinch out;' that is, the walls of the crevice came nearer together, and the ore sheet became thinner, and ceased to produce ore enough to pay for the cost and labor of taking it out. The owners of the range, as partners, at that time were, as I have stated, John Anthony, Sr., one of the discoverers, Robert Raisbeck, the land-owner, and this plaintiff. Robert Raisbeck at that time desired John Dixon, an old and experienced miner, to come and work his interest in the mine, and told him that his son, this plaintiff, had not much experience as a miner, and that if he (Dixon) would work for him (Robert Raisbeck) on the range at $1.25 per day, which was less than regular miner's wages, he would likely, after a time, give him his interest in the range. Dixon accepted the offer, and went to work. After working for a time, and the mine appearing no better, Robert Raisbeck told

him that he might have his interest if he would pay him
the expense he had been to for powder, etc. To this Dixon
agreed, and he became the owner of Robert Raisbeck's interest. At that time the range had almost ceased to yield
ore. Dixon went into the mine to work in the hope that
by working ahead paying ore would be discovered. He
testifies that Robert Raisbeck gave him his interest in the
range, naming no limit, and that he knew of no limit, and
that it was his understanding that if he and his partners
could strike paying ore that they might follow it indefi-
nitely in Raisbeck's field. It is certain from the testimony
that Robert Raisbeck did not want work upon the range to
stop, but, on the contrary, that he was anxious in the interests of his son *William*, as well as himself as land-owner,
that efforts should be made to find upon it valuable ores.
After Dixon became the owner, the range was followed
about one hundred feet, some zinc ore being taken out, when
it became barred up; that is, a solid wall of rock was struck
against, at which the crevice they were following abruptly
ended, and the yield of ore stopped. I have no question
that Robert Raisbeck knew this, and there is no proof that
he desired, much less expressed a desire, that the work
within the field should stop. A surveyor was then employed to determine, as near as possible, a point where a
shaft should be sunk to strike the lost crevice, if it extended
beyond the bar. A point was designated forty-five feet
ahead of the place where the work had stopped. A shaft
was sunk there. It did not strike the crevice, but from it
a crevice was found by drifting, but it contained no ore at
the place the drift struck it. They drifted ahead, and at
length, after having worked for several months without
obtaining paying ore, and after John Anthony, Sr., and
this plaintiff had become so disheartened that they proposed to abandon the range, and would have done so but
for Dixon's persistence, ore was again found in paying

quantities, and that ore was followed until work was
stopped by the preliminary injunction. John Dixon sold
his one-third interest in the mine, as stated heretofore, about
1881, and received for it $600. The testimony of John
Dixon, as above substantially given, was not contradicted.

"I find the facts above stated to be true. From them I
can but conclude that, whatever talk there was of a limit
when the work in the field began, there was no purpose
upon the part of Robert Raisbeck to limit the work upon
the range when he requested John Dixon to come and
work upon it, and that Dixon and John Anthony, Sr., and
this plaintiff, who together worked the range as owners of
it, did not understand from the time Dixon became an
owner that their rights were limited by a point 300 yards
from the fence. Nearly half of this distance had been
worked when they struck the bar, and it seems to me im-
probable that they would after that work hard for months,
without remuneration, to develop a range that had ceased
to yield ore, if they believed that they could not follow beyond a point not far in advance the ore their persistence
might discover. The land-owner must have understood
that they were not then working under a belief that they
were limited, and I think it a fair conclusion that he had
abandoned the intention of insisting upon a limit. It would
be altogether unlikely, in view of the hard and unpaid
work that was being done and that he must have known
of, that he could have had the purpose of insisting upon a
limit as to his son, and, under the circumstances, it would
have been manifestly unfair to have applied a harsher restriction upon the partners of the son than to him.

"I find that the crevice they struck beyond the bar was
practically a new crevice, and that the ore they finally
found in it was in fact a new and valuable discovery; that
the land-owner, Robert Raisbeck, knew that after they
struck the bar they were working to find a new crevice;

that he did not object; that it was with his sanction and license that they prosecuted the work; and that no limit was imposed upon them beyond which, in said field, they should not work any crevice or valuable discovery of ore they might strike.

"As final conclusions of fact I find that the plaintiff and the defendants are the owners of the range which was being worked by them upon the lands of the plaintiff at the time this action was commenced; that the plaintiff owns the one-half of said range and the defendant *John Anthony* owns the other half thereof, as the heir of his father, John Anthony, Sr., subject to the rights in said half of his co-defendant, *Louisa Anthony*, as the widow of John Anthony, Sr.; that the defendants, as the owners of one half of said range, and as tenants in common thereof with the plaintiff, were in the lawful possession of said range at the same time this action was commenced, and that they had the right, as such tenants, to work thereon, subject to the payment of the ground rent to the plaintiff as landlord; that the right of the defendants to work said range is not limited by a point 300 yards west of said fence.

"And as conclusions of law that judgment be entered, dismissing the plaintiff's complaint upon the merits with costs, and dissolving the preliminary injunction that has been granted in this action."

For the appellant there was a brief by *Orton & Osborn*, and oral argument by *P. A. Orton*.

For the respondents there was a brief by *Bushnell & Watkins*, and oral argument by *A. R. Bushnell*.

The following opinion was filed December 22, 1888:

Lyon, J. We think the testimony is sufficient to sustain the finding of fact that John Anthony, Sr., and Wallace Dixon discovered the range of mineral in controversy, on the land of Robert Raisbeck, about the year 1872. We are also of the opinion that it is sufficiently alleged in the answer, by necessary implication at least, and proved, that Anthony and Dixon entered upon and prospected the lands in which the range of mineral was found by the consent and license of Robert Raisbeck, the owner thereof. This appears from the allegations that they made such discovery of the range and paid the rent for the mineral obtained therefrom to such owner, who accepted the same, and from the proofs of those facts and the presumptions fairly deducible from the evidence that they so entered peaceably and with the knowledge of the owner, who made no objection thereto.

This brings the case within the provisions of ch. 260, Laws of 1860, as amended by ch. 117, Laws of 1872, being sec. 1647, R. S., except in so far as the statutory rights of the discoverers may have been restricted by special contract between Anthony and Dixon and the owner of the land. If there was no such restriction, the discovery of the range or the crevice which contained the mineral rendered the license irrevocable by the land-owner, and vested in the discoverers the title to the ores in the range or crevice on the lands of the licensor, subject only to the rent due him. If such title so vested in the discoverers, it necessarily results that neither a sale of the land by the licensor or of the range by the licensees, nor the death of either or all parties, would operate to revoke such license. If the licensor limited the right of the discoverers to work the range or crevice only to a certain point, such limitation is binding, and the statute gives the discoverers no right therein beyond the point of limitation.

The statute above mentioned is as follows: "Sec. 1647. Where there is no contract between the parties, or terms established by the landlord to the contrary, the following rules and regulations shall be applied to mining contracts and leases for the digging of ores or minerals, viz.: (1) No license or lease, verbal or written, made to a miner, shall be revocable by the maker thereof after a valuable discovery or prospect has been struck, unless the miner shall forfeit his right by negligence, such as establishes a forfeiture according to mining usages. (2) The discovery of a crevice or range containing ores or minerals shall entitle the discoverer to the ores or minerals pertaining thereto, subject to the rent due his landlord, before as well as after the ores or minerals are separated from the freehold; but such miner shall not be entitled to recover any ores or minerals, or the value thereof, from the person digging on his range in good faith, and known to be mining thereon, until he shall have given notice of his claim; and he shall be entitled to the ores or minerals dug after such notice. (3) Usages and customs among miners may be proved in explanation of mining contracts to the same extent as usage may be proved in other branches of business."

The contention of the plaintiff is that Anthony and Dixon were limited by their agreement with Robert Raisbeck to a point 300 yards west of the stone fence, beyond which point their license gave them no authority to mine, while that of the defendants is that there was no limitation upon their right to work the range or crevice entirely across Raisbeck's land, if the same extended across it.

The circuit judge found that when the license was given it was not in the contemplation of the parties that the range extended west beyond the stone fence; that when the fence was reached there probably arose a question between them as to the right of the licensees to proceed further; and that the work was suspended, and negotiations were had which resulted in an agreement limiting the right of the latter to mine the range to a point 300 yards west of the stone fence, and no farther. A careful perusal of the testimony satisfies us that these facts were correctly found. The judge commented somewhat upon the intrinsic weakness of the testimony upon which the above findings rest, and doubtless there is some force in his observations. But it must be remembered that the transactions rested in parol, and the original parties thereto had all deceased before the cause of action arose; hence the testimony was the best that could be obtained. In our view it quite satisfactorily establishes the facts thus found. The judge also expresses some doubt as to whether the limitation was not contingent upon the failure to find mineral in paying quantities beyond the 300-yards point to the westward. Without stating the testimony bearing upon the doubt thus suggested, or going into any discussion of it, it must suffice to say we think the evidence is that the limitation was absolute. There having been an uncertainty as to the extent of the original license, and probably a controversy between the parties in respect thereto, the 300-yards limit settled upon by them when the stone fence was reached removed such uncertainty and terminated the controversy, and the limitation thus agreed upon became, by relation, a part of the original contract or license, and settled conclusively what were the terms thereof.

Were the foregoing facts all there is of the case, there can be no doubt the plaintiff would be entitled to the relief he demands; for, standing alone, they demonstrate that the defendants have no rights in the range west of the 300-yards point, and inasmuch as they persist in working the range beyond that point the plaintiff would be entitled to a perpetual injunction restraining them from so doing. But the circuit judge made two deductions from the testimony, upon which he based the judgment for the defendants. These are (1) that after the crevice had been worked to the point where it pinched out, and Robert Raisbeck had employed John Dixon to prospect ahead for the purpose of again finding it, and after Dixon had become a part owner of the range, it was the understanding of all the parties interested

that the limitation to the point 300 yards west of the stone
fence was no longer binding upon the owners of the range,
but that they were at liberty to work the crevice across the
lands of Robert Raisbeck west of that point; and (2) that
the crevice discovered by John Dixon beyond the point
where the original crevice pinched out was a new one, and
the ore which Dixon and his associates found therein was a
new and valuable discovery, made under a license from the
land-owner which contained no limitation of their right to
mine the crevice entirely across his land, should it extend
so far. Whether the above deductions were correctly made
and, if so, their effect, will now be considered.

1. The limitation in question was created by contract,
and the discoverers of the range and those claiming under
them could be relieved therefrom only by contract. The
learned circuit judge scarcely finds that any contract removing the limitation was ever made. He speaks of the
purpose of Robert Raisbeck and the understanding of the
owners of the range; also of the improbability that such
owners would search for the crevice after the bar had been
struck, and perform the labor they did in finding the mineral west of the bar, had they supposed they were restricted
by the limitation. But he does not say that the parties
agreed that the limitation should be removed. We fail to
find any sufficient evidence in the record to prove that any
such contract was made. The owners of the range at the
time were John Anthony, Sr., John Dixon, and the plaintiff. John Anthony, Sr., was a party to the contract of
limitation, and must have known that it was made. John
Dixon knew, also, that there was a limitation. He purchased his interest of Robert Raisbeck, and testified on the
trial that before he so purchased Raisbeck told him there
was a limit, but not where it was. Knowing the existence
of a limitation, they could only avoid it by a contract with
Robert Raisbeck rescinding it. They obtained no such

contract from him. True, John Dixon testified that Robert Raisbeck told him to go where he pleased on the range and work it as he pleased; but this was not sufficient to relieve the parties from the limitation which they knew they were subject to. It must be held that the evidence fails to show that the limitation in question was ever abrogated.

2. It only remains to consider the question, Was the crevice which John Dixon found west of the point where the original crevice pinched out, a distinct crevice, and the discovery of the ore therein a new discovery; or was it a continuation of the original crevice and vein of mineral therein? It was not a new crevice and a new discovery merely because the original crevice ceased to yield ore and pinched out. This may have occurred, and still the crevice or vein be the same throughout. In *Iron Silver Mining Co. v. Cheesman*, 116 U. S. 529, this subject was considered, and the following definition of a lode or vein (which we understand to be the equivalent of a range or crevice, as those terms are employed in this case) is given: " In general it may be said that a lode or vein is a body of mineral, or mineral body of rock, with defined boundaries, in the eneral mass of the mountain." This is the definition given by Judg ᴶᴬLLETT, in *Stevens v. Williams*, 1 McCrary, 480, 488. Speaking of obstructions to a vein or lode, Mr. Justice MILLER, who delivered the opinion of the court in the case first above cited, said: "Now, a vein containing the precious metals is by no means always a straight line of uniform dip, or thickness, or richness of mineral matter throughout its course. Generally the veins are found in what, when the mineral is taken out of them, constitute clefts or fissures in the surrounding rock, with a well-defined wall above and below of different kinds of rock, as porphyry on one side, above or below, and limestone on the other. So long as these inclosing walls can be distinctly and continuously traced and the mineral matter of the same

character found between them, there can be no doubt that it is the same vein. But sometimes the cleft between the inclosing rocks, called in mining parlance the country rock, diminishes so as to be scarcely perceptible. Sometimes for a short distance the fissure disappears entirely and again is found distinctly to exist a little further on. Again it is seen that, though the underlying and superposing country rock is there, the mineral deposit ceases to be found, but, following the fissure, it reappears again very soon. It also happens that both fissure and mineral come to an end, and are found no more in that direction, or, if found, so far off or so deflected from the original line as to constitute no part of that vein. Of course, it is sometimes easy to see that it is the same vein all through. 'It is also easy to see, in some instances, that the vein is run out,— is ended." The court there sustain the following instruction given to the jury by the trial judge: "With well-defined boundaries, very slight evidence of ore within such boundaries will prove the existence of a lode. Such boundaries constitute a fissure, and if in such fissure ore is found, although at considerable intervals and in small quantities, it is called a lode."

In the present case it appears by the testimony of John Dixon and the defendant *John Anthony* that at a point about 100 feet west of the second shaft beyond the stone fence the crevice pinched out; that is, the walls thereof came nearly together. As the latter witness expressed it, "they barred up very narrow to a seam." The owners of the range thereupon sunk another shaft to the westward, in the general direction of the range, hoping to strike the lost crevice. The circuit judge found that this shaft was forty-five feet ahead of the place where the work had stopped. The evidence does not clearly show the location of such shaft, but it was probably not many yards west or southwest of the point where the crevice had pinched out.

From this shaft a drift was made in the same general direction, and finally a crevice was struck in which mineral was again found. It does not satisfactorily appear how far this drift was run before the crevice was struck, nor how far the latter point is from the point where the crevice pinched out. The fair inference from all the testimony, however, is that it could not have been more than a few rods. The parties working the range, especially John Dixon, who had the principal direction of the work, supposed that they had found the original crevice, and none of them seem to have thought they had found a new vein of mineral. Dixon uniformly speaks of the last-alleged discovery as "striking up the diggings again," and says that he expressed the opinion, when they came to the obstruction, that the vein was "split up," and he was determined to explore further for it. The idea of a new discovery seems first to have taken shape on the trial in the circuit court. So far as the testimony shows, the crevice, before it reached the barrier, and after the barrier was passed, was of the same general character — no change in the rock, or in general direction of the crevice, is indicated. Besides, the mineral found on both sides of the barrier was alike.

The above considerations have impelled our minds to the conclusion that, within the definition of a lode or vein above given, the crevice east of the barrier which cut the same off, and that discovered west of the barrier, which extends to the 300-yards limit, is one and the same crevice or range, and that the finding of the mineral therein west of the barrier is not in any correct sense a new discovery.

It follows from the foregoing views that the plaintiff is entitled to judgment.

By the Court. — The judgment of the circuit court is reversed, and the cause will be remanded with directions to that court to give judgment for the plaintiff granting a perpetual injunction as prayed, and awarding him compensation for the mineral taken by the defendants from the crevice west of the 300-yards point and appropriated to their own use.

A motion for a rehearing was denied March 12, 1889.

===

THE STATE, Plaintiff in error, vs. GROTTKAU, Defendant in error.

December 8, 1888 — March 12, 1889.

CRIMINAL LAW AND PRACTICE. *(1) Stay of execution: When term of imprisonment begins. (2) Discharge on* habeas corpus: *Writ of error.*

1. G., having been convicted of riot, was, on May 7, 1887, sentenced to confinement in the house of correction for one year. Before execution of the sentence, and on May 14, a stay was granted, and G. was released on bail, pending the determination of the case on writ of error. The judgment of conviction was affirmed, and the *remittitur* from the appellate court was filed in the trial court on March 13, 1888. On April 5, 1888, G. was committed to the house of correction pursuant to the sentence. *Held*, that the term of his imprisonment commenced on the date last mentioned.

2. When a person convicted and imprisoned for crime is discharged from custody in a *habeas corpus* proceeding by a court of competent jurisdiction, the state cannot obtain a review of the order or judgment in that behalf by writ of error. And it is immaterial whether such court issues the *habeas corpus* in the first instance, or adjudicates the matter on *certiorari* to a court commissioner who issued the writ. *State ex rel. McCaslin v. Smith*, 65 Wis. 93, distinguished.

ERROR to the Circuit Court for *Milwaukee* County.

Paul Grottkau was indicted, tried, and convicted in the municipal court of Milwaukee county of the offense of riot, and on May 7, 1887, was sentenced to confinement at hard labor for one year in the house of correction. Before execution of such sentence, and on May 14, 1887, that court granted a stay of execution of the judgment, pending the determination of the case by this court, to which it was brought by writ of error. *Grottkau* gave the required security, and was released from custody. This court affirmed the judgment of the municipal court. The *remittitur* from this court was filed in the municipal court March 13, 1888.

On or about April 5, 1888, *Grottkau* was committed to the house of correction pursuant to the sentence. May 8, 1888, he was brought before Court Commissioner Hugh Ryan, Esq., by virtue of a writ of *habeas corpus* duly issued, and a hearing was had. On May 12th the commissioner made an order remanding *Grottkau* to the custody of the keeper of the house of correction, and dismissed the proceeding. The matter was removed by *certiorari* to the circuit court, and.that court, by its order and judgment bearing date May 21, 1888, discharged *Grottkau* from custody. The state thereupon sued out a writ of error, by virtue of which such order and judgment and all the proceedings preliminary thereto have been certified to this court for review.

For the plaintiff in error there was a brief by the *Attorney General* and *L. K. Luse,* Assistant Attorney General, and oral argument by the *Attorney General.* A writ of error will lie to review the determination of the circuit court in discharging the prisoner. *In re Crow,* 60 Wis. 371; *Yates v. People,* 6 Johns. 337; *Holmes v. Jennison,* 14 Pet. 561; *Ex parte Lafonta,* 2 Rob. (La.), 495; *People v. Lincoln,* 62 How. Pr. 412; 2 Parker's Crim. R. 650; *People v. Bennett,* 49 N. Y. 137; *Bagnall v. Ableman,* 4 Wis. 170; Hurd's Habeas Corpus, 572; *In re Eldred,* 46 Wis. 530. The term of his imprisonment had not expired when the prisoner was discharged. The time when a sentence shall be carried into effect is not necessarily a part of the sentence, and is to a great extent within the control of the court, and execution of the sentence may be stayed or ordered to be carried out at some future time. *Reinex v. State*, 51 Wis. 152; *Petition of McCormick*, 24 id. 492; 1 Bish. Crim. Proc. sec. 1310; *Hollon v. Hopkins*, 21 Kan. 638–646; *Dolan's Case*, 101 Mass. 219; *People v. Reiley*, 53 Mich. 260; *Allen v. State*, Martin & Yerg. 294; *Miller's Case*, 9 Cow. 730; *State v. Cockerham*, 2 Ired. Law, 204; *State v. Cardwell*, 95 N. C. 643; *Fults v. State*, 2 Sneed, 232; *Johnson v. People*, 83 Ill. 431; *Rex v. Reader*, 1 Strange, 531; *People v. Hobson*, 48 Mich. 27; *People ex rel. King v. McEwen*, 62 How. Pr. 226. A prisoner who is admitted to bail is in the custody of his sureties. *Nicholls v. Ingersoll*, 7 Johns. 155; *Ex parte Gibbons*, 1 Atk. 237; *Comm. v. Brickett*, 8 Pick. 138.

[No appearance for the defendant in error.]

The following opinion was filed December 22, 1888:

LYON, J. We have not been favored with an argument or brief in behalf of defendant in error, and for that reason shall not indulge in any extended discussion of the questions which might be raised upon the record before us. Indeed, we shall consider but one of those questions, and that but briefly.

Doubtless the circuit court discharged *Grottkau* from custody because the year for which he was sentenced to imprisonment had expired when the writ of *habeas corpus* was issued. Hence that court must have held that his term of imprisonment commenced when judgment and sentence were pronounced, and that the commencement of such term was not postponed nor the running thereof suspended by the stay of execution and his release on bail pending the decision of this court. Whether this is a correct view of the law or not is the single question we propose now to determine.

In the case of *Petition of McCormick*, 24 Wis. 492, a

sentence to imprisonment on a conviction for crime, not to commence until the expiration of another sentence of the same person on a conviction for another crime, was upheld. There seems to be little doubt that, in the absence of statutory provision to the contrary, the trial court may lawfully appoint a future day after judgment for the commencement of the term of imprisonment. The *McCormick Case* sustains that doctrine, and cases elsewhere to the same effect are cited by the attorney general. We have no statute on the subject in respect to misdemeanors, and hence, in such cases (this being one of them), the court may appoint a future day for the punishment to commence.

Sec. 4733, R. S., which was first enacted in the present Revision, provides that on sentences to imprisonment in the state prison the term of imprisonment shall commence on the day of sentence, but the section excludes from the computation "any time which may elapse after such sentence while such convict is confined in the county jail, or while he is at large on bail, or while his case is pending in the supreme court upon writ of error or otherwise." In most, if not all, cases the effect of this statute seems to be to make the term of imprisonment commence when the convict is committed to the state prison. It is doubtful whether it operates to change the law which existed before its enactment, but it makes the law certain in the cases covered by it, and that was the declared object which the revisers sought to attain when they incorporated it in the Revision. (See Revisers' Notes.) Sec. 4733, however, does not rule this case. If any argument can be deduced from it affecting the present case it is that the legislature was of the opinion that without the statute the term of imprisonment, even in a conviction for a felony, did not necessarily commence on the day of sentence.

The stay of execution granted by the municipal court before *Grottkau* was committed to the house of correction, was substantially an order of that court that his term of imprisonment should not commence, in any event, until after the case should be determined by this court, and is as potent to postpone the commencement of the term of imprisonment as though the court had fixed April 5, 1888, as the day for the commencement thereof.

It follows that Commissioner Ryan properly remanded *Grottkau,* and that the circuit court erred in discharging him from custody.

By the Court.— The order and judgment of the circuit court, discharging the defendant in error from custody, is reversed.

Upon a motion for a rehearing there was a brief signed by the defendant in error, and by *Moritz Wittig, Jr.,* and *C. E. Monroe,* of counsel. They argued, *inter alia,* that there is no authority, statutory or otherwise, for allowing a writ of error to issue on behalf of the state as against a prisoner who has been lawfully discharged from his imprisonment by order of the circuit court, after sentence, on the ground that the term of sentence had expired. *People v. Conant,* 59 Mich. 565; *People v. Fairman,* id. 568; *Ex parte Jilz,* 64 Mo. 205. By sec. 8, art. I, Const., it is enjoined that "no person for the same offense shall be twice put in jeopardy *of punishment.*" Under this provision it is held that a writ of error will not lie at the suit of the state to reverse a judgment in favor of a defendant in a criminal action. *State v. Kemp,* 17 Wis. 669, citing *People v. Corning,* 2 N. Y. 9, and *Comm. v. Cummings,* 3 Cush. 212. *Habeas corpus* proceedings, though not technically criminal actions, may be so related to a criminal action as to come within the same rule. See sec. 3437, R. S. As to the question of jeopardy, see 1 Bish. Crim. Law (7th ed.), secs. 991-3; *Ex parte Lange,* 18 Wall. 163, 169, 173; *U. S. v. Choteau,* 102 U. S. 603; *Ex parte McGehan,* 22 Ohio St.

442, 445; *Comm. v. McBride,* 2 Brewst. 545. The day on which a prisoner is sentenced is the first day of his term of imprisonment. Bish. Stat. Crimes, sec. 218; *Comm. v. Keniston,* 5 Pick. 420; *Nigotti v. Colville,* 14 Cox's Crim. Cas. 263; *In re Crow,* 60 Wis. 349, 368; *Ex parte Meyers,* 44 Mo. 280; *Hollon v. Hopkins,* 21 Kan. 638, 646. When the term has by law begun to run it does not cease running so long as the person sentenced has been guilty of no wrong to occasion a delay. *In re Crow,* 60 Wis. 370, and cases cited; *Hollon v. Hopkins, supra.*

In opposition to the motion there was a brief by *L. K. Luse,* Assistant Attorney General. He contended, *inter alia,* that the constitutional rule forbidding the placing of a person twice in jeopardy simply embodies the principle of the common law that no man shall be placed in danger of legal penalties more than once upon the same accusation. Chitty's Crim. Law, 451. It has no bearing upon the inquiry whether he has suffered punishment in accordance with the judgment of the court having jurisdiction, upon a single conviction. That is the sole inquiry here. *Ratzky v. People,* 29 N. Y. 135; *McKee v. People,* 32 id. 244; *Shepherd v. People,* 25 id. 406; *Mitchell v. State,* 42 Ohio St. 383, 391. To the point that the writ of error would lie in this case, he cited, besides cases cited in the former brief, *Ableman v. Booth,* 21 How. 506; *State ex rel. McCaslin v. Smith,* 65 Wis. 93; R. S. sec. 4724; *Milwaukee v. Gross,* 21 Wis. 241; *Boscobel v. Bugbee,* 41 id. 59; *Platteville v. McKernan,* 54 id. 487; *State v. Mushied,* 12 id. 561; *State v. Jager,* 19 id. 235; *In re Tarble,* 25 Wis. 394, 13 Wall. 397.

The following opinion was filed March 12, 1880:

LYON, J. This case was decided at the last term on the argument of the attorney general alone. For that reason we determined only the single question, When did *Grott-*

kau's term of imprisonment commence? On that question we adhere to the ruling then made.

The defendant in error now moves for a rehearing of the cause, and his counsel, in their argument, raise the question whether a writ of error lies at the suit of the state to bring to this court for review the order or judgment of the circuit court reversing the order of Commissioner Ryan and discharging the defendant in error from custody.

It was decided by this court twenty-five years ago, and the rule has never been questioned or doubted since, that a writ of error does not lie at the suit of the state to reverse a judgment for the defendant in a criminal prosecution, whether upon a verdict of acquittal or upon an issue involving a question of practice, as where final judgment was rendered for the defendant on a demurrer to a plea in abatement of the indictment. *State v. Kemp*, 17 Wis. 669. The case overrules, to some extent, the doctrine of *United States v. Salter*, 1 Pin. 278, wherein it was said that if the court quashes the indictment or arrests judgment erroneously the prosecution may have a writ of error to reverse such decision.

Is the rule of *State v. Kemp* applicable to this case? We have concluded, after much deliberation, that the question must be answered in the affirmative. We can perceive no difference in principle between a case where, as in that case, the accused is discharged from custody without a trial because an issue of law on the pleadings had been determined in his favor, and the present case, in which the defendant in error was discharged from custody by the final order of the circuit court made in a proceeding on *habeas corpus*. The reasons why the state is remediless in the former case, apply with equal force to the latter. To illustrate, suppose that, in a criminal prosecution, the trial court arrests judgment after conviction and dismisses the case on the ground that it has no jurisdiction thereof. So far as that prosecution is concerned the order in that behalf, which results in the discharge of the accused from custody, is final, and the state is remediless. But suppose the court holds it has jurisdiction, and proceeds to sentence the accused to imprisonment, and some court of competent jurisdiction thereafter discharges him upon *habeas corpus* because, in its opinion, the trial court had no such jurisdiction. Both discharges in the cases supposed rest upon precisely the same ground. It being the settled law that the state cannot have a writ of error in the one case, it seems logically to follow that it ought not to have the writ in the other.

The only adjudication by this court which is claimed to be a direct authority for allowing a writ of error in the present case, was made in *State ex rel. McCaslin v. Smith*, 65 Wis. 93. In that case a judgment had been rendered against Smith for the costs of a prosecution for larceny, instituted by him against one Davis, which had failed. The judgment was so rendered pursuant to sec. 4791, R. S. Smith was imprisoned under an execution against his goods and person, issued on such judgment. On a *habeas corpus* he was discharged from custody by a court commissioner, and the circuit court, on *certiorari*, affirmed the order of discharge. McCaslin then sued out a writ of error from this court to obtain a review and reversal of the order of affirmance. It was held that he was entitled to the writ.

The judgment in the above case under which Smith was imprisoned is nominally in favor of the state, but really in favor of the county which was chargeable with such costs. It is a mere judgment for money, and is not distinguishable in principle from an ordinary judgment for tort in a civil action between individuals, or from a case in which a person is imprisoned for violation of or non-compliance with an order made for the enforcement of a private right or remedy, as distinguished from imprisonment for a criminal contempt. For a discussion of this distinction, see *In re Murphey*, 39 Wis. 286; *In re Pierce*, 44 Wis. 411, and cases cited.

In the present case the imprisonment of the defendant in error was for crime of which he had been duly convicted. This distinguishes it from the case of *State ex rel. McCaslin v. Smith*, and renders the application of a different rule entirely proper. Hence, while we do not question the accuracy of the judgment in that case, but rather re-affirm it, we hold that when, as in the present case, a person convicted and imprisoned for crime is discharged from custody in a *habeas corpus* proceeding by a court of competent jurisdiction, the state cannot obtain a review of the order or judgment in that behalf by writ of error. And it is immaterial whether such court issues the *habeas corpus* in the first instance, or adjudicates the matter on *certiorari* to a court commissioner who issued the writ.

Inasmuch as the judgment of this court herein can only be upheld on the assumption that the writ of error was properly issued at the suit of the state, and that assumption now being negatived, it follows that the motion for a rehearing must be granted.

The question here decided is one of considerable general interest, but has probably ceased to be of any importance in this particular case. *Grottkau's* term of imprisonment commenced April 5, 1888, and his sentence is for one year. If the time he has been at large since his discharge on *habeas corpus* is not deducted from such term, the same will expire April 5, 1889. While we do not here decide the point, we are strongly inclined to the opinion that the term of *Grottkau's* punishment, after having once commenced, was not interrupted by such discharge, and hence that it will expire April 5, 1889.

The proposition upon which the motion for a rehearing is granted has been fully and ably argued by the learned assistant attorney general, as well as by the learned counsel for the defendant in error, and has been much considered by the court. It is not at all probable that further argument will change our opinion. Hence, after the order for rehearing is entered, the clerk will enter a further order quashing the writ of error and dismissing the case.

By the Court.— Ordered accordingly.

THE STATE, Respondent, vs. LOGUE, Appellant.

January 31 — March 12, 1889.

Highways: Notice of proceedings to lay out.

1. Under sec. 1208, R. S., an order laying out a highway is only *prima facie* evidence of the regularity of the proceedings, and its invalidity may be shown by proof that the notices required by sec. 1267 were not given.

2. Though the owner of land over which it was attempted to lay out a highway signed the petition therefor and hence was not entitled to notice of the meeting of the supervisors, yet he may avail himself of the want of notice to the public and other owners, to invalidate the proceedings.

APPEAL from the Circuit Court for *La Fayette* County. The facts are stated in the opinion.

For the appellant there was a brief by *Orton & Osborn,* and oral argument by *P. A. Orton.*

For the respondent the cause was submitted on the brief of *D. S. Rose.*

TAYLOR, J. This is an action brought by the state to recover the penalty prescribed by sec. 1326, R. S. 1878, for obstructing a public highway. The action was tried in the court below by the court, a jury trial having been waived by the parties. The only controversy in the case was upon the question whether the *locus* was a public highway, the defendant, by his answer, having denied the existence of any highway at the place of the alleged obstruction.

After hearing the evidence the learned circuit judge made and filed the following findings of fact and conclusions of law: "That the highway described in the complaint in this action was duly laid out by the supervisors of the town of Willow Springs in La Fayette county, Wisconsin, on the 11th day of March, 1882. That said highway was lawfully opened by said supervisors in the month of September, 1882, and highway labor performed thereon, under the direction of the overseer of highways, in each year thereafter. That the defendant removed his fences from such highway, or caused the same to be removed in the year. That said highway was worked, used and traveled as such, from the time it was opened as aforesaid until the month of April, 1885, when it was obstructed and closed by the defendant, who built a fence across the same. That the defendant, from the time said highway was opened as aforesaid, treated the same as a public highway by removing his fences therefrom, doing highway labor thereon under the direction of the overseer of highways, and by using the same as a public highway up to the time he obstructed it as aforesaid. As conclusions of law, the court finds that there was a lawful highway existing at the place mentioned in the complaint in this action, in the month of April, 1885, and that the defendant at that time unlawfully obstructed the same, and is liable to the penalty prescribed in sec. 1321, ch. 52, R. S., and that the plaintiff is entitled to the judgment demanded in the complaint to the amount of $1, with costs."

The defendant duly excepted to each of the findings of fact, and to the conclusions of law. The court entered judgment in favor of the state for the penalty and costs. The defendant appealed to this court, and alleges as error that the evidence in the case does not sustain the finding of the learned circuit judge, "that the highway described in the complaint was duly laid out by the supervisors of the town of Willow Springs in La Fayette county, Wisconsin, on the 11th day of March, 1882."

After a careful reading of all the evidence in the case, we are forced to the conclusion that there is clearly a failure of evidence to support this finding. The only evidence introduced on the part of the state to show that the alleged highway was ever laid out by the supervisors of said town, was a certified copy of an order made by said supervisors on the 11th day of March, 1882, which purports on its face to be an order laying out a highway over the place where the obstruction complained of was placed by the defendant; a survey of said highway; an award of damages to the owners; and a petition for the highway in due form. The name of the defendant appeared on this petition, written in pencil. There was also some evidence given tending to show that the alleged highway had been opened for public use and had been used as such previous to the commencement of this action, and that some highway work had been performed on portions thereof before this action was commenced. The action was commenced in April, 1885, and according to the findings of the court the road was not lawfully opened or any highway labor performed thereon until the month of September, 1882.

Upon the evidence introduced by the state there was a legal presumption that the supervisors had regularly laid out a highway over the *locus in quo*. This presumption is, however, a mere presumption of fact, declared to be such by statute. Sec. 1298, R. S. Without the aid of this section it could not be contended that the proofs of the state had established such fact. The only question for the consideration of the court was whether this presumption of fact had been overcome by the evidence of the defendant. The evidence of the defendant which is clearly uncontradicted shows that although the name of the defendant ap-

The State vs. Logue.

peared on the petition for the highway, he did not place it there, nor did any other person place it there with his knowledge or assent. The evidence of the defendant also establishes the fact that the notices of the application for laying out the highway and of the time and place when and where they would meet to consider such application, which are required to be given by sec. 1267, R. S., were not in fact given. That the failure to give the notice required by said section is fatal to the proceedings of the supervisors in laying out a highway has been frequently decided by this court. *Williams v. Mitchell,* 49 Wis. 284, 288; *State v. Langer,* 29 Wis. 68, 71; *Austin v. Allen,* 6 Wis. 134; *Babb v. Carver,* 7 Wis. 124; *Roehrborn v. Schmidt,* 16 Wis. 519. As said in *Williams v. Mitchell,* 49 Wis. 288, sec. 1298, R. S., makes the order of the supervisors laying out a highway *prima facie* evidence that the proper notice was served, and all that is necessary for the party denying such service is to show by competent evidence that such notices were not in fact served or given. It seems very clear to us that the evidence of the defendant in this case is sufficient to overcome the presumption of the statute, and leaves the state in the position it would have been in had not the statute been enacted. *Roehrborn v. Schmidt,* 16 Wis. 519, 522.

But it is urged that the defendant signed the petition for the highway, and so was not entitled to notice of the meeting of the supervisors. Admitting this to be true, it would not dispense with notice to the public and other owners, and he may avail himself of such want of notice to other parties to invalidate the proceedings. See *Roehrborn v. Schmidt, supra.* There is, however, no evidence in the case that the defendant ever signed the petition. There was no proof that the signature was his, but the contrary. There was no presumption raised against the defendant that he authorized the signature. In order to bind him by a signature admitted not to be in his handwriting, the state would be bound to show affirmatively that he authorized such signature. No such evidence was offered; on the contrary, the evidence in the case shows that the signature was attached without his consent or direction. It being clearly shown that the proceedings of the supervisors in laying out the road in question were irregular and void, no case was made in favor of the state unless there is evidence establishing a highway by prescription, or by use for three years or more under sec. 1295, R. S., or by dedication by the defendant. There is no evidence to sustain a highway by prescription at common law, and the evidence fails to sustain a highway under sec. 1295 by three years' use, as the court finds that the road was not opened or worked until in September, 1882, and this action was commenced in April, 1885. The court has not found that the defendant had dedicated the *locus in quo* as a public highway, and we do not think there is sufficient evidence in the case upon which such a finding could be sustained.

By the Court.— The judgment of the circuit court is reversed, and the cause is remanded with directions to said court to render judgment for the defendant.

In re O———.

February 4 — March 12, 1889.

Attorney at law: Disbarment: Evidence: Good moral character: Conversion of client's money: Findings: Acting against former client: Jurisdiction.

1. Even where the charges of professional misconduct upon which an attorney is disbarred are not of a criminal nature, they should be established by a preponderance of satisfactory evidence.

2. As "good moral character" is a condition precedent to admission to the bar, so it is a requisite condition for the rightful continuance in the practice of the profession.

In re O——.

3. The fact that an attorney collected and wrongfully converted moneys belonging to his clients, and then failed to pay them over after repeated demands, especially where his attempt to retain such moneys was a subterfuge and in bad faith, is sufficient to authorize his suspension if not disbarment.

4. The misconduct which will warrant the suspension of an attorney is not limited to acts committed strictly in a professional character, but extends to all such misconduct as would have prevented an admission to the bar.

5. In proceedings to disbar an attorney the court may find the facts proved by evidence admitted without objection, even though such facts were not stated in the formal charges filed.

6. It is sufficient to warrant the disbarment of an attorney that, having acted for the claimant in a contest concerning the validity of a homestead claim, he afterwards instigated and conducted in behalf of another person a second contest against his former client, involving the same subject matter and based largely upon the same facts, and in such second contest testified as a witness against his former client and used the information acquired by means of his former employment.

7. In proceedings instituted in the court of his residence, such court may disbar or suspend an attorney for professional misconduct before officers of the United States land office.

APPEAL from the Circuit Court for *Eau Claire* County. The following statement of the case was prepared by Mr. Justice CASSODAY:

It appears from the record that prior to August 6, 1888, *O——* was a member of the bar of Eau Claire county; that between July 27, 1887, and September 10, 1887, the bar association of that county investigated certain charges of improper and unprofessional conduct of said *O——*, and thereupon directed three of its members, *Thomas F. Frawley, Lelon A. Doolittle,* and *Louis R. Larson* to present such matter to the circuit court for that county; that the said *Frawley, Doolittle,* and *Larson* thereupon presented to the judge of said court their verified petition in said matter, September 14, 1887, whereupon the said judge ordered said *O——* to show cause before said court September 26, 1887, why his license to practice as such attorney should not be revoked and he be disbarred and his name stricken from the roll of attorneys; that said petition and order to show cause was served on said *O——* September 15, 1887; that said petition contained a general charge and thirteen specific charges; that within the time required the said *O——* put in a verified answer to said several charges; that upon the trial of the issues so formed the court found in favor of said *O——* on all of such specific issues except the third, fourth, sixth, ninth, and twelfth, upon each of which he was convicted; that the said general charge and specific charges upon which he was so convicted, were and are as follows:

"General Charge: That said *O——* is an attorney at law, residing in the city and county of Eau Claire, duly licensed and admitted to practice and actively practicing as such in the circuit court of Eau Claire county and in the circuit and inferior courts of this state, and is a member of the bar association of Eau Claire county, and that while so residing in said Eau Claire county and a member of said bar association, and while engaged in the practice of law, has been guilty of general unprofessional conduct, of numerous acts unbecoming an attorney and member of said association, and among others, in particular instances, as follows:"

"Charge 3. That said *O——*, while engaged in practice as an attorney at Eau Claire, Wisconsin, on or about the middle of February, 1885, in an action pending in the circuit court for said county, wherein one Jules Jacobson was plaintiff and Adolph Hoffman was defendant, and George H. Murray was garnishee, and wherein said *O——* was attorney for said plaintiff, procured and induced said Murray to intrust and pay to him, said *O——*, the sum of $30, the same being the alleged liability of Murray in said action. That the same was paid to *O——* by said

Murray upon the representation made to him by said O——
as an attorney that he would represent him as his attorney
in said matter and look out for and guard his interests
therein, and that payment to him of said sum would discharge said Murray's liability therein and liquidate and pay
the indebtedness of said Murray to said Hoffman, and that
he, said O——, would in all respects as attorney protect
and defend the rights of said Murray in said action, and so
use and apply the said money so received by him as to discharge and pay the said indebtedness due to said Hoffman.
That in March, 1885, said action aforesaid was discontinued
and dismissed. That said O—— did not look out for and
protect the interests of said Murray therein, and did not
use or employ said money so received by him or any part
thereof to pay or discharge the indebtedness in favor of
said Hoffman, and said Murray was compelled to pay to
said Hoffman the entire amount of his indebtedness to him,
and said O—— has ever since neglected and refused to re-
fund or pay to said Murray the sum of $30 or any part
thereof, except the sum of $2, and although the same of
him has been frequently demanded he unlawfully and
wrongfully converted the same to his own use.

"Charge 4. That on or about the 24th day of November,
1885, and while practicing as an attorney in said county
of Eau Claire, said O——, as an attorney, was intrusted
by one Manley Harriman with the sum of $30 for the
express purpose of safely keeping and holding the same
for him, said Harriman, until he should call for the same.
That said O—— unlawfully and wrongfully converted the
same to his own use, and has refused and neglected to return the same or any part thereof to said Harriman, although of him often demanded, except the sum of $24.50,
which part has been so repaid by him in small sums varying
from one to ten dollars, and the greater portion whereof
has been so returned within a short time last past."

"Charge 6. That said *O*——, while practicing as an attorney in said city of Eau Claire in the year 1885, was retained and employed by one Charles Erickson to render and perform for him generally the services of an attorney, and was by said Erickson specially employed to prepare and conduct for him his defense in a contest before the register and receiver of the United States land office in the city of Eau Claire, instituted by one Chris Brown against him, said Erickson. That in pursuance of said retainer and employment said *O*—— counseled with said Erickson and his witnesses in said matter, and appeared before said register and receiver and conducted the defense of said contest on the day fixed for the hearing thereof, on the 26th day of August, 1885. That for the said services so rendered and performed by said *O*—— for said Erickson in said matter, said *O*—— received of said Erickson pay therefor. That thereafter, on the 24th day of November, 1885, said *O*—— procured one Adelbert D. Moon to file an affidavit of contest before the register and receiver of the United States land office against said Erickson on his said homestead aforesaid, upon the same grounds and for the same reasons on which the said contest of August, 1885, was based. That thereafter, in December, 1885, said *O*—— appeared in said land office, and as attorney conducted the contest on the part of said Moon in said matter, and was sworn and testified as a witness in the proceedings on the part of said Moon to facts and circumstances that came to his knowledge while attorney and counsel of said Erickson as aforesaid. That from an adverse decision rendered against said Moon by the register and receiver on said hearing, said *O*—— appealed on behalf of said Moon to the commissioner of the United States land office, before whom said matter is now pending on said appeal, and undetermined."

"Charge 9. That said *O*——, unmindful of the duties of

an officer of the court and in violation of his oath of office, while practicing as an attorney at Eau Claire, Wisconsin, during the fall of 1882 and the winter of 1882 and 1883, was guilty of unprofessional and criminal conduct as an attorney in that he did during said time collect for one Alfred Kahn of said city, and from August Rahn of Altoona in said county, the sum of $79.59, which said sum so collected was the property of said Alfred Kahn; and that he converted the same to his own use. That the collection of said sum was intrusted to him by said Kahn with the understanding and agreement that said sum was to be collected for a commission of ten per cent. That said O—— collected the same without any action therefor, and after collecting and converting said sum to his own use denied that he collected the whole or any part thereof. That said Kahn has since succeeded in collecting from said O——, through the efforts of A. C. Larson, Esq., and L. M. Vilas, Esq., a portion of said sum of $79.59, but that over $30 thereof is still retained by said O——."

"Charge 12. That on or about the 10th day of April, 1884, said O——, while acting in his professional capacity as the attorney of Andrew Hegdale, collected for said Andrew Hegdale, of one Peter Truax, the sum of $18.43. That said sum when collected was the property of said Andrew Hegdale, but that O—— on the day aforesaid converted the same to his own use."

The answer of O—— to these several charges consisted of denials and explanations which if true would have expurgated him of the several offenses thus charged. Upon the trial of such issues, the court on May 1, 1888, filed its findings in writing, as follows:

"As to charge three, I find the facts as follows: In February, 1885, one Jules Jacobson commenced an action against Adolph Hoffman, in which George H. Murray, with others, was summoned as garnishee. That in said

In re O——,

action respondent appeared as attorney for the plaintiff. That upon the service of the garnishee summons upon Murray, it appears that he, Murray, was indebted to defendant, Hoffman, in the sum of $30, and, not questioning his indebtedness and desiring to avoid trouble, he paid over to the respondent the said sum, who received it for the purpose of paying it upon the judgment it was expected would be obtained in the original action. For some defect in the proceedings no such judgment was obtained and such garnishee proceedings were dismissed. It then became the clear duty of respondent to return to Murray the $30. Instead of doing so, however, he converted the same to his own use. He repeatedly promised to repay the money to Murray, and Murray having since died he has repeatedly promised to pay his widow, but has failed to keep his promise, and as a result, Murray, who is a man of very limited means, was compelled to pay the debt to Hoffman or his representatives. The respondent attempts to justify his cause by saying that he got Jacobson's consent to use the money. This is no excuse. The money belonged to Murray and not to Jacobson. Respondent received it, as his receipt shows, as attorney for both parties, that is, to hold it for Murray until it was legally applied to the payment of Jacobson's judgment, when it would become the money of Jacobson, and Murray would thereby be relieved from his debt to Hoffman. Respondent's conduct in this particular has caused a serious loss to a man who could illy afford to sustain it, and deprived his widow of greatly needed means of support. I therefore find respondent guilty of dishonest and unprofessional conduct as charged.

" As to charge four, the evidence shows the facts to be as follows: On or about the 24th day of November, 1885, one Manley Harriman came into the office of respondent, having in his possession about $35 in money. That respondent suggested to him that it would not be safe to carry that

amount of money, and that it would be better to leave it
with him, he promising to lock it in his safe, keep it, and
return it when called for. That said Harriman, agreeable
to such suggestion, did leave $30, and took from respondent
a receipt reading as follows: 'November, 24, 1885. Received of Manley Harriman $30. (Signed) ———. O———.'
That almost immediately after such money was deposited
the respondent took it and spent it without Harriman's
consent, and did not repay it until he was repeatedly importuned for payment, and then making payments in small
sums, the last payment, $5.50, not being made until after
the commencement of these proceedings. The respondent
claims that this transaction was a loan from Harriman to
him. The evidence fails to sustain that theory. All the
circumstances appearing show a bailment and not a loan.
Had it been an honest loan there is no reason why the receipt should not have said so, and many reasons why it
should. It is clear that Harriman did not understand it to
be a loan, and equally clear that respondent did not intend
to have him so understand it. The receipt is artfully written by respondent, as it would seem, so as to conceal respondent's real intention to use the money and thereafter
claim it as a loan. It looks as if there was a premeditated
design to obtain the money ostensibly as a bailor, and then
to justify its use by calling it a loan. The respondent's
counsel insists that whatever the moral aspect of this transaction may be, this court has no power to entertain the
charge, because the respondent's acts were not in his professional character, as the relation of attorney and client
did not exist between respondent and Harriman at the
time. I do not so understand the law. I understand that
if an attorney is shown to be guilty of such gross misconduct as shows him to be unfit for the honest discharge of
the trust reposed in him, it is the right and duty of the court
to interfere.

" As to charge six, there is but little real conflict in the testimony as to the main facts. It appears that on the 20th day of July, 1885, one Erickson was in possession of, claiming under the homestead law, the E. ¼ of the S. E. ¼ of section 8, township 27, range 18, his claim dating from June 20, 1884. That on the 20th day of July a contest was initiated by one Christ Brown against Erickson to procure a cancellation of such homestead claim. In such proceedings respondent appeared as counsel for Erickson, receiving as part payment for his services $10 in cash. That while so employed respondent, at the request of Erickson, in order to ascertain the condition of the premises, visited them on two occasions pending such contest, for which services he charged Erickson. That during the pendency of such contest he had repeated conferences with his client as to his residence and, as incidental to that question, where he had cast his vote at previous elections. Such contest never came to a hearing, but was settled or abandoned, thus leaving Erickson in the enjoyment of possession under his homestead claim; that respondent presented a bill of $—— for balance on his services, which Erickson declined to pay, claiming that respondent had been fully paid, whereupon respondent threatened, in case such bill was not paid, that he would take measures to deprive him of his homestead. Such threats not proving effectual for compelling payment, a second contest was on the 2d day of November, 1885, inaugurated in the name of Adelbert Moon against Erickson, on complaint being made alleging an abandonment of such homestead. In this latter contest the respondent changed sides, and appeared for the contestant Moon. The two contests were concerning the same property, and involved in part at least the same questions of fact, because between the ending of the first contest and the beginning of the second six months had not elapsed, and under the provisions of the homestead law a charge of abandonment

In re O——.

can only be sustained by showing nonresidence for at least six months at one time.

"The affidavit on which the Moon contest was initiated was made by the respondent, and upon the case coming on for trial it was conducted by respondent on the part of Moon against the objections of Erickson, and not only that but the respondent on the part of Moon went on the stand as a witness. There is some conflict as to precisely what he swore to, but there is no dispute that he swore to the condition of the premises as he saw them at the time he was paid by Erickson to go and see them, thus using the information acquired at Erickson's expense against him. The evidence satisfied me that he swore directly to statements claimed to have been made by Erickson to him while the relation of counsel and client existed between them, or that he called attention by way of interrogatories to such statements claimed to have been made at the time. The witnesses are not very clear on this point, but enough appears to show that he used the information acquired by the confidence of Erickson to defeat him in the second contest. He was a principal witness for Moon, giving extended testimony, a great part of which referred directly to matters said to have transpired during the first contest. The evidence further clearly shows that the second contest was not only conducted but was instigated by the respondent, and that but for him it would have never been commenced. That he was influenced in such action by the fact that Erickson had not paid him his fees, and was using the contest in pursuance of previous threats to extort such payment, thus being guilty of a species of blackmail. We cannot countenance such methods of collecting debts, but must hold the conduct of defendant to have been unprofessional and disgraceful, violating every principle of legal ethics, and tending to impair the confidence of the public in the members of the legal profession.

" As to charge nine, I find the respondent, during the fall and winter of 1882 and 1883, collected for one Alfred Kahn $79.59, said collections having been paid in small sums. That by the contract with Kahn he was to receive ten per cent. of the amount collected for his fees. That after such collection was made he failed to pay it over, but used the same as his own. That he subsequently paid $30, still leaving due and unpaid $49.59. The respondent's claim is that no bargain was made as to the amount of his fees, and that his services were worth fifty per cent. of the amount collected; and he alleges that he has always been ready and willing to settle on that basis. Were this a *bona fide* difference between the respondent and his former client, this court would have no right to interfere, but should leave the parties to settle their dispute in the usual way by action. But Mr. Kahn's testimony is positive that ten per cent. was the agreed rate of compensation, and the subsequent conduct of the respondent tends strongly to corroborate him and to show that the claim now made by respondent is an afterthought and not made in good faith. It seems that for years after the collection was made counsel in behalf of Mr. Kahn endeavored to induce respondent to settle the claim, and even threatened him with a prosecution for embezzlement, and during all that time no claim was made such as is here made, and no one disputed the amount due from respondent to be as now claimed by the testimony of Kahn. This conduct on the part of respondent is entirely inconsistent with the version he now gives of the transaction.

"Charge number twelve is fully sustained by the evidence. The respondent collected of Peter Truax for one Ole Hegdale $68.43, and instead of paying it over used it for his own purposes without the consent of his client. Respondent admits making this collection, but alleges that after it was made and before the money was used Hegdale

In re O——.

came into his office and loaned it to him. The absence of
any note, receipt, or other paper showing this transaction,—
this change in their relation from attorney and client to
that of debtor and creditor,— is very suspicious. An attorney borrowing money already in his hands from a client
in the absence of witnesses should certainly, as a matter of
ordinary prudence, make some clear record of the transaction, so as to show that the matter was fully understood
between them. But the subsequent conduct of the respondent, to my mind, clearly establishes the falsity of this
claim. Soon after the collection Hegdale put the matter in
the hands of counsel, who has testified to repeated interviews on the subject. He says that after asking for the
money, as money collected by the respondent, for, he
thinks, as much as a dozen times, he commenced a suit for
trover and conversion in the municipal court, and that on
the trial of that action he learned for the first time that respondent claimed to have borrowed the money. The issue
was tried in municipal court and decided against the respondent's claim, and a judgment in tort rendered against
him. I therefore find there was a conversion by respondent of the money so collected.

"It is not necessary to mention the other charges, as I do
not find them sustained.

"Finding as I do as to the above facts, it follows that
the respondent must be held to have testified falsely in regard to the several transactions above named. He would
have stood much better in the estimation of the court had
he frankly told the truth in regard to them, instead of trying to shield himself by falsehood, as I am compelled to believe he has. The chief object of this proceeding is not to
punish the respondent but to protect the public from imposition. An attorney bears with him the certificate of the
court that he is of good moral character and a fit person to
be trusted with the delicate and responsible duties of a mem-

ber of the legal profession. This certificate the public has
a right to rely upon, and to presume its holder to be a person of integrity and honor. Hence, when it is made to appear that he has been guilty of acts which show him to be
so deficient in honesty as to be unworthy of confidence, it
is the duty of the court to withdraw its certificate. We
owe this duty alike to the public and to the bar. I am
not unmindful of the serious consequences to respondent of
an order disbarring him, nor lacking in sympathy for those
who must suffer with him, but the evidence shows such repeated acts of unprofessional conduct on his part that I do
not feel at liberty to pass them by and to continue to hold
him out to the world as a fit and proper person to practice law. It will therefore be ordered that the respondent O—— be expelled from the bar of this court, and
that his name be stricken from the roll of attorneys. It
is, however, further ordered that after the lapse of two
years from the date of entry of this order, said O—— may
make application to be reinstated, and upon a satisfactory
showing to the court of good conduct between the said date
of filing and the said application he may be so reinstated;
and let it be ordered accordingly."

From the order entered thereon accordingly, the said
O—— appeals.

For the appellant there was a brief by *James Wickham*,
and oral argument by *Mr. Wickham* and *B. W. Jones.*
They contended, *inter alia,* that to warrant a conviction in a
proceeding of this kind upon charges of a criminal nature
a mere preponderance of evidence is not sufficient. *In re
Baluss,* 28 Mich. 507; *In re Houghton,* 67 Cal. 511; *State
v. Tunstall,* 51 Tex. 81; *People ex rel. Shuffeldt v. Barker,*
56 Ill. 299; Weeks on Attorneys, 156; *People ex rel. Miller
v. Harvey,* 41 Ill. 277; *In re Orton,* 54 Wis. 386. The misconduct complained of in the fourth charge was not committed in a professional capacity, and in such case the

attorney's name should not be stricken from the roll unless the charge is of a criminal nature and of such a character as to render him totally unfit to be an officer of the court, as in cases of forgery, perjury, or theft; and then he cannot be disbarred, if he does not admit the offense, without being indicted, tried, and convicted. *Anonymous*, 7 N. J. Law, 162; *People ex rel. Hughes v. Appleton*, 105 Ill. 474; *People ex rel. Noyes v. Allison*, 68 id. 151; *Dickens' Case*, 67 Pa. St. 169, 5 Am. Rep. 420; *Ex parte Steinman*, 95 Pa. St. 220; *In re Husson*, 62 How. Pr. 358, and cases cited; Weeks on Attorneys, 135. From the finding on the sixth charge it is very difficult to ascertain just what the court considered was the improper conduct of the appellant in relation thereto. Such a finding cannot sustain an order for disbarment, for an attorney has a right to know on what ground he is disbarred. *State v. Watkins*, 3 Mo. 480; *Perry v. State*, 3 Greene (Iowa), 550. No charge had been made against the appellant to justify a finding of blackmail, and he cannot be disbarred on a charge for which he has never been tried. *In re Orton*, 54 Wis. 379. The sixth charge, and in fact the whole proceeding, reduces itself to the question whether the appellant had the right to act as the attorney for Moon on the second contest, having been retained as the attorney for Erickson in the former contest, which was abandoned before trial. Even if it appeared that he had, in the course of his employment, obtained knowledge which he could use against his former client, that fact would not even be ground for restraining him from acting against such former client. Weeks on Attorneys, 221; 1 Wait's Act. & Def. 448; *Price v. G. R. & I. R. Co.* 18 Ind. 137. And even if there was ground for restraining him from acting as attorney on that second contest, it by no means follows that such action is ground for disbarment. An attorney may not be disbarred for every mistake in law or in professional ethics, but only for such gross acts of unprofessional conduct as render his continuance in practice incompatible with a proper respect of the court for itself, and render the attorney totally unfit to be an officer of the court. Weeks on Attorneys, 143; *In re Orton*, 54 Wis. 382. As to the conduct of the appellant in proceedings before the land officers, the state courts have no jurisdiction, except in so far as it affects his moral character. *In re Knott*, 71 Cal. 584.

T. F. Frawley, for the respondents (the petitioners), argued, among other things, that the appellant was guilty of gross dishonesty and unprofessional conduct in procuring from Murray and Harriman the sums of money in the charges specified, and converting the same to his own use; and for this dishonest and corrupt practice his name should be stricken from the roll. *In re Davies*, 93 Pa. St. 116; *In re Percy*, 36 N. Y. 651; *Baker v. Commonwealth*, 10 Bush, 592; *People ex rel. Cutler v. Ford*, 54 Ill. 520. He violated his official oath and was guilty of dishonest conduct in refusing to pay to Kahn and Hegdale, his clients, the money belonging to them. *Slemmer v. Wright*, 54 Iowa, 164; Weeks on Attorneys, 263; *Voss v. Bachop*, 5 Kan. 67. He violated his official oath and betrayed the confidence reposed in him as an attorney by accepting fees from conflicting parties in the Erickson case, and by improperly and to the prejudice of Erickson employing the knowledge which had been confidentially entrusted to him. *In re Cowdery*, 69 Cal. 82; 1 Monell's Pr. 182, 183, and cases cited; *In re Whittemore*, 69 Cal. 67; *Herrick v. Catley*, 1 Daly, 514; Weeks on Attorneys, 152; *Mason's Case*, 1 Freem. 74; *Berry v. Jenkins*, 3 Bing. 423; *State v. Halstead*, 73 Iowa, 376; *Henry v. Raiman*, 25 Pa. St. 354; *Galbraith v. Elder*, 8 Watts, 81; *Dietrich v. Mitchell*, 43 Ill. 40; *Brown v. Payson*, 6 N. H. 443; *Robson v. Kemp*, 5 Esp. 52; *Price v. G. R. & I. R. Co.* 18 Ind. 137; *White v. Huffaker*, 27 Ill. 349; *Gaulden v. State*, 11 Ga. 47; *State ex rel. McCormick v. Winton*, 11 Oreg. 456; *Ex parte Wall*, 107 U. S. 266. As to the jurisdiction of the court, see *Ex parte Wall, supra; Anderson v. Bosworth*, 15 R. I. 443; *In re Aitkin*, 4 Barn. & Ald. 47, 49; *Grant's Case*, 8 Abb. Pr. 357; *Ex parte Saäts*, 4 Cow. 76; *Ex parte Cripwell*, 5 Dowl. Pr. Cas. 689; *De Woolf v. ——*, 2 Chit. 68; *In re Knight*, 1 Bing. 91; *Tharratt v. Trevor*, 7 Exch. 161. The power to remove an attorney is incidental to all courts, and unless it be clearly exceeded and abused by the circuit court, this court should not interpose, as it cannot decide with the same means of information that the court below was possessed of. *Rice v. Commonwealth*, 18 B. Mon. 472; *Ex parte Burr*, 9 Wheat. 529; *In re Secombe*, 19 How. 9.

CASSODAY, J. This court has held, in effect, that where the charges of professional misconduct upon which the accused is disbarred are such as would, if true, subject him to criminal prosecution, the same "should be established by clear and satisfactory evidence, and cannot rest in doubtful and uncertain inferences." *In rè Orton*, 54 Wis. 386. But even where such charges are not of a criminal nature, yet we apprehend that, in order to justify disbarment, they should be established by a preponderance of satisfactory evidence. Here the charges were specific. The hearing was adjourned from time to time. The accused had ample opportunity for defending himself against the several charges made. In the conflict of evidence the trial court had advantages for ascertaining the truth which we do not possess. The findings of fact, therefore, in so far as they seem to be supported by evidence, must be received as verities in the case. Such facts need not be repeated nor stated in detail. It is enough to say, that a careful examination of all the testimony forces us to the conclusion that the several findings of fact against the accused given above are substantially supported by the evidence.

Th& difficulties and perplexities which frequently beset an attorney in active practice are not underestimated. In the language of another court: "His professional life is full of adversaries. Always in front of him there is an antagonist, sometimes angry and occasionally bitter and venomous. His duties are delicate and responsible, and easily subject to misconstruction." *In re Eldridge*, 82 N. Y. 167. But we feel constrained to add that there is a spirit of fairness and magnanimity among members of the bar, not surpassed in any other profession. Besides, experience and observation warrant the assertion that no respectable bar, as a body, would for a moment tolerate the persecution of one of its members. There would, as a general thing, be more danger of laxity in the opposite direction.

To entitle a person to practice law in Wisconsin, he must, in addition to the other requisites, be "of good moral character." Subd. 3, sec. 2586, R. S.; ch. 144, Laws of 1881; ch. 63, Laws of 1885. As a good moral character is a condition precedent to admission to the bar, so it is a requisite condition for the rightful continuance in the practice of the profession. *Ex parte Brounsall*, 2 Cowp. 829; *Penobscot Bar v. Kimball*, 64 Me. 146; *Strout v. Proctor*, 71 Me. 290; *Delano's Case*. 58 N. H. 5, 42 Am. Rep. 556; *In re Davies*, 93 Pa. St. 120; *Ex parte Wall*, 107 U. S. 280. The words "good moral character" are general in their application, but of course they include all the elements essential to make up such a character. Among these are common honesty and veracity, especially in all professional intercourse. The several acts of which the accused was found guilty all related to such intercourse. The ninth and twelfth findings are each to the effect that the accused collected and wrongfully converted moneys belonging to his clients, and then failed to pay them over after repeated demands. Besides, it was in effect found that his attempt to retain such moneys was a subterfuge and in bad faith.

These things of themselves were sufficient to authorize suspension if not disbarment. *In re Davies, supra; In re Temple,* 33 Minn. 343; *Jeffries v. Laurie,* 23 Fed. Rep. 786; *S. C.* 27 Fed. Rep. 195; *In re Treadwell,* 67 Cal. 353; *Slemmer v. Wright,* 54 Iowa, 164; *People ex rel. Hungate v. Cole,* 84 Ill. 327; *People ex rel. Att'y Gen. v. Murphy,* 119 Ill. 159; *State ex rel. McCormick v. Winton,* 11 Oreg. 456; *In re Moore,* 72 Cal. 359.

As to the third finding, it is said that the money was used by the consent of his client. But the money did not belong to his client. The accused received it from the garnishee by reason of the confidence reposed in him as an attorney in the case. That confidence was misplaced, and by reason of it the garnishee was compelled to pay the money over again. Such professional misconduct is just as reprehensible as though he had used his client's money without consent and then failed to pay it over when demanded.

As to the fourth finding, it is said that the accused did not receive the money in the course of his business as an attorney, but merely as bailee, and hence that his wrongful conversion of it does not subject him to disbarment or suspension. Cases are cited which seem to sustain such contention, but we decline to follow them. The better rule seems to be, that the misconduct requisite for such suspension is not limited to acts committed strictly in a professional character, but extends to all such misconduct as would have prevented an admission to the bar. This is sustained by one class of the cases above cited. See, also, *Re Hill,* L. R. 3 Q. B. 543; *In re Blake,* 3 Ellis & Ellis, 34.

But the most serious finding against the accused is to the effect that after having successfully defended his client Erickson against a contest for the cancellation of his claim to his homestead, before the register and receiver of the United States land office at Eau Claire, made by one

In re O——.

Brown, and received part payment for his services, he threatened Erickson that in case the balance of his bill for such services should not be paid he would take measures to deprive him of his homestead, and that, as such threats were ineffectual, and for the purpose of coercing such payment, he inaugurated a new contest against Erickson in the name of one Moon for the cancellation of the same homestead claim, based largely on the same facts, and in which second contest he appeared not only as attorney but as a witness for Moon and against his former client. Exception is taken because such threats and attempted coercion were not contained in the charges. Proofs were made of such threats, however, without objection, and hence the court was justified in making such findings. But the mere finding that the accused thus turned against his client is sufficiently serious for the purposes of this case. The rights of litigants and the ends of justice demand the most implicit confidence in all legitimate professional intercourse between attorney and client. *Queen v. Cox,* 14 Q. B. Div. 153. In such intercourse the client should feel free to disclose the weak points of his case as well as the strong ones. This he cannot feel at liberty to do if his attorney is liable to turn up against him in a similar case based on substantially the same facts.

It may be said that an attorney is not obliged to continue in the service of his client without pay. However this may be, he certainly is not at liberty to desert his client and take up against him in the same cause or a similar cause based upon substantially the same facts, for the purpose of getting better pay or even any pay. To allow such change of sides would reduce the attorney to a mere mercenary, always open for employment by the highest bidder. It would compel the poor man to surrender his supposed rights without contest, or enter into competition as a bidder for any legal talent with his more wealthy opponent. It would supplant the confidence which clients rightfully have in their counsel by a baneful suspicion and distrust. Eminent professional learning and ability will naturally command appropriate compensation; but professional integrity is not the subject of purchase, sale, or traffic. Such integrity is absolutely essential to the continued usefulness of the profession. Its untarnished preservation is as essential to the honor of the bar as it is beneficial to the public. These views are well supported by the authorities. *State v. Halstead*, 73 Iowa, 376; *People v. Spencer*, 61 Cal. 128; *In re Cowdery*, 69 Cal. 32; *In re Whittemore*, 69 Cal. 67; *Comm. v. Gibbs*, 4 Gray, 146.

It is strenuously urged that the trial court had no jurisdiction to disbar or suspend for unprofessional conduct before the officers of the United States land office. But this is not a proceeding for contempt. The issues involved the accused's professional conduct, instituted in the court of his residence. In such a case we perceive no good reason for such limitation upon such jurisdiction. It has been held that an appellate court may take original jurisdiction for professional misconduct in the trial court or before a judge thereof. *In re Whitehead*, 28 Ch. Div. 614; *People ex rel. Elliott v. Green*, 7 Col. 237, 49 Am. Rep. 351. The findings of the trial court are sufficient to properly justify the condemnation of the accused in taking up against his client. As indicated by the trial court, these proceedings are not so much to punish the accused as to protect the public from imposition. The true lawyer has been rightfully termed a minister of justice, and he should never forget the requirements of his calling, nor allow his professional integrity to be tampered with.

In view of the conditions imposed by statute upon admission to the bar, the small amounts converted under claims of right, the payment of some of them, the age of the accused, and the confidence entertained of his reformation, this court has concluded to so far modify the order appealed from as only to suspend him from practice during the two years named therein.

By the Court.— The order of the circuit court is reversed, and the cause is remanded with directions to enter such modified order as indicated. No costs allowed to either party in this court, except the appellant is to pay the clerk's fees.

PEDRICK and others, Appellants, vs. THE CITY OF RIPON and others, Respondents.

February 19 — March 12, 1889.

Equity: Injunction: Municipal corporations.

Where nothing has been done further than the adoption by the common council of a resolution that the mayor and city clerk take immediate steps to let a contract for the construction of waterworks for the city, a court of equity will not interfere, at the suit of tax-payers, to enjoin the threatened enforcement of such resolution, even though its adoption by the council was unauthorized.

APPEAL from the County Court of *Winnebago* County. The facts are sufficiently stated in the opinion.

For the appellants there was a brief by *Henry J. Ger-pheide* and *J. Dobbs,* and oral argument by *Mr. Gerpheide.* To the point that plaintiff, on behalf of himself and others similarly situated, can maintain this action to restrain defendants from enforcing the resolution, they cited High on Injunctions, secs. 367, 793-4; *Dean v. Madison,* 9 Wis. 402; *Heywood v. Buffalo,* 14 N. Y. 534; *Mayor v. Gill,* 31 Md. 375; *New London v. Brainard,* 22 Conn. 555; *Scofield v. Eighth School Dist.* 27 id. 499; *Delaware Co. v. McClintock,* 51 Ind. 325; *People v. Mayor,* 32 Barb. 35; *Perry v. Kinnear,* 42 Ill. 164; *People v. Mayor,* 32 Barb. 102; *Pullman v. Mayor,* 49 id. 57; *Whiting v. S. & F. du L. R. Co.* 25 Wis. 167; *Peck v. School Dist.* 21 id. 516; *Willard v. Comstock,* 58 id. 565.

For the respondents there was a brief by *Stark & Sutherland,* and oral argument by *Geo. E. Sutherland.* Besides cases referred to in the opinion, they cited *Milwaukee Iron Co. v. Hubbard,* 29 Wis. 51, 59; *Smith v. Oconomowoc,* 49 id. 694, 697.

COLE, C. J. This is an appeal from an order dissolving a temporary injunction. The suit is brought by the plaintiffs for themselves and others similarly situated, to restrain the officers of the defendant city from entering into a contract with any corporation or person for the construction of a system of water-works to supply the city and its inhabitants with water. The plaintiffs are residents and taxpayers of the city, and aver that their taxes will be greatly increased if the city is allowed to carry into execution the purposes and things contemplated and resolved upon as set forth in the complaint. It is alleged that the common council, at a regular meeting in August, 1888, adopted a resolution to the effect that the mayor and city clerk take immediate steps for the letting of a contract to some reliable company for the construction of a system of waterworks, and that the officers of the city threaten and declare that they intend to enforce this resolution and let a contract in pursuance thereof. This is as far as the officers of the city had proceeded in the matter of constructing waterworks, and the question is, Do these facts present a case for the interference of a court of equity, at the suit of a tax-payer, before something further has been done in the premises? It seems to us that these facts furnish no grounds for such interference by way of injunction.

It is said on behalf of the plaintiffs that the common council had no authority to decide upon and erect water-works, or to enter into a contract for the construction of a system of water-works, without first submitting the question of the construction of such water-works to the voters of the city, as provided by ch. 100, Laws of 1887, and in case a majority of the votes cast should be in favor of the project. It may be conceded that this view is correct; that the common council has no authority either to undertake on behalf of the city the construction of a system of water-works or to enter into a contract with any company or person for the construction thereof, without the electors of the city first vote in favor of such works; but, still, can a tax-payer interfere and arrest the proceedings of the common council before anything has been done to carry the resolution into effect, as by levying and assessing an illegal tax which may be an apparent lien upon real property?

It is very obvious that a court of equity does not sit as a court of errors to review and correct the proceedings of a municipal body, unless they are productive of a peculiar or irreparable injury to the plaintiff. The law upon this subject is well stated by DIXON, C. J., in *Judd v. Fox Lake*, 28 Wis. 583, where, among other things, he says: "The general principle that equity possesses no power to revise, control, or correct the action of public, political, or executive officers or bodies, is, of course, well understood. It never does so at the suit of a private person, except as incidental and subsidiary to the protection of some private right or the prevention of some private wrong, and then only when the case falls within some acknowledged or well-defined head of equity jurisprudence." There has been no assessment of an illegal tax in this case, assuming that the common council would have no authority to assess a tax for the expense of constructing a system of water-works without a vote; nor has that body done anything in the matter except to adopt a resolution that the mayor and city clerk take immediate steps for the letting of a contract to some reliable company for the construction of such works. This is all that has been done by the municipal officers. True, it is alleged that the officers threaten and declare that they intend to enforce this resolution and let a contract for the construction of water-works. But in the *Judd Case* it was held that the fact of voters at a town meeting having voted an illegal tax did not constitute a sufficient ground for enjoining the town officers from assessing or collecting the tax. The reasons why a court of equity will not interfere in such a case are very cogently stated by the chief justice. " The grounds," he says, "are too remote, intangible, and uncertain, and the public inconvenience which would ensue from exercise of the jurisdiction would be enormous. It would lie in the power of every taxpayer to arrest all proceedings on the part of the public officers and political bodies in the discharge of their official duties, and, assuming to be the champion of the community, to challenge them in its behalf to meet him in the courts of justice to defend and establish the correctness of their proposed official acts before proceeding to the performance of them. A pretense more inconsistent with the due execution of public trusts and the performance of official duties could hardly be imagined."

· The doctrine laid down in *Judd v. Fox Lake* rests upon sound principles, and the case has been approved and affirmed in subsequent causes which have come before this court. See *West v. Ballard*, 32 Wis. 168; *Nevil v. Clifford*, 55 Wis. 161; *Roe v. Lincoln Co.* 56 Wis. 66; *Gilkey v. Merrill*, 67 Wis. 459; *Sage v. Fifield*, 68 Wis. 546. These decisions are decisive of this appeal. The resolution of the common council, of itself, does the plaintiffs no damage; nor is it clear that that body will proceed to do any unauthorized act under it which will result in injury to their property. Of course such cases as *Peck v. School Dist.* 21 Wis. 516; *Whiting v. S. & F. du L. R. Co.* 25 Wis. 167; and

Nevil v. Clifford, supra, stand upon quite different grounds, and the relief granted came within well-settled principles of equity jurisprudence. But here, assuming that the common council would have no power to construct water-works or enter into a contract for such an improvement without a favorable vote of the electors of the city first had, still no tax has been levied or assessed, and at most a mere anticipated or threatened contract has been contemplated, which has ripened into nothing injurious to the plaintiffs or their property, and which may never do so. The aid of a court of equity cannot be invoked in advance to restrain the city officers founded on such a state of facts.

We were requested to construe ch. 100, Laws of 1887, and determine its validity and whether it was binding upon the common council in the matter of contracting for or in constructing water-works on behalf of the city. The validity of that law is not necessarily involved in this appeal, though we have assumed, for the purposes of the case, that the common council should submit the question of constructing water-works to a vote of the electors. But even on that assumption we hold the complaint states no ground for the interference of equity by its writ of injunction. It follows from these views that the order dissolving the injunction was correct and must be affirmed.

By the Court.— Order affirmed.

JANUARY TERM, 1889.   627

The La Fayette County Monument Corporation vs. Magoon.

THE LA FAYETTE COUNTY MONUMENT CORPORATION, Respondent, vs. MAGOON, Appellant.

February 19 — March 12, 1889.

Contracts: Subscription: Consideration: Payment by check: Parol evidence to vary written contract: Condition subsequent: Discharge of judgment recovered prior to breach.

1. The defendant stated, in writing, to the county board that if within two years $2,000 should be raised by tax from the county and paid to a certain corporation to aid in the erection of a soldiers' monument, he would himself pay to said corporation $1,000 for the same purpose. *Held,* that the raising of the $2,000 by the county by tax, and the payment thereof to the corporation, was a good consideration for the defendant's subscription, which, not having been previously withdrawn, thereby became absolute.

2. Afterwards, in a communication to said corporation, the defendant stated that, in conformity with his agreement with the county board, he did thereby "subscribe and hand to the treasurer of said corporation $1,000 in money, to be used . . . in the erection of a soldiers' monument," on condition that the net cost thereof should not be less than $6,000, and that the full amount of $6,000 should be in the treasury of the corporation on or before March 1, 1888, "and if said amount of $6,000 is not in the hands of said treasurer by March 1, 1888, the said $1,000, so by me subscribed and hereby paid, shall be at once returned and refunded and paid back to me." The board of directors of the corporation approved of such communication and all its conditions, and the defendant thereupon gave to the treasurer his check for $1,000, and a receipt was given to him, signed by the treasurer and approved by the directors, as follows: "Received of [defendant] the sum of $1,000 according to the foregoing letter, its terms and conditions; and if the sum of $6,000 in money is not in my hands as treasurer . . . on March 1, 1888, then the said sum of $1,000 is to be refunded to said [defendant] forthwith." Subsequently, by direction of the defendant, payment of his check was refused. *Held:*

(1) The check was given upon sufficient consideration.

(2) The check was given and received *as money,* and was a *payment* of the subscription.

(3) Parol evidence of a contemporaneous agreement that the check was to be paid by a bond to be given by the defendant for the payment of the $1,000 upon the conditions specified in his com-

munication, was inadmissible to vary the contract evidenced by the communication, check, and receipt.

(4) The failure of the corporation to raise $6,000 by March 1, 1888, could not be a defense to an action upon the check brought and prosecuted to judgment before that date.

(5) If the condition as to the raising of such $6,000, contained in the contract between the defendant and the corporation, is valid (a question not determined), and there has been a breach thereof, the trial court may, on defendant's motion, discharge the judgment recovered before March 1, 1888, on the check.

APPEAL from the Circuit Court for *Grant* County.

The action is upon an unpaid bank check which is as follows: " $1,000. DARLINGTON, WIS., April 6, 1887. *Citizens' National Bank:* Pay to Joseph Blackstone, Treasurer of the La. Co. M. Ass. One Thousand Dollars, and charge account. HENRY S. MAGOON." On the back of the check was written, "Payable, May 3, 1887. HENRY S. MAGOON."

The complaint alleges that when such check was given the plaintiff was and still is a duly organized corporation under the laws of this state; that the check was given to the payee therein named as treasurer thereof; that the plaintiff is the holder and owner of the check; that payment thereof was demanded of said bank on May 3, 1887, and the bank refused to pay the same; and that the check was duly protested for nonpayment May 4, 1887, and notice thereof forthwith given the defendant.

On the trial of the cause the plaintiff proved by undisputed evidence all the above allegations of the complaint, and proved further that the check was given for and on account of the plaintiff, and that payment thereof was refused by the bank pursuant to directions given it by the defendant. When the plaintiff rested its case the defendant moved for a nonsuit, which motion was denied by the court.

The answer of defendant alleges generally want of consideration for the check in suit, and also payment thereof by the tender of a certain bond which the plaintiff agreed to receive as such payment. The answer then proceeds to allege an agreement by the plaintiff with the defendant to erect, at its own expense, a monument to the deceased soldiers and sailors of La Fayette county, whether of the war of the rebellion, or the revolutionary war, or the last war with Great Britain, or the Mexican or Black Hawk war, which monument should be suitable and beautiful, and appropriately inscribed, and should contain the names of such deceased soldiers and sailors. That the plaintiff further irrevocably agreed that such monument should stand in the center of the public square in Darlington, should cost not less than $6,000, should be completed by January 1, 1889, and that plaintiff should raise and have in its treasury on March 1, 1888, $6,000 in money for monument purposes on or before said March 1, 1888.

It is admitted in the answer that upon the faith of such agreement, and not otherwise, the defendant subscribed $1,000 to the monument fund, and at the request of plaintiff gave the check in suit therefor, but upon the agreement that the same should be payable by the bond of defendant conditioned to pay such subscription on or before March 1, 1888, if by that date the plaintiff had in its treasury $5,000, exclusive of defendant's subscription, for the erection of the monument, and if the plaintiff would ever after adhere to and fulfil all its agreements with defendant above stated. It is also alleged that such bond was tendered to plaintiff on May 3, 1887, and repeatedly thereafter, and the check demanded, but that plaintiff refused to accept the bond or surrender the check. It is claimed that the tender of the bond pursuant to such agreement operates as a payment of the check in suit.

The defendant offered testimony on the trial to prove the agreement alleged in the answer, and the tender of the bond and demand of the check as alleged therein, but the court rejected the testimony.

The following additional facts are proved by the testimony, mainly by that introduced by the defendant:

Under date of January 8, 1885, the defendant addressed the following communication to the board of supervisors of La Fayette county: " *Gentlemen:* Respecting the proposition to raise by tax $2,000 from La Fayette county to aid in the erection of the soldiers' monument to the memory of the deceased and wounded soldiers of said county, I will on the receipt by the monument organization of said sum of $2,000 so raised by tax from said county, myself pay to said organization $1,000 of my funds towards the erection of said soldiers' monument. Provided, that said sum of $2,000 be so raised by tax and paid to said monument organization within two years from this date. HENRY S. MAGOON." On the same day the board passed a resolution submitting to a vote of the electors of the county at the ensuing April election or town meeting, the question of raising by tax $2,000, toward the erection of such monument — $1,000 to be raised in that year, and the remaining $1,000 to be raised in 1886. A majority of the electors voted at such election in favor of such proposition, and the tax was duly levied, collected, and paid into the county treasury pursuant to such vote.

In November 1885, the plaintiff was organized as a corporation. The defendant is a signer of the articles of incorporation, and upon its organization became a director for three years, and its president. On January 6, 1887, the county board of supervisors by resolution ordered the county treasurer to pay over to the plaintiff corporation the $2,000 thus raised, and such treasurer executed the order on the same day by paying that amount to the treasurer of the plaintiff, who duly receipted therefor. On the following day the county treasurer notified the defendant of such payment.

April 6, 1887, the defendant presented to the plaintiff's board of directors the following communication signed by him: " *To the Officers, Directors and Members of the La Fayette County Monument Corporation, and to said Corporation:* I, *Henry S. Magoon,* in conformity with and based upon the charter and by-laws of said corporation and the vote of the people and resolution of the county board and the agreement of *Henry S. Magoon* to said county board, hereby subscribe and hand to the treasurer of said corporation, the sum of one thousand dollars in money, to be used for the purposes of said corporation in the erection of a soldiers' monument in the center of the public square in the city of Darlington, on the condition that the net cost of said monument and its foundation shall not be less than $6,000, and on the further condition that the full amount of $6,000 shall be in the treasury of said corporation on or before March 1, 1888. And likewise that the monument shall be of approved design and materials. And if said amount of $6,000 is not in the hands of said treasurer by March 1, 1888, then said $1,000, so by me subscribed and hereby paid, shall be at once returned and refunded and paid back to me, said *Henry S. Magoon,* by said treasurer and said corporation, without default. *Dated, Darlington, Wisconsin, April 6, 1887.*" The board approved of the communication and all its conditions. Thereupon the defendant made and delivered to the plaintiff's treasurer the check in suit, and the following receipt was then signed by such treasurer, approved by the board of directors, and delivered to the defendant: " Received from *Henry S. Magoon* the sum of one thousand dollars, according to the foregoing letter, its terms and conditions; and if the sum of $6,000 in money is not in my hands as treasurer of said corporation, belonging to said corporation, on March 1,

1888, then the said sum of $1,000 is to be refunded to said *Magoon* forthwith by me and by said corporation." It is recited in the record of the directors' meeting of April 6, 1887, that the defendant handed such check to the treasurer on the faith and condition that all the agreements and conditions contained in his communication to the board would be faithfully observed and carried out by the plaintiff.

The court directed the jury to return a verdict for the plaintiff for the amount of the check and interest thereon from May 3, 1887, and the verdict was returned accordingly. Subsequently a motion for a new trial was denied by the court, and on February 24, 1888, judgment for the plaintiff was entered pursuant to the verdict. The defendant appeals from the judgment.

For the appellant there were briefs signed by *Henry S. Magoon*, in person, and by *A. R. Bushnell, J. T. Mills*, and *M. M. Cothren*, of counsel, and the cause was argued orally by *Mr. Mills* and *Mr. Magoon*. They contended, *inter alia*, that the uncontradicted evidence proved that the check was wholly without consideration and intended simply to evidence a promised gift; that the check was only *deposited* on a condition to be fulfilled by the plaintiff, which condition it never fulfilled and thereby never became the owner of the check; and that by the law of *depositum* the plaintiff never was owner of the check, but ought to have surrendered it to the defendant at his request.

For the respondent there was a brief by *Orton & Osborn*, and oral argument by *P. A. Orton*.

LYON, J. 1. We cannot doubt that the transactions between the parties of April 6, 1887, evidenced by the communication of the defendant to the plaintiff corporation, and the receipt which was approved and accepted by the defendant (both of which will be found in the foregoing statement of facts), show conclusively that the check in suit was given and received as a payment of the defendant's subscription to the monument fund. The language of the defendant to the plaintiff in such communication is: " I, *Henry S. Magoon*, . . . hereby subscribe and hand to the treasurer of said corporation one thousand dollars in money to be used," etc., and that of the receipt is: "Received from *Henry S. Magoon* the sum of one thousand dollars according to the foregoing letter," etc. It is therefore a receipt for $1,000 in money. We cannot conceive how the parties could have expressed in stronger terms their intention that the check was given and received *as money*, and hence that it paid the defendant's subscription as effectually as though the payment had actually been made in cash. Had the plaintiff brought an action upon the subscription instead of the check, we think a defense that the subscription had been paid would be proved by the transactions of April 6, 1887. Possibly this view of the case removes from it the question whether there was a valid consideration for the subscription, but it is deemed proper to determine that question.

2. The communication of January 8, 1885, addressed by the defendant to the board of supervisors of La Fayette county, was a conditional subscription to the monument fund. The county performed all the conditions prescribed therein by the defendant within the required time. The defendant not having withdrawn his proposition to the county, his subscription thereupon became absolute. The raising of the $2,000 by the county by tax, and the payment thereof to the plaintiff corporation, is a good consideration for the defendant's subscription. This has been held in numerous cases in this court and elsewhere, and really is elementary doctrine. In *Lathrop v. Knapp*, 27 Wis. 214, the prevailing opinion by DIXON, C. J., goes further, and asserts the rule to be that where several persons mutually promise to contribute to a common object, the promise of

each is a good consideration for the promise of each of the others. The present chief justice filed an opinion holding the above rule too broad. He said, however, "I concede that the doctrine is well established that where such advances have been made or expenses and liabilities incurred by others, upon the credit of such a subscription, before any notice of withdrawal, then it becomes obligatory and binding upon the promisor, although he may not have derived any pecuniary advantage from the enterprise." The subscription of the defendant in the present case is within the qualified rule laid down in the latter opinion. The subject is so fully discussed in both opinions in *Lathrop v. Knapp* that further consideration of it here is uncalled for. It must be held that the defendant's subscription, as well as the check in suit, is supported by a valid consideration.

3. The testimony offered by defendant to prove the agreement to accept a bond in place of the check in suit and to surrender the check, also to prove a tender of the bond and demand of the check by defendant, as alleged in the answer, was properly rejected. There is no claim of any fraud or mistake in the written instruments which evidence the contract of the parties of April 6, 1887, and hence parol proof is not admissible to vary or add to the contract thus expressed in writing. This has been so frequently and so uniformly held by this court, and is so thoroughly well settled, that it is quite unnecessary to cite adjudications upon the subject.

4. The failure to raise $6,000 for the monument fund by March 1, 1888 (if such failure has occurred), is not a defense to this action, although had the action been pending after that date such failure might, perhaps, have been interposed by leave of court, as a counterclaim arising *puis darrein continuance*, provided the stipulation between the parties in that behalf is valid and binding upon the plaintiff — a proposition not here determined. On the hypothe-

sis that it is a valid condition, it need only be said of it, that it is in the nature of a condition subsequent, which could not have been broken until long after the check became payable by its terms, and after judgment actually recovered upon it. Until such breach the right of action upon the check was as complete and perfect as though no such condition existed. Thus, in ejectment by a grantee of land who holds his title upon condition subsequent, against his grantor who, before breach of the condition, has evicted him, the unbroken condition subsequent is not available to the defendant either as a defense or in abatement of the action. All the defendant stipulated for was that in case of a breach of the condition the same sum should be refunded to him — not the same money or the same check. Hence the law of bailments, invoked by the defendant, has no application to the case.

It is believed that the foregoing views cover the whole case, and that they necessarily result in an affirmance of the judgment.

5. It has already been suggested that if the condition contained in the contract between the parties of April 6, 1887, is valid, and if there has been a breach thereof, the defendant can recover of the plaintiff, in any proper action or proceeding, the amount paid upon his subscription. In such case, the judgment herein not having been paid, it would be against equity and good conscience to require the defendant to pay it. Under the old practice, he could probably be relieved of the judgment by a suit in equity to restrain its collection. But if entitled to relief, the present practice gives him a simpler and more summary remedy, that is, by a motion to the circuit court, upon a proper showing, to discharge the judgment. If such a motion be made after the cause shall have been remitted to that court, and the defendant can satisfy the court that such condition is a valid and binding one upon the plaintiff,

and that it has been broken, and the defendant shall pay the costs of this action, we think the motion should be granted. If the circuit court should be of the opinion that the condition is invalid because not a part of the original subscription, and because the county of La Fayette is not a party thereto, or for any other reason, the motion will necessarily be denied. We leave the circuit court to pass upon the question above suggested, without intimating any opinion as to how it should be determined.

Since the argument of the appeal, and since the foregoing opinion was prepared, the members of this court have learned with profound regret that the able and scholarly defendant who had long been an honored and prominent member of the bar of this court, has departed this life. It is necessary, however, in order to facilitate the settlement of his estate, that judgment should be entered upon this appeal.

By the Court.— The judgment of the circuit court is therefore affirmed as of February 19, 1889, that being the day on which the cause was argued in this court.

HAGENAH and another, Appellants, vs. GEFFERT, Respondent.

February 20 — March 12, 1889.

Reformation of written instrument: Mistake: Pleading: Demurrer ore tenus.

1. The complaint alleges that, upon the dissolution of a partnership between the parties with relation to a certain business, it was agreed that the plaintiffs should assume all the debts of the firm relating to such business, and, to carry out such arrangement, they executed to the defendant a bond conditioned, by its terms, that they should pay all the debts of the firm and save him harmless therefrom; that at that time the individual members of the

firm held stock in a certain manufacturing company, and there was then outstanding a note executed in the firm name (and by other makers) which was not given for any debt of the firm and was not in any way connected with its said business, but was given for the benefit of such manufacturing company, the makers of the note being in reality sureties for said company: that said note was not intended or understood by the parties to be included among the liabilities of the firm assumed by the plaintiffs or covered by the conditions of their bond, and that if the bond is so written as to bear such construction and so as to apparently require the plaintiffs to save the defendant from all liability thereon, it was so written by mistake, and said bond, so written and construed, does not express the real agreement, understanding, and intentions of the parties. It is further alleged that plaintiffs have paid a judgment on said note, one third of which ought, in equity, to be paid by the defendant. Judgment is demanded for a reformation of the bond and for one third of the amount so paid by the plaintiffs. *Held*, ou demurrer *ore tenus*, that the complaint sufficiently alleges a mistake in the bond, and not a mere misunderstanding of the words employed therein.

2. Upon a demurrer *ore tenus* a greater latitude of presumption will be indulged to sustain a complaint than upon a regular demurrer thereto.

APPEAL from the Circuit Court for *Sauk* County.

The following statement of the case was prepared by Mr. Justice CASSCDAY:

The complaint in this action alleges, in effect, that on and prior to February 13, 1883, the parties were partners doing business in the name of Hagenahs & Geffert, and engaged in the hardware and agricultural implement business. That they were also engaged in carrying on a brewery, and the individual members also held stock in the Reedsburg Woolen Mills. That, at the date aforesaid, "it was mutually agreed by and between the several members of said firm that said firm should be dissolved, so far as related to the said hardware and agricultural implement business, by the retirement of the said defendant therefrom, they, the said plaintiffs, paying to the said defendant the sum of $500 for his interest in said business, and assuming all of the debts of said firm relating thereto." That to carry out such arrangement plaintiffs paid to the defendant the $500, and executed to the defendant a bond, of which the following is a copy: " Know all men by these presents that we, *John H. Hagenah* and *Peter Hagenah*, of Reedsburg, Wisconsin, as principals, and Henry Meyer, of Westfield, as surety, are held and firmly bound unto *Henry Geffert*, of Reedsburg, Wisconsin, in the sum of ten thousand dollars, to be paid to the said *Henry Geffert*, his heirs and adminis trators, to which payment, well and truly to be made, we do bind ourselves, our heirs and administrators, and each of them, firmly by these presents. Sealed with our seals, and dated this 13th day of February, 1883. The condition of this obligation is such that if the above-bounden *John H.* and *Peter Hagenah*, and Henry Meyer, their heirs and ad- ministrators, shall in all things stand to and abide by, well and truly keep, perform, and pay all the liabilities, debts, obligations, and contracts, in any manner contracted, out- standing, or against the late firm of Hagenahs & Geffert, and shall see that the same are duly discharged, and shall keep and save harmless the said *Henry Geffert* from any and all costs, expense, and trouble on account of the same, then the above obligation shall be void; else to remain in full force and virtue." And the defendant executed to the plaintiffs a bill of sale of all his "right, title, and interest in all the joint property, real and personal, notes, credits, book accounts, and everything of every nature belonging to the said firm of Hagenahs & Geffert." That at the time of the dissolution of said firm and the execution of said bond, there was outstanding and unpaid a promissory note for $10,000, executed by David B. Rudd, Eli O. Rudd, Silas J. Seymour, Joseph L. Green, and the firm of Harris & Hasler, and purporting also to be executed by the said firm of Hagenahs & Geffert. That said note was not given for any indebtedness of the said firm of Hagenahs & Geffert, nor in anywise connected with the business of hardware and agricultural implements of said firm, but was given for the benefit of the Reedsburg Woolen Mill, and that all of the makers of the note were in reality sureties for the Woolen Mill, and co-sureties for each other. "That it [the note] was not included nor understood nor intended by the parties or any of them to be included among, or as constituting a part of, the liabilities of said firm of Hagenahs & Geffert, nor any part of the liabilities to be assumed by the said plaintiffs, nor to be included in nor covered by the conditions of said bond." That suit was afterwards brought upon said note, and judgment rendered thereon in the circuit court, which was afterwards affirmed by this court. (*Morse v. Hagenah*, 68 Wis. 603.) That the sole question litigated in that action was whether or not all the members of the firm of Hagenahs & Geffert were liable upon said note by reason of the signature of the firm name thereon. That in addition to said note there were two other notes of $10,000 each, made by the same parties to the same payee for the same purposes, outstanding and unpaid at the time of the dissolution. That plaintiffs have paid the judgment upon said note, paying therefor the sum of $2,273.53 (the other joint makers having paid their just proportion of the note before suit brought), one third of which ought, in equity, to be paid by the defendant, but the defendant refuses to pay any portion thereof, claiming that by the terms of said bond the plaintiffs are bound to pay the whole thereof. "But said plaintiffs aver and expressly charge that if the said bond is so written as to bear such construction, and so as to apparently require these plaintiffs to pay the whole of said judgment, or to indemnify the said defendant from liability upon said note, the same was so written by mistake; that it was not so agreed between the parties; and that said bond, so written and so construed, does not express the real and true agreement, understanding, and intentions of the parties thereto."

The complaint demands that the bond be reformed and corrected so as to conform to and express the agreement and contract actually made; and demands judgment for one third of the amount paid by the plaintiffs in paying off said judgment.

The defendant answered upon the merits, forming an issue, and the case was brought on for trial at the September, 1888, term of the court for Sauk county, when the defendant objected to the reception of any evidence under the complaint, upon the ground that the complaint did not state facts sufficient to constitute a cause of action. That objection was sustained by the court, and judgment dismissing the complaint with costs was rendered. From that judgment the plaintiffs appeal.

G. Stevens, for appellants, cited *Menominee L. Mfg. Co. v. Langworthy,* 18 Wis. 444; *Benson v. Markoe,* 37 Minn. 30, and cases cited; Kerr on Fraud and Mistake, 398 *et seq.*

For the respondent there was a brief by *Gregory, Bird & Gregory,* and oral argument by *J. C. Gregory.* They contended that to justify the reformation of a written instrument the mistake must be in the language used, either by inserting words not agreed to or by omitting words intended to be used. If the language used was that intended to be used, the writing cannot be changed on the ground of misunderstanding as to its meaning or effect. *Nelson v. Davis,* 40 Ind. 366; *Allen v. Anderson,* 44 id. 395; *Barnes v. Bartlett,* 47 id. 98; *Toops v. Snyder,* 70 id. 554; *Treacy v. Hecker,* 51 How. Pr. 69; *Kelly v. Turner,* 74 Ala. 513; *Oswald v. Sproehnle,* 16 Bradw. 368; *Webster v. Stark,* 10 Lea, 406; *Easter v. Severin,* 78 Ind. 540; *Grubb's Appeal,* 90 Pa. St. 228; *Eastman v. St. Anthony Falls W. P. Co.* 24 Minn. 437; *Nevius v. Dunlap,* 33 N. Y. 676.

CASSODAY, J. It is claimed that no mistake of fact is alleged in the complaint, but only a misunderstanding as to the meaning of the words employed. Had the question arisen upon regular demurrer, we might possibly have reached that conclusion. But no such demurrer was interposed. The defendant answered upon the merits. The cause was regularly noticed for trial, and the plaintiffs appeared with the expectation of trying it. They were met by a demurrer *ore tenus*. It has long been settled in this court that, where the sufficiency of the complaint is thus raised for the first time, more latitude of presumption will be indulged to sustain it than where the objection is taken by regular demurrer. *Teetshorn v. Hull*, 30 Wis. 162; *Hazleton v. Union Bank*, 32 Wis. 34. Without further citing cases, it is sufficient to say that this rule has since been frequently sanctioned by this court. By indulging in such liberal presumption in favor of the complaint, the court is inclined to hold that it alleges, in effect, that by mistake the bond was so written as to make the plaintiffs assume " all the debts " of the firm, instead of limiting such liability to such debts of the firm as had been incurred in the " hardware and agricultural implement business," as was intended by the parties. Especially is this so in view of the liberal rule for the reformation of contracts on the ground of mistake, adopted by this court in *Green Bay & M. Canal Co. v. Hewitt*, 62 Wis. 329 *et seq.* The discussion of the question by Mr. Justice ORTON in that case is too recent and too exhaustive to be here renewed. See, also, *Silbar v. Ryder*, 63 Wis. 109. The case comes clearly within the ruling of that decision. It is true the allegations are vague and indefinite, and might have been made more certain on motion; but such defect cannot be reached on demurrer *ore tenus*. Not wishing to embarrass a trial upon the merits, we refrain from any further discussion.

By the Court.— The judgment of the circuit court is reversed, and the cause is remanded for a new trial.

ANDRUS and another, Respondents, vs. THE HOME INSUR-
ANCE COMPANY OF NEW YORK, Appellant.

February 21 — March 12, 1889.

Reference: Account: Insurance against fire.

Where there is no *account* between the parties in the ordinary acceptation of that term, a reference cannot be directed, without the
consent of the parties, merely because there may be many items
of damage. So *held* in an action upon an insurance policy where,
to ascertain the amount of the loss, it would be necessary to examine bills of sale, inventories, and accounts consisting of numerous items.

APPEAL from the Circuit Court for *Dane* County.
The case is sufficiently stated in the opinion.

H. W. Chynoweth, for the appellant, cited, besides cases
referred to in the opinion, *Dean v. Empire S. M. Ins. Co.* 9
How. Pr. 69; *Lewis v. Irving F. Ins. Co.* 15 Abb. Pr. 303;
Batchelor v. Albany City Ins. Co. 1 Sweeny, 346; *Samble
v. Mechanics' F. Ins. Co.* 1 Hall, 560.

For the respondents there was a brief by *Luse & Wait*,
attorneys, and *C. E. Estabrook*, of counsel, and oral argument by *L. K. Luse*. In addition to cases referred to in the
opinion, they cited *Druse v. Horter*, 57 Wis. 644; *Cameron
v. Freeman*, 18 How. Pr. 310; *M'Cullough v. Brodie*, 13 id.
346; *Kain v. Delano*, 11 Abb. Pr., N. S., 29; *Van Rensse-
laer v. Jewett*, 6 Hill, 373; *Thomas v. Reab*, 6 Wend. 503;
Levy v. Brooklyn F. Ins. Co. 25 id. 687; *McLean v. East
River Ins. Co.* 8 Bosw. 700; *Brink v. Republic F. Ins. Co.*
2 T. & C. 550; *Magown v. Sinclair*, 5 Daly, 63; *Seigel v.
Heid*, 36 How. Pr. 506.

COLE, C. J. Was the court below right in refusing to
order a compulsory reference in this case? The action is
upon a policy of insurance upon a stock of drugs, paints,
oils, medicines, stationery, books, wall-paper, and such

other merchandise as is usually kept in a retail country drug-store. The stock was wholly destroyed by fire within the life of the policy. The motion for the reference was founded upon affidavits which tended to show that it will be necessary to examine bills of sale, inventories, or accounts consisting of 1,200 or 1,500 items, to ascertain the amount of the loss of the assured. Does such a case come within the statute authorizing the court, without the consent of the parties, to direct a reference on the ground that the trial of the issue requires the examination of a long account on either side, within the meaning of sec. 2864, R. S.? It seems to us it does not. Though the examination of numerous items may be necessary to ascertain the amount of damage, yet that does not involve directly the examination of a long account. The value of the property destroyed is only collaterally involved as affecting the measure of damages. *Stacy v. M., L. S. & W. R. Co.* 72 Wis. 331. That case was an action for the negligent burning of the plaintiff's property. It was claimed the trial of the issues would involve the examination of a long account, and that a compulsory reference could be ordered. But the court overruled this position, holding that the value of the merchandise, lumber, and other property burned was only collaterally involved.

Substantially the same ruling was made in *Camp v. Ingersoll*, 86 N. Y. 433, which was an action upon an award for the failure of the defendants to deliver certain stock; and it was insisted that to ascertain the value of the stock the examination of a long account would be necessary. But the court say: "Though the examination of numerous items of damage may be involved, they do not constitute an account, technically and properly speaking, between the parties." An account implies dealings and transactions between the parties, and where the action is based upon such an account, which has to be examined and investigated in order to settle the rights of the parties, a reference can be made. But it is where the action is based upon the account itself that a compulsory reference can be made. But it does not follow, because a variety of items has to be examined to ascertain the amount of damage recoverable, that the same rule obtains. There the examination of the account is merely an incidental matter, not the main issue in the cause. We therefore hold that the inquiry as to the list of articles or items destroyed by the fire, though it may be necessary and proper to determine the amount of loss or the damages recoverable on the policy, still, in a legal sense, does not require the examination of a long account, as where the action is upon the account itself, which is the real subject of investigation. This view of the law is sustained by the weight of authority in New York, where the question has arisen. In *Untermyer v. Beinhauer*, 105 N. Y. 521, the action was to recover damages for the breach of a building contract. The court held that neither the fact of the bill of particulars furnished by the plaintiff, nor the counterclaim in the answer which required the examination of a long account, made the action a proper one for a compulsory reference. The court say: "These items of damages did not constitute an account. It has repeatedly been held that where there is no account between the parties in the ordinary acceptation of the term, the cause cannot be referred, although there may be many items of damage. This rule has been applied in actions on policies of insurance where there are many items of loss." The cases of *Freeman v. Atlantic Mut. Ins. Co.* 13 Abb. Pr. 124; *Ryan v. Atlantic Mut. Ins. Co.* 50 How. Pr. 321; *S. C. 66 N. Y. 628*,— may be somewhat in conflict with this rule, but we think the law is correctly stated in *Camp v. Ingersoll* and *Untermyer v. Beinhauer, supra.* See, also, *Keep v. Keep*, 58 How. Pr. 139; *Dane v. Liverpool & L. & G. Ins. Co.* 21 Hun, 259; *Bell v. Mayor*, 11 Hun, 511.

In *Littlejohn v. Regents*, 71 Wis. 437, the court went as far as it has gone in any case to sustain a reference. The action was to recover the balance due on a building contract and for extra work and materials. The court held the issues might be referred, as the question what was due the plaintiff on the contract and for extra work and materials involved an accounting, which was the main issue. The cases of *Dane Co. v. Dunning*, 20 Wis. 210, and *Cairns v. O'Bleness*, 40 Wis. 469, are clearly distinguishable from the case before us. In those cases it would be absolutely necessary to examine the treasurer's accounts to ascertain the amount of the deficiency and to determine the extent of the liability of the sureties upon the official bond. In both cases the examination of the treasurer's account was a matter directly involved in the issue. But these decisions cannot apply here, where the issue is as to the amount and value of the merchandise destroyed by the fire. If a compulsory reference could be ordered in this cause, of course it could be ordered in every action on a policy of insurance where there were many items of loss. But, as we have said, the examination of the accounts or bills of sale is an incidental inquiry merely, to determine the amount of damages recoverable on the policy. We therefore think the reference was properly denied.

By the Court.— The order refusing the reference is affirmed.

LANE, Appellant, vs. DUCHAC and others, Respondents.

February 21 — March 12, 1889.

(1-3) Registry of deeds: Indexes: Omission of description of land: Time of making entries and of recording: Presumptions. (4) Married woman: Use of baptismal name in contracts. (5) Taking securities in name of person not interested. (6-8) Mortgages: Non-negotiable note: Parol transfer: Payment to person not authorized: Release.

1. Though the general index in the office of register of deeds does not contain the description of the land affected by a mortgage entered therein, yet where such mortgage is transcribed in the proper record book the defect is cured, and the registry is complete from the time the instrument is so transcribed; and, in the absence of evidence to the contrary, it will be presumed that the entry in the general index and the actual recording of the instrument were simultaneous acts.

2. Though the entries in the general index were not made in the consecutive order of the numbers or the dates of receipt of the instruments,— thus showing that an instrument was not entered therein immediately upon its receipt, as required by sec. 759, R. S.,— that fact does not necessarily so impeach the index as to destroy the validity of the registry. If it is made to appear that the entry of such instrument was made at a later date, the same presumption arises that the instrument was transcribed upon the records and the registry completed at that date.

3. The statute (sec. 760, R. S.) does not require the entries in the grantee index to be made in the order in which the instruments were received.

4. Obligations and conveyances executed by and to a married woman in her baptismal name are valid.

5. The fact that securities were taken by one person in the name of another who had no interest in them, does not invalidate the securities or prevent the person beneficially interested from enforcing payment of them by action.

6. After loaning money and taking a note and mortgage as security, a loan agent charged the amount thereof to a client whose money (exceeding such amount) he held with authority to invest it in his discretion. *Held*, in an action by the client to foreclose the mortgage, that the note and mortgage were thereby transferred to the

client, although the papers remained in the hands of the agent and he did not report the transaction to the client until long after.

7. A valid sale and transfer of a non-negotiable note secured by mortgage may be made by parol, and such a sale carries with it the mortgage as an incident of the debt. A defect in the acknowledgment of the formal assignment of the mortgage is therefore immaterial.

8. A mortgagor paid the amount of the mortgage debt to loan agents through whom he had borrowed the money, for the purpose of discharging the mortgage. He knew that the mortgage and the note secured thereby were not in the hands of such agents but had been sent to another person for whom they had acted. The agents had no general authority to collect money for such other person, and the mortgagor had no right to assume that such authority had been given to them. They did not attempt to release the mortgage, but only undertook to procure a release from or through such other person. *Held*, that the payment to such agents did not discharge the debt.

APPEAL from the Circuit Court for *Langlade* County. The action is to foreclose a mortgage executed by the defendants *Joseph Duchac* and wife to Barbara M. Rhyner, on certain lands in Langlade county, to secure the payment of an unnegotiable promissory note for $300, and interest, given by said *Joseph Duchac* to said Barbara. The note and mortgage were given for a loan of money, and bear date May 29, 1883. The mortgage purports to have been recorded May 31, 1883, in the office of the register of deeds of that county. The loan was made to *Duchac* by one Louis Schintz, of Appleton, a land and loan agent, through the firm of Deleglise & Hutchinson, which firm was engaged in a similar business at Antigo.

Barbara M. Rhyner was the maiden name of the wife of one Ferdoline Zentner, a client of Schintz. The latter had loaned money for Zentner at different times, and for some of those loans had taken securities in the maiden name of Mrs. Zentner, with her consent and by the direction of her husband. Schintz was verbally authorized by both of them to execute receipts, etc., in her maiden name. Schintz was also accustomed to make other loans in the name of Barbara M. Rhyner, with her consent.

The money loaned to *Duchac* did not belong to Zentner or his wife, and was not loaned as the money of any particular client of Schintz. The latter had in his hands when this loan was made more than $300 of the money of the plaintiff, who was also one of his clients, to be loaned for him, and from whom Schintz had a general authority to invest the money in his discretion. On June 5, 1883, which was almost immediately after he received the note and mortgage from D. & H., Schintz charged the amount of such note to the plaintiff, and at the same time assigned, or attempted to assign, the mortgage to the plaintiff by a written assignment executed by him in the name of said Barbara. He attested such assignment and attached thereto his certificate, as a notary public, of the acknowledgment thereof by Barbara. He retained the papers in his hands until after the action was commenced, and until that time plaintiff was not informed of the transaction. On August 15, 1883, *Duchac* refunded the $300 to D. & H., who agreed to obtain the note and mortgage then in the hands of Schintz, and a release of the mortgage, but failed to do so. *Duchac* then mortgaged the same land to one Barnes, who knew of the mortgage in suit. Barnes afterwards foreclosed his mortgage, purchased in the land at the foreclosure sale, and conveyed the same by warranty deed to the defendant *McCully*. The latter had no actual notice, when he purchased the land, of the existence of the mortgage here in suit.

The general index kept in the office of the register of deeds, pursuant to sec. 759, R. S., contains an entry of the mortgage, in compliance with the statute, except a description of the land thereby mortgaged is omitted therefrom, and except also certain apparent irregularities in the order of the entries therein, which are referred to in the following opinion. The index first mentioned in sec. 760, and the grantee index provided for therein, were kept in such office, and contain entries of the mortgage as required by the statute. The mortgage was recorded in full in the proper record book, at the place specified in the indexes, and the register indorsed upon it the time it was received for record, etc., pursuant to subd. 5, sec. 758. When the mortgage was thus recorded at length does not affirmatively appear.

Defendant *McCully*, and two others who were made defendants as alleged subsequent incumbrancers, answered in the action. The other defendants defaulted. The answers need not be stated here, because no question arises on the pleadings. It is sufficient to say that they present the questions considered and determined in the opinion. The transactions out of which this action arose are somewhat numerous and involved, but it is believed the foregoing statement of facts contains all that is necessary to an intelligent understanding of the material points in the case.

The circuit court held that there was no valid registry of the mortgage, and, because the defendant *McCully* had no actual notice of the mortgage when he purchased and paid for the land, that his rights were paramount to those of the plaintiff under his mortgage. The court thereupon gave judgment dismissing the complaint upon the merits. The plaintiff appeals from the judgment.

For the appellant there was a brief by *Kennedy & Schintz*, attorneys, and *Thos. Lynch*, of counsel, and oral argument by *Mr. Lynch*. To the point that the interest of a mortgagee can be transferred by parol, and that a mere transfer of the debt to secure which the mortgage is given transfers the interest of the mortgagee in the mortgaged premises, unless it be otherwise expressly agreed, they cited *Brinkman v. Jones*, 44 Wis. 498; *Croft v. Bunster*, 9 Wis.

503; Jones on Mortg. sec. 831; *Carpenter v. Longan*, 16
Wall. 271, and cases cited; *Kennicott v. Supervisors*, id. 452;
Cornell v. Hichens, 11 Wis. 353; *Andrews v. Hart*, 17 id.
297; *Crosby v. Roub*, 16 id. 616; *Maxwell v. Hartmann*, 50
id. 660; *Kelley v. Whitney*, 45 id. 110; *Perkins v. Sterne*,
76 Am. Dec. 72, and notes.

For the respondents there was a brief by *G. G. Sedgwick*
and *Nash & Nash*, and oral argument by *L. J. Nash*.

Lyon, J. I. On all objections to the validity of the
mortgage in suit and the right of the plaintiff to maintain
this action to foreclose it, the court held with the plaintiff,
except upon the question of the validity of the registry
thereof. In view of the undisputed fact that the defendant *McCully* took a conveyance of the mortgaged land
adversely to the mortgage, without actual notice of its existence, the question of the validity of the registry goes to
the right of the plaintiff to a judgment of foreclosure as
against him, and is therefore a vital one in the case.

1. One defect in the registry of the mortgage which it is
claimed invalidates such registry is that the general index
required by sec. 759, R. S., to be kept in the office of the
register of deeds, and in which the mortgage is entered,
does not contain a description of the mortgaged land, as
required by the statute. But where (as in this case) the
mortgage has been transcribed in the proper record book
of the office, this court held in *Oconto Co. v. Jerrard*, 46
Wis. 317, and again at the present term, in *St. Croix L. &
L. Co. v. Ritchie, ante*, p. 409, that the defect is cured and
the registry is complete from the time the instrument is so
transcribed; and further, that, in the absence of proof to
the contrary (and there is none in this case), it will be presumed that the entry in the general index and the actual
recording of the instrument were simultaneous acts. These
decisions rule this case as to the defect under consideration,

and lead to the conclusion that (unless there is some other defect fatal to the validity of the registry) the mortgage in suit was effectually recorded May 31, 1883. The grounds upon which the above decisions are placed are sufficiently stated in the opinions therein.

2. Sec. 759 requires the entry in the general index to be made immediately upon receipt of the instrument for registry, and, because there is a column in the prescribed form of such index headed "Number of Instrument," the requirement may fairly be implied that all instruments so received must be numbered as received in consecutive order. In the present case that portion of the general index wherein the mortgage in suit is entered contains intrinsic evidence that the first of the above requirements was not complied with, for the entries therein were not made in the consecutive order either of their numbers or the dates of the receipt of the instruments. This fact, however, does not necessarily so absolutely impeach the index as to destroy the validity of the registry. If it is made to appear that the entry of the mortgage therein was made at a later date, the same presumption arises that the mortgage was transcribed upon the records and the registry completed at that date. If thus completed before an adverse title was conveyed to the defendant *McCully*, such registry was constructive notice to him of the plaintiff's mortgage. These are fair deductions from the case of *Hay v. Hill*, 24 Wis. 235. There an entry had been written in the proper index, "with a different ink from the entries immediately before and after, and was interlined between the ruling, and was written in after the entry of the minutes below it, and with different ink from the other entries on that page." There was no explanatory proof, and nothing on the face of the index to show when the entry was thus interlined, or that it was there at any particular time. Adverse rights in the land affected by the instrument intervened, and it was held

there could be no presumption that the entry was made before such adverse rights accrued. A perusal of the opinion in that case, prepared by the present chief justice, will, we think, satisfy any one that, had it been shown the entry was in fact made before such rights accrued, although a considerable time after the instrument was delivered for record, the registry would have been held valid from that time, and constructive notice to such adverse claimant.

The entry of plaintiff's mortgage in the general index (as well as of three other mortgages executed by the defendants *Duchac* and wife to the same mortgagee, and received for record at the same time) is between an entry of a deed received for record June 2, 1883, at 9 A. M., and another deed so received on the same day at 4 P. M. So far as appears from the portion of the general index preserved in the bill of exceptions, no entry of any other instrument received for record on or after May 31, 1883, precedes the entries of such mortgages. Next after the entry of these mortgages we find other entries of instruments received for record at the following dates: April 14th, May 29th, June 7th, and no others received earlier than June 11th. We think from these facts that the entry of plaintiff's mortgage must have been made either on June 2d, or within a very few days thereafter, and hence that the registry thereof was completed long before the defendant *McCully* acquired his adverse title to the mortgaged land. The present case is entirely unlike that of *Lombard v. Culbertson*, 59 Wis. 433, where it was held that an entry in the general index of the receipt of an instrument for record is essential to make the record thereof constructive notice of the instrument to a subsequent purchaser of the land affected thereby.

The index of records and files required by sec. 760 is in compliance with the statute. That of grantees shows on its face (as does the general index) that the entries therein were not made in the order in which instruments were received. But the statute does not require that they shall be so entered.

We reach the conclusion, therefore, that, when *McCully* acquired the title to the land covered by the plaintiff's mortgage, such mortgage was effectually recorded in the register's office of Langlade county; and hence that *McCully* is chargeable with constructive notice of its existence. It follows that, if such mortgage is otherwise valid, *McCully's* title is subordinate and subject to it. As to the answering defendants other than *McCully,* it is sufficient to say that they occupy no better position in respect to the plaintiff's mortgage than does *McCully.*

II. The question of the validity of the registry of the mortgage being thus determined in favor of the plaintiff, the defendants who have interposed answers maintain that the judgment is correct on other grounds, and they seek to uphold it on those grounds, under the rule of *Maxwell v. Hartmann,* 50 Wis. 660, and other cases, that the exceptions of the respondent are available on appeal to save the judgment. Such exceptions raise, in this case, and we think arc all presented in, three questions. These are: (1) Is the mortgage void because the name of Barbara M. Rhyner (which it is claimed is a fictitious name) is inserted therein as mortgagee? (2) Does the evidence show any effectual assignment of the mortgage to the plaintiff? and (3) Did the payment of the amount of the mortgage debt by the mortgagor *Duchac* to Deleglise & Hutchinson satisfy such debt? These questions will now be considered in their order.

1. An examination of the testimony satisfies us that the $300 loaned by Schintz to the defendant *Duchac,* although Schintz may have received the money from his clients to be loaned, was, in contemplation of law, the money of Schintz, and that as between him and *Duchac* he was the

owner of the note and mortgage given therefor. He was responsible for the money so received by him, and it does not appear that he used the funds of any particular client or any person other than himself in making the loan. Had the securities been executed to him in his own name, we do not doubt he could have maintained an action upon them.

It is not true that a fictitious payee and mortgagee is named in the note and mortgage. Barbara M. Rhyner is not a fictitious person, but a person *in esse.* True, since her marriage she is entitled to the name of her husband, Zentner, but we are aware of no law that will invalidate obligations and conveyances executed by and to her in her baptismal name, if she choose to give or take them in that form. Hence, were she the owner of the note and mortgage in suit, it would be no defense to her action upon them that they were executed to her by her baptismal name. Neither is it a defense in an action upon them by any other owner that Schintz, with her consent, took them in her baptismal name for a loan made by himself. It is not unusual for a person to take securities in the name of another who has no interest in them, but that does not invalidate the securities or prevent the person beneficially interested from enforcing payment of them by action.

2. Schintz, being the owner of the note and mortgage, was competent to transfer the same to the plaintiff. In view of the course of business between them, as disclosed in the testimony, we think when he charged the amount of the mortgage debt to the plaintiff such transfer was made. It is not important that the papers remained in the hands of Schintz, or that he did not report the transaction to the plaintiff until long after. The relations between them were such that Schintz could lawfully make the transfer without consulting the plaintiff. If ratification by the plaintiff is essential to the validity of such transfer, the bringing of this action founded upon the transfer, or the failure to re-

pudiate it, is a sufficient ratification by the plaintiff of the acts of Schintz. Moreover, Schintz had authority from the mortgagee to sign her baptismal name to the assignment of the mortgage to the plaintiff. Of course he was not competent to attest the same instrument, and certify her acknowledgment thereof before himself as a notary. But neither attestation nor acknowledgment, nor even a written assignment, are essential to the validity of the transfer of the note and mortgage to the plaintiff. A valid sale and transfer of the note could be made by parol so as to vest the same and the mortgage debt of which it is the evidence in the purchaser, and such sale would carry with it the mortgage, as the incident of the debt, without any written assignment thereof. The adjudications in this state and elsewhere to this effect are very numerous. Some of the cases are cited in the brief of counsel for plaintiff.

It is immaterial that the note is not negotiable. A sale of it transfers to the purchaser the mortgage given to secure its payment as effectually as though the note were negotiable. It must be held that the plaintiff was the owner of the mortgage when this action was commenced.

3. When the mortgagor *Duchac* paid D. & H. the $300 for the purpose of discharging the mortgage in suit, he knew that the note and mortgage were not in the hands of that firm, but had been sent to Schintz. D. & H. did not attempt to release the mortgage, but only undertook to procure a release from or through Schintz. *Duchac* took the risk of getting the release in that manner. Had the securities been in the hands of D. & H., and had they surrendered them to *Duchac*, or discharged the mortgage, we should have the question of their authority to do so to determine. But D. & H. assumed to do nothing of the kind, and the question of their authority to discharge the debt is not here. We also think the testimony insufficient to prove that the firm had general authority to collect money for

Schintz before the same became due, or that the course of business between them was such, to the knowledge of *Du-chac*, that he had the right to assume that such authority had been given by Schintz.

Our conclusion is that the defendant's exceptions are insufficient to sustain the judgment. The judgment of the circuit court must therefore be reversed, and the cause will be remanded with directions to that court to give judgment to the plaintiff of foreclosure and sale as demanded in the complaint.

By the Court.— Ordered accordingly.

THE NORTH WISCONSIN LUMBER COMPANY, Appellant, vs. THE AMERICAN EXPRESS COMPANY, Respondent.

February 21 — March 12, 1889.

Collection of draft by express company: Payments: Application.

In an action to recover the amount of a draft alleged to have been collected by the defendant, it appeared that before receiving said draft the defendant had received other drafts upon the same debtor for collection, and that the debtor in making payments had not directed the application thereof. *Held,* that to maintain the action the plaintiff must show that the debtor had paid to the defendant a sum more than sufficient to satisfy the other drafts.

APPEAL from the Circuit Court for *Chippewa* County. The case is sufficiently stated in the opinion.

For the appellant there was a brief by *Jenkins & Jenkins,* and oral argument by *John J. Jenkins.* They cited *Bardwell v. Am. Exp. Co.* 35 Minn. 344.

For the respondent there was a brief by *Rusk & Boland,* and oral argument by *L. J. Rusk.*

TAYLOR, J. This action was brought to recover of the respondent the amount due upon a draft or bill of exchange drawn by the appellant upon one W. S. Craig, and delivered by appellant to the express company for collection. The complaint charged that the said W. S. Craig paid the amount of the draft to the said express company for the use of the plaintiff, and that the company has failed to pay the amount or any part thereof to the plaintiff. The answer was a denial of all the material allegations of the complaint. On the trial in the circuit court the learned circuit judge directed a verdict for the defendant, and from the judgment entered upon such verdict the plaintiff appealed to this court.

The appellant alleges that it was error for the court to direct a verdict against it upon the evidence offered by the respective parties on the trial. After reading the evidence contained in the bill of exceptions, it seems to us that the plaintiff failed to show by any satisfactory evidence that the said W. S. Craig, or any other person for him, had paid said draft or any part of it to the express company. This was the only issue in the case. The burden of proof was on the plaintiff to show that said Craig had paid the amount of the draft or some part thereof to the company before the commencement of this action, in order to entitle it to recover. Craig was the only witness called by the appellant to establish the fact that the company had collected the draft in question. On the direct examination of this witness he testified that he paid the amount of this draft to one Burns, the agent of the express company, on the 25th of February, 1884. On his cross-examination, he testified that he paid it by a check delivered to said agent on said day for the sum of $425, and in no other way. It appeared on the trial that Burns, the agent of the company, absconded on the same day or in the evening after said alleged payment.

The evidence in the case clearly shows that on and before the 20th of February, 1884, the express company had in its hands for collection three other drafts drawn upon said Craig, one by the Chicago Lumber Company for $993.39, one by Bardwell, Robinson & Co. for $351.81, and one by Max Meyer for $25. These three drafts had been received by said express company previous to the date of the receipt of the draft in question in this case, and were entitled to preference in payment, out of any money delivered or paid to the express company by Craig, to the draft of the plaintiff. The evidence clearly shows that on the 20th of February, 1884, there was due and unpaid on the Chicago Lumber Company draft $593.39, and that nothing had been then paid on the Bardwell, Robinson & Co. draft, or on the Meyer draft. It also appears from the evidence that the express company had been sued by the Chicago Lumber Company for the $593.39 due on their draft, and by Bardwell, Robinson & Co. for the amount of their draft for $351.81, and that the plaintiffs in each of these actions had recovered of the defendant the amounts claimed by them in their several actions. The witness Craig gave no positive testimony showing any payments upon either of the three drafts, amounting in all to the sum of about $1,229, except a check for $350, paid February 20, and a check for $425, paid February 25, 1884.

We think it was necessary, in order to charge the defendant company with the amount of the draft in question, that the plaintiff should show by his evidence that Craig had paid into the hands of the company a sum more than sufficient to satisfy the other drafts which had preference in payment to the draft in question in this case. It is clear that this was necessary, because Craig does not pretend to testify that any part of the two checks of which he speaks in his testimony were paid to the agent of the defendant to be applied in the payment of any particular draft in the hands of the company, but were to be applied in the payment of any drafts held by the company for collection, and in such case it would be the duty of the company to apply them upon the drafts in the order of their receipt as to time.

We find no evidence showing the receipt of any money by the company from Craig which they ought to have applied in payment of the draft of the plaintiffs.

By the Court.— The judgment of the circuit court is affirmed.

LUNDGREEN, Appellant, vs. STRATTON and another, Respondents.

February 21 — March 12, 1889.

Vendor and purchaser of land: Mistake in description: Practical location: Specific performance.

The defendant S. owned lots 11 and 12 in a village block, and sold to the defendant T. what they both supposed to be lot 11, but which was in fact lot 12. T. went into possession of the lot purchased and made improvements thereon. Afterwards S. sold to the plaintiff, who had actual notice of T.'s purchase, possession, and improvements, what the plaintiff and S. supposed was lot 12, and the contract of sale described it as such, but in fact the land so sold was all situated in a public street which adjoined the real lot 12 but had not yet been opened for travel. Plaintiff went into possession of the land in such street and built a house thereon. In an action to enforce specific performance of the contract of sale by the conveyance to him of the real lot 12, it is *held* that the plaintiff has no equity against T., and his only remedy against S. lies in the recovery of damages.

APPEAL from the Circuit Court for *Washburn* County. The facts are sufficiently stated in the opinion.

For the appellant there were briefs by *A. L. Bugbee* and *Jenkins & Jenkins,* and oral argument by *Mr. Bugbee.*

For the respondents there was a brief by *L. H. Mead* and *J. F. Coe*, and oral argument by *Mr. Coe.*

ORTON, J. The facts of this case, as established by the evidence, the report of the referee, and by the admissions of the complaint, are substantially as follows:

Block No. 3, in the village of Spooner, Washburn county, is bounded on the north by Walnut street, and on the west by River street. Lot No. 12 is in the northwest corner of said block, and lot No. 11 adjoins it on the east. In November, 1883, River street on the west had not been opened, and it was not known by the defendants *Stratton* and *Thomas* just where lot 12 lay, but it was supposed that said lot was where it was afterwards discovered said River street was located, and that lot 11 was on the east side of it. The defendant *Stratton* had purchased and paid for lots 11 and 12, but had no deed, and he went into actual possession of lot 12, supposing it to be lot 11, and built a store building upon it, and occupied it as a store. At the above date he sold the said lot and improvements to the defendant *Thomas* for the consideration of $525, and received $300 paid, and the balance was to be paid in the near future, with interest; and *Stratton* agreed to put a cellar under the store building, and build a warehouse adjoining it; and *Thomas* went into immediate possession of said lot, and received a contract for a deed therefor, supposing it to be lot 11, and it was so described. It was afterwards found that said lot was lot 12, and the mistake was corrected by *Stratton* deeding to *Thomas* said lot as lot 12, its correct description, and *Thomas* paid *Stratton* an additional $70 for the same. *Thomas* has continued in the actual occupancy of said lot 12 until the present time, and has made improvements upon the same of about $100, making the lot cost him about $700.

In July, 1884, the plaintiff proposed to *Stratton* to purchase what they both supposed was the vacant lot No. 12, and it was pointed out, identified, and measured as lot 12, and the plaintiff purchased it for $65, and paid down $25, and was to have a deed upon the payment of the balance and interest at a future time. The plaintiff went into the actual occupancy and possession of that tract of ground, by the mutual mistake and description, as lot 12, and built a house upon it, which he still occupies. But, as before stated, it was afterwards discovered that the lot or tract of land actually sold to the plaintiff was entirely in River street, opposite lot 12 in block 3, and did not embrace any part of it. The plaintiff worked as a carpenter on the store building purchased by *Thomas*, and personally knew that *Thomas* had actually purchased and gone into posses- sion of lot 12, and knows that he made improvements thereon and has continued in possession thereof.

It follows, as a matter of course, that the defendant *Stratton* sold to the plaintiff a tract of land that he did not own. At the time of the sale *Stratton* gave the plaintiff a receipt for the $25, "for lot in Spooner, B. 3, lot 12," and specifying when the subsequent payments were to be made. The plaintiff brings this suit for specific performance of this contract, having demanded a conveyance of said lot by that description, which was refused. The defendant *Stratton* failed to answer, but the defendant *Thomas* an- swered, setting up substantially the above facts. The plaintiff averred in his complaint that *Stratton* pointed out to him the tract as lot 12, block 3, and that he took posses- sion of the land that he pointed out to him as such lot, and has made improvements thereon of the value of $400, and "that in fact and in truth the tract of land pointed out by said *Stratton* as lot 12 of block 3 was not lot 12 in block 3 of the village of Spooner, but said tract of land is in the street of the village of Spooner known," etc., "as 'River street.' "

These admissions show substantially the real facts about his purchase. The referee found the facts as above stated, and reported that the complaint be dismissed as to the defendant *Thomas*, and that the plaintiff recover in damages the consideration paid by him, and interest and costs, of the defendant *Stratton;* and the circuit court confirmed the report of the referee, and rendered judgment accordingly.

There was a mutual mistake of description in the number of the lot by *Thomas* and *Stratton*, and a mutual mistake by *Stratton* and the plaintiff of the location of lot 12. But there was no mistake whatever as to the actual premises which both *Thomas* and the plaintiff purchased and have been in possession of ever since. The plaintiff had notice of the rights of *Thomas* in lot 12 a long time before he purchased the tract which was misnamed as lot 12; so that whatever equity he might have as against *Stratton* in lot 12 must be deferred to the right or equity of *Thomas*. 1 Story's Eq. Jur. § 64*d;* 2 Pom. Eq. Jur. §§ 729–753; Adams, Eq. 161. *Qui prior est in tempore, potior est in jure. Martin v. Morris,* 62 Wis. 418; *Meade v. Gilfoyle,* 64 Wis. 18; *Honzik v. Delaglise,* 65 Wis. 494. The land contracts to both the plaintiff and *Thomas* must be construed to give effect to the actual intention of the parties at the time, and the facts and circumstances at the time are to be considered to show what such intention really was. *Parkinson v. McQuaid,* 54 Wis. 473. The intention of *Stratton* and *Thomas* was that *Stratton* purchased the tract of land which finally proved to be lot 12, and he went into possession of that tract; and the intention of *Stratton* and the plaintiff was that the plaintiff purchase the identical tract of land which afterwards proved to be in River street, and he went into possession of that tract. It certainly was not the intention of *Stratton* to sell to him, or of the plaintiff to purchase, for $65, a lot worth nearly $1,000 with improvements, and which the plaintiff knew *Thomas* had purchased the year before and was in the actual possession of. Both the plaintiff and *Thomas* went into possession of the lots or tracts of land which they respectively purchased, and there was no mistake about what they did purchase. The only difficulty is that *Stratton* did not own the tract of land he sold to the plaintiff. He did own the lot he sold to *Thomas*, and he has rightfully conveyed the same to him.

Where there is an obvious mistake or ambiguity in the numbers or description of land purchased, resort may then be had to its practical location at the time by the parties by going into and retaining possession of it and making improvements thereon. *Bader v. Zeise,* 44 Wis. 96; *Messer v. Oestreich,* 52 Wis. 684; *Tobey v. Secor,* 60 Wis. 310; *Thompson v. Jones,* 4 Wis. 106. Where the description is by mistake or is doubtful, a practical location of the premises by the agreement, acts, conduct, or declarations of the parties, followed by exclusive possession, may be sufficient to remove the doubt and give certainty to the description. *Whitney v. Robinson,* 53 Wis. 314; *McMillan v. Wehle,* 55 Wis. 694; *Coe v. Manseau,* 62 Wis. 82. *Meade v. Gilfoyle,* 64 Wis. 18, is in point as to misdescription, and its correction by a practical location of the premises by the parties at the time, and going into possession.

In view of these well-established principles, this is really a very plain case. The plaintiff has not the slightest equity against the defendant *Thomas,* and as against the defendant *Stratton* all the relief he can possibly have is his compensation in damages in consequence of *Stratton's* inability to convey to him the tract of land he sold by reason of a want of title to it. The plaintiff does not complain of the amount of the damages recovered against the defendant *Stratton.*

By the Court.— The judgment of the circuit court, both as to the dismissal of the complaint as to the defendant *Thomas,* and as to damages allowed to the plaintiff against the defendant *Stratton,* is affirmed.

THE STATE, Appellant, vs. POMEROY, Respondent.

February 28 — March 12, 1889.

Highways: Obstruction or encroachment? Penalty.

1. The penalty prescribed by sec. 1326, R. S., for the obstruction of a highway cannot be recovered for a mere encroachment.
2. A fence intruding into a highway, but not hindering or rendering dangerous the travel thereon, is a mere encroachment.

APPEAL from the Circuit Court for *Rock* County.

Action to recover the penalty prescribed by sec. 1326, R. S., for the obstruction of a highway. The facts will sufficiently appear from the opinion. The plaintiff appeals from a judgment in favor of the defendant.

For the appellant there was a brief by *Winans & Hyzer,* and oral argument by *John Winans.*

For the respondent there was a brief by *Smith & Pierce,* and oral argument by *Chas. E. Pierce.* They argued, among other things, that even if the *locus in quo* is a highway this action cannot be maintained, because the fence is but an encroachment and not an obstruction. This fence had stood where it now does for many years, and the highway has at all times been sufficient to accommodate all the public travel that there was on the road. *Wyman v. State,* 13 Wis. 663, 667; *Godsell v. Fleming,* 59 id. 52; Thompson on Highways, 340; *Harrower v. Ritson,* 37 Barb. 301; *Griffith v. McCullum,* 46 id. 561; *McCarthy v. Syracuse,* 46 N. Y. 194.

COLE, C. J. For the purpose of this appeal it is assumed that the *locus in quo* where the defendant's fence stood was a public highway, either by being originally legally laid, or had become so by user. On this assumption, how does the case stand? The action is brought under sec. 1326, R. S., to recover the penalty for obstructing a highway. If the fence in question really was in the highway as claimed by the plaintiff, it was an encroachment as defined in sec. 1330 and subsequent sections. It will be noticed that the statute makes a clear distinction between an obstruction and an encroachment upon a highway. It speaks of a highway lawfully opened being encroached upon "by a fence, building, or other fixture," and points out the method of proceeding to determine whether it is an encroachment or not, and fixes the penalty for failure to remove it on notice. In the statutory sense, an encroachment is a fixture which intrudes into or invades the highway, but does not necessarily prevent public travel. An obstruction may prevent or hinder and delay travel in a greater or less degree, or render the use of the highway dangerous. The legislature has seen fit to make this distinction in the law, and the court has endeavored to maintain it in the construction of this statute. Thus, in *State v. Leaver*, 62 Wis. 387, Mr. Justice Lyon says: "It is difficult to lay down any general rule by which to determine, in any given case, whether an object placed in a highway is an *obstruction* within sec. 1326, or only an *encroachment* within the meaning of sec. 1330. It may safely be said that an object or structure, to be an obstruction, need not necessarily be such as to stop travel on the highway. A man may wilfully place a load of hay or a pile of wood in the middle of the street and leave it there. This would not be an encroachment within sec. 1330, because it is not a 'fence, building, or other fixture.' Yet it would undoubtedly be an obstruction within the meaning of sec. 1326, although room was left on either side of it for travelers on the highway to pass." See, also, *Pauer v. Albrecht*, 72 Wis. 416, where the same distinction is observed. Now, it is very obvious that there could be no recovery of the penalty given by sec. 1326, for what was properly an encroachment within the meaning of the other sections. To sustain such a recovery would be confounding and disregarding all the marked distinctions between an "obstruction" and an "encroachment," which we have just dwelt upon. It would be a plain perversion of the provisions of the statute to allow a recovery of the penalty for an encroachment which is given for an obstruction. This, it seems, is too plain to require argument. The legislature has treated the two things as different in their nature and consequences. The overseer of the proper district is authorized to cause an obstruction to be summarily removed, while, as we have said, a method is pointed out for determining the question whether an encroachment has been made, and penalty is prescribed where the occupant suffers the encroachment to continue after its character has been determined.

In this case, it appears, the supervisors made an order under sec. 1330, declaring that the fence encroached upon the highway, and requiring the defendant to remove it. A copy of this order was served upon the defendant, who denied, in writing, within thirty days, the encroachment, as provided in secs. 1331 and 1332. This denial was addressed to the supervisors, and served upon one of them. The supervisors should then have taken steps which the statute points out to determine whether an encroachment had been made. This proceeding is made very plain by the subsequent provisions, which afford an ample remedy for removing such an encroachment. But, instead of pursuing this remedy, this action was brought to recover the penalty given for obstructing a highway. The court below held upon the evidence that there never had been a public highway where the fence stood, and gave judgment for the defendant. We have assumed that the *locus in quo* was a highway, but hold that the fence does not constitute an obstruction within the meaning of the statute. On that ground the judgment of the circuit court is affirmed.

By the Court.— Judgment affirmed.

BLAKE OPERA HOUSE COMPANY and another, Respondents, vs. THE HOME INSURANCE COMPANY, Appellant.

February 23 — March 12, 1889.

Reformation of written contract: Evidence: Insurance.

To show that a policy of insurance issued to, and upon the property of, a corporation was so written by mistake and was intended to be issued to, and to cover only the interest of, a stockholder to whom the loss was made payable, the proofs must be entirely plain and convincing beyond reasonable controversy; otherwise the writing will be held to express correctly the intention of the parties.

APPEAL from the Circuit Court for *Rock* County.

The following statement of the case was prepared by Mr. Justice CASSODAY:

The complaint is upon a policy of insurance issued by the defendant to the plaintiff company, with the loss payable to the plaintiff *Blake* as his interest might appear. The answer, among other things, alleged as a counterclaim, in effect, that the contract was wholly between the defendant and *Blake*, who paid the premium, and was to insure his interest as a stockholder of the company, and that the policy should have run to him accordingly, but that by mistake it was issued as stated, and by reason of such mistake a reformation of the policy was prayed. The plaintiffs replied to such counterclaim.

The cause was tried by the court, and the testimony taken was voluminous. At the close of the trial of the equitable cause of action alleged in the counterclaim, the court found as matters of fact, in effect, that at the times mentioned *Blake* was a large stockholder of the company; that the company owed him $700, and he was liable as indorser on its paper to the amount of $30,000; that February 6, 1884, the defendant, in consideration of $30 to be

paid, made and delivered to the company its policy, whereby
it insured the company against loss or damage by fire for
the period of one year in the sum of $1,000, payable as
stated; that said _Blake_ did not apply to the defendant's
agent for such insurance to him as such stockholder, nor
represent to such agent that he was such stockholder, nor
request insurance to protect him as such; that _Blake_ at the
time, in fact, owned one fourth of the stock, and the same
was known to such agent; that the company had at the
time other insurance to the amount of $48,000 in various
companies; that as he was a director of the company, and
was about to go out of the state, he applied to the defendant's agent for additional insurance on the company's real
and personal property in the amount of the policy as stated
in the complaint, with the "loss, if any, by request of assured, payable to _L. S. Blake;_" that it had previously been
agreed by the directors of the company that any of them
might take out such additional insurance upon the property
of the company, payable to himself, by paying the premium, as the company had no money to pay the same; that
Blake took such insurance and paid for the same in pursuance of such agreement; that the contract was in fact between the defendant and the company; that there was no
mistake made in the wording of the policy; that it was
never intended by the defendant, or its agent, or _Blake,_
that the policy should be written as insuring _Blake's_ interest in the company; that _Blake_ made no other contract of
insurance with the defendant than the one thus found; that
the main object of _Blake_ in so obtaining said insurance was
to protect his own interest as such stockholder and creditor
of and indorser for the company.

As conclusions of law, it was found that said policy
should not be reformed nor changed in any manner, but
that the same should stand and remain in all of its terms
and conditions as it was when issued and delivered; that

the plaintiffs were entitled to the costs of the trial of said equitable issue, and to judgment for said costs; and judgment was therein ordered accordingly.

Thereupon the other issues were tried by the court without a jury, and upon such trial the court found as matters of fact, in effect, that the policy was made and delivered as above stated; that December 28, 1884, the property thereby insured was totally destroyed by fire; that January 22, 1885, the plaintiffs made and forwarded by mail to the defendant due and formal proofs of loss under the policy and in accordance with its terms, and that no part of said insurance had been paid; that the value of the property insured exceeded the total amount of insurance thereon; that *Blake's* interest in the property so destroyed was, *first*, as a stockholder of the capital stock to the amount of $15,000; and, *secondly*, as a creditor of the company to the amount of $1,240 at the time of the loss, and interest. And as conclusions of law the court found, in effect, that the defendant was indebted to the plaintiffs in the sum of $1,000, with interest from March 22, 1885, and that the plaintiffs were entitled to judgment therefor, with costs. From the judgment entered in the case in accordance with such conclusions the defendant appeals.

For the appellant there was a brief signed by *Winkler, Flanders, Smith, Bottum & Vilas* and *Edwin White Moore*, of counsel, and oral argument by *F. C. Winkler.*

For the respondents there was a brief by *Fish, Dodge & Fish*, and oral argument by *John T. Fish.*

Cassoday, J. It was certainly competent for the parties to make the contract of insurance in the form it was executed. This is, in effect, conceded. Undoubtedly, it would have been competent for the defendant to have insured *Blake's* interest in the company as a stockholder by a policy issued directly to him, if such had been the contract.

It is claimed that such was in fact the contract made, but that by reason of a mistake in writing the policy it was issued to the company and insured its property against loss by fire, with the "loss, if any, by request of the assured, payable to *L. S. Blake*," aforesaid. Until reformed, the policy as drawn was certainly conclusive upon all the parties that the contract was with the plaintiff company and insured its property against loss by fire. *Gillett v. Liverpool & L. & G. Ins. Co., ante,* p. 203. The learned counsel for the defendant concedes such to have been the presumption until overborne by the testimony. It is, moreover, conceded that such proofs, to overcome such written evidence, "must be entirely plain and convincing beyond reasonable controversy; otherwise, the writing will be held to express correctly the intention of the parties." This reduces the whole question involved to one of fact, to be determined from the evidence. After a very careful reading of the printed case we are unable to hold that there is any such clear preponderance of evidence of mistake as would authorize us to disturb the findings; on the contrary, we are forced to the conclusion that the findings are supported by the evidence. A discussion of the facts would be of no benefit to any one.

By the Court.— The judgment of the circuit court is affirmed.

INDEX.

ABATEMENT of action. See APPEAL, 2.

ACCEPTANCE of deed. See VENDOR, ETC. OF LAND, 4.

ACCOUNT STATED.

See APPEAL, 5.

In an action for a balance alleged to be due upon an account stated, the plaintiff attempted to prove a settlement of all matters between the parties. The court charged the jury that if all matters were settled, and the defendant, knowing just how the plaintiff had performed the contract upon which his claim was based, had talked over that matter, and the parties agreed as to the amount due, then they were bound by the settlement: that no advantage could be taken, but the parties must have fully understood and agreed that any claim for a breach of the contract was included in the matters settled, otherwise such claim was still open and unadjusted. *Held*, sufficiently favorable to the defendant. *Garvin v. Gates,* 513

ACCOUNTING. See PARTNERSHIP, 1, 4.

ACKNOWLEDGMENT. See MORTGAGES, 6.

ACTION.

Cause of Action. See CONTRACTS, 1, 3, 4, 6, 8. DIVORCE. EQUITY. EXCISE LAWS, 1. HIGHWAYS, 3. INSURANCE, 1, 2. LIENS, 2–5, 10, 12. MUNICIPAL CORPORATIONS, 2, 3. NEGLIGENCE. PARTNERSHIP, 3–5. PAYMENT. PLEADING, 6, 8–10. RELIGIOUS SOCIETIES, 6–11. RES ADJUDICATA. SLANDER. TOWNS, 1, 2. VENDOR, ETC. OF LAND, 1, 5.

By whom to be brought — Who may maintain. See CONTRACTS, 9. MORTGAGES, 3, 5, 6. PARTIES, 3. RECEIVERS. RELIGIOUS SOCIETIES, 6.

Condition precedent to maintenance. See MUNICIPAL CORPORATIONS, 2. RELIGIOUS SOCIETIES, 6. TOWNS, 1.

Commencement. See LIMITATION OF ACTIONS, 2, 3.

Limitations. See LIMITATION OF ACTIONS.

Abatement. See APPEAL, 2.

Law or Equity? See INSURANCE, 6. PLEADING, 6.

Tort or Contract? See PLEADING, 8, 9.

Various Actions and Proceedings.
　Against the United States.
　　For flowage of land, 363.

For slander, 131.
For a conspiracy, 870.
Ejectment, 89, 137, 385, 468, 542.
Replevin, 409, 548, 557.
Attachment, 184.
Garnishment, 20, 70, 854.
For penalty for obstructing highway, 598, 664.
Certiorari to review action of board of review, 806, 816.
Mandamus to compel state treasurer to make certain application of
  moneys paid in, 211.
Habeas corpus proceedings, 589.
Proceedings to disbar attorney at law, 602.
Petition of insolvent debtor for discharge, 851.
Probate of will, 78.
Settlement of final accounts, distribution of estates, etc.. 126, 445,
  497.
For a divorce, 59, 84.
For contribution from joint maker of note, 636.
For contribution from heirs, etc., of deceased partner, 583.
For dissolution of partnership, accounting, etc., 52.
For dissolution of partnership. receiver, etc., 142.
To enforce liens for building materials, etc., 1, 217, 520.
To enforce liens on logs for supplies, 14, 233.
To foreclose mortgage, 111, 482, 486, 646.
To cancel conveyance of land, 191.
To quiet title and have deed declared valid, 238.
To have judgment declared not a lien and restrain sale on execu-
  tion, 113.
To restrain mining and for damages, 572.
To restrain interference with water rights, etc., 229.
To restrain trustees of religious society from acting as such, and to
  recover possession of property, 258.
To restrain city officers from making contract for water-works,
  622.
To restrain town supervisors from allowing bills or levying taxes
  for water-works, etc., in village, 294.
To restrain manufacture and sale of certain medicine, 401.
To reform written contract, 636, 667.
For specific performance of land contract, 659.
Information for allowing girl under twenty-one to resort to place for
  unlawful purpose, 248.
Complaint for unlicensed sale of liquors, 251.
Information for riot, 589.
Writ of error to review discharge on *habeas corpus*, 589.

ADMINISTRATORS AND EXECUTORS. See EVIDENCE, 1. ESTATES OF DE-
  CEDENTS. PARTNERSHIP, 3-5. WILLS.

ADVERSE POSSESSION.

See BOUNDARIES, 2. EJECTMENT, 1.

1. The continued occupancy or possession of land by one who has conveyed it, or by persons claiming under him subsequent to the
   conveyance, will be presumed to have been in subordination to the
   title of the grantee; and to rebut such presumption there must be
   shown some clear, unequivocal act which would amount to an
   open denial of the grantee's title. *Schwalbach v. C., M. & St. P.
   R. Co.*   187

2. One who by prescription acquires the right to maintain a vault or cellar under another's land does not thereby acquire any right to the surface over such vault. *Koenigs v. Jung,* 178

8. One entering into possession of land under a conveyance from the holder of a life estate only, cannot hold adversely to the remainder-man during the continuance of the life estate. *Barrett v. Stradl,* 885

4. But where the conveyance from the tenant for life purports to convey an estate in fee, and the grantor intended to convey the fee, and the grantee supposed he was getting the fee, the possession of the person entering under such conveyance becomes adverse to the remainder-man immediately upon the death of such life tenant. *Ibid.*

5. Findings that during a certain time a person had the exclusive possession of land, that he claimed to be the sole owner of the premises under and by virtue of a deed thereof to him, and that he asserted his title founded on said deed in good faith, are *held* equivalent to a finding that he was in possession holding adversely under color of title asserted in good faith. *Ibid.*

6. If the defendant in ejectment was at one time in possession of the land, holding adversely to the plaintiff under color of title asserted in good faith, and his possession continued down to the commencement of the action, it will be presumed to have continued to be adverse, in the absence of any evidence showing a change in the character of the possession in that respect. *Ibid.*

AGENCY.

See CARRIERS, 2. ESTOPPEL. EVIDENCE, 8. MORTGAGES, 5, 7.

An instruction that "the idea that if you appoint an agent who is incompetent he can charge you two or three times the amount of the claim, if he chooses to make such expenses, is not tenable in the law," is not erroneous, there being evidence to which it is applicable. *Best v. Sinz,* 243

ALIENATION, Suspension of power of. See RELIGIOUS SOCIETIES, 5.

ALIMONY. See DIVORCE, 4–6.

ALLOWANCES. See DIVORCE, 4–6.

AMENDMENT.
Of pleading. See LIENS, 7, 8, 11.
Of summons. See LIMITATION OF ACTIONS, 8.

ANSWER. See BILLS AND NOTES, 1, 2. CONTRACTS, 8 (4). EQUITY, 8. PLEADING, 5, 7.

APPEAL.

To Supreme Court. See APPEALABLE ORDER. CIRCUIT COURTS. DAMAGES, 4–6. DIVORCE, 4. EVIDENCE, 5. EXCISE LAWS, 2. GARNISHMENT. INSTRUCTIONS TO JURY. MORTGAGES, 1, 2, 4. PARTNERSHIP, 4. PLEADING, 8, 7.

1. An action upon sixty-eight town orders for about $2,000 was barred by the statute of limitations as to all but one order for $15. The judgment dismissed the action. In the argument on appeal no special point was made as to that one order as distinguished from

the others. *Held*, that the judgment would not be reversed for an error affecting a sum so comparatively small. *Schriber v. Town of Richmond.* 5

2. The entry of judgment dismissing an action upon the merits instead of abating it is an immaterial error where another action would be barred by the statute of limitations and it is manifest that that defense would be interposed. *Ibid.*

8. Where the plaintiff recovers substantial damages upon one cause of action and merely nominal damages upon another, the judgment will not be reversed on defendant's appeal for an error relating only to the nominal recovery, if that recovery does not affect the question of costs. *Middleton v. Jerdee,* 39

4. Where the violation by one partner of the partnership agreement has caused great confusion and conflict in the accounts, findings of a referee and the trial court, in an action for an accounting, against allowing items in favor of such partner, will not be disturbed unless contrary to the clear weight of evidence. *Carroll v. Little,* 52

5. In such a case, it not being shown that an item for which the appellant was entitled to credit was overlooked by the referee in footing up the various sums in the statement of an account, the court declines to disturb the account stated. *Ibid.*

6. An exception "to the allowance of each and all the items mentioned in Schedule A, and the charging of each of them to the defendant," where such schedule contains a large number of items many of which are not disputed, is not sufficiently specific, and the court will not review the evidence thereon. *Ibid.*

7. The printed case herein containing a mass of immaterial testimony, but as to the points in dispute being so lacking in fullness and accuracy that resort must be had to the manuscript bill of exceptions, this court declines to review the alleged errors. *Ibid.*

8. An error in permitting a witness to be questioned on cross examination as to matters not inquired of on the direct examination, and to be contradicted afterwards as to such matters by the party so questioning him, will not work a reversal where the matters so inquired about were merely collateral and it is not apparent that the error could have had any influence with the jury upon the issues of fact found by them. *Stutz v. C. & N. W. R. Co.* 147

9. The refusal of the trial court to submit certain questions or give certain instructions to the jury will not be reviewed on appeal unless such questions and instructions, the rulings thereon, and the exceptions to such rulings are made part of the record by the bill of exceptions. Merely filing them with the clerk is insufficient. *Koenigs v. Jung,* 178

10. In an action in which the defendant's goods had been attached the plaintiff failed to file security for costs as required. The court made an order denying defendant's motion to dismiss the action and for judgment for his damages, etc., but afterwards made a second order dismissing the action but denying defendant's motion for judgment for his damages, etc., and also a third order dismissing the action and denying defendant's motion and request for judgment in his favor and to have a jury impaneled to assess his damages, etc. The defendant took one appeal from the first and third orders, and a separate appeal from the second order. *Held,* that each of the several orders was appealable, but, as all might

APPEALABLE ORDER.

See APPEAL, 10.

ATTACHMENT.

See RECEIVERS.

ATTORNEYS AT LAW.

See CONTRACTS, 2. MORTGAGES, 2.

established by a preponderance of satisfactory evidence. *In re* O——, 602

2. As "good moral character" is a condition precedent to admission to the bar, so it is a requisite condition for the rightful continuance in the practice of·the profession. *Ibid.*

3. The fact that an attorney collected and wrongfully converted moneys belonging to his clients, and then failed to pay them over after repeated demands, especially where his attempt to retain such moneys was a subterfuge and in bad faith, is sufficient to authorize his suspension if not disbarment. *Ibid.*

4. The misconduct which will warrant the suspension of an attorney is not limited to acts committed strictly in a professional character, but extends to all such misconduct as would have prevented an admission to the bar. *Ibid.*

5. In proceedings to disbar an attorney the court may find the facts proved by evidence admitted without objection, even though such facts were not stated in the formal charges filed. *Ibid.*

6. It is sufficient to warrant the disbarment of an attorney that, having acted for the claimant in a contest concerning the validity of a homestead claim, he afterwards instigated and conducted in behalf of another person a second contest against his former client, involving the same subject matter and based largely upon the same facts, and in such second contest testified as a witness against his former client and used the information acquired by means of his former employment. *Ibid.*

7. In proceedings instituted in the court of his residence, such court may disbar or suspend an attorney for professional misconduct before officers of the United States land office. *Ibid.*

AUTHENTICATION of judgment. See CIRCUIT COURTS.

BILL OF EXCEPTIONS. See APPEAL, 9, 13. COSTS.

BILL OF PARTICULARS. See PLEADING, 2, 3.

BILLS AND NOTES.

See CONTRACTS, 9. MORTGAGES, 3, 5, 6. TAXATION, 6.

1. Where shares of stock in a corporation are pledged as collateral security to a note, the payee of which is a director and officer of such corporation, the negligence of the payee in the performance of his duties as such director and officer, whereby the stock depreciated or became worthless, is no defense to an action by him on the note. So *held* where the defense was sought to be interposed by one who indorsed the note at the time of its execution and who owned a part of the stock pledged. *Palmer v. Hawes,* 46

2. In such action it was alleged that some months after the stock was so pledged the plaintiff had falsely represented to the indorser that the affairs and business of the corporation were in good condition, when in fact they were being so carelessly and wastefully managed by the plaintiff and the other officers that the stock was rapidly depreciating; that the indorser relied on such representations and was thereby lulled into inactivity and rest concerning her liability on the note when, but for such representations, she might have secured herself from loss. *Held,* that such facts did not constitute a defense. *Ibid.*

3. In an action against the indorsers of an instrument for the payment of money, made and payable in another state, the court will

not, on demurrer, take judicial notice of laws of that state relating to the liability of indorsers, which have not been pleaded. *Continental Nat. Bank v. McGeoch,* 832

4. A written instrument for the payment of a specified sum of money at a time specified, is rendered non-negotiable by an alternative contract therein that the payee may sell the collateral securities mentioned therein, and, if these decline in value, may sell them before the money for which the instrument was given would otherwise become due, in which case the proceeds of the sale, less the expenses thereof, shall be applied in payment or part payment of the debt, and if a deficiency remains the amount thereof shall become due forthwith. *Ibid.*

BOARD OF REVIEW. See TAXATION, 1–5.

BOUNDARIES.

1. A finding of the jury fixing the line of a street is *held* to be sustained by evidence that the street was originally located on such line more than thirty years ago and has been maintained thereon ever since, although a recent survey tends to show that another line is the true one. *Koenigs v. Jung,* 178

2. Plaintiff owns the east half, and defendant the west half, of a quarter section. While the premises were occupied by their respective grantors, the plaintiff's grantor had objected that the fence between the tracts was too far east, and had procured a survey, which, however, showed that the true division line was still further east; whereupon he had importuned the defendant's grantor to allow the fence to be rebuilt on the old line, and the latter had finally consented to do so "for the present." The fence had been rebuilt accordingly, and had remained on the old line without further question for more than twenty years, when the plaintiff, being dissatisfied because the fence was too near his house, asked the defendant to join him in having a new survey made. The defendant declined to do so, and the plaintiff himself procured a new survey. which substantially agreed with the former one, showing the true line to be east of the fence. Thereupon the defendant, with the consent and by the direction of the plaintiff, proceeded to build a fence upon the line fixed by the surveys. The plaintiff afterwards brought suit to recover possession of the strip between the old fence and the new one. *Held,* that the possession of such strip by the plaintiff and his grantor had not been adverse to the defendant and his grantor, and that the line of the old fence had not been established as the division line by agreement or acquiescence. *Fairfield v. Barrette,* 463

3. Evidence as to how the old fence would agree with the fence on the division line of a corresponding quarter section to the north, owned by a third person, was immaterial. *Ibid.*

BUILDING CONTRACTS. See CONTRACTS, 3.

BURDEN OF PROOF. See ADVERSE POSSESSION, 1, 6. APPEAL, 5. ESTATES OF DECEDENTS, 2. EVIDENCE, 2. HIGHWAYS, 1. NEGLIGENCE, 2. PAYMENT. WILLS, 1, 5.

CAPITOL BUILDING. See CONTRACTS, 3.

CARRIERS.

See RAILROADS, 1.

1. An agent of the defendant company gave a receipt for goods shipped in the following form: "Milwaukee ——— 188-. — Shipped by Roundy, Peckham & Co. the following articles, in good order, to be delivered in like good order, as addressed, without unnecessary delay.— Consigned to Hansen & Kirsh, Onekama, Mich." On the face of the receipt the agent stamped and wrote: "F. & P. M. R. R. Co.— Rec'd. Nov. 2. 1887.— By agent, P., Milwaukee." *Held*, that this imported a contract to carry the goods through to Onekama, and that defendant's liability did not cease on the delivery of the same. at the end of its line, to a connecting carrier. *Hansen v. F. & P. M. R. Co.*   346

2. Express authority of the agent to make such contract need not be shown, he having acted as such agent in the proper place for receiving goods for the company, and having been in possession of the company's stamp to be used on such receipts, and the company having taken possession of the goods and caused them to be shipped, presumably with knowledge of the receipt.   *Ibid.*

CASES DISTINGUISHED, ETC.

1. *Benware v. Pine Valley*, 58 Wis. 527. See No. 28.

2. *Cairns v. O'Bleness*, 40 Wis. 469. See No. 3.

3. *Dane Co. v. Dunning*, 20 Wis. 210; *Cairns v. O'Bleness*, 40 id. 469 (as to reference), distinguished. *Andrus v. Home Ins. Co.*   645

4. *Duffy v. Hickey*, 68 Wis. 380 (as to remission of excessive allowance of costs), followed. *Killops v. Stephens*,   112, 113

5. *Esslinger v. Huebner*, 22 Wis. 632 (as to lien for materials used by vendee on land of another), distinguished. *North v. La Flesh*,   526-7

6. *Hamilton v. Fond du Lac*, 40 Wis. 47. See No. 20.

7. *Hay v. Hill*, 24 Wis. 235. See No. 18.

8. *Heath v. Solles*, 73 Wis. 217 (as to lien for materials), followed. *North v. La Flesh*,   520, 529

9. *Hilgers v. Quinney*, 51 Wis. 62 (as to registry of deed), distinguished. *St. Croix L. & L. Co. v. Ritchie*,   413

10. *Hurley v. Texas*, 20 Wis. 637. See No. 20.

11. *Lombard v. Culbertson*, 59 Wis. 437 (as to registry of deed), distinguished. *St. Croix L. & L. Co. v. Ritchie*, 414. *Lane v. Duchac.*   652

12. *Messer v. Oestreich*, 52 Wis. 690 (as to practical construction of uncertain description of land), distinguished. *Morse v. Stockman*,   94

13. *Nevil v. Clifford*, 55 Wis. 161. See No. 16.

14. *Oconto Co. v. Jerrard*, 46 Wis. 317 (as to registry of deed), followed. *St. Croix L. & L. Co. v. Ritchie*, 413-4. *Lane v. Duchac*,   650

15. *Parmelee v. Western Transp. Co.* 26 Wis. 439 (as to liability of carriers), distinguished. *Hansen v. F. & P. M. R. Co.*   351

CHATTEL MORTGAGES.

1. When the mortgagee of chattels delays the filing of his mortgage at the request of the mortgagor and in order that the credit of the latter may not be injured, he is estopped to assert such mortgage as against creditors who, after the execution of the mortgage and before its filing, gave credit to the mortgagor upon the faith that his property was unincumbered; and this is so although the mortgagee had no actual intent to defraud any creditor. *Standard Paper Co. v. Guenther*, 67 Wis. 101, followed. *Sanger v. Guenther*.   354

2. The fact that a creditor who took the note of the mortgagor before the mortgage was filed, required such note to be signed also by other persons, is not conclusive that he did not rely upon the property of the mortgagor ultimately to pay it. *Ibid.*

3. The fact that the creditor permitted the mortgagee to take possession and dispose of the mortgaged property does not estop him from requiring the latter to account therefor. *Ibid.*

CHECKS. See CONTRACTS, 8.

CIRCUIT COURTS

See ATTORNEYS, 7.

Where in an action in the circuit court for one county judgment is rendered at a special term of that court held in another county, the want of proper authentication of the judgment by the clerk of the latter county (sec. 2428, R. S.) is not a jurisdictional defect, but, at most, a mere irregularity which will not be corrected on appeal unless an opportunity is first given to the circuit court to supply the alleged defect in the record. *Morris v. Peck,* 482

CITIES. See MUNICIPAL CORPORATIONS.

CLAIMS.
Against assignor. See VOLUNTARY ASSIGNMENT, 4.
Against decedent. See PARTNERSHIP, 3-5.
Against town. See TOWNS, 1.

CLERICAL ERRORS. See PRACTICE. REGISTRY OF DEEDS, 1.

COLLECTION of draft by express company. See PAYMENT.

COMMON CARRIERS. See CARRIERS. RAILROADS, 1.

COMPLAINT. See APPEALABLE ORDER, 3. EXCISE LAWS, 1. LIENS, 1, 7, 8, 11. LIMITATION OF ACTIONS, 1. MORTGAGES, 3. PLEADING, 1-3, 6-10. SLANDER.

CONDITIONS.
Precedent. See MUNICIPAL CORPORATIONS, 2. PLEADING, 5.
Subsequent. See CONTRACTS, 8 (4, 5). EVIDENCE, 3, 4.

CONDONATION. See DIVORCE, 3.

CONFLICT OF LAWS. See BILLS AND NOTES, 3.

CONSIDERATION. See CONTRACTS, 7, 8.

CONSPIRACY. See PLEADING, 9.

CONSTITUTIONAL LAW. See CRIMINAL LAW, 2. TOWNS, 4, 5.

CONTINGENT CLAIMS against decedents. See PARTNERSHIP, 3, 5 (3).

CONTINUANCE. See APPEALABLE ORDER, 1.

CONTRACTS.

See ACCOUNT STATED. AGENCY. BILLS AND NOTES. CARRIERS. CHATTEL MORTGAGES. DEED. DURESS. EQUITY, 1, 3. EVIDENCE, 8. FALSE REPRESENTATIONS. INSURANCE. LIENS, 1-3. LIMITATION OF ACTIONS, 1, 4. LOGS AND TIMBER, 3. MARRIED WOMEN. MINES AND MINING. MORTGAGES. PARTIES, 1, 3. PARTNERSHIP. PAYMENT. PLEADING, 8, 9. RAILROADS, 1. VENDOR, ETC. OF LAND. VOLUNTARY ASSIGNMENT.

1. By the terms of a written contract the defendants were to cut and haul to their saw-mill all the down timber and slashings on lands of the garnishee and manufacture the same into timber and shingles, and for all lumber so manufactured and safely piled in their mill-

yard the garnishee was to pay them $6 per thousand feet. Defendants cut and hauled a large quantity of logs and put them in their pond, but, before any of them were sawed into lumber, their mill was burned. *Held:*

(1) A finding of the trial court that the contract had not been modified so that the defendants should be paid a certain sum for getting out and hauling the logs, irrespective of sawing them into lumber, is sustained by the evidence, although it appears that the garnishee had made advances to aid in getting out the logs.

(2) The contract was entire, and there could be no recovery *quantum meruit* for its part performance in getting out the logs.

(3) The fact that the garnishee took possession of the logs more than a year after the defendants had abandoned them and were insolvent, does not show a waiver of complete performance of the contract. *McDonald v. Bryant,* 20

2. In an action by an attorney for a balance claimed to be due for several distinct services, the defendant alleged a contract whereby, for all of the services except one, the plaintiff was to receive nothing unless successful, and that he was unsuccessful. On the trial it appeared that such alleged contract could have related to but one of the services rendered. *Held,* that it was error to instruct the jury that it was for them to determine to what services the contract, if made, applied. *Gough v. Root,* 82

3. Ch. 252, Laws of 1882, authorizing the construction of two transverse wings to the capitol, provided for a board of commissioners who should procure "suitable and proper plans, drawings, and specifications for the construction" of said wings, and let the contract for their erection. It also authorized them to employ an "architect or superintendent to superintend the work on said building" as it progressed, and to certify to the board monthly estimates of all materials furnished and labor performed. Pursuant to such act the board procured plans, engaged an architect, and entered into a contract with the plaintiffs whereby all the materials were to be furnished and all the work done according to the plans and specifications furnished by the board, and under the direction and to the entire satisfaction of the architect. The contract further provided that the architect might vary from such plans, and that any doubt as to the quality of materials or workmanship, or as to allowances for extras, should be determined and adjusted solely by the architect. After the plaintiffs had in good faith constructed a large portion of one wing, and the materials and work had been approved by the architect, accepted by the board, and paid for by the state, the wing fell by reason of latent defects in the plans. At the special request of the state the plaintiffs restored the wing according to amended plans and specifications furnished by the board. *Held,* that the state warranted the sufficiency of the original plans, and was liable to the plaintiffs for the expense of restoring the portion of the building so destroyed. *Bentley v. State,* 416

4. The plaintiff agreed to take entire charge of all engines, boilers, and pumps in the defendants' saw-mill, to keep them in good repair and running order, and to keep in repair "all other machinery located and situated in said saw-mill," for a certain sum for one year. During the year the plaintiff superintended the digging of a well and the putting in of a pump, water-pipes, and hydrants in the mill-yard, constituting a system of water-works for the protection of the property against fire. In an action to recover extra compensation therefor, it is *held* that the contract did not in terms

cover such work, and, there being evidence tending to show an implied contract that plaintiff should be paid therefor, a verdict in his favor will not be disturbed. *Reiser v. Stauer,* 477

5. There being evidence of declarations of the plaintiff that he considered the work as embraced in his contract, a charge that if, at the time it was being done, plaintiff assumed that it came within the contract and that it was his right and duty to superintend it under the contract, and defendants understood that he was doing the work as part of his duty under the contract, he could not recover, was sufficiently favorable to the defendants. *Ibid.*

6. In an action upon a contract which the plaintiff had not fully performed and which the defendant had employed a third person to complete, the defendant may recoup what such completion was fairly worth, but not necessarily all he paid therefor. *Garvin v. Gates,* 513

7. The defendant stated, in writing, to the county board that if within two years $2,000 should be raised by tax from the county and paid to a certain corporation to aid in the erection of a soldiers' monument, he would himself pay to said corporation $1,000 for the same purpose. *Held,* that the raising of the $2,000 by the county by tax, and the payment thereof to the corporation, was a good consideration for the defendant's subscription, which, not having been previously withdrawn, thereby became absolute. *La Fayette Co. Monument Corp. v. Magoon,* 627

8. Afterwards, in a communication to said corporation, the defendant stated that, in conformity with his agreement with the county board, he did thereby "subscribe and hand to the treasurer of said corporation $1,000 in money, to be used . . . in the erection of a soldiers' monument," on condition that the net cost thereof should not be less than $6,000, and that the full amount of $6,000 should be in the treasury of the corporation on or before March 1, 1888, "and if said amount of $6,000 is not in the hands of said treasurer by March 1, 1888, the said $1,000, so by me subscribed and hereby paid, shall be at once returned and refunded and paid back to me." The board of directors of the corporation approved of such communication and all its conditions, and the defendant thereupon gave to the treasurer his check for $1,000, and a receipt was given to him, signed by the treasurer and approved by the directors, as follows: "Received of [defendant] the sum of $1,000 according to the foregoing letter, its terms and conditions; and if the sum of $6,000 in money is not in my hands as treasurer . . . on March 1, 1888, then the said sum of $1,000 is to be refunded to said [defendant] forthwith." Subsequently, by direction of the defendant, payment of his check was refused. *Held:*

(1) The check was given upon sufficient consideration.

(2) The check was given and received *as money,* and was a *payment* of the subscription.

(3) Parol evidence of a contemporaneous agreement that the check was to be paid by a bond to be given by the defendant for the payment of the $1,000 upon the conditions specified in his communication, was inadmissible to vary the contract evidenced by the communication, check, and receipt.

(4) The failure of the corporation to raise $6,000 by March 1, 1888, could not be a defense to an action upon the check brought and prosecuted to judgment before that date.

(5) If the condition as to the raising of such $6,000, contained in the contract between the defendant and the corporation, is valid (a

question not determined), and there has been a breach thereof, the trial court may, on defendant's motion, discharge the judgment recovered before March 1, 1888, on the check. *Ibid.*

9. The fact that securities were taken by one person in the name of another who had no interest in them, does not invalidate the securities or prevent the person beneficially interested from enforcing payment of them by action. *Lane v. Duchac,* 646

CONTRIBUTION. See PARTNERSHIP, 8, 4.

CONTRIBUTORY NEGLIGENCE. See RAILROADS, 8, 4.

CONVERSION. See PLEADING, 8.

CONVEYANCE. See ADVERSE POSSESSION, DEED. DURESS. EJECTMENT, 1. EQUITY, 1. EVIDENCE, 2–4. FOX AND WISCONSIN RIVER IMPROVEMENT. INSOLVENCY, 2. MARRIED WOMEN. PARTIES, 2. REGISTRY OF DEEDS. RELIGIOUS SOCIETIES, 1–5, 8, 9, 11. VENDOR, ETC. OF LAND.

COPY served, of order to show cause: Defects. See PRACTICE.

CORPORATIONS. See BILLS AND NOTES, 1, 2. INSURANCE, 5. MUNICIPAL CORPORATIONS. RELIGIOUS SOCIETIES.

COSTS.

See APPEAL, 3, 10. LOGS AND TIMBER, 2. MORTGAGES, 2. PLEADING, 5.

Under sec. 2921, R. S., fees for drafting a bill of exceptions used on appeal to this court may be taxed as costs in the trial court. *Schwalbach v. C., M. & St. P. R. Co.* 187

COUNTERCLAIM. See CONTRACTS, 6.

COUNTIES.

By ch. 155, Laws of 1878, and ch. 197, Laws of 1879, Burnett county was authorized to borrow from the trust funds of the state, $20,000, to be used in aiding the construction of a railroad, and to be repaid, with interest, in fifteen annual instalments. Until the whole amount should be repaid the railroad company was required to pay annually into the state treasury, in lieu of all license fees, a sum equal to five per cent. of its gross earnings, which sum was to be applied upon the indebtedness of the county. By ch. 172, Laws of 1883, Washburn county was formed out of part of the territory of Burnett, and, pursuant to that act, the existing debt was apportioned, and new certificates of indebtedness issued to the state by the respective counties. No provision was made by the act for the application of the sums paid into the treasury by the railroad. *Held,* that such sums should be applied upon the certificates of the two counties, ratably and in proportion to the amount of the indebtedness assumed by each. *State ex rel. Burnett Co. v. Harshaw,* 211

COURT AND JURY. See INSOLVENCY, 2. LOGS AND TIMBER, 8. MUNICIPAL CORPORATIONS, 1. NEGLIGENCE. RAILROADS, 2. VERDICT.

CRIMINAL LAW AND PRACTICE.

See EVIDENCE, 10. EXCISE LAWS.

1. G., having been convicted of riot, was, on May 7, 1887, sentenced to confinement in the house of correction for one year. Before ex-

ecution of the sentence, and on May 14, a stay was granted, and G. was released on bail, pending the determination of the case on writ of error. The judgment of conviction was affirmed, and the *remittitur* from the appellate court was filed in the trial court on March 13, 1888. On April 5, 1888, G. was committed to the house of correction pursuant to the sentence. *Held*, that the term of his imprisonment commenced on the date last mentioned. *State v. Grottkau,* 589

2. When a person convicted and imprisoned for crime is discharged from custody in a *habeas corpus* proceeding by a court of competent jurisdiction, the state cannot obtain a review of the order or judgment in that behalf by writ of error. And it is immaterial whether such court issues the *habeas corpus* in the first instance. or adjudicates the matter on *certiorari* to a court commissioner who issued the writ. *State ex rel. McCaslin v. Smith*, 65 Wis. 93, distinguished. *Ibid.*

DAMAGES.

1. The car in which the plaintiff was riding on defendant's railroad having stopped, in the night time, several hundred feet distant from the platform of the depot at her destination, she was directed by the conductor to leave the train at that place, and was compelled to walk up along a side track in which there was an open culvert or cattle-guard. Not knowing of such culvert she fell into it, in the darkness, and was injured. While she was trying to extricate herself, those in charge of the train switched some cars towards her on the side track, greatly frightening her. The conductor knew of the culvert in the track along which the plaintiff would be compelled to walk, and that cars would be switched upon such track. *Held*, that in assessing the plaintiff's damages the jury might consider the fright to which she was subjected by reason of the wrongful act of the conductor. *Stutz v. C. & N. W. R. Co.* 147

2. In an action by a married woman to recover for personal injuries, evidence that by reason thereof she was unable to perform her work as she had previously done is admissible to show the extent of her injuries, the jury being instructed that she could not recover for loss of time. *Ibid.*

3. Where there is evidence tending to show that the plaintiff had not, at the time of the trial, fully recovered from her injuries, it is not error to instruct the jury that "she is entitled to recover for any further physical suffering which you may find from the evidence is reasonably certain to result from the injury complained of." *Ibid.*

4. The trial court having refused to set aside a verdict for the reason that the damages were excessive, this court will not interfere on that ground unless it is apparent from the evidence that the jury were actuated by passion or prejudice. *Ibid.*

5. A verdict for $299.54 damages for injury to the feelings of a passenger wrongfully ejected from a railroad train and called a liar by the conductor, is *held* not excessive. *Wightman v. C. & N. W. R. Co.* 169

a case of cruel and inhuman treatment, within the meaning of subd. 5, sec. 2356, R. S. *Crichton v. Crichton,* 59

2. Though the testimony of the parties is in conflict, and there is corroborating testimony on each side, the unimpeached testimony of the three children of the parties in support of the allegations of cruelty and habitual drunkenness is *held* to create such a clear preponderance of evidence against the findings of the trial court that its judgment denying a divorce is reversed. *Ibid.*

3. After condonation, former injuries will be revived by subsequent similar misconduct. *Ibid.*

4. Questions of allowances, alimony, or division of estate, will not be considered by this court until they have been passed upon by the trial court. *Ibid.*

5. A judgment of divorce giving to the plaintiff wife all the property, real and personal, and confirming in her the title to the homestead (the title to which had been taken in her name although the husband had bought and paid for it), makes a final division and distribution of the estate of the husband, within the meaning of sec. 2364, R. S., although it also directs that the plaintiff pay to the defendant the sum of $42 per year until further order, and that the same be a lien upon the homestead. [Whether the court had power to make such allowance to the husband, the divorce having been granted on the ground of his drunkenness and cruelty, not determined.] *Thompson v. Thompson,* 84

6. A modification of such judgment after the term and more than one year after its rendition, requiring the plaintiff to pay an additional $600 to the defendant and to give a mortgage of the homestead to secure such payment, is without jurisdiction and void. And although such modification is afterwards vacated and then again re-established, it does not become *res adjudicata,* but may be set aside at any time. *Ibid.*

DURESS.

The evidence in this case is *held* (contrary to the finding of the trial court) to show that the mortgage sought to be foreclosed was executed, as to the homestead embraced therein, by the defendant wife under duress and undue influence exerted by means of threats that unless she so executed it the plaintiff would cause the imprisonment of her son for a crime of which the latter was not in fact guilty. The mortgage is therefore void as to such homestead. *McCormick H. M. Co. v. Hamilton,* 486

EJECTMENT.

See Adverse Possession. Boundaries.

1. Where the defendant in ejectment entered upon the possession of the premises under color of title asserted in good faith, and has held adversely to the plaintiff, he is entitled (under sec. 3096, R. S.) to recover for improvements made by him, even though they were made after he had notice of the plaintiff's claim. *Barrett v. Stradl,* 885

2. Under sec. 3098, R. S., if the plaintiff in ejectment fails to pay the amount of the assessment for improvements and taxes within three years from the date of the verdict assessing the same, he is barred of his recovery whether the judgment so providing has

been entered or not; and if the judgment has not been entered within such three years the plaintiff is not thereafter entitled to have it entered, but the defendant may have it entered *nunc pro tunc* and then declared absolute in his favor. *Neeves v. Eron,* 542

ELKHORN, Village of. See TAXATION, 4.

ENCROACHMENTS. See HIGHWAYS, 3, 4.

EQUITY.

See COUNTIES. DIVORCE. DURESS. ESTOPPEL. INSURANCE. 5, 6. LIENS. MORTGAGES. PARTIES, 2. PARTNERSHIP, 1, 3–5. PLEADING, 6. RECEIVERS. RELIGIOUS SOCIETIES, 6, 10, 11. RES ADJUDICATA. VENDOR, ETC. OF LAND, 5.

1. A judgment setting aside a conveyance of land from the plaintiff to the defendants is affirmed, the evidence being *held* to sustain the findings of the trial court that the plaintiff was a woman about seventy-five years old and unable, by reason of ignorance and mental weakness, to make a sale of her land or to comprehend the effect of such a sale, and that the defendants, upon whose counsel and advice she was accustomed to depend, took advantage of her ignorance and weakness of mind to obtain such conveyance for a grossly inadequate consideration. *Kelly v. Smith,*   191

2. Where nothing has been done further than the adoption by the common council of a resolution that the mayor and city clerk take, immediate steps to let a contract for the construction of waterworks for the city, a court of equity will not interfere, at the suit of tax-payers, to enjoin the threatened enforcement of such resolution, even though its adoption by the council was unauthorized. *Pedrick v. Ripon,*   622

3. The complaint alleges that, upon the dissolution of a partnership between the parties with relation to a certain business, it was agreed that the plaintiffs should assume all the debts of the firm relating to such business, and, to carry out such arrangement, they executed to the defendant a bond conditioned, by its terms, that they should pay all the debts of the firm and save him harmless therefrom; that at that time the individual members of the firm held stock in a certain manufacturing company, and there was then outstanding a note executed in the firm name (and by other makers) which was not given for any debt of the firm and was not in any way connected with its said business, but was given for the benefit of such manufacturing company, the makers of the note being in reality sureties for said company; that said note was not intended or understood by the parties to be included among the liabilities of the firm assumed by the plaintiffs or covered by the conditions of their bond, and that if the bond is so written as to bear such construction and so as to apparently require the plaintiffs to save the defendant from all liability thereon, it was so written by mistake, and said bond, so written and construed, does not express the real agreement, understanding, and intentions of the parties. It is further alleged that plaintiffs have paid a judgment on said note, one third of which ought, in equity, to be paid by the defendant. Judgment is demanded for a reformation of the bond and for one third of the amount so paid by the plaintiffs. *Held,* on demurrer *ore tenus,* that the complaint sufficiently alleges a mistake in the bond, and not a mere misunderstanding of the words employed therein. *Hagenah v. Geffert,* 636

ESTATES OF DECEDENTS.

See EVIDENCE, 1. PARTNERSHIP, 3–5. WILLS.

1. An administrator who retains money of the estate in his hands long after the time limited by law for the settlement of the estate, is liable for it if stolen. *Black v. Hurlbut,*   126
2. Under the laws of this state (R. S. secs. 3258, 3800, 3933, 3934) the executor of a deceased executor cannot be compelled to render and settle the account of the latter. Under sec. 3934 such account may be settled by the county court upon the application of any person interested, but the moving party must furnish the proofs to enable the court to state and settle it. *Reed v. Wilson,*   497

ESTOPPEL.

See BOUNDARIES, 2. CHATTEL MORTGAGES.

Where a husband has charge of his wife's business which consists in dealing in horses, the fact that in looking after the horses he treats them as his own with her knowledge ought not to estop her from asserting her title to them as against his creditors. *Green v. Walker,*   548

EVIDENCE.

See APPEAL, 8, 11, 12. ATTORNEYS, 1. BILLS AND NOTES, 3. BOUNDARIES. 1, 3. CHATTEL MORTGAGES, 2. CONTRACTS, 8 (3). DIVORCE, 2. LIMITATION OF ACTIONS, 2, 3. NEW TRIAL. RAILROADS, 5. VENDOR, ETC. OF LAND, 3, 4. .WILLS, 1, 5.

1. The final judgment or decree of a county court, construing a will, assigning the real estate of which the testator died seized, and settling his estate, recited, among other things, that the wife of the testator had died since his decease. *Held,* in an action of ejectment affecting a part of the real estate devised, that it sufficiently appears from such decree that the testator and his widow had previously died, and that the will had been admitted to probate. *Morse v. Stockman,*   89
2. Under sec. 4154, R. S., a sheriff's deed of land is presumptive evidence that the title, estate, or interest which it purports to convey, of every person whom it purports to affect, passed to and vested in the grantee, without proof of the judgment upon which the execution issued by virtue of which the sheriff sold the land. *Ibid.*
3. Conversations, had after the date of an absolute deed to a railroad company, with persons connected in some way with such company, but not shown to have had authority to speak for or bind it, are not admissible in evidence to prove that the grant was upon condition that a depot should be built on the premises. *Schwalbach v. C., M. & St. P. R. Co.*   137
4. Nor is a writing, drawn up at the instance of the grantor after the date of the deed, and stating that the deed was made upon that condition, admissible to prove such fact, where such writing was never signed by or on behalf of the company and there is no evidence that the company ever admitted that the real facts were stated therein. *Ibid.*

EXCISE LAWS.

2. On appeal from a justice's court in a prosecution for selling liquor without a license, the accused gave an undertaking, with surety, in the form used in civil cases, and not as required by secs. 4714, 4717, R. S. In the circuit court he was again found guilty, and judgment was entered that he pay a fine of $50 and costs. and that in default of payment he be committed to the county jail until the fine and costs should be paid, his imprisonment, however, not to exceed six months. It was further ordered that the state have judgment against the accused and his surety for the amount of the fine and costs. A writ of error was sued out by the accused alone. *Held:*

(1) The judgment against the accused was not in excess of the authority given by the statute.

(2) Any supposed grievance of the surety cannot be considered.
Ibid.

EXECUTIONS.

See GARNISHMENT. VOLUNTARY ASSIGNMENT, 2, 8.

Money loaned to be used in purchasing certain property and actually so used by the borrower, is "purchase money" within the meaning of subd. 20, sec. 2982, R. S., and the property so purchased is not exempt from execution issued upon a judgment in an action by the lender to recover the money lent. *Houlehan v. Russler*, 557.

EXECUTORS AND ADMINISTRATORS. See EVIDENCE, 1. ESTATES OF DECEDENTS. PARTNERSHIP, 8–5. WILLS.

EXEMPTIONS. See EXECUTIONS. VOLUNTARY ASSIGNMENT, 2, 8.

EXPERT TESTIMONY. See EVIDENCE, 5, 7.

FALSE REPRESENTATIONS.

See BILLS AND NOTES, 2.

In an action for false representations alleged to have been made to induce the plaintiffs to lease land from the defendants, an instruction that if the defendants in making the contract for the lease made positive statements as to the character of the land, etc., without knowing them to be true, and they were not true and were relied upon by the plaintiffs, then the plaintiffs could recover, is *held* fairly to imply that such statements must have been made for the purpose of inducing the plaintiffs to enter into the lease, and the failure expressly so to state will not work a reversal of the judgment where such instruction was immediately followed by others to the effect that there could be no recovery unless the false representations were made with intent to deceive. *Middleton v. Jerdee*, 89

FEELINGS, Injury to. See DAMAGES, 5.

FEES of referee. See REFERENCE, 1.

FENCES. See RAILROADS, 2–4.

FINDINGS OF FACT. See ADVERSE POSSESSION, 5. ATTORNEYS, 5. DIVORCE, 2. PARTNERSHIP, 4. WILLS, 2.

FIRE INSURANCE. See INSURANCE, 1–5.

FLOWAGE OF LAND. See FOX AND WISCONSIN RIVER IMPROVEMENT.

FORECLOSURE. See LIENS. MORTGAGES.

FOX AND WISCONSIN RIVER IMPROVEMENT.

1. The lands granted to this state by the act of Congress of August 8, 1846, to aid in the improvement of the Fox and Wisconsin rivers, were not granted merely as a location for the improvements, but to be sold and the proceeds used in making the improvements. And where such lands were sold by the state without any express reservation of the right to flood them, if necessary in making the improvements, without making compensation therefor, no such reservation can be implied from the mere fact that the lands were granted to the state to aid in making such improvements. *Zemlock v. United States,* 863

2. Nor is any such reservation created by the act of the legislature of August, 1848 (Laws of 1848, p. 58). Sec. 16 of that act, providing that when any lands appropriated by the board of public works to the use of such improvements shall *belong to the state* they shall be absolutely reserved to the state, refers to an ownership by the state at the time of the appropriation, and not to an ownership of which the state had lawfully divested itself prior to the taking of the lands by the board. *Ibid.*

FRAUD. See BILLS AND NOTES, 2. CHATTEL MORTGAGES. EQUITY, 1. FALSE REPRESENTATIONS. INSOLVENCY. PARTNERSHIP, 5. VOLUNTARY ASSIGNMENT, 1-3.

FRAUDS, Statute of. See VENDOR, ETC. OF LAND, 1.

FRAUDULENT CONVEYANCES. See CHATTEL MORTGAGES. INSOLVENCY. VOLUNTARY ASSIGNMENT, 1-3.

FRAUDULENT REPRESENTATIONS. See BILLS AND NOTES, 2. FALSE REPRESENTATIONS.

GARNISHMENT.

An affidavit for garnishment stating that an execution has been issued on a judgment against the principal defendant and has not been returned, is sufficient to give the court jurisdiction over the proceeding; and where the fact that an execution had been issued was not contested in the trial court it cannot be objected, on appeal, that there was no proof of that fact. *Sanger v. Guenther,* 854

HABEAS CORPUS. See CRIMINAL LAW, 2.

HIGHWAYS.

See MUNICIPAL CORPORATIONS.

1. Under sec. 1298, R. S., an order laying out a highway is only *prima facie* evidence of the regularity of the proceedings, and its invalidity may be shown by proof that the notices required by sec. 1267 were not given. *State v. Logue,* 598

2. Though the owner of land over which it was attempted to lay out a highway signed the petition therefor and hence was not entitled to notice of the meeting of the supervisors, yet he may avail himself of the want of notice to the public and other owners, to invalidate the proceedings. *Ibid.*

3. The penalty prescribed by sec. 1326, R. S., for the obstruction of a highway cannot be recovered for a mere encroachment. *State v. Pomeroy,* 664

4. A fence intruding into a highway, but not hindering or rendering dangerous the travel thereon, is a mere encroachment.   *Ibid.*

HOLIDAYS. See EVIDENCE, 15.

HOMESTEAD. See DIVORCE, 5, 6. DURESS. INSOLVENCY, 1. VOLUNTARY ASSIGNMENT, 2.

HUSBAND AND WIFE. See DIVORCE. ESTOPPEL. LIENS, 2, 3.

IMPRISONMENT, When term begins. See CRIMINAL LAW, 1.

IMPROVEMENTS. See EJECTMENT.

INDEFINITENESS in pleading. See LIENS, 1, 9. PLEADING, 1-3, 9.

INDEXES to records. See REGISTRY OF DEEDS, 2-6.

INJUNCTION. See EQUITY, 2. PLEADING, 6. RES ADJUDICATA.

INSOLVENCY.

1. The homestead of an insolvent debtor was mortgaged for $10,000. It contained a narrow strip, valued at $637.50, in excess of one fourth of an acre. The title had been in his wife for nine years before he applied for a discharge from his debts. *Held,* that the failure to include said strip in the inventory of his estate was not sufficient to bar a discharge. *In re Mabbett,*   351

2. Upon an application by an insolvent debtor for a discharge from his debts, the question whether a previous conveyance or mortgage of his property was made with intent to defraud his creditors is a question of fact and should be passed upon as such by the jury or court.   *Ibid.*

INSTRUCTIONS TO JURY.

See ACCOUNT STATED. AGENCY. APPEAL, 9. CONTRACTS, 2, 5. DAMAGES, 3. FALSE REPRESENTATIONS. LIMITATION OF ACTIONS, 4. NEGLIGENCE.

1. It is not error to refuse to give instructions the substance of which has been given in the general charge. *McGrath v. Bloomer,*   29

2. The jury were repeatedly told that the defendant was entitled to reasonable compensation for collecting a claim, and that they must fix the same from all the testimony. The judge remarked that if he had charged ten per cent. this would be about the amount expended for railroad fares in making the collection. The jury allowed the defendant ten per cent. *Held,* that the hypothetical allusion to that amount was not error prejudicial to the defendant. *Best v. Sinz,*   243

3. Where the trial court would have been justified in directing a verdict for the defendant, the plaintiff was not injured by omissions in the instructions given or by the refusal to give others. *Fairfield v. Barrette,*   463

INSURANCE.

Fire Insurance. See REFERENCE, 2.

1. The agent of an insurance company agreed orally with the plaintiff to write a policy insuring certain property to the amount of $500, for six months from a certain time, for an agreed premium, but said that the company might be unwilling to carry the risk after he had reported it. He did not write any policy or report the risk to the company. *Held,* that, although the premium was not in

fact paid, there was a valid contract to insure, upon which, in case of a loss during the six months, the plaintiff might recover from the company the value of the property destroyed not exceeding the $500. *Campbell v. American F. Ins. Co.* 100

2. The plaintiff having given the company notice of the loss, it is no defense to the action that he did not make proofs of loss in the manner which the policy, had one been issued according to the agreement, would have required, especially where the defendant has denied all liability on the ground that it never insured or agreed to insure the property. *Ibid.*

3. The agent not having questioned the plaintiff as to what the building contained besides the property to be insured, it is no defense that it contained other property which increased the risk, unless the plaintiff fraudulently concealed that fact. *Ibid.*

4. A mortgage provided that if the mortgagors failed to insure the property the mortgagee might insure the same, the expense thereof being added to the mortgage debt. The mortgagee applied to the defendant company for insurance on the property to secure his interest therein. The defendant issued the policy in suit, insuring the *mortgagors* against loss, but providing that the loss, if any, should be payable to the mortgagee as his interest should appear. The policy also provided that it should be void if the assured obtained other insurance on the property or any part thereof without consent, etc. This policy was delivered to the mortgagee, who paid the premium, and retained the policy without objection for nearly a year before the property was burned. *Held:*

(1) The mortgagee was bound by the stipulations of the policy.

(2) Subsequent insurance upon the property, obtained by and insuring the interest of *one* of the mortgagors, avoided the policy. *Gillett v. Liverpool & L. & G. Ins. Co.* 203

5. To show that a policy of insurance issued to, and upon the property of, a corporation was so written by mistake and was intended to be issued to, and to cover only the interest of, a stockholder to whom the loss was made payable, the proofs must be entirely plain and convincing beyond reasonable controversy; otherwise the writing will be held to express correctly the intention of the parties. *Blake Opera House Co. v. Home Ins. Co.* 667

Life Insurance.

6. By the terms of a contract of life insurance the company agreed to pay to the beneficiary, upon the death of the insured, " eighty per cent. of an assessment levied and collected therefor, not exceeding $4,000," etc. *Held,* that for a breach of such contract by neglect and refusal to make the assessment the beneficiary may maintain an action at law and, if it appears that such an assessment would have produced a substantial sum, may recover substantial damages. *Jackson v. N. W. Mut. Relief Ass'n,* 507

INTEREST. See LOGS AND TIMBER, 1. PARTNERSHIP, 1.

INTERPLEADER. See PARTIES, 1.

INTERVENTION. See RECEIVERS.

INTOXICATING LIQUORS. See EXCISE LAWS.

JOINDER.

Of causes of action. See PARTIES, 2. PLEADING, 6, 9.

Of parties. See LIENS, 5. PARTIES, 2, 3. PARTNERSHIP, 5 (2). RES ADJUDICATA.

Of several orders in one appeal. See APPEAL, 10.

JUDGMENT.

Offer of judgment. See LOGS AND TIMBER, 2.
Motion for judgment on pleadings. See PLEADING, 4.
In divorce action: Division of estate. See DIVORCE, 5.
In action to enforce lien. See LIENS, 5.
In ejectment. See EJECTMENT, 2.
In prosecution for unlicensed sale of liquors. See EXCISE LAWS, 2.
For too large an amount. See MORTGAGES, 2, 4.
Modification. See DIVORCE, 6.
Authentication. See CIRCUIT COURTS.
As evidence of matters recited. See EVIDENCE, 1.
Res adjudicata. See DIVORCE, 6. RES ADJUDICATA.
Vacating.
 Under sec. 2832, R. S., the circuit court may, at a subsequent term
 within one year, relieve a party from a judgment against him
 through his surprise or excusable neglect. *Black v. Hurlbut,* 126
Reversal on appeal. See APPEAL, 1–9, 11, 12. CIRCUIT COURTS., DAM-
 AGES, 4. EVIDENCE, 5. EXCISE LAWS, 2. FALSE REPRESENTA-
 TIONS. GARNISHMENT. INSTRUCTIONS TO JURY. MORTGAGES, 2,
 4. PARTNERSHIP, 4.
Discharge. See CONTRACTS, 8 (5).

JUDICIAL NOTICE. See BILLS AND NOTES, 3.

JURISDICTION. See ATTORNEYS, 7. CIRCUIT COURTS. DIVORCE, 6.
 GARNISHMENT.

JUSTICES' COURTS. See LIMITATION OF ACTIONS, 3.

LAND CONTRACT. See VENDOR, ETC. OF LAND.

LANDLORD AND TENANT. See FALSE REPRESENTATIONS.

LANDS SOLD FOR TAXES. See REGISTRY OF DEEDS, 1.

LICENSE to mine, etc. See MINES AND MINING.

LICENSE LAWS. See EXCISE LAWS.

LIENS.

Of Mechanics, Material-men, etc.
1. In an action to enforce a lien for machinery and materials furnished
 and labor performed, a complaint to which is annexed a copy of
 an agreement under which certain specified articles were to be
 furnished for a certain price, and a bill of particulars of all charges,
 including, as one item, the articles furnished under the specific
 contract, is *held* to be sufficiently definite and certain, although it
 does not state separately a cause of action for the articles furnished
 under the written agreement, and one for the other articles furnished and labor performed. *Barnes v. Stacy,* 1
2. Under sec. 3314. R. S., as amended by ch. 349, Laws of 1885, one who
 furnishes materials for a house which a husband is building on his
 wife's land with her knowledge and consent, may have a lien
 therefor upon such land although it was understood that the husband should pay the entire cost of the house. *Heath v. Solles,* 217

8. Under sec. 3314, R. S., as amended by ch. 349, Laws of 1885, one who furnishes materials for a house which a husband is building on his wife's land with her knowledge and consent, may have a lien therefor upon such land, although the materials were purchased by the husband upon credit without the authority of his wife. *Heath v. Solles, ante,* p. 217, followed. *North v. La Flesh,* 520

4. The fact that such materials are charged in one continuous account with non-lienable goods sold to the husband, does not impair the right to a lien therefor, where the value of the lienable materials can easily be ascertained from the account itself without a restatement thereof. *Ibid.*

5. In such a case, in an action against both husband and wife, the plaintiff may have a judgment against the husband for the whole amount of his account, and a further judgment making a portion of that amount a lien upon the land of the wife. *Ibid.*

6. In such a case the non-lienable items in the account against the husband included more than $280 which the plaintiff had advanced without charge, for the accommodation of the husband, to pay freights chargeable to the latter. Payments amounting to about $310 had been made on the general account, no application thereof being made by the parties. *Held,* that it was equitable to apply all such payments on the non-lienable items. *Ibid.*

7. The fact that the petition for the lien states that the materials were sold to both the husband and the wife, while the complaint and the proofs show that they were sold to the husband alone, is immaterial. The petition might be amended at any time to correspond with the complaint and proofs. *Ibid.*

8. So it is an immaterial variance that the petition states that the materials were used in the erection of a certain building on the land in question, while the complaint alleges that they were used in the erection of a house and barn thereon. *Ibid.*

9. In the petition for a lien it is sufficient to describe the building for which the materials were furnished as " a certain building," if the land on which the building stands is accurately described. *Ibid.*

On Logs and Timber.

10. Under secs. 1, 2, ch. 469, Laws of 1885, the vendor of supplies to be used in a logging camp, and which were in fact used in such camp by the vendees in getting out logs, is entitled to a lien on the logs for the amount due, although the supplies, before being so used, were placed by the vendees in their store to be sold at a profit to their employees and others. *Stacy v. Bryant,* 14

11. In an action to enforce a lien upon logs the description of the logs in the complaint and the petition for a lien may be amended to conform to the evidence which was admitted without objection, when it is evident that the defendant is not surprised by such amendment and no injustice is done thereby. *Ibid.*

12. Under sec. 1, ch. 469, Laws of 1885, a lien is given where supplies are furnished to be used, and are in fact used, in the cutting. etc., of logs in any of the counties named; and the residence of the person furnishing the supplies, or the place where they are delivered to the person who uses them, is wholly immaterial. *Patten v. N. W. Lumber Co.* 233

LIFE INSURANCE. See INSURANCE, 6.

LIMITATION OF ACTIONS.

See ADVERSE POSSESSION. APPEAL, 1, 2. PARTNERSHIP, 3, 5 (3). TOWNS, 2.

1. A complaint alleging that between September 1 and December 1, 1873, the plaintiff rendered services for the defendant which were reasonably worth $4,000, "which sum became due some time in September, 1884," is *held*, on demurrer, to show that the cause of action accrued as early as December 1, 1873. The allegation that the sum became due in 1884 is a mere conclusion of law, unsupported by the facts stated, and must be disregarded. *Tucker v. Lovejoy*, 66

2. No record evidence of the time when a summons issued by a justice of the peace was delivered to the sheriff for service being required by statute, such time may be proved by parol. *Town of Woodville v. Town of Harrison*, 360

3. If after a summons issued by a justice of the peace is delivered to the sheriff for service the return day fixed therein is changed, such alteration makes another and entirely different process of it, which, in contemplation of law, the sheriff did not and could not receive until the alteration was made. And the fact and time of such alteration may be proved by parol. *Ibid.*

4. The question whether the plaintiff's claim was "for the balance due upon a mutual and open account current" (sec. 4226, R. S.) and therefore not barred by the statute of limitations, is *held*, on defendant's appeal, to have been fairly submitted to the jury by instructions to the effect that such an account must contain credits as well as debits, that the burden of proof was upon the plaintiff, and that the jury must determine whether it was such an account and, if so, the amount due thereon. *Dunn v. Estate of Fleming*, 545

LIVE STOCK. See RAILROADS, 2–4.

LOGS AND TIMBER.

See CONTRACTS, 1. LIENS, 10–12.

1. Where, in an action for the wrongful cutting of timber, the plaintiff recovers as damages, under sec. 4269, R. S., the highest market value of such timber while in the possession of the defendants, he is not entitled to recover interest on such value. *Smith v. Morgan*, 375

2. In an action for the wrongful cutting of timber an offer of judgment under sec. 4269, R. S., is only available to the defendant to prevent further costs, in cases where "the jury find such cutting was by mistake." An offer of judgment under that section is not available under sec. 2789. *Ibid.*

3. By the terms of a contract logs were to be delivered into a certain stream "in good driving water," and landed "so that they could be easily started through the dam in the spring." It appeared that at the point where the logs were landed the stream, at its ordinary stage, really had no good driving water, but that at times of high water logs could be run therefrom by means of the water set back from a flooding dam below; and the evidence tended to show that the logs might have been run down the stream had not the dam below been choked with other logs. *Held*, that it was not error to submit to the jury the question whether the logs were delivered in good driving water. *Garvin v. Gates*, 513

MARRIED WOMEN.

See DAMAGES, 2. DIVORCE. ESTOPPEL.

Obligations and conveyances executed by and to a married woman in her baptismal name are valid. *Lane v. Duchac,* 646

MASTER AND SERVANT.

1. The risk from an uncovered saw projecting over its frame and partly across a narrow passage-way along which a servant in a mill is obliged to go in the performance of his duties, being apparent, is assumed by the servant in accepting and remaining in the service. *Stephenson v. Duncan,* 404

2. A servant having the right to abandon the service because it is dangerous may refrain for a reasonable time from so doing in consequence of assurances by the master that the danger shall be removed, and will not be held to have thereby assumed the risk. But if he continues in the service for a time longer than it is reasonable to allow for the performance of the master's promise he will be deemed to have waived his objection and assumed the risk. *Ibid.*

MAXIMS.

De minimis non curat lex, 13, 42.

Persona conjuncta æquiparatur interesse proprio, 494.

Qui prior est in tempore, potior est in jure, 662.

Stare decisis, 414.

MECHANICS' LIENS. See LIENS, 1–9.

MEDICAL BOOKS. See EVIDENCE, 5.

MILLS AND MILL DAMS. See PLEADINGS, 6.

MINES AND MINING.

1. By the terms of a mining license a range of mineral was not to be worked beyond a point 300 yards west of a certain fence. When it had been worked for nearly half of the distance the crevice pinched out and became barred by a solid wall of rock. A shaft was then sunk about forty-five feet ahead, and by drifting from it a few rods in the same direction a crevice was struck in which mineral was again found. The crevice, before it reached the barrier, and after the barrier was passed, was of the same general character, and there was no change in its general direction or in the rock or the mineral found. *Held,* that the crevice west of the barrier was a continuation of the crevice or range east of it, and that there was no new discovery such as would give rights not limited by the terms of the original license. *Raisbeck v. Anthony,* 572

2. The limitation on the right to work the range having been created by contract, the discoverers of the range and those claiming under them could be relieved therefrom only by contract; and the evidence (showing, among other things, that the land-owner told one of the owners of the range to go where he pleased upon the range and work it as he pleased) is *held* insufficient to show that the limitation was ever abrogated. *Ibid.*

MISTAKE. See EQUITY, 3. INSURANCE, 5. VENDOR, ETC. OF LAND, 5.

MORTGAGES.

MUNICIPAL CORPORATIONS.

See COUNTIES. EQUITY, 2. PLEADING, 1. TOWNS.

1. It is not error for the trial court to assume that an excavation several feet deep in the line of a sidewalk is a defect in the walk unless properly guarded. *McGrath v. Bloomer,* 29

2. A provision in a city charter that no action against the city for injuries sustained by reason of any defect in any street shall be maintained unless written notice of the injury was given to the proper officers within five days of the occurrence thereof, does not apply where the injury was caused by a nuisance created by the positive acts of the city's agents, such as leaving a large wooden roller in the street. [*Quære,* whether the provision requiring notice to be given within *five days* is not invalid, as fixing a time unreasonably short.] *Hughes v. Fond du Lac,* 380

3. The board of street commissioners of a city, disregarding the requirement of the charter that all work for the city should be let by contract, resolved that the work of repairing and reconstructing a bridge should be done by themselves under the supervision of their committee and a superintendent appointed by them. *Held,* that for injuries to a person, caused by the negligence of the employees of the board engaged in doing the work in pursuance of such resolution, the street commissioners were liable individually, and the city was not liable. *Robinson v. Rohr,* 486

MUTUAL BENEFIT SOCIETIES. See INSURANCE, 6.

NAME. See MARRIED WOMEN.

NEGLIGENCE.

See BILLS AND NOTES, 1. MUNICIPAL CORPORATIONS. RAILROADS, 3-5. VERDICT, 2.

1. An accident to a railroad train was caused by the breaking of the side-rods of the engine. The speed at which the train was running was not unlawful or unusual, and it was not shown that it would tend to contribute to such breakage. *Held,* that it was not error to instruct the jury that the speed of the train had no connection with the accident and could not be considered on the question of negligence. *Beery v. C. & N. W. R. Co.* 197

2. An instruction that the jury should feel "reasonably certain" as to what they should find to be the cause of an accident, is *held* not erroneous. *Ibid.*

NEGOTIABLE INSTRUMENTS. See BILLS AND NOTES. CONTRACTS, 9.

NEW TRIAL.

To support a motion for a new trial on the ground of newly discovered evidence that the breaking of the side-rods on defendant's engine was the result of negligence, the plaintiff filed affidavits of two section men that on the day after the accident they picked up pieces of the strap or iron frame which held the brasses of the side-rod in place, and now have such pieces in their possession. The plaintiff's own affidavit stated that he had examined such pieces since the trial, and that one of them plainly showed that it had been cracked for some time before the final break. Plaintiff's description of this piece was adopted in the affidavits of the section men, but in none of the affidavits was there any attempt to describe the appearance of the piece when it was picked up, but only its appearance after it had been lying about exposed to the air and dirt for several months. *Held*, that it was not error to refuse to grant the new trial, the appearance of the piece after such exposure not warranting any inference that there was an old crack therein at the time of the accident. *Beery v. C. N. W. R. Co.* 197

NOTICE.
Of trial. See APPEALABLE ORDER, 1.
Of proceedings to lay out highway. See HIGHWAYS, 1, 2.
Of injury on street. See MUNICIPAL CORPORATIONS, 2.
Of motion to strike out demurrer. See PLEADING, 5.
Of meeting of board of review. See TAXATION.
Constructive notice of conveyances. See REGISTRY OF DEEDS.

NUISANCE. See MUNICIPAL CORPORATIONS, 2.

OBSTRUCTIONS. See HIGHWAYS, 3, 4.

OFFER of judgment. See LOGS AND TIMBER, 2.

OFFICERS.
Assessors. See TAXATION, 5.
Attorneys at law. See ATTORNEYS.
Board of review. See TAXATION, 1-5.
Of city. See EQUITY, 2. MUNICIPAL CORPORATIONS, 2, 3.
Of corporation. See BILLS AND NOTES, 1, 2. RELIGIOUS SOCIETIES, 6.
Receivers. See RECEIVERS.
Register of deeds. See REGISTRY OF DEEDS.
Sheriff. See LIMITATION OF ACTIONS, 2, 3.

OPINIONS. See EVIDENCE, 5, 7.

OUSTER. See RELIGIOUS SOCIETIES, 6.

PARENT AND CHILD. See DURESS. EVIDENCE, 9.

PARTIES.

See CONTRACTS, 9. LIENS, 5. MORTGAGES, 3, 5, 6. MUNICIPAL CORPORATIONS, 3. PARTNERSHIP, 5 (2). RES ADJUDICATA.

1. Sec. 2610, R. S. (providing that a defendant against whom an action is pending upon a contract may apply for an order substituting in his place a person, not a party to the action, who makes against him a demand for the *same debt*), does not apply to a defendant sued for the purchase price of logs to which the persons sought to be substituted claim title adverse to that of his vendor, the plaintiff. *Baxter v. Day*, 27

2. In an action to quiet title to land and to have a certain deed declared valid, all persons claiming interests in the premises hostile to such deed and which would be affected by a judgment affirming its validity, may be made parties, although they claim separate parcels of the land: and there is no misjoinder of causes of action, although it is asked that the plaintiff's title under such deed be established as against the claims of all the defendants. *Leinenkugel v. Kehl*, 238

3. Though two have joined in a power of attorney authorizing a third person to collect their respective shares on the distribution of an intestate estate, one may sue alone to recover his share so collected. *Best v. Sinz*, 243

PARTNERSHIP.

See APPEAL, 4, 5. EQUITY, 3. RECEIVERS. VOLUNTARY ASSIGNMENT, 1-3.

1. The allowance of interest in taking partnership accounts depends upon the circumstances of each particular case. Upon the facts in this case, there having been no agreement between the parties as to allowing or charging interest prior to the ascertainment of balances, it is *held* that the plaintiff should have interest on the amount found due him from the commencement of the suit. *Carroll v. Little*, 52

2. The business of a copartnership may be transacted without the use of a firm name, and it may be agreed that the names of the individual partners or any one or more of them shall be used and bind the firm. *Severson v. Porter*, 70

3. The claim of surviving partners against the estate of a deceased partner for contribution for losses sustained by the firm is a contingent claim which does not become absolute until the business of the firm is settled, the assets converted, and the debts paid, and which (under sec. 3860, R. S.) need not be presented for allowance until it so becomes absolute. If, before such claim becomes absolute, the estate of the deceased partner has been settled and the assets distributed, the claim is not barred by sec. 3844, R. S., but the surviving partners may pursue their remedy against the heirs and distributees under ch. 141, R. S. *Logan v. Dixon*, 533

4. To establish a claim for contribution from the estate of a deceased partner, the state of the accounts of the several partners with the firm should be shown, as well as the fact that upon the closing up of the business there were losses which were paid by the surviving partners out of moneys not belonging to the firm. But where, in an action to enforce such contribution, it was admitted in the pleadings that each partner had an equal interest in the business, and the trial proceeded throughout on the implied understanding that neither partner had contributed more than his share to the capital stock and that if there were any losses upon the closing up of the business each was liable to contribute equally to pay the same, and the trial court was not requested to take proofs or make findings on that subject, and on appeal it is not claimed that the appellants would be in any way benefited by the taking of an account to show the *status* of each partner with the firm, a judgment rendered on the theory of the equal liability of the partners will not be reversed for the want of a formal finding on that subject. *Ibid.*

5. W. & L., as partners, holding mortgages on certain logs and lumber, took possession thereof and proceeded to manufacture and sell the same under an agreement with the mortgagors to apply the proceeds on the mortgage debts, the residue if any to be returned to such mortgagors. The value of the property largely exceeded the debts. L. assumed charge of the property and of the execution of the agreement with the mortgagors, one S. being employed by the firm to do the work. Without the knowledge of W., L. became a secret partner with S., and they together, fraudulently and to the injury of W., mismanaged the business of executing the agreement with the mortgagors, converting large quantities of the mortgaged property and its proceeds to their own use without accounting therefor to W. or the firm of W. & L. Afterwards the firm of W. & L. was dissolved, and in the division of assets

the mortgages and mortgaged property were transferred to L., who took all the rights and assumed all the obligations, liabilities, and duties of the firm in respect thereto. L. having died, the mortgagors brought suit to compel W., as surviving partner, to account for the mortgaged property and its proceeds. The administrators of L. refused to assume the defense, and W. was compelled to defend the suit and afterwards to pay a judgment rendered against him therein. *Held:*

(1) After the mortgaged property and the rights and obligations pertaining thereto were transferred to L., the same ceased to be partnership property, and as between L. and W. the latter became a mere surety for the faithful performance by L. of the agreement with the mortgagors. The amount of the judgment which W. was compelled to pay by reason of L.'s failure to perform such agreement, is, therefore, a proper claim against the estate of L. without reference to other partnership matters. [Whether W. has a right to be reimbursed by said estate for his expenses incurred in defending the suit brought by the mortgagors, not determined.]

(2) The fact that S. may also be liable to W. by reason of his participation in the fraudulent mismanagement of the business as aforesaid, does not interfere with the right of W. to present his claim against the estate of L.

(3) Such claim of W. was a contingent claim which did not become absolute until he paid the judgment, and (under sec. 3860, R. S.) it might be presented at any time within one year after it so became absolute. *Webster v. Estate of Lawson,* 561

PAYMENT.

See CONTRACTS, 8 (2). COUNTIES. LIENS, 6. MORTGAGES, 1, 7.

In an action to recover the amount of a draft alleged to have been collected by the defendant, it appeared that before receiving said draft the defendant had received other drafts upon the same debtor for collection, and that the debtor in making payments had not directed the application thereof. *Held,* that to maintain the action the plaintiff must show that the debtor had paid to the defendant a sum more than sufficient to satisfy the other drafts. *North Wis. Lumber Co. v. Am. Exp. Co.* 656

PERPETUITIES. See RELIGIOUS SOCIETIES, 5.

PERSONAL PROPERTY. See APPEAL, 1, 10. ATTACHMENT. BILLS AND NOTES. CARRIERS. CHATTEL MORTGAGES. CONTRACTS, 1, 9. ESTATES OF DECEDENTS, 1. ESTOPPEL. EVIDENCE, 8, 12, 13. EXCISE LAWS. EXECUTIONS. GARNISHMENT. LIENS, 10–12. PLEADING, 8. RECEIVERS. TAXATION, 3, 6. VOLUNTARY ASSIGNMENT, 8. WILLS, 4, 5.

PLEADING.

See APPEALABLE ORDER, 3. ATTORNEYS, 5. CONTRACTS, 8 (4). EQUITY, 8. EXCISE LAWS, 1. LIENS, 1, 7–9, 11. LIMITATION OF ACTIONS, 1. MORTGAGES, 3. PARTIES, 2. SLANDER.

1. In an action for injuries sustained by reason of a defective sidewalk, a general allegation that the walk was defective or out of repair at the place named, or at most briefly stating in what the defect consisted, is sufficient without describing the defect in detail. *Barney v. City of Hartford,* 55

(2) The action is upon contract for money had and received. The allegation of a conversion does not, in view of the other allegations, render it a tort action. *Ibid.*

9. A complaint sets forth the employment of the plaintiff as a minister, under a written contract, by the officers of an unincorporated religious society, his salary, perquisites, etc., and alleges that the members of the society were satisfied with him and desired his continuance as such minister, but that the defendants (two of whom were trustees of the society, who signed the contract of employment and had control of the temporal affairs of the church), wrongfully *conspiring* and contriving together to injure the plaintiff and drive him from his position as such minister, did various acts, which are fully set forth. Then follows a statement of plaintiff's damages by reason of such acts. *Held,* on motion to make more definite and certain, that the complaint is in tort for a conspiracy, and states but one cause of action. *Fisher v. Schuri,* 370

10. Upon a demurrer *ore tenus* a greater latitude of presumption will be indulged to sustain a complaint than upon a regular demurrer thereto. *Hagenah v. Geffert,* 636

POLLING THE JURY. See VERDICT, 8.

POSSESSION. See ADVERSE POSSESSION.

POWER OF ATTORNEY. See PARTIES, 3.

PRACTICE.

See APPEAL. APPEALABLE ORDER. ATTACHMENT. ATTORNEYS. BILLS AND NOTES, 3. CIRCUIT COURTS. COSTS. CRIMINAL LAW. ESTATES OF DECEDENTS, 2. EVIDENCE. EXECUTIONS. GARNISHMENT. INSOLVENCY, 2. INSTRUCTIONS TO JURY. JUDGMENT. LIMITATION OF ACTIONS, 2, 3. NEW TRIAL. PARTIES. PLEADING. RECEIVERS. REFERENCE. VERDICT.

In the copy served of an order to "show cause why an order should not be entered dismissing the action," etc., the word *dismissing* had a pen-mark drawn through it. *Held,* that the motion should not have been denied merely for that reason. *Harrison Machine Works v. Hosig,* 184

PRESCRIPTION. See ADVERSE POSSESSION.

PRESUMPTIONS. See ADVERSE POSSESSION, 1, 6. PLEADING, 10. REGISTRY OF DEEDS, 3-5. WILLS, 1, 5.

PRINCIPAL AND AGENT. See AGENCY.

PRINCIPAL AND SURETY. See EXCISE LAWS, 2. PARTNERSHIP, 5.

PRINTED CASE. See APPEAL, 7.

PROCESS. See LIMITATION OF ACTIONS, 2, 3.

PROMISSORY NOTES. See BILLS AND NOTES. CONTRACTS, 9. MORTGAGES, 3, 5, 6. TAXATION, 6.

PROXIMATE CAUSE. See VERDICT, 2.

PUBLIC LANDS. See FOX AND WISCONSIN RIVER IMPROVEMENT.

PUBLIC POLICY. See TOWNS, 6.

QUO WARRANTO. See RELIGIOUS SOCIETIES, 6.

RAILROADS.

Municipal Aid. See COUNTIES.

Carriers. See CARRIERS. DAMAGES, 5.

1. A round-trip railroad ticket, punctured for separation into two parts, and having on the " going " part the words "Not good for passage," and, on a line therewith, on the "returning" part the words " if detached," is nevertheless good for passage where the parts have become separated by accident, if both parts are in good faith presented to the conductor on the outward trip. *Wightman v. C. & N. W. R. Co.* 169

Fences.

2. At a certain point on defendant's railroad there was a station building, but for several years no agent had been kept there, and the building had been closed up and had gone to decay. Freight, if taken on at that place, was not billed until it arrived at the first station beyond. There was a side track there, where trains sometimes passed each other, and where the company received charcoal to be transported, but there were no grounds for a depot outside of the usual right of way. A cattle-guard had been put in about 350 feet south of the station building, and another about 721 feet north of it and about 350 feet north of the north end of the side track. Beyond these points the road was fenced. In an action for the killing of horses which, as the jury found, got upon the track near the north cattle-guard where the track was not fenced, the court, assuming that there were depot grounds where the station building was located, submitted to the jury the question whether the point at which the horses got upon the track was within the limits of such depot grounds, and the jury found that it was not. *Held,* that there was no error in thus submitting to the jury the question of the extent of the depot grounds, and that the evidence showing the foregoing facts, among others, justified the finding. *McDonough v. M. & N. R. Co.* 223

3. Under sec. 1810, R. S., as amended by ch. 193, Laws of 1881, if fences have been duly erected in good faith along the right of way of a railroad, although they are afterwards destroyed or become defective, an action for an injury alleged to have been caused by the lack of or defects in the fence will be defeated if it appears that the plaintiff was guilty of contributory negligence. *Martin v. Stewart,* 553

4. The plaintiff turned his colt into a pasture beside a railroad track, knowing that there was nothing to prevent the animal from going upon the track, and using no precaution to prevent it from doing so. The animal went upon the track and was killed by a passing locomotive. *Held,* that the plaintiff was guilty of contributory negligence. The fact that he had no other pasturage for the colt is of no importance. *Ibid.*

Negligence — Evidence. See DAMAGES, 1. NEGLIGENCE. NEW TRIAL.

5. In an action for the negligent burning of a building alleged to have been fired by sparks from a locomotive, the testimony of defendant's inspector that the screen on the engine was the same as on the defendant's other engines does not entitle the plaintiff to show in rebuttal that other fires had been set by the other engines. *Allard v. C. & N. W. R. Co.* 165

RECEIVERS.

One who has attached partnership property in the hands of a receiver
appointed in an action for dissolution of the partnership may intervene in such action for the purpose of asserting his claim under
the attachment, and may attack the validity of the appointment of
the receiver by a petition setting forth the facts, upon which an issue
may be made and determined. He cannot, however, attack such
appointment in a summary proceeding by motion. *Jacobson v.
Landolt,* 142

REFERENCE.

1. Under a stipulation in a garnishment proceeding "that the referee
   herein on the trial of the issue against the garnishee shall receive
   $10 per day for his services as such referee, in lieu of any and all
   other fees or perquisites," it is *held* that the *per diem* compensation
   of the referee was not limited to the time actually occupied by
   the trial itself. *McDonald v. Bryant,* 20

2. Where there is no *account* between the parties in the ordinary acceptation of that term, a reference cannot be directed, without the
   consent of the parties, merely because there may be many items
   of damage. So *held* in an action upon an insurance policy where,
   to ascertain the amount of the loss, it would be necessary to examine bills of sale. inventories, and accounts consisting of numerous items. *Andrus v. Home Ins. Co.* 642

REGISTRY OF DEEDS.

1. The registry of a conveyance of land is not invalidated by a mere
   clerical error in transcribing the instrument, not affecting the
   sense or obscuring its meaning. So *held*, where in copying upon
   the record a tax deed in the statutory form, the word *is* was
   omitted from the formula " as the fact is," where it occurs the
   second time in such deed. *St. Croix L. & L. Co. v. Ritchie,* 409

2. The omission from the general index of the description of the land
   affected by the instrument entered therein for record, is cured by
   correctly recording the instrument at length in the proper record
   book, and from the time the instrument is so recorded at length
   the registry is valid and effectual. *Ibid.*

8. Nothing appearing to the contrary, the presumption is that a conveyance was recorded at length on the day it was received for record in the register's office. *Ibid.*

7. The dismissal of one minister and the employment of another is a matter pertaining to the temporalities of a church, and does not necessarily operate as a change of faith or doctrine. When done by the majority of a religious society in accordance with the statute and the constitution and by-laws of the society, it does not operate as a wrongful exclusion of the minority who adhere to the former minister. *Ibid.*

8. Land was conveyed in trust for the erection thereon of a church building for the use of the members of a certain church "according to the rules of said church, and according to the rules of said church" which might thereafter "be adopted from time to time by their authorized synods." The synod to which the church was attached was a mere confederation of local self-governing churches, acting, so far as the local organization was concerned, merely as an advisory body. *Held,* that the mere withdrawal of the church from such synod was not a violation or perversion of the trust. *Ibid.*

9. Land was conveyed to trustees in trust for the erection thereon of a church building "for the use of the members of the Norwegian Evangelical Church of St. Paul's on Liberty Prairie, according to the rules of said church," etc. The grant was, presumably, made with reference to the articles of faith previously adopted by said church. The church was subsequently incorporated, the certificate of incorporation simply giving the name of the church. *Held,* that the trustees and officers of the corporation could not lawfully devote the church building to purposes other than those specified in the grant. *Ibid.*

10. It is not the province of courts of equity to determine mere questions of faith, doctrine, or schism, not necessarily involved in the enforcement of an ascertained trust. To call for equitable interference there must be such a real and substantial departure from the designated faith or doctrine as will be in contravention of such trust. *Ibid.*

11. Where the adoption of certain articles of faith by the majority of a religious society is claimed by the minority to be such a departure from the faith referred to in a trust deed as to result in a perversion of the use of the property granted, the fact that such minority remained united with the majority for more than two years after the adoption of such articles, constitutes an additional reason why, in the absence of a clearly established violation of the trust, a court of equity should not interfere. And the fact that before suit was brought the majority repealed such articles and substantially reaffirmed those previously adopted, is still another reason why the action should not be maintained. *Ibid.*

RES ADJUDICATA.

See Divorce, 6.

In an action to restrain the preparation and sale of an imitation of plaintiff's medicine, and for damages, the plaintiff's husband was joined with her, and she claimed to derive her right to the medicine from another as the inventor. *Held,* that a judgment against her in that action is conclusive and binding upon her in a subsequent suit by her alone in the same court against the same defendant, in which she alleges that she is the inventor, but in which the matters involved are otherwise the same. *Marshall v. Pinkham,*   401

INDEX. 711

REVERSAL OF JUDGMENT. See JUDGMENT, Reversal.
RIVERS. See PLEADING, 6.
ROUND-TRIP TICKETS. See RAILROADS, 1.
RULES OF COURT.
Supreme Court Rule XX (Motions for rehearing), 37.
SALE OF CHATTELS. See EXECUTIONS. LIENS, 10, 12. MORTGAGES,
3, 6. PLEADING, 8.
SALE OF LANDS. See ADVERSE POSSESSION. DEED. EQUITY, 1. EVI-
DENCE, 2–4. FOX AND WISCONSIN RIVER IMPROVEMENT. PAR-
TIES, 2. REGISTRY OF DEEDS. VENDOR, ETC. OF LAND.
SALE of liquor without license. See EXCISE LAWS.
SECURITY for costs. See APPEAL, 10.
SERVICE OF SUMMONS. See LIMITATION OF ACTIONS, 2, 3.
SETTLEMENT. See ACCOUNT STATED.
SHERIFF. See LIMITATION OF ACTIONS, 2, 3.
SIDEWALKS. See PLEADING, 1.

SLANDER.

The words, "My father-in-law [the plaintiff] has used my wife for
eleven years. The children are not mine; they are from him,"
are capable of the meaning, ascribed to them in innuendoes, that
the plaintiff had been guilty of the crimes of incest and adultery.
Guth v. Lubach,   131

SPECIAL VERDICT. See VERDICT.
SPECIFIC PERFORMANCE. See VENDOR, ETC. OF LAND, 5.
STATUTE OF FRAUDS. See VENDOR, ETC. OF LAND, 1.
STATUTE OF LIMITATIONS. See ADVERSE POSSESSION. APPEAL, 1, 2.
PARTNERSHIP, 3, 5 (3). TOWNS, 2.
STATUTES.
Constitutionality. See TOWNS, 4, 5.
Construction. See ATTACHMENT. CIRCUIT COURTS. CONTRACTS, 3.
COSTS. COUNTIES. DEED, 2. DIVORCE, 1, 5. EJECTMENT. ES-
TATES OF DECEDENTS, 2. EVIDENCE, 2, 15. EXCISE LAWS. EXE-
CUTIONS. FOX AND WISCONSIN RIVER IMPROVEMENT. HIGHWAYS,
1, 3. JUDGMENT. LIENS, 2, 3, 10, 12. LIMITATION OF ACTIONS, 4.
LOGS AND TIMBER, 1, 2. MUNICIPAL CORPORATIONS, 2. PARTIES,
1. PARTNERSHIP, 3, 5 (3). PLEADING, 5. RAILROADS, 3. REFER-
ENCE, 2. REGISTRY OF DEEDS, 5, 6. RELIGIOUS SOCIETIES, 3–5.
TAXATION, 3, 6. TOWNS. VOLUNTARY ASSIGNMENT, 5. WILLS, 4.

STATUTES CITED, ETC.

CONSTITUTION OF WISCONSIN.

Art. IV, sec. 23	-	295, 299, 302
" VIII, " 1	- - -	324
" XI, " 3	-	295, 301

SESSION LAWS.

1848. Page 58, - 363–365, 367
1848. " 61, sec. 15 - 367, 369
1848. " 62, " 16 363, 367, 369

SESSION LAWS — con.

1848. Pages 62, 63, secs. 17–20 368
1848. Page 67, sec. 43 - - 368
1857. P. & L. Ch. 153, sec. 1 - 322
1858. " " 133, sec. 1 - 322
1860. Ch. 215 - - - - 236
1860. " 260 - - - - 582
1860. " 337 - - - 281, 282
1860. " 337, sec. 1 - - 283

STATUTES CITED, Etc.—con.

STIPULATIONS construed. See APPEAL, 13. EVIDENCE, 11. REFERENCE, 1.

STREETS. See BOUNDARIES, 1. HIGHWAYS. MUNICIPAL CORPORATIONS. PLEADING, 1.

SUBROGATION. See COUNTIES.

SUBSCRIPTION. See CONTRACTS, 7, 8.

SUBSTITUTION of parties. See PARTIES, 1.

SUMMONS. See LIMITATION OF ACTIONS, 2, 3.

SURETYSHIP. See EXCISE LAWS, 2. PARTNERSHIP, 5.

SURVIVORSHIP. See WILLS. 4, 5.

SUSPENSION of power of alienation. See RELIGIOUS SOCIETIES, 5.

TAXATION.

See Towns, 6.

TOWNS.

See APPEAL, 1. TAXATION, 4.

tion can be maintained thereon against the town so becoming liable unless a claim thereon has been filed with its town clerk to be laid before the town board of audit. *Schriber v. Richmond,* 5

2. Although, before the enactment of ch. 240, Laws of 1881, an action on a town order could be maintained only after demand and refusal of payment, yet the statute of limitations began to run from the date of the order, not from the date of the demand. [The court inclines to the opinion, but does not decide, that the effect of ch. 240, Laws of 1881, so far as the statute of limitations is concerned, is only to extend the period of limitation thirty days.]
Ibid.

3. Ch. 292, Laws of 1883,—providing that "all powers relating to villages and conferred upon village boards by ch. 40, R. S., and all acts amendatory thereof, excepting those the exercise of which would conflict with the provisions of law relative to towns and town boards, are conferred upon towns and town boards of towns containing one or more unincorporated villages of not less than 1,000 inhabitants, and are made applicable to such villages, and may be exercised therein when directed by a resolution of the electors of the town." etc.,— is not void for uncertainty. *Land, Log & Lumber Co. v. Brown,* 294

4. Said act does not incorporate the villages as separate municipalities, and is not in violation of sec. 3, art. XI, Const. The power given to the legislature to incorporate villages does not deprive it of power to legislate for their control and government before they are incorporated. *Ibid.*

5. The fact that the law is applicable only to towns containing villages of a certain population does not render it a violation of sec. 23, art. IV, Const., providing that the legislature shall establish but one system of town and county government. *Ibid.*

6. Nor is the act void under any rule of public policy which forbids the taxation of property for any purpose not benefiting it. It is for the legislature, not for the courts, to fix the limits of the taxing district. *Ibid.*

. TOWN ORDERS. See TOWNS, 1, 2.

TRESPASS. See DAMAGES, 6.

TRUST FUNDS. See COUNTIES.

TRUSTS AND TRUSTEES. See RELIGIOUS SOCIETIES.

UNDERTAKING on appeal. See EXCISE LAWS, 2.

VALUE, Evidence of. See VENDOR, ETC. OF LAND, 8.

VARIANCE. See ATTORNEYS, 5. LIENS, 7, 8.

VENDOR AND PURCHASER OF LAND.

See ADVERSE POSSESSION. DEED. EQUITY, 1. EVIDENCE, 2–4. FOX AND WISCONSIN RIVER IMPROVEMENT. PARTIES, 2. REGISTRY OF DEEDS.

1. Where a conveyance has been executed and accepted in pursuance of an oral contract for the sale of land, an action may be maintained for a breach of the promise to pay the contract price. The statute of frauds does not apply to such an executed agreement. *Niland v. Murphy,* 326

2. The measure of damages in such case is the amount promised to be paid, and interest. And though it was not all due presently at the time of the sale, yet the whole amount may be recovered

where it is all due before the trial and the grantee has from the
outset refused to execute the notes and mortgage which he agreed
to give for the deferred payments. *Ibid.*

8. Evidence of the value of the land is properly excluded in such a
case, the value having been fixed in the deed. *Ibid.*

4. Evidence that after receiving a deed the grantee directed a sale of
the premises, shows an acceptance of the deed. *Ibid.*

5. The defendant S. owned lots 11 and 12 in a village block, and sold to
the defendant T. what they both supposed to be lot 11, but which
was in fact lot 12. T. went into possession of the lot purchased
and made improvements thereon. Afterwards S. sold to the
plaintiff, who had actual notice of T.'s purchase, possession, and
improvements, what the plaintiff and S. supposed was lot 12, and
the contract of sale described it as such, but in fact the land so
sold was all situated in a public street which adjoined the real lot
12 but had not yet been opened for travel. Plaintiff went into
possession of the land in such street and built a house thereon. In
an action to enforce specific performance of the contract of sale by
the conveyance to him of the real lot 12, it is *held* that the plaintiff has no equity against T., and his only remedy against S. lies in
the recovery of damages. *Lundgreen v. Stratton,* 659

VERDICT.

See APPEAL, 9.

1. The trial court may, in its discretion, submit for a special verdict
questions material to the issues. *McGrath v. Bloomer,* 29

2. In an action to recover for personal injuries, it being a disputed
question whether the injuries were the proximate result of the
negligence complained of or of some independent and intervening
cause for which the defendant was not responsible, it was error to
refuse to submit that question to the jury for a special finding.
Kreuziger v. C. & N. W. R. Co. 158

3. Where the findings of a special verdict upon the subject of damages
are inconsistent and manifestly made under a misapprehension of
the instructions, the court may decline to receive the verdict and,
after explaining the instructions previously given, direct the jury
to retire for further consultation; and a request that the jury be
polled before they so retire may be denied. *Wightman v. C. & N.
W. R. Co.* 169

4. Where the request for a special verdict is not made until after the
commencement of the argument to the jury, it is not error to refuse it. *U. S. Exp. Co. v. Jenkins,* 471

VIEW. See EVIDENCE, 10.

VILLAGES. See TAXATION, 4. TOWNS, 3–6.

VOLUNTARY ASSIGNMENT.

1. A voluntary assignment by a firm doing business in the names of
the individual partners, treating all their property as firm property and all debts as firm debts, is not fraudulent as to creditors
although they did not know of the copartnership. *Severson v.
Porter,* 70

2. The reservation of the homesteads of partners in an assignment by
the firm does not render such assignment void. *Ibid.*

8. In an assignment by a firm a reservation to each partner of personal
property (specifically described in the inventory) claimed to be ex-

empt from execution, and which had, by prior agreement, been
allotted to each in severalty and actually separated from the partnership assets, does not invalidate the assignment.   *Ibid.*

4. In the absence of fraud a creditor who files his claim in the manner
prescribed by law thereby waives all objections to the regularity
of the assignment and to the title of the assignee to the assets.
Littlejohn v. Turner,   113

5. The court may, under sec. 1698, R. S., in a proper case, authorize
the assignee to sell the assigned property free from all incumbrances.   *Ibid.*

6. One who had notice of the application for an order authorizing the
sale of the assigned property free from incumbrances, but failed to
appear and object, or, if he did object, has taken no steps to have
the order set aside or reversed, cannot attack it in a collateral proceeding, except for fraud.   *Ibid.*

WAIVER.
Of specificness in exceptions. See APPEAL, 13.
Of objections to evidence. See ATTORNEYS, 5.   EVIDENCE, 5.
Of performance of contract. See CONTRACTS, 1 (8).
Of right to judgment. See EJECTMENT, 2.
Of proof of issuance of execution. See GARNISHMENT.
Of notice of meeting of supervisors. See HIGHWAYS, 2.
Of proofs of loss. See INSURANCE, 2.
Of lien. See LIENS, 4, 10.
Of objection to risks. See MASTER AND SERVANT.
Of finding of fact. See PARTNERSHIP, 4.
Of notice of meeting of board of review. See TAXATION, 1.
Of right to special verdict. See VERDICT, 4.
Of objections to regularity of assignment, sale, etc. See VOLUNTARY
ASSIGNMENT, 4, 6.

WARRANTY of sufficiency of building plans. See CONTRACTS, 8.

WATERCOURSES. See PLEADING, 6.

WILLS.

1. The signatures of witnesses to a will, following an attesting clause
stating that they signed in the presence of the testator, raises a
strong presumption of that fact, which will be overcome only by
clear and satisfactory proof to the contrary. So *held* in a case
where the witnesses, while verifying their signatures, had no recollection of attesting the will. *Will of O'Hagan,*   78

2. A finding by the trial court that the will was executed by the testator in the city of B. on the day it bears date, and was at the
same time subscribed by the attesting witnesses in his presence, is
sufficiently specific, and it was unnecessary to find at what place
in the city the testator executed and the witnesses subscribed the
instrument, or whether the testator could and did leave his house
on the day of its date.   *Ibid.*

3. A testator devised "all of [his] real estate" to his son J. for life, remainder to J.'s three infant children in fee. The will then states
that "the land so devised consists of 160 acres" in the town of
G., and directs that upon the death of J. it shall be divided into
three portions by lines running from north to south, each portion
containing 53⅓ acres, and that the western third, embracing the
buildings, shall belong to A., one of said children, and the other
two thirds shall belong to the other two children respectively.

The testator died seized of 260 acres of land in a compact form, 240 rods in length and 178¼ rods in width. *Held:*

(1) Even if there was a sufficient description of the 160 acres to be divided, the devise of *all* the testator's real estate was not limited to that amount by the later clause of the will. The 100 acres not to be divided would go to the infant devisees as tenants in common.

(2) It being impossible to determine from the will the exact location of the 160 acres to be divided, the direction as to division is void for uncertainty. *Will of Ehle,*   445

4. The testator, his son J., and the wife and three infant children of the latter perished in a fire which consumed the testator's house. The evidence (fully stated in the opinion), showing the arrangement of the house, the probable origin of the fire, the location of the bodies when found, etc., is *held* to sustain the findings of the circuit court that the testator died first and that J. died before his wife or either of the three children. The title to the testator's real estate therefore vested, under the will, in the three children, and its descent must be traced from them. If the mother survived them. the land descended to her and, upon her death, to her parents, under subd. 2, sec. 2270. R. S.; but if the children, or any of them, survived their mother the land descended to their next of kin (in this case their mother's parents aforesaid) under subd. 4 of that section. The personal estate of J. also passed to and through his widow and children.   *Ibid.*

5. In such case those claiming the real estate by descent from J., on the ground that it descended to him from his children, had the burden of showing that he survived such children. But those claiming the personal property of J. under and through his widow and children had the burden of showing that they or some of them survived him.   *Ibid.*

WITNESSES. See DEED, 2.

WORDS AND PHRASES.
Account, in statute. See REFERENCE, 2.
The assured, in policy. See INSURANCE, 4.
Bills of exceptions, in statute. See COSTS.
Belong to the state, in statute. See FOX AND WISCONSIN RIVER IMPROVEMENT.
Corner, in deed. See DEED, 1.
Cruel and inhuman treatment, in statute. See DIVORCE, 1.
Depot grounds, in statute. See RAILROADS, 2.
Detached, on ticket. See RAILROADS, 1.
Division of estate, in statute. See DIVORCE, 5.
Encroachment, in statute. See HIGHWAYS, 8, 4.
Fractional part, in deed. See DEED, 1.
Furnishing supplies in —— county, in statute. See LIENS, 12.
Holding adversely under color of title asserted in good faith, in statute. See ADVERSE POSSESSION, 5. EJECTMENT, 1.
Mutual account, in statute. See LIMITATION OF ACTIONS, 4.
Obstruction, in statute. See HIGHWAYS, 8, 4.
Persons in being by whom an absolute fee in possession could be conveyed, in statute. See RELIGIOUS SOCIETIES, 5.
Property in this state, in statute. See TAXATION, 6.
Purchase money, in statute. See EXECUTIONS.
Same debt, in statute. See PARTIES, 1.
Trial, in stipulation. See REFERENCE, 1.
Used a woman. See SLANDER.

WRIT OF ERROR. See CRIMINAL LAW, 2.